Microsoft

Microsoft®
SharePoint™
Portal Server 2001

Resource Kit

IT Professional

PUBLISHED BY
Microsoft Press
A Division of Microsoft Corporation
One Microsoft Way
Redmond, Washington 98052-6399

Library of Congress Cataloging-in-Publication Data
Microsoft SharePoint Portal Server 2001 Resource Kit / Microsoft Corporation.
　　　　p. cm.
　　Includes index.
　　ISBN 0-7356-1562-4
　　1. Intranets (Computer networks)　2. Web servers.　3. Microsoft Corporation.　I.
Microsoft Corporation.

　　HD30.385 .M52　2001
　　004.6--dc21　　　　　　　　　　　　　　　　　　　2001044544

Printed and bound in the United States of America.

1 2 3 4 5 6 7 8 9　QWT　6 5 4 3 2 1

Distributed in Canada by Penguin Books Canada Limited.

A CIP catalogue record for this book is available from the British Library.

Microsoft Press books are available through booksellers and distributors worldwide. For further information about international editions, contact your local Microsoft Corporation office or contact Microsoft Press International directly at fax (425) 706-7329. Visit our Web site at www.microsoft.com/mspress. Send comments to *rkinput@microsoft.com.*

Acquisitions Editor: Juliana Aldous Atkinson
Project Editors: Maureen Williams Zimmerman, Julie Miller

Body Part No. X08-51295

Contents

Chapter 4   Introducing the Dashboard Site   29

Part 6   Case Studies   455

Chapter 26   T-Systems: Technology Center Bids Piles of Files a Final Farewell   457

Chapter 27   Migrating from Site Server 3 to SharePoint Portal Server 2001 for Enterprise Search at Microsoft   461

Contributors to this book include the following:

User Education Group Manager
Allan Risk

User Education Content Manager
Gail Burke

User Education Program Manager
Caroline Briggs

User Education Production Lead
Sean Hyde

Program Managers
Jim Boyle
Andrew Datars
Jeremy Mazner
April Pierson
Daniel Witriol

Technical Editing Lead
Kelly Bowen

Contributing Writers
Mark Adolf, Tami Amador, Kelly Bowen, Jim Boyle, Reza Chitsaz, Andrew
Datars, Dennis Dwyer, Marc Faerber, Jeff Finn, Mike Fitzmaurice, Karen
Guilbeault, Geir Hanson, David Holladay, Shannon Joyner, Sreeram Krishnan,
Margaret Li, Matt Masteller, Harry Miller, Jennifer Moser, Allan Risk, Emily
Schroeder, Viki Selca, Simon Shepherd, Joe Sherman, Manendra Sheokand,
Margaret Sherman, Avi Shmueli, Tony Soper, Emily Schroeder, Heidi Steen,
Steve Tullis, Zac Woodall

Technical Editors
Tami Amador, Kelly Bowen, Gail Burke, Erik Heino, Tamara Kaplan,
Emily Schroeder

Technical Contributors

Mark Adolf, Vikas Ahuja, John Begley, Robert Alexander-Carew, Uri Barash, Gary Barnes, Gunther Beersaerts, Jim Boyle, Jason Browne, Andrew Datars, Andrew DeBruyne, Marti Emerson, Mike Fitzmaurice, Enrico Giordani, Garry Gross, Karen Guilbeault, Dean Halstead, Steve Hansen, Scott Hay, Sid Hayutin, Scott James, Jeremy Jameson, Dean Justus, Prakash Sundra Krishnamoorthy, Sreeram Krishnan, Dwight Kruger, Bernard Lam, David Lee, Rob Lefferts, Margaret Li, Teresa Linder, Ajay Malhotra, Tom Minty, Jennifer Moser, Brian Murphy, Shailja Nair, Mircea Neagovici-Negoesc, Wayne Roseberry, Manendra Sheokand, Joe Sherman, Avi Shmueli, Jing Tan, Ying Tao, Steve Tullis, Radu Vaduva, Vishnu Varadaraj, Alex Wade, Rich Woods

Graphic Designer

Gavin Schmitz

S&T Consulting: Dan Ballard, Jarrod Jackson

Copy Editors

S&T Consulting: Jan Backstrom, Linda Caputo, Gina Craig, Carolyn Emory, Elliot Graff, Beth Harmon, Shawn Jackson, Bill Jones

Introduction to Microsoft SharePoint Portal Server 2001

This section provides a general overview of key concepts and features of Microsoft®
SharePoint™ Portal Server 2001, including the dashboard site. It describes the overall
SharePoint technologies and presents an overview of the various search solutions offered
by Microsoft.

CHAPTER 1

Introducing the Resource Kit

Welcome to the Microsoft® SharePoint™ Portal Server 2001 Resource Kit. This resource kit is designed for people who want helpful tips, advanced techniques, and useful tools and samples to enhance their work with SharePoint Portal Server.

If you are responsible for administering or designing SharePoint Portal Server workspaces, or developing applications that work with SharePoint Portal Server, this resource kit is for you. Members of the SharePoint Portal Server product team and Microsoft Consulting Services wrote this resource kit with the intention of extending the information provided in the online documentation included with SharePoint Portal Server 2001. The information in this resource kit addresses specific questions from customers, and includes helpful tips for using SharePoint Portal Server that were not available at the time SharePoint Portal Server 2001 was released.

In addition to the information in this resource kit, the enclosed SharePoint Portal Server 2001 Resource Kit CD-ROM contains various tools, utilities, and code samples for SharePoint Portal Server. It also contains an online version of the SharePoint Portal Server Resource Kit in eBook format for Microsoft Windows® CE devices.

Inside the Resource Kit

The resource kit is divided into six parts. These parts are designed to assist you in all phases of deployment from initial planning and deployment to developing custom solutions with SharePoint Portal Server.

Part One: Introduction to Microsoft SharePoint Portal Server 2001

This section provides a general overview of key concepts and features of Microsoft SharePoint Portal Server 2001, including the dashboard site. It describes the overall SharePoint technologies and presents an overview of the various search solutions offered by Microsoft.

Part Two: Planning and Installation

This section provides detailed planning information including planning server capacity, security concepts, taxonomy planning information, and more.

Part Three: Deployment

This section provides in-depth deployment information including detailed installation instructions. It describes possible deployment solutions including deploying in an extranet environment, in a multilingual environment, and across multiple dashboard sites using RapPort.

Part Four: Administration and Management

This section provides general strategies for optimizing performance and includes information to add value to your SharePoint Portal Server installation.

Part Five: Development

This section provides tools and information for developers who want to customize SharePoint Portal Server. It provides key strategies for mapping custom properties, how to develop Web Parts for business applications, and how to enhance searching.

Part Six: Case Studies

This section provides specific examples of SharePoint Portal Server as it is deployed in real-world scenarios. These case studies provide ideas and information for how SharePoint Portal Server can assist you to develop a custom portal solution for your own environment.

Part Seven: Appendixes

This section provides additional relevant information for use in planning, deploying, and maintaining SharePoint Portal Server. It includes a description of the CD-ROM contents, including the tools and a list of additional resources that are available to further assist you.

Additional Sources of Information

Users can view Help documentation from the User's Help page in the workspace or from the Tours and User's Help quick link on the default home page of the dashboard site. There is an additional link to Help documentation from the Getting Started page in the Management folder. You must be a member of the local administrators group or be assigned to the role of coordinator to access the Management folder. A link to Getting Started also appears on the default home page of the dashboard site.

Documentation Provided with SharePoint Portal Server

Managing Content. An overview of the product along with information about planning and configuring the workspace and the dashboard site.

Planning and Installation. Basic information about installation, product use, and features.

Administrator's Help. Online documentation providing information about SharePoint Portal Server Administration in Microsoft Management Console (MMC). Additional information is provided about maintenance, performance, and troubleshooting.

Dashboard Site Help. Online documentation providing information about configuring and managing the dashboard site and searching for and using documents.

User's Help. Online documentation providing procedures for configuring and using the workspace. Describes how to use Web folders to access SharePoint Portal Server.

SharePoint Portal Server Tours. An introduction to SharePoint Portal Server, highlighting key document management and search features.

Readme. Important information that may not be covered in other documentation.

Product Overview for International Customers. An overview of the product for use in countries and regions that do not have a localized version of SharePoint Portal Server.

Internet Sites

Microsoft Product Support Services. Latest service packs, fixes, white papers, and frequently asked questions (FAQs), plus a searchable knowledge base that contains technical support information and self-help tools. See http://support.microsoft.com.

SharePoint Portal Server Web site on www.microsoft.com. A central source of information about SharePoint Portal Server. See http://www.microsoft.com/sharepoint.

Training and Certification. Information about training and certification. See http://www.microsoft.com/trainingandservices.

Course 2095, "Building Knowledge Management Solutions Using Microsoft SharePoint Portal Server," is a three-day, instructor-led, Microsoft Official Curriculum course. The course provides students with the architectural concepts and the skills necessary to deploy SharePoint Portal Server as a search and document management solution as well as a dashboard site.

To take this course in the United States and Canada, find a training provider on the Web site and register with a Microsoft Certified Technical Education Center (Microsoft CTEC). Outside the United States and Canada, contact your Regional Education Service Center.

Microsoft Developer Network (MSDN) Newsgroups. Web-based forums in which you can share information about developing with Microsoft products, including SharePoint Portal Server. See http://msdn.microsoft.com/newsgroups.

TechNet. Web-based resource to help you deploy, maintain, and support SharePoint Portal Server. See http://www.microsoft.com/technet.

Software Development Kit. Information about developing applications for SharePoint Portal Server will be available after product release. It will be part of the MSDN® Platform Software Development Kit. See http://msdn.microsoft.com.

Digital Dashboard Resource Kit. Technical reference guide with tools. See http://www.microsoft.com/business/digitaldashboard.

Conventions Used in This Resource Kit

To help you locate and interpret information easily, this guide uses the following typographic conventions.

Convention	Description
ALL CAPITALS	Acronyms, names of certain commands, and keys on the keyboard.
Bold	Menus and menu commands, command buttons; tab and dialog box titles and options; command-line commands, options, and portions of syntax that must be typed exactly as shown.
Initial Capitals	Names of applications, programs, files, servers, and named windows; directory names and paths.
Italic	Information that you provide, terms that are being introduced, and book titles.
`Monospace`	Examples, sample command lines, program code, and program output.

Figures used to illustrate concepts show views in Windows 2000, Microsoft Internet Explorer, or Microsoft Office 2000. Users can access SharePoint Portal Server from different operating systems, different browsers, or Office 2000. Depending on your method of access, your view may differ from figures in this book.

Examples and scenarios used to clarify key concepts in this guide refer to a fictional company called Adventure Works. Adventure Works is an outdoor equipment company that specializes in outdoor clothing. Several departments, including Manufacturing, Sales, and Marketing, serve as examples for deploying SharePoint Portal Server.

Resource Kit Support Policy

Microsoft does not support the software supplied in the SharePoint Portal Server Resource Kit. Microsoft does not guarantee the performance of the tools, response times for answering questions, or bug fixes for the tools. However, Microsoft does provide a way for customers who purchase the SharePoint Portal Server Resource Kit to report any problems with the software and receive feedback for such issues. To report any issues or problems, send e-mail to *rkinput@microsoft.com*. This e-mail address is only for issues related to SharePoint Portal Server Resource Kit. For issues related to the SharePoint Portal Server product, see the support information included with the product.

CHAPTER 2

Introducing SharePoint Technologies

No matter the size of their organizations, customers are looking for better, more efficient ways to share information within their organizations and with outside key suppliers, partners, and clients. Microsoft® SharePoint™ is a set of two new technologies from Microsoft, SharePoint Portal Server 2001, and SharePoint Team Services, that facilitate information sharing both within organizations and over the Internet. The SharePoint technologies are a direct result of customer feedback and research on information sharing practices within organizations. These technologies address the information sharing needs of entire organizations.

Small or improvised workgroups need informal means to work together on group deliverables, share documents, and communicate status with one another. These groups need to share information effortlessly. Web sites created by using SharePoint Team Services allow them to do that.

Large workgroups with structured processes need greater management over their information. They require features such as formal publishing processes and the ability to search for and aggregate content from multiple data stores and file formats. SharePoint Portal Server 2001 provides this structure and formality.

When an organization offers SharePoint Team Services and SharePoint Portal Server 2001 in combination, they can address the information-sharing challenges for both the large and small groups within their enterprise. Together, the SharePoint Technologies give users the ability to organize information, readily access that information, manage documents, and enable efficient collaboration—all in a familiar, browser-based environment integrated with Microsoft Office.

Comparing Sharepoint Team Services and Portal Server

Feature	Team Services	Portal Server
Web site	Team Web sites (5-75 users)	Portal Web sites (75+ users)
Search Capabilities	Documents within Web site and sub Webs created using SharePoint Team Services	Across multiple servers and data types
Discussion & Notifications	Discussions, Notifications, Surveys	Discussions, Notifications, Subscriptions

continued

Comparing Sharepoint Team Services and Portal Server *continued*

Feature	Team Services	Portal Server
Customization	Browser-based, Microsoft FrontPage® 2002, and Software Development Kit (SDK)	Web Parts and SDK
Document Management	Publishing	Check-in and check-out, Versioning, Routing, Publishing
Client applications	Browser, Office XP, FrontPage 2002	Browser, Microsoft Windows® Explorer, Office 2000 or Office XP
Roles-based security	Customizable roles: Administrator, Advanced Author, Author, Contributor, and Browser Administrator, Coordinator, Author, and Reader	
Storage	SQL Server™	Web Storage System
Licensing	Covered in base Windows Server licensing	Server license and client access licenses

Microsoft SharePoint Portal Server 2001

SharePoint Portal Server is the complete portal solution for content aggregation and document management. SharePoint Portal Server creates a portal Web site, called a *dashboard site*, which allows users to share documents and search for information across the organization and enterprise, including Web sites based in SharePoint Team Services—all within one extensible portal interface. SharePoint Portal Server includes robust document management features that allow companies to incorporate business processes into their portal solution.

Small workgroups often use a combination of e-mail, file servers, and hard disks to store and share information. This type of information sharing has become the status quo for team information sharing because all members can participate easily and equally, but it does not create an organized record of a team's efforts. Using a Web site based on SharePoint Team Services gives teams an easy and informal way to centralize and share project and team information with team members and other interested parties within the organization.

At an organization or business division level, however, information-sharing requirements become more sophisticated. By using SharePoint Portal Server 2001, organizations can aggregate content from across the organization into a corporate portal so that their users can find the information they need to make better business decisions, regardless of where the data resides. This requires comprehensive search capabilities and the ability to manage large volumes of information across a great number of data stores. Business units also need advanced document management, including structured publishing processes to ensure the information they are sharing is complete and up to date.

Together SharePoint Team Services and SharePoint Portal Server 2001 can provide an end-to-end solution that addresses the information sharing needs for organizations of all sizes. SharePoint Team Services provides a solution for workgroup information sharing that requires little in the way of information technology (IT) support. SharePoint Portal Server effectively aggregates corporate knowledge across file servers, databases, public folders, and Internet sites in addition to Web sites created by using SharePoint Team Services.

SharePoint Team Services

With SharePoint Team Services, users can quickly create and contribute to team-focused or project-focused Web sites from within their Web browser or Office XP applications. Teams can quickly create a Web site for sharing information such as documents, calendars, announcements, and other postings. Web sites created with SharePoint Team Services are easy to customize and manage, even for those who have never created a Web site before. SharePoint Team Services is included with the Web site creation and management tool in FrontPage 2002, and versions of Office XP that contain FrontPage. Microsoft plans to include the technology in upcoming releases of the Windows Server operating system and other Microsoft products.

SharePoint Technologies Highlights

SharePoint Team Services is the team Web site solution that allows teams to create improvised workspaces to manage group activities, work together effectively, and advance on shared deliverables.

The following table describes key features in SharePoint Team Services and SharePoint Portal Server 2001.

SharePoint Team Services Features

Feature	Description
Team Web site template	Out of the box, SharePoint Team Services creates fully functional, fully designed, and configured team Web sites.
Browser-based document creation	Team members with appropriate permissions can create documents directly on the Web site from Internet Explorer 4 or later.

continued

11

SharePoint Team Services Features *continued*

Feature	Description
Pre-formatted team lists	Share team information in a structured and uniform way using built-in lists such as events, announcements, discussions, and tasks.
Document Libraries	Document libraries allow you to upload documents, assign templates to libraries, and custom properties to documents within libraries.
Subscriptions and Notifications	Subscribe to lists and document libraries and receive notification when changes meet the criteria you specify.
Document discussions	Team members can use the Web discussions feature to conduct inline discussions on documents and other Web pages without affecting the original document.
Surveys	Get a sense of where your team stands on issues that affect them by creating a team survey.
Delegated administration	Site owners and those with administrative privileges can set up user accounts for team Web sites through the browser.
Three click installation	SharePoint Team Services automatically installs the software required to search (Index Server) Web sites created with SharePoint Team Services. It stores data by using Microsoft Data Engine (MSDE).
Roles-based memberships	Web sites created with SharePoint Team Services allow site owners to assign five different levels of permissions to users according to roles. In addition, they can customize the permissions within those roles.
Browser-based customization	Members can customize existing lists using the browser by adding new properties to lists and document libraries, specifying custom views, or creating entirely new lists and document libraries with unique properties.
Integration with Office XP	Office XP integration gives users the ability to easily share information from their desktop to their team Web site and from their team Web site to their desktop.
Integration with FrontPage 2002	FrontPage 2002 provides additional opportunities for advanced customization of Web sites created with SharePoint Team Services.
ISP/ASP Support	Web Presence Providers for FrontPage support SharePoint Team Services.

SharePoint Portal Server is the flexible portal solution that lets you easily find, share, and publish information.

SharePoint Portal Server 2001 Features

Feature	Description
Enterprise Search Engine	Includes a probabilistic ranking algorithm to ensure accurate search results and adaptive crawling of content sources for up-to-date indexes. Also includes ability to tag "Best Bets" and use document profiles for easier discovery. Includes content from file servers, Web servers, Lotus Domino, or Microsoft Exchange Public Folders in an index.
Data Access and Index Services	Crawl and search file and Web servers, Microsoft Exchange Server Public Folders, Lotus Notes servers, and remote servers for SharePoint Portal Server.
Subscriptions	Subscribe to a document, folder, category, or search query so you are notified when changes are made in the dashboard site. You can also choose to be notified by e-mail.
Categories	Classify content under a set of customer-defined categories for better content management and discoverability.
High Performance Crawling	Support manual and scheduled crawls, as well as adaptive and incremental crawling, to ensure that your search results contain all the most recent information.
Search Extensibility	Search protocol handlers allow connection to custom data sources. Support custom content types through IFilters.
Office 2000, Office XP, and Windows Integration	A complete set of document management functionality is accessible directly from the Office 2000 toolbar and Windows Explorer. This helps users manage documents with familiar tools.
Check-in and Check-out	Enables optional enhanced Web folders so that individual users can reserve documents for updating.
Document Versions	Document changes, including metadata such as keywords, are tracked and assigned different version numbers for auditing and rollback.
Document Profiles	This captures optional and required metadata about customer-defined document types.
Security	Uses roles built on Microsoft Windows NT® security. SharePoint Portal Server ensures that only users with appropriate access can see a given document.

continued

SharePoint Portal Server 2001 Features *continued*

Feature	Description
Document Collaboration	Use the Web Discussions feature in Office and HTML documents for inline, content review.
Digital Dashboard-Based Portal	Digital dashboard-based user interface is built on Internet and industry standards, such as Extensible Markup Language (XML) and can be customized using Web Parts.
Integration with Enterprise System	Use pre-existing Web Parts or build your own to integrate existing enterprise systems into your corporate portal. Pre-built Web Parts are available from Microsoft for a variety of Microsoft and third party enterprise systems.

Summary

This chapter presents an overview of the features of SharePoint Portal Server 2001 and SharePoint Team Services, in addition to an overview of how the SharePoint technologies are best used together to provide the appropriate level of information management across an enterprise. For more information about SharePoint Team Services, see Appendix B, "For More Information."

CHAPTER 3

Introducing SharePoint Portal Server

Microsoft® SharePoint™ Portal Server 2001 extends the capabilities of Microsoft Windows® and Microsoft Office by offering knowledge workers a powerful new way to organize, find, and share information. For system architects and developers, SharePoint Portal Server is a solution that delivers dramatic new value by combining the ability to create corporate Web portals with document management, enterprise content indexes, and team collaboration features.

The goal of this chapter is to help you understand how SharePoint Portal Server can help you solve the content management needs of your organization.

SharePoint Portal Server Overview

As an organization creates and collects information, people spend increasing amounts of time searching, organizing, and managing that information. SharePoint Portal Server combines the ability to create corporate Web portals with searching, document management, and collaboration options. SharePoint Portal Server tightly integrates with the tools that you use every day—Windows Explorer, Office applications, and Web browsers—to help you create, manage, and share content throughout your organization.

Introducing the Dashboard Site—A "Portal in a Box"

Web portals are quickly becoming a popular means of aggregating information from many different sources into one convenient place. SharePoint Portal Server provides an easy way to create corporate Web portals and integrate document management and search.

SharePoint Portal Server creates a Web portal—known as the *dashboard site*—automatically during installation. The dashboard site offers a centralized access point for finding and managing information. By using a browser to view the dashboard site, users can perform document management tasks and find information. The dashboard site allows users to

- Browse through information by categories.

- Search for information.

- Subscribe to new or changing information.

- Check in and check out documents.

- Review a document's version history.

- Approve documents for publication.

- Publish documents.

The dashboard site provides access to information that is stored both inside and outside your organization, which allows users to find and share documents regardless of the location or format of those documents. In addition, you can customize the home page of the dashboard site to display organizational news and other important information.

The dashboard site uses Microsoft Digital Dashboard technology to organize and display information. A digital dashboard consists of reusable, customizable Web Parts that can present information from a wide variety of sources, including Office documents and Web sites. You can add or remove Web Parts to customize the dashboard site for your organization.

In addition to providing a default, organization-wide dashboard site, you can allow users to create customized "personal" dashboards to organize and present information that is especially relevant to them, such as project-specific or workgroup-specific information. Users can add content to dashboards by creating Web Parts directly from Office XP or by importing Web Parts from a catalog.

Managing and Publishing Documents

Large and complex information sources, such as a collection of file shares, can be difficult to navigate and use because there is little or no organizational framework to direct users. File shares, for instance, provide only a hierarchical directory structure as a means of organizing content. There is only one navigation path to any given document, and users must know the name of the server that the document is stored on, in addition to the directory structure of folders on the server. When you add other sources of information, such as Web sites, e-mail servers, and databases to the mix of information sources, finding the correct information can be difficult.

SharePoint Portal Server offers a number of features to help streamline your document management, such as the following:

- Version tracking to record the history of documents.

- Application of descriptive, searchable information (*metadata*) to identify a document.

- Document publishing control.

- Automated approval routes for documents to be reviewed.

- Web discussions for online comments by multiple document reviewers.

- Control of document access based on roles.

Version Control

SharePoint Portal Server records a document's history to help you track changes and eliminate the possibility of someone overwriting another user's modifications. To edit a document, you must check it out first. This prevents others from changing the document until you check it in again. Every time you check in a document, SharePoint Portal Server assigns a new version number to the document and archives the previous version. When you check out a document, you retrieve the most recent version unless you specifically select an earlier version.

Document Profiles

Document profiles provide a way to add searchable information that pertains to a document. This information, known as *metadata*, can help describe or identify the document. By default, a document profile includes basic properties, such as Author and Title. You can easily add custom properties to capture additional information that makes it easier to organize and find documents.

Document Publishing

SharePoint Portal Server can store both "private" and "public" versions of a document. You can automatically publish a document each time you check it in or you can choose to check in private drafts and publish the document only when it is complete. You can generate as many drafts as you want before you publish a version of a document. Only published documents are available for users to search or view on the dashboard site.

Approval Routes

You can use approval routes to ensure adequate review of documents before publishing. When an author chooses to publish a document, SharePoint Portal Server can send it automatically to one or more people for review before publishing it. Each of these people, called *approvers*, has the option of approving or rejecting the document.

Approvers receive e-mail notification when a document requires review. SharePoint Portal Server supports two approval routes: *One after another* (serial) and *All at once* (parallel). Figure 3.1 illustrates both models.

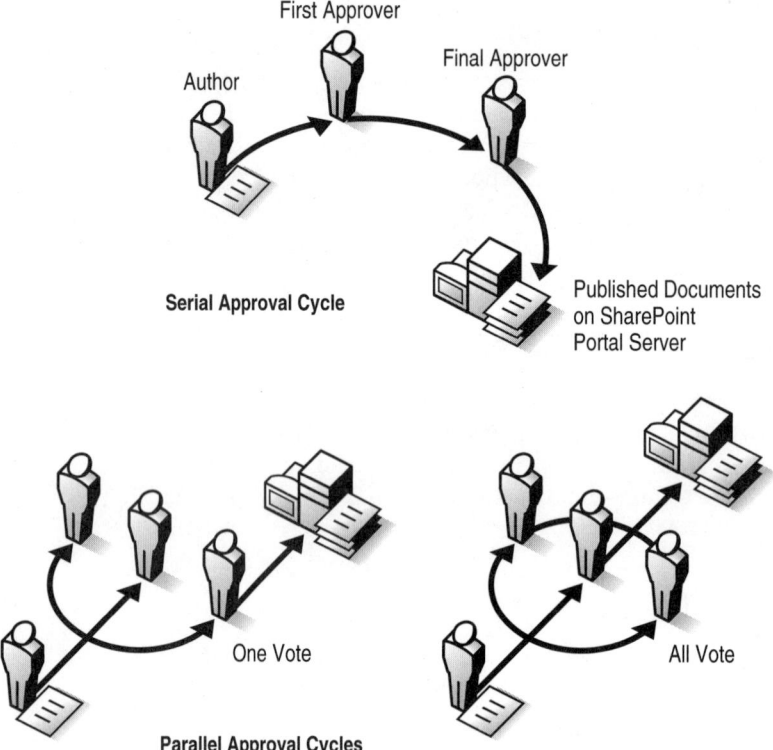

Figure 3.1. Approval routes

Web Discussions

Web discussions allow you to conduct online discussions about a document without modifying the document. Instead of using e-mail to discuss a document or trying to capture conversations about a document, authors and reviewers can now communicate with each other through Web discussions. Simultaneous discussions about a document can occur even if one person has the document checked out. Comments are stored as threaded conversations, grouping comments and replies together. With all comments grouped into a single place, authors no longer need to compile hand-written comments from reviewers or comments sent through individual e-mail messages.

Role-Based Security

SharePoint Portal Server uses *roles* to control access to content. You can assign the *coordinator*, *author*, and *reader* roles to users based on the tasks they perform. Each role identifies a specific set of permissions: coordinators handle management tasks, authors add and update files, and readers can read published documents. SharePoint Portal Server also offers the option of denying a user access to specific documents.

Searching Content and Creating Indexes

An organization's information is usually stored in multiple locations, in a variety of formats. Even if a server infrastructure allows searches across multiple data stores, often only limited text searches are available. It can also be difficult to determine whether the results that these simple searches provide are relevant.

Whether you are searching for a specific document or you just want to browse through a group of related documents, SharePoint Portal Server has several features that help you find information quickly and easily.

To make information easier to find, SharePoint Portal Server offers

- A single location to search for information stored in many different places.

- Keyword searches that query the full text of a document and the document's properties.

- Browsing by topic (categories) to find information.

- Automatic categorization of documents.

- Best Bet classification for documents that are highly relevant to a search.

- Subscriptions to keep you updated on useful information.

Full-Text Search

The dashboard site provides a full-text search option so that you can search document text and document properties for the keywords that you type. SharePoint Portal Server finds all documents that match your search and returns a list of results. For a more specific search, you can use the advanced search option to add document properties, such as Author, to your search criteria. You can also narrow your search scope to search only a specific set of documents, such as a folder for press releases or a supplier's Web site. In addition to searching from the dashboard site, you can also search content that is included in the index by SharePoint Portal Server from within Office XP applications.

Content Sources

Organizations keep information in a variety of places such as Web sites, file systems, public folders on mail servers, and databases. SharePoint Portal Server improves search efficiency by enabling you to search across all of these information sources at the same time. In SharePoint Portal Server, each of these information sources is known as a *content source*. By using a wizard to add a content source, you identify the location of the content that you want to make available for searching and link that content to your dashboard site. SharePoint Portal Server then includes information from each content source in the index. Users can perform quick searches on this content from the dashboard site. With the addition of content sources, the dashboard site is the easiest place to find information, regardless of its location or format.

Categories

You can organize information on the dashboard site by using categories to group similar documents. This allows users to browse through information by topic. For users who do not know where documents are stored, categories help them find what they need. Another advantage is that a document can appear in several different categories. Categories can include documents that are stored in SharePoint Portal Server and information from additional content sources.

Category Assistant

Categories are an excellent way to organize your information. However, if you have a large number of documents, categorizing them can be a time-consuming task. To simplify the process, SharePoint Portal Server provides an automated categorization tool called Category Assistant. After you have categorized a few representative documents for each category, Category Assistant compares those sample documents to the uncategorized documents, and then selects the best category matches based on the content in the uncategorized documents.

Best Bets

Best Bets guide users by directing them to documents that are particularly relevant to their search. A *Best Bet* is a document that is selected as the best recommendation for a category or specific keyword. SharePoint Portal Server displays Best Bets at the top of a search results list.

Subscriptions

Subscriptions notify you about new or updated information on topics that match your interests. You can subscribe to content you find useful: a specific document, all documents in a folder, all documents assigned to a category, or a set of search results. After you subscribe to content, SharePoint Portal Server notifies you when the content is modified, if a new document matching your criteria is available, or if Web discussion comments about the content are added. You can view your subscription notifications on the dashboard site. You can also choose to receive notifications by e-mail.

SharePoint Portal Server Architecture

SharePoint Portal Server integrates with and makes use of key Microsoft technologies, including Windows, digital dashboards, Office, Microsoft Internet Explorer, the Microsoft Exchange Server Web Storage System, and Microsoft Search Service. Figure 3.2 represents an overview of the SharePoint Portal Server product architecture.

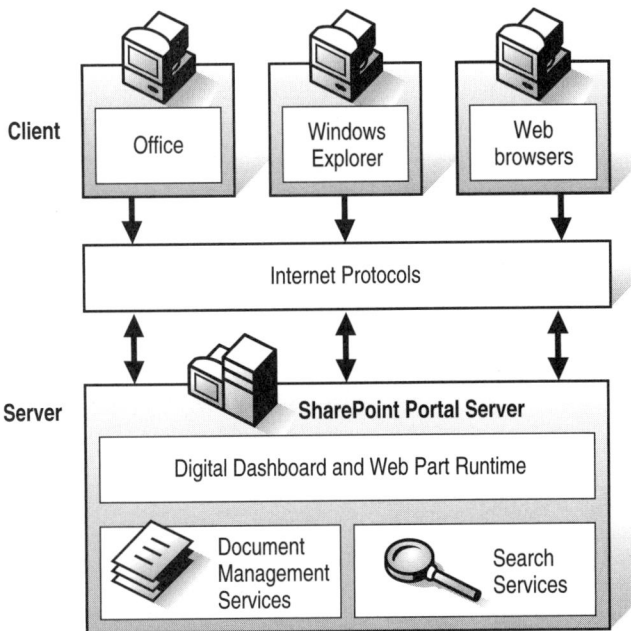

Figure 3.2. SharePoint Portal Server architecture overview

The client components consist of extensions to Office applications and Windows Explorer. These components allow users to perform document management and search tasks within those applications. The dashboard site, viewed through a browser, provides a Web-based view of the document management and search services the product provides. The core server components include document management services, search services, and the Digital Dashboard and Web Part run-time environment.

Client Components

The client components of SharePoint Portal Server consist of functional extensions to Office and Windows Explorer that enable document management functions within those applications. For example, after you modify a Microsoft Word document that you checked out from a SharePoint Portal Server workspace, you can go to the **File** menu in Word and select the **Check In** command. Alternatively, you can use Windows Explorer to view and perform document management operations on files contained in a SharePoint Portal Server workspace. The rich search capabilities of SharePoint Portal Server are also available from within Office XP when you connect to the workspace that you want to search through Web folders.

> **Note** Office XP includes the client components of SharePoint Portal Server. Users of earlier versions of Office must run a simple client setup program that is provided with SharePoint Portal Server to add document management functionality.

In addition to providing an aggregation point for a wide variety of content, the dashboard site also provides access to the document management and search capabilities of SharePoint Portal Server. Users can interact with the dashboard site by using their favorite browser.

These client components communicate with the server components using standard Internet protocols.

Server Components

The server components of SharePoint Portal Server provide the services for document management and search. In addition, the Digital Dashboard and Web Part runtime provide the functionality that allows administrators and users to create their own dashboard sites to aggregate content into a single source.

Document Management Services

The document management services consist of a store (based on Microsoft Web Storage System technology) and the services that facilitate document management functions like check-in, check-out, and document versioning.

Search Services

SharePoint Portal Server makes use of Microsoft Search—the Microsoft world-class search technology for creating indexes, searching, and retrieving content in the local document store, in addition to external content sources.

The Microsoft Search Service has four main components that perform the following functions:

- Crawl the collected content of a set of URLs for inclusion in an index.

  The *Gatherer* component can find its way to a wide variety of content sources, including SharePoint Portal Server workspaces, Web servers, file servers, Exchange 2000 public folders, and Lotus Notes databases. Customers can extend the reach of SharePoint Portal Server to additional types of content by using the product's software development kit (SDK) to create custom *protocol handlers* that tell the product how to retrieve data from specific sources.

- Parse or filter the document to extract the relevant metadata and content.

  SharePoint Portal Server includes filters for a variety of document types, including HTML, Office documents, text files, and Tagged Image File Format (TIFF) image files. Developers can learn how to create custom filters, known as *IFilters,* from the Microsoft Search section of the product's SDK.

- Include the data retrieved by the Gatherer component in an index.

  The *Indexer* component uses language-specific word breakers and stemmers to extract words from the content. Then "noise" words, (for example, a, the, of) are filtered out, and the content index is generated. SharePoint Portal Server provides specific-language support for English, French, Spanish, Italian, German, Traditional Chinese, Simplified Chinese, Korean, Thai, Dutch, Swedish, and Japanese. SharePoint Portal Server uses a "neutral" word breaker for all other languages.

  Note You do not need to have a localized version of SharePoint Portal Server to take advantage of this language-specific support for indexes. SharePoint Portal Server supports all the languages listed previously in each language version of the product.

- Perform searches for content. Users can submit search queries from the Search page of the dashboard site or from Office XP applications. In addition, developers can issue searches programmatically in the form of Microsoft ActiveX® Data Objects (ADO) or WebDAV SQL search queries.

Digital Dashboard and Web Part Runtime

These server components manage all functions related to presenting the SharePoint Portal Server dashboard site through a browser. It displays the user interface and enables dashboard site customization by administrators and coordinators. In addition, this run-time component services requests from Web Parts that are displayed on the dashboard site.

Configuration Flexibility

Different organizations can use SharePoint Portal Server in different ways. Some want to make use of the product's document management features, whereas others want to take advantage of the sophisticated search capabilities to provide access to documents that are stored across multiple information stores. SharePoint Portal Server provides the flexibility to handle the following scenarios:

- Hundreds of thousands of documents stored in a single server, single document management workspace.

- Hundreds of thousands of documents using a similar single server configuration where a majority of the content is stored on external information stores.

- Millions of documents when dedicated SharePoint Portal Server content index and search server configurations are used to crawl external content stores for inclusion in an index.

The scenarios that follow are examples of how the configuration flexibility of SharePoint Portal Server accommodates each of these distinct sets of requirements.

Group Collaboration

In this scenario, illustrated in Figure 3.3, a department's primary requirements include the ability to create documents, implement version control, and publish documents within the group.

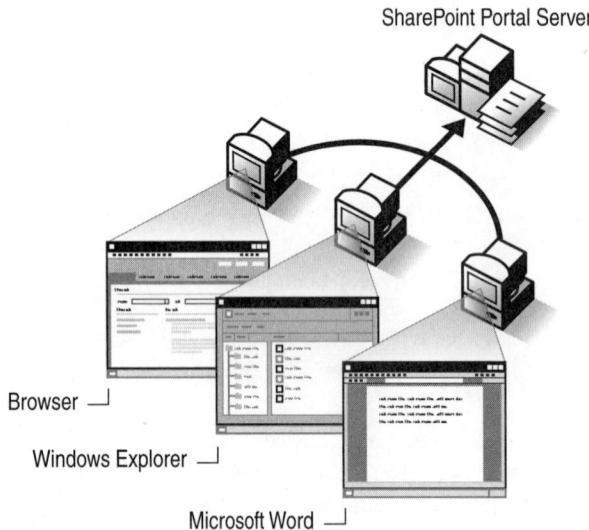

SharePoint Portal Server

Browser ⌐

Windows Explorer ⌐

Microsoft Word ⌐

Figure 3.3. Single server configuration for document management

In this example, the team sets up a single SharePoint Portal Server computer with a workspace that consists almost entirely of content stored locally. The amount of content stored outside the workspace is small and consists of content sources pointing to one or two competitors' Web sites. The emphasis is on the document management capabilities of SharePoint Portal Server rather than its search capabilities.

Information Search Services

In this scenario, illustrated in Figure 3.4, a group uses SharePoint Portal Server to search content stored on its file servers, database servers, and an Internet Web site. The dashboard site also displays organization-wide communication such as announcements, holiday schedules, and human resources information.

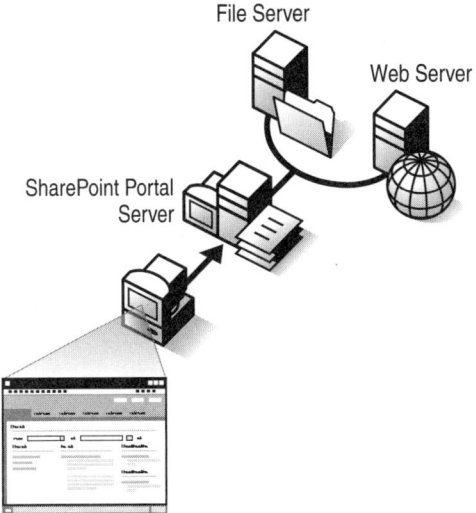

Figure 3.4. Single server configuration for search services

The SharePoint Portal Server computer stores indexes for the configured content sources and makes them available to the dashboard site associated with the workspace. In addition to the content sources that link to documents that are stored outside the workspace, the workspace itself can contain documents. The group primarily searches its own content, with limited searching on Internet sites. Document management is required only for the documents stored in the workspace. The only users performing document management tasks are those responsible for updating the dashboard site.

Aggregated Search and Document Management

When your organization needs division-wide or enterprise-wide search capabilities across a wide variety of content sources, you can increase performance and efficiency by deploying SharePoint Portal Server on multiple servers that perform dedicated tasks. For example, you can configure one server to be dedicated to creating indexes and another to function as a search and dashboard site server.

The configuration shown in Figure 3.5 supports an intranet site for an organization that needs extended search functionality but has limited document management needs. This deployment uses two SharePoint Portal Server computers: a server dedicated to creating and maintaining indexes and a server dedicated to searching. One server performs the tasks that relate to the creation and maintenance of indexes through an *index workspace*; the other server, which is used for searching, stores workspace content and provides the dashboard site that is associated with the workspace.

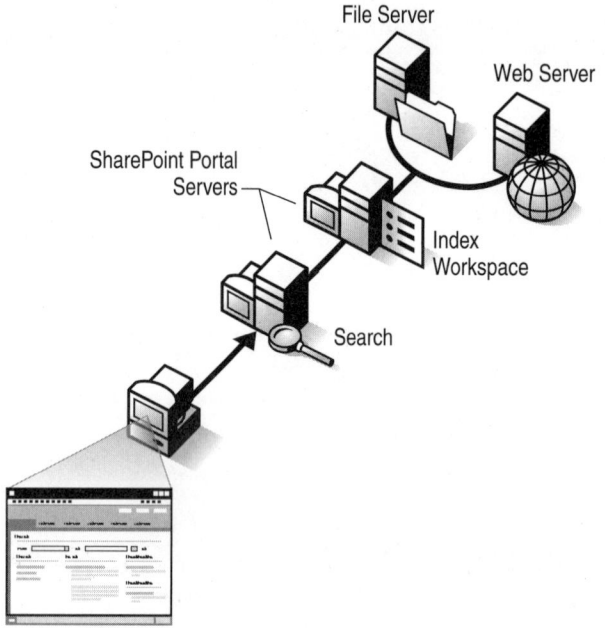

Figure 3.5. Multiple-server configuration for enterprise-level search services

For example, an organization uses SharePoint Portal Server to search content stored on its file servers, Lotus Notes database servers, intranet sites, and the Web sites of several competitors. The server with the index workspace creates an index of this content and then propagates the index to the search server. The search server provides the dashboard site that is used for searching this content and stores the documents that are displayed on the dashboard site, such as announcements, holiday schedules, and company press releases.

The *index workspace*, located on the server that creates and maintains indexes, is dedicated to the resource-intensive task of creating an index of content stored outside the workspace. This index workspace stores only indexes that are associated with content sources. After SharePoint Portal Server creates the index, it propagates the index to the server that is used for searching. SharePoint Portal Server can propagate the index immediately after creating it, or you can schedule propagation to coincide with periods of low network traffic.

On the server that is dedicated to search services and the dashboard site, search queries encompass both intranet and Internet content. Only users who are responsible for configuring and updating the dashboard site can perform document management tasks.

This deployment configuration supports an intranet site for an organization that needs extended search functionality but has limited document management needs. This deployment uses two SharePoint Portal Server computers: a server dedicated to creating and maintaining indexes and a server dedicated to searching. The server with the index workspace performs the tasks relating to creating and maintaining indexes; the search server stores workspace content and provides the dashboard site associated with the workspace.

The configuration shown in Figure 3.6 supports an organization that requires both document management features and robust search capability. This deployment includes at least three SharePoint Portal Server computers: a server dedicated to searching, a server dedicated to creating and maintaining indexes, and one or more document management servers. It is important to include a sufficient number of document management servers to support users who require the document management functionality. For example, each division in a large organization might have a document management server.

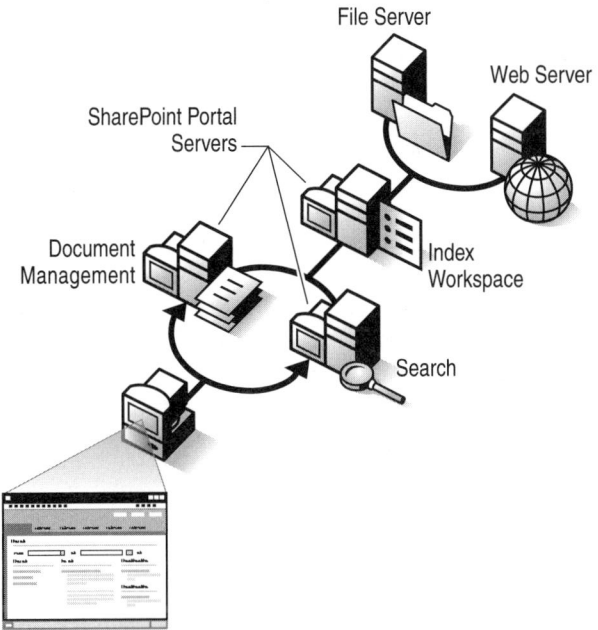

Figure 3.6. Multiple-server configuration for enterprise-level document management and search services

The document management server stores documents in its workspace. The index workspace, located on the server that is dedicated to creating and crawling indexes, creates an index of all the content on each document management server, in addition to other content from the intranet and Internet. The index workspace propagates its index to the search server. The search server provides the dashboard site that is used for searching this content and stores documents that are displayed on the dashboard site, such as announcements, holiday schedules, and organization information.

Organizations can also choose to duplicate read-only versions of the search server in this topology to provide improved response time across a geographically dispersed network. For example, you could have a search server located in your company's headquarters in Geneva duplicated to Singapore, New York, and Vancouver. Users in those locations would be able to view the dashboard site and perform searches without having response times slowed by low-bandwidth network connections.

Summary

This chapter describes how SharePoint Portal Server can help you solve the content management needs of your organization. It introduces the document management and search features, presents an overview of the product architecture, and presents basic configuration options.

CHAPTER 4

Introducing the Dashboard Site

This chapter presents the dashboard site, the Web-based component of Microsoft® SharePoint™ Portal Server 2001. It introduces the default dashboard site and presents information about customizing the dashboard site to suit your organization's needs. It provides an overview of the components of the dashboard site and describes the primary management tasks and security issues associated with it.

Based on Microsoft Digital Dashboard technology, the dashboard site offers a single customizable source for accessing information drawn from a wide variety of content sources while it maintains the security of the documents. Because the dashboard site is composed entirely of Web Parts, you can easily customize it for your business needs. By using Digital Dashboard technology, you can also manage common resources, such as your contacts, calendars, and messages.

Key Concepts and Terminology

The dashboard site is part of the total portal solution provided by SharePoint Portal Server. Designed to provide flexibility, the dashboard site provides the primary view of the portal. With SharePoint Portal Server, you create a portal that uses Web Parts and digital dashboards to present content. You can use third-party Web Parts or create your own Web Parts.

SharePoint Portal Server relies on the following:

- **Web Storage System.** Built-in services for building Web-based collaborative applications.

- **Standard Tools.** Develop solutions by using familiar tools like Microsoft Visual Studio®.

- **Standard Interfaces.** Use common interfaces like Microsoft ActiveX® Data Objects (ADO), Extensible Markup Language (XML), and Hypertext Transfer Protocol (HTTP) Web Distributed Authoring and Versioning (WebDAV).

For more information about developing additional solutions for SharePoint Portal Server, see Appendix B, "For More Information."

SharePoint Portal Server Terminology

The dashboard site offers a single customizable source for accessing information drawn from a wide variety of content sources while maintaining the security of the documents. External content sources can include other SharePoint Portal Server workspaces, intranet or Internet sites, Microsoft Exchange 2000 and Microsoft Exchange Server 5.5 public folder hierarchies, Lotus Notes 4.6a+ and R5 databases, local file systems, and network file servers.

Workspace. The workspace is an organized collection of documents, content sources, management folders, categories, document profiles, subscriptions, and discussions. It provides a central location to organize, manage, and publish content.

Dashboard site. The dashboard site is a specialized Web site that SharePoint Portal Server creates at the same time as the associated workspace. The dashboard site provides a Web view of the workspace and enables users assigned to appropriate roles to search for, view, and manage documents in the workspace and to search for and view content from other sources. The dashboard site contains a number of pages, or dashboards, and includes customization pages and custom Web Part forms.

Dashboard. A dashboard is a Web page on the dashboard site. Each dashboard contains a collection of Web Parts in a modular view that SharePoint Portal Server presents to users in a Web browser.

Web Part. A Web Part is a customizable, reusable component used to display specific information on a dashboard. SharePoint Portal Server uses Web Parts to associate Web-based content (such as XML, HTML, and scripting) with a specific set of properties in an organizational framework.

Folders for Web Parts. Located under the Portal Content folder, SharePoint Portal Server associates these folders with specific default Web Parts on the dashboard site. SharePoint Portal Server applies a specific document profile to documents according to the folder in which it is stored. For example, the Quick Links folder is associated with the Quick Links Web Part and applies the Quick Links document profile to all of the documents it contains.

For more information about Digital Dashboard technology, see Appendix B, "For More Information."

Reviewing the Default Dashboard Site

The dashboard site is composed of multiple dashboards. The first default dashboard is called the home page. Figure 4.1 shows the default home page of the dashboard site.

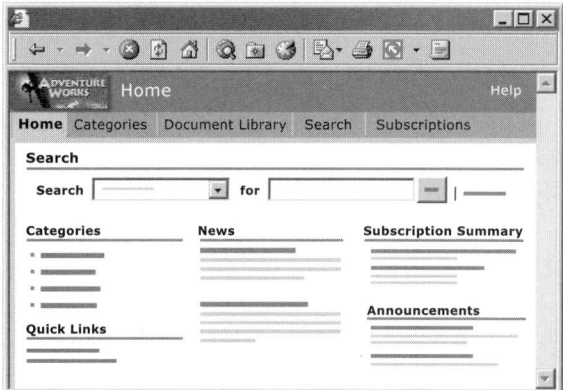

Figure 4.1. The home page of the dashboard site

The home page is the first page you see when browsing the default dashboard site. From this page, you can access all of the other dashboards on the site, and view information in the Web Parts.

The default dashboard contains the following items:

- A customizable site title

- A customizable dashboard site logo

- A Search Web Part containing a search bar with a drop-down menu from which users can select search scopes, and a text box in which users can type search terms

- A set of site navigation buttons that link to other dashboards: Home, Document Library, Categories, Subscriptions, and Help

Depending on your role, other links that allow you to perform management tasks may be available.

The default home page contains four additional default Web Parts—News, Announcements, Quick Links, and Subscriptions Summary:

- **The News Web Part.** Displays general items of interest, such as company news, departmental news, or stories from news services. For example, the News Web Part on the home page of a sales and marketing group might display quarterly sales figures or press releases.

- **The Announcements Web Part.** Displays company announcements, departmental events, and so on. For example, the Announcements Web Part in the dashboard site of a sales and marketing group might contain announcements regarding a new employee or a reminder about a department meeting.

- **The Quick Links Web Part.** Displays links to other information of interest, such as company resources. For example, the Quick Links Web Part in the dashboard site of a human resources group might contain links to job openings or benefits information.

- **The Subscriptions Summary Web Part.** Provides a summary of the current user's subscription notifications. If you find a document, folder, category, or a set of search results useful, you can subscribe to the content and SharePoint Portal Server notifies you of changes.

You can add value to your dashboard site by adding Web Parts that display business information such as news headlines and stock tickers, collaboration tools such as Microsoft Outlook®, or general information such as weather or driving directions.

Access the Dashboard Site

Users access the dashboard site through a Web browser, such as Microsoft Internet Explorer or Netscape Navigator. The user is not required to install the client components to access SharePoint Portal Server through the dashboard site.

For the Microsoft Windows® operating system, you can use the following browsers:

- Microsoft Internet Explorer 4.01 or later

- Netscape Navigator 4.51 or later (for Italian and Spanish versions of SharePoint Portal Server)

- Netscape Navigator 4.7x or later (for English, French, German, and Japanese versions of SharePoint Portal Server)

No other operating systems or Web browsers are currently supported.

In addition, you must enable Microsoft JScript® or Netscape JavaScript support in your browser for the dashboard site to function.

To use the dashboard site with Netscape Navigator, you must use Internet Services Manager to enable Basic authentication for the workspace on the default Web site. To enable discussions to work with Netscape Navigator, you must also enable Basic authentication for the MSOffice node.

Find Additional Pages from the Home Page

Navigation links appear at the top of every dashboard page.

All users can access the following sub-dashboards or pages of the default dashboard site:

- **Home.** Return to the Home page. Because this is a customizable link, the name may change.

- **Categories.** View a list of categories and subcategories.

- **Document Library.** View the folders and subfolders containing the contents of the workspace. Users associated with the proper role can manage their documents from the Document Library.

- **Search.** Conduct simple and advanced search queries.

- **Subscriptions.** View all of your current subscriptions in detail.

- **Help.** Access the Dashboard Site Help.

Users assigned to the role of coordinator can access the following additional sub-dashboards or pages.

- **Management.** Manage another user's subscriptions, manage Web discussions on the workspace, and empty the application cache for the dashboard site.

- **Content.** Customize and manage the Web Parts that appear on the pages of the dashboard site, and then specify the content that appears in those Web Parts.

- **Settings.** Customize and manage dashboard settings.

- **Layout.** Customize dashboard layout.

In addition, if your coordinator has enabled this option, you may also be able to access additional personal dashboards.

Security and the Dashboard Site

SharePoint Portal Server uses role-based security to control access to content, regardless of whether the user is accessing content by using a Web browser, Web folders, or a Microsoft Office application. SharePoint Portal Server uses a fixed set of three roles to offer a flexible and secure method for controlling user access to content. You cannot modify the permissions associated with a specific role. Although you can assign roles at the top level of the workspace, you generally assign roles on folders in the workspace. In addition, you can completely deny a user or group access to a specific document.

- **Specify security in the workspace.** By using Web folders, you assign users to roles for specific folders and documents in the workspace.

    Note You cannot specify security from the dashboard site.

- **Security on the dashboard site.** Users accessing content from the dashboard site only view content for which they are assigned an appropriate role.

The role-based security model provided with SharePoint Portal Server allows you to customize access to content for viewing on the dashboard site. For more information about role-based security in SharePoint Portal Server, see Chapter 8, "Planning Security."

Modifying Security to Allow Personal Dashboards

Only users who are authors or coordinators on the **Dashboards** folder can create new personal dashboards. A coordinator at the workspace level must change the assigned roles for users on this folder if they are not already authors or coordinators.

If, as a workspace coordinator, you want to allow several people in the organization to create personal dashboards, it is recommended that you assign roles that use domain groups rather than individuals. For example, if you want everybody in your organization to have the ability to create a personal dashboard, you could add the Windows 2000 Everyone group to the **Dashboards** folder and assign the author role to that group.

Understanding Folder Inheritance Settings and Personal Dashboards

By default, the **Dashboards** folder does not inherit security settings from the workspace. As a result, to allow users to create or modify personal dashboards, you must assign the user an appropriate role to the **Dashboards** folder.

Content Access from the Dashboard Site

The dashboard site offers a centralized access point for finding and managing information. Through the dashboard site, users with appropriate permissions can search for and share documents, regardless of location or format.

Enhancing Search Results

To improve the quality of search results on the dashboard site, you can customize and use the following features.

Create Document Profiles

Document profiles help organize folders and documents and enhance searching on the dashboard site.

You can create document profiles by using the Add Document Profile Wizard in the **Document Profiles** folder, which is located in the top-level **Management** folder.

Users can assign document profiles to their documents by using the **Profiles** tab on the Properties page of each document, or, for documents stored in an enhanced folder, by selecting a document profile on the check in form. Users can also modify and assign document profiles from the dashboard site.

Identify Content Sources

Content sources serve as starting places from which dashboard site users can search for and view documents that are stored outside the workspace in sources such as Web sites, file shares, and databases. Figure 4.2 illustrates the variety of possible content sources.

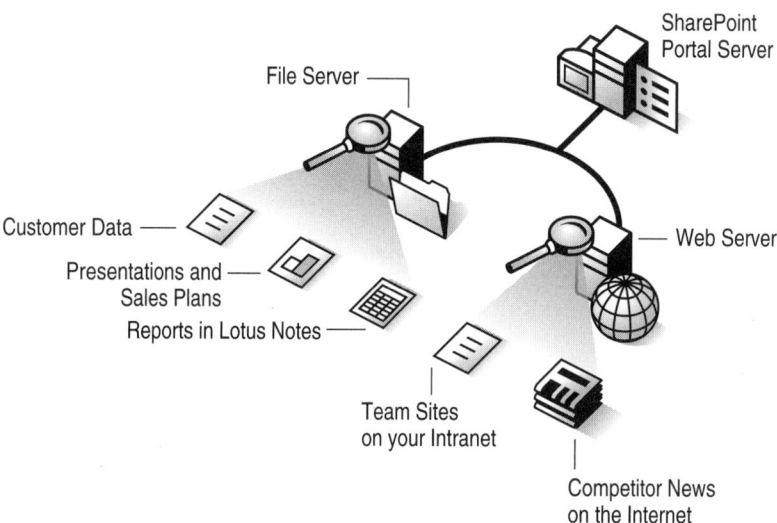

Figure 4.2. Possible content sources

You use the Add Content Source Wizard to create and store content sources in the **Content Sources** folder, which is located in the **Management** folder.

Use Categories to Organize Documents

Categories provide an easy way to locate documents on the dashboard site and organize documents into a hierarchy of topics and subtopics. Categories serve two purposes. First, they provide a centralized structure for information browsing. Categories direct readers to the information they seek through an organized hierarchy of topics. Second, they provide a consistent, controlled set of values that you can add as document metadata. Categories provide a flexible way both to describe and to find documents.

You can create categories to use in the workspace by using the **New Category** command in the **Categories** folder. You can categorize large numbers of documents by using the Category Assistant. You train and start the Category Assistant from the Properties page of the **Categories** folder in the workspace.

Identify Best Bets

Best Bets enhance search efficiency and provide guidance to users by directing them to documents considered particularly relevant to their search. A Best Bet is a document selected as the best recommendation for a category or specific keyword. SharePoint Portal Server displays Best Bets at the top of a search results list.

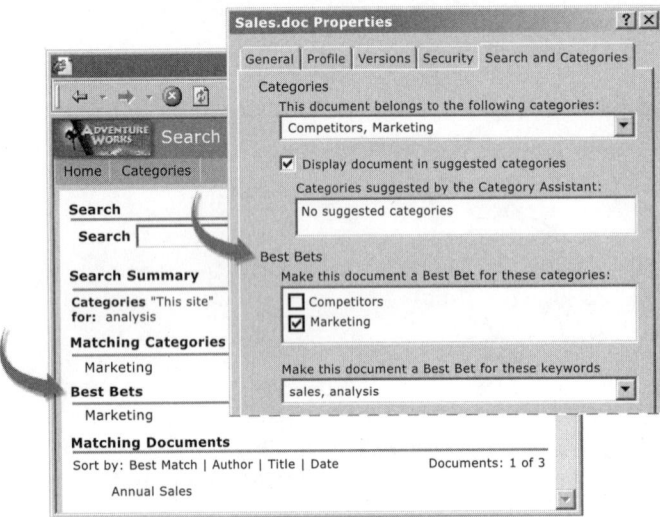

Figure 4.3. Best Bets

Keyword Best Bets

A Keyword Best Bet is highly relevant to a keyword. It appears in search results when a user enters that keyword in a query. For example, a coordinator might select the Manufacturing home page as a Best Bet for the keyword "inventory." If someone then searched for "inventory," the search results page would display a link to the Manufacturing home page at the top of the search results.

Category Best Bets

A Category Best Bet is a document that is highly relevant to a particular category. For example, the Marketing category for competitor case studies might have a product analysis of Clocktower Sporting Goods as a Category Best Bet. SharePoint Portal Server prominently displays category Best Bets in category listings on the dashboard site, just as SharePoint Portal Server prominently displays Keyword Best Bets in search results.

You can select a document as a Best Bet for more than one category or keyword. You can also select multiple documents as Best Bets for the same category or keyword. You can select a document as a Best Bet only if you have coordinator privileges for the folder in which the document is stored.

> **Important** You can include an external document in categories or identify it as a Best Bet by creating a shortcut to the document within the **Documents** folder. When you add the shortcut to the **Documents** folder, SharePoint Portal Server prompts you with a profile form. Depending on the document profile you choose, you can add keywords and category information. This allows SharePoint Portal Server to include the external document in categories or as a Best Bet.

Customizing Search Results

In addition to providing default search scopes, SharePoint Portal Server allows you to create custom search scopes for use on the dashboard site. You can also affect search results by modifying the thesaurus.

For more information about customizing search results, see Appendix B.

Create Custom Search Queries

You can create custom search queries by using your preferred application programming interface (API) and programming application.

You can create an Active Server Pages (ASP) page, a Web Part for the digital dashboard, or a Microsoft Visual Basic® or Microsoft Visual C++® application containing a specific search query tailored to the needs of your organization. The dashboard site included with SharePoint Portal Server is a collection of digital dashboards that communicates with the Web Storage System by using the Distributed Authoring and Versioning (DAV) protocol with the XMLHTTPRequest object. SharePoint Portal Server displays results in XML. You can use ADO to access the OLEDB Provider for Internet Publishing to create custom search queries.

Use the Thesaurus to Expand a Search Query

You can use the thesaurus included with SharePoint Portal Server to adjust search results for the benefit of your users. To improve search results on the dashboard site, you can edit the thesaurus to expand queries. This means that a user can enter one word in a search query and receive search results for a similar word. For example, the user can search for "IE" and receive matches to "Internet Explorer" in the search results.

Sharing Information as an Author

SharePoint Portal Server offers a number of features to help streamline document development. Once the coordinator prepares the workspace and makes information accessible, you can perform most tasks directly from the dashboard site by using your Web browser:

- Adding and Removing Documents
- Check-in and Check-out
- Publishing
- Approving and Rejecting Documents

For more information about how to perform these tasks, see Appendix B.

Finding Information as a Reader

SharePoint Portal Server provides a flexible solution for users to find information. As a reader, you can use the dashboard site for the following:

- Conducting Search Queries
- Accessing Content Sources
- Performing Full-Text Search Queries
- Finding Information Based on Document Profiles
- Browsing Categories
- Browsing the Document Library
- Using Best Bets
- Creating Subscriptions

These features allow you to direct your users to the most appropriate method for finding information based on their knowledge and skill level.

Management of the Dashboard Site

With SharePoint Portal Server you can decide your own level of customization for the dashboard site. The default dashboard site lets you quickly deploy an out-of-the-box total portal solution that facilitates finding, creating, and sharing all of your mission-critical data.

You can access the Management page on the dashboard site only if you are a coordinator on the **Portal** folder in the workspace. By using this page, you can manage other users' subscriptions, manage discussions on the workspace, and flush the application cache for the dashboard site.

In addition, you must be a coordinator on the **Portal** folder in the workspace to customize the dashboard site and the Web Parts that make up the content of the individual dashboard pages. The Content, Layout, and Settings management pages, accessed through links at the top right of the dashboard site, provide the tools for dashboard customization. In order to customize a personal dashboard, you must be a coordinator for the individual dashboard folder.

Customizing the Appearance of Your Dashboard Site

You can customize the appearance of the dashboard site for your organization by modifying the following elements:

- Dashboard title

- Dashboard description

- Dashboard image and logo

- Font style, size, and color

- Web Part layout

Coordinators at the workspace level have access to three management pages on the dashboard site to update the content and appearance. You can change the style settings (colors and fonts on the dashboard) by using the Settings management page. You can view and modify the layout of Web Parts on a dashboard by using the Layout management page. To add new Web parts, use the Content management page.

Modify Settings

To edit the settings for a particular dashboard, on the navigation bar of the home page, click the link for that dashboard. To open the Settings management page for that dashboard, click **Settings**. Use the controls on the Settings management page to edit the following settings for the dashboard:

- Dashboard Name, Caption, and Description

- Predefined Style

- Refresh Rate

For more information about dashboard settings, see Appendix B.

Change the Layout

SharePoint Portal Server creates a dashboard from a customizable assortment of Web Parts, which are discrete units that contain specific sets of information. You can view and modify how these Web Parts appear by using the Layout management page.

SharePoint Portal Server arranges the dashboard in a framework that consists of five different sections. This framework and the sections that it contains appear in an outline on the Layout management page. Each section can contain several Web Parts. If a section is empty or does not contain any Web Parts, that section does not appear on the dashboard.

Although you can configure the dashboard to support a framework with any number of sections, a given dashboard implementation can support only a single framework at a time. You can change the basic default framework only by rewriting the dashboard implementation. Only a developer familiar with the Microsoft Digital Dashboard architecture should perform this task. Consider the following points when configuring the layout of a dashboard:

The position and order in which SharePoint Portal Server displays the Web Parts contributes to the effectiveness and usability of your dashboard. Experiment with different Web Part arrangements to make the best use of your dashboard space.

You cannot add new Web Parts to the dashboard from the Layout management page. To add new Web Parts, go to the Content management page.

> **Important** You must use Internet Explorer 5 or later to access the link to the Layout management page. For Internet Explorer 4 and for Netscape Navigator, SharePoint Portal Server does not display the Layout link because these browsers do not fully support required actions on the Layout management page.

Modifying Default Content

To configure Web Parts for a particular dashboard, on the navigation bar of the home page, click the link for that dashboard. To open the Content page for that dashboard, click **Content**.

- **Add content to existing Web Parts.** You can add content to default Web Parts.

- **Add or Remove Web Parts.** You can add and remove Web Parts from a dashboard.

For more information about customizing dashboard content, see Appendix B.

Add Content to Default Web Parts

The coordinator configures the links to the content that appears in the default Web Parts by adding documents to the News, Announcements, or Quick Links subfolders in the **Dashboard Site** folder in the workspace.

- The News Web Part lists general items of interest, such as company news, departmental news, stories from news services (for example, the Associated Press), and so on. For example, the News Web Part in the dashboard site of a sales and marketing group might contain links to all of the current press releases.

- The Announcements Web Part lists company announcements, departmental events, and so on. For example, the Announcements Web Part in the dashboard site of a sales and marketing group might contain announcements regarding a new employee, exceptionally high quarterly sales figures, or a departmental picnic.

- The Quick Links Web Part contains links to other content of interest, such as company resources. For example, the Quick Links Web Part in the dashboard site of a human resources group might contain links to employee information, project schedules, or benefits information.

   Important If you associate the Link property with an item, SharePoint Portal Server renders the hyperlink for that item as a hyperlink to the link target rather than a hyperlink to the item itself. SharePoint Portal Server crawls the Link target and makes the content of the Link target available for full-text searching.

Add and Remove Web Parts

Use the Content page to choose the Web Parts that appear on the dashboard. To configure Web Parts for a particular dashboard, click the link for that dashboard on the navigation bar of the home page. To open the Content management page for that dashboard, click **Content**. Use the controls to select the Web Parts that appear on the dashboard.

Importing and Creating Web Parts

There are three ways to add Web Parts to a dashboard. You can choose from the following:

- **Import from a Catalog.** SharePoint Portal Server provides a default catalog. As a coordinator, you can add additional catalogs.

- **Create from Office XP.** By using Microsoft Office XP, you can create Web Parts quickly and easily.

- **Create Custom Web Parts.** You can develop your own Web Parts and import them to a dashboard.

Import Web Parts from a Catalog

Add Web content to your dashboard by using Web Parts from a pre-existing catalog of Web Parts.

To import a Web Part from a catalog to your dashboard:

   1. From your Web browser, open the dashboard to which you want to add a Web Part.

   2. Click **Content**.

   3. In the **Web Part Catalogs** section, click **Microsoft Web Part Gallery**.

   Note Depending on whether a coordinator has customized the dashboard site, there may be other catalogs available as well.

4. Select the Web Parts you want to add to the dashboard.

5. Click **Import**. SharePoint Portal Server adds the new Web Part.

> **Note** If necessary, you can change the layout and settings for these parts on your dashboard from the Layout and Settings links. You can also change dashboard content at any time by clicking **Content** on the dashboard title bar.

Create Web Parts from Office XP Documents

Office XP documents that you save to a dashboard folder automatically become Web Parts for that dashboard.

To save a document from an Office XP application as a Web Part for a dashboard:

1. On the **File** menu of an Office XP application, click **Save As Web Page**.

2. In the dialog box, click **Web folders**, and then double-click a Web folder linked to a workspace to open it.

3. Click the folder, and then double-click the appropriate folder to select it as the destination folder for the document.

> **Note** To save a Web Part to an existing dashboard, choose the **Portal** folder and then the appropriate subfolder. By default, the **Portal** folder is hidden. You must be assigned to the coordinator role at the workspace level to add or modify content in the **Portal** folder. To save a Web Part to a personal dashboard, choose the **Dashboards** folder and then the appropriate subfolder. You must be assigned to the coordinator or author role to add or modify content in the **Dashboards** folder.

4. Verify the file type and file name for the Web Part, and then click **Save**.

SharePoint Portal Server displays a form to specify a title and a description for the Web Part along with the position on the page in which it should appear on the dashboard.

5. Click **OK**.

The new Web Part appears on the dashboard.

> **Note** If necessary, you can change the layout and settings for these parts on your dashboard from the Layout and Settings links. You can also change dashboard content at any time by clicking **Content** on the dashboard title bar.

Create Custom Web Parts

You can create your own Web Parts in many different ways. One of the easiest ways is to create one from existing Web content by using a URL. You can also create a Web Part that uses embedded Microsoft Visual Basic Scripting Edition (VBScript) or JavaScript to generate the content to display on your dashboard.

To create a Web Part from SharePoint Portal Server:

1. From your Web browser, open the dashboard to which you want to add a Web Part.

2. Click **Content**.

   Important Only the original creator of the dashboard or a coordinator on the folder for the personal dashboard can access the Content link.

3. Click **Create a New Web Part**. Type the name and description of the Web Part, and then choose the layout position.

4. Click **Save**.

Enabling Personal Dashboards

You can create your own custom dashboards using the Personal Dashboard Web Part. For example, you can use the Personal Dashboard Web Part to create a dashboard for a specific project, team, or collection of data.

Personal dashboards are dashboards created by users that consist of one or more Web Parts chosen by the creator. You can import Web Parts from a catalog, create Web Parts by saving content from Office XP as a Web Part, or create custom Web Parts directly from SharePoint Portal Server.

Personal dashboards are stored as folders in the **Dashboards** folder at the root of the workspace (http://server/workspace/Dashboards). All Web Parts that appear on the personal dashboard are stored as items in the personal dashboard folder.

Create a Personal Dashboard

If you are a coordinator at the workspace level, you can allow users who are authors on the **Dashboards** folder in the workspace to create their own personal dashboard from the home page of the dashboard site. To do this, you can either create the personal dashboard for each user or add the Personal Dashboards Web Part to the page on the dashboard site from where you want to allow users to create their own dashboards.

   Note If you allow users to create their own dashboards, those users can also create their own Web Parts that run script on the server. Since the server is a shared resource and the Web Part code can affect the server function (though only the user's security limitations), you should examine server resources and security policy before implementing this feature.

To enable personal dashboard creation:

1. On the dashboard site, click the **Management** link to open the Management dashboard, and then click the **Content** link at the top of the page.

2. On the Content management page, select the Personal Dashboards Web Part, and then click **Export**.

3. Choose a location on your hard drive to save the exported Web Part.

4. Click **OK**.

> **Note** SharePoint Portal Server saves the Web Part as a .dwp file on your hard drive.

5. Go the page on the dashboard site where you want the Personal Dashboards Web Part to appear, and then click the **Content** link at the top of the page.

6. Click **Import a Web Part File.**

7. On your hard drive, locate the .dwp file for the Personal Dashboards Web Part that you exported, and then click **OK**.

> **Note** The Web Part appears on the page you selected.

8. In the workspace, right-click the **Dashboards** folder, and then click **Properties**.

9. Click the **Security** tab.

10. Allow appropriate users to create personal dashboards by making them Authors on the **Dashboards** folder.

11. Click **OK**.

Users who are Authors or Coordinators on the **Dashboards** folder can create personal dashboards from the Personal Dashboards Web Part on the dashboard site.

> **Tip** To disable personal dashboard creation for a single user, change the user's role from Author to Reader on the **Dashboards** folder.

To disable personal dashboard creation for all users, remove the Personal Dashboards Web Part from the dashboard site, and change the appropriate users from Authors to Readers on the **Dashboards** folder.

To create a personal dashboard:

1. From the dashboard site, click **Create a new personal dashboard**.

2. Type a unique name for the dashboard, a caption, and a description. Each of these fields is described as follows:

   - **Name.** The title that appears at the top of each dashboard. The name you select for the dashboard must be unique. If you select a name that is already in use for another dashboard on your network, an error message appears, and SharePoint Portal Server prompts you to select another name.

   - **Caption.** A brief descriptor or tagline that displays above the title. The caption should be brief, no more than a few words. You can use it to give a collection of dashboards a unifying theme. For example, you might have several dashboards to present Web content for different manufacturing facilities, and use the caption "Production" to indicate to users that they are all related.

- **Description.** A brief textual description of the dashboard or other beneficial information for dashboard users.

     Note There are other advanced settings where you can specify things such as the style sheet to use for the dashboard, or the name of a Help file.

3. Click **Save**. SharePoint Portal Server saves the new dashboard to the **Dashboards** folder, and the dashboard appears on your dashboard site. You can now add Web Parts to your personal dashboard.

     Note Users can also create additional sub-dashboards from a personal dashboard. This allows a user to create multiple dashboards under one single navigation structure.

Access Personal Dashboards

Once they are created, you can view personal dashboards by using a Web browser by typing the Uniform Resource Locator (URL) that corresponds to the specific personal dashboard in the **Dashboards** folder. For example, if you create a personal dashboard called "Production" in the Manufacturing workspace on the server called "Adventure," you would use http://Adventure/Manufacturing/Dashboards/Production as the URL in your Web browser to display the Production dashboard.

     Note Users assigned to the Reader role for the folder containing the personal dashboard can view the dashboard from their Web browser. If you want to restrict access to your personal dashboard, you must manually change the roles assigned to specific users or groups for the folder that contains the dashboard.

Delete a Personal Dashboard

You can only delete personal dashboards from the Web folder for the workspace in which they are stored. You cannot delete them from the dashboard site of the workspace.

To delete a personal dashboard:

1. In Windows 2000, open Web folders and double-click a Web folder that links to the workspace.

2. In the workspace, double-click the **Dashboards** folder.

3. Right-click the folder for the specific dashboard you want to delete, and then click **Delete**.

Administering Discussions and Subscriptions

You can access the Management page on the dashboard site only if you are a coordinator on the **Portal** folder in the workspace. By using this page, you can manage other users' subscriptions, manage Web discussions, flush the application cache for the dashboard site, and create personal dashboards.

For more information about implementing Web discussions, see Chapter 10, "Planning Web Discussions."

Summary

This chapter introduces the default dashboard site and presents information about customizing the dashboard site. It reviews the components of the dashboard site and describes the primary management tasks and security issues associated with it.

The dashboard site offers a single customizable source for accessing information drawn from a wide variety of content sources. Because the dashboard site is composed entirely of Web Parts, you can easily customize it for your business needs. You can also manage common resources, such as your contacts, calendars, and messages.

CHAPTER 5

Introducing Microsoft Full-Text Search Technologies

This chapter reviews the concept of full-text search and explains how different Microsoft® products implement full-text search. This information can help you to determine which Microsoft products are best for your information retrieval needs.

Microsoft full-text search technology contributes to a number of server and client products. Search functionality varies, depending on the requirements of each product. However, all products benefit from the common advantage of efficient retrieval of unstructured, textual data by means of a full-text index.

The following Microsoft products use variants of Microsoft full-text search technology:

- Index Server, Indexing Service for Microsoft Windows®
- Microsoft SharePoint™ Portal Server 2001
- Microsoft SQL Server™ 7 and SQL Server 2000
- Microsoft Exchange Server 2000
- Microsoft Site Server 3
- Microsoft Office XP

The product you choose depends on your needs. For example, you might want to search intranet sites, Internet sites, or Exchange public folders, or you might want to search over-structured or unstructured data. You might need to cater to an internal team, or you might need to serve the needs of customers over your extranet site. These and other considerations help you determine which product is best for you.

For more information about full-text search technology or these products, see Appendix B, "For More Information."

Full-Text Search

Full-text search provides relevant information from a collection of sources in response to a user's need. This need is typically expressed as a textual query that looks for each, or any, of the query terms in each of the documents in the collection. A simple approach opens and scans each document when a query is processed, looking for each of the query terms. However, opening every document at query processing time and searching for the query terms can be very time consuming. This approach is impractical beyond the individual user searching a small number of documents.

The simple solution is to do much of the work ahead of time. This is done by extracting information about the terms in each document and storing the information in a way that is easy to retrieve. When the search engine processes a query, there is no need to scan each document. The search engine only needs to compare the documents to each other by using the inverted index. The search engine then chooses the documents that are most relevant to the query.

The principle of doing much of the work ahead of query time serves as the foundation of all full-text search technologies, including Microsoft full-text search. To be effective, a search technology must

- Get documents from various document stores.

- Extract text from various document formats.

- Update the index with the document terms.

- Rank the documents, bringing the most relevant documents to the top of a list.

Good search technology performs these tasks for documents in various languages, over many different types of formats, and across documents stored in a variety of document repositories. Good search technology returns those documents that are truly relevant to a user's need. At its best, full-text search technology fits into a complete knowledge solution, where direct textual query is the user's last resort. Full-text search technology should interpret the information the user needs by using advanced mechanisms, and it should answer the query with a combination of structured and unstructured information.

The following components of Microsoft full-text search technology provide an excellent full-text search solution:

- **Protocol handlers.** A protocol handler accesses data over a particular protocol or from a particular store. Common protocol handlers include the file protocol, Hypertext Transfer Protocol (HTTP), Messaging Application Programming Interface (MAPI), and HTTP Distributed Authoring and Versioning (HTTPDAV). The protocol handler processes URLs passed to it by the Gatherer.

- **Gatherer.** The Gatherer maintains the queue of URLs to access across protocols. For example, a Web site crawl may include hundreds of pages and create network traffic by accessing each Web page one at a time. To increase efficiency, the Gatherer interleaves URLs from a remote Web location with URLs from other Web locations or with access to file system documents or other stores. The Gatherer may use additional logic to improve crawl efficiency, such as SharePoint Portal Server adaptive crawling. The Gatherer balances the load that the gathering process imposes on crawled servers. The Gatherer maintains the queue of URLs to be processed and manages the combined crawl. For each document accessed, the Gatherer fetches the stream of content from the protocol handler and passes it on to the appropriate filter.

- **Filters.** Filters (also known as IFilters) extract textual information from a specific document format, such as Microsoft Word documents or text files. For example, Microsoft provides the Microsoft Office filter, which can extract terms from Word, Microsoft Excel, and Microsoft PowerPoint® files. Other filters work with HTML or e-mail messages. There are also third-party filters, such as the PDF filter provided by Adobe.

  The filter extracts a stream of textual information from a document, discarding all non-textual and formatting information. The filter produces strings of text and property/value pairs to pass in turn to the index engine. All filters are written to an application programming interface (API). For more information about filters, see Appendix B.

- **Word breakers and stemmers.** A word breaker is a component that determines where the word boundaries are in the stream of characters in the query or in the document being crawled. A stemmer extracts the root form of a given word. For example, "running," "ran," and "runner" are variants of the word "run." In some languages, a stemmer expands the root form of a word to include alternate forms.

  SharePoint Portal Server provides word breakers for English, French, Spanish, Japanese, Thai, Korean, Traditional Chinese, and Simplified Chinese. SharePoint Portal Server uses the Windows 2000 Server Indexing Service word breakers for Dutch, Italian, Swedish, and German. When SharePoint Portal Server crawls documents that are in multiple languages, the customized word breaker for each language enables the resulting terms to be more accurate for that language. When there is a word breaker for the language family, but not for the specific sub-language, the major language is used. For example, SharePoint Portal Server uses the French word breaker to handle text that is French Canadian. If no word breaker is available for a particular language, SharePoint Portal Server uses the neutral word breaker. Words are broken at neutral characters, such as spaces and punctuation marks. The code for determining where words are broken is built into the Microsoft Search (MSSearch) service and cannot be changed. You cannot create custom word breakers.

- **Index engine.** The function of the index engine is to prepare an inverse index of content. An inverse index is a data structure with a row for each term. In this row, there is information about the documents in which the term appears and the number of occurrences and relative position of the term within each document. The inverse index provides the ability to apply statistic and probabilistic formulas to compute the relevance of documents quickly.

  Applications that do not have full-text search enabled, such as Windows or Microsoft Outlook®, access each document at query time. These applications traverse each document and use a filter or other outdated technology to find query terms. This process is very slow when compared to an inverse index. The inverse index provides the ability to go directly into a ranking formula instead of going to sources.

- **Ranking.** Ultimately, the task of evaluating a query results in a set of relevant documents. In relational databases, each row either is in the result set or is not. For example, when a user queries for "all accounts with a balance lower than or equal to $30,000", it is easy to tell which rows in the accounts table to return. The task of full-text search, by contrast, is subtler. The queries are imperfect representations of an information need, and the documents retrieved vary in their relevance. Full-text search ranks the most relevant documents at the top of the result set. Less relevant documents are still valuable to the user, however. Full-text search ranks these documents further below.

Microsoft full-text search products differ in the algorithm used for this ranking. Index Server and Site Server 3 use vector-based ranking algorithms, while later products employ an advanced probabilistic algorithm.

Query Languages

To express the information request to the system, the user depends on a language that describes the restrictions and conditions over the terms. For example, a user may be interested in all documents published in the previous week. To query for this, the user must express both the concept of "publishing" a document and the precise time range. For example, the time range might start on the previous Monday and end on the previous Sunday.

Microsoft full-text search products evolved through three different query languages:

- Query Dialect 1

- Query Dialect 2

- Structured Query Language (SQL) full-text extensions

The following sections discuss Microsoft products that incorporate Microsoft full-text search technology. Each section includes an overview of the product, its target user, and the way in which full-text search integrates with the product. For more information about these products and the related technologies, see Appendix B.

Microsoft SharePoint Portal Server

SharePoint Portal Server is the flexible portal solution with which you can find, share, and publish information easily. With SharePoint Portal Server, you can use existing information effectively and capture information in new ways that are appropriate for your business. In addition, you can rapidly deploy a prepackaged dashboard site and easily use Web Parts technology to customize a Web-based view of your organization.

SharePoint Portal Server targets dashboard site solutions, starting with the team portal and ending at the enterprise portal.

SharePoint Portal Server presents the most current and the richest set of search and information discovery features. Figure 5.1 illustrates components of the SharePoint Portal Server Search architecture.

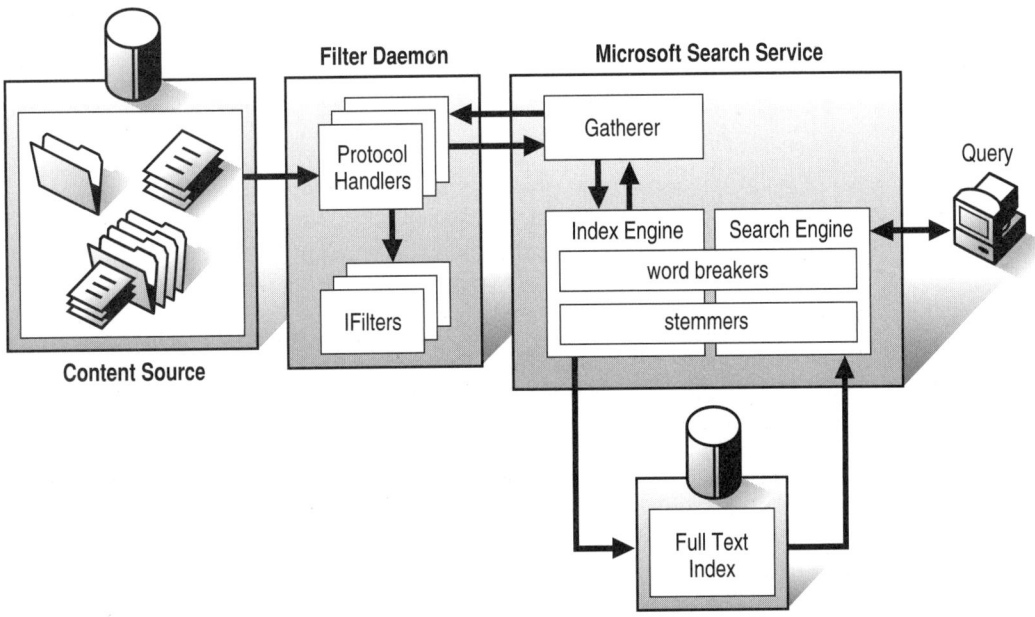

Figure 5.1. SharePoint Portal Server content crawling and search architecture

The following list describes the components of the SharePoint Portal Server Search architecture.

- **Search Engine.** Component of MSSearch that runs queries written in the SQL full-text extension syntax against the full-text index.

- **Index Engine.** Component of MSSearch that processes chunks of text and properties filtered from content sources, and determines which properties are written to the full-text index.

- **Gatherer.** Component of MSSearch that manages the content crawling process and that has rules that determine what content is crawled.

- **Word breakers.** Components shared by the Search and Index engines that break up compound words and phrases.

- **Stemmers.** Components shared by the Search and Index engines that generate inflected forms of a word.

- **Filter Daemon.** Component that handles requests from the Gatherer. Uses protocol handlers to access content sources, and IFilters to filter files. Provides the Gatherer with a stream of data containing filtered chunks and properties.

- **Protocol Handlers.** Open content sources in their native protocol and expose documents and other items to be filtered.

- **IFilters.** Open documents and other content source items in their native format and filter into chunks of text and properties.

- **Content sources.** Collection of data MSSearch must crawl, and specific rules for crawling items in that content source. Items in content sources are identified by URLs. The protocol portion of the URL is what distinguishes different types of content sources.

- **Data Access.** SharePoint Portal Server uses protocol handlers and the Gatherer to crawl and provide search results over data from diverse content sources. Without modification, SharePoint Portal Server can crawl documents from file systems, Web sites, Exchange 2000 Server and Exchange Server 5.5 computers, Lotus Notes servers, and other SharePoint Portal Server workspaces.

Although it does not provide direct access to OLE DB, Open Database Connectivity (ODBC), or other relational data access standards, SharePoint Portal Server can crawl information from databases by using HTTP. To do this, you must create an Active Server Pages (ASP) page that renders information from each row in the database.

The Microsoft SharePoint Portal Server SDK describes the protocol handler interface. The protocol handler interface enables developers to write a protocol handler for document repositories with other, proprietary, data access methods, such as document management systems or archiving solutions. For more information about this interface, see Appendix B. The Microsoft SharePoint Portal Server Resource Kit CD-ROM includes protocol handlers that you can use to crawl File Transfer Protocol (FTP) sites and SharePoint Team Services sites. You can access these protocol handlers in the \Tools directory of the CD. For a complete listing of tools and Web Parts available on the CD, see Appendix A, "Tools, Samples, eBooks, and More."

- **Filters.** SharePoint Portal Server includes filters for Microsoft Office documents, HTML files, Tagged Image File Format (TIFF) files, and text files. The TIFF filter enables SharePoint Portal Server to crawl the textual content of saved fax data based on Optical Character Recognition (OCR) technology. When filtering messages from Exchange public folders, SharePoint Portal Server uses the Multipurpose Internet Mail Extensions (MIME) filter that is included with Windows 2000. SharePoint Portal Server also supports third-party and custom file types, such as the Adobe PDF filter. For more information about the Adobe PDF filter, see Appendix B.

- **Ranking.** SharePoint Portal Server offers an advanced probabilistic ranking algorithm, which is based on achievements in information retrieval accomplished by Microsoft Research. This algorithm guarantees that SharePoint Portal Server returns the documents that are most relevant to a user's query at the top of the list of search results, providing increased user efficiency and satisfaction.

  Stephen Robertson, Microsoft researcher, City University professor, and winner of the prestigious Association for Computing Machinery Special Interest Group on Information Retrieval (ACM SIGIR) 2000 Salton Award, developed the formula for ranking. The ranking formula adopted and used by Microsoft full-text search is a direct result of this research. In computing the likely relevance of a document, the formula uses the following factors: the length of the document, the frequency of the query term in the entire collection of documentsthe number of documents containing the query term, andthe number of documents in the entire collection of documents.

- **Best Bets.** This feature enables users with appropriate permissions to tag individual documents as most appropriate for specific queries or categories. Even in the most advanced probabilistic ranking environment, certain documents lack the textual information to be prominent in search results for particular terms. The Best Bets feature addresses this problem most effectively, either by advancing the specially tagged documents to the top of the results list or by displaying them prominently when browsing categories. The default query included with SharePoint Portal Server also nominates Best Bet documents when the rank of the document is very high. For more information about the default query, see Chapter 24, "Analyzing the Default Query for the Dashboard Site."

- **Automatic Categorization.** In addition to simple search, SharePoint Portal Server provides automatic categorization. This feature enables the user to define a category hierarchy and then use a sample set of documents within the hierarchy as a training sample. After training, SharePoint Portal Server automatically tags documents stored on the server and crawled documents. After they are tagged, these documents appear in the category hierarchy.

- **Schema Support.** SharePoint Portal server provides simplified schema management facilities that are compatible with Office by using promotion and demotion. Users define document profiles and associated properties. During promotion, SharePoint Portal Server copies property values in the Office document to the properties of a document profile. During demotion, SharePoint Portal Server copies property values found in a document profile to the Office document. SharePoint Portal Server tightly integrates full-text search with that schema. Advanced search uses properties and document profiles.

- **Extensibility and Programmability.** The SharePoint Portal Server dashboard site uses Microsoft Digital Dashboard technology. Microsoft Digital Dashboard technology enables easy integration of business applications and custom content with the built-in search features of SharePoint Portal Server. SharePoint Portal Server provides query submission and search results as Web Parts, which can easily coexist on the dashboard site with custom Web Parts. However, the Web Parts for query submission and search results rely on each other for functionality and therefore must reside on a SharePoint Portal Server computer. You can manipulate search by using Microsoft ActiveX® Data Objects (ADO), OLE DB, or the Web-based Distributed Authoring and Versioning (WebDAV) protocol. SharePoint Portal Server does not provide automation interfaces for management of its search, document management, or dashboard site features. For more information about developing customized search solutions for SharePoint Portal Server, see Appendix B.

- **Query Languages.** SharePoint Portal Server uses SQL full-text extensions. Queries are submitted using Distributed Authoring and Versioning Searching and Locating (DASL) requests, part of WebDAV, also called HTTPDAV.

- **Subscriptions.** The SharePoint Portal Server subscriptions feature enables users to subscribe to changes in documents, folders, categories, and search results. SharePoint Portal Server maintains subscriptions as persistent queries. SharePoint Portal Server sends notifications to the subscriber whenever a change occurs. SharePoint Portal Server implements subscriptions by using Persistent Query Service (PQS) rules. PQS is a reverse-query processor. It evaluates a large set of queries against a single document to determine which queries match the document. This allows SharePoint Portal Server to identify matching subscriptions as each new document arrives in the document store. Subscriptions provide this "push" model to match the "pull" model of full-text search.

- **Adaptive Crawling.** Site Server 3 introduced incremental crawling, which uses time stamp comparisons to include only documents that have changed since the previous update of the index. Incremental updates reduce the amount of time involved in repeated crawls. However, incremental updates do not eliminate the need to inspect the time stamp of each document previously crawled each time a crawl occurs. Adaptive crawling reduces the time required for crawling even further. During crawls, the algorithm for adaptive crawling compiles statistics about the rate of change for each document. In subsequent adaptive crawls, the algorithm targets only documents likely to have changed.

SharePoint Portal Server does not replace all of the functionality of Site Server, but the search technology used in SharePoint Portal Server is more recent than the search technology used in Site Server. In addition, SharePoint Portal Server uses an advanced ranking algorithm. You can use the advanced features of the algorithm to conduct a search from the dashboard site. These advanced features include Best Bets, categories, and Office schema integration.

When creating indexes, SharePoint Portal Server offers significantly better performance than Site Server 3 by providing a multi-threaded index engine. The introduction of adaptive crawling also reduces the amount of time it takes to perform incremental crawling when updating indexes.

Microsoft Indexing Service

Indexing Service is a Microsoft Windows 2000 base service for file systems and Web servers. Formerly known as Index Server, its original function was to crawl and create a catalog—similar to the index created by SharePoint Portal Server—of the content of Internet Information Services (IIS) Web servers. Indexing Service now creates catalogs for the contents and properties of both file systems and virtual Web sites.

As an operating system component, Indexing Service targets the same wide range of customer scenarios that Windows targets. Indexing Service targets the desktop experience. It provides an enhanced search experience for individual users covering information stored on local disks. You access Indexing Service in Windows when you click the **Search** button in the **Start** menu, when you press CTRL+F, when you click the **Search** button in Windows Explorer, and when you click the search task pane in Office XP. Indexing Service exposes management and query objects that allow rapid development of custom search applications. You can expand Indexing Service catalogs to contain information from remote file shares. Such custom applications can serve vertical applications or groups of users. These custom applications can crawl information from multiple locations.

Indexing Service also offers full-text search from Internet sites. You can use Indexing Service to drive custom search Web applications. In addition to query language support, Indexing Service offers a full range of programmability features targeted for the custom-application developer: scripting objects for query and administration, an OLE DB provider, and ADO compatibility.

The following list describes the components of Indexing Service.

- **Data access.** Indexing Service does not include a cross-protocol gathering component. It can access any data that is available from the file system, including local file systems and shared file systems on remote computers. Indexing Service facilitates crawling of Web site content to create an index by using the IIS metabase to understand which files map to Web site content. Indexing Service then follows the information from the IIS metabase to crawl the local Web sites. Indexing Service does not use the HTTP protocol to crawl Web sites. Therefore, Indexing Service cannot crawl content that is rendered dynamically, such as ASP pages referencing a database or personalized content that changes for each user.

- **Filters.** Indexing Service uses filters installed on the operating system, including the MIME filter for news and e-mail, the Office filter for Office documents, and the HTML filter.

- **Ranking.** Indexing Service uses ranking algorithms based on the vector space model. The default algorithm used is the Jaccard formula. For more information about the specific algorithms, see Appendix B.

- **Schema support.** Indexing Service provides rich, broad schema support. By using SharePoint Portal Server Administration in Microsoft Management Console (MMC), users can view all properties indexed from documents and can indicate which properties to store in the property cache for fast retrieval.

- **Extensibility and programmability.** Indexing Service provides a platform for full-text search applications. It includes a full set of programming interfaces, including scripting interfaces for administration and query and an OLE DB provider for searches. For information about Indexing Service programming interfaces, see Appendix B.

- **Query languages.** Indexing Service provides rapid access to files through flexible querying language. Indexing Service supports Query Dialect 1, Query Dialect 2, and SQL full-text extensions.

For a list of features new to Indexing Service 3 included with Windows 2000, see Appendix B.

Indexing Service is the performance solution for the need in custom application development to provide full-text search over content of an Internet site. It is less appropriate for applications where the data is primarily structured. Developers of such applications should consider Microsoft SQL Server 2000. For ease of use without need for customization, or for applications that require aggregation of content from various sources and source types, SharePoint Portal Server is the appropriate choice.

Indexing Service is an optional operating system component. The initial creation of indexes of file system contents can be resource-intensive and can affect desktop application performance. Therefore, Windows does not enable Indexing Service by default.

Microsoft SQL Server 2000

SQL Server 2000 is a family of products that meets the data storage and analysis requirements of the largest data processing systems and commercial Web sites. SQL Server 2000 can provide easy-to-use data storage and analysis services to an individual or a small business.

Full-text search in SQL 2000 focuses on searching data that is primarily structured, but also includes textual, unstructured information.

SQL Server 2000 uses the same search engine technology used by SharePoint Portal Server, benefits from the same advanced ranking algorithm, and uses a subset of the full-text extensions to SQL used by SharePoint Portal Server. The following list describes the components of SQL Server.

- **Data access.** You can use full-text search in SQL server only over content stored in SQL columns.

- **Filters.** SQL Server 2000 uses filters installed on the server to handle documents stored in database columns. Users use IMAGE-type columns to store documents, and then specify a second column to indicate the document type. Full-text search then applies the appropriate filter, such as HTML, Office, or third-party filters, based on the document type. In addition, you can apply full-text search to the contents of columns of type [N]CHAR, [N]VARCHAR, and [N]TEXT.

- **Extensibility and programmability.** Full-text search SQL extensions are integrated into the T-SQL language. Users can specify SQL queries that span structured data from SQL tables, unstructured data from SQL columns, from documents embedded in the columns, and from the file system.

SQL Server 7 first introduced full-text search as a feature of SQL Server.

Microsoft Site Server

Site Server is designed to help you get the most usability from your corporate intranet. Site Server enables users to publish, find, and share information quickly and easily. Features include extensive search capabilities and tools to perform thorough analyses of your intranet's usage and effectiveness.

Site Server Commerce Edition is a comprehensive, Internet commerce server that enables you to engage customers, transact business, and analyze commerce Web sites. Highly scalable and secure, Site Server Commerce Edition streamlines and integrates your online dealings with distributors and suppliers.

Since the introduction of Site Server 3 Standard Edition and Site Server 3 Commerce Edition in May 1998, the Web marketplace has evolved rapidly. Site Server 3 Standard Edition targets the intranet space, allowing users to find, share, and publish information to their corporate intranets. In comparison, Site Server 3 Commerce Edition targets the Internet space, with the ability to conduct a financial transaction online, analyze transactions, and conduct a personalized interaction with the consumer.

Since then, the needs of the intranet market have changed substantially and have evolved into the portal market, with greater need for core services and application integration as well as a continued requirement for robust enterprise-wide search. As a result, product focuses have shifted accordingly. The search technology of Site Server 3 Standard Edition is expanded in SharePoint Portal Server.

The following list describes the components of Site Server.

- **Data access.** Site Server introduced the concept of gathering and the concept of protocol handlers. Site Server can crawl Exchange Server 5.5 computers and Web sites. The Gatherer can process both hierarchical (file system) and Web spaces (HTTP). Site Server does not support custom protocol handlers. The interface is not extensible to support new document stores. Site Server can crawl information from databases by using an ASP page that renders the information from rows in a database.

- **Filters.** Site Server uses the same filters as Indexing Service. Site Server uses filters installed on the operating system, including the MIME filter for news and e-mail, the Office filter for Office documents, and the HTML filter.

- **Ranking.** Site Server uses the same ranking as Indexing Service. Site Server uses ranking algorithms based on the vector space model. The default algorithm used is the Jaccard formula. For more information about the specific algorithms, see Appendix B.

- **Schema support.** Site Server provides rich, broad schema support. Users can define properties over OLE DB data types by using a proprietary management interface.

- **Extensibility and programmability.** Site Server has its own object model.

- **Query language.** Site Server uses Query Dialect 1 and SQL full-text extensions.

Microsoft Exchange 2000 Server

Exchange 2000 Server integrates seamlessly with the Windows 2000 operating system. It is designed to meet the messaging and collaboration needs for businesses of all sizes. Together with its client software, Outlook 2000, Exchange provides a highly reliable, scalable, and easy-to-manage messaging and collaboration infrastructure.

If your primary need is to crawl e-mail messages, use Exchange 2000 Server. By using Exchange 2000 Server full-text search, servers can search messaging items in personal mailboxes and public folders to all users.

To aggregate searches from e-mail and other sources, use SharePoint Portal Server. However, SharePoint Portal Server does not support crawling private mailboxes.

Exchange 2000 Server uses the same search technology that SharePoint Portal Server uses. Exchange 2000 Server uses a version with proven clustering capability. The following list describes the components of Exchange 2000 Server.

- **Data access.** Data access is restricted to information stored in Exchange public folders and mailboxes.

- **Filters.** Exchange 2000 Server full-text search uses the MIME filter to crawl messaging items. Attachments are processed by using available filters according to their content type.

- **Ranking.** Exchange 2000 Server uses the same advanced probabilistic ranking algorithm that SharePoint Portal Server uses. This algorithm guarantees that Exchange 2000 Server returns the documents most relevant to a query at the top of the list of search results, providing increased user efficiency and satisfaction.

- **Extensibility and programmability.** Exchange 2000 Server uses the HTTPDAV protocol, specifically DASL, for searching.

- **Query language.** Full-text search in Exchange 2000 Server uses and supports SQL full-text extensions through the Distributed Authoring and Versioning (DAV) protocol. When using Exchange 2000 Server, Outlook Advanced Search takes advantage of Exchange 2000 Server full-text search. Exchange 2000 Server submits the natural language queries directly to the server. There is no client-side support for the SQL query language.

Microsoft Office XP Search

The world's leading suite of productivity software, Microsoft Office helps you complete common business tasks, including word processing, e-mail, presentations, data management and analysis, and much more.

If you are an Office user and you want to work from your desktop, use Office XP search. Office XP enables you to search not only the local hard disk but also file shares and SharePoint Portal Server computers. The following list describes the components of Office XP.

- **Data access.** If you enable Indexing Service on a computer running Windows 2000, Indexing Service creates an index of local disks. On computers running Microsoft Windows NT® version 4, Windows 98, or Windows Millennium Edition, Microsoft Office XP provides a version of the search engine used in SharePoint Portal Server for local disk crawling. You must choose to activate Indexing Service or the Office search index engine. If you do not enable indexing, Office XP provides a slower, non-indexed form of search.

- **User Interface.** Office XP provides a search task pane accessible from Word, Excel, and PowerPoint.

- **Advanced Features.** The task pane provides federated search of the user's local hard drives, remote servers through Indexing Services, SharePoint Portal Server computers, SharePoint Team Services sites (which use Indexing Service for their full-text search feature), and Outlook mail (PST files or Exchange mailboxes). A query broker component dispatches search commands to the search providers for each of these stores.

- **Extensibility and programmability.** Office applications can program to the search query broker through an API that is similar to the FindFast API.

Full-Text Search Comparison Tables

The tables on the following pages show a technology and feature comparison of the Microsoft products that implement full-text searching, including the following:

- SharePoint Portal Server
- Indexing Service
- Site Server
- SQL Server 2000
- Exchange 2000 Server
- Office XP

Technology Comparison

	SharePoint Portal Server	Indexing Service	Site Server	SQL Server 2000	Exchange 2000 Server	Office XP on Windows 2000	Office XP on Windows 98 or Millennium Edition
Full-text search using proprietary query language		✔	✔			✔	✔
Full-text search using SQL full-text extensions	✔	✔	✔	✔	✔		
Boolean ranking algorithm	✔	✔	✔				
Advanced probabilistic ranking algorithm	✔			✔	✔		✔
Uses multiple data access protocols	✔		✔				

Feature Comparison

	SharePoint Portal Server	Indexing Service	Site Server	SQL Server 2000	Exchange 2000 Server	Office XP on Windows 2000	Office XP on Windows 98 or Millennium Edition
Crawls							
File system	✔	✔	✔			✔ Local only	✔ Local only
Web sites	✔	✔ Local only, through file system	✔				
Lotus Notes	✔						
Exchange 5.5	✔ Public folders		✔				
Exchange 2000	✔ Public folders				✔ Public folders and private mail boxes		
SQL tables	✔ Through ASP		✔ Through ASP	✔			
SharePoint Portal Server workspaces	✔					✔	✔
3rd party protocols	✔						
Best Bets	✔						
Categories	✔						
End user UI	Dashboard	Windows Explorer on Windows 2000 and custom	Custom	Custom	Outlook through Advanced Find, custom	Office search task pane	Office search task pane

Summary

This chapter describes full-text search technology that is used in a variety of Microsoft products. This chapter can help you to choose the Microsoft products that are best suited for your information retrieval needs.

Planning and Installation

This section provides detailed planning information including planning server capacity, security concepts, taxonomy planning information, and more.

CHAPTER 6

Planning a Deployment

Microsoft® SharePoint™ Portal Server can help your organization manage its information. A deployment plan outlines ways to streamline your document management processes and create an effective dashboard site to deliver valuable information to the users in your organization. You can develop a successful deployment plan by understanding what the people in your organization need, how they are most likely to search for information, and what content your organization produces. A SharePoint Portal Server deployment includes establishing the appropriate security for your organization's information, preparing the workspace, and organizing the dashboard site.

Organization Needs and Goals Analysis

Your deployment of SharePoint Portal Server is a good opportunity to evaluate document management practices and content organization. Before you begin configuring your workspace, take some time to assess your existing content, identify the needs and habits of your users, and outline your deployment goals. This information can help you decide how to streamline your document management processes and create an effective dashboard site to deliver valuable information to your organization.

If you are deploying SharePoint Portal Server for a group or organization that you know well, you may already be familiar with the current practices and needs of the organization. Consultations with group members about key goals can help you identify which SharePoint Portal Server features you want to deploy. Coordination with others is especially important if your deployment fits into a larger information management system in your organization. If this is the case, you may want to form a team of key people who understand the goals and requirements of your organization to help you plan an effective deployment.

Reviewing Your Content

An organization often stores data in many different places, such as file servers, Web sites, and mail servers. If you are uncertain about the location and purpose of the content used by your organization, a content review can help you identify them. Knowing the types of documents that exist in your organization helps you determine the best way to organize your content.

A content review addresses the following questions:

- **Who produces content? Who manages it?** Content managers can provide information about the people who create the content. They are also the best people to suggest ways to improve the organization of content.

- **Where is content stored?** Identify the location of each server used to store content. For example, your group may store discussions about new advertising campaigns in public folders on an Exchange server. Your system administrator can identify the servers used in your organization.

- **What is the purpose of the content? How is it structured?** Learn who uses the content and what format is used. For example, you might discover that the product development department stores product specifications as Microsoft Word documents but the marketing department uses Lotus Notes to maintain customer profiles.

Knowing where information is stored and how your organization uses it helps you to clarify your deployment goals.

Assessing User Needs and Habits

If you are uncertain about the needs of your organization, a survey can capture information about the habits and concerns of your users. It can also identify other useful information for planning your deployment.

You can ask users to identify the types of content they find valuable. A user survey could include the following questions:

- **What are the five most useful information sources, content types, or groups of documents for your job?** Users might list a call-tracking database, spreadsheets listing sales figures, or a folder of design specifications.

- **Are there additional information sources, content types, or groups of documents that would benefit from increased exposure?** Users might list documents produced in another department or industry publications on the Internet.

- **What information is missing from the current portal? Why is this information important to include?** Users might list a Web site that offers free tutorials for a software application or a request that the employee handbook be available on the portal.

Responses to these questions help to identify the content that users want to access, even if it is not currently available to them. Users might provide a variety of answers to the same question. For example, some users might identify certain tasks as easy that other users identify as difficult. In this case, consider differences in knowledge between the two groups. Assess whether your dashboard site needs to address each group separately or if you need to redefine your target audience.

You can also ask users how they prefer to find information. Responses to this question help to prioritize your goals for deploying search features. With SharePoint Portal Server, users can locate content by:

- **Performing a keyword search.** By using a specific word or phrase, a keyword search query can produce numerous results. This method appeals to users who want to see all possible content related to a specific query.

- **Browsing or searching through categories.** Categories group documents by topic and provide an organized view of the information. This method is especially valuable for users who do not know the location of content.

- **Navigating through the folder structure.** Users find information based on file location. This method may be especially suitable for authors who are familiar with the folder structure in the workspace.

- **Viewing information posted on the home page.** When information is visible on the home page, users immediately see it without needing to perform a search. This method works well for content that is relevant to many users.

You can conduct a survey by distributing a questionnaire with detailed questions, and analyzing the answers with your planning team. You can also survey your organization by meeting with users to discuss existing practices, work styles and habits, and potential deployment goals. Whether your process is formal or informal, the scope of your deployment and the structure of your organization determine the approach that you take.

Identifying Your Goals

Your initial research helps you identify your organization's information management processes and may uncover some common problems. Analyzing these problems can help you clarify your goals. The following table describes a few typical problems and suggests some of the SharePoint Portal Server features to include in your configuration plan to solve those problems and achieve your information management goals.

SharePoint Portal Server Solutions

Common Problem	Solution
It is difficult to track revisions to documents with multiple authors.	Use version control to save changes made to a document and to eliminate the possibility of people overwriting each other's documents.
Information for the organization is not widely circulated.	Display news, announcements, quick links, and other information on the home page of the dashboard site.
The group lacks control over who accesses content.	Use roles for flexible control over access to content.

continued

SharePoint Portal Server Solutions *continued*

Common Problem	Solution
There is no process to maintain a private view of a document.	Select a document publication process to ensure that drafts are not visible to readers until the appropriate time.
It is time-consuming to enforce review cycles for documents.	Use an approval process to route documents automatically to designated reviewers.
Information is hard to find on the current portal.	Use categories and Best Bets to organize and highlight relevant content.
Searches are slow because servers are queried one at a time.	Add content sources to create an index of multiple information sources, such as Web servers, file servers, Exchange servers, Lotus Notes databases, and other SharePoint Portal Server workspaces.

Security Plan Implementation

Security is essential, both for document management tasks and for the integrity of the search function. In document management, it is important to restrict access to sensitive information. In some cases, it is important to restrict the viewing of a document to those who edit or approve it, until it is ready for a larger audience. In search scenarios, it is important that when users view the results of searches, SharePoint Portal Server does not display documents to which they do not have access.

SharePoint Portal Server security uses standard Windows-based encrypted authentication to ensure password security. In addition, you can control access to documents by using a fixed set of three roles. SharePoint Portal Server roles offer a flexible and secure method to control access to documents. A role is a way to configure permissions for users based on the kinds of tasks they perform. SharePoint Portal Server roles add actions such as check-in, check-out, publish, and approve to traditional file-access permissions, such as Read, Write, and Change. Roles group users who have the same permissions and tasks with specific titles: coordinator, author, and reader.

Each role identifies a specific set of permissions: coordinators handle management tasks, authors add and update files, and readers have read-only access to published documents. Access permissions for the three roles are fixed and cannot be modified. SharePoint Portal Server also offers the option of denying users access to specific documents. Roles are usually specified at the folder level, although you can add coordinators at the workspace level for management tasks.

SharePoint Portal Server recognizes any security policies that you currently apply to your organization's servers, file shares, and databases. For example, when SharePoint Portal Server crawls documents stored on your organization's servers, SharePoint Portal Server enforces the security policy on each document when it displays search results.

Note SharePoint Portal Server enforces file-level security, not share-level security.

Assigning a user to a particular role gives the user the ability to perform specific tasks in the workspace. You must assign a user to a role at the workspace level before that user can have access to the workspace. The user can be an individual user or a group, where a group is a list of users who collectively have the same rights and permissions. For detailed information about roles and security, see Chapter 8, "Planning Security."

Workspace Preparation

Examine how your organization creates and uses information before you decide how to store content in the document library. Configuring the Documents folder is a large part of preparing the workspace for document management and group collaboration. It is important to understand your current document management practices so that you can decide which SharePoint Portal Server features meet the needs of your organization.

Designing Your Folder Structure

Careful planning of your folder structure ensures the most benefit from your new workspace.

For example, you might answer the following questions:

- How does the group currently organize their documents?

- Who has permission to add documents and edit them?

- Which folders contain documents that may have multiple authors?

- What should occur before publishing a document?

Talk to the people in your organization. They can help you understand existing processes and identify areas that need improvement. You can then begin to design the folder structure of your document library.

Enabling Enhanced Folders

SharePoint Portal Server provides two types of folders for document storage. Enhanced folders support all content management features, including document profiles, public and private views for workspace items, check-in and check-out functions, document version history, and document publishing and approval processes. If you disable enhanced folder settings, you disable check-in, check-out, and versioning for that folder, which changes the enhanced folder to a standard folder. SharePoint Portal Server immediately publishes all documents added to standard folders,

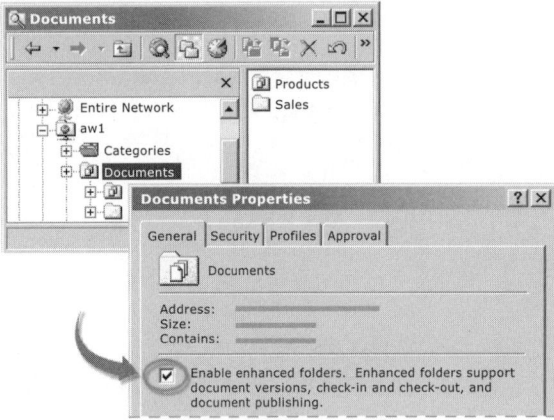

Figure 6.1. Enabling enhanced folders

SharePoint Portal Server records a history for each file stored in enhanced folders. This helps you track editorial cycles and prevents a user from overwriting another user's modifications. To edit a document, you must check it out first. This prevents others from changing it until you check it in. Every time you check in or publish a document, SharePoint Portal Server assigns a new version number to the document and archives the previous version. When you check out a document, you retrieve the most recent version unless you select a previous version. SharePoint Portal Server displays the version history on the Properties page of the document.

Enhanced folders require users to check out documents for editing and to use the **Publish** command to make a document visible to readers. Use enhanced folders for documents that require editing, review, or approval before you make them available to users associated with the reader role on the folder. For example, you can store a marketing plan created by a team of people in an enhanced folder. You can see who is working on the file at any time and ensure that it receives management approval before it is published.

The following table compares the SharePoint Portal Server features supported by each folder type.

Standard and Enhanced Folders

Feature	Standard folder	Enhanced folder
Roles	Yes	Yes
Document version history	No	Yes
Check-in/check-out	No	Yes
Private draft versions	No	Yes
Approval routing	No	Yes
Profile metadata	Yes	Yes
Indexed documents	Yes	Yes
Categories	Yes	Yes

Both standard and enhanced folders support SharePoint Portal Server roles. Published documents from both types of folders are included in the index and made available for users to search and read on the dashboard site.

SharePoint Portal Server supports compound, or multi-part, documents only in standard folders. Examples of compound documents are HTML files with relative links, a Word document with a linked Excel spreadsheet, and a master document created in Word.

> **Caution** You can enable or disable enhanced folder settings only on an empty folder. If you want to change these settings on a folder that contains documents, you must empty the folder first.

Understanding Folder Inheritance

All folders inherit folder settings from their parent folder unless otherwise specified. The Documents folder in the workspace is an enhanced folder, by default. When you create a new folder in the Documents folder, it inherits this setting. Folder inheritance also occurs when you drag a folder from your computer to the workspace. The folder you drag into the workspace inherits the folder settings of the new parent folder. For example, if the new parent folder is a standard folder, the folder that you drag into the workspace automatically becomes a standard folder. To break the folder inheritance setting, create a new folder in the workspace and enable or disable the folder inheritance setting before moving documents into the new folder.

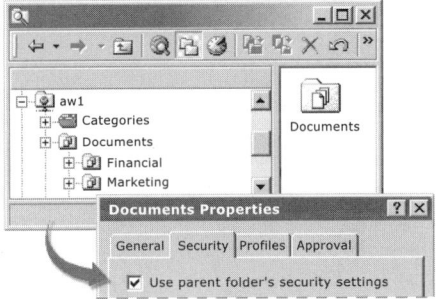

Figure 6.2. Security inheritance

Creating Your Folder Structure

After deciding what type of folder to use for each group of documents, you must create the folder hierarchy in the workspace. You can duplicate your existing folder structure in the workspace or design a new folder structure.

The quickest method is to duplicate your existing folder structure and make any modifications (combining or dividing folders) necessary to accommodate the desired document management processes. You can drag a folder and its contents into the workspace. The top-level Documents folder is an enhanced folder. Because a folder inherits its settings from the parent folder, any folder you drag into the Documents folder has enhanced folder settings. To break the folder setting inheritance, create a new folder in the workspace, enable or disable the folder setting inheritance as appropriate, and then move the documents into the new workspace folder.

Alternately, you can redesign your structure to take the greatest advantage of SharePoint Portal Server features. This method requires more planning but can yield greater benefits by eliminating redundancy, clarifying processes, and improving document discovery.

You can use folders to decide where a document is stored, and what policies apply to that document. Three key factors influence how you organize your documents in the workspace:

- Security and management requirements

- Document publishing processes

- Document profiles

These factors determine whether you combine folders or separate the documents in a folder into different folders.

Assigning Roles for Security

Each role identifies a specific set of permissions: coordinators handle management tasks, authors add and update files, and readers have read-only access to published documents. Roles offer a flexible and secure way to control user access to workspace documents. You can assign roles to users selected from your existing Microsoft Windows 2000 domain users and groups. SharePoint Portal Server role-based security combines traditional file-access permissions such as Read, Write, and Change, with an extended set of actions such as Check-out, Publish, and Approve. You control access to each folder by assigning roles to the appropriate users or groups.

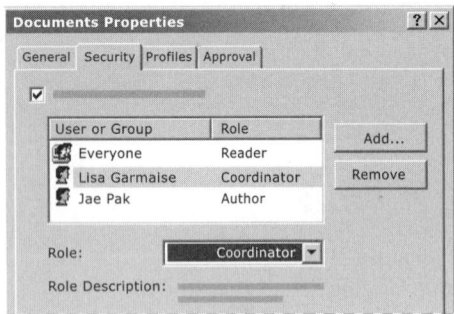

Figure 6.3. Assigning users to roles

When deciding whether content should be stored in one folder or several, assess security requirements, and evaluate how you can delegate coordinator responsibilities. For example, you may create a folder for each project within a department and assign a project manager as the coordinator on each folder. For detailed information about roles and security, see Chapter 8, "Planning Security."

Choosing a Publishing Process

Identifying the publication process best suited to your documents helps you decide what folder type to use. Publishing a document creates a public version that is available to readers of a folder. Review the types of documents used in your organization. Which document types can you publish immediately? Which document types should remain private until ready for a larger audience of readers?

If folders contain a mixture of potentially public content and content that is restricted to a specific group, consider separating the two types of content into different folders. Evaluate the needs of your document publishing processes when creating the folder structure for your document library.

When you save a document to a standard folder, SharePoint Portal Server publishes it immediately. Therefore, all documents stored in a standard folder are, by default, available for public view. For example, meeting agendas could be stored in standard folders.

In an enhanced folder, unpublished document versions, or drafts, are accessible only to other authors and coordinators for the folder. The Publish action allows you to control when a document changes from a private view to a public view. For example, you can store presentation slides in an enhanced folder to restrict the audience until they are reviewed for accuracy.

Add Approval Routes

Often one or more people must review and approve a document's content. In this situation, consider adding approval routing to the document publishing process. In approval routing, a document is sent to one or more people, and each person can approve or reject the document. Each step in the approval process is complete when the required people approve or reject the document. An approver receives an e-mail notification when a document requires his review.

You can store published documents in standard or enhanced folders, but only enhanced folders have the option for approval routing. In enhanced folders, you can choose to have a document undergo an approval process before publishing. After an author chooses to publish a document, SharePoint Portal Server can automatically route the document to a list of reviewers for approval before successfully publishing it. Each of these people, called *approvers*, may approve or reject the document. Approval routing provides an easy way to ensure that a document receives adequate review before publication.

> **Important** When you create subfolders, they do not inherit approval process settings from their parent folders. You must configure an approval process for each folder.

Types of Approval Routes

SharePoint Portal Server offers two routing options for reviewing a document before publishing it:

- One after another, called *serial approval routing*

- All at once, called *parallel approval routing*

Both types of approval routing are a series of steps that lead to publication.

A serial approval route (One after another) identifies a list of successive approvers. Each person must approve the document before the next person in the route receives an approval request notification. When the last person on the list approves the document, SharePoint Portal Server publishes the document and makes it available to readers. If any person on the list rejects the document, the approval process ends and the document's status returns to checked in. A serial route works well in highly structured organizations that use sequential review processes.

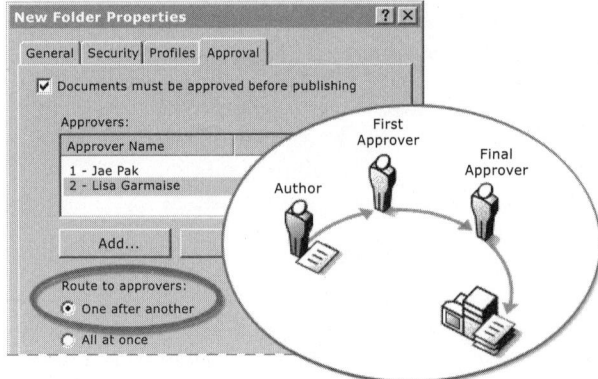

Figure 6.4. Using a serial approval route

A parallel approval route (All at once) sends an e-mail message about the document to all approvers at the same time. Parallel routing notifies all approvers simultaneously, instead of the sequential approver notifications used in serial routing. Any approver can approve or reject the document at any time.

Before using a parallel route, you must define the number of approvals required to publish the document. When you establish a parallel approval route for a folder, you can require approval from only one approver or from all of the approvers to publish the document.

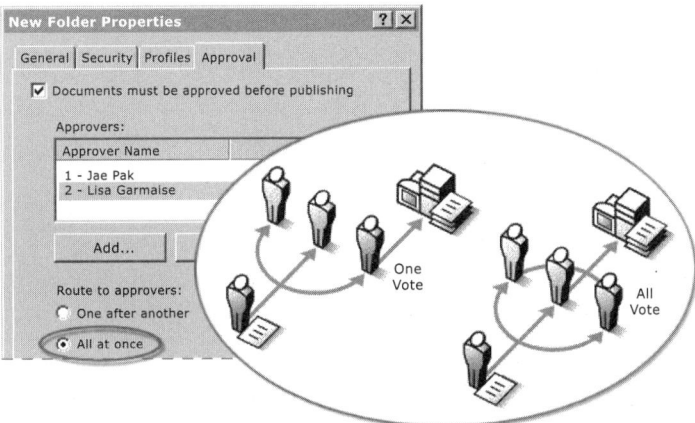

Figure 6.5. Using a parallel approval route

For example, you can route a document to three approvers. If only one approval is required, SharePoint Portal Server automatically publishes the document after the first approval. This is especially useful for time-sensitive documents that cannot tolerate delay because a single approver is unavailable. This option suits an informal approval style for a document that does not require everyone on the list to review and approve it.

Requiring unanimous approval is an option that is especially suitable for confidential or very important documents in which you must track each approver's vote. Because this information requires unanimous agreement, SharePoint Portal Server does not publish the document unless all members of the board approve it.

Creating Document Profiles

Planning for document profiles and properties depends on how you structure the folders in the workspace. You can create document profiles based on how you group documents in your current structure.

To prepare deployment of document profiles and properties in your workspace, consider these planning steps:

1. Decide whether the properties on the Base Document profile are sufficient or whether you want to create new document profiles with custom properties.

   SharePoint Portal Server supplies a template called the Base Document profile, which you can use to create new document profiles and properties. The Base Document profile consists of the Title, Author, Keywords, and Description properties. If you currently have a simple folder structure in which all documents contain similar content, you can apply the Base Document profile to all your documents. However, to aid in successful searching, you can create new document profiles with custom properties to better identify your documents.

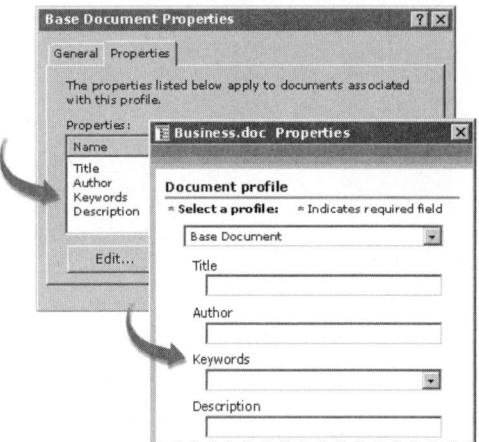

Figure 6.6. Adding custom properties to the document profile

2. Examine your content for descriptive patterns. For each pattern, choose a document profile name.

Do you see any patterns that suggest how you can group certain documents together with a profile? Look for types of documents found in more than one folder. Plan a profile name for each group of documents. For example, you may have separated your folders by competitor name but you see a group of documents that you could describe as competitor product analyses. Although you stored the documents in folders for different competitors, you can create a document profile called Competitor Product Analysis and apply it to all of those documents.

3. For new properties, use a word or phrase that people would be likely to use to search for these documents.

When you add new properties, try to anticipate the word or phrase that users may choose in a search query for each document. Talk to the people who create the content and ask which words or phrases they would use to describe it. Choose the properties you need from the words or phrases that people suggest. You can add the specific answers as values for the properties. For example, because you can apply the document profile Competitor Product Analysis to content in folders for two different competitors, you add a new property called Competitor to the document profile. The property values are the names of specific competitors.

4. Mark essential properties as required. Decide which properties can have multiple values.

You can make a property required or leave it as an optional field on the document profile. When a property is required, the user must enter a value before checking in a document. Be aware that authors do not consistently enter values for optional properties.

> **Note** Requiring property values improves discovery of your documents but slows the process of checking documents in. Consider your authors when deciding how many required values to include on your document profiles.

You can also permit a user to enter multiple values for the same property. For example, in the document profile Competitor Product Analysis, an author could enter the names of two competitors as values for the Competitor property.

5. For required properties, decide whether values are predetermined or added as needed by authors.

You can restrict property entries to an established list or allow authors to enter free-text property values. When you add a property to a document profile, you must decide whether to restrict the property values to an approved list.

Allowing authors to add a value as needed is appropriate if your group is small and if users maintain a common vocabulary throughout all content. However, inconsistencies can appear when users enter values in an unrestricted manner. Consider designating one person in your group to review all values entered on document profiles. For example, as part of the editorial process, an editor can evaluate the appropriateness of the property values selected by the author on the document profile.

Preventing authors from adding new values ensures consistency throughout all document profiles and improves search success. Restricting entries to an established list requires some planning to create a controlled vocabulary for selected properties. However, this task is more manageable if you consult the people who create the content.

Using Document Profiles to Apply Metadata

In many organizations, it is difficult to find documents that contain similar subject matter, especially if the words used in a search query are not in the text of the document. To overcome this problem, you can apply metadata to documents using document profiles. Metadata supplies additional descriptive information for a document, including additional search keywords that may not appear in the text of a document. During a search, SharePoint Portal Server searches a document's metadata in addition to the text of the document.

Metadata matches a property with a value. For example, you can associate a number of values, such as *London* or *Tokyo*, with a property called City. A document profile is a collection of properties that provides a consistent way to describe and classify documents. For example, you can create a Marketing Analysis profile to define your market-trend analyses. Document profiles include system-generated metadata such as the file size and modification date.

You can modify a document profile to include custom properties, such as sales region, product, and competitor. A workspace can contain multiple document profiles. After you add a document profile to the workspace, you can assign it to any folder by using the **Profiles** tab on the Properties page of the specific folder. Every document in the workspace must have a document profile assigned to it.

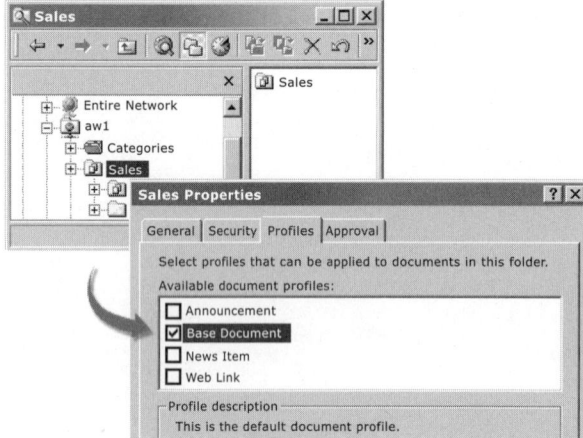

Figure 6.7. Selecting document profiles

For example, Eva writes an analysis of a competitor's product. This product will compete in the market with her organization's product, the Kodiak coat. Although she does not mention the Kodiak in her document, she decides to include this product name as a key-word property value. After Eva publishes the document, Carol uses *Kodiak* in a search query on the dashboard site. Her search results include Eva's analysis because the search query found a match in the keyword property value in the document's metadata.

Emphasize Subjects with Keywords

A keyword is one of the properties available on document profiles. When a search query matches a value in the Keywords property of a document, the document appears toward the top of a search results list, because SharePoint Portal Server weights a match in the Keywords property more heavily than it weights a match in the document body text.

You have two options for allowing authors to add keyword values to a document profile:

- Authors can add values as needed for the property on the profile form. SharePoint Portal Server enables this method by default.

- Authors must select values from a predetermined list in the property on the profile form.

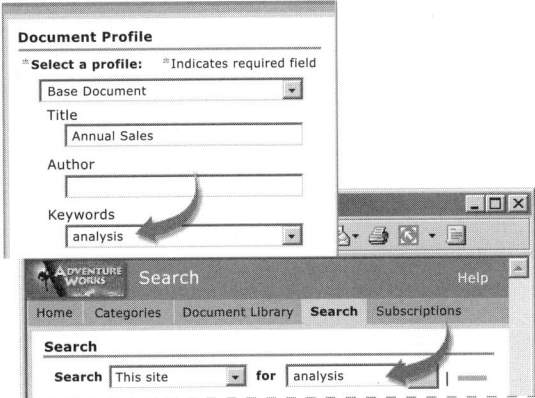

Figure 6.8. Identifying key words for searching

Like other document profile properties, SharePoint Portal Server displays the values for the Keywords property as a list of terms an author can select when completing the profile form. If this list is not restricted, an author may either choose a term from the list or enter a new one. Regardless of the method you choose for designating these values, try to keep this list short and manageable so authors can select the correct keyword quickly and accurately.

Identifying Content Sources

A content source represents a location outside the workspace where content is stored. A URL for this content is stored in the workspace. This content can be located in a different workspace on the same server, on another server on your network, or on the Internet. Examples of content sources include Web sites, file systems, databases, and other workspaces. SharePoint Portal Server creates a searchable index of all content in the workspace and the information available from the content sources that you add. On the dashboard site, users can search for and view information from these content sources.

Important Users cannot check out or edit items from content sources.

Content sources are stored in the Content Sources folder, found in the Management folder of the workspace. To create and manage content sources, you must be designated as a coordinator for the Management folder. You can add a content source at any time by using the Add Content Source Wizard.

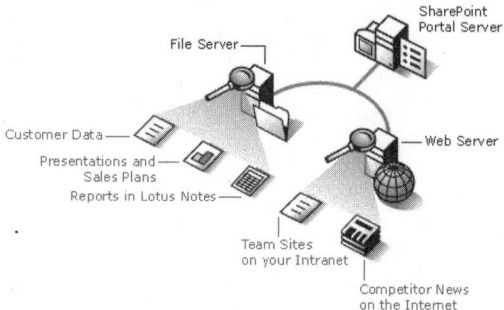

Figure 6.9. Different content sources that SharePoint Portal Server can crawl

You can add the following types of information as content sources:

- Web site

- File share

- Microsoft Exchange 2000 public folders

- Microsoft Exchange 5.5 public folders

- Lotus Notes databases

- SharePoint Portal Server workspaces

Determine what content is most useful to your users when before adding content sources. A content review and user survey are helpful to learn where content is stored and what information users need to access.

Adding Content Sources

Each workspace contains an index of content stored in the workspace and content from the content sources that you add. The Content Sources folder contains the Additional Settings tool. Use this tool to configure settings for this index. By using the Additional Settings tool, you can create a schedule to update the index and choose a method for crawling content sources. You can also customize the index settings for a specific content source or apply the same settings to all content sources.

After you create a content source, you can complete the following management tasks related to the index by using the Additional Settings tool located in the Content Sources folder:

- **Schedule updates.** Indicate how often SharePoint Portal Server should update the index to include new material in existing content sources and any content sources that you added since the last update.

- **Create search scopes.** Provide a way for users to limit what is included in dashboard site searches, in order to improve the speed of searches and yield shorter search results lists.

- **Add rules.** Indicate what types of information you want SharePoint Portal Server to include in or exclude from the index.

Scheduling Updates to the Index

You can apply one schedule to update the index for all content sources or customize the schedules to update individual content sources at different times. There are four update methods. Each update method suggests a default schedule to update index content, although you can customize the schedule settings.

The four update methods are:

- **Full update.** During a full update, SharePoint Portal Server updates links to all content in the content source. A full update includes refreshing the index for unchanged content, adding new content, modifying changed content, and removing deleted content from the index. This is the most time-consuming and resource-intensive type of update.

- **Incremental update.** An incremental update of a content source includes only changed content. SharePoint Portal Server removes deleted content from the index, but does not modify the index for unchanged content. For this reason, performing an incremental update is faster than performing a full update.

  You can perform an incremental update if you know that content has changed but you do not want to create a full update. A periodic (for example, daily) incremental update creates the index without using the time or resources required for a daily full update. By using incremental updates, you can perform full updates less frequently.

- **Adaptive update.** An adaptive update is an incremental update that uses a statistical formula to improve performance. An adaptive update records how often content changes, and then crawls only the content that is statistically most likely to have changed. The more frequently you perform an adaptive update, the more efficiently SharePoint Portal Server processes the content. For this reason, an adaptive update is faster than a full or incremental update.

  Important Although an adaptive update is faster than an incremental or full update, SharePoint Portal Server could miss some updated content. For this reason, SharePoint Portal Server always crawls documents that it has not retrieved for two weeks, even if they have not been updated.

- **Notification update.** A notification update is the most efficient type of update. SharePoint Portal Server uses this method by default when possible. If a content source supports notification updates, it automatically sends a notification of any changes to the index. This notification triggers an update of the individual content source in the index.

  Note Notifications are available only for SharePoint Portal Server computers and for file shares located on an NTFS file system partition on a computer running Windows NT 4 or Windows 2000. Your system administrator can provide you with additional information.

You can customize how often SharePoint Portal Server updates the information for a specific content source or how often it updates the entire index. The default schedule for the Content Sources folder, which contains all content sources, is a daily adaptive update Monday through Thursday at 10:00 P.M. and an incremental update on Friday at 10:00 P.M. This schedule allows SharePoint Portal Server to update information in the index about the content sources daily based on the frequency with which users access the content and for SharePoint Portal Server to include all changes to content sources in the index on Fridays.

Creating Search Scopes

When you configure a search scope for a content source, dashboard site users can narrow their searches to information from a specific content source. For example, if press releases from a competitor's Web site are included in the index, you can apply a search scope called Competitor Press to this content source. SharePoint Portal Server displays the scope as an option next to the keyword search box on the dashboard site. A user can select this search scope and search for a keyword match in the press release content only.

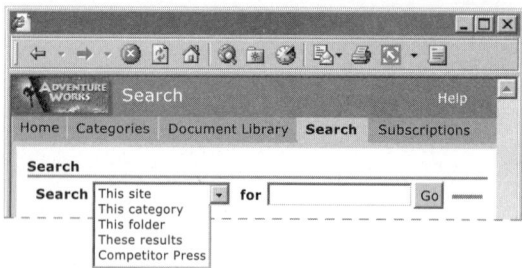

Figure 6.10. Selecting a search scope

If your index includes many content sources, search scopes can enhance server performance by applying a search query to a specific subset of the content in the index. Search scopes work well when you give them a descriptive, functional name such as Customer Profiles, Finance Department, or Competitor Press.

Modifying Content Source Rules

When adding a content source, you need to determine how much content from each source to include in the index. The amount of content varies depending on the type of information with which you are working. For example, you can restrict Web site content included in the index to a single Web page or an entire site.

You can use rules to specify the content that SharePoint Portal Server includes in the index. You can configure content source rules to avoid specific sites or document types when creating the index for a content source.

Supporting Web Discussions

Discussions are an excellent way for groups to collaborate on a document. Web discussions allow users to add remarks about a document without modifying the document itself. Discussions are threaded—replies to a discussion remark appear directly underneath the original remark. In addition, multiple discussions about the same document can occur at the same time. SharePoint Portal Server consolidates comments in a single location, allowing you to review them easily.

Discussions are stored separately from the document they reference. Even if you delete the document, the discussions remain in the workspace until you specifically delete them. SharePoint Portal Server maintains only one set of discussions for each document, even though there may be several versions of that document.

Discussion items are not secure. They will appear in search results if you enable the search feature for discussions. Discussion items may be visible to users who do not have access to the document under discussion. For this reason, SharePoint Portal Server disables the search feature for discussions by default. Disabling the search feature for discussions does not prevent users from adding discussion remarks. Evaluate the security requirements of your documents before enabling the search feature for discussions.

For detailed deployment information about Web discussions, see Chapter 10, "Planning Web Discussions."

Dashboard Site Preparation

When creating a workspace, SharePoint Portal Server also creates an associated Web site. By using a Web browser, a user can perform document management tasks and search for information. This is especially valuable if you have users working on operating systems other than Windows 98, Windows NT 4, or Windows 2000. Those users do not need to upgrade or change their software to benefit from your SharePoint Portal Server deployment.

You can add value to your dashboard site by adding Web Parts that display business information such as news headlines and stock tickers, collaboration tools such as Microsoft NetMeeting®, or general information such as weather or driving directions. You can also tailor the dashboard to meet the specific needs of your organization by creating custom Web Parts. For example, you could add a Web Part that displays an Excel spreadsheet with your quarterly sales figures. You can also export Web Parts from SharePoint Portal Server to another digital dashboard site. For example, you could use the Search Web Part or Subscription Notifications Web Part in your existing corporate portal.

Posting information on the home page is an important step in preparing the dashboard site for your organization. The home page highlights information that is especially important to users. You can also add new Web Parts to display additional information of interest to your readers. For example, a dashboard site for a group or department would include information relevant to the group's work. It might contain a Web Part called Project Status to display project information such as status reports and schedules. In contrast, the dashboard site for a company typically highlights information relevant to all departments of that company. For example, the human resources department learns that searches for information about employee benefits are common. They decide to post information about employee benefits on the home page under a Web Part called Benefits. To keep employees informed about product changes, the marketing department creates a Web Part called Product News with information about a new product line.

For more information about the dashboard site and ways in which you can customize it, see Chapter 4, "Introducing the Dashboard Site."

Using Categories for Organization

The success of a search for information usually depends on the volume of content available for searching, the skill of the user who is attempting to find the information, and the user's access permissions. For example, browsing through 10,000 documents can be overwhelming. If a user does not know exactly what he is searching for or where information is stored, finding a specific document can be time-consuming and frustrating.

You can organize information in the dashboard site by using categories to group similar documents. This allows you to browse through information by topic. For users who are unfamiliar with where documents are stored, categories help them find what they need. Another advantage is that a document may appear in several different categories. Categories accommodate users outside a group without changing the existing folder structure and processes that the group uses. Creating an effective category structure requires planning and some understanding of how others might organize the content.

Creating Your Category Structure

Every workspace contains a category hierarchy. SharePoint Portal Server labels the top level of the hierarchy Categories, with subcategories nested under it. To a user browsing the workspace using Windows Explorer, categories operate like folders. By using Windows Explorer, a user can expand the category hierarchy and browse through the associated document links for each category. The dashboard site displays the categories as a Web Part on the home page.

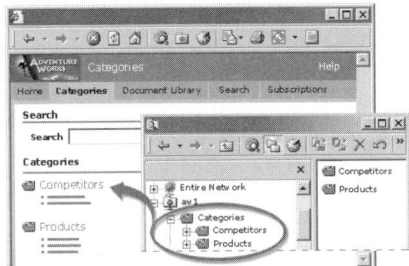

Figure 6.11. Viewing the category hierarchy

After you decide which content to categorize, plan your category structure by considering how users choose to organize the content. For example, do users organize content by department, by project, or by subject matter? If the users organize content by subject matter, what are the top-level categories? What are the subcategories? How many levels of subcategories do you want users to navigate?

You can use SharePoint Portal Server to define as many category levels as you want. However, the more levels you establish, the more likely it is that a user may have difficulty finding content. If you have not organized content in this way before, begin with a shallow structure of one to three levels. You can add more subcategories after users have tested the initial category structure. It is recommended that you use no more than 500 categories in a single workspace.

As with planning for keywords, a user survey facilitates the design of the category structure. You do not need to configure and implement categories, but they can serve as an excellent tool to help dashboard site users find information. Any user with the appropriate permissions can search for and view a published document. However, the category structure offers a way to direct users to a core group of documents that represent that topic. When you decide which categories to use, create the structure in the Categories folder of the workspace. For more information about implementing categories, see Chapter 17, "Using Categories."

Categorizing Your Content

After you establish a group of categories, the next step is to assign the appropriate categories to documents. You can manually assign categories on each document or you can assign them automatically by using the Category Assistant.

Manually Categorize Documents

You can manually categorize a document by using the **Search and Categories** tab on the Properties page of the document. If the document is stored in an enhanced folder, you must check out the document before you can change the document's category assignments. If you have only a small number of documents to categorize, you can use this method of manual categorization exclusively.

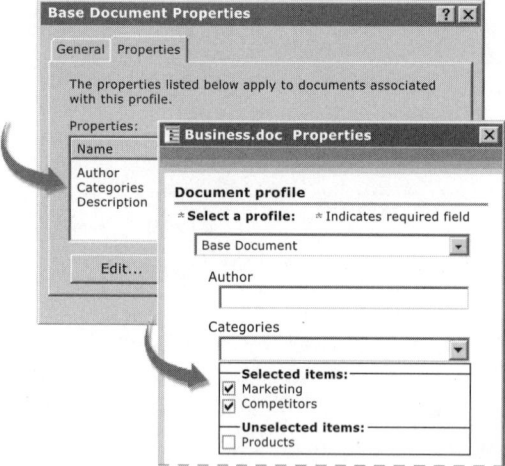

Figure 6.12. Categorizing document from the document profile

You can associate a document with specific categories by using document profiles. Adding the Categories property to document profiles provides a way to enforce category assignment when authors check in a document. Allowing authors to assign categories on the profile form at check-in also distributes the task of document categorization among multiple authors.

Automatically Categorize Documents

The Category Assistant is a tool that automatically assigns categories to documents. If you plan to use categories for a large number of files, the Category Assistant can efficiently assign categories to existing documents and add categories automatically to new documents. This reduces the time required to implement categories for your users. Before using it, you must manually apply categories to a selection of documents for the Category Assistant to use as training examples. Documents used as training examples help the Category Assistant learn the definition of a category. The Category Assistant compares training documents assigned to a category with training examples from other categories to identify the most characteristic features (words). Ultimately, the definition of a category is the list of words that best distinguish documents in one category from documents in other categories.

The Category Assistant automatically categorizes new documents by comparing the list of words for each category to the list of words contained in each new document encountered. SharePoint Portal Server will often automatically categorize a single document into multiple categories.

If the Category Assistant does not select the appropriate categories for a document, a co-ordinator can override the Category Assistant by using the following methods:

- **For a single document.** The coordinator may enable the Category Assistant for the workspace but occasionally override automatically chosen categories for specific documents. For example, the Category Assistant may place a document about hats in the Coats category. The coordinator can correct the category assignment by editing the document's properties.

- **For all documents.** If the Category Assistant is not performing as expected, the co-ordinator can disable it and neutralize all automatically assigned categories.

Improving Search Results with Best Bets

Best Bets enhance search efficiency and provide guidance to users by directing them to documents considered particularly relevant to their search. A Best Bet is a document selected as the best recommendation for a category or specific keyword. SharePoint Portal Sever displays Best Bets at the top of a search results list.

You can use Best Bets to enhance the search efficiency on your portal. You can identify two types of Best Bets:

- A *Keyword Best Bet* is highly relevant to a keyword. It appears in search results when a user enters that keyword in a query.

- A *Category Best Bet* is a document that is highly relevant to a particular category.

To identify a document as a Best Bet, you update the **Search and Categories** tab on the Properties page of the document. The **Search and Categories** tab has two controls: a simple text field for specifying Keyword Best Bets and a Category selection control for selecting Category Best Bets.

In addition, SharePoint Portal Server identifies documents as Best Bets if it finds a very strong match in the search results.

Administration and Maintenance

When you plan your deployment of SharePoint Portal Server, it is recommended that you designate an administration team to perform important system administration and mainte-nance tasks as the system grows to meet your organization's needs. Depending on the size of your organization, the administration team may consist of one or more individu-als. In smaller organizations, the server administrator and the coordinator on the top level of the workspace may be the same person.

Identifying Administrative Tasks

The administrator works with the users responsible for content to determine the number and type of SharePoint Portal Server computers required and the number of workspaces required on each server. For example, in a deployment in which SharePoint Portal Server primarily crawls content sources to make content available for search, you might configure a server that is dedicated to searching and a server that is dedicated to creating and updating indexes. In a deployment in which you use SharePoint Portal Server primarily for document management, you might configure only one server with up to 15 workspaces. When determining how many workspaces to place on each server, the administrator takes into consideration the number of users for each workspace and the quantity of documents stored in the workspace. In a larger deployment, you might configure multiple servers with multiple workspaces on each server. This type of planning is important to ensure that servers are capable of handling the load that users are likely to place on them.

You must use SharePoint Portal Server Administration in MMC to manage the SharePoint Portal Server computer. One administrator can perform tasks for both SharePoint Portal Server and Microsoft Windows 2000 Server, or you can manage these resources separately.

The administrator determines how to best meet customer needs and balance the server load. Administrative tasks include:

- Attaching the server to an organization-wide security infrastructure and linking the server to an organization-wide directory.

- Configuring the server. In conjunction with the user responsible for the content found in the workspace, the administrator must determine the type of server configuration needed.

- Creating workspaces on the server. The administrator monitors disk space available and the number of workspaces per server to determine when additional servers are required for additional workspaces. Although a server can store multiple workspaces, the recommendation is to have no more than 15 workspaces per server.

- Configuring security on the top level of the workspace. You can do this by using SharePoint Portal Server Administration or by using Workspace Settings in the Management folder of the workspace. The administrator must identify one or more users who should have the coordinator role on the top level of the workspace. Coordinators configure security directly on folders and documents in the workspace. This decentralizes security configuration from a single administrator to one or more coordinators.

- Maintaining a list of index workspace names, the server on which they are stored, and the server and workspace to which they are propagated.

- Propagating an index from an index workspace to a workspace on another server, while ensuring that there is sufficient disk space on the destination server for propagated indexes.

- Managing servers by using SharePoint Portal Server Administration. During installation, SharePoint Portal Server automatically installs the console on the server.

- Manually performing full, incremental, or adaptive updates to an index, if required.

- Backing up and restoring the server.

- Duplicating a server.

- Installing and registering IFilters. If you want to crawl documents that have proprietary file extensions, you must register the IFilter for that file type. SharePoint Portal Server includes filters for Office documents, HTML files, Tagged Image File Format (TIFF) files, and text files. SharePoint Portal Server also supports third party and custom file types. The procedure you use to register an IFilter depends on the particular IFilter you are registering. See the documentation that accompanies the IFilter to learn the proper procedure for registering it.

- Modifying the noise word and thesaurus files and creating custom search queries. A *noise word* is a word, such as *the* or *an,* that is not useful for searches. The thesaurus is a query-expansion tool that allows the user to type one word in a search query and receive results on a similar word.

- Configuring the server to crawl Microsoft Exchange Server 5.5 and Lotus Notes content sources.

- Maintaining the server and keeping it available for users, which includes monitoring usage levels of the server, disk space, and performance counters.

Planning for System Maintenance

Maintaining your system includes monitoring the performance of your servers. You can use performance counters to assist you in troubleshooting, capacity planning, and monitoring performance. Administrators can maintain and use historical copies of the gatherer log to collect statistics or perform trend analysis. Each time SharePoint Portal Server updates an index, it creates a gatherer log file for the workspace. This file contains data on the URLs that SharePoint Portal Server accesses while creating an index. You can specify that you want to log successful accesses, documents excluded by rules, and the number of days to keep log files by using SharePoint Portal Server Administration.

Preparing for Disaster Recovery and Server Propagation

This section discusses backing up, restoring, and duplicating the server running SharePoint Portal Server. The SharePoint Portal Server backup and restore process enables you to recover the entire server. The server duplication process enables you to create a copy of a master dashboard site on multiple computers distributed across the network.

The backup and restore process has the same operating system requirements as the server. All dashboard sites, document management, search, subscription, and discussion functionality is available during the backup process. However, you cannot add or remove workspaces or content sources during the backup process. You cannot perform the backup and restore process from any client computer, nor can you back up individual workspaces or documents.

You can create scripts to automate the backup and restore process of the server or to duplicate the server. SharePoint Portal Server installs the backup and restore script automatically.

Back up the Server

You can back up the server by running a script at the command prompt. You cannot back up individual workspaces or documents. You must have local administrator permissions to back up the server.

The backup process creates an image of the server. You can use this image to create a fully functioning instance of the server that is identical to the server at the time you created the backup image.

The image also includes any shortcuts or content sources that reference the local file system. However, these shortcuts and content sources do not work if the referenced content does not exist on the computer on which you perform the restore. In addition, you must restore any shortcuts to workspaces in My Network Places.

You can back up a server to another hard disk on the same server or to a share on a remote disk.

Restore the Server

You can restore a server by running a script at the command prompt. You cannot restore individual workspaces or documents. You must have local administrator permissions to restore the server. You can restore a server from a hard disk on the same server or from a remote file share. You can perform restorations on any computer, regardless of whether you used the computer to produce the backup image. If you used a utility to save the backup image to tape, you must restore the image from tape to disk by using that same utility before you can use the SharePoint Portal Server restore procedure. During the restore process, the server is offline.

Restoring a server destroys all SharePoint Portal Server data currently on that server. The server is unavailable during the restore process and may be unusable if the restore process fails.

Duplicate the Server

The server duplication process enables you to deploy multiple copies of a master SharePoint Portal Server computer across an organization's global network. You can use the SharePoint Portal Server backup and restore process to make multiple copies of the master server by restoring server backup images remotely to other servers in the same domain.

You can duplicate a server by using the backup and restore process as follows:

- Back up your server to a local or remote hard disk.

- Restore from the backup image to the remote server.

You can write scripts to automate the server backup process and create scheduled jobs to create a backup image of the master server for duplication. You can also configure a scheduled duplication process to restore the image on the target server.

Summary

You can deploy SharePoint Portal Server in a department or across an entire organization. Your SharePoint Portal Server deployment can help you use existing content effectively and capture information in new ways that make sense for your business.

When your initial SharePoint Portal Server deployment provides value for one component of the organization, you will likely discover other uses for SharePoint Portal Server. You can easily add workspaces for different groups or create a corporate dashboard site with links to group dashboard sites. You can scale your use of SharePoint Portal Server from a single dashboard site to a network of organizational and departmental dashboard sites. Whether your deployment goal is building a corporate dashboard site to consolidate your information services or a creating a workspace to help a department manage its documents, you will find SharePoint Portal Server a versatile solution.

As you find additional uses for SharePoint Portal Server, it is important to coordinate your deployment efforts with other groups in your company to maintain an efficient system of information management. Maintaining your deployment ensures its effectiveness over time. After your deployment is in place, evaluate it periodically to ensure that it remains useful.

CHAPTER 7

Planning Server Capacity

This chapter identifies the technical boundaries of Microsoft® SharePoint™ Portal Server 2001 to assist you in planning for maximum capacity usage. It also provides suggestions about where to increase resources to scale SharePoint Portal Server to maintain optimal performance. To make effective use of this chapter, it is important that you have a clear understanding of your business requirements.

The following terms are used in this chapter:

- **Corpus.** The corpus includes the collection of documents stored and crawled by SharePoint Portal Server, the categories and folders, document profiles, document versions, and role principals.

- **Role principal.** A role principal is a unique Microsoft Windows NT® security identifier. For example, if you have four unique Windows NT user accounts and three Windows NT group accounts assigned to a role, you have seven role principals.

  Important Microsoft is working on enhancements that should improve performance measurably. For information about the latest performance improvements, see the SharePoint Portal Server Web site at http://www.microsoft.com/SharePoint/.

Deployment Options

There are many issues to consider for capacity planning. Not every statistic is relevant to your deployment scenario. Some issues to consider include:

- When you expand your deployment by adding workspaces to a single server, the additional server load due to increased user activity can cause unacceptable user performance. What is the maximum user activity your server can support?

- The more documents you have, the longer it takes to propagate the index. When is an index too large to propagate efficiently?

- Use of the document management features consumes hard disk space at a fast rate if there is high document versioning activity.

Hard disk space, network, and CPU costs are associated with specific tasks. You must determine which configurations provide the most beneficial user experience. Similarly, there are benefits to increasing specific resources. You must identify which resources could have the greatest impact in your environment.

SharePoint Portal Server is a flexible and efficient solution that can provide portal services to thousands of users. Depending on your organization, you may want to deploy SharePoint Portal Server on one server or on multiple servers.

Deploying a Single Server

Most organizations initially plan for deploying a portal from a single server. Many organizations often address growth and geographical distribution issues after the initial deployment. The following general recommendations apply if you are planning to deploy SharePoint Portal Server on a single server:

- **1 million document versions stored.** A single SharePoint Portal Server computer can store 1 million document versions. You must make choices about several deployment details (such as the extent of the category hierarchy) to achieve, or exceed, this metric. For information about the performance characteristics of such a site, see the "Detailed Recommendations" section in this chapter.

- **3.5 million documents included in the index.** A single SharePoint Portal Server computer can crawl 3.5 million documents. A large, search-oriented site would typically employ several servers dedicated to crawling content to remove the load of crawling content from the server dedicated to searching. For more information, see the "Detailed Recommendations" section in this chapter.

- **10,000 licensed users per server.** Estimating the number of licensed users that a specific server can support is difficult. For many common deployment scenarios, it is possible to support 10,000 licensed users with a single SharePoint Portal Server computer. For information about estimating user support levels, see the "Hardware Requirements" section in this chapter.

If your implementation exceeds the recommended boundaries shown, you may want to deploy additional servers in one or more geographical locations.

Deploying Multiple Servers

Many organizations can benefit from deploying several servers. Reasons for considering multiple server deployments include:

- Geographic user dispersion separated by slow network connections.

- Differing functional goals such as team collaboration, business unit and divisional workspaces and enterprise search servers.

- Distinct organizational goals such as manufacturing, marketing, sales, finance, etc.

SharePoint Portal Server makes it easy to deploy several different servers within an organization and have them all work together to help users find information.

A common approach for larger organizations is to deploy multiple servers for various geographic regions. Later, the organization may provide an additional master search portal. This master portal makes it possible to search over all geographic portals, file servers, Web sites, and other resources.

Hardware Requirements

Selecting an appropriate server platform is an extremely important component of a successful portal deployment. The key hardware requirements are the CPU speed, amount of RAM, and hard disk space:

- Sufficient CPU resources allow SharePoint Portal Server to provide an excellent user experience to large numbers of users during peak usage periods.

- If there are insufficient CPU resources, users experience unacceptable server response times during peak usage periods.

- Additional RAM and hard disk space allow SharePoint Portal Server to provide improved user performance.

- If there is insufficient RAM, users experience unacceptable server response times regardless of the number of active users.

- If there is insufficient hard disk space, users are not able to search for or save additional documents.

An important step in determining your server hardware requirements is establishing clear performance and scalability requirements. Unfortunately, it is frequently difficult to establish clear and detailed performance and scalability requirements for portal deployments. Most organizations find it difficult to predict the level or type of use that the site receives. To complicate matters, this level of use frequently changes and grows over time.

Most organizations can estimate accurately the following important deployment metrics:

- **Number of users.** This is the total number of users who may have access to the site.

- **Percent of active users per day.** This percentage represents the total number of users who might use the dashboard site during any particular day. Typically, this figure ranges from 10 percent to 100 percent. This number is frequently overestimated and is commonly around 30 percent.

- **Number of operations per active user per day.** This is the number of operations that a typical user does from the dashboard site during a typical day. An operation is an action such as viewing the home page, searching, retrieving documents, etc. This number usually ranges from 1 to 10. It is frequently possible to estimate the number of operations by analyzing the Web server log of an existing portal deployment, if one exists. Note, however, that when analyzing the Web server log it is only necessary to consider page views, not site hits. Site hits are frequently significantly higher than the number of page views.

- **Number of hours per day.** This is the number of hours during which most activity occurs. This number typically ranges between 10 and 24 hours.

- **Peak factor.** This is an approximate number that estimates the extent to which the peak throughput for the dashboard site exceeds the average throughput. This number typically ranges from 1 to 5.

You can use the quantitative descriptions of a portal deployment to estimate the required peak throughput. The following formula yields the peak throughput in operations per second.

Peak Throughput Formula

$$\frac{number\ of\ users \times percent\ of\ active\ users\ per\ day \times number\ of\ operations\ per\ active\ user\ per\ day \times peak\ factor}{360{,}000 \times number\ of\ hours\ per\ day}$$

The number 360,000 is determined by:

100 (for percent conversion) X 60 (number of minutes in an hour) X 60 (number of seconds in a minute)

SharePoint Portal Server uses Hypertext Transfer Protocol (HTTP) for all communication between the client and the server. The HTTP protocol is a connectionless protocol. Therefore, it is not possible to identify the number of concurrent users. The most important measurement of server throughput is the operations per second. The following examples illustrate applying the formula to a sample deployment for three sites.

Deploying a Small Group Site

The following is an example of how you can use the preceding formula to determine the requirements for a product group portal for 200 people. The product group contributes more than 90 percent of the site traffic. Although there might be thousands of other users who occasionally use the site, the number is insignificant compared to the product group usage.

For such a deployment, the following characteristics are reasonable.

Small Group Site Deployment

Number of users	200
Percent of active users per day	90
Number of operations per active user per day	10
Number of hours per day	12
Peak factor	5

These estimates yield a predicted peak throughput of 0.21 operations per second.

Predicted Peak Throughput

$$\frac{200 \quad X \quad 90 \quad X \quad 10 \quad X \quad 5}{360,000 \qquad X \qquad 12} = 0.208$$

You could successfully deploy such a site with a server such as a 500 megahertz (MHz) Pentium III with 512 megabytes (MB) of RAM.

Deploying a Large General Site

Another common deployment scenario is a divisional or enterprise portal for approximately 2,000 users. Such a site usually differs from the small group site as follows:

- A more diverse set of workers uses the site.

- The user community is frequently not as focused on document publishing or document collaboration.

In this scenario, there is usually a broad mix of user needs. The average user is typically a less-focused user who might access the site to find a document or to read the morning news or announcements.

The following characteristics for such a site are typical.

Large General Site Deployment

Number of users	2,000
Percent of active users per day	90
Number of operations per active user per day	5
Number of hours per day	12
Peak factor	5

These estimates yield a predicted peak throughput of 1.0 operations per second. Such a site would probably require a server such as a quad processor 500 MHz Pentium III with 1 gigabyte (GB) of RAM.

Deploying a Large Search Site

One final deployment example is the corporate search portal. In this scenario:

- The organization uses the portal predominantly to search over content that was crawled from other sources within the organization.

- The organization does not manage a large number of documents from the site.

- Users are more infrequent than users of the large general site.

- Usage spreads out more during the day due to time zone distribution.

The following are common characteristics for such a deployment.

Large Search Site Deployment

Number of users	10,000
Percent of active users per day	50
Number of operations per active user per day	5
Number of hours per day	16
Peak factor	3

These estimates yield a predicted peak throughput of 1.3 operations per second. Such a site would probably require a server such as a quad processor 700 MHz Pentium III with 2 GB of RAM.

A large search site that includes more than 100,000 documents in the index benefits from using a server dedicated to crawling content to improve performance for users of the server dedicated to searching.

Summary of Requirements

The following table presents a summary of the operations per second and the recommended hardware requirements for the three configurations discussed previously.

Deployment Configuration Comparison

	Small Group Site	Large General Site	Large Search Site
Number of users	200	2,000	10,000
Percent of active users per day	90	90	50
Number of operations per active user per day	10	5	5
Number of hours per day	12	12	16
Peak factor	5	5	3
Operations per second	.21	1.0	1.3
Recommended processor	500 MHz Pentium III	Quad processor 500 MHz Pentium III	Quad processor 700 MHz Pentium III
Recommended RAM	512 MB	1 GB	2 GB

Optimal Throughput with Acceptable Performance

All successful portal deployments share one attribute—the users do not complain about the server being slow. This might seem like an obvious statement, but it is important to consider this requirement and understand in more detail what acceptable performance really means before discussing the details of the performance characteristics of SharePoint Portal Server.

User operations fall into four general categories when measuring performance and throughput:

- **Common operations.** Common operations include viewing the home page on the dashboard site, browsing folders, browsing categories, retrieving documents, and simple search.

- **Rare operations.** Rare operations include creating document profiles, creating categories, and creating content sources.

- **Long-running operations.** Long-running operations include moving, copying, or deleting folders; deleting or renaming categories; and changing inherited security.

- **Uncommon operations.** Uncommon operations include all other operations such as check-in, check-out, publish, and approve.

Defining Acceptable Performance

Performance recommendations are for configurations that pass the following stringent set of user latency criteria:

- All common operations must have a mean latency less than three seconds.

- All uncommon or rare operations must have a mean latency less than five seconds.

- No single operation (excluding potentially long-running operations) can have a latency exceeding 10 seconds.

To determine the latency criteria, all latency measurements were performed multiple times in a variety of load, corpus, and network configurations. The latency criteria provided ensure that, for a typical deployment, users experience excellent performance.

Measuring Optimal Throughput

Recommendations for maximum throughput are the result of an extensive series of laboratory tests and real-world deployment experience. The laboratory tests generated a simulated user activity load against the server and measured a broad set of latencies under varying load rates. Reported maximum throughput rates satisfy the acceptable performance criteria outlined previously.

Profiling User Activity

A broad series of tests show that the exact mix of user operations (such as viewing the home page of the dashboard site, retrieving documents, checking in documents, etc.) does not have a significant impact on the maximum throughput recommendations. Although certain operations are more costly for the server to perform, throughput recommendations use a user activity mix that is representative of the majority of portal deployments. The user activity profile for all laboratory tests was:

- 95 percent for common operations (evenly distributed among the constituents).

- 5 percent for uncommon operations (evenly distributed among the constituents).

- Random occasional testing of all long-running and rare operations.

Detailed Recommendations

Microsoft conducted extensive testing of SharePoint Portal Server to ensure that you can perform detailed planning prior to deployment and to ensure that deployment plans deliver a portal that truly makes users more effective. It is not possible to characterize all server performance without providing an extraordinary amount of data. To help customers focus on the most relevant data, the testing efforts focused on scenarios that experience has shown to be common.

The detailed capacity planning recommendations fall into three broad categories:

- **Corpus characteristics.** Corpus limits describe maximum recommended values for several important characteristics such as the number of documents per workspace, etc.

- **Maximum throughput.** Maximum throughput results describe the expected optimal throughput for a given server. This information can help you plan an optimal deployment.

- **Resource consumption.** Resource consumption recommendations allow you to make detailed predictions of the future server requirements for CPU resources, RAM, and hard disk storage.

Identifying Corpus Characteristics

Each of the recommended limits in this section was obtained by starting with the test workspace shown and modifying it with the characteristic in question until end-user latencies were no longer acceptable.

The base workspace for the tests had the following characteristics.

Workspace Characteristics

Number of documents	50,000
Number of document versions	100,000
Average number of versions per document	2
Document profiles	50
Categories	75
Number of documents per folder or category	Up to 20
Number of categories per document	Up to 3
Average number of documents per folder or category	10
Average number of role principals	20
Average file size	100 kilobytes (KB)
Number of subscriptions	1,000
Number of subscription results	2,000

Summary of Recommendations

The following table displays a summary of the recommendations presented in this section. These recommendations do not represent the limit for support from Microsoft Product Support Services. The recommendations can help you plan your deployment. Your specific requirements may vary, and you should adequately test performance and usability. For details and caveats regarding these limits, read the sections that follow this table.

Recommendations

Maximum number of documents stored per server	500,000
Maximum number of document versions per server	1,000,000
Maximum number of documents included in the index per server	3,500,000
Maximum number of documents per folder	200–3,000*
Maximum document size	50 MB
Maximum number of versions per document	1,000
Maximum number of subscriptions per workspace	100,000

continued

Recommendations *continued*

Maximum number of document profiles	500
Maximum number of content sources	100
Maximum number of role principals per folder	150–600
Maximum number of categories	500

* Maximum recommended is 200 documents per folder. However, it is possible to store up to 3,000 documents per folder if rendering time is not a gating factor.

The following list provides more detail about the recommended maximums.

- **Maximum number of documents stored per server.** The maximum recommended number of documents stored per server is 500,000, with 1 million document versions (an average of two versions per document). This number is the same regardless of the number of workspaces on the server. Therefore, if a workspace requires storage for 1 million document versions, then it should be the only workspace on the server.

- **Maximum number of documents included in the index per server.** The maximum recommended number of documents included in the index per server is 3.5 million. The primary resource constraint for this limit is memory consumption due to database cache growth to support searches over both full-text and document metadata. It is possible to crawl and search over a larger corpus if you use a custom query to search only document text and not document metadata.

- **Maximum number of documents per folder.** The maximum recommended number of documents per folder is 200. This limitation is due to long rendering times for Web browser pages when listing the folder contents. Typical clients can require more than 10 seconds rendering the list of documents in the folder. It is possible to store up to 3,000 documents in a folder if rendering time is not a concern. This might be true if you do not expect users to browse to the contents of the folder from a Web browser, or if users are predominantly using Web folders for folder browsing.

- **Maximum document size.** The maximum recommended document size stored in SharePoint Portal Server is 50 MB.

- **Maximum number of versions per document.** The maximum recommended number of versions per document is 1,000.

- **Maximum number of subscriptions per workspace.** The maximum recommended number of subscriptions per workspace is 100,000. The SharePoint Portal Server subscription technology is extremely efficient. Even with 100,000 subscriptions, there is a negligible impact on server performance. Testing is continuing in this area, and it is likely that this number will increase in the future.

- **Maximum number of document profiles.** The maximum recommended number of document profiles is 500. The number of document profiles does not significantly affect the performance of the server.

- **Maximum number of content sources.** The maximum recommended number of content sources is 100.

- **Maximum number of role principals per folder.** The maximum number of role principals per folder can vary depending on the role. The maximum size of a security descriptor is 64 KB. This size limitation determines the maximum number of role principals. The maximum number of coordinators is 150, and the maximum number of readers is 600. Note that role principals can actually be groups. Therefore, it is possible to allow a very large number of users access to a document.

- **Maximum number of categories.** The maximum recommended number of categories is 500. However, this number of categories can have a negative impact on performance with certain corpus types. Key factors affecting performance are the total number of categories and the total number of documents in all categories. If the average number of documents per category is 20, then the maximum recommended number of categories is 200.

Speed of Long-Running Operations

The following operations can take a long time to complete because the operation must update information on a large number of resources:

- Changing role members on a folder affects the role memberships on all the folders that inherit from that folder. Role membership inheritance completes at a rate of approximately three folders per second.

- Copying a folder also copies all of the documents and folders that belong to that folder. The typical file-copying rate is two files per second. If the number of documents copied causes the task to take more than one hour, Microsoft Windows® Explorer reports a time-out error. The server continues executing the move operation, and it ultimately completes successfully if there is enough hard disk space. If there is not enough hard disk space, then the operation partially completes, terminating at the point where disk space is exhausted.

- Renaming categories requires updating the categorization data on all the documents that belong to the affected categories. Categorizing documents typically completes at a rate of five documents per second. SharePoint Portal Server can rename a category hierarchy of 100 categories, with 10 documents in each category, in approximately 3 minutes 20 seconds.

Determining Maximum Throughput

Throughput testing was accomplished by progressively increasing the rate of user requests until latencies were no longer acceptable. The test server was a multi-processor 500 MHz Pentium III with 2 GB of RAM, a typical large general site configuration.

- **User activity profile.** The user load for all throughput testing was 95 percent common operations and five percent uncommon operations.

- **Maximum number of operations per second.** The maximum throughput on a quad processor 500 MHz Pentium III is 10 operations per second for access using Web folders. The maximum throughput is 1.5 operations per second for access using the Web browser. During these tests, the server is always using 100 percent of its CPU resources. The quad processor server achieved 3.7 times more throughput than an otherwise identical single processor server did for both browser and Web folder access. These results indicate that a server with more and faster CPUs should be able to achieve even greater throughput.

- **Crawling.** The rate of crawling can vary tremendously depending on file types and network conditions. For common document types stored on Web servers and file servers, a typical quad processor server is capable of crawling 12-18 documents per second. For example, crawling 1 million external documents at a rate of 12 documents per second would take 23 hours initially. An adaptive update can reduce crawling time by a factor of six—in this case, it would take four hours to crawl 1 million documents, assuming a typical pattern of changes and updates.

- **Search.** The optimal throughput of searches from the dashboard site varies depending on the number of documents included in the index. It is important to ensure sufficient RAM for the database cache to achieve optimal throughput for searches. A quad processor 500 MHz server with 2 GB of RAM and 3.5 million documents included in the index can respond to 95 percent of all searches in less than five seconds, with a maximum throughput of 20 searches per minute.

- **Propagation.** The amount of time required to propagate an index to the dashboard server can vary depending on the kinds of documents included in the index, and the amount of metadata in the index. Typically, propagation takes one minute for every 20,000 documents in the index.

Calculating Resource Consumption

It is very important to ensure that the server has sufficient amounts of key resources to prevent a suboptimal user experience.

CPU

The CPU resources of the server are consumed during periods of maximum usage. It is possible to ensure that there is sufficient CPU capacity on the server by following the detailed user model recommendations and maximum throughput recommendations outlined previously.

The processing required for adding documents to the index can also consume CPU resources. If the server has more than 100,000 documents in the index, it is recommended that you use a separate server dedicated to crawling content to improve the experience of users.

Hard Disk

As SharePoint Portal Server stores more documents or adds more documents to the index, document storage consumes hard disk space. The following detailed guidelines help you to calculate your storage requirements depending on the particular balance of the number of documents stored within the server or available for searching:

- **Base installation and workspace creation.** The base installation of SharePoint Portal Server without creating a workspace consumes approximately 150 MB. The creation of the first workspace consumes an additional 50 MB. Each additional workspace consumes an additional 20 MB.

- **Document and version storage.** The rate of hard disk consumption varies depending on several criteria.

  Documents stored in standard folders using a document profile with 10 properties consume disk space equal to the sum of 12 KB for metadata storage, 30 percent of the document size for index storage, and the size of the document.

  Standard folder space = 12 KB + (1.3 X document size)

  Documents stored in enhanced folders using a document profile with 10 properties consume 12 KB for metadata storage for each version. In addition, index storage after the document is published accounts for 30 percent of the document size. You must also calculate 100 percent of the document size for each stored version of the document.

  If the document was never checked out (that is, the document is checked in and then immediately approved), then you can calculate the following:

  Enhanced folder space = 12 KB + (1.3 X document size)

  If the document was checked out, then the following is true:

  Enhanced folder space = (number of versions + 1) X (document size + 12 KB) + (0.3 X document size)

- **Index growth.** The index can grow at a widely varying rate depending on the types of documents that you add to the index. The growth rate also depends on the number of searchable words in the document. Text files and HTML files increase the size of the index faster than Microsoft Word files or Microsoft Excel files. Typical mixes of HTML files and Microsoft Office documents expand the size of the index at approximately 30 percent of the size of the original documents. The index increases in size due to documents stored on SharePoint Portal Server and documents stored elsewhere but made available for searching by use of content sources.

  A server dedicated to searching that uses an index from a server dedicated to crawling must have twice the total size of the index available as free space on the disk volume prior to the first index propagation. After the first propagation, it is necessary to have the total size of the index available as additional free space.

- **Log files.** SharePoint Portal Server stores all documents and metadata using database technology that supports both transactions and circular logging. The log files consume a maximum of 25 MB of hard disk space.

RAM

The optimal amount of RAM depends on the number of documents stored and the number of documents included in the index. In general, plan for a server that has base RAM of 256 MB, plus an additional 100 MB for every 100,000 documents either stored on the server or available in the index.

Backup and Restore

The total size of the backup file is the size of the data stored on the server. You can determine the size by calculating the size of the wss.mdb file and the full-text index. The rate of writing the backup file varies depending on the speed of the hard disks. The backup process does not consume a large quantity of RAM or CPU resources. A quad processor 500 MHz Pentium III server with a 40 MB per second Redundant Array of Independent Disks (RAID) 5 disk array can write the backup file at about 5 MB per second. This server can complete an online backup process for 28 GB of data in slightly over one hour.

Future Planning

Capacity planning is an ongoing process. It requires continually monitoring the use of the server to ensure that there are sufficient resources for an optimal user experience. Over time, most deployments experience a significant growth in both the number of users and the amount of content accessed.

Monitoring Performance Counters

You can use performance counters to help you monitor the performance of the SharePoint Portal Server computer, to assist you in troubleshooting, and to assist you in capacity planning.

The *% Processor Time* counter on the **Processor** performance object is an excellent general mechanism for monitoring the current level of activity on the server. This counter should be below 80 percent during periods of peak usage. If the counter exceeds this amount, the user experiences poor performance. In this case, it is likely that your server has inadequate resources to provide peak performance. Either you can deploy a server with more CPU resources, or you deploy an additional server to host an index workspace.

The *Available Mbytes* counter on the **Memory** performance object should always exceed 5 MB. If this counter is below 5 MB, the server experiences dramatically increased disk activity causing severely reduced user performance.

The disk volumes storing the SharePoint Portal Server documents and indexes should have more than 10 MB of free space at all times. If the free space falls below this amount, it is necessary to add more disk space to accommodate additional documents.

If you want to monitor the average time taken to perform a document management function such as check-in, copy, or publish, see the **SharePoint Portal Document Management Server** object, *Successful Checkins Latency*, *Successful Copies Latency*, and *Successful Publishes Latency* counters. For more information about the SharePoint Portal Document Management Server object and related counters, see Appendix B, "For More Information."

Managing Resources

SharePoint Portal Server includes resource usage controls for the two resource-intensive processes that SharePoint Portal Server computers commonly perform. These processes are searching and index creation. You can configure the server to give each process a higher or a lower priority.

You can balance resource usage to optimize performance according to your server configuration. If you plan to distribute searching and index creation across multiple servers, dedicate resources on one or more servers to searching and resources on another server or servers to index creation. If you are using one server to accomplish both tasks, you must balance your settings. By default, SharePoint Portal Server distributes resources evenly between the search resource usage and the indexing resource usage controls.

With the Background usage setting, the server gives higher priority to other applications. With the Dedicated usage setting, the server reserves most of the system resources for searching or creating an index. For example, if the server is primarily dedicated to creating and updating indexes, adjust Search resource usage to Background and Indexing resource usage to Dedicated.

Note If you use this server to run other applications, such as Microsoft SQL Server™, avoid adjusting the controls to Dedicated or near-Dedicated usage for either searching or index creation because this setting may affect resources that are dedicated to those applications.

For more information about setting resource usage, see Appendix B.

Summary

This chapter describes how to calculate the resources you will need to deploy SharePoint Portal Server to best meet your organization's needs. A single server deployment of SharePoint Portal Server can store 1 million document versions and crawl 3.5 million documents. A quad processor server can issue 1.5 dashboard site pages per second, which should provide a portal solution for approximately 10,000 users.

CHAPTER 8

Planning Security

This chapter presents an overview of the advantages of using Microsoft® Windows® 2000 security features with Microsoft SharePoint™ Portal Server 2001. It reviews the elements of Windows 2000 security that allow you to secure access to content on your corporate portal and the role-based security model for SharePoint Portal Server. Although this chapter primarily reviews Windows 2000 security, SharePoint Portal Server supports use of a Microsoft Windows NT® version 4 domain structure. This chapter describes the SharePoint Portal Server security architecture including the publishing model and provides suggestions for securing content for search and content aggregation. For more information about security-related topics, see Appendix B, "For More Information."

Extending the Distributed Security Model

SharePoint Portal Server extends the distributed security model supported by Windows 2000. With role-based security, SharePoint Portal Server simplifies content management by allowing you to distribute administrative tasks to content owners. Instead of relying on a complex and customized system of access rights and permissions, SharePoint Portal Server associates users with roles according to tasks. SharePoint Portal Server modifies their access to a specific document based on the state of the document. The roles create a more flexible and dynamic security model.

Combining the security features available in Windows 2000 and SharePoint Portal Server results in a powerful and flexible security infrastructure that puts significant new capabilities into the hands of content experts.

Assigning Traditional NT Security

With a server based on a traditional NTFS file system, administrators could define groups of users for the local system or within the domain, but could not customize these memberships to specify security policies on content folders. In this situation, the person responsible for securing content must choose among a difficult set of strategies:

- Make continual requests of the local system/domain administrator to manage group memberships.

- Manage many different permission settings on a large number of folders.

- Settle for a compromise on security policy that is either overly restrictive or overly permissive.

SharePoint Portal Server solves these issues by using roles as the primary mechanism for controlling access to content.

Using Role-Based Security

Coordinators can give users or groups access to content by adding them to the security policy on a folder and classifying them into one of three roles: **Reader**, **Author**, or **Coordinator**. On enhanced folders, you can also classify a user as an **Approver**. SharePoint Portal Server then manages security automatically on all content within the folder to ensure that a user has the appropriate level of access to each document. In the case of enhanced folders, SharePoint Portal Server updates the security settings as the document traverses the publishing model. As a document goes through the typical document lifecycle of check-in, check-out, check-in and approval, SharePoint Portal Server gives users the appropriate level of access to the document based on their role membership on the folder.

Role-Based Security

SharePoint Portal Server uses a fixed set of three roles to offer a flexible and secure method for controlling user access to content. You cannot modify the permissions associated with a specific role. You can assign roles both at the individual folder level and on the workspace node, which is the top level of the workspace. In addition, you can completely deny a user (or users) access to a specific document. SharePoint Portal Server uses role-based security to control access to content regardless of whether the user is accessing content by using a Web browser, Web folders, or Microsoft Office.

> **Important** Security settings in SharePoint Portal Server restrict access only to document contents. Members of the Windows 2000 Everyone group can view all metadata associated with a document, such as keywords or other custom properties. Consequently, it is recommended that you refrain from including potentially sensitive information such as password information or program code within the metadata of a document.

The role-based security model provided with SharePoint Portal Server allows you to customize access to content easily.

Reviewing SharePoint Portal Server Roles

Figure 8.1 illustrates SharePoint Portal Server roles.

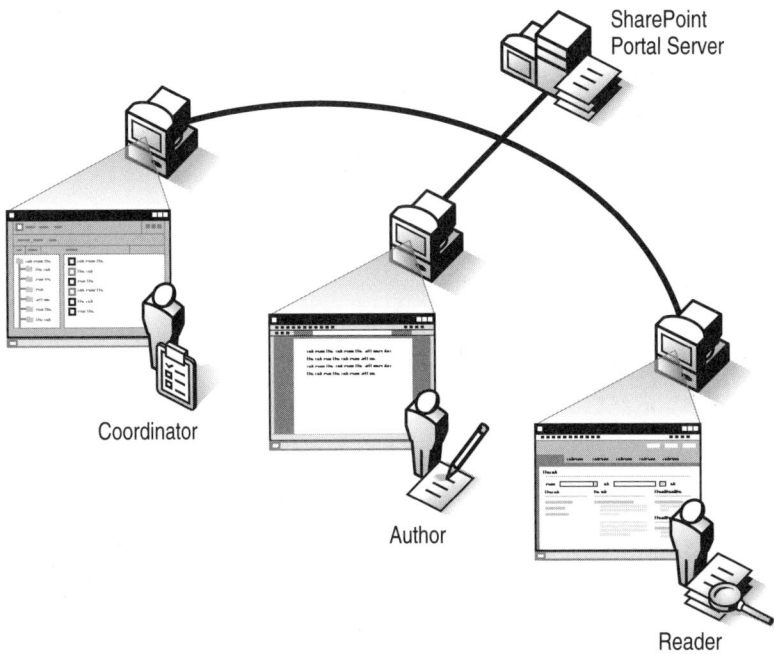

Figure 8.1. SharePoint Portal Server roles

SharePoint Portal Server includes the following roles.

Reader

A reader can search for and read documents but cannot add them to the workspace. By default, all folder users have Read permissions. In an enhanced folder, readers can only view folders and published versions of documents. Enhanced folders provide increased document management functions, including approval routing and version control. A reader cannot check out, edit, or delete documents and cannot view draft document versions.

By default, SharePoint Portal Server assigns the Windows 2000 Everyone group to the reader role for all folders in the workspace when it creates the workspace.

Author

An author can add new documents to a folder, edit all documents in the folder, delete any document or subfolder from the folder, and read all documents in the folder. An author can also delete the folder itself. In an enhanced folder, authors can also submit any document for publishing.

An author can create, rename, and delete folders. When you create a new folder, it inherits the security settings, including role and folder policies, from the parent folder. However, the author cannot change the roles or the approval policy on folders that he creates.

Coordinator

A workspace coordinator manages content in the top-level folder and performs a set of administration tasks that pertain to the entire workspace. These tasks include managing content sources, document profiles, categories, discussions and subscriptions, and customizing the dashboard site. The coordinator creates indexes of updated content when necessary or schedules this to occur automatically.

A coordinator on a specific folder assigns user roles on the folder. The coordinator creates subfolders. In addition, the coordinator adds, edits, and deletes documents from the folder. Coordinators can also read and delete a document that is created but is not yet checked in. For enhanced folders, the coordinator selects the appropriate approval process. In addition, the coordinator can undo the check-out of a document or end the publishing process by using the Cancel Publishing or Bypass Approval actions.

> **Note** SharePoint Portal Server automatically assigns the administrator who creates the workspace to the coordinator role on the top level of the workspace and on each folder.

SharePoint Portal Server provides the Deny Access security option on documents only. This setting supersedes all access permissions except those of the local Administrators group. You can deny access to a document for a specific user or group if you do not want that user or group to view that document. When you deny access to a document, the document is no longer visible to the denied user or group. The user can no longer view the document in lists nor does the document appear in search results. Denying access to a document does not affect the local Administrators group's access to that document.

In addition, the following set of folders and their subfolders support workspace management functions: Management, Portal, System, Shadow, and Categories folders. You must be a coordinator on the top level of the workspace to manage these folders. You cannot directly configure security on these folders. Except for the Management folder, these folders are generally not visible to users of the workspace.

The Windows 2000 local Administrators group has permission to read documents and specify security on any folder or document in a workspace. The ability to configure security provides a way to access every folder and document in the event that, through accident or malicious intent, the folder or document is made unavailable to those who should have access to it. The local Administrators group can restore permissions for individual folders. Denying access to a document does not affect the local Administrators group's access to that document.

> **Important** If you install SharePoint Portal Server on a domain controller, there is no local Administrators group. Consequently, only users assigned to the coordinator role can specify security on folders. If a coordinator makes an error, there is no local administrator to resolve security issues.

Example

Susan, an employee of an outdoor sports company, manages the server in her branch office. The server not only stores the office's workspace, but also serves as the domain controller for the office.

As the server administrator, Susan makes Paul the coordinator for the Finance folder on the regional workspace. As the coordinator, Paul then specifies other roles for the folder, including removing Susan from the list of coordinators. Several months later, Paul leaves the company. Because Susan is no longer a coordinator, and the domain controller has no local administrators group, Susan no longer has access to the Finance folder and cannot modify the security to add a new coordinator for the folder.

> **Note** It is recommended that you plan carefully if you choose to install SharePoint Portal Server on a domain controller. Implementing a specific security practice can help to prevent security lockouts such as the one described in the previous example.

Managing Access to Content

SharePoint Portal Server includes a versatile set of features that allow you to define when and how users can access documents. To help you manage documents, SharePoint Portal Server offers the following:

- Version tracking to record the history of documents.
- Application of descriptive, searchable information to identify a document.
- Document publishing control.
- Automated routing of documents to reviewers.

Version History

SharePoint Portal Server records a document's history to help you track changes and eliminate the possibility of people overwriting another user's modifications. To edit a document, you must first check it out. This prevents others from changing the document until you check it in.

> **Note** To check out a document, you must be assigned to the role of author or coordinator.

Every time you check in a document, SharePoint Portal Server assigns a new version number to the document and archives the previous version. When you check out a document, you retrieve the most recent version unless you specifically select an earlier version.

Document Profiles

Document profiles offer a way to add searchable information, called metadata, pertaining to a document. This information can help describe or identify the document more clearly. By default, a profile includes basic properties such as Author and Title. As a coordinator, you can easily add custom properties such as Account Number or Project Manager to capture additional information that makes it easier to organize and find documents in your organization.

> **Note** Security settings in SharePoint Portal Server restrict access only to document contents. Members of the Windows 2000 Everyone group can view all metadata associated with a document, such as keywords, and other custom properties. Consequently, it is recommended that you refrain from including potentially sensitive information, such as password information or program code, within the metadata of a document.

Document Publishing

SharePoint Portal Server supports both private and public versions of a document. Published documents are available for users to search or view on the dashboard site. As an author or coordinator, you can publish a document automatically each time you save it to the server or you can choose to maintain private document drafts and publish the document when it is complete. You can generate as many drafts as you want before publishing a version of a document.

Approval Routes

As a coordinator, creating approval routes is an easy way to ensure that a document is adequately reviewed before publishing. When an author chooses to publish a document, you can choose to route it automatically to one or more persons for review before publishing it. Each of these individuals, called approvers, has the option of approving or rejecting the document. Approvers receive e-mail notification when a document requires review.

Traditional Windows NT Security

SharePoint Portal Server extends the traditional Windows NT security model of Windows 2000. This section reviews Windows 2000 security concepts that pertain to SharePoint Portal Server security architecture.

Although Windows 2000 is fully backward compatible with previous versions of Windows NT, Windows 95, and Windows 98, Windows 2000 enhances the security model considerably, notably by the introduction of Kerberos version 5 protocol. Windows 2000 security is easier to use than earlier versions of Windows and provides improved support for distributed applications. These changes allow much greater scalability and increased ease of administration compared with earlier versions of Windows NT. Many of the enhancements directly support the Microsoft Active Directory™ directory service. SharePoint Portal Server adds value to the customer experience by further simplifying the administration process.

Using Access Control Lists

Windows 2000 security relies on Access Control Lists (ACLs) to control access to resources. Windows NT stores an ACL with every file and folder on an NTFS partition. The ACL contains a list of all user accounts, groups, and computers that are granted access for a file or folder and the type of access granted to them. For a user to access a file or folder, the ACL must contain an entry—called an access control entry (ACE)—for the user account, group, or computer to which the user belongs. The entry must specifically allow the type of access the user is requesting for the user to be able to gain access to the file or folder.

If no ACL exists, Windows 2000 grants all users Read access. If no ACE exists in the ACL, Windows 2000 denies the user access to the resource. If you apply an empty ACL, then Windows 2000 denies access to all users. If multiple ACEs exist for a user, Windows 2000 applies the first one. Consequently, it is recommended that you grant permissions first to an individual user, and then to any groups. This ensures that specific users are granted any appropriate permissions that might supercede their group permissions.

Figure 8.2 illustrates how access is granted based on an ACL.

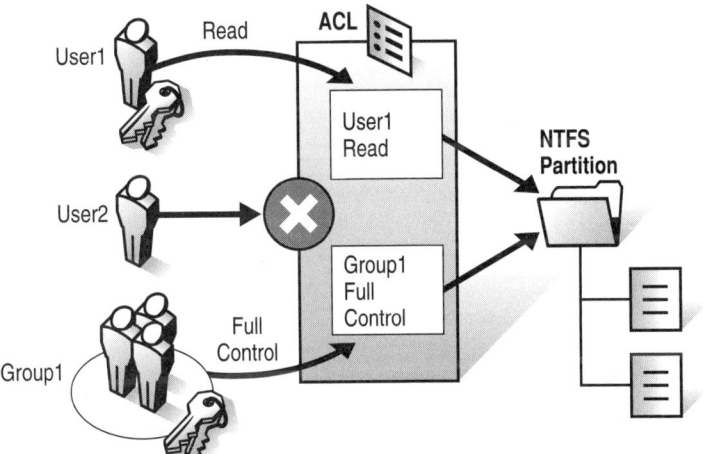

Figure 8.2. Access control lists

In this figure, User2 does not have an ACE. Consequently, User2 is not granted access to the resources on the NTFS partition.

SharePoint Portal Server uses ACLs extensively to ensure secure and appropriate access to content.

Highlighting Windows 2000 Security

The Windows 2000 Distributed Security Services provides flexible solutions for building secure and scalable distributed applications. Security administration and management have richer features for delegation and detailed account control. Active Directory supports domains with a much higher number of accounts in a structured naming environment of organizational units. Inter-domain trust management is simpler, providing greater flexibility to use domains in ways that reflect the needs of the enterprise. You can use SharePoint Portal Server in an Active Directory environment.

Windows security APIs for network authentication, data privacy, digital signatures, and encryption support secure application development for the enterprise and the Internet. The Microsoft Security Support Provider Interface (SSPI) and CryptoAPI interfaces, in addition to higher-level Component Object Model (COM) and distributed version of COM (DCOM) interface abstractions, make all the integrated security features of Windows 2000 available for SharePoint Portal Server to use. SharePoint Portal Server uses the robust security architecture of Windows NT consistently across all system components and extends to support strong authentication and public-key security.

Windows 2000 Distributed Security integrates mature Internet standards for authentication while introducing new public-key security technology based on industry direction and available standards. Many of the Internet public-key security standards are still forming. Microsoft is involved in the development of these standards but recognizes that they are likely to change over time. The Windows 2000 security architecture is specifically designed to incorporate new security technology in the form of protocols, cryptographic service providers, or third-party authentication technology. Customers deploying Windows 2000 have choices about which security technology to use, how to integrate security into their application environment with minimum impact, and when to migrate to new technology as it becomes available.

Together, these factors make the Windows 2000 Distributed Security Services the best foundation for secure Internet-distributed computing. For the latest information about secure Internet-distributed computing with SharePoint Portal Server, see Chapter 12, "Deploying SharePoint Portal Server in an Extranet Environment."

Honoring Windows 2000 Authentication Methods

SharePoint Portal Server honors all the various types of authentication by accepting the appropriate access token based on a user's security identifier (SID). However, there are some scenarios where you may use certificate authorities (CAs) that do not work with SharePoint Portal Server. SharePoint Portal Server security uses SIDs. A user without a valid SID does not gain access to content using SharePoint Portal Server.

In SharePoint Portal Server, workspace access is restricted to valid Windows NT users and groups, whether they are domain users or local server users. When you deploy SharePoint Portal Server within a Windows NT domain and the user logs into the domain, SharePoint Portal Server uses the domain security services for authentication. This enables a single logon for users. Where you deploy SharePoint Portal Server in non-Windows NT domains, SharePoint Portal Server collects and authenticates the user name and password. It does this by using basic authentication against accounts maintained on the server running SharePoint Portal Server.

Note Using Basic Authentication, Windows 2000 sends user accounts and passwords as clear text.

You must assign a user a Windows NT account in order to receive a SID. SharePoint Portal Server uses SIDs to assign roles. You must assign users a role to access content. For anonymous access, Windows 2000 security provides a specific SID for use in ACLs. Consequently, you can assign anonymous users to roles.

Important If you enable anonymous access to the document library, then by default, SharePoint Portal Server gives all users anonymous access. In order to allow anonymous readers access to the document library, it is recommended that you create a separate virtual server for this type of access.

For more information about creating a separate virtual server, see Chapter 12.

Windows 2000 manages the network security credentials for a user transparently after a single instance of signing on successfully. The user is not concerned about whether a connection to a network server uses NT LAN Manager (NTLM), Kerberos protocol, or a public-key-based security protocol. Users simply sign on to the system and have access to a wide variety of network services.

Within the enterprise, Windows 2000 determines access to resources by the rights granted to users' accounts or by group memberships. Across the Internet, Windows 2000 determines users' access based on their identity proven by a private-key signature operation and the corresponding public-key certificate. All the security protocols rely on some form of user credentials, which the client computer presents to a server when a connection is established. Windows 2000 manages these user credentials and automatically uses the appropriate set of credentials, based on the security protocol involved.

The Windows 2000 Active Directory service supports multiple security credentials as part of the secure portion of user account information. Windows 2000 uses these credentials for enterprise authentication services that use the domain controller for online user authentication. Advanced application servers can support integrated Windows 2000 authentication by using the Security Service Provider Interface for network authentication.

Reviewing Windows 2000 Security Group Scopes

The scope of a group determines whether you can use a group across one or more domains. The group scope affects group membership and group nesting. Nesting is adding a group to another group as a member. Windows 2000 provides three group scopes: global, domain local, and universal.

Global Group Scope

Use this group scope to organize users who share similar network access requirements. You can use a global group to grant permissions to gain access to resources that are located in any domain.

- Global groups have limited membership. Add user accounts and global groups only from the domain in which you create the global group.

- You can nest global groups within other groups. This function allows you to add a global group to another global group in the same domain or to universal and domain local groups in other domains.

Domain Local Group Scope

Use this scope to grant permissions to domain resources that are located in the same domain in which you created the domain local group. The resource does not have to reside on a domain controller.

- Domain local groups have open membership. Add user accounts, universal groups, and global groups from any domain.

- You cannot nest domain local groups within other groups. Consequently, you cannot add a domain local group to any group, even groups in the same domain.

Universal Group Scope

Grant permissions to related resources in multiple domains. Use a universal group to grant access permissions to resources that are located in any domain.

- Universal groups have open membership. All domain user accounts and groups can be members.

- You can nest universal groups within other domain groups. This capability allows you to add a universal group to domain local or universal groups in any domain.

  Important Security groups with a universal group scope are only available when the domain is in native mode. Native mode is when all domain controllers are running Windows 2000.

In addition, you can create local groups only on member servers and on computers running Windows 2000 Professional, and you use them to assign permissions to resources only on the local computer. The membership rules for local groups include the following:

- Local groups can only contain local user accounts from the computer on which you create the local groups.

- A local group cannot be a member of any other group.

Guidelines for using local groups include:

- Define local groups only on computers that do not belong to a domain.

  You can use local groups only on the computer where you create the local groups. Although you can set up local groups on domain client computers and member servers, it is not recommended. Using local groups on domain computers prevents you from centralizing group administration. Local groups do not appear in Active Directory services, and you are required to administer local groups separately for each computer.

- Use local groups to control access to resources on the local computer and to perform system tasks for the local computer.

In order to allow SharePoint Portal Server to crawl content, you must carefully plan your group strategy for securing content and domain structure.

> **Important** SharePoint Portal Server limits you to 200 SIDs that you can associate with a given role on a folder. Consequently, in large deployments, strategic planning of groups allows you to grant users appropriate access to content.

Using Security Groups in Windows 2000

Figure 8.3 illustrates the recommended strategy for granting users permission to resources.

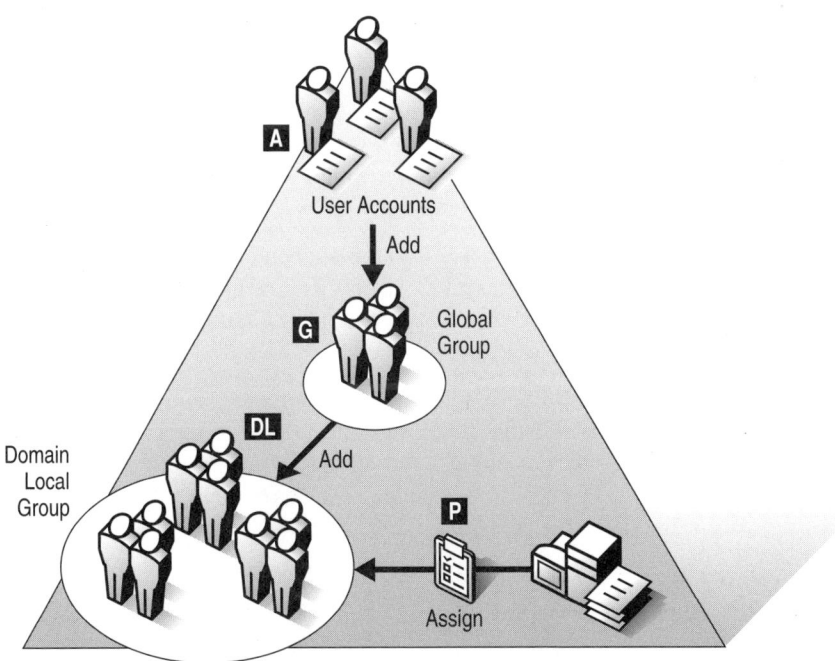

Figure 8.3. Applying group strategy in a single domain

When you use groups in a single domain, you use the *AGDLP* strategy. You can describe the AGDLP strategy as follows: You put user accounts (A) into global groups (G), put the global groups into domain local groups (DL), and then grant permissions (P) to the domain local group.

When you create the groups, Windows 2000 recommends the following strategy:

- Identify users with common responsibilities and add the user accounts to a global group. For example, in a sales department, add user accounts for all sales employees that use the same resources to a global group called Sales.

- Determine whether you can use a built-in domain local group, or if you need to create one to provide users with access to domain resources. For example, if you want users to be able to print to a shared color printer in the domain, create a domain local group called Color Printer Users.

- Make all global groups that share the same access needs for resources members of the appropriate domain local group. For example, add the appropriate global groups, including Sales, to the domain local group Color Printer Users.

- Grant the required permissions to the domain local group on the domain controller. You grant permissions at the resource. For example, grant the necessary permissions to use color printers to the Color Printers Users domain local group.

  Note If there are parallel groups in multiple domains, make sure that the names are parallel and that they reflect the domain names. For example, if there is a group for managers in each domain, these groups should use a similar naming scheme, such as Managers USA and Managers Australia.

Windows 2000 allows you to customize the type of access a specific user or group has to a specific resource. It also allows you to customize how a given resource inherits access rights from parent resources. Although this provides you with maximum flexibility and control, it can lead to increasingly complex security configurations.

Important SharePoint Portal Search secures searching across remote content sources, so that search results only include documents that users are actually allowed to view and access. In order to provide this functionality, the computer running SharePoint Portal Server must be able to resolve an ACE used to grant access.

If you use local groups to grant permissions to documents stored on remote NTFS file shares, SharePoint Portal Server cannot resolve the local group ACE. Therefore, SharePoint Portal Server does not return documents from those file shares in search results. You must grant permission through another mechanism, such as domain local groups or global groups, to allow access to the content.

You must secure content on remote NTFS file shares by using a compatible group strategy.

Applying Security Groups to SharePoint Portal Server

SharePoint Portal Server simplifies administration by allowing you to assign users and groups to a specific set of roles according to task. This approach provides more flexibility for the content owner. You can use large, natural grouping where appropriate. Some groups lend themselves to roles. For example, you may assign the Windows 2000 Users group to the role of author. Depending on your security model, you may assign smaller global groups to the role of coordinator.

With enhanced folders, SharePoint Portal Server modifies the specific access that a user has for a document according to the state of the document.

Security Groups in a Single Domain

You can apply the AGDLP strategy when deploying SharePoint Portal Server within a single domain whether operating in a native or mixed-mode environment.

In this situation, you put user accounts (A) into global groups (G), put the global groups into domain local groups (DL), and then grant permissions (P) to the domain local group.

Security Groups across Multiple Domains

When deploying SharePoint Portal Server across multiple domains in a native-mode environment, you can secure content by using universal groups as part of the group strategy. You put user accounts (A) into universal groups (U), put the universal groups into domain local groups (DL), and then grant permissions (P) to the domain local group.

When deploying SharePoint Portal Server across multiple domains in a mixed-mode environment, you must establish an appropriate trust relationship across domains. For SharePoint Portal Server to access content in another domain, you must establish a one-way trust where the other domain trusts the domain where you deploy SharePoint Portal Server. In addition, you must modify the group memberships to include the account used by SharePoint Portal Server.

> **Note** In this case, SharePoint Portal Server successfully crawls content on a different domain. However, users from that domain have only limited access to content on SharePoint Portal Server. To provide these users with a different level of access, you must establish a two-way trust.

Example

For example, suppose Server A is in Domain A, and you want to crawl content located on Server B in Domain B. Server B could be another SharePoint Portal Server computer, a Web server, or a file share.

- In a native-mode environment, you can use universal groups to grant access permissions to resources that are located in either domain. This greatly simplifies the administration process.

  In this situation, Server A can crawl content from Server B and make it available to users from Domain A who are members of the appropriate universal group.

- In a mixed-mode environment, you want to establish a one-way trust where Domain B trusts Domain A.

  In this situation, Server A can crawl content from Server B and make it available to users from Domain A assigned to the appropriate security groups.

For information about establishing trust relationships in a Windows NT 4 environment, see Appendix B.

SharePoint Portal Server Security Architecture

SharePoint Portal Server provides significant new features for controlling access to documents, in addition to a state machine for structured approval of a document. When an event occurs with a state machine, the object responds by changing its state to reflect the new history of the object. SharePoint Portal Server uses a complex and extensible permissions system that builds upon the traditional Windows NT security model, while providing the ability to control access to operations in a way that does not conflict with the publishing model.

Viewing Role States and Actions

The following table shows the document states and user actions and which roles can perform these actions in the given state. The list of allowed roles is the following:

- **Lock Holder.** The last person to check out the document
- **Submitter.** The person who submitted the document for approval.
- **Reader.** A person viewing the document.
- **Author.** A person creating or modifying the document.
- **Approver.** The current approver of the document (as opposed to all the members of the approver role).
- **Coordinator.** A person who specifies security for a given folder or document.

Note These roles are not visibly apparent in the user interface but describe how SharePoint Portal Server modifies access as a document traverses the publishing model. From the perspective of the user, SharePoint Portal Server features three roles: Reader, Author, and Coordinator. In addition, you can also specify a list of approvers for a folder within the workspace.

The following table shows the different states of a document during the publishing model, the various actions that can be performed, and who is given the access rights on the source folder to perform the action.

Role States and Actions

State/Action	Created/ Checked Out	Checked In	Checked Out	Under Approval	Approved
Save			Lock Holder		
Check In	Creator		Lock Holder		
Check Out		Author; Coordinator			Author; Coordinator
Undo Check Out			Lock Holder; Coordinator		
Submit		Author; Coordinator			
Approve				Approver	
Reject				Approver	
Bypass Approval				Coordinator	
Cancel Approval				Submitter, Coordinator	
Move	Creator; Coordinator	Author; Coordinator	Lock Holder		Author; Coordinator
Copy	Creator; Coordinator	Reader; Author; Approver; Coordinator	Reader; Author; Approver; Coordinator	Reader; Author; Approver; Coordinator	Reader; Author; Approver; Coordinator
Delete	Creator; Coordinator	Author; Coordinator	Lock Holder		Author; Coordinator

continued

Role States and Actions *continued*

State/Action	Created/ Checked Out	Checked In	Checked Out	Under Approval	Approved
Read Draft	Creator; Coordinator	Author; Coordinator	Author; Coordinator	Author; Approver; Coordinator	Author; Approver; Coordinator
Read Approved		Reader; Author; Coordinator	Reader; Author; Coordinator	Reader; Author; Approver; Coordinator	Author; Coordinator

Defining the Publishing Model

Figure 8.4 presents a simplified publishing model for SharePoint Portal Server. In addition, it demonstrates the path a document traverses from a published state to a newly published version.

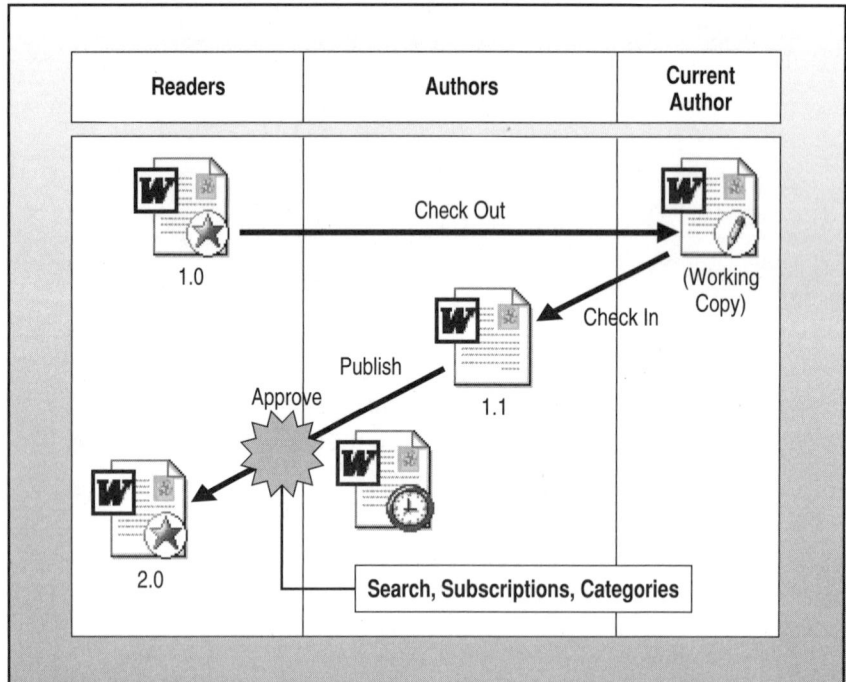

Figure 8.4. Publishing model

In this illustration, a reader or approver may view the last approved version (1.0), while the author is working on the latest unapproved version (working copy) of a document. The current author, as the person who checked the document out, is the lock holder and consequently has the working copy of the document. As the author checks in the document, SharePoint Portal Server assigns the version number 1.1 to it. After publishing and approval, the document becomes version 2.0.

Enabling Role Membership Inheritance

Many SharePoint Portal Server deployments incorporate a large number of folders, while requiring a relatively small number of distinct security policies. SharePoint Portal Server allows you to enable inheritance of role membership so that coordinators can manage security policies across large numbers of folders by making changes to role memberships on a single parent folder. You can configure every folder to adopt the security settings of its parent folder (similar to the ACL inheritance provided in Windows 2000). When a folder inherits security from its parent folder, all role memberships on the folder match the parent folder. It is not possible to alter role membership on the folder. The server applies all changes to role membership on the parent to inheriting children at the time you change the security settings for the parent folder.

If you choose to cancel inheritance, you have the option of copying the role membership from the parent folder, or removing all role memberships from the folder. If you enable inheritance after it is cancelled, SharePoint Portal Server completely replaces the current role membership with the role membership of the parent. When you create a new folder, it inherits security settings from its parent by default.

> **Note** Because the state of approver is not a security role, subfolders do not inherit approval policies: Subfolders inherit neither the role settings nor the approval topology. You must specify approval policies on each folder.

It is possible to reset the inheritance on all subfolders. This resets inheritance recursively on all descendants. Resetting the security on subfolders is only successful on those folders for which you are assigned the role of coordinator.

Viewing Folder Hierarchies

In order to discover a document by browsing the folder hierarchy, the user must be a member of at least one role on the parent folder. In order to view a list of subfolders within a folder, the user must be a member of at least one role on both the parent folder and the subfolder.

In order to list the contents of a folder, the user must be assigned to a role on the folder. SharePoint Portal Server modifies the list of all items in that folder so that the user only sees items that he actually has access to read. In other words, any documents for which a user is denied access or any subfolders on which the user has no role membership are not visible in the list of contents. Search results only include documents that users are granted permission to view and access.

As described previously, local administrators always have implicit read access to all contents.

Assigning Default Role Membership

By default, when you create a workspace, SharePoint Portal Server assigns the following default role membership for all visible folders:

- Reader: Everyone
- Coordinator: Workspace Creator

Selecting Users from Directory Sources

When roles are used, the coordinator populates each role's membership list with actual Windows NT users and groups in the specific domain. You select users, groups, and roles from the standard Windows NT user picker. You can select users and groups from the following locations.

Windows 2000 Active Directory Domains

The contents of a role's membership list are the users and groups from the Windows 2000 directory structure.

Windows NT 4 Domains

In a Windows NT 4 domain, Windows stores SIDs in the security accounts manager (SAM) database. When a coordinator needs to add users to a role, she selects users from the directory. In this case, SharePoint Portal Server lists the user and group SIDs from the SAM database and allows the person to place them in the Role membership list.

The Windows NT 4 SID structure is the same as Windows 2000 SIDs. No special handling needs to occur for users and group collected from a Windows NT 4 domain.

Local Windows NT Accounts

In addition to domain groups, coordinators may select from local groups and users on the server running SharePoint Portal Server. This option is particularly helpful in an environment where you do not employ Windows NT domains. In this situation, SharePoint Portal Server collects and authenticates the username and password against local accounts maintained on the local SharePoint Portal Server computer running Windows 2000.

> **Important** In general, you should not allow local user or group accounts to secure content because other servers running SharePoint Portal Server cannot resolve local accounts on individual computers. Consequently, content secured by using local accounts on other servers cannot be included in an index nor viewed by users on the dashboard site.

Authenticating with SharePoint Portal Server

SharePoint Portal Server workspace access is restricted to valid Windows NT users and groups, whether they are domain users or local server users. When you deploy SharePoint Portal Server within a Windows NT domain and the user logs into the domain, SharePoint Portal Server uses the domain security services for authentication. This enables single logon for users. When you deploy SharePoint Portal Server and you do not implement Windows NT domains, SharePoint Portal Server collects and authenticates the username and password against accounts maintained on the computer running SharePoint Portal Server.

Note Windows 2000 assigns anonymous users an SID that allows them to be included in ACLs. Consequently, you can also assign anonymous accounts to roles. However, if you choose to enable anonymous accounts, Windows 2000 treats all users as anonymous users. It is recommended that you create a separate virtual server, or vroot, for this type of access.

For more information about creating a separate virtual server, see Chapter 12, "Deploying SharePoint Portal Server in an Extranet Environment."

Ensuring Dashboard Site Security

SharePoint Portal Server relies on Internet Information Services (IIS) Web server to enforce security. SharePoint Portal Server supports URL access to the Web Storage System. All access to the dashboard site is through a vroot, controlled by IIS, which uses Windows NT permissions to enforce security. Windows NT requires the basic set of rights that are embodied by the Web Storage System. IIS relies on the underlying storage system, such as NTFS or the Microsoft Web Storage System, to provide ACLs that contain the users who have access to the requested object.

Ensuring Search Security

The user search experience requires security in two aspects of search processing:

- **Default content access account.** SharePoint Portal Server crawls external content within the context of a user account. You provide a default content access account for SharePoint Portal Server to use to access external content. In addition, you can specify an access account for an individual content source. This account information is stored as a property of the crawl seed item.

- **Search results access.** In search results, that is, logical views of documents, a user cannot view a document or folder unless he has access to read the file.

Unless an appropriate trust relationship is established, the default content access account or the access account for a particular content source must be a member of the appropriate group in the domain where the content is located in order to crawl the content and include it in an index. In addition, the user must also be a member of the appropriate security group in order to view the content.

In a native-mode environment, universal groups can facilitate the security administration. In a mixed-mode environment, you must establish the appropriate trust relationship as well as implement a compatible group strategy.

Ensuring Access to Security Tasks

Coordinators specify content security and assign roles. The predefined set of roles provides the appropriate level of control and flexibility.

SharePoint Portal Server Administration

A computer running SharePoint Portal Server may contain one or more workspaces. When you create a workspace, SharePoint Portal Server prompts you to designate a workspace owner. SharePoint Portal Server assigns this owner to the coordinator role for the workspace.

Workspace Lockout

SharePoint Portal Server allows coordinators to control the access to a document for both reading and viewing. Someone who does not have access to a document or folder cannot discover its existence through search or folder browsing. In addition, it is possible to configure the security membership on a folder to be completely distinct from the role membership of the parent folder. As a result, you could configure security so that no users can view the secured object. In this situation, it would be impossible to change the role membership on the folder again, because it would be impossible for anyone to browse to the parent folder and access the Properties page of the subfolder to modify the security settings.

To address this possibility, SharePoint Portal Server assigns the local Administrators group the permissions to read and browse every document and every folder in all workspaces. This is a nonconfigurable, nonrevocable right of the local Administrators group. It takes precedence over the No Access role on individual items. The local Administrators group also has the permissions to specify role membership on all folders and all documents. Therefore, if a folder becomes inaccessible due to the scenario outlined previously, anyone who is a member of the local Administrators group on the server can resolve the problem. Any user who is a member of the local Administrators group can assign role membership on all files and folders, regardless of the user's role membership on specific folders

> **Important** SharePoint Portal Server does not grant a member of the local Administrators group full privileges for all coordinator operations. For example, although a member of the local Administrators group can attempt operations such as changing Web Part settings or layout of the dashboard site, those operations silently fail. SharePoint Portal Server does not report the failures. To complete these operations successfully, the local Administrator must add herself to the coordinator role on the appropriate folder.

Content Security for Searching and Document Management

The server administrator and the workspace coordinator must consider the organization's security policy when planning to make content available through the dashboard site. In the past, information across an organizational structure was often secure by virtue of being difficult to find. With SharePoint Portal Server, obscurity no longer acts as a deterrent for information access. After you identify a source of content, SharePoint Portal Server includes it in an index and makes it available to users across the organization who are associated with the appropriate role.

If information is not properly secured, it could potentially be visible to an unintended audience. For example, confidential information stored on an unsecured file server within one department of a financial institution could be visible to users from a different department through the dashboard site.

SharePoint Portal Server offers several features that make searches faster and more successful for users. These features could also potentially give access to inappropriately secured content. These features include:

- A single location to search for information stored in many different places

- Keyword searches that search the full text of a document and the document's properties

- Advanced search on specific document profiles, properties, or date

- Browsing by topic (categories) to find information

- Automatic categorization of documents

- Best Bet classification for documents that are highly relevant to a search

- Subscriptions to keep you up to date on useful information

When deploying SharePoint Portal Server, you should take steps to ensure that information is available only to the intended audiences by securing content across all information sources.

SharePoint Portal Server reveals all information to the appropriate users according to Windows NT security settings. A lack of clearly defined NTFS security policy can pose a dramatic security risk.

> **Tip** Review your organizational security policy and identify possible security risks. Revise the security policy for each potential hazard to ensure accurate and sufficient permissions for the appropriate groups of people.

There are two sources of content to consider when configuring security: content stored in the workspace and content stored outside the workspace. You must also consider how the dashboard site displays these content sources.

Securing Content in the Workspace

Content stored in the workspace includes documents in standard and enhanced folders. There are several issues to consider when securing content in the workspace.

Security Settings Inheritance

When you create a new subfolder, it inherits security settings from its parent folder by default. If you do not want to use the security settings of the parent folder, you can customize the role settings on the subfolder. If you change the settings for a parent folder, you can specify that all subfolders use the new settings. In this case, you override any modified role settings on the subfolders.

Folders inherit only the role settings. For enhanced folders, SharePoint Portal Server copies the approvers and the approval route to the subfolder when it is created; however, subsequent changes to this setting on the parent folder are not passed to the subfolders.

Control Access with Roles

Roles can assist you in controlling how users access information in a folder hierarchy. For example, if a coordinator does not want the user to infer information based on the folder structure, she can structure the roles so that users can search for particular documents and view them, but the user cannot view parent folders.

To browse the folder hierarchy to locate a document, you must assign a user to at least one role on the parent folder. To browse to a subfolder of a parent folder, you must assign a user to at least one role on both the parent folder and the subfolder.

If a user has access to a subfolder but not the parent folder, he can access that subfolder directly through its URL, even though the parent folder is not visible in Windows Explorer. In this case, documents in the subfolder appear in search results.

Compound Documents

SharePoint Portal Server supports compound documents (the set of files and folders created when you save a document as a Web page from an Office application) only on standard folders. Only coordinators can configure security on a subfolder of a compound document. Enhanced folders do not support any structures similar to compound documents (for example, HTML files with relative links or a Microsoft Word document with a linked Microsoft Excel spreadsheet where both are stored in the workspace). If you attempt to check in a compound document to an enhanced folder, SharePoint Portal Server displays a warning message.

Using Subscription Notifications with Windows 2000 Authentication

When a user creates a subscription, the user does not receive a subscription notification if her right to read the document is assigned through a Windows 2000 Authenticated Users SID, which is inside a domain or local group. Note that the Windows 2000 Everyone group is not one of the SIDs in this category.

For example, ADVENTURE\user falls into the category of Authenticated Users in the ADVENTURE domain. The SharePoint Portal Server computer Marketing is in the same domain. ADVENTURE\user creates a subscription on Marketing to the search results for "specification." Any document that is included in the index and contains the word "specification" should generate a notification.

- ADVENTURE\user receives a notification if a document that contains the word "specification" is in the Projects folder and that folder has Everyone in the Reader role.

- ADVENTURE\user receives a notification if a document that contains the word "specification" is crawled on a Web server.

- ADVENTURE\user does not receive a notification if a document that contains the word "specification" is in the SpecialCase folder, on which the only Reader is the domain group AuthPeople and that domain group contains Authenticated Users.

A user does not receive notifications if his only access to the document is assigned through an Authenticated Users or other special SID such as:

- ANONYMOUS LOGON

- BATCH

- DIALUP

- INTERACTIVE

- NETWORK

- TERMINAL SERVER USER

If an access control list (ACL) contains a group whose members consist of both ADVENTURE\user and Authenticated Users, the user receives a notification.

Using IFS and IIS to Access Content

Installable file system (IFS) and Internet Information Services (IIS) can fully access workspace folders. SharePoint Portal Server workspaces have an associated vroot or virtual directory created in IIS under the Default Web Site. You can manage security for the dashboard site here.

Users can access the IFS by using Windows Explorer on the SharePoint Portal Server computer. SharePoint Portal Server typically maps IFS to network drive M, unless there is already a mapping that uses that drive. Although you can use IFS to view the contents of the Microsoft Web Storage System used by SharePoint Portal Server, this access is read-only.

> **Important** It is not recommended to use IFS (network drive M) to create SharePoint Portal Server folders or documents, assign security to folders or documents, or edit properties on folders or documents. SharePoint Portal Server roles and configuration options are available through the supported Web folders interface. Manipulating the IFS security attributes may interfere with the roles information associated with SharePoint Portal Server, which results in data loss. Workspace management functions, such as creating document profiles, are also available through the Web folders interface only.

Do not use Microsoft ActiveX® Data Objects (ADO) or OLE DB to configure security on SharePoint Portal Server folders or documents.

Securing Content Outside the Workspace

SharePoint Portal Server recognizes user-level security policies currently assigned to your organization's servers, file shares, and databases. SharePoint Portal Server does not enforce share-level security.

Security Mapping

- SharePoint Portal Server maps the security scheme for a content source to Windows 2000 security and applies the security scheme when it crawls the content and when a user searches the content.

- If you plan to crawl content located on a server in a different domain, do not use local group accounts on the server being crawled to secure content. SharePoint Portal Server may not recognize the local group accounts, which results in the user not being able to view the crawled content.

  > **Note** SharePoint Portal Server can recognize universal group accounts, global group accounts, and domain local group accounts.

For example, suppose Server A is in Domain A, and you want to crawl content located on Server B in Domain B. Server B could be another SharePoint Portal Server computer, a Web server, or a file share.

- The content on Server B is secured by using a local group account.

- When Server A crawls Server B, the SIDs associated with the content are those for the local group account on Server B.

- When a reader in Domain A tries to access the crawled content on Server A, Server A is unable to recognize the security on this content because the SIDs are associated with Server B.

- The reader is unable to view the content, even if the user is an authenticated user from Domain B.

Security Enforcement for Types of Content Sources

Security for the different types of content sources works as follows:

- **Web sites.** SharePoint Portal Server does not enforce security at query time. SharePoint Portal Server specifies a per-path logon for crawling, but everyone has access to the results. Secure Socket Layer (SSL) shares (preceded by https://) cannot be crawled.

- **File shares.** SharePoint Portal Server enforces user-level security at query time. There is no share-level security on file allocation table (FAT) and other file systems that do not have user-level security. SharePoint Portal Server specifies a per-path logon for crawling, which allows access through share-level security. Encrypted documents are not crawled.

- **SharePoint Portal Server computers.** SharePoint Portal Server enforces user-level security at query time.

- **Microsoft Exchange 2000 servers.** SharePoint Portal Server enforces message-level security at query time. Encrypted messages are not crawled.

- **Microsoft Exchange 5.5 servers.** SharePoint Portal Server enforces message-level security at query time. Encrypted messages are not crawled.

- **Lotus Notes servers.** A mapping from the Lotus Notes user identification (ID) to the Windows NT user ID allows record-level security at query time.

Before you can create Exchange Server 5.5 and Lotus Notes content sources, you must configure the server to crawl Exchange Server 5.5 and Lotus Notes content sources.

SharePoint Portal Server can access a UNIX system by using the network file system (NFS) protocol. SharePoint Portal Server can also access Novell NetWare by using a NetWare client. You must install the corresponding client for the UNIX or NetWare file system on the SharePoint Portal Server computer.

SharePoint Portal Server does not understand the security descriptors on the remote file systems that are not NTFS file systems, such as UNIX, NetWare, or similar foreign file systems. Per-file security on non-NTFS file systems is lost, but SharePoint Portal Server maintains per-share security. In the absence of security mapping, SharePoint Portal Server logs on as anonymous (or guest) and does not have access to any content that is not accessible to anonymous users. In this case, SharePoint Portal Server crawls the documents and then stamps them with read access for the Windows 2000 Everyone group. This means that all crawled documents are searchable by any user. Administrators should be aware of this to avoid disclosing information that is secured in a way that is not compatible with Windows NT.

SharePoint Portal Server can send security credentials while accessing foreign file systems, such as UNIX or NetWare. You can specify that the account and password in the site path rules for the remote file system path requiring Basic authentication. A failure to get the security descriptor causes SharePoint Portal Server not to include the item in the index.

> **Important** SharePoint Portal Server can include any Windows File Share (SMB) in an index, but does not have built-in support for any other network file system protocol. These file systems can be included in the index using an emulator that exposes them as a Windows File Share, but security on the file share is enforced only as well as it is exposed by the emulation software. In general, all documents included in the index from a non-NTFS file system are searchable by all readers on the SharePoint Portal workspace.

Summary

This chapter presents an overview of the advantages of using Windows 2000 security features with Microsoft SharePoint Portal Server 2001. It reviews the elements of Windows 2000 security that allow you to secure access to content on your corporate portal and the role-based security model for SharePoint Portal Server. It presents an overview of SharePoint Portal Server security architecture, including the publishing model and provides suggestions for securing content for search and content aggregation.

SharePoint Portal Server delivers a powerful and flexible security infrastructure that puts significant new capabilities into the hands of content experts. SharePoint Portal Server extends the distributed security model supported by Windows 2000. With role-based security, SharePoint Portal Server simplifies content management by allowing you to distribute administrative tasks to content owners. SharePoint Portal Server associates users with roles according to tasks. SharePoint Portal Server modifies access to a specific document based on the state of the document. The roles create a more flexible and dynamic security model.

CHAPTER 9

Planning Taxonomies

This chapter describes the tools available in Microsoft® SharePoint™ Portal Server 2001 that help organize information for delegated coordination, collaboration, and browsing. It also presents a method that coordinators can use to import an existing folder hierarchy into a workspace in a way that takes advantage of the capabilities provided by SharePoint Portal Server.

Information Organization

In traditional file systems, users organize information by using folders and descriptive file names. Folders and file names must accommodate all the possible reasons that one would separate, categorize, secure, or enforce business policy on various types of information. This type of folder structure can result in folder proliferation and arbitrary, subjective nesting of subfolders. At the same time, the file system offers few, if any, mechanisms to locate information within an ever-expanding folder tree, and few built-in clues as to the content or purpose of documents after they are found.

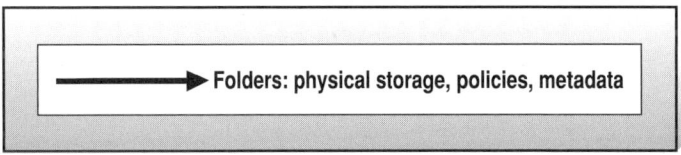

Figure 9.1. Traditional folders: single axis of organization

SharePoint Portal Server provides a richer set of tools for organizing your information. Instead of the single axis of organization represented by traditional folders, illustrated in figure 9.1, SharePoint Portal Server offers the following three axes:

- Folders

- Properties and document profiles

- Categories

Each of these axes, shown in Figure 9.2, enhances the overall view of information within the workspace. Each provides a different benefit to SharePoint Portal Server users.

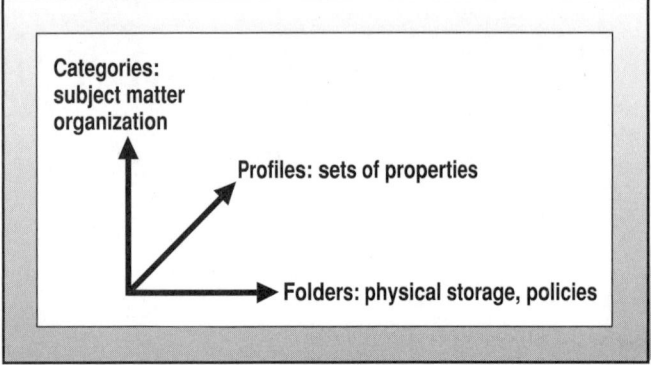

Figure 9.2. SharePoint Portal Server: three axes of organization

Using Folders

Within SharePoint Portal Server, you can use folders to store documents, a very familiar concept. Because SharePoint Portal Server presents three axes of organization, folders need not proliferate to address every organizational need. In fact, minimizing the number of folders has its advantages for those who manage in addition to those who use the folder hierarchy. Very few instances require the creation of new folders. You can use folders to decide where a document is stored, and what policies apply to that document.

Folders are useful for

- Delegating management (coordination) of a subset of content in the workspace.

- Applying different security to a subset of content.

- Applying a different versioning choice to a subset of content.

- Excluding a subset of content from inclusion in an index.

- Avoiding redundancy in naming documents.

New SharePoint Portal Server users may feel most comfortable using folders because they represent a familiar organizational tool. However, folders need not carry the same overloading of purpose as traditional file system folders. In cases where none of the previous reasons applies, use of one of the other organizing tools can minimize the depth and expansion of the folder hierarchy, making folders easy to find and manage.

Users who create or import content into the workspace use folders most heavily. In order to store new documents in the workspace, a contributor must select a folder for that document. You should consider this when designing the structure of folders.

Adding Properties and Profiles

Properties store metadata, or information about content, in the workspace. Facts about a document such as who created it, how it is described, and which customer it pertains to are stored as properties of those documents. Each document in the workspace has its own set of properties associated with it. Properties help an organization define what information they know about a particular document.

You can designate properties as mandatory or optional. An author must supply a value for mandatory properties of a document before successfully publishing the document.

The use of properties enhances the ability to locate documents within the workspace. Within the detailed view of Microsoft Windows® Explorer, properties head the columns. You can sort documents in a folder according to these properties.

Documents that have a related purpose often share a common set of properties. For example, the invitation to a meeting, its agenda, and its minutes all share common properties such as the meeting place, the time, and the list of attendees. A *document profile* is a named group of properties that you can apply to a document. Document profiles apply to documents with a common purpose, rather than a common file type or a common storage location. Coordinators select the list of profiles that are available for documents within a given folder, and users use that list to associate a specific document profile with a document. You can make a single document profile available simultaneously within any number of folders.

A coordinator designing the set of document profiles within a workspace must make trade-offs concerning profile sizes and the number of profiles per folder. Larger document profiles that have more properties, especially mandatory properties, provide richer information to locate and organize documents. However, very large document profiles burden users, making publishing troublesome and discouraging use of the workspace. The proper balance depends heavily on the culture of the organization, the type of users, the importance of the metadata, and other unique considerations.

Likewise, coordinators must determine how many document profiles to create in the workspace, and how many to make available within any given folder. A coordinator can create a large number of very specific document profiles. In this case, each document profile targets a particular purpose, simplifying the choice for authors who must select a document profile to apply to a document at the time of publishing. It is recommended that you keep the number of properties in each document profile low and primarily mandatory. However, authors would have to sort through a large list of document profiles to find the correct one when publishing content. Conversely, a coordinator can choose a smaller set or more broadly targeted document profiles, but this choice can expand the number of properties in each document profile, and force many of them to remain optional so that you can apply the document profile more flexibly to a broader set of documents. Users tend to ignore optional properties, which reduces the ability to locate content.

As a simple example, a coordinator might need to choose between creating Design Specification and Test Specification document profiles, each targeted to the particular function, or a single Specification document profile that serves both functions.

Creating Categories

Categories represent a subject matter view of content in the workspace. Like folders, the workspace features a hierarchy of categories. However, unlike its folder location, a document can be simultaneously placed in any number of categories. Categories help an organization identify what a document is about, and how a reader might search for it.

Categories stand completely independent of folders, properties, and profiles. All categories are available for tagging all documents in the workspace. As a result, the category hierarchy can aggregate content by subject matter regardless of its location inside (or outside) the workspace, providing the third axis of organization. Users performing searches also receive matching categories.

Just as you design a folder hierarchy with the needs of authors in mind, you design a workspace category hierarchy according to the needs of readers. Visitors to the workspace who are unfamiliar with the content or organization of the workspace can use categories to search for content. Because different readers approach searching differently, using multiple category tagging allows the coordinator to anticipate more than one way of searching for content, leading users to the most relevant documents through different paths.

Comparing Folders and Categories

When creating an initial set of workspace categories, some coordinators start by copying the folder hierarchy. Although this structure functions adequately, it fails to take the fullest advantage of SharePoint Portal Server. Search results match both folder and category names, so having folders and categories with the same name directs searchers to the same content and yields redundant search results. Instead of enhancing the ability to locate relevant content, such a category structure adds no value.

Coordinators should take advantage of the ability of categories to aggregate content across folders—a purpose quite different from that of folders. Categories free coordinators from the concerns about security policy that drive the folder layout, allowing a purer, subject-matter view of content in the workspace. In addition, coordinators should think about the diverse audiences that use folders and categories: folders primarily serve authors, while categories primarily serve readers, especially those unfamiliar with the structure and contents of the workspace.

Equating Folders and Properties

The expansion of folder names beyond the very short Microsoft MS-DOS™–supported format has allowed those names to be more descriptive. This ability to describe the folder completely by using its name is a boon to an organization that uses a traditional file structure. By using SharePoint Portal Server terms, however, many such names contain information more appropriately stored as properties within the folder.

In addition to a folder name storing embedded properties, coordinators often rely on the relationship between parent folders and subfolders to store implicit information. By using SharePoint Portal Server, a user can capture this information as properties. For example, you may organize a database of actors' filmographies by actors' names, each containing subfolders for the decades of that actor's career. The fact that many actor folders contain subfolders called "1970s" causes no ambiguity due to the position of those subfolders beneath their parent folders.

In the previous example, the information presents a naturally hierarchical organization. Although you could find some value in having a folder for each decade, and the list of active actors below it, few people design a folder hierarchy in this manner. However, many folder hierarchies present no such clear choice. Consider a file share that holds documents concerning airplane parts that were used in particular aircraft in particular years. You could easily encounter either of the two folder organizations shown in Figure 9.3.

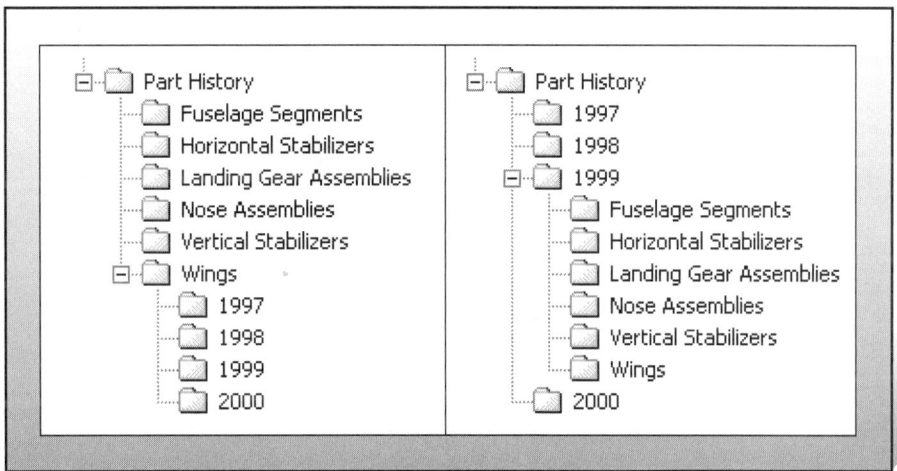

Figure 9.3. Two possible folder organizations

The traditional single axis of organization of a folder hierarchy forces the arrangement of folders that have no intrinsic hierarchical relationship. Because of this, either organizational structure has equal validity. In fact, the needs of a given user at a given time primarily determine the usefulness of each choice.

In SharePoint Portal Server, properties—rather than folders—contain information about content. SharePoint Portal Server can recognize that the name of the aircraft part and the year it was installed are in fact properties of the documents stored in the folders of this hierarchy. Because properties provide far richer search capabilities than folder names and relationships, you can make the best use of SharePoint Portal Server by extracting implicit properties and turning them into explicit ones. In fact, you can readily convert sets of folders into a smaller number of folders plus a set of properties and property values. This conversion retains all information in the original folder hierarchy and leaves fewer folders in the workspace, making it easier for authors to decide where content should be stored.

Revisiting the previous example, Figure 9.4 illustrates how you can represent the original 11 folders as a single folder, within which each document has two properties. The following method presents a systematic way to apply this principle to a full hierarchy, yielding a content organization better oriented for use in a workspace.

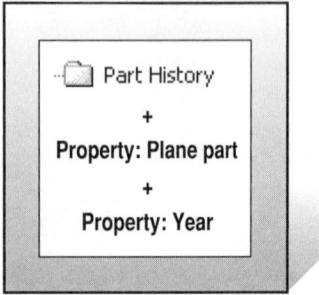

Figure 9.4. The new content organization

Folder Adaptation Method

The following method of adapting folder hierarchies to create taxonomies for a workspace originated from project management within Microsoft that used SharePoint Portal Server. This method requires organization, subject expertise, and intuition. The method assumes an existing folder hierarchy as a starting point. An organization that starts a workspace taxonomy from scratch may find that some of these methods still apply with modification.

Many organizations have already undertaken significant taxonomy efforts as part of a knowledge management initiative. You should use the results of those efforts before turning to this folder adaptation method. Other organizations have no resources to create the tailored structure that this method yields. Simply dragging and dropping an existing folder hierarchy into the workspace still functions but lacks optimization.

Converting Folder Hierarchies

The overall goal of folder adaptation is to convert a folder hierarchy into a set of folders, document profiles, properties, and property value lists (dictionaries) that capture all the information embedded in the original folder hierarchy, and then extend that taxonomy to capture richer information. The resulting taxonomy

- Has fewer folders than the original hierarchy.

- Creates a set of workspace document profiles, properties, and dictionaries.

- Exposes implicit metadata as explicit properties.

- Produces a workspace that looks familiar to users.

Building taxonomies requires human expertise. Although you can automate some of the organization, you derive decisions from knowledge of the content and its purpose and how various compromises occur within an organization.

This author-focused method creates no categories. For more information about creating taxonomies by using categories, see the section "Categories" later in this chapter.

Creating Document Profiles

The first goal is to attach a document profile to each document in each folder in the original hierarchy.

To achieve this goal, you must perform an audit of the content migrating into the workspace. Review each folder in the original hierarchy and examine each file. For each one, attach a document profile that roughly describes what the document is. Choose whatever level of detail seems appropriate. You can modify this information later in this process.

For example, a folder might contain two test specifications, a presentation, and a set of meeting notes. The next folder might contain a sales invoice, a personnel report, and another presentation. You should reuse document profiles when documents with the same purpose appear in multiple folders.

As the audit progresses, the number of reused document profiles from previous folders increases, while the number of new document profiles decreases.

This step requires at least recognition of the purpose of everything in the folder hierarchy. Accomplishing this step may require consultation with subject matter experts more familiar with a particular region of the hierarchy.

Adapting Folders into Properties

The second goal is a reduced folder list. You might apply security policies to some folders. Also, you have populated document profiles with mandatory and optional properties and dictionaries for some of the properties.

The second step addresses the idea that you can represent implicit metadata explicitly as properties in the workspace. Each folder receives an evaluation of its reasons for existence. From this evaluation, you can either convert this implicit purpose into properties on a document profile or tag the folder with an appropriate security policy. Later, you can decide whether to retain the folder based on its stated purpose.

To do this, apply the following algorithm to the subfolders of each parent folder:

- For each subfolder, determine whether the folder needs to exist for security reasons (such as to limit access, to delegate coordination, to specify approval routes, etc.).

- If the subfolder has a reason for existing, tag it with that reason.

- If the subfolder does not have a security reason for existing, add the folder information as a mandatory property to all document profiles in that folder, and add the folder name as a value for the dictionary of the new property. Then, move all subfolder content to the parent folder, add all subfolder document profiles to the parent folder's document profile set, and remove the subfolder.

  For example, if you have a folder called "1998," add a mandatory property called "year" to all document profiles in the folder, and a value "1998" to the dictionary for the property "year." If the property already exists from another document profile, reuse it and add the dictionary value to the existing dictionary for that property.

Reducing the List of Document Profiles

For this step, your goal is to reduce the list of document profiles and to change some mandatory properties to optional.

Because the audit produced just a list of document profiles, an examination of the results of converting folder information into properties shows redundancies between document profiles where closely related profiles have similar names and/or similar sets of properties. You can combine these redundant document profiles to reduce the list of document profiles to be managed by coordinators and used by authors.

If two document profiles contain identical sets of mandatory and optional properties, you can combine them. To do so, create a new document profile. After combining them into one document profile, you associate the relevant folders and documents with the new profile. If you must combine two document profiles with different property sets, you may choose to change properties from mandatory to optional as you aggregate them. Any property that applies to only one of the document profiles must become an optional property in the aggregated document profile.

As an example, consider two document profiles, Development Specification and Test Specification. Test Specification contains a mandatory property called Test Case Number. That property does not appear in the Development Specification document profile. A single document profile called Specification that aggregates the two original document profiles cannot contain a mandatory Test Case Number property since that property has no value for Development Specifications. It becomes an optional property in the aggregated document profile.

Although a reduced document profile list is easier for coordinators and authors, users tend to ignore optional properties. The decisions on aggregating document profiles must take into account the metadata enforcement policies of the organization. If the organization insists on mostly mandatory properties in document profiles, the opportunities for aggregating document profiles are reduced.

Even without strong metadata enforcement, over-aggregation of document profiles results in document profiles with a large number of properties. Because authors see a document profile form each time they publish content in the workspace, a large document profile burdens users, reducing their willingness to publish content. The coordinator designing the document profiles must consider this.

Extending the Document Profiles

In this step, you include additional properties in some document profiles in order to represent new metadata.

This step recognizes that the previous steps have accomplished nothing more than, change the representation of the information already contained in the original folder hierarchy. However, document profiles allow the capture of more information to aid in searching, approval, sorting, etc. You can extend the document profiles created in the previous steps with additional properties.

This step relies on business knowledge and a bit of intuition. Coordinators extend document profiles by adding mandatory and optional properties that "make sense." Some of these originate from an inspection of the implicit metadata captured in file names. Some originate from the requirements of approvals, where approvers must know certain information to make an approval decision. Some originate from outside considerations and business needs.

Starting with a New Workspace

Not all workspaces derive from existing file hierarchies. Starting with a new workspace requires more research and thought, but the ideal outcome remains the same: a folder hierarchy that focuses on authors and maps to appropriate document profiles and properties while capturing the needs of the organization using the workspace. Starting with a new workspace requires the same knowledge of the intended content, the organization, and the business needs as building from an existing hierarchy does.

One challenge faced when starting with a new workspace is recognizing when you complete the task. In the method presented previously, the process is complete when you apply the four steps to the entire existing hierarchy. When starting with a new workspace, you must gather requirements to understand how the workspace will be used, and use those requirements to build a taxonomy. The analysis may not fully cover all needs on the first pass, either because they cannot be easily anticipated or are simply missed. The full set of factors affecting folder usage may remain unclear. Starting with a new workspace often requires a more iterative approach, involving an initial taxonomy that develops into an ideal solution over time.

Without an existing hierarchy, the analysis starts by reviewing the flow of relevant information within the organization. Typically, the workspace must support some specific business processes. You can try to answer questions such as the following:

- What key documents do we handle?

- What steps do we execute to produce or approve key documents?

- What key processes do we use, and what information supports these processes?

- What have other groups in my organization built to solve similar problems?

- What taxonomy elements exist within other systems in the organization?

The answers to these and other questions uncover business policies that the workspace must support, and identify information that must be stored and accessed. Security policies of folders, such as role information, identified coordinators, and approval routes, form the motivation for a set of folders. Information about those folders suggests properties and document profiles.

After you answer these questions and identify an initial taxonomy, you can use the method described previously to optimize the results.

Considering Limitations of Modifying Folder Hierarchies

The four-step method presented in this chapter produces a taxonomy for your workspace that derives from an existing folder hierarchy and produces a workspace tailored to the population accustomed to using the original folders. This method does have some drawbacks and limitations.

How much time do you have? The method rigorously ensures that your workspace loses no information when compared to the original folder hierarchy, but the process is time-consuming. For hierarchies that contain a few hundred folders and a few thousand files, the effort is manageable. Beyond that size, the resources required to be thorough might exceed the value of the effort. In some cases, it may be more realistic to take a representative segment of the original folders and use that segment to derive a starting taxonomy. This starting point risks missing key document profiles, properties, or dictionary values, but you can extend it during the life of the workspace to accommodate these omissions.

Garbage in, garbage out. Basing the workspace taxonomy on an existing folder hierarchy preserves familiarity, but it also propagates into the workspace all the structural weaknesses of the original hierarchy. If the hierarchy grew organically to include redundancies, dead ends, and illogical organization, the workspace also exhibits some of these qualities in its folder structure. Fortunately, the ability to aggregate content across folders by using categories, and to search by properties, mitigates the effects on the workspace, but you should consider more extensive folder reorganization when faced with a set of folders in extreme disarray.

Categories

Categories, representing the subject matter view of the content in your workspace, differ from the taxonomy structures addressed by the folder adaptation method. As stated before,

- Categories are reader-focused.

- Categories follow no security policy restrictions.

- Documents in the workspace can be placed in multiple categories.

The readers who use categories could be the content authors who are very familiar with the workspace, readers who have a basic view of the workspace without intimate knowledge, or casual exploring visitors who have no knowledge of the workspace structure or content. These latter groups most need the browsing guidance that categories provide, so they should remain the primary focus when designing category structures.

As stated earlier, the folder hierarchy is not the optimal basis from which to derive categories. As the folder adaptation method shows, the concerns that drive folders are not the concerns that drive readers. Categories should adopt an external view of the information in the workspace. One way to gain an external view is to look at materials designed for external consumption. Another way is to listen to the questions people outside the organization ask about the material in the workspace, and design categories that guide those people to the answers.

As an example, one team reviewed marketing presentations and external reviews about their projects to understand how to organize information for consumption outside of the team. Because people whose expertise lies in communicating project concepts to unfamiliar audiences had built the presentations, using the materials leveraged the work that they had already done. Then they used the information breakdown from the presentations to guide the formation of the initial set of categories.

Unlike folders, where it should be as easy as possible to identify the single location where a document belongs, categories should not shy away from redundancy. Multiple categorizations allow the category designer to anticipate and respond to the many ways that different readers search for information. Having multiple category paths to a given document increases the odds that the reader locates a document of interest. For example, a reader searching for content about the U.S. Congress might start with Government, then Federal Government as opposed to state or local, then Congress, while another reader might start with National Legislatures, then U.S. Congress as opposed to the Japanese Diet, Israeli Knesset, or Russian Duma.

Every level of the category tree can point to content. Beware of intermediate categories that provide no value and force users to browse through before they can find anything. Each intermediate category represents additional layers of navigation standing between readers and the content they seek. At worst, they increase the complexity of navigation through the category tree. In addition, although you can organize information into categories to an arbitrary depth, excessive category depths challenge readers. Any category structure deeper than three or four levels merits review. You should limit the maximum depth to that with which your readers are comfortable.

The categories defined on the first day of the workspace design do not remain static. Expect that the categories evolve over time in response to the needs of the users. Beyond responding to specific requests from users, you can explicitly capture the real needs of users by monitoring the most frequent searches, and striving to turn those search terms into categories.

Implementation

After you create a folder hierarchy and a category structure, you must create an overall security policy and identify further sources of content. This section highlights the remaining tasks.

Adapting Folders

It is recommended that you track your process as you adapt existing folder hierarchies to a workspace. The decision on each folder combination remains a manual process, but you can automate much of the process. You can build a spreadsheet that contains a mapping from the original folder hierarchy to the workspace structure. Then, build a script to parse the spreadsheet, build the taxonomy in an empty workspace, and import and tag the content. For more information about this, see Appendix B, "For More Information."

Applying Security Policies

After building the workspace structure, you should complete the following tasks:

- **Map security into workspace.** After creating the structure, you still must assess security. You may choose to break security inheritance and specify actual permissions on secured folders.

- **Specify content sources.** The workspace contains only native content, but you may consider including external content also.

- **Designate folder coordinators.** From the planning stage, you identified coordinators, however, you still must assign them to the appropriate folders.

- **Specify approval routes.** Again, you must identify and implement approval routes and approvers.
- **Identify Best Bets.** Categories and search keywords become much more useful after you define Best Bets, but much of that definition comes from authors rather than co-ordinators, and evolves over time.

Recommendations

The best way to get started building taxonomies is to start the process and learn as you go. Experiment with the trade-offs, build a prototype, put it in use with some users to see how it functions, and then throw it away. The second and third ones that you build will be better-optimized and easier for all to use.

The initial taxonomy continues to evolve for a variety of reasons. The folder creation rate is probably slower than in traditional file systems, but does not stop. Business needs may require more document profiles. Properties add dictionary values. Usage expands and molds categories. Be prepared to constantly modify and update the work of setting up the initial workspace.

The following table summarizes the results of applying the method described in this chapter and demonstrates the scale of folder reduction, and the volume of created entities such as document profiles and properties.

Summary of Results

	Visual SourceSafe folders	SharePoint Portal Server workspace
Folders	240	72
Properties	—	11
Document profiles	—	68 reduced to 10
Properties per document profile	—	3–5
Dictionaries	—	8

Summary

This chapter describes the tools available in SharePoint Portal Server that help organize information for delegated coordination, collaboration, and browsing. This chapter also presents a method that coordinators can use to import an existing folder hierarchy into a workspace in a way that takes advantage of the capabilities provided by SharePoint Portal Server.

CHAPTER 10

Planning Web Discussions

Microsoft® SharePoint™ Portal Server 2001 extends Web discussions, a feature of Microsoft Office. Web discussions allow any user who has Read access to a document to read and create comments (discussion items) that are related to the specific document without having to modify the document. To implement Web discussions successfully, you must consider the interactions among Office, your existing Web browser, and SharePoint Portal Server. When you deploy Web discussions, you must address certain incompatibilities to achieve flexibility in various customer scenarios. This chapter describes the relationships among Office, your existing Web browser, and SharePoint Portal Server and assists you in addressing incompatibilities.

This chapter includes the following sections to assist you in achieving the optimum implementation of Web discussions for your organization:

- Variables affecting Web discussions

- Typical Web discussion configurations

- Strategies for Web discussion configurations

- Specific steps required for implementing a strategy

- Troubleshooting issues and incompatibilities

Variables Affecting Web Discussions

This section presents a list of the variables that affect Web discussions, including settings for SharePoint Portal Server, choice of client for using Web discussions, and choice of Web discussions server.

Choosing Web Discussions Settings

When you deploy SharePoint Portal Server, you must choose a setting for the following items (note that the default settings are in parentheses):

- Enable Web discussions in this workspace (Enabled).

- Enable searching and indexing of discussion items (Disabled).

   Caution If you include Web discussions in your index, SharePoint Portal Server may return them in a search results list. The discussion items are visible to users with Read access to any folder in the workspace, even if the users do not have access to the document to which the discussion items pertain. This may compromise the security of the content in a document. To prevent this, SharePoint Portal Server disables the option to include Web discussions in search scopes and the index by default.

- Restrict Web discussions to items that are stored in workspaces on this server (Enabled).

SharePoint Portal Server does not include Web discussions in the index when crawling other SharePoint Portal Server computers or other workspaces on the same server. Therefore, although SharePoint Portal Server returns documents from those servers or workspaces in search results, and these documents may contain Web discussion items, the discussion items are not included in the search results.

A matrix of SharePoint Portal Server Web discussions settings follows. This matrix identifies typical configurations and the effects of the possible settings.

Possible Web Discussions Configurations for SharePoint Portal Server

Web discussions server	SharePoint Portal Server			SharePoint Portal Server		Other Office Web discussions server
	Documents stored inside the current workspace			Documents stored outside any workspace on the server		n/a
Web Enabled discussions	Disabled*	Enabled†			Disabled	Enabled†
Searching and indexing of discussion items*	Disabled	Disabled†	Enabled	n/a	n/a	n/a

Web discussions server	SharePoint Portal Server			SharePoint Portal Server		Other Office Web discussions server
	Documents stored inside the current workspace			Documents stored outside any workspace on the server		n/a
Configuration A		Yes			Yes	No
Storage location(s)	n/a	n/a	Workspace**	n/a	External**	n/a
Notifications for Web discussions: on the dash-board site and optional e-mail	n/a	None	n/a	n/a	None	None
Search discussions	n/a	None	n/a	n/a	None	None
Configuration B			Yes		Yes	No
Storage location(s)	n/a	n/a	Workspace	n/a	External	n/a
Notifications for Web discussions: on the dash-board site and optional e-mail	n/a	n/a	Yes	n/a	None	None
Search discussions	n/a	n/a	Yes	n/a	None	None
Configuration C	Yes			Yes		Yes
Storage location(s)	None	n/a	n/a	None	n/a	Other server

continued

Possible Web Discussions Configurations for SharePoint Portal Server *continued*

Web discussions server	SharePoint Portal Server			SharePoint Portal Server		Other Office Web discussions server
	Documents stored inside the current workspace			Documents stored outside any workspace on the server		n/a
Notifications of Web discussions: on the dash-board site and optional e-mail	n/a	None	n/a	None	n/a	E-mail only from other server
Search discussions	n/a	None	n/a	None	n/a	None

† Default SharePoint Portal Server Installation

---

* For information about how to enable or disable Web discussions settings for SharePoint Portal Server, see "Typical Web Discussions Configurations" later in this chapter.

** SharePoint Portal Server stores discussion items for documents in two locations, based on whether the document is located inside or outside of a workspace on that server:

- Document stored in the workspace: http://Server_Name/Public/Workspaces/Workspace_Name/System/Discussions

- Document stored outside the workspace: http://Server_Name/Public/Workspaces/System/Discussions

Using Web Discussions with Office 2000 Installed

If Office 2000 is installed on your computer and you use Microsoft Internet Explorer as your Web browser, you can add Web discussions items from Office by using the **Online Collaboration** toolbar, or from Internet Explorer by using the **Online Collaboration** toolbar or the **Web Discussions** toolbar, depending on how you start discussions. If you use Netscape as your Web browser, you can use the **Web Discussions** toolbar, which is available from a **Discuss** link that is displayed below the document title in the dashboard site.

Using Web Discussions with Office XP Installed

If Office XP is installed on your computer and you use Internet Explorer as your Web browser, you can add Web discussion items from Office or Internet Explorer by using the **Online Collaboration** toolbar. If you use Netscape as your Web browser, you can use the **Web Discussions** toolbar, which is available from a **Discuss** link that is displayed below the document title in the dashboard site.

Using Web Discussions from a Web Browser Client

If Office is not installed on your computer and you use Internet Explorer or Netscape as a Web browser, you can only insert Web discussions about the document on the dashboard site that has a **Discuss** link displayed below the document title.

When you click the **Discuss** link, the **Web Discussions** toolbar (a custom SharePoint Portal Server Active Server Pages (ASP) toolbar) is displayed with the SharePoint Portal Server computer assigned as the discussion server.

Note To use Web discussions from a computer that does not have Office installed, you must choose to enable Web discussions in this workspace. By default, SharePoint Portal Server enables Web discussions. For more information, see "Variables Affecting Web Discussions" earlier in this chapter.

Inserting Web Discussions Items

Office allows two types of discussion items:

- **Items about the Document.** These items are related to each discussion item and any subsequent replies to the target document in general.

- **Items Inserted in the Document.** These items, available with Microsoft Word and Internet Explorer, are associated with a specific discussion item and any subsequent replies with a specific paragraph in the target document.

  Note In Word, you can insert inline discussion items for Word documents and Hypertext Markup Language (HTML) files. In Internet Explorer, you can insert inline discussion items only for HTML files.

To insert an inline Web discussions item in a document from Word:

1. Point to the paragraph for which you want to add an inline discussion item.

2. On the **Online Collaboration** toolbar, click the **Insert discussion in the document** icon.

To insert an inline Web discussions item in a document from Internet Explorer:

1. On the **Online Collaboration** toolbar, click the **Insert discussion in the document** icon.

2. Click the document icon at the end of the paragraph in which you want to insert your comment.

Choosing a Web Discussions Server on the Client

To use Web discussions, you must specify a Web discussions server the first time you choose to discuss a document.

After you specify a Web discussions server, type comments inline (in a document), or about the document (in your browser window), depending on the document type. You can also subscribe to be notified of changes to the document or folder. In addition, you can add additional Web discussions servers from the **Online Collaboration** toolbar.

> **Caution** You can select any of the available Web discussions servers. If the discussion server you choose differs from the one in use by other users, your discussions are stored on a different server. Consequently, other users cannot view your discussion items.

Specify the Web Discussions Server in Office 2000

The first time you open the **Online Collaboration** toolbar, you must enter a Web discussions server. Type the name of the Web discussions server in the text box, and then click **OK**.

Specify the Web Discussions Server in Office XP

The first time you use Web discussions, the active document's server is automatically selected as the Web discussions server.

> **Note** This behavior only occurs if the server of the active document is a valid Office Web discussions server, such as a computer running SharePoint Portal Server with Web discussions enabled.

By default, the **Online Collaboration** toolbar uses the last manually specified Web discussions server, regardless of where a document is stored. For more information, see "Using Web Discussions with Office XP Installed" later in this chapter.

Depending on the combination of settings for the SharePoint Portal Server computer and the location of the document that is open, you may not be able to designate the SharePoint Portal Server computer as a Web discussions server. For more information about possible incompatibilities, see the "Issues and Incompatibilities" section of this chapter.

Modify the Default Web Discussions Server

You can use the **Online Collaboration** toolbar to add additional Web discussions servers and to specify which Web discussions server to use.

To add a Web discussions server by using the Online Collaboration toolbar:

1. On the **Online Collaboration** toolbar, click **Discussions**.

2. Click **Discussion Options**, and then click **Add**.

3. Type the name of the SharePoint Portal Server computer where the document is located (for example, http://Adventure-Works/).

   Note If you specify a SharePoint Portal Server computer as the Web discussions server, do not include any workspace name in the URL.

4. Click **OK**.

   Note If you use the **Web Discussions** toolbar, you cannot specify a Web discussions server. When you use the **Web Discussions** toolbar, the active server is automatically chosen as the Web discussions server.

Planning Additional Factors

You must consider several factors when you decide how to implement Web discussions, including the following:

- **Enabling Web discussions on external content may log user activity.** If you do not restrict Web discussions to items stored in workspaces on this server, leaving the **Online Collaboration** toolbar open in Internet Explorer causes SharePoint Portal Server to log the Internet browsing activity of each user's computer.

  When a user accesses the dashboard site to discuss a document that is stored in a workspace, the **Online Collaboration** toolbar is started to access the Web discussions feature. If the **Online Collaboration** toolbar remains open when the user later navigates to other Web sites, SharePoint Portal Server logs the URL of any Web site the user visits, in addition to the user name, in the Microsoft Internet Information Services (IIS) logs that are stored on the system disk. Depending on the log settings on the server, this could potentially affect the Event Viewer system log size.

- **Including Web discussions in an index can allow users to view discussions on content to which they do not have access.** If you include Web discussions in your index, SharePoint Portal Server may return them in a search results list. The discussion items are visible to users on the dashboard site even if the users do not have access to the document to which the discussion items pertain. All existing discussion items for all versions of a document are viewable by any individual with Read access to a document, regardless of whether the version is published. This may compromise the security of the content in a document. To prevent this, SharePoint Portal Server disables the option to include Web discussions in search scopes and in the index by default.

  SharePoint Portal Server does not include Web discussions in the index when crawling other SharePoint Portal Server computers or other workspaces on the same server. Thus, although SharePoint Portal Server returns documents from those servers or workspaces in search results, and these documents may contain discussion items, the discussion items are not included in the search results.

- **Users may not search for discussions on high-ASCII or double-byte character set (DBCS) URLs created by using the Online Collaboration toolbar in Internet Explorer.** For Office users who discuss documents on high-ASCII or DBCS URLs, SharePoint Portal Server saves discussions created using the **Online Collaboration** toolbar in Internet Explorer in the following location, regardless of whether the document is stored in the workspace:

  http://*Server_Name*/Public/Workspaces/System/Discussions

  The process of retrieving Web discussions that contain European (high-ASCII) and Japanese/Chinese (DBCS) characters in the related document's URL is unpredictable because of the URL encoding schemes of Web browsers. The encoding schemes generally expect to have URLs provided in low-ASCII character sets. Depending on the combination of methods that are used for accessing the Web discussions from their Office client version or for accessing a document from the workspace, SharePoint Portal Server may not recognize the document's URL as residing in the document store.

  Because SharePoint Portal Server does not recognize these discussions correctly, they are not searchable, and you cannot subscribe to these discussions. To enable users to search for and subscribe to discussions, use the **Web Discussions** toolbar for high-ASCII or DBCS URLs.

- **The locale of the client and server must match during a high-ASCII/DBCS URL discussion.** This applies whether you are using the **Web Discussions** toolbar or the **Online Collaboration** toolbar.

- **The Close Discussion Items feature is not supported.** SharePoint Portal Server uses the Office 2000 implementation of the Web discussions server for administering discussion items. Consequently, SharePoint Portal Server does not support the Close Discussion Items feature of Office XP.

Typical Web Discussions Configurations

The following sections describe typical user configurations and the interaction between SharePoint Portal Server, Office, and the Web browser. Depending on your deployment, you can use Web discussions from the dashboard site by using a Web browser or from Office.

Important If Office is not installed on your computer, clicking the **Discuss** link under a document title on the dashboard site activates the **Web Discussions** toolbar, a custom SharePoint Portal Server ASP toolbar. If you are using Office XP, clicking the **Discuss** link activates the **Online Collaboration** toolbar. If you are using Office 2000, clicking the **Discuss** link activates the **Web Discussions** toolbar.

Using Web Discussions with Office 2000 and Internet Explorer

In Office 2000, you have the option of using either the **Online Collaboration** toolbar that is included with Office and added to Internet Explorer, or the **Web Discussions** toolbar that is included with SharePoint Portal Server.

To enable the Online Collaboration toolbar, use either of the following methods:

- On the **Internet Explorer** toolbar, click the **Web Discussion** button.

- On the **View** menu, point to **Explorer Bar**, and then click **Discussion**.

To enable the Web Discussions toolbar:

- Click the **Discuss** link under a document title on the dashboard site.

    Caution The **Online Collaboration** toolbar and the **Web Discussions** toolbar may use different Web discussions servers, resulting in multiple discussions. For more information about how to prevent this behavior from happening, see "Strategies for Web Discussions Configurations."

If you enabled the **Online Collaboration** toolbar the last time you used Internet Explorer, both the **Web Discussions** toolbar and **Online Collaboration** toolbar may be open simultaneously. This may be confusing, but in general, you can view and modify Web discussions that you create with either version of the toolbar.

Adding Discussion Items

This section describes the variety of ways you can add discussion items to a document by using Office 2000 and Internet Explorer.

- If you open the document from the dashboard site and then choose to add discussion items in Internet Explorer, clicking the **Web Discussion** button on the toolbar opens the **Online Collaboration** toolbar. You can then insert Web discussions items inline or insert Web discussions items about the document.

    Note In Internet Explorer, you can only insert inline discussion items for HTML files.

- If you click the **Discuss** link under a document title on the dashboard site or the link from a discussion item subscription, the **Web Discussions** toolbar opens with the SharePoint Portal Server computer assigned as the Web discussions server.

- You can add a discussion item directly from Office or Windows Explorer.

To add a discussion item from the Online Collaboration toolbar in an Office application:

- On the **Tools** menu, point to **Online Collaboration**, and then click **Web Discussions**.

Using Web Discussions with Office XP Installed

In Office XP, you can use the **Web Discussion** button from Internet Explorer or any Office application to open the **Online Collaboration** toolbar. When you click the **Discuss** link under the document title in the dashboard site, the **Online Collaboration** toolbar opens. Regardless of how you choose to access the Web discussion, Office XP automatically specifies the active document's server as the Web discussion server if it can identify that server as a valid Web discussions server. In the case of a document that is stored on a SharePoint Portal Server computer, the associated computer depends on the combination of Web discussions settings on the server in addition to the location of the document. If Office determines that the server on which the document is located is not a valid Web discussions server, you are prompted to provide the name of a valid Web discussions server when you attempt to add a new discussion item. For more information about Web discussions settings, see "Variables Affecting Web Discussions" earlier in this chapter.

> **Important** Office XP uses the designated server for all subsequent Web discussions items, regardless of the document locations, without displaying a prompt to you. This behavior continues for the current and future Office and Internet Explorer sessions. After you choose a Web discussions server, Office XP continues to specify this server until you manually choose a different server. It does not choose the active document's server for the next document.

Adding Discussion Items

This section describes a variety of ways that you can add discussion items to a document using Office XP and Internet Explorer.

To add discussion items to a document, use any of the following methods:

- Open a document from the dashboard site, and then choose to add discussion items in Internet Explorer. On the **Internet Explorer** toolbar, click the **Web Discussion** button to open the **Online Collaboration** toolbar. You can then insert Web discussions items inline or about the document, depending on the file type.

- Under a document title on the dashboard site or from a discussion item subscription, click the **Discuss** link to open the **Online Collaboration** toolbar. You can then insert Web discussions items inline or about the document, depending on the file type.

- On the **Tools** menu in Office, point to **Online Collaboration**, and then click **Web Discussions**.

Using Web Discussions Only from a Web Browser

If Office is not installed on your computer or if you use Netscape as your Web browser, you can click the **Discuss** link under a document on the dashboard site to open the **Web Discussions** toolbar. By using this toolbar, you can insert comments about a document, but you cannot insert inline discussion items.

> **Note** To use Web discussions from a computer without Office installed, you must enable Web discussions in this workspace. For more information, see "Variables Affecting Web Discussions" earlier in this chapter.

In Internet Explorer, you can insert Web discussions items for HTML documents directly in the browser window. For other file types (such as .bmp files), you are prompted to open or save the file. If you choose to open the file, it is opened in a separate discussion window by using the associated application. You can then discuss the file in your browser using the **Web Discussions** toolbar while viewing the file in the separate window.

In Netscape, you are prompted to open or save the file. If you choose to open the file, it is opened in a separate window by using the associated application. You can then discuss the file in your browser using the **Web Discussions** toolbar while viewing the file in the separate window.

Strategies for Web Discussions Configurations

The following section reviews key strategies and decisions you must make based on your configuration. It is recommended that you decide which toolbar you want users to use and identify the Web discussions servers in your deployment.

Choosing a Toolbar

The **Online Collaboration** toolbar and the **Web Discussions** toolbar offer different features. The **Online Collaboration** toolbar offers slightly more flexibility and customizability, but is not available to users who are not using Office and Internet Explorer. The **Web Discussions** toolbar provides a way for users who do not have Microsoft Internet Explorer 5 and Office 2000 installed on their systems to participate in Web discussions. A brief overview of each kind of Web discussions follows:

Online Collaboration Discussions. For users who have Internet Explorer 5 or Office 2000 installed on their computer, the **Online Collaboration** toolbar provides access to discussions from these applications.

> **Note** Users who have Office XP installed on their computer can also access the **Online Collaboration** toolbar by clicking the **Discuss** link below the document title on the dashboard site.

Browser-Based Discussions. Browser-based discussions using the **Web Discussions** toolbar are available when you click the **Discuss** link below a document title on the dashboard site. Browser-based discussions allow users who do not have Internet Explorer 5 and Office installed on their computer to read and add discussion remarks.

It is recommended that Internet Explorer and Office users choose the **Online Collaboration** toolbar for maximum flexibility. From the **Online Collaboration** toolbar, users can subscribe to be notified of changes to the document or folder. Users can also specify which Web discussions server and insert inline discussion items in a Word or HTML document.

> **Note** From Internet Explorer, you can only insert inline discussion items for HTML documents.

For more information, see "Variables Affecting Web Discussions" earlier in this chapter.

Choosing a Web Discussions Server

It is important to determine a strategy for choosing a Web discussions server before you implement Web discussions. Computers running SharePoint Portal Server are valid Web discussions servers. Consider the following conditions when you choose a Web discussions server:

- **All computers are running Office XP.** You can choose to centralize your Web discussions on any valid Web discussion server. In this case, have your users specify the same Web discussions server from the **Online Collaboration** toolbar, so that Office consolidates all discussions on a single Web discussions server.

- **Some computers are running earlier versions of Office.** You can choose to centralize your Web discussions on any valid Web discussions server. However, instruct any user accessing discussions from a computer running an earlier version of Office to avoid using the **Discuss** link to discuss documents.

  > **Important** Users must specify the same Web discussion server from the **Online Collaboration** toolbar. In this scenario, Office consolidates all discussions on a single Web discussions server.

- **Some computers are not running Office and Internet Explorer.** Organizations with a mix of client environments, including computers without Office installed and computers with Office 2000 or Office XP installed, that plan to implement Web discussions are at increased risk of having Web discussions for the same document located on different Web discussions servers.

  > **Important** You must specify a server running SharePoint Portal Server as the Web discussions server to allow non-Office clients to participate in Web discussions for any documents or to search for or subscribe to Web discussions.

You may want to instruct Office users to specify the name of the server on which the document is stored or accessed from the Web discussions server each time they choose to participate in or view a discussion. Otherwise, users may inadvertently distribute discussions across multiple Web discussions servers. In this case, you may want to disable the ability to discuss documents that are stored outside the workspace and store all documents that you want to be available for Web discussions in a workspace. This forces Office users to use the active document's server as the Web discussions server and minimizes the risk of multiple discussions.

By implementing a specific strategy, you can ensure that all users can view and participate in Web discussions.

Avoiding Multiple Discussions for the Same Document

It is possible to create two separate discussions for the same document if users specify an alternate Web discussions server with the **Online Collaboration** toolbar. When you specify an alternate Web discussions server, SharePoint Portal Server stores the Web discussion in the external discussion location on the alternate Web discussion server rather than in the internal discussion location on the server where the document is stored.

Implementation Strategy

To use Web discussions with SharePoint Portal Server, it is recommended that you implement a specific strategy. After you identify your strategy, you must modify the Web discussions settings to match your deployment plan.

Considering Key Factors

To use Web discussions, you must consider the following issues:

- What servers in your environment are valid Web discussions servers?

- Do you want to enable Web discussions?

- Do you want to discuss documents that are stored outside the workspaces of the SharePoint Portal Server computer?

- Do you want users to search for and view discussion items on documents?

- Do you need to recommend a specific Web discussions server to your users?

- What variables affect your implementation of Web discussions?

- Are there any incompatibilities or troubleshooting issues that you need to address?

Modifying Web Discussion Settings for SharePoint Portal Server

The following section provides detailed procedures about how to modify the Web discussions settings for SharePoint Portal Server. You must specify these settings for each workspace on the server.

Enable or Disable Web Discussions of Items Stored Outside Workspaces

You can restrict Web discussions to items that are stored in workspaces on the SharePoint Portal Server computer.

To specify discussion settings for the SharePoint Portal Server computer:

1. In the console tree, select the server for which you want to specify Web discussions settings.

2. On the **Action** menu, click **Properties**,
   -or-
   right-click the server name, and then click **Properties**.

3. On the **Other** tab, click to select the **Restrict Web discussions to items stored in workspaces on this server** check box if you want to restrict Web discussions only to documents that are stored in workspaces on the current server. If you do not want to restrict Web discussions, clear the check box.

4. Click **Apply**.

Enable or Disable Searching and Indexing of Web Discussions Items

You can restrict searching and index crawling of Web discussion items.

To specify discussion settings for the workspace:

1. In the console tree, select the server that contains the workspace discussion settings that you want to specify.

2. Click to expand the server, and then select the workspace that contains the discussion settings.

3. On the **Action** menu, click **Properties** (you can also right-click the workspace name, and then click **Properties**).

4. On the **Subscriptions/Discussions** tab, click to select the **Enable Web discussions in this workspace** check box.

5. If you want to include discussions in the index and make them available for searching, click to select the **Enable search and indexing of discussion items** check box.

> **Important** Discussion items are not secured and may be visible to a user, even if that user does not have access to the document to which they pertain.

6. Click **Apply**.

Issues and Incompatibilities

The following sections review troubleshooting issues and incompatibilities you may encounter when you use Web discussions with SharePoint Portal Server.

Storing Web Discussions

SharePoint Portal Server stores Web discussions according to URLs. SharePoint Portal Server directs you to a specific URL for a Web discussion, based on the location of the document:

- Discussions for documents that are in the workspace are in the following location:

    http://*Server_Name*/Public/Workspaces/*Workspace_Name*/System/Discussions

    Following the earlier example, the URL for a Web discussion of a document located in the workspace:

    http://Adventureworks/Public/Workspaces/Adventure/System/Discussions

- Discussions for documents that are stored outside the workspace are in the following location:

    http://*Server_Name*/Public/Workspaces/System/Discussions

    Following the earlier example, the URL for a Web discussion of a document stored outside the workspace:

    http://Adventureworks/Public/Workspaces/System/Discussions

    By default, discussions that are stored in this location are not searchable.

    > **Note** You must display hidden folders to view these folders.

Consequently, users cannot retrieve discussions for a document that is moved or renamed. When you move or rename a document, or any portion of its path, the document is disassociated from its discussion items.

Deleting Discussions

Although Web discussions are typically managed from the Management dashboard of the dashboard site, you may have difficulty deleting discussions for documents that are stored outside the workspace, those created by using the **Online Collaboration** toolbar accessed from Internet Explorer, and those created from Office applications for documents with high-ASCII or DBCS URLs.

To delete these discussions, an administrator must use the installable file system to access the Web storage system drive. For more information about the Web storage system drive, see Appendix B, "For More Information."

Viewing Web Discussions

If you experience difficulties viewing all the associated Web discussions for a document, confirm that your users are all using the same Web discussions server. If Office users have specified a different Web discussions server than the server that is specified on the **Web Discussions** toolbar, more than one Web discussion about the same document can occur.

There are two steps to confirm which servers have been chosen.

- On the **Web Discussions** toolbar, available from the **Discuss** link, confirm that the correct Web discussions server is the active server.

- On the **Online Collaboration** toolbar available from Office applications and Internet Explorer, you can choose a Web discussions server and should confirm that you chose the same server as the one used for the **Web Discussions** toolbar.

For more information, see "Choosing a Web Discussion Server on the Client" earlier in this chapter.

Installing SharePoint Portal Server and SharePoint Team Services Together

If Microsoft SharePoint Team Services is installed on the computer on which you want to install SharePoint Portal Server, you must uninstall SharePoint Team Services before you install SharePoint Portal Server. In addition, you must delete the following registry key:

HKEY_LOCAL_MACHINE\Software\Microsoft\Office\9.0\Web Server

Caution Incorrectly editing the registry may severely damage your system. Back up the current version of the registry before making any changes. You should also back up any valued data on the computer.

Installing SharePoint Team Services after you install SharePoint Portal Server changes the the way Web Discussions work in the following ways:

- Discussion items are not included in the index and are not available for search.

- You do not receive notifications for subscriptions to documents or folders in the workspace when you subscribe by using the **Online Collaboration** toolbar. The **Online Collaboration** toolbar is available from Office and Internet Explorer.

- Subscriptions made by using the **Online Collaboration** toolbar and all discussions are stored in SharePoint Team Services. SharePoint Portal Server does not include these subscriptions and discussions in the backup image.

Installing SharePoint Portal Server and Office XP Together

If you install Office XP on a computer running SharePoint Portal Server, the **Online Collaboration** toolbar does not allow you to specify a Web discussions server from Internet Explorer. This prevents you from using the **Online Collaboration** toolbar in Internet Explorer to add discussion items and create subscriptions from this computer.

To discuss a document from a computer running SharePoint Portal Server and Office XP, open the document with Office XP instead of with Internet Explorer. You have the option of using the active document's server or choosing a different Web discussions server as appropriate for your deployment.

Summary

This chapter describes how to implement and use Web discussions with SharePoint Portal Server. This chapter describes the relationships among Office, your existing Web browser, and SharePoint Portal Server, and assists you in troubleshooting and addressing any incompatibilities.

PART 3

Deployment

This section provides in-depth deployment information, including detailed installation instructions. It describes possible deployment solutions including deploying in an extranet environment, in a multilingual environment, and across multiple intranet portals by using RapPort.

Installing SharePoint Portal Server

This chapter provides information about the hardware and software required to install Microsoft® SharePoint™ Portal Server 2001 and how to install the server and client components on one or more computers in an organization.

When you insert the SharePoint Portal Server compact disc (CD) into your compact disc read-only memory (CD-ROM) drive, the Start page appears automatically. The page includes:

- A shortcut to Server Installation, which starts the SharePoint Portal Server Setup Wizard.

- A shortcut to Client Installation, which starts the Client Components for SharePoint Portal Server Setup Wizard.

- A shortcut to the SharePoint Portal Server Tours, which are interactive introductions to SharePoint Portal Server.

- A shortcut to Help, which links to the SharePoint Portal Server online Help, including the *Planning and Installation* and the *Managing Content* guides.

- A shortcut to the SharePoint Portal Server Readme file.

This chapter includes procedures for installing SharePoint Portal Server and the client components for SharePoint Portal Server. Major sections are devoted to hardware and software requirements, server setup, and client setup. In addition, the following sections are provided:

- **Troubleshooting.** Includes information to assist you in diagnosing installation problems.

- **Other Installation Issues.** Includes instructions for changing the proxy settings for the SharePoint Portal Server computer at some time after installation. In addition, it includes information about the installable file system (IFS) and the Microsoft Web Storage System.

To install the server and client components of SharePoint Portal Server:

- Review the hardware and software requirements. This section also includes information about coexistence issues, including coexistence with Microsoft SQL Server™.

- Install SharePoint Portal Server on the server by running the SharePoint Portal Server Setup Wizard.

- Create a workspace on the server.

- Install the client components of SharePoint Portal Server on user computers. Do this by running the Client Components for SharePoint Portal Server Setup Wizard.

- On client computers, add a Web folder that points to the workspace. The address of the workspace is http://*server_name/workspace_name*.

Hardware and Software Requirements

Before you install SharePoint Portal Server, make sure that your computer meets the following recommended hardware and software requirements.

Server Requirements

The following are the requirements for each server running SharePoint Portal Server:

- Intel Pentium III–compatible processor minimum recommended.

- 256 megabytes (MB) minimum of RAM recommended.

- 550 MB minimum of available disk space. The drive must be formatted as NTFS file system.

- Microsoft Windows® 2000 Server or Windows 2000 Advanced Server operating system, and Windows 2000 Service Pack 1 (SP1) or later.

  Installing SharePoint Portal Server on a system that has been upgraded from Microsoft Windows NT® version 4 can cause install failures. It is recommended that you install SharePoint Portal Server on a clean Windows 2000 Server. If you are installing on a Windows 2000 system that was upgraded from Windows NT 4, manually register the Oledb32.dll file before installation to avoid installation failure. Go to the Program Files\Common Files\System\Ole DB folder and type **regsvr32 oledb32.dll** to register the file.

- Internet Information Services (IIS) 5.

- Simple Mail Transfer Protocol (SMTP) Service. This is a Windows 2000 Server component.

In addition to the requirements listed previously, install the following Windows 2000 updates before installing SharePoint Portal Server. These updates are available at http://support.microsoft.com/. These issues will be addressed in subsequent Windows 2000 service packs.

If you are installing on Windows 2000 Server with Service Pack 1, install the following updates:

- Windows 2000 Patch: Token Handle Leak in LSASS. Note that this new version of the hotfix replaces the previous hotfix (Q288861) release.

  For this hotfix, see Q291340: Token Handle Leak in LSASS Using Basic Authentication.

- Windows 2000 Patch: GetEffectiveRightsFromAcl Causes ERROR_NO_SUCH_DOMAIN. Addresses a problem that can cause subscription notifications to fail when the access control list (ACL) on a document contains a Domain global group.

  For this hotfix, see Q286360: GetEffectiveRightsFromAcl() Function Causes "ERROR_NO_SUCH_DOMAIN" Error Message.

If you are installing on Windows 2000 Server with Service Pack 2, install the following update:

- Windows 2000 Patch: Token Handle Leak in LSASS. Note that this new version of the hotfix replaces the previous hotfix (Q288861) release.

  For this hotfix, see Q291340: Token Handle Leak in LSASS Using Basic Authentication.

The following prerequisites must be met before installing SharePoint Portal Server:

- Windows 2000 Hot fix (Pre-SP2) Q269862 cannot be installed on the computer. If it is installed, remove it before installing SharePoint Portal Server.

- The Windows Remote Registry service must be running. This service is started by default.

To start the service manually:

1. On the taskbar, click **Start**, point to **Programs**, point to **Administrative Tools**, and then click **Services**.

2. Right-click **Remote Registry Service**, and then click **Start**.

   - IIS configuration: Ensure that World Wide Web Publishing Service (W3SVC/1), the Default Web Site in IIS, is started. SharePoint Portal Server setup performs a simple test to warn of potentially invalid IIS settings. This test checks the configuration of W3SVC/1 (the Default Web Site) to ensure that the Web Site Identification TCP Port is "80" with IP Address "(All unassigned)". If multiple entries were configured in Advanced Settings, setup checks only the first entry. Other configurations may be acceptable, as long as "localhost" on port "80" is a valid way to connect to W3SVC/1 (the Default Web Site) on the computer. If necessary, you can alter the configuration by opening **Internet Services Manager** under **Administrative Tools** and selecting **Properties** on the Default Web Site.

   - SharePoint Portal Server requires the Default Web Site in IIS to use port 80 as the TCP port for localhost. Before installing SharePoint Portal Server, ensure that you specify 80 as the TCP port. In addition, do *not* change the port to an alternative HTTP port (such as 8000 or 8080) after installation. Ensure that port 80 is specified and remains as the primary port for the server.

Coexistence Issues

The following software does not coexist with SharePoint Portal Server:

- Exchange 2000 Server

- Exchange 2000 Enterprise Server

- Exchange Server version 5.5 and earlier

- Microsoft Site Server (any version)

- Microsoft Office Server Extensions

SharePoint Portal Server setup checks for the existence of this software and fails if this software is already installed. If you install this software after installing SharePoint Portal Server, SharePoint Portal Server will stop functioning properly.

SharePoint Portal Server is not supported in a clustered environment. You cannot install SharePoint Portal Server in a clustered environment, and you must not add the server to a clustered environment.

SharePoint Portal Server and Microsoft SQL Server

If you install SharePoint Portal Server on a computer running SQL Server 7 or SQL Server 2000, SharePoint Portal Server upgrades the existing Microsoft Search (MSSearch) service. In addition, SharePoint Portal Server upgrades the full-text index format of all of the existing indexes on that computer the next time that MSSearch starts. For the upgrade to succeed, there must be enough disk space on the computer to accommodate 120 percent of the size of the largest full-text index on the drive. Upgrading the full-text index format can take several hours, depending on the number and size of the existing indexes. During the SharePoint Portal Server setup, a message informs you that the service will be upgraded.

Because SharePoint Portal Server upgrades MSSearch and full-text indexes, do not install SharePoint Portal Server on a server that participates in a SQL Server clustering environment or add a computer running SharePoint Portal Server to a clustered environment.

You can install SQL Server on a computer already running SharePoint Portal Server. In this instance, SQL Server uses MSSearch installed by SharePoint Portal Server. If you remove SharePoint Portal Server from a computer that has SQL Server installed, SharePoint Portal Server will not remove the upgraded MSSearch because it is a shared service with SQL Server.

SharePoint Portal Server and SharePoint Team Services

If SharePoint Team Services from Microsoft is installed on the computer on which you want to install SharePoint Portal Server, you must uninstall SharePoint Team Services before installing SharePoint Portal Server. In addition, you must delete the following registry key:

HKEY_LOCAL_MACHINE\Software\Microsoft\Office\9.0\Web Server

Caution Incorrectly editing the registry may severely damage your system. Back up the current version of the registry before making any changes. You should also back up any valued data on the computer.

If you install SharePoint Team Services after installing SharePoint Portal Server, you lose the following functionality from SharePoint Portal Server:

- Discussion items are not included in the index and are not available for search.

- You do not receive notifications for subscriptions to documents or folders in the workspace when you subscribe by using the Microsoft Office collaboration toolbar. The Office collaboration toolbar is available from both Office and Microsoft Internet Explorer.

- Subscriptions made by using the Office collaboration toolbar and all discussions are stored in SharePoint Team Services. These subscriptions and discussions are not backed up during the SharePoint Portal Server backup process.

Installing SharePoint Portal Server on a Domain Controller

If you install SharePoint Portal Server on a domain controller:

- There is no local Administrators group. Consequently, only users assigned to the co-ordinator role can specify security on folders. If a coordinator makes an error, there is no possibility for a local administrator to resolve security issues.

- You may need to restart the domain controller after installing SharePoint Portal Server.

Renaming a SharePoint Portal Server Computer

You can rename a SharePoint Portal Server computer at any time. After renaming the server, you must restart it. In addition, SharePoint Portal Server Administration installed by setup prompts for authentication and displays an error before opening, after you rename the server. To remedy this situation, manually add the SharePoint Portal Server snap-in to Microsoft Management Console (MMC).

Client Requirements

The following are the requirements for each computer running the client components of SharePoint Portal Server:

- Intel Pentium-compatible 200 megahertz (MHz) or higher processor recommended.

- 64 MB of RAM minimum recommended.

- 30 MB of available disk space on Windows 2000 systems; 50 MB of available disk space on all other systems.

- Windows 98, Windows Millennium Edition, Windows NT 4 with SP6A, or Windows 2000 Professional, Windows 2000 Server, or Windows 2000 Advanced Server. Coordinator functions require Windows 2000 Professional, Windows 2000 Server, or Windows 2000 Advanced Server.

- Internet Explorer 5 or later. Microsoft Visual Basic® Scripting Edition (VBScript) support is required. This is included in the default installation of Internet Explorer 5.

- Microsoft Outlook® Express version 5.01 or later.

- SharePoint Portal Server Office extensions require Office 2000 or later.

Dashboard Site Requirements

Accessing SharePoint Portal Server through the dashboard site does not require the user to install the client components. For the Windows operating system, you can use the following browsers:

- Internet Explorer 4.01 or later

- Netscape Navigator 4.51 or later (for Italian and Spanish versions of SharePoint Portal Server)

- Netscape Navigator 4.75 or later (for English, French, German, and Japanese versions of SharePoint Portal Server)

Macintosh and Solaris operating systems are not supported.

In addition, you must enable Microsoft JScript® or Netscape JavaScript support in your browser for the dashboard site to function.

To use the dashboard site with Netscape Navigator, you must use Internet Services Manager to enable Basic authentication for the workspace node on the Default Web Site. To enable discussions to work when the browser is Netscape Navigator, you must also enable Basic authentication for the MSOffice node on the Default Web Site.

Operating System and Browser Support Summary

The following table summarizes the operating system and browser support for SharePoint Portal Server.

Operating System and Browser Support for SharePoint Portal Server

Operating system	Server support	Client support	Browser support (for dashboard site/Web access only)
Microsoft Windows 95	No	No	Yes
Windows 98	No	Yes (limited)*	Yes
Windows NT 4 (SP6A)	No	Yes (limited)*	Yes
Windows 2000 Professional	No	Yes	Yes
Windows 2000 Server or Windows 2000 Advanced Server	Yes (requires SP1)	Yes	Yes
Windows 2000 Datacenter Server	No	No	Yes
Windows Millennium Edition (includes Internet Explorer 5.5)	No	Yes (limited)*	Yes
Systems with Internet Explorer 5 or later	Yes	Yes	Yes
Systems with Office XP	Yes	Yes	Yes

* Supported Browsers (dashboard site/Web access only):

- Internet Explorer 4.x and later running on the Windows operating system
- Netscape Communicator 4.7x running on the Windows operating system

Note Windows 98, Windows Millennium Edition, and Windows NT 4.x computers do not support coordinator functions such as scheduling updates and configuring content sources, tasks performed by using MMC, or Web views. In addition, on computers running Windows 98 or Windows NT 4.x, you cannot access User's Help from the workspace by using F1 or the Help menu. To access User's Help when using these operating systems, click the User's Help page in the workspace, and then click the User's Help link on that page.

Server Installation

You can install SharePoint Portal Server by running the SharePoint Portal Server Setup Wizard. The wizard guides you through the installation process. Before running the setup wizard on your server, plan how you will use SharePoint Portal Server in your organization. For more information about planning your deployment, see Appendix B, "For More Information."

To install SharePoint Portal Server on the server:

1. Review the server hardware and software requirements, including coexistence issues, outlined earlier in this chapter.

2. Install SharePoint Portal Server on the server by running the SharePoint Portal Server Setup Wizard.

3. Create a workspace on the server.

If you have Terminal Services, you can use it in remote administration mode to install SharePoint Portal Server. If you are running in Terminal Services in application mode, run **chgusr /install** in **Command Prompt** before attempting to install SharePoint Portal Server.

You can also use group policy to install the server in attended or unattended mode by using ZAP files. For more information about using ZAP files, see the following resources:

- Knowledge Base Article Q231747: How to Publish non-MSI Programs with .zap Files (http://support.microsoft.com/support/kb/articles/Q231/7/47.ASP)

- Microsoft Windows 2000 Server Resource Kit (http://mspress.microsoft.com/prod/books/1394.htm)

- "Step-by-Step Guide to Software Installation and Maintenance" on Microsoft TechNet (http://www.microsoft.com/TechNet/win2000/instmain.asp)

If you want to install SharePoint Portal Server on the server in unattended mode, see "Using Unattended Server Installation" later in this section. If you want to uninstall or repair a SharePoint Portal Server computer, see "Uninstalling or Repairing SharePoint Portal Server" later in this section.

Installing SharePoint Portal Server

To install SharePoint Portal Server:

1. Log on to the computer running Windows 2000 Server or Advanced Server as a local or domain administrator.

2. Stop all anti-virus software. If anti-virus software is running during SharePoint Portal Server installation, the workspace creation step at the end of the setup process fails.

3. Ensure that there is at least one free network drive letter on the computer. The setup process requires at least one free network drive letter on the computer.

4. Configure the proxy server settings for Internet access:

   - On the taskbar, click **Start**, point to **Settings**, and then click **Control Panel**.

   - Double-click **Internet Options**. The **Internet Properties** dialog box appears.

   - Click the **Connections** tab, and then click **LAN Settings**.

   - Clear both check boxes under **Automatic configuration**.

   - If you use a proxy server, select the **Use a proxy server** check box, type a valid proxy server address and port number, and then select the **Bypass proxy server for local addresses** check box. If you do not use a proxy server, clear all check boxes.

   - Click **OK** to apply the changes, and then click **OK** to close **Internet Properties**.

5. Insert the SharePoint Portal Server CD into your CD-ROM drive.

6. Click **Server Installation**. The SharePoint Portal Server Setup Wizard appears. You can also go to the Server folder on the CD, and then double-click **Setup.exe**.

7. Follow the instructions that **appear** in the setup wizard.

8. On the **Product Identification** page, type the CD Key in the spaces provided. The CD Key uniquely identifies your copy of SharePoint Portal Server and enables you to receive technical support. The CD Key is located on the back of your SharePoint Portal Server CD case. If the number that you type is not accepted, check the following:

   - If you are using the keypad to the right of your keyboard, ensure that NUM LOCK is on.

   - Ensure that you are not using the letter I for the number one.

   - Ensure that you are not using the letter O for the number zero.

9. On the **SharePoint Portal Server Installation Folders** page, specify the location on the server's disk where you want to install the SharePoint Portal Server program files and data files. You can change the installation location for these files by clicking **Change Folder**. SharePoint Portal Server also installs additional required files on the operating system drive. Click **Disk Information** for information about the amount of disk space required and the amount remaining. If there are existing files in the installation paths, setup removes these files. Note the following restrictions for the path:

   - The path name can have a maximum length of 100 characters.

   - The path name can contain only characters in the lower ASCII range.

   - The path cannot point to a root directory. For example, E:\ is not allowed, but E:\Installation is allowed.

10. On the **SharePoint Portal Server Indexing Settings** page, specify the default content access account and the Gatherer e-mail address. SharePoint Portal Server uses the default content access account to crawl content sources. The Gatherer e-mail address is an e-mail address that an external site administrator can contact if problems occur when SharePoint Portal Server crawls the external site. SharePoint Portal Server uses these settings to crawl content stored outside the workspace and include it in an index. If you choose not to specify these settings during installation, you can specify them later by using the Properties page of the server in SharePoint Portal Server Administration.

Administrators can manage servers and workspaces from SharePoint Portal Server Administration. To open SharePoint Portal Server Administration, click **Start**, point to **Programs**, point to **Administrative Tools**, and then click **SharePoint Portal Server Administration**.

Creating a Workspace on the Server

After you run SharePoint Portal Server setup, the New Workspace Wizard appears. This wizard helps you create a workspace. If you click **Cancel** to close the New Workspace Wizard, you can create a workspace later by using SharePoint Portal Server Administration.

To create a workspace by using the New Workspace Wizard:

1. Stop all anti-virus software. If anti-virus software is running during workspace creation, the process may fail.

2. On the first page of the wizard, click **Next**.

3. On the **Workspace Definition** page:

   - In the **Workspace name** box, type the name of the workspace that you are creating. Workspace names can consist of characters from lower ASCII except for the following:

     # : \ ? * < > % / | " { } ~ [ ] Space ! ( ) = ; . , @ & +

     The lower ASCII code set includes the characters with codes 32–127. The workspace name cannot exceed 25 characters in length.

     The wizard verifies that the workspace name is unique and does not conflict with any other workspace names or propagated index names on the server. If the name is already in use, the wizard prompts you to enter a unique name. You cannot edit a workspace name after you create the workspace. If you are creating an index workspace, the name of the workspace that you are creating must be different from that of the destination workspace.

   - In the **Description** box, type an optional description of the workspace.

4. If you are *not* creating an index workspace, omit this step. If you are creating an index workspace, click **Advanced**. Select the **Configure as an index workspace** check box. In the **Specify the destination workspace address** box, type the destination workspace for the propagated index. The name of the destination workspace is http://*server_name/ workspace_name*. Click **OK**. The wizard prompts you to provide the name of a propagation access account, which is required before you can propagate an index. This account must have local administrator permissions on the destination server.

   The destination workspace must exist before you create the index workspace. The wizard ensures that a workspace with the same name as the index workspace does not already exist on the destination. You cannot change the destination workspace after you have created the index workspace. If the destination server is not a SharePoint Portal Server computer, the wizard logs an error in the Application Log in Windows 2000 Event Viewer (commonly referred to as the Windows 2000 event log).

   You can create index workspaces with the same name (and propagating to the same destination) on multiple servers dedicated to creating and updating indexes. The last index to propagate has its index active on the destination. You can use this setup to continually update the destination by appropriately scheduling the crawls for each index workspace.

   It is recommended that you maintain a list of index workspace names, the servers on which they are stored, and the servers and workspaces to which they are propagated.

   Note that to use fully qualified domain names and index workspace propagation together, both the server dedicated to indexes and the destination server must be in Windows 2000 domains.

5. Click **Next**.

6. On the **Workspace Contact** page:

   - In the **Workspace contact name** box, type the name of the user or group that you are assigning as the workspace contact. The workspace contact is the individual user or group with overall responsibility for the workspace.

   - In the **Workspace contact e-mail address** box, type the e-mail address for the workspace contact. The contact e-mail address can be that of an individual user or a group.

   - Click **Next**.

7. Click **Finish** to complete the wizard and create the new workspace. After SharePoint Portal Server creates the workspace, it displays a message stating that the wizard will open the workspace and create a link to it in **My Network Places**.

8. Click **OK**. The link is created, the **Configure Your Workspace** page opens, and the dashboard site opens. For index workspaces, an introduction page opens and the link points to the **Content Sources** folder within the workspace.

After you create the workspace, you must configure security on the workspace node by using SharePoint Portal Server Administration or Web folders. The Windows 2000 local Administrators group has permission to read documents and configure security on any folder or document in a workspace.

The SharePoint Portal Server Setup Wizard automatically installs the client components. After installing the client, you must add a Web folder that points to the workspace. The address of the workspace is http://*server_name/workspace_name*.

Using Unattended Server Installation

If you are installing a large number of servers or want to customize your installation, you can run SharePoint Portal Server setup in unattended mode by using an .ini file. When you install SharePoint Portal Server by using an .ini file (also called silent install), no dialog boxes or error messages that require user intervention are displayed unless prerequisites are missing. This setup lets you install identical configurations of SharePoint Portal Server on multiple computers.

Before running this unattended setup, you must create an .ini file that contains the default installation settings that you want to use, such as the installation directory. After you create the .ini file, you can edit it by using a text editor. By editing the .ini file, you specify additional options and gain more control over your installation.

To create the .ini file used for unattended setup, you must run the SharePoint Portal Server Setup Wizard. However, instead of installing SharePoint Portal Server, the wizard stores the settings that you specify in the .ini file.

Double-byte character set (DBCS) or high-ASCII characters cannot be used in installation paths when performing an unattended installation. If you use these characters, the installation fails. In addition, no path in the .ini file should be longer than 140 characters.

To install SharePoint Portal Server by using an .ini file:

1. Create an .ini file:

   - On the taskbar, click **Start**, and then click **Run**.

   - In the **Open** box, type *path_to_server_setup_file* **setup** / **CreateUnattend** *path filename*.**ini** where *filename* is the name of the .ini file that you want to create. For example, if the setup file is in the Setup directory on drive D and you want to create sample.ini on drive E, type **D:\Setup\setup** / **CreateUnattend E:\sample.ini**

   - Click **OK**.

- Follow the instructions that appear in the SharePoint Portal Server Setup Wizard. All settings that you choose are included in the .ini file that you create.

  One additional parameter is available for use with /CreateUnattend: /EncryptedMode. This parameter enables you to create an .ini file with the password for the default content access account hidden. To do this, type:

  path_to_server_setup_file **setup** /**CreateUnattend** *path file_name***.ini** / **EncryptedMode**

2. Edit the .ini file:

   - In a text editor, such as Microsoft WordPad, open *filename***.ini** where *filename* is the name of the .ini file that you created.

   - Modify parameters in the file for the settings that you want SharePoint Portal Server setup to use.

     If you plan to use an unattended installation file on servers with varying storage configurations, ensure that hard-coded paths are valid for each server configuration before starting the installation. An example of a hard-coded path reference is "C:\." You can force the installer to automatically choose the correct default path by removing an entry line completely.

     You can modify only the following paths:

     - **InstallDirectory.** You can specify the installation location for SharePoint Portal Server program files. By default, the program files are stored on the operating system drive in Program Files\SharePoint Portal Server.

       There are two other InstallDirectory paths. One path is for the Microsoft Web Storage System and the other is for MSSearch. Altering these paths is not recommended. This is the recommended option for the MSSearch and Web Storage System installation directories:

       InstallDirectory=*operating_system_drive*\Program Files\Common Files\Microsoft Shared\Web Storage System

       InstallDirectory=*operating_system_drive*\Program Files\Common Files\Microsoft Shared\MSSearch

       By default, the Microsoft Web Storage System files are stored on the operating system drive in Program Files\Common Files\Microsoft Shared\Web Storage System. However, if you are running unattended server installation and you delete all lines containing a hard-coded path reference, the location defaults to Program Files\Exchsrvr on the operating system drive.

- **Search Gatherer Log Directory.** Each time that SharePoint Portal Server creates an index, it creates a log file for that workspace. This log file contains data about crawling content sources and records access errors. After installation, you can use SharePoint Portal Server Administration to change this path. By default, the log is stored on the operating system drive in Program Files\SharePoint Portal Server\Data\FTData\SharePointPortalServer\GatherLogs.

  The Gatherer log contains data about URLs that SharePoint Portal Server accesses while it creates an index. The file records successful accesses, access errors, and accesses disallowed by rules (in case the user needs to debug the index restrictions). Coordinators can view this log from a user-friendly Active Server Pages (ASP) page in the workspace.

- **Search Index Directory.** When creating a workspace, SharePoint Portal Server creates an index under this root node. SharePoint Portal Server also creates all indexes propagated to the server under this root node. After installation, you can use SharePoint Portal Server Administration to change this path. By default, the indexes are stored on the operating system drive in Program Files\SharePoint Portal Server\Data\FTData\SharePointPortalServer\Projects. If you want to move existing indexes to a new location, you must use a tool that is included on the SharePoint Portal Server CD. For more information, see ToolsHowTo.txt in the Support\Tools directory on the SharePoint Portal Server CD.

- **Search Property Store Database Directory.** You can specify the location of the property store file. The property store file contains the metadata from documents. After installation, you cannot modify the file location by using SharePoint Portal Server Administration. By default, the property store file is stored on the operating system drive in Program Files\SharePoint Portal Server\Data\FTData\SharePointPortalServer. To modify the file location, you must use a tool that is included on the SharePoint Portal Server CD. For more information on ToolsHowTo.txt, see ToolsHowTo.txt in the Support\Tools directory on the SharePoint Portal Server CD. For optimal performance, the property store and property store log files should be on dedicated physical volumes. SharePoint Portal Server shares this file across all workspaces.

- **Search Property Store Log Directory.** You can specify the location of the property store log files. The property store log files are the log files for the property store. After installation, you cannot modify the location of these files by using SharePoint Portal Server Administration. By default, the property store log files are stored on the operating system drive in Program Files\SharePoint Portal Server\Data\FTData\SharePointPortalServer. To modify the file location, you must use a tool that is included on the SharePoint Portal Server CD. For more information on ToolsHowTo.txt, see ToolsHowTo.txt in the Support\Tools directory on the SharePoint Portal Server CD. For optimal performance, the property store and property store log files should be on separate dedicated physical volumes. SharePoint Portal Server shares these files across all workspaces.

- **Web Storage System Database Directory.** You can specify the location of the Web Storage System Database file. Every SharePoint Portal Server computer contains one public store (wss.mdb). All workspaces hosted on the server reside on the Web Storage System. After installation, you can use SharePoint Portal Server Administration to change this path. If this location changes, the existing file moves to the new location. By default, the database file is stored on the operating system drive in Program Files\SharePoint Portal Server\Data\Web Storage System.

- **Web Storage System Streaming Database Directory.** You can specify the location of the WSS-Streaming Database file. Used for streaming files, the WSS-Streaming Database file (wss.stm) contains data and is a companion to the WSS-Database file (wss.mdb). Together, these two files form the database. SharePoint Portal Server document streams make up a sizable part of the total amount of data. You might want to move this file to a larger drive (ideally a dynamic disk that you can easily resize) because it can increase substantially over time. After installation, you can use SharePoint Portal Server Administration to change this path. If this location changes, the existing file moves to the new location. By default, the streaming database file is stored on the operating system drive in Program Files\SharePoint Portal Server\Data\Web Storage System.

- **Web Storage System Database Log Directory.** You can specify the location of the WSS-Database Log files. These are the log files for the Web Storage System. For optimal performance, place the log files on a dedicated physical volume. After installation, you can use SharePoint Portal Server Administration to change this path. If this location changes, the existing files move to the new location. By default, the log files are stored on the operating system drive in Program Files\SharePoint Portal Server\Data\Web Storage System.

> **Caution** Do not modify other paths.

You can modify the parameter "apply indexing settings" in the .ini file to set the default content access account and Gatherer e-mail address during the unattended installation. SharePoint Portal Server uses the default content access account to crawl content outside the workspace. SharePoint Portal Server provides the Gatherer e-mail address to each Web site it crawls when creating an index. If a problem occurs while crawling (for example, the crawler is hitting the site too much), the Web site's administrator can contact this address.

If the "apply indexing settings" parameter is equal to zero (0), the default content access account and Gatherer e-mail address are not set when you run the unattended installation. You can set these options after installation by using SharePoint Portal Server Administration.

To specify the account and e-mail address:

- Set **apply indexing settings=1**
- Set **Default Content Access Account=***user_name,domain,password*
- Set **gatherer e-mail address=***someone@microsoft.com*

1. Run setup by performing the following tasks:

   - On the taskbar, from the server on which you want to run setup, click **Start**, and then click **Run**.

   - In the **Open** box, type *path_to_server_setup_file* **setup** /**UnattendFile** *path filename*.**ini** where *filename* is the name of the .ini file that you created.

   - Click **OK**. You do not see the finish page or the **New Workspace Wizard** page.

Uninstalling or Repairing SharePoint Portal Server

The SharePoint Portal Server Setup Wizard installs the client components of SharePoint Portal Server. If you uninstall SharePoint Portal Server, it removes the client components. If you repair SharePoint Portal Server, it repairs the client components as well.

If you remove SharePoint Portal Server from a computer that has SQL Server installed, SharePoint Portal Server does not remove the upgraded MSSearch because it is a shared service with SQL Server.

During the uninstall process, SharePoint Portal Server requires access to the original installation point to uninstall the Microsoft Embedded Exchange files. If the original installation point has moved, you can insert the SharePoint Portal Server CD into the CD-ROM drive to continue uninstalling. You can also point to the Server\Web Storage System directory at the installation point.

Before uninstalling SharePoint Portal Server, you must:

- Verify that all command prompts are closed.

- Remove any additional virtual roots mapped to the Web Storage System drive. The Web Storage System is mapped to network drive M by default.

  If network drive M is already in use when you install SharePoint Portal Server, the Web Storage System is mapped to another network drive.

  By default, this drive is disabled (it is not visible in My Computer). For more information about enabling this drive, see "Using the IFS Drive and the Microsoft Web Storage System" later in this chapter.

When you uninstall SharePoint Portal Server, all files and folders located in the installation directories are removed, including any user-created or modified files. The uninstall process also removes all workspaces. It is highly recommended that you restart the server after you uninstall SharePoint Portal Server.

The repair process requires at least one free network drive letter on the computer. If no drive is available, repair fails.

You can uninstall or repair a server by running SharePoint Portal Server setup. Alternatively, you can use Add/Remove Programs in the Control Panel.

Client Component Installation

After you run SharePoint Portal Server setup, you can install the client components of SharePoint Portal Server on client computers across your network. The client functionality of SharePoint Portal Server is included with Office XP.

The client components are extensions to Windows Explorer and Office applications. There is no individual client application. These extensions integrate SharePoint Portal Server commands with Windows Explorer and Office applications. Note that to take advantage of the Microsoft Office integration features of SharePoint Portal Server, Office 2000 or later is required. You can use other applications to create documents, but you cannot access SharePoint Portal Server commands from the menus within those applications. You must use Windows Explorer or a Web browser to perform SharePoint Portal Server document management tasks on documents created by using those applications.

You can install the client components by running setup either from the server or from the SharePoint Portal Server CD. By default, the SharePoint Portal Server Setup Wizard installs client installation files to the following location on the server: Program Files\SharePoint Portal Server\ClientDrop\Languages*Lang*, where *Lang* corresponds to the language of the client. For information about installing additional languages, see "Installing the Client Components in Additional Languages" later in this chapter.

To install the client components:

1. Review client hardware and software requirements outlined earlier in this chapter.

2. Install the client components by running the Client Components for SharePoint Portal Server Setup Wizard from one of the locations described previously.

3. Add a Web folder that points to the workspace.

There is a setup.ini file for the client components in Program Files\SharePoint Portal Server\ClientDrop\Languages*Lang*. You can edit this file to specify the location of the SPSClient.msi file. You can also edit this file to specify the path and file name for the log file.

If you want to install the client components of SharePoint Portal Server in unattended mode, see "Using Unattended Installation Options for the Client" later in this section. If you want to uninstall or repair the client components, see "Uninstalling or Repairing Client Components" later in this section.

Installing the Client Components

The following steps describe how to install the client components.

To install the client components:

1. Log on to the client computer as a user with administrator privileges.

2. Connect to the location on the server where the client installation files are located. These files must be shared or otherwise available. By default, these files are located at Program Files\SharePoint Portal Server\ClientDrop\Languages*Lang*, where *Lang* corresponds to the language of the client. If you want to install the client components from the CD, see the comments following this procedure.

3. Double-click **Setup.exe**. The Client Components for SharePoint Portal Server Setup Wizard appears.

4. Follow the instructions that appear in the wizard.

If you want to install the client components from the SharePoint Portal Server CD, insert the SharePoint Portal Server CD into your CD-ROM drive, and then click **Client Installation**. The Client Components for the SharePoint Portal Server Setup Wizard appears. You can also go to the Client folder on the CD, and then double-click **Setup.exe**.

The client components require Microsoft Data Access Components (MDAC) version 2.5 or later. If this is not already present on the computer, the client installation process installs MDAC 2.5 SP1.

Adding a Web Folder

After you install the client components, you must add a Web folder that points to the workspace. The address of the workspace is http://*server_name/workspace_name*.

The procedure for adding a Web folder varies depending on your operating system. For detailed instructions, see your operating system Help. For example, in Windows 2000 Professional, go to **My Network Places** and use the Add Network Place Wizard to add a Web folder that points to http://*server_name/workspace_name*. In Windows 98, go to **Web Folders** in **My Computer**, and use **Add Web Folder** to add a Web folder that points to http://*server_name/workspace_name*.

Using Unattended Installation Options for the Client

By default, you can install the client components by running the Client Components for SharePoint Portal Server Setup Wizard, which guides you through the installation process. You can also use Systems Management Server to install a client remotely on multiple computers in your organization. In addition, you can use Windows Installer directly to conduct an unattended installation of the client components.

If your server and client computers are both running Windows 2000 and are on a Windows 2000 domain, you can use the Active Directory™ directory service to make the SharePoint Portal Server client setup program available to your users automatically.

Systems Management Server

SharePoint Portal Server provides a .pdf file that can be used with Systems Management Server to install the client components on multiple computers. The file SPSClient.pdf is located in the Client directory on the SharePoint Portal Server CD. SharePoint Portal Server also installs it on the server by default in Program Files\SharePoint Portal Server\ClientDrop\Languages*Lang*, where *Lang* corresponds to the language of the client.

For more information about Systems Management Server, see Appendix B.

After you install the client components, you must add a Web folder that points to the workspace. The address of the workspace is http://*server_name/workspace_name*.

Windows Installer

You can use Windows Installer to conduct an unattended installation of the client components if you are running Windows 2000 or Windows Millennium Edition, or if Windows Installer is present. By default, Windows Installer is installed with Office 2000 or later. Windows Installer is also installed by some other applications.

To install the client by using Windows Installer:

1. On the taskbar, click **Start**, and then click **Run**.

2. In the **Open** box, type **msiexec /qn /I "***path***\SPSClient.msi"**

   The quotation marks are required only if the path contains spaces. For example, if SPSClient.msi is on a file share called \\ServerName\SharePoint Portal Server Client Setup, quotation marks are required because of the spaces in "SharePoint Portal Server Client Setup." You would type the following:

   msiexec /qn /I "\\ServerName\SharePoint Portal Server Client Setup\ SPSClient.msi"

   If your operating system is Windows 98 and Windows Installer is present, include the path to Msiexec.exe. For example, if Msiexec.exe is located in C:\Windows\System, type:

   C:\Windows\System\msiexec /qn /I "C:\SharePoint Portal Server Client\ SPSClient.msi"

   You can also add the directory that contains Msiexec.exe to the system path.

3. Click **OK**. SharePoint Portal Server installs the client without displaying user interface messages. Note that if the computer must be restarted, it is restarted automatically.

After you install the client components, you must add a Web folder that points to the workspace. The address of the workspace is http://*server_name/workspace_name*.

For more information about Windows Installer, including options other than unattended installations, see Appendix B.

Supported Command Line Parameters

The following table documents additional parameters available for both attended and un-attended installation.

The command line parameters in the following table are supported for installing the client components of SharePoint Portal Server setup. No other parameters are supported.

> **Note** Specifying *path_to_SPSClient.msi* is optional if Setup.exe, Setup.ini, and SPSClient.msi are all in the same directory, and you execute the setup command from within that directory.

Command Line Parameters

To do this	Type this at the command prompt
Install from the Setup.ini file, which you have modified. User interaction is required.	*"path_to_client_setup.exe"* **/settings** *"path_to_setup.ini"*
Install the client components. User interaction is required.	*"path_to_client_setup.exe"* **/i** *"path_to_SPSClient.msi"*
Repair the installation of the client components. For this option to work properly, you must specify the *path_to_SPSClient.msi* or you receive an error.	*"path_to_client_setup.exe"* **/f** *"path_to_SPSClient.msi"*
Uninstall the client components. User interaction is required.	*"path_to_client_setup.exe"* **/x** *"path_to_SPSClient.msi"*
Display no user interface. Optionally, display completion notice. No user interaction is required unless you choose to display the completion notice.	With any of the previous parameters, **insert /qn[+]**. For example, *"path_to_client_setup.exe"* **/qn+ /i** *"path_to_SPSClient.msi"*
Display basic user interface. Optionally, display completion notice.	With any of the previous parameters, **insert /qb[+]**. For example,

To do this	Type this at the command prompt
No user interaction is required unless you choose to display the completion notice. You see a status bar as the process progresses.	*"path_to_client_setup.exe"* **/qb** **/f** *"path_to_SPSClient.msi"*
Display reduced user interface. No user interaction is required. You see the user interface, but it automatically progresses through the steps.	With any of the previous parameters, **insert** **/qr**. For example, *"path_to_client_setup.exe"* **/qr** **/x** *"path_to_SPSClient.msi"*
Specify logging modes.	With any of the previous parameters, insert **/L**[*logging_modes*|*] *path_to_the_log_file* to specify logging modes. For more information about logging modes, see Windows Help. Use * to log all information except for the v option. Using /Lv* *path_to_the_log_file* creates the most verbose logging available. For example, *"path_to_client_setup.exe"* **/qr** **/i** *"path_to_SPSClient.msi"* **/Lv*** *"path_to_the_log_file"*
Access help for using the parameters.	*"path_to_client_setup.exe"* **/?**

Group Policy and Active Directory

If you are a domain administrator on a Windows 2000 domain, you can use Group Policy and Active Directory to make the Client Components for the SharePoint Portal Server setup program available to users. The program appears in the Control Panel under Add/Remove Programs. Both the server and the client computers must be running Windows 2000.

Group Policy settings define the various components of the user's desktop environment that a system administrator can manage. To create a specific desktop configuration for a particular group of users, you use the Group Policy snap-in. Group Policy settings that you specify are contained in a Group Policy object, which is in turn associated with se-lected Active Directory objects—sites, domains, or organizational units.

Group Policy includes settings for User Configuration, which affects users, and Computer Configuration, which affects computers.

- User policy settings are located under **User Configuration** and are obtained when a user logs on.

- Computer policy settings are located under **Computer Configuration** and are obtained when a computer starts up.

You can use Group Policy to publish the client under User Configuration or Computer Configuration.

To publish the client under User Configuration:

When you publish the client under User Configuration, the user can then install the client components by using Add/Remove Programs in the Control Panel.

Read the following known issues before publishing the client under User Configuration:

- After one user on a particular computer adds the client by using Add/Remove Programs in the Control Panel, the client files are present on the computer. However, another user cannot access Web folders until she adds the client also; the user receives an error stating that the folder entered does not appear to be valid even for valid folders.

- If one user on a particular computer adds the client, and a new user attempts to add the client on that computer, the new user may see a screen prompting for uninstall or repair. The user sees this screen if you select **Maximum** for the Installation user interface options on the **Deployment** tab of the Properties page of the client package. Choosing repair activates client functionality for the new user. If you select **Basic** for the user interface option, the user sees only a progress bar when the client repairs. Each user of the computer must perform this action once. By default, only members of the local Administrators group can add the client.

- If any user on the computer uninstalls the client, each user experiences automatic client repair upon the next access of the client components by opening a Web folder pointing to the workspace. If the user examines Add/Remove Programs in the Control Panel prior to this automatic repair, the client is present, but the **Change** button is disabled (therefore preventing manual repair). The user corrects this by triggering the automatic repair, which is triggered by opening a Web folder. The user who uninstalled the client will still be unable to access client functionality unless he installs the client components again.

- To see the client entry in Add/Remove Programs, the user may need to log off and then log on to the computer.

- You can exclude specific users by denying them read access to the client package. See the following procedure to learn how to do this. The excluded users will not see the client components package in the Add Programs portion of Add/Remove Programs. Excluding computers in this way, for this type of deployment, has no effect (users on that computer can see and add the client). For computer exclusion, see "To assign the client under Computer Configuration" later in this section.

- If the client is manually installed on a computer (for example, from the SharePoint Portal Server CD) prior to the client being published, the client functionality is accessible to all users on the computer. If any user adds the program, they are prompted for repair or uninstall.

To use Active Directory (User Configuration) to make the client setup program available to users:

1. Read the preceding known issues.

2. Copy the folder containing the client files to the domain controller computer.

   You can copy the Client folder from the SharePoint Portal Server CD.

   You can also find the folder containing the client files on the SharePoint Portal Server computer. SharePoint Portal Server installs this folder by default on the operating system drive under Program Files\SharePoint Portal Server\ClientDrop\Languages*Lang*, where *Lang* corresponds to the language of the client. For example, on an English version of SharePoint Portal Server, you would copy the "enu" directory to the domain controller.

3. Share the folder containing the client files. When sharing, specify that anyone installing from the share has read access to it. You can use standard Windows 2000 security groups, or you can create your own specific groups. You can optionally enable or disable the other privileges, depending on the policy of your organization.

4. Add the Group Policy snap-in:

   - On the taskbar, click **Start**, and then click **Run**.

   - In the **Open** box, type **MMC** and then click **OK**. The MMC console opens.

   - On the **Console** menu, click **Add/Remove Snap-in**. The **Add/Remove Snap-in** dialog box appears.

   - On the **Standalone** tab, click **Add**. The **Add Standalone Snap-in** dialog box appears.

   - Under **Available Standalone Snap-ins**, click **Group Policy**, and then click **Add**. The **Select Group Policy Object** dialog box appears.

   - Click **Browse**. The **Browse for a Group Policy Object** dialog box appears.

   - On the **Domains/OUs** tab, click **Default Domain Policy**, and then click **OK**.

   - Click **Finish** to close the **Select Group Policy Object** dialog box. The Group Policy Object (Default Domain Policy) appears on the **Standalone** tab in the **Add/Remove Snap-in** dialog box.

   - Click **Close** to close the **Add Standalone Snap-in** dialog box.

   - Click **OK**.

5. Add the SharePoint Portal Server client package by using the Group Policy snap-in.

- Expand the **Default Domain Policy** node.
- Expand the **User Configuration** node.
- Expand the **Software Settings** node.
- Right-click **Software installation**, point to **New**, and then click **Package**.
- Type the path to the folder that you copied in step 2, and then click **Open**.

  Do not use local references such as C:\share. Type a share location, such as \\server\share. Otherwise, some users may not be able to access the deployed application.

  Do not browse to this path.

- Double-click **SPSClient.msi**. The **Deploy Software** dialog box appears.
- Click **Published**, and then click **OK**.

  Note Do not choose the **Assign** option for the package. This option causes a program to be automatically installed when a shortcut to its application, or an associated file type, is accessed. The client components of SharePoint Portal Server do not have associated file types, nor is there any shortcut to activate the installation. Therefore, the installation would never be triggered. If you want to automatically install the client for all users, see the next section, "To assign the client under Computer Configuration."

To exclude specific users:

1. Expand the **Default Domain Policy** node.

2. Expand the **User Configuration** node.

3. Expand the **Software Settings** node.

4. Click **Software installation**.

5. In the details pane, right-click **Client Components for Microsoft SharePoint Portal Server 2001**, and then click **Properties**.

6. Click the **Security** tab, and then click **Add**.

7. Click the user to exclude, click **Add**, and then click **OK**.

8. On the **Security** tab, click the excluded user, select the **Deny** check box for the **Read** permission, and then click **Apply**.

9. Click **Yes** to continue when the caution message appears.

10. Click **OK** to close the **Properties** page.

To install the client components, the user uses **Add/Remove Programs** in the Control Panel.

After installing the client components, the user must add a Web folder that points to the workspace. The address of the workspace is http://*server_name/workspace_name*.

To assign the client under Computer Configuration:

When you assign the client under Computer Configuration, the client software installs the next time that any computer managed by this group policy is restarted.

Read the following known issues before assigning the client under Computer Configuration:

- If the client is deployed in this way, it is not installed on any computer affected by the deployment until that computer is restarted. It is recommended that only one application be assigned per restart in this way. Therefore, to deploy three applications, you would deploy one, restart the computer, deploy another, restart, deploy the third, and restart. This minimizes any interactions between the deployments.

- You must exclude the following from the deployment by creating an excluded group: computers with SharePoint Portal Server installed; computers on which you want to install SharePoint Portal Server; other computers on which you do not want to install the client components.

  After creating the group, you must deny access to it from the client package. See the following procedures for an explanation of how to do this.

- If you do not add current SharePoint Portal Server computers to the excluded group and you deploy the client, the server functions properly until the next restart. After restarting, you cannot access properties on workspaces while working on the server. In addition, the Web folders on the server will lack SharePoint functionality. To correct this situation, add the server to the excluded group. Repair the server that was impaired, and then restart it. The server should now function properly.

- If you add a SharePoint Portal Server computer to the domain without adding it to the excluded group, the server will not function properly when you restart it. You must add the server to the excluded group, repair the server, and then restart the server.

- If you want to install SharePoint Portal Server on a computer that already has the client installed, you must add the computer to the excluded group, ensure that the excluded group is denied access to the client package, and then restart the computer before installing SharePoint Portal Server.

To use Active Directory (Computer Configuration) to make the client setup program available to users:

1. Read the preceding known issues.

2. Copy the folder containing the client files to the domain controller computer.

   You can copy the Client folder from the SharePoint Portal Server CD.

   You can also find the folder containing the client files on the SharePoint Portal Server computer. SharePoint Portal Server installs this folder by default on the operating system drive under Program Files\SharePoint Portal Server\ClientDrop\Languages*Lang*, where *Lang* corresponds to the language of the client. For example, on an English version of SharePoint Portal Server, you would copy the "enu" directory to the domain controller.

3. Create the excluded group.

- On the taskbar, click **Start**, point to **Programs**, point to **Administrative Tools**, and then click **Active Directory Users and Computers**. If the **Active Directory Users and Computers** does not appear under **Administrative Tools**, you can add it manually.

- Expand the **Active Directory Users and Computers** node.

- Right-click the domain name, point to **New**, and then click **Group**.

- In the **Group name** box, type a name for the group.

- Do not change the default **Group scope** and **Group type**.

- Click **OK**.

- Click the domain name node. The new group appears in the details pane.

4. Add members to the excluded group.

- Right-click the group that you created in the previous step, and then click **Properties**.

- Click the **Members** tab, and then click **Add**.

- Select the computer to add, and then click **Add**. Add any servers on which you intend to install SharePoint Portal Server. In addition, add any servers on which you have already installed SharePoint Portal Server. You can also add other computers on which you do not want the client to install.

- Click **OK**.

- Click **OK** to close the **Properties** page.

- Close **Active Directory Users and Computers**.

5. Add the Group Policy snap-in.

- On the taskbar, click **Start**, and then click **Run**.

- In the **Open** box, type **MMC** and then click **OK**. The MMC console opens.

- On the **Console** menu, click **Add/Remove Snap-in**. The **Add/Remove Snap-in** dialog box appears.

- On the **Standalone** tab, click **Add**. The **Add Standalone Snap-in** dialog box appears.

- Under **Available Standalone Snap-ins**, click **Group Policy**, and then click **Add**. The **Select Group Policy Object** dialog box appears.

- Click **Browse**. The **Browse for a Group Policy Object** dialog box appears.

- On the **Domains/OUs** tab, click **Default Domain Policy**, and then click **OK**.

- Click **Finish** to close the **Select Group Policy Object** dialog box. The Group Policy Object (Default Domain Policy) appears on the **Standalone** tab in the **Add/Remove Snap-in** dialog box.

- Click **Close** to close the **Add Standalone Snap-in** dialog box.

- Click **OK**.

6. Add the SharePoint Portal Server client package by using the Group Policy snap-in.

- Expand the **Default Domain Policy** node.

- Expand the **Computer Configuration** node.

- Expand the **Software Settings** node.

- Right-click **Software installation**, point to **New**, and then click **Package**.

- Type the path to the folder that you copied in step 2, and then click **Open**.

  Note Do not use local references such as C:\share. Type a share location, such as \\server\share. Otherwise, some users may not be able to access the deployed application. Do not browse to this path.

- Double-click **SPSClient.msi**. The **Deploy Software** dialog box appears.

- Click **Advanced published or assigned**, and then click **OK**. The **Properties** page for the new package appears.

  Note If you close the Properties page at this point, you can later configure the settings in the steps described in the following procedure by reopening the Properties page.

- On the **Properties** page, click the **Deployment** tab, and then click **Advanced**.

- Clear both check boxes under **Advanced deployment options**, and then click **OK**.

- Click the **Security** tab, and then click **Add**.

- Click the excluded group that you created in step 3, click **Add**, and then click **OK**.

- On the **Security** tab, click the excluded group, select the **Deny** check box for all permissions, and then click **Apply**.

- Click **Yes** to continue when the caution message appears.

- Click **OK** to close the **Properties** page.

The client software is installed the next time the computer is restarted.

After installing the client components, you must add a Web folder that points to the workspace. The address of the workspace is http://*server_name*/*workspace_name*.

Uninstalling or Repairing Client Components

You can uninstall or repair client components of SharePoint Portal Server by using Add/Remove Programs in the Control Panel. You can also use the command line to remove or repair client components.

To remove or repair the client components by using the command line:

1. On the taskbar, click **Start**, point to **Programs**, point to **Accessories**, and then click **Command Prompt**.

2. Type "*path***setup**" *switch* "*path***SPSClient.msi**" where *path* is the path to the Setup.exe and SPSClient.msi files. Use the /x *switch* to uninstall the client components. Use the /f *switch* to repair the client components.

   For example, to remove the client components, where Setup.exe and SPSClient.msi are in E:\Client Files, you would type

   "E:\Client Files\setup" /x "E:\Client Files\SPSClient.msi"

   To repair the components in the preceding example, you would type

   "E:\Client Files\setup" /f "E:\Client Files\SPSClient.msi"

When you uninstall the client components, the *User's Help* (webfoldr.chm) file remains. It replaces the original Web folders Help file.

> **Note** If you remove one or more of the installation prerequisites, you cannot uninstall or repair the client components unless you disable the prerequisite check.

You disable the prerequisite check by adding DISABLEPREREQ=1 to the command line. To disable the prerequisite check in the preceding examples:

- To remove the client components, type

  "E:\Client Files\setup" /x "E:\Client Files\SPSClient.msi" DISABLEPREREQ=1

- To repair the client components, type

  "E:\Client Files\setup" /f "E:\Client Files\SPSClient.msi" DISABLEPREREQ=1

Installing the Client Components in Additional Languages

SharePoint Portal Server includes a client install for a single language. Users can install any language of the client to operate against a server. You can download client installations for additional languages from http://www.microsoft.com/Sharepoint.

> **Important** If you install Office XP in one language and the client components of SharePoint Portal Server in another language, the user interface may appear in either of the two languages.

Troubleshooting

The following sections address problems and possible solutions associated with installing SharePoint Portal Server. The first section reviews problems and possible solutions for server installations. The second section presents problems and possible solutions for client component installations.

Troubleshooting Server Installations

This section addresses problems and possible solutions associated with installing SharePoint Portal Server on a server computer.

Gather Information from the Server Installation Logs

You can examine the following logs for information about server installation:

- **Errorlog.txt file.** This file is located in Program Files\Microsoft Integration\ SharePoint Portal Server\Logs. For failed installations, this file may be located in the %temp% directory instead, depending on the stage of the installation process when the failure occurred. The error "VAIfy Failed" tells you that the portion of setup that configures default SharePoint Portal Server settings in the Microsoft Web Storage System failed.

    Setup may experience a nonfatal error that documents an ordering problem. The errors in the log may report one or more lines of the following:

    [Date, Time] Dependency Manager: [2] Ordering problem: Microsoft SharePoint Portal Server Microsoft Search

    The ordering problem could originate from MSSearch, SharePoint Portal Server, or a combination of these. The installation program is simply informing you that the order in which things are installing is different from the order SharePoint Portal Server requested. This error message is benign and is safe to ignore.

    If you are running unattended server installation, the log reports the following two errors, which are benign and safe to ignore:

    [Date, Time] Setup.exe: [2] ISetupManager::AddGlobalCustomProperty() called with an existing custom property (GUID)

    [Date, Time] Setup.exe: [2] ISetupManager::AddGlobalCustomProperty failed in ISetupManager::LoadPersistantData()

- **Eventlog.txt file.** This file is located in Program Files\Microsoft Integration\ SharePoint Portal Server\Logs. For failed installations, this file may be located in the %temp% directory instead, depending on the stage of the installation process when the failure occurred. This file contains a detailed list of the actions performed during the installation. Lines that contain errors are copied to Errorlog.txt.

  Some of the events in this log appear in English even on non-English systems. The events are useful to Microsoft Support for diagnosis of reported problems. In most cases, users can safely ignore these events.

- **Setup.log file.** This file is located in Program Files\Microsoft Integration\ SharePoint Portal Server\Logs.

- **Spsclisrv.log file.** This file is located in Program Files\Microsoft Integration\ SharePoint Portal Server\Logs for successful server installations.

- **Exchange Server Setup Progress.log file.** This file is located at the root of the operating system drive. This log tells you if the Web Storage System installed correctly. It can help you identify issues such as:

  - A server name has an illegal character.

  - IIS 5 is not installed, so the Web Storage System cannot be installed.

  - SMTP service is not installed. This is a Windows 2000 Server component.

    Note When you install SharePoint Portal Server on a Japanese operating system, the Exchange Server Setup Progress log is unreadable when opened with Microsoft Notepad, which is the typical association for .log files. To view the log, open it as a Unicode file in Microsoft Word.

For more information about VAIfy errors, see Appendix B.

If SharePoint Portal Server Does Not Install on Your Computer

SharePoint Portal Server does not install if any of the following are on the computer:

- An unsupported operating system. Only Windows 2000 Server and Advanced Server, SP1 or later, are supported.

- Windows 2000 Hot fix (Pre-SP2) Q269862. This hotfix cannot be installed on the computer. If it is installed, remove it before installing SharePoint Portal Server.

- Exchange 2000 Server or Exchange 2000 Enterprise Server.

- Exchange Server version 5.5 and earlier.

- Microsoft Site Server (any version).

- Microsoft Office Server Extensions.

  Note SharePoint Portal Server is not supported in a clustered environment. You cannot install SharePoint Portal Server in a clustered environment, and you must not join the SharePoint Portal Server computer to a clustered environment.

For information about the server requirements, see "Hardware and Software Requirements" earlier in this chapter.

The setup process (for both installation and repair) requires at least one free network drive letter on the computer. If no drive is available, setup fails. The Exchange Server Setup Progress.log file notes that no free drive was available.

If Server Installation Fails

SharePoint Portal Server requires the Default Web Site in IIS to use port 80 as the TCP port for localhost. Before installing SharePoint Portal Server, ensure that you specify 80 as the TCP port. Additionally, do *not* change the port to an alternative HTTP port (such as 8000 or 8080) after installation.

To ensure that port 80 is specified and remains as the primary port for the server:

1. On the taskbar, click **Start**, point to **Programs**, point to **Administrative Tools**, and then click **Internet Services Manager**.

2. Expand the node for the computer on which you want to install SharePoint Portal Server.

3. Right-click **Default Web Site**, and then click **Properties**.

4. On the **Web Site** tab, click **Advanced**.

5. Ensure that under **Multiple identities for this Web Site**, **(All Unassigned)** is specified as TCP port 80. If it is specified as port 80, click **Cancel** and go to step 7. If it is not specified as port 80 or is not listed, do one of the following:

   - If (All Unassigned) is not set to port 80, select **(All Unassigned)**, and then click **Edit**. In the **TCP Port** box, type **80** and then click **OK**.

   - If (All Unassigned) is not listed, click **Add**. In **IP Address**, select **(All Unassigned)**. In the **TCP Port** box, type **80** and then click **OK**.

6. Click **OK**.

7. Click **OK** to close the **Properties** page.

8. Restart the server before installation. You do not need to restart the server if you did not change any settings in step 5.

   Note Other configurations may be acceptable, as long as "localhost" on port "80" is a valid way to connect to W3SVC/1 (the Default Web Site) on the computer.

If Setup Is Very Slow or Fails After Long Periods of Inactivity

Setup may slow due to insufficient memory or excessive network traffic. Consider the following possibilities:

- Are you installing from a CD with a slow CD-ROM drive?

- Does your system meet the recommended processor and RAM requirements?

- If you are installing over a network, is your network experiencing slow or impaired operations?

If Setup Fails When Installing on a System Upgraded from Windows NT 4

Installing SharePoint Portal Server on a system that has been upgraded from Windows NT 4 can cause install failures. You should install SharePoint Portal Server on a clean Windows 2000 Server. If you are installing on a Windows 2000 system that was upgraded from Windows NT 4, you must manually register the Oledb32.dll file before installation to avoid installation failure.

To manually register the Oledb.32.dll file:

1. On the taskbar, click **Start**, point to **Programs**, point to **Accessories**, and then click **Command Prompt**.

2. Go to Program Files\Common Files\System\Ole DB on the operating system drive.

3. Type **regsvr32 oledb32.dll**

If Setup Fails with a VAlfy Error

Installing SharePoint Portal Server may result in VAIfy errors in Errorlog.txt. There are several troubleshooting steps that you can take to investigate this problem.

To troubleshoot a "VAlfy failed" error in Errorlog.txt:

1. Verify that MDAC is installed correctly by running the Component Checker tool (ComCheck.exe) available at http://www.microsoft.com/data/download.htm - ccinfo. Use this tool to verify that the MDAC version is 2.5 or later and the MDAC dynamic-link libraries (DLLs) are correct.

   If you find an error and need to reinstall MDAC 2.5 on your Windows 2000 server, do the following:

   - Display hidden files.

   - On the operating system drive, right-click winnt\inf\mdac.inf, and then click **Install**. You may be prompted for your Windows 2000 installation disc or service pack files location.

     If you are running MDAC 2.6 and need to reinstall it, install it from the original source or download it from http://www.Microsoft.com.

2. Ensure that W3SVC/1 (the Default Web Site in IIS) is started:

   - On the taskbar, click **Start**, point to **Programs**, point to **Administrative Tools**, and then click **Internet Services Manager**.

   - Expand the node for the SharePoint Portal Server computer.

- Right-click the Web site located at W3SVC/1. By default, this site is named Default Web Site.

- Click **Start**. If Start appears dimmed, W3SVC/1 is already started.

You can also find information about VAIfy errors in the Application Log in Windows 2000 Event Viewer (commonly referred to as the Windows 2000 event log).

If Workspace Virtual Directories Show the Error "Stop Sign" Symbol in the IIS Snap-In

This is a benign error. If W3SVC starts before Microsoft Exchange Information Store (MSExchangeIS), "stop sign" symbols appear under the Default Web Site folder of the Internet Information Services console in MMC.

There is a dependency between the local paths of the SharePoint Portal Server virtual directories and MSExchangeIS. You must start MSExchangeIS first, followed by W3SVC.

To prevent the stop signs from appearing each time you restart, complete the following steps:

1. Change the **Startup type** for W3SVC to **Manual**.

2. Restart the server. The MSExchangeIS service starts automatically.

3. Start W3SVC.

If the Server No Longer Functions

- Did you uninstall any of the server prerequisites after installing SharePoint Portal Server? SharePoint Portal Server requires:

  - Windows 2000 Server or Advanced Server SP1 or later operating system.

  - IIS 5.

  - SMTP service. This is a Windows 2000 Server component.

- Did you install software that does not coexist with SharePoint Portal Server after installing SharePoint Portal Server?

- Are all required services running?

- Did you attempt to configure security by using the IFS drive?

For more information about server requirements, see "Hardware and Software Requirements" earlier in this chapter.

Troubleshooting Client Installations

This section addresses problems and possible solutions associated with installing the client components for SharePoint Portal Server.

If Client Installation Fails

The client installation can fail if the computer does not meet the basic installation requirements. Consider the following possibilities:

- Do you have Internet Explorer 5 or later installed on the client computer? Internet Explorer 5 or later is required.

- Do you have Outlook Express 5 or later installed on the client computer? Outlook Express 5 or later is required.

- Are you attempting to install the client components of SharePoint Portal Server on Windows 95? The client components do not install on Windows 95.

- If you are attempting to install the client components on Windows NT 4, do you have SP6A or later installed?

- Are you an administrator on the client computer?

For more information about client requirements, see "Hardware and Software Requirements" earlier in this chapter.

If You Experience Recurring Installation Errors

If you experience recurring errors, a detailed log file can help you diagnose the problem.

To run setup with a detailed log file:

1. Go to the directory containing Setup.exe for the client components.

2. On the taskbar, click **Start**, point to **Programs**, point to **Accessories**, and then click **Command Prompt**.

3. Type **setup /L*v** "*path_and_file_name_for_the_log_file*"

    For example, if you want to store the log file named Clientsetup.log in the Client Setup directory on drive C, type **setup /L*v** "**C:\Client Setup\clientsetup.log**"

If you require assistance interpreting the information in the log file, you can call Microsoft Product Support Services.

If You Do Not See the SharePoint Portal Server Client in the Programs Menu

This is by design. The client components of SharePoint Portal Server are extensions to Windows Explorer and Office applications. There is no individual client application. Instead, SharePoint Portal Server commands are integrated into the menus of Windows Explorer, Word, Microsoft Excel, and Microsoft PowerPoint®.

Note You can use other applications to create documents, but you cannot access SharePoint Portal Server commands from the menus within those applications.

You must use Windows Explorer or a browser to perform SharePoint Portal Server document management tasks on documents created from within other applications.

Other Installation Issues

The following section describes other issues related to installation. It reviews how to modify proxy server settings after installation. It also describes the interaction between the IFS drive and the Web Storage System.

Modifying Proxy Server Settings

You need to specify your proxy server settings in SharePoint Portal Server. The following section describes how to modify these settings in your Web browser and how to correct settings that SharePoint Portal Server modified during setup.

Modifying Proxy Server Settings in Your Web Browser

You may need to change your proxy server settings for SharePoint Portal Server if your proxy server configuration has changed.

To change your proxy settings for the SharePoint Portal Server computer at some time after installation:

1. Configure the proxy server settings for your SharePoint Portal Server computer.

   - On the taskbar of the computer on which you are installing SharePoint Portal Server, click **Start**, point to **Settings**, and then click **Control Panel**.

   - Double-click **Internet Options**. The **Internet Properties** dialog box appears.

   - Click the **Connections** tab, and then click **LAN Settings**.

   - Clear both check boxes under **Automatic configuration**. Do one of the following:

     - If you use a proxy server, select the **Use a proxy server** check box, type a valid proxy server address and port number, and then select the **Bypass proxy server for local addresses** check box.

     - If you do not use a proxy server, clear all check boxes. For more information about the use of SharePoint Portal Server without a proxy server, see step 3.

   - Click **OK** to apply the changes, and then click **OK** to close **Internet Properties**.

2. Configure the proxy server settings used by the Gatherer. SharePoint Portal Server uses this setting when it creates indexes of external Web sites.

   Use **SharePoint Portal Server Administration** to configure this setting on the **Proxy Server** tab of the **Properties** page for the server. For more information about configuring the proxy server settings used by the Gatherer, see "Specify Proxy Server Options" under "Managing Servers" in *Administrator's Help*.

3. Configure the proxy server settings for the dashboard site.

   - To enable SharePoint Portal Server to import Web Parts to the dashboard site, the server administrator must use a tool called Proxycfg.exe, located under the SharePoint Portal Server \Bin directory. The location of this directory depends on the location of the SharePoint Portal Server installation directory.

   Note You must run Proxycfg.exe even if you are not using a proxy server.

   Using SharePoint Portal Server with a Proxy Server

   If you are using a proxy server, run the following command, which uses the settings specified in step 1: **proxycfg –u**

   For more information about Proxycfg.exe, see "Configure the Dashboard Site to Work with a Proxy Server" under "Advanced Topics" in *Administrator's Help*.

   Using SharePoint Portal Server without a Proxy Server

   By default, SharePoint Portal Server is not configured to run with direct Internet connectivity. SharePoint Portal Server is initially configured for use with a proxy server. For more information about the proxy settings if you are not using a proxy server, see Chapter 12, "Deploying SharePoint Portal Server in an Extranet Environment."

4. When using Fully Qualified Domain Names (FQDNs) on an intranet (this does not apply to the extranet), users must configure browser proxy server settings on client computers to bypass the proxy server for local addresses on each client computer accessing the dashboard site if:

   - Your network does not natively support FQDN.

   - You are running Windows Internet Naming Service (WINS).

   - Users experience errors navigating to the dashboard site by using FQDN.

   In addition, server administrators must configure the Internet Explorer proxy settings on the SharePoint Portal Server computer to include the domain of the local computer on the bypass list.

   Each user and the server administrator can configure the proxy server settings by using the following procedure. This procedure applies when your browser is Internet Explorer 5. To do this on other browsers, consult the browser documentation.

5. Restart the server after configuring the proxy settings.

To configure the proxy server settings when using Internet Explorer:

1. On the **Tools** menu, click **Internet Options**.

2. On the **Connections** tab, click **LAN Settings**.

3. Select the **Use a proxy server** and **Bypass proxy server for local addresses** check boxes.

4. Specify the address and port number of the proxy server, and then click **Advanced**.

5. In the **Do not use proxy server for addresses beginning with** box, type *domain* where *domain* is the domain of your SharePoint Portal Server. For example, if the domain is Adventure-works.com, type:

   *Adventure-works.com

6. Click **OK**, and then close the remaining dialog boxes.

Undoing Proxy Settings Modified by Setup

During the installation of SharePoint Portal Server, the setup process changes the proxy settings for the server from per-user to per-computer.

If you later uninstall SharePoint Portal Server, you can change the proxy settings back to per-user on the computer. This allows each individual user on the server to configure specific proxy settings.

To change proxy settings to per-user:

1. Open Group Policy as a stand-alone MMC snap-in:

   - On the taskbar, click **Start**, and then click **Run**.

   - Type **MMC** and then click **OK**. The MMC console opens.

   - On the **Console** menu, click **Add/Remove Snap-in**. The **Add/Remove Snap-in** dialog box appears.

   - On the **Standalone** tab, click **Add**. The **Add Standalone Snap-in** dialog box appears.

   - In **Available Standalone Snap-ins**, click **Group Policy**, and then click **Add**. The **Select Group Policy Object** dialog box appears. By default, the Group Policy Object is specified as Local Computer.

   - Click **Finish** to close the **Select Group Policy Object** dialog box. The Group Policy Object (Local Computer Policy) appears on the **Standalone** tab in the **Add/Remove Snap-in** dialog box.

   - Click **Close** to close the **Add Standalone Snap-in** dialog box.

   - Click **OK**.

2. Use the Group Policy snap-in to change the proxy settings per-user:

- Expand the **Local Computer Policy** node.

- Expand the **Computer Configuration** node.

- Expand the **Administrative Templates** node.

- Expand the **Windows Components** node.

- Click **Internet Explorer**.

- In the details pane, right-click **Make proxy settings per-computer (rather than per-user)**, and then click **Properties**.

- On the **Policy** tab, click **Not Configured**.

- Click **OK** to close the **Properties** page.

3. Each individual user on the server must reconfigure his proxy settings.

Using the IFS Drive and the Microsoft Web Storage System

The IFS provides access to the Microsoft Web Storage System that SharePoint Portal Server uses. By default, IFS is not mounted during the installation of SharePoint Portal Server.

You can use IFS access for the following tasks:

- Read-only access to the document library

- Microsoft FrontPage® Server Extensions

- Web Storage System development through IFS

Server administrators can access the IFS by using Windows Explorer on the SharePoint Portal Server computer. SharePoint Portal Server typically maps IFS to network drive M, unless there is already a mapping that uses that drive. Although you can use IFS to view the contents of the Microsoft Web Storage System that is used by SharePoint Portal Server, this access is read-only.

Note It is strongly recommended that you do *not* use IFS (network drive M) to create SharePoint Portal Server folders or documents, assign security to folders or documents, or edit properties for folders or documents. SharePoint Portal Server roles and configuration options are available through the supported Web folders interface. Manipulating the IFS security attributes may interfere with the roles information associated with SharePoint Portal Server, which results in data loss. Workspace management functions, such as creating document profiles, are also available through the Web folders interface only. In addition, do not use Microsoft ActiveX® Data Objects (ADO) or OLE DB to configure security on SharePoint Portal Server folders or documents.

SharePoint Portal Server setup uses drive M during setup and repair. This has the following issues:

- Drive M is added to the backup exclusion list for Windows NT backup. You will not see any drives mounted as M: under the Windows NT backup utility. You can reset this by using the backup utility for Windows NT.

- If there are no free drive letters, the repair option of setup fails. For the repair option to succeed, you must disconnect another drive.

You can mount drive M temporarily by doing the following:

To temporarily mount drive M:

1. On the taskbar, click **Start**, point to **Programs**, point to **Accessories**, and then click **Command Prompt**.

2. Type **subst M: \\.\backofficestorage** and then press ENTER. If drive M is already mapped, you can use any available drive letter. If the drive does not appear after running this command, restart the server and run the command again.

You can access the drive until you restart the server. To permanently mount drive M, you must edit the registry.

To permanently mount drive M:

1. On the taskbar, click **Start**, and then click **Run**.

2. In the **Open** box, type **regedit**, and then click **OK**.

   Caution Incorrectly editing the registry may severely damage your system. Back up the current version of the registry before making any changes. You should also back up any valued data on the computer.

3. In **Registry Editor**, go to HKEY_LOCAL_MACHINE\SYSTEM\CurrentControlSet\ Services\EXIFS\ Parameters.

4. Click **Parameters**.

5. In the details pane, right-click **DriveLetter**, and then click **Modify**.

6. In the **Value data** box, type **M** and then click **OK**. If drive M is already mapped, you can use any available drive letter.

7. Close **Registry Editor**.

8. Restart the server.

Summary

This chapter provides installation procedures and troubleshooting information. In addition, this chapter provides information about the operating system and browser support, the IFS drive and the Microsoft Web Storage System, and proxy server settings used by SharePoint Portal Server.

CHAPTER 12

Deploying SharePoint Portal Server in an Extranet Environment

This chapter provides the procedures for deploying Microsoft® SharePoint™ Portal Server 2001 across an *extranet*. This chapter defines an extranet as intranet resources that are accessible from the Internet, usually through a firewall. These procedures apply to a SharePoint Portal Server computer with one network interface card (NIC). The extranet deployment is not supported for dual-homed servers.

This chapter also defines the key terms used to describe deploying SharePoint Portal Server in an extranet environment, the various ways to access a workspace on your SharePoint Portal Server computer, and the tasks necessary to deploy SharePoint Portal Server in an extranet environment.

Deployment Tasks

The chapter organizes this procedure into multiple sections according to the tasks in the following list. Optional tasks are labeled as such.

- **Configure proxy settings on the server.** Configure the proxy setting on the SharePoint Portal Server computer.

- **DNS entry creation.** Create a Domain Name System (DNS) entry.

- **Web Site creation.** Create a new Web site in Internet Information Services (IIS).

- **Enable Web discussions.** Enable discussions on the new Web site.

- **Modify security settings.** Modify the security settings on the new Web site.

- **Configure proxy server settings.** Configure the proxy server settings.

- **Extranet testing from the Intranet.** Test the extranet from the intranet.

- **Extranet testing from the Internet.** Test the extranet from the Internet.

- **E-mail notifications.** Specify the server URL to use in e-mail notifications.

- **Secure Sockets Layer.** Optionally, enable Secure Sockets Layer (SSL).

- **Internal FQDN mapping.** Optionally, specify an internal Fully Qualified Domain Name (FQDN) for the SharePoint Portal Server computer.

- **Settings for crawling Web sites on the Internet.** Optionally, enable SharePoint Portal Server to crawl sites on the Internet.

- **Settings for crawling another SharePoint Portal Server site on the Internet.** Optionally, enable SharePoint Portal Server to crawl another SharePoint Portal Server computer across the Internet.

In addition to the tasks specified previously, the following sections are provided:

- **Troubleshooting.** Includes information to assist you in diagnosing any configuration problems.

- **Extranet features.** Describes SharePoint Portal Server featuresavailable when you deploy the server across an extranet.

Understanding Key Terms

This chapter uses following terms:

- **NetBIOS name.** The network basic input/output system (NetBIOS) name is the computer name of your server. You can find the computer name on the Properties page of My Computer. Right-click **My Computer**, and then click **Properties**. On the **Network Identification** tab, click **Properties**. You can view the computer name of the server in **Computer name**. In this chapter, examples use a NetBIOS name of AdvWks.

- **Internal domain name.** The internal domain name is the domain name you use on your intranet. It can be the same as the external domain name, or it can be different. In this chapter, examples use an internal domain name of corp.adventure-works.com.

- **Internal Fully Qualified Domain Name (FQDN).** The internal FQDN is the name you want to use for the server on your intranet. It is in the form *NetBIOS_name.internal_domain_name*. Users must use the internal FQDN to access the server if you do not enable your network for Microsoft Windows® Internet Name Service (WINS) resolution, or if you do not configure the Domain Name System (DNS) to support NetBIOS throughout the domain. In this chapter, examples use an intranet FQDN of AdvWks.corp.adventure-works.com.

- **External server name.** The external server name (host name) is the name you use for the server on the extranet. If your internal and external domain names are the same, the external server name must be different from the NetBIOS name. Add this name to the external domain name to form the external FQDN. In this chapter, examples use an external server name of AdventureWorks.

- **External domain name.** The external domain name is the domain name you use on the extranet. It can be the same as the internal domain name, or it can be different. In this chapter, examples use an external domain name of adventure-works.com.

- **External FQDN.** The external FQDN is in the form *external_server_name.external_domain_name*. In this chapter, examples use an external FQDN of AdventureWorks.adventure-works.com.

Internal and external FQDNs must be unique, as described here:

- If the internal and external domain names are the same, for example, adventure-works.com, the external server name must differ from the NetBIOS name. For example, you could have AdventureWorks.adventure-works.com and AdvWks.adventure-works.com as the external and internal FQDNs, respectively.

- If the internal and external domain names are different, the external server name can be the same as the NetBIOS name. For example, you could have AdvWks.adventure-works.com and AdvWks.corp.adventure-works.com as the external and internal FQDNs, respectively.

Accessing SharePoint Portal Server

The following table shows different ways to access a workspace on your SharePoint Portal Server computer. Examples use a workspace name of Marketing.

Workspace Access Points

To access by	Use
NetBIOS (computer name for the server)	http://*server_name/workspace_name* This is the way that you access SharePoint Portal Server out of the box. Example http://AdvWks/Marketing to access the workspace
Internal FQDN	http://*NetBIOS_name.internal_domain_name/workspace_name* Example http://AdvWks.corp.adventure-works.com/Marketing
External FQDN	http://*external_server_name.external_domain_name/workspace_name* Example http://AdventureWorks.adventure-works.com/Marketing
Internet Protocol (IP) address and port	**Important** You *cannot* access the SharePoint Portal Server computer by typing its Internet Protocol (IP) address and port number. For example, you *cannot* use http://10.0.0.X/*workspace_name* or http://10.0.0.X:8080/*workspace_name*.

Proxy Settings on the Server

The dashboard site uses a special server-side object called ServerXMLHTTP to make Hypertext Transfer Protocol (HTTP) requests. These requests are necessary to return the correct page to the client. The ServerXMLHTTP object has its own proxy settings. If the dashboard site is behind a proxy server, you must configure the ServerXMLHTTP object with the proxy server name to access data that is located beyond the intranet. The proxy settings are important when the dashboard site must access resources on a different server, such as when you use the Content management page to import new Web Parts.

Note For more information about changing proxy settings on the server, see Chapter 11, "Installing SharePoint Portal Server."

Specifying the Bypass List

When you configure the proxy settings on your server, you can specify a bypass list. This section reviews the most common options that you can choose. If the virtual directory for the workspace has NTLM enabled, you must set the proxy server and bypass list. The ServerXMLHTTP object attempts NTLM authentication against the virtual directory for the workspace.

You can separate multiple bypass addresses with a semicolon. A *bypass address* is an address for which you do not want to use the specified proxy server.

If You Are Using a Proxy Server

If you are using a proxy server, run:

> **proxycfg –d –p** *proxy_name:port_number "root_domain_name;<local>"*

In the preceding line, *root_domain_name* is the bypass address. Root_domain_name is the FQDN of the base root domain in which the computer is a member, with a wildcard exception prefixed to the root_domain_name. The bypass address is in the form *domain, such as *adventure-works.com. Include the brackets <> around **local** when you type the command.

Example. If your proxy server name is Proxy1, the port number is 80, and you want to bypass the proxy server for the SharePoint Portal Server computer in the domain adventure-works.com, type proxycfg –d –p Proxy1:80 "*adventure-works.com;<local>"

If You Are Not Using a Proxy Server

If are not using a proxy server in your environment, you must specify a fake proxy server to force SharePoint Portal Server to use integrated Windows 2000 authentication. Integrated Windows 2000 authentication is most commonly used in an intranet environment. If you do not specify a fake proxy server, network components on your SharePoint Portal Server computer default to Basic authentication. As a result, SharePoint Portal Server does not work correctly. To configure a fake proxy server, you must configure both the dashboard site and Microsoft Internet Explorer.

Note If you are using Basic or Anonymous authentication methods, you do not need to specify the proxy settings.

To configure the proxy settings on your SharePoint Portal Server computer, run:

proxycfg -d -p *fake_proxy_name***:80 "*;<local>"**

Example. If you do not have a proxy, specify any non-existent proxy and bypass for all addresses by using the wildcard (*). To do so, type:

proxycfg –d –p FakeProxy1234:80 "*;<local>"

Testing has indicated that this option works for most customers and that the preceding syntax should be used first, if you are not using a proxy. However, further options are provided later in this section.

To configure the proxy settings for Internet Explorer:

1. Open Internet Explorer.

2. On the **Tools** menu, click **Internet Options**.

3. Click the **Connections** tab, and then click **LAN Settings**.

4. Select the **Use a proxy server** check box.

5. Type *fake_proxy_name* in **Address**.

6. Type **80** in **Port**.

7. Select the **Bypass proxy server for local addresses** check box.

8. Click **Advanced**.

9. In **Exceptions**, type one of the following:

    "******root_domain_name*" or "*internal_FQDN*"

   For example, for a server with a NetBIOS name of AdvWks, you would type one of the following:

    *adventure-works.com

   or

    AdvWks.corp.adventure-works.com

10. To close the **Proxy Settings** dialog box, click **OK**.

11. To close the **Local Area Network (LAN) Settings** dialog box, click **OK**.

12. To close the **Internet Options** dialog box, click **OK**.

13. Restart the computer.

> **Note** You must configure the proxy settings for Internet Explorer on all client computers that access the server by using an FQDN (not the computer name) and integrated Windows 2000 authentication. You can configure all your client computers to use these proxy settings by using the Internet Explorer Administration Kit. If you do not configure each client computer, each user will be prompted for authentication for each session.

If you are not using a proxy server, and if the configuration specified earlier does not work for you, you can run one of the following configurations as an option:

- **To prevent downloading of Web Parts from any site, including the Microsoft Web Part Gallery, run:**

  proxycfg –d –p *fake_proxy_name***:80 "<local>"**

  This setting enables NTLM on the computer and on the subnet mask. This setting has no known security issues because all traffic is local.

- **To allow downloading of Web Parts from the Microsoft Web Part Gallery, run:**

  proxycfg –d –p *fake_proxy_name***:80 "*microsoft.com;<local>"**

  With this option, you can download Web Parts from the Microsoft Web Part Gallery. You cannot download Web Parts from any other site. This setting enables NTLM on the computer and on the subnet mask. This setting may increase the security vulnerability because traffic going to *www.microsoft.com* may send NTLM packets. This depends on the Internet service provider (ISP) configuration. In addition, it depends on whether the ISP enables ports to send and receive NTLM packets.

- **To download Web Parts from any Web site, run:**

  proxycfg –d –p *fake_proxy_name***:80 "*;<local>"**

  This setting enables NTLM on the computer and on the subnet mask. With this option, you can send NTLM traffic to any site on the Internet. This depends on the ISP configuration. In addition, it depends on whether the ISP enables ports to send and receive NTLM packets.

- **To run the computer directly on the extranet, run:**

  proxycfg –d

  You cannot download Web Parts from any Web site. This setting enables NTLM only on the computer, not on the subnet mask. Some SharePoint Portal Server functionality may be disabled. You must create a new Web site in IIS that uses Basic authentication. NTLM remains enabled on the Default Web Site in IIS. For more information about creating a new Web Site in IIS, see the section, "Web Site Creation" later in this chapter.

> **Caution** Running a computer directly on the extranet with no proxy server has inherent security vulnerabilities, and is therefore not recommended. However, using Basic authentication with SSL enabled on the new Web site in IIS is the most secure SharePoint Portal Server configuration available when the computer runs directly on the extranet.

Configuring the Proxy Settings on the Server

During the SharePoint Portal Server installation, the setup process automatically configures the proxy settings for ServerXMLHTTP by using the proxy settings specified for the server. If you need to change these proxy settings at some time after installation, or if you want to use SharePoint Portal Server across the extranet without a proxy server, use the following procedure.

To configure the proxy settings:

1. On the **Start** menu, point to **Programs**, point to **Accessories**, and then click **Command Prompt**.

2. Change to the SharePoint Portal Server \Bin directory. For example, if you installed SharePoint Portal Server in the Installation directory on drive E, change to E:\Installation\Bin. If you installed SharePoint Portal Server on drive D under Program Files\SharePoint Portal Server, change to the following directory:

   D:\Program Files\SharePoint Portal Server\Bin.

3. To see the current proxy settings, type **proxycfg.**

4. To configure the proxy appropriately, type one of the options specified in the preceding section.

5. Restart the computer.

   Important SharePoint Portal Server does not support direct Internet connectivity out of the box. By default, SharePoint Portal Server is initially configured for use with a proxy server.

DNS Entry Creation

You must create a DNS entry for the external server name. The procedure for this varies, depending on the DNS server software. If DNS is running on a computer running Windows 2000 Server, use the following procedure. For more information about DNS, see Appendix B, "For More Information."

Before performing the following procedure, you must have a static external IP address that you can assign to your SharePoint Portal Server computer. This is not the same IP address as the static internal IP address for the server. You receive a range of static external IP addresses when you first establish Internet access through Network Solutions or through another company authorized by the Internet Corporation for Assigned Names and Numbers (ICANN).

The external static IP address is used when you map the external static IP address to the internal static IP address on the proxy server to create a "server publish." For more information, see the "Proxy Server Settings" section later in this chapter.

Note You should not need to create a DNS entry if the SharePoint Portal Server computer is on the Internet with no proxy server. If the server is directly on the Internet, the domain controller should already have an entry for the NetBIOS name. In this case, the NetBIOS name is also the external (host) name.

To create a DNS entry on a Windows 2000 server:

1. On the **Start** menu, point to **Programs**, point to **Administrative Tools**, and then click **DNS**.

2. Expand the node for one of the *external* DNS computers.

3. Expand the node for **Forward Lookup Zones**.

4. Right-click the correct zone file, and then click **New Host**. For example, if you are creating a DNS entry for the external server name of your SharePoint Portal Server computer, right-click adventure-works.com.

5. In **Host**, type the external server name. For example, if the external server name is AdventureWorks, type **AdventureWorks.**

6. In **IP address**, type the external static IP address of the SharePoint Portal Server computer. This is not the same as the static internal IP address for your server.

7. Select the **Create associated pointer (PTR) record** check box.

8. Click **Add Host**.

9. Click **OK**, and then click **Done**.

10. Replicate to all DNS computers or wait 15-30 minutes for replication.

Web Site Creation

You must create a new Web site for each authentication model that you want to use. For example, if you want to have both Anonymous access and Basic authentication, you must create two Web sites. On one Web site, you specify Anonymous access, and on the other site, you specify Basic authentication.

Note You should not modify settings on the Default Web Site. Specifically, SharePoint Portal Server requires the Default Web Site to use port 80 as the TCP port. Do not change the port to an alternative HTTP port (such as 8000 or 8080) after installation. Ensure that you specify port 80 and that it remains the primary port for the server.

To create a new Web site:

1. On the **Start** menu, point to **Programs**, point to **Administrative Tools**, and then click **Internet Services Manager**.

2. Expand the node for the SharePoint Portal Server computer.

3. Right-click the name of the SharePoint Portal Server computer, point to **New**, and then click **Web Site**. The **Web Site Creation Wizard** appears.

4. Click **Next**, and then follow the instructions in the wizard.

5. On the **Web Site Description** page, type a description of the Web site, and then click **Next**. The description appears in the tree view of the console. For example, if you want to use this Web site to provide Anonymous access, you could type AdventureWorksAnon as the description.

6. On the **IP Address and Port Settings** page, complete the following steps:

   - Select the IP address. Do *not* select (**All Unassigned**).

   - Type **80** for the TCP port number.

   - Type the external FQDN as the host header. The host header is of the form *external_server_name.external_domain_name*. For example, if the external server name for your SharePoint Portal Server computer is AdventureWorks, and the external domain name is adventure-works.com, you would type AdventureWorks.adventure-works.com as the host header.

   - Click **Next**.

7. On the **Web Site Home Directory** page, complete the following steps:

   - Type the path for your home directory.

     Important It is strongly recommended that the home directory be under the Inetpub directory. For example, the path can be C:\Inetpub\AdventureWorks. For more information about creating a default Web page, see the section "Extranet Testing from the Intranet" later in this chapter.

   - If you do not want to allow Anonymous access to SharePoint Portal Server, clear the **Allow anonymous access to this Web site** check box. For detailed information about specifying security on the new Web site, see the section "Security Settings" later in this chapter.

   - Click **Next**.

8. On the **Web Site Access Permissions** page, click **Next**. Do not change the default access permissions.

9. Click **Finish**. The new Web site appears.

10. Expand **Default Web Site**, and then note the following five virtual directories (nodes on the tree): **Exchweb**, **SharePoint Portal Server**, **Public**, **MSOffice**, and **YourWorkspace**, where **YourWorkspace** represents the name of the virtual directory for your workspace. Write down the local path for each virtual directory, or use copy and paste while performing the steps. You need this path to complete the following steps.

For example, if you name your workspace Marketing, look at the Marketing virtual directory.

> **Note** To find the local path, complete these steps for each of the five virtual directories.

- Right-click the virtual directory, and then click **Properties**.
- On the **Virtual Directory** tab, note or copy the path shown in **Local Path**.
- Close the **Properties** page.

11. Right-click the new Web site that you created in steps 3 through 9, point to **New**, and then click **Virtual Directory**. The **Virtual Directory Creation Wizard** appears.

12. Click **Next**, and then follow the instructions in the wizard.

13. On the **Virtual Directory Alias** page, type **Exchweb** in **Alias**, and then click **Next**.

14. On the **Web Site Content Directory** page, type or paste the path for Exchweb from step 10 in **Directory**, and then click **Next**.

15. On the **Access Permissions** page, click **Next**. Do not change the default access permissions.

16. Click **Finish**.

17. To create a virtual directory for **SharePoint Portal Server**, **Public**, **MSOffice**, and **YourWorkspace**, where **YourWorkspace** represents the name of the virtual directory for your workspace, repeat steps 11 through 16.

> **Important** The names of the new virtual directories must exactly match the names of the original virtual directories under the Default Web Site. Do *not* rename the virtual directories.

18. After creating the virtual directories, for the **Public** and **YourWorkspace** virtual directories on the new Web site that you created, use the following procedure:

- Right-click the virtual directory, and then click **Properties**.
- Click the **Virtual Directory** tab.
- In **Application Protection**, select **Low** (IIS Process).
- On the **Virtual Directory** tab, click **Configuration**.
- On the **App Mappings** tab, click **Add**.

- In **Executable**, type the path to the msdmisap.dll file. You can also browse to the msdmisap.dll file. By default, this file is located in the SharePoint Portal Server \Bin directory. For example, if you installed SharePoint Portal Server to Program Files\SharePoint Portal Server, this file is in Program Files\SharePoint Portal Server\Bin.

  Important In **Executable**, ensure that path entered follows the 8.3 naming convention. For example, if the msdmisap.dll file is in the Program Files\SharePoint Portal Server\Bin directory on drive D, type the path in **Executable** as the following:

  D:\Progra~1\ShareP~1\Bin\msdmisap.dll

- In **Extension**, type * and then click **OK**.

- Clear the **Check that file exists** check box.

- To close **Application Configuration**, click **OK**.

- To close the **Properties** page, click **OK**.

19. For the **YourWorkspace** virtual directory on the Web site that you created, use the following procedure:

    - Right-click the virtual directory, and then click **Properties**.

    - On the **Virtual Directory** tab, select the **Write** check box.

    - Click the **HTTP Headers** tab, and then click **Add**.

    - In **Custom Header Name**, type **MicrosoftTahoeServer**.

    - In **Custom Header Value**, type **1.0**.

    - Click **OK**.

    - To close the **Properties** page, click **OK**.

20. For the **MSOffice** virtual directory on the Web site that you created, complete the following steps:

    - Right-click the virtual directory, and then click **Properties**.

    - Click the **Virtual Directory** tab.

    - In **Execute Permissions**, click **Scripts** and **Executables**.

    - To close the **Properties** page, click **OK**.

21. Right-click **YourVirtualWeb**, where **YourVirtualWeb** is the name of the new Web site you just created, and then click **Start**.

    Note If the computer already started **YourVirtualWeb**, omit this step.

22. Restart the server.

Web Discussions

To use Web discussions on your SharePoint Portal Server computer from the extranet, you must modify the registry.

You can use Web discussions to discuss a document with other users. Web discussions allow users to add remarks about a document without modifying the document. Discussions are threaded, which means that replies to a discussion remark appear directly underneath the original remark. In addition, multiple discussions about the same document can occur simultaneously. SharePoint Portal Server consolidates comments in a single location, allowing you to review them easily. For detailed information about using Web Discussions with SharePoint Portal Server, see Chapter 10, "Planning for Web Discussions."

To enable discussions on the new Web site:

1. On the **Start** menu, click **Run**.

2. Type **regedit** and then click **OK**.

   Caution Incorrectly editing the registry may severely damage your system. Back up the current version of the registry before making any changes. You should also back up any valued data on the computer.

3. In **Registry Editor**, move to HKEY_LOCAL_MACHINE\SOFTWARE\ Microsoft\Office\9.0\Web Server\1.

4. On the **Registry** menu, click **Export Registry File**.

5. Save the file as **EnableDiscussions** on your desktop.

6. Move to HKEY_LOCAL_MACHINE\SOFTWARE\Microsoft\Office\9.0\Web Server\1.

7. Right-click **1**, and then click **Rename**.

8. Type *number* and then press ENTER. *Number* is determined from the following procedure:

   - On the **Start** menu, point to **Programs**, point to **Accessories**, and then click **Command Prompt**.

   - Move to the directory where adsutil.vbs is located. Typically, this is in the Inetpub\AdminScripts directory on the operating system drive.

   - Type **cscript adsutil.vbs enum W3SVC/***number*, where *number* is 1, 2, etc. Type each number in order until the properties display the name of the new Web site. Typically, W3SVC/1 is the Default Web Site, W3SVC/2 is the Administration Web Site, and W3SVC/3 is the new Web site. If W3SVC/3 is the new Web site, type 3 as *number* when renaming the registry key in this step.

9. Click **Web Server**.

10. On the **Registry** menu, click **Import Registry File**.

11. Import **EnableDiscussions** that you saved to the desktop previously.

12. Click **OK**.

13. Click **3**, right-click **Server Root Url** in the right pane, and then click **Modify**.

14. In **Value data**, type the external FQDN of the server, and then click **OK**. For example, type http://AdventureWorks.adventure-works.com.

15. Close **Registry Editor**.

16. Restart the server.

Security Settings

By default, SharePoint Portal Server uses NTLM authentication (on the Default Web Site in IIS). To use SharePoint Portal Server on the extranet, you must modify the security settings on the new Web site to Basic authentication or Anonymous access.

> **Caution** Do *not* specify both Basic authentication and Anonymous access on the same Web site. If you want Basic authentication and Anonymous access, create two Web sites.

If you want to use Basic authentication and Anonymous access, configure the security settings as follows:

- For the Default Web Site in IIS, leave the default of NTLM authentication.

- Create a new Web Site in IIS and specify Basic authentication access.

- Create a second new Web Site in IIS and specify Anonymous access.

SharePoint Portal Server does not support both NTLM and Anonymous authentication on the same Web site. If you modify the security setting to Anonymous access, users cannot create subscriptions from the dashboard site.

> **Caution** Do *not* run the **Windows 2000 Internet Server Security Tool** after installing SharePoint Portal Server. Running this tool may disable the dashboard site.

To modify the security settings on the new Web site:

1. On the **Start** menu, point to **Programs**, point to **Administrative Tools**, and then click **Internet Services Manager**.

2. Expand the node for the SharePoint Portal Server computer.

3. Right-click **YourVirtualWeb**, where **YourVirtualWeb** is the name of the new Web site you created, and then click **Properties**.

4. Click the **Directory Security** tab.

5. In **Anonymous access and authentication control**, click **Edit**.

6. In **Authentication Methods**, select the authentication method you want for the new Web site:

   - To enable Anonymous access, select the **Anonymous access** check box. Clear all other check boxes. Do *not* specify both Anonymous access and Basic authentication on the same Web site.

   - To enable Basic authentication, select the **Basic authentication (password is sent in clear text)** check box, and then click **Yes** when prompted. Clear all other check boxes. Do *not* specify both Basic authentication and Anonymous access on the same Web site.

     Note All information, including passwords, sent over the Internet is in a readable format. To secure your transmissions, use SSL. For more information about SSL, see the section "Secure Sockets Layer" later in this chapter.

7. Click **OK**.

8. To close the **Properties** page, click **OK**.

If you use Anonymous access, you must also assign the Internet Guest Access account to the reader role on each workspace for which you want Anonymous access. If you are configuring Basic authentication only, you do not need to assign the Internet Guest Access account to the reader role.

To assign the Internet Guest Access account to the reader role:

1. On the **Start** menu, point to **Programs**, point to **Administrative Tools**, and then click **SharePoint Portal Server Administration**.

2. In the console tree, click to expand the server, and then select the workspace.

3. On the **Action** menu, click **Properties**. You can also right-click the workspace name, and then click **Properties** on the shortcut menu.

4. Click the **Security** tab.

5. Click **Add**.

6. From **Select Users or Groups**, select the name of your server from **Look in**.

7. From the list of names, select the name IUSR_server_name, where server_name is the NetBIOS name of your server.

8. Click **Add**, and then click **OK**.

9. Click **Apply**. SharePoint Portal Server adds the account to the Reader role.

If you close the **Properties** page, open it, and then click the **Security** tab, SharePoint Portal Server lists the account you just entered as Internet Guest Account.

> **Important** SharePoint Portal Server licensing requires that all devices accessing the server have a valid license. Nothing in this chapter waives or modifies any rights or requirements under the end user license agreement or other applicable license agreement for SharePoint Portal Server.

Proxy Server Settings

If you want to use SharePoint Portal Server across the extranet and you have a proxy server, you must:

- Ensure that you add the external IP address of your SharePoint Portal Server computer to the proxy server.

- Map the internal static IP address of the server to an external static IP address. Microsoft Internet Security and Acceleration (ISA) Server 2000 calls this *server publishing*. The proxy server must pass permissions through and must not modify the host header file.

If you are not using ISA Server, you must configure your proxy server as follows:

- The proxy server must allow password and authentication information to pass through to the SharePoint Portal Server computer inside the firewall.

- The host header name must stay intact when passing through.

- Do not use SSL bridging.

Before performing the following procedures, you must know the static external IP address that is assigned to your SharePoint Portal Server computer. This is not the same IP address as the static internal IP address for the server. You must also have a subnet mask. You receive a range of static external IP addresses and a subnet mask when you first establish Internet access through Network Solutions or through another company authorized by the ICANN.

The following procedures apply if you are using ISA Server as your proxy server. Note that the following steps assume that you have already enabled the firewall and reverse proxy for ISA Server. Additionally, your ISA Server must allow internal users to access the Internet by using the proxy server without authentication. If you have a proxy server that requires a server to provide authentication to access the Internet from your intranet, you cannot download a Web part from the Internet. This is because the ServerXMLHTTP object cannot access the Internet if authentication is required.

To ensure that the external static IP address of your server is added to the proxy server:

1. On the desktop on the proxy server, right-click **My Network Places**, and then click **Properties**.

2. Right-click the NIC that is connected to the Internet, and then click **Properties**.

3. Under **Components checked are used by this connection**, click **Internet Protocol (TCP/IP)**, and then click **Properties**.

4. Click **Advanced**.

5. Under **IP addresses**, scroll through the list of IP address to ensure that it lists the external static IP address for the SharePoint Portal Server computer. This external static IP address is the same one used to create the DNS entry for the server.

6. If the IP address appears in the list, no further action is required. If the external static IP address does not appear in the list of IP addresses, you must complete steps 7 through 12.

7. Click **Add**. The **TCP/IP Address** dialog box appears.

8. In **IP address**, type the external static IP address.

9. In **Subnet mask**, type the subnet mask for the IP address.

10. Click **Add** to close the **TCP/IP Address** dialog box, and then click **OK**.

11. Click **OK**, and then click **OK** again to close the **Properties** page.

12. Restart the server.

You have now successfully added the external static IP address of your server to the proxy server.

To map an external IP address to an internal IP address:

1. On the **Start** menu, point to **Programs**, point to **Microsoft ISA Server**, and then click **ISA Management**.

2. Expand **Servers and Arrays**.

3. Expand the name of your proxy server.

4. Expand **Publishing**.

5. Right-click **Server Publishing Rules**, point to **View**, and then click **Taskpad**.

6. Click **Publish a Server**. The **New Server Publishing Rule Wizard** appears.

7. In **Server publishing rule name**, type a name to identify the new publishing rule, and then click **Next**.

8. On the **Address Mapping** page, type the internal static IP address of the server in **IP address of internal server**.

9. On the **Address Mapping** page, type the external static IP address in **External IP address on ISA Server**.

10. Click **Next**.

11. On the **Protocol Settings page** under **Apply the rule to this protocol**:

    • Select **HTTP Server** if you have not enabled SSL.

    • Select **HTTPS Server** if you have enabled SSL.

    Note You must enable these protocols on the proxy server. For procedures used to enable the protocols, see the documentation for your proxy server.

12. Click **Next**.

13. On the **Client Type** page, click **Any request**, and then click **Next**.

14. Click **Finish**.

15. Double-click the rule you just created, and on the **General** tab, ensure that you select the **Enable** check box.

    Note It may take up to 15 minutes for the mapping to be effective. If the mapping has not become effective after 15 minutes, perform steps 16 through 24.

16. On the **Start** menu, point to **Programs**, point to **Microsoft ISA Server**, and then click **ISA Management**.

17. Expand **Servers and Arrays**.

18. Expand the name of your proxy server.

19. Expand **Monitoring**.

20. Right-click **Services**, point to **View**, and then click **Taskpad**.

21. Select the Web proxy service, and then click **Stop a Service**.

22. Select the Firewall service, and then click **Stop a Service**.

23. Select the Web proxy service, and then click **Start a Service**.

24. Select the Firewall service, and then click **Start a Service**.

If the mapping has not taken effect within 30 minutes after this procedure, restart the proxy server.

Extranet Testing from the Intranet

Use this procedure to confirm that you have set up your server correctly to access it from the extranet.

Important Perform the following procedure from the server.

To test the extranet from your intranet:

1. Create a test file in the home directory for the new Web site:

   - Create default.htm and place it in the home directory. Your home directory should be under the Inetpub directory. For example, the home directory can be C:\Inetpub\AdventureWorks.

   - Type some text in default.htm and save the file. For example, type <H1>*some text, such as the external FQDN*</H1>.

2. Create an entry in the **hosts** file on the server:

   - Move to the **hosts** file. Typically, this file is located in WINNT\system32\drivers\etc on the operating system drive.

   - Open the **hosts** file in Microsoft Notepad.

   - Add the SharePoint Portal Server computer (internal static) IP address along with the external name of your server to the hosts file. For example, add 10.0.0.X AdventureWorks.adventure-works.com.

   - Save the file.

3. Modify the proxy settings for Internet Explorer on the server:

   - Open **Internet Explorer**.

   - On the **Tools** menu, click **Internet Options**.

   - Click the **Connections** tab, and then click **LAN Settings**.

   - Select the **Use a proxy server** and **Bypass proxy server for local addresses** check boxes.

   - Type the address and port number for the proxy server, and then click **Advanced**.

   - In **Do not use proxy server for addresses beginning with**, type *root_domain_name* and then click **OK**. For example, if the root domain is adventure-works.com, you type *adventure-works.com.

   - Click **OK**, and then click **OK** to close **Internet Options**.

4. In **Internet Explorer**, type **http://***external_server_name.external domain name* in **Address**. You should see the text that you typed in default.htm. For example, if you typed AdventureWorks in default.htm, AdventureWorks displays.

If you can access the server, you have specified the external FQDN correctly. If you cannot access the server, ensure that the Web site started.

To ensure that the Web site started:

1. On the **Start** menu, point to **Programs**, point to **Administrative Tools**, and then click **Internet Services Manager**.

2. Expand the node for the SharePoint Portal Server computer.

3. Right-click **Your VirtualWeb**, where **Your VirtualWeb** is the name of the new Web site you created, and then click **Start**.

If you still cannot access the server, see the section "Troubleshooting" later in this chapter. After you successfully access the extranet from your intranet, you should test access from the Internet.

Extranet Testing from the Internet

Use this procedure to confirm that you have set up your server correctly to access it from the Internet.

Important Perform the following procedures from a computer that is not connected to your corporate LAN or WAN, either directly or by dialing in to the network.

To test the extranet from the Internet:

1. From the computer connected to the Internet through an ISP, type **http://***external_FQDN*.

   For example, type http://AdventureWorks.adventure-works.com.

   The default Web page (default.htm) that you created in the previous section should appear.

2. If the default Web page appears, type **http://***external_FQDN/workspace_name*

   For example, type http://AdventureWorks.adventure-works.com/Marketing.

   The dashboard site for the Marketing workspace appears.

If you cannot access the dashboard site, see the section "Troubleshooting" later in this chapter.

E-Mail Notifications

SharePoint Portal Server sends e-mail notifications for document approval requests and subscription notifications. The URLs in the notification mails can use the NetBIOS name, the internal FQDN, or the external FQDN of the server. If you are using FQDN without WINS, SharePoint Portal Server cannot automatically choose which form of the server name is appropriate for a particular e-mail recipient.

For example, assume you are in one domain and you approve a document by accessing the document through the NetBIOS name. The next person to receive the approval e-mail is in another domain (either a parent domain or another domain entirely). The link this person receives in the approval e-mail contains the NetBIOS name for the link (href). Because the recipient is in another domain, the name used in the link does not resolve and the recipient cannot access the document by clicking the link.

SharePoint Portal Server allows administrators to control the form of the name by adding a property to the folder that contains all the workspaces on the server. You can edit this property by using Web Storage System Explorer in the *Web Storage System Software Development Kit* (SDK). For more information about the Web Storage System SDK, see Appendix B, "For More Information." The administrator can specify that the URL use the internal FQDN or the external FQDN.

- If you specified the external FQDN, users on both the intranet and the extranet need to use Basic authentication or SSL, depending on how you configure the server. In addition, each user must modify the hosts file on her computer, or the network infrastructure must be able to resolve the external name and force the user out to the Internet and back into the intranet through the proxy.

- If you specified the internal FQDN, everyone on the intranet can click any links sent. However, users on the extranet receive an error when they attempt to click the link in the subscription or approval e-mail. If you have a small percentage of extranet users, you might choose to specify the internal FQDN so that the majority of your users do not need to modify the hosts file.

To specify the URL of the server name:

1. Open **Web Storage System Explorer**.

2. Connect to http://*NetBIOS_name*/SharePoint Portal Server/workspaces:

   - Type *username*.

   - Type *password*.

   - In **Web Storage System URL**, type **http://***NetBIOS_name***/SharePoint Portal Server/workspaces**. For example, to connect to a server named AdvWks, type http://AdvWks/SharePoint Portal Server/workspaces.

3. Click the node for http://*NetBIOS_name*/SharePoint Portal Server/workspaces to display its schema detail view.

4. Right-click in **Detail View**, and then click **Add Property**.

5. In **Add Property**:

   • In **Name**, type **urn:schemas-microsoft-com:publishing:ServerUrl**

     Important The property name is case-sensitive. Type the property name exactly as specified.

   • In **Datatype**, select **string**.

   • If you always want to use the NetBIOS name in e-mail, in **Value**, type **http://***NetBIOS_name*. If you always want to use the internal FQDN in e-mail, type **http://***internal_FQDN*. If you always want to use the external FQDN in e-mail, type **http://***external_FQDN*.

   • Click **OK**.

6. Close **Web Storage System Explorer**.

7. Restart **MSSearch**. To do so:

   • On the **Start** menu, point to **Programs**, point to **Administrative Tools**, and then click **Services**.

   • Right-click **Microsoft Search**, and then click **Restart**.

Secure Sockets Layer

If you want to secure your transmissions over the extranet, you must enable SSL. After enabling SSL, you must access the workspace by using https://*external_server_name.external_domain_name/workspace_name*.

You should ensure that http:// is working properly before enabling SSL.

Enabling SSL requires several steps:

• Request a new certificate, and then submit the text file that you generated to your SSL vendor.

• Install the certificate file that you receive from your vendor.

• Assign a certificate.

• Specify the secure bindings value.

• Remove port 443 from multiple SSL identities.

• Require SSL.

The following procedures provide the steps for completing this process.

To request a new certificate:

1. On the **Start** menu, point to **Programs**, point to **Administrative Tools**, and then click **Internet Services Manager**.

2. Expand the node for the SharePoint Portal Server computer.

3. Right-click **YourVirtualWeb**, where **YourVirtualWeb** is the name of the new Web site you created, and then click **Properties**.

4. Click the **Directory Security** tab, and then click **Server Certificate** under **Secure communications**. The **Welcome to the Web Server Certificate Wizard** appears.

5. Click **Next**.

6. Click **Create a New Certificate**, and then click **Next**.

7. Click **Prepare the request now, but send it later**, and then click **Next**.

8. In **Name**, type *YourVirtualWeb* where *YourVirtualWeb* is the name of your new Web site.

9. In **Bit length**, select **512** or **1024**. For server performance, it is recommended that you select 512.

10. If required, select the **Server Gated Cryptography (SGC) certificate (for export versions only)** check box.

    Important It is recommended that you do not change the default (the check box is not selected).

11. Click **Next**.

12. Type your organization's information on the **Organization Information** page, and then click **Next**.

13. In **Common name**, type the external FQDN of your server (which includes the domain name), and then click **Next**. For example, type AdventureWorks.adventure-works.com.

14. Type your geographical information on the **Geographical Information** page, and then click **Next**.

15. Specify a file name for the certificate request, and then click **Next**.

16. On the **Request File Summary** page, click **Next**.

17. Click **Finish**.

18. Click **OK** to close the **Properties** page.

You have now completed the certificate request process. Submit the text file that you generated to your SSL vendor.

After you receive the certificate file from your vendor, you must install the certificate.

To install the certificate that you receive from your vendor:

1. On the **Start** menu, point to **Programs**, point to **Administrative Tools**, and then click **Internet Services Manager**.

2. Expand the node for the SharePoint Portal Server computer.

3. Right-click **YourVirtualWeb**, where **YourVirtualWeb** is the name of the new Web site you created, and then click **Properties**.

4. Click the **Directory Security** tab, and then click **Server Certificate** under **Secure communications**. The **Welcome to the Web Server Certificate Wizard** appears.

5. Click **Next**.

6. Click **Process the pending request and install the certificate**, and then click **Next**.

7. Specify the path and file name for the certificate file on the **Process a Pending Request** page, and then click **Next**.

8. On the **Certificate Summary** page, click **Next**.

9. Click **Finish**.

10. Click **OK** to close the **Properties** page.

To assign a certificate to the Default Web Site:

This step enables you to remove port 443 from **Multiple SSL identities for this Web Site** in a later step. If you do not remove port 443, SharePoint Portal Server may experience unexpected behaviors because the Default Web Site and any new Web sites you create are trying to use port 443.

1. Right-click **Default Web Site**, and then click **Properties**.

2. Click the **Directory Security** tab, and then click **Server Certificate** under **Secure communications**. The **Welcome to the Web Server Certificate Wizard** appears.

3. Click **Next**.

4. Click **Assign an existing certificate**, and then click **Next**.

5. On the **Available Certificates** page, select a certificate, and then click **Next**.

6. On the **Certificate Summary** page, click **Next**.

7. Click **Finish**.

8. To close the **Properties** page, click **OK**.

To specify the secure bindings value to include the host header for the new Web site:

1. On the **Start** menu, point to **Programs**, point to **Accessories**, and then click **Command Prompt**.

2. Move to the directory where adsutil.vbs is located. Typically, this is in the Inetpub\AdminScripts directory on the operating system drive.

3. Type **cscript adsutil.vbs set W3SVC/*number*/securebindings** "*IP_address_of_the_server*:**443**:*external_FQDN_in_lowercase*"

   where *number* is the number for **YourVirtualWeb**. Typically, W3SVC/1 is the Default Web Site, W3SVC/2 is the Administration Web Site, and W3SVC/3 is the new Web site. To find the number, you can type **cscript adsutil.vbs enum W3SVC/***number* until you find the number for **YourVirtualWeb**. Type each number in order until the properties display the name of **YourVirtualWeb**.

If you do not remove port 443 from Default Web Site, SharePoint Portal Server may experience unexpected behaviors because the Default Web Site and any new Web sites you create are trying to use port 443.

To remove port 443 from Multiple SSL identities for this Web Site on the Default Web Site:

1. On the **Start** menu, point to **Programs**, point to **Administrative Tools**, and then click **Internet Services Manager**.

2. Expand the node for the SharePoint Portal Server computer.

3. Right-click **Default Web Site**, and then click **Properties**.

4. On the **Web Site** tab, click **Advanced**. The **Advanced Multiple Web Site Configuration** dialog box appears.

5. In **Multiple SSL identities for this Web Site**, click the IP address for SSL port 443, and then click **Remove**.

6. To close the **Advanced Multiple Web Site Configuration** dialog box, click **OK**.

7. To close the **Properties** page, click **OK**.

To require SSL:

You must choose to require SSL before you can access SharePoint Portal Server by using https://.

1. Right-click **YourVirtualWeb**, and then click **Properties**.

2. On the **Directory Security** tab, under **Secure communications**, click **Edit**.

3. Select the **Require secure channel (SSL)** check box, and then click **OK**.

4. To close the **Properties** page, click **OK**.

   Important After completing these procedures, restart the server.

You should now test access to the extranet from your intranet by using https:// instead of http://.

Internal FQDN Mapping

If you want to use SharePoint Portal Server on your intranet with an internal FQDN, you must map the internal FQDN of the server to an IP address. If you do not want to enable internal FQDN support, you can skip this section.

To map the SharePoint Portal Server computer name to an IP address:

1. On the **Start** menu, point to **Programs**, point to **Administrative Tools**, and then click **Internet Services Manager**.

2. Expand the node for the SharePoint Portal Server computer.

3. Right-click **Default Web Site**, and then click **Properties**.

4. On the **Web Site** tab, click **Advanced**. The **Advanced Multiple Web Site Configuration** dialog box appears.

   Important Do *not* remove (**All Unassigned**) from port **80** under **Multiple identities for this Web Site**.

5. Map the internal FQDN for the server to an IP address:

   • Click **Add**. The **Advanced Web Site Identification** dialog box appears.

   • Select your IP address from **IP Address**. Do *not* select (**All Unassigned**).

   • Type **80** in **TCP Port**.

   • Type the internal FQDN for the server in **Host Header Name**, and then click **OK**. The internal FQDN is of the form *NetBIOS_name.internal_domain_name*. For example, if the NetBIOS name for your SharePoint Portal Server is AdvWks, and the internal domain name is corp.adventure-works.com, you would type AdvWks.corp.adventure-works.com as the host header name.

6. To close the **Advanced Multiple Web Site Configuration** dialog box, click **OK**, and then to close the **Properties** page, click **OK**.

If your network does not natively support FQDN, you are running WINS, or users experience errors navigating to the dashboard site by using FQDN, each user and the server administrator must perform an additional step.

- Users must configure proxy server settings for the browser to bypass the proxy server for local addresses on each client computer accessing the dashboard site.

- The server administrator must configure the proxy settings for Internet Explorer on the SharePoint Portal Server computer to include the domain of the local computer on the bypass list.

Each user and the server administrator can configure the proxy server settings by using the following procedure. This procedure applies when your browser is Internet Explorer 5. To do this on other browsers, consult the browser documentation.

To configure Internet Explorer 5 to bypass the proxy server for local addresses:

1. Close all current Internet Explorer 5 windows and Microsoft Windows Explorer windows.

2. On the SharePoint Portal Server computer, **Start** menu, point to **Settings**, and then click **Control Panel**.

3. Double-click **Internet Options**. The **Internet Properties** dialog box appears.

4. On the **Connections** tab, click **LAN Settings**.

5. Select the **Use a proxy server** and **Bypass proxy server for local addresses** check boxes.

6. Specify the address and port number of the proxy server, and then click **Advanced**.

7. In **Do not use proxy server for addresses beginning with**, type *domain* where *domain* is the domain of your SharePoint Portal Server. For example, if the domain is adventure-works.com, type *adventure-works.com

8. Click **OK**, and then to close the remaining dialog boxes, click **OK** again.

Settings for Crawling Web Sites on the Internet

If you want SharePoint Portal Server to crawl Web sites on the Internet, it is recommended that you modify the time-out settings both for connecting to a Web site or server and for waiting for request acknowledgment. Specify 60 seconds for the wait time for connecting to a Web site or server, and specify 30 seconds for the wait time for request acknowledgment from a Web site or server. You can modify these settings from SharePoint Portal Server Administration.

If you have a proxy server that requires authentication to access the Internet from your intranet, SharePoint Portal Server cannot crawl sites on the Internet.

To modify the time-out settings:

1. On the **Start** menu, point to **Programs**, point to **Administrative Tools**, and then click **SharePoint Portal Server Administration**.

2. In the console tree, select SharePoint Portal Server computer.

3. On the **Action** menu, click **Properties**. You can also right-click the server name, and then click **Properties** on the shortcut menu.

4. Click the **Load** tab.

5. In **Number of seconds to wait for a connection**, type **60**.

6. In **Number of seconds to wait for request acknowledgment**, type **30**.

7. Click **Apply**.

Depending on the connection speed and other factors, such as Internet loss, Internet latency, and Internet jitter, you may need to increase the previous settings.

Settings for Crawling Another SharePoint Portal Server Site on the Internet

There may be instances when you want to expose your server, by using HTTP, to the Internet to allow other sites to crawl your server. The instructions in this section enable a SharePoint Portal Server computer with access to the Internet to crawl another SharePoint Portal Server computer across the Internet. Currently, SharePoint Portal Server only supports HTTP crawling. HTTPS crawling is not supported.

SharePoint Portal Server cannot use the default content access account to access another SharePoint Portal Server over the Internet. You can only specify an NTLM trusted domain account as the default content access account, and you cannot use NTLM for Internet crawls. You must specify an access account for the site path to the SharePoint Portal Server you want to crawl.

>**Important** If the workspace you want to crawl has enabled Anonymous access (the Internet Guest Account is assigned to the reader role on the workspace), you do not need to use Basic authentication and do not need to perform the following procedure. You need only create a content source to the workspace on the other server. For information about assigning the Internet Guest Account to the reader role on a workspace, see the section, "Security Settings" earlier in this chapter.

To configure the server to crawl another SharePoint Portal Server computer across the Internet:

1. Navigate to the **Content Sources** folder located in the **Management** folder in the workspace.

2. Double-click **Additional Settings**.

3. On the **Rules** tab, click **Site Paths**.

4. Click **New**. The **Create New Site Path Rule** dialog box appears.

5. In **Path**, type the URL to the SharePoint Portal Server to be crawled. The URL must be the external FQDN of the server.

6. Click **Include this path**, and then click **Options**. The **Options** dialog box appears.

7. Click **Account**. The **Account Information** dialog box appears.

8. Under **Account**, specify the account information for the account that is valid for Basic authentication.

9. Under **Authentication type**, click **Basic authentication (password is sent in clear text)**.

10. To close the **Account Information** dialog box, click **OK**, and then to close the **Options** dialog box, click **OK**.

11. To close the **Create New Site Path Rule** dialog box, click **OK,** and then, to close the **Site Paths** dialog box, click **OK**.

12. If prompted to start a full update, click **Yes**.

13. Click **OK**.

After completing the preceding steps, create a content source to the workspace on the SharePoint Portal Server computer that you want to crawl.

Troubleshooting

This section describes specific error messages or issues you may encounter when deploying SharePoint Portal Server across an extranet. It also provides suggestions for how to address each issue.

Features Do Not Function

For a table showing features of SharePoint Portal Server that are available when you deploy the server across an extranet, see the section "Extranet Features" earlier in this chapter.

Server Access Denied

If you cannot access the server, ensure that you have specified security on the new Web site. Until you specify either Anonymous access or Basic authentication, you cannot access the server from the extranet.

Error 401

If you have specified Anonymous access on the new Web site, you may receive error 401 (Unauthorized) when attempting to access the dashboard site. If this happens, ensure that the Internet Guest Access account is a reader on the hidden Portal folder in the workspace. For the procedure to add the Internet Guest Account as a reader on the workspace, see the section "Security Settings" earlier in this chapter.

> **Note** If the Portal folder in the workspace does not inherit the security settings of the parent folder, you must add the Internet Guess Access account as a reader on the Portal folder.

Error 424

If you receive error 424 when attempting to access the dashboard site, try the following:

- Restart IIS Admin Service or restart the SharePoint Portal Server computer. Possible cause: you did not restart the server after configuring the proxy settings.

- Ensure that you are typing http://*external_FQDN*/*workspace_name* (or https:// if you enabled SSL). Possible cause: from the server, you are typing http://localhost/*workspace_name* for the URL. By default, SharePoint Portal Server does not support localhost out of the box.

You may receive error 424 when trying to navigate to the dashboard site by using HTTPS, but you might not receive the error when using HTTP. In this case, on the new Web site, ensure that you specify IIS Application Protection as low for the virtual directory for the workspace.

To specify IIS Application Protection:

1. On the **Start** menu, point to **Programs**, point to **Administrative Tools**, and then click **Internet Services Manager**.

2. Expand the node for the SharePoint Portal Server computer.

3. Expand **YourVirtualWeb**, where **YourVirtualWeb** is the name of the new Web site you created.

4. Right-click **YourWorkspace** under **YourVirtualWeb**, where **YourWorkspace** represents the name of the virtual directory for your workspace, and then click **Properties**.

5. Click the **Virtual Directory** tab.

6. In **Application Protection**, select **Low (IIS Process)**.

7. Click **OK**.

Error 500

If you receive error 500 (internal server error) on the dashboard site, ensure that you have not selected the **Check that file exists** check box when configuring the Public and YourWorkspace virtual directories on the new Web site. If the **Check that file exists** check box is selected, clear the check box, and then restart IIS Admin Service.

To restart the IIS Admin Service:

1. On the **Start** menu, point to **Programs**, point to **Administrative Tools**, and then click **Internet Services Manager**.

2. Expand the node for the SharePoint Portal Serve computer.

3. Expand the node for the new Web site that you created.

4. For the **Public** and **YourWorkspace** virtual directories on the new Web site that you created:

   - Right-click the virtual directory, and then click **Properties**.

   - On the **Virtual Directory** tab, click **Configuration**.

   - On the **App Mappings** tab, select the entry for the * extension displaying the path to msdmisap.dll, and then click **Edit**.

   - Clear the **Check that file exists** check box.

   - Click **OK**, and then to close **Application Configuration,** click **OK** again.

   - To close the **Properties** page, click **OK**.

5. Restart IIS Admin Service.

Error 503

If you attempt to access the dashboard site and you receive error 503 (Service Unavailable), the server is restarting and the services have not yet started. Wait several minutes and try accessing the dashboard site again.

Error 519

If you receive error 519 when attempting to discuss a document, ensure that you have enabled discussions on the new Web site. To use Web discussions on your SharePoint Portal Server computer from the extranet, you must modify the registry. For the procedure to modify the registry, see the section "Web Discussions" earlier in this chapter. For detailed information about using Web discussions with SharePoint Portal Server, see Chapter 10, "Planning Web Discussions."

Unable to Map Web Folder to Workspace

If you are unable to map a Web folder to the workspace, ensure that you have not selected the **Check that file exists** check box when configuring the Public and YourWorkspace virtual directories on the new Web site. If the **Check that file exists** check box is selected, clear the check box and restart IIS Admin Service.

To restart the IIS Admin Service:

1. On the **Start** menu, point to **Programs**, point to **Administrative Tools**, and then click **Internet Services Manager**.

2. Expand the node for the SharePoint Portal Serve computer.

3. Expand the node for the new Web site that you created.

4. For the **Public** and **YourWorkspace** virtual directories on the new Web site that you created:

   - Right-click the virtual directory, and then click **Properties**.

   - On the **Virtual Directory** tab, click **Configuration**.

   - On the **App Mappings** tab, select the entry for the * extension displaying the path to msdmisap.dll, and then click **Edit**.

   - Clear the **Check that file exists** check box.

   - Click **OK**, and then to close **Application Configuration,** click **OK** again.

   - To close the **Properties** page, click **OK**.

5. Restart IIS Admin Service.

Discussion Error

If you see a server execution or server unavailable error inside a discussion panel, ensure that the execute permissions are set to Scripts and Executables on the virtual directory for MSOffice on the new Web site.

To set permissions on the virtual directory:

1. On the **Start** menu, point to **Programs**, point to **Administrative Tools**, and then click **Internet Services Manager**.

2. Expand the node for the SharePoint Portal Server computer.

3. Expand the node for **YourVirtualWeb**, where **YourVirtualWeb** is the name of the new Web site you created.

4. Right-click the **MSOffice** virtual directory, and then click **Properties**.

5. Click the **Virtual Directory** tab.

6. In **Execute Permissions**, select **Scripts and Executables**.

7. To close the **Properties** page, click **OK**.

Script Execution Error

If you receive a script execution error, the custom header name (MicrosoftTahoeServer) for the new Web site is either not specified or specified incorrectly. For information about specifying the custom header name, see the section "Web Site Creation" earlier in this chapter.

No Access Externally

If you cannot access the SharePoint Portal Server computer from the extranet, try the following:

- Shut down the SharePoint Portal Server computer.

- Attempt to access the server from the Internet. The proxy server should return a message that the host is not available. This validates that access from the Internet to the proxy server is operating correctly.

If this test succeeds, the problem is possibly in the proxy server configuration for server publishing. For more information about server publishing, see the section "Proxy Server Settings" earlier in this chapter.

Host Not Found

If you receive error 11004 (host not found), ensure that your DNS server has an entry for the host you are trying to access.

If the entry exists, check the spelling of the URL that you are typing in the browser.

Page Cannot Be Displayed

If SSL is enabled and you receive this error, run adsutil.vbs. For more information, see the section "Secure Sockets Layer" earlier in this chapter.

Dashboard Site Settings Cannot Be Saved

If you cannot save settings on the dashboard site, you may not have write permissions on the workspace.

To specify write permissions:

1. On the **Start** menu, point to **Programs**, point to **Administrative Tools**, and then click **Internet Services Manager**.

2. Expand the node for the SharePoint Portal Server computer.

3. Expand the node for the new Web site you created.

4. For the **YourWorkspace** virtual directory on the Web site that you created, where **YourWorkspace** represents the name of the virtual directory for your workspace, do the following:

   - Right-click the virtual directory, and then click **Properties**.

   - On the **Virtual Directory** tab, select the **Write** check box.

   - Click **Apply**.

   - To close the **Properties** page, click **OK**.

Blank Page Displays

If a blank page displays when attempting to access the dashboard site from the extranet:

- The proxy server may be offline.

- You may need to map the internal static IP address and the external static IP address on the proxy server. For more information, see the section "Proxy Server Settings" earlier in this chapter.

Crawling a Web Site Fails

If you cannot crawl a Web site on the Internet, you may need to reconfigure the time-out settings or the proxy settings. For more information, see the sections, "Settings for Crawling Web Sites on the Internet" and "Proxy Server Settings" earlier in this chapter.

Subscriptions Do Not Function Properly

You cannot subscribe to folders by using the collaboration toolbar from Microsoft Office or Internet Explorer in the extranet scenario. You must subscribe to the folder from the dashboard site.

Server URL in E-Mail Notifications Is Incorrect

You can modify the URL that SharePoint Portal Server uses in e-mail notifications by following the procedure shown in the section "E-mail Notifications" earlier in this chapter.

If SharePoint Portal Server does not display the modified URL as expected, ensure that you have:

- Typed the property name correctly. The property name is case-sensitive. Type the property name exactly as specified in the procedure shown in the section "E-mail Notifications."

- Restarted MSSearch.

Access Problems When Using HTTPS – Client Certificate Issues

If you have enabled SSL and are accessing the dashboard site of SharePoint Portal Server by using https://*external_FQDN*/*workspace_name*, you might experience sporadic functionality failure such as navigation failures or access violations. This indicates a possible problem with the security certificate—specifically, you may need to install the full certificate chain.

You may need to install the full certificate chain on the client computers if either of the following applies:

- You are using an internal certificate server to generate your own certificates.

- You are using a certificate that is not distributed with a Microsoft operating system.

To confirm that the security certificate is the problem:

1. When attempting to access the dashboard site, you receive a **Security Alert** dialog box stating that the security certificate was issued by a company you have not chosen to trust.

2. Click **View Certificate** on this box, and then click the **Certification Path** tab.

3. In **Certification path**, there is a red circle with an X in it next to one or more nodes.

4. When you click the node identified in step 3, the **Certificate status** displays the message that the certificate cannot be verified up to a trusted certification authority.

To fix this problem, install the full certificate chain on all client computers.

If you suspect that the certificate chain might be the cause of the problem, you can view the certificates on client computers.

To view the certifications on client computers:

1. On the client computer, click the **Start** menu, and then click **Run**.

2. Type **mmc** and then click **OK**.

3. On the **Console** menu, click **Add/Remove Snap-in**.

4. Click **Add**.

5. Select **Certificates** from the list, and then click **Add**.

6. Select **Computer account**, and then click **Next**.

7. Select **Local computer**, and then click **Finish**.

8. Click **Close**, and then click **OK**.

Access Problems When Using HTTPS – Server Certificate Issue

The common name specified for the SSL certificate *must* match the external FQDN of your server. For more information, see the section "Secure Sockets Layer" earlier in this chapter. For example, if the external FQDN is AdventureWorks.adventure-works.com (accessed by typing https://AdventureWorks.adventure-works.com), the SSL certificate must have a common name of AdventureWorks.adventure-works.com.

The dashboard site appears incorrectly and does not function if the common name does not match the external FQDN.

Note This also applies to internal SSL certificates.

IFrame Error When Using Netscape Navigator

If you designate that a Web Part run in its own process, separate from other processes, you receive an IFrame error when using Netscape Navigator.

To correct the IFrame error:

1. On the dashboard site, click **Content**.

2. Click the Web Part that runs in its own process. The **Settings** page for the Web Part opens.

3. Click **Show Advanced Settings**.

4. Clear the **Isolate this Web Part's content from the other Web Parts** check box.

5. To close the **Settings** page, click **Save**, and then to close the **Content** page, click **Save**.

Dashboard Site Appears Incomplete

When accessed, the dashboard site may appear complete when you use the HTTP protocol but incomplete when you use the HTTPS protocol. If you have previously accessed the site by using http://*external_FQDN*/*workspace_name* and then you enable SSL (so that you access the site using https://), the dashboard site may open with no style sheet applied (the background is white) and with broken links. To fix this problem, restart the server. You must restart the server after enabling SSL.

Dashboard Site Stops Functioning

Your dashboard site may stop functioning if you attempt to secure your server by running **Windows 2000 Internet Server Security Tool** (available for download from http://www.microsoft.com/TechNet/security/tools.asp). For the latest information about implementing IIS security configurations to secure your server, see http://www.microsoft.com/SharePoint/.

Extranet Features

The following table shows features of SharePoint Portal Server that are available when you deploy it across an extranet.

Extranet Features of SharePoint Portal Server

Area	Feature
Dashboard Site	
Site Search	Advanced
	Simple
Search	Best Bets
	Categories
	Categories Best Bets
	Click through to items on server
	Click through to items on Internet
Misc.	Approval Mail
	Discussions
	Notifications
	Subscriptions
Dashboard Site (Document Management)	
Enhanced Folders	Add document
	Add folder
	Approve document
	Check in document
	Check out document
	Delete document

Area	Feature
Dashboard Site (Document Management) *continued*	
Enhanced Folders *continued*	Delete folder
	Download document
	Publish document
	Rename document
	Rename folder
Standard Folders	Add document
	Add folder
	Delete document
	Delete folder
	Download document
	Rename document
	Rename folder
Web Folders	
All Web folders Items	Copy
	Move
	Rename
Document Management	Add document
	Add folder
	Approve document
	Check in document
	Check out document
	Delete document
	Delete folder
	Publish document
Categories	Add category
	Delete category
Folder Properties	General tab
	Profiles tab

continued

Extranet Features of SharePoint Portal Server *continued*

Area	Feature
Web Folders *continued*	
Document Properties	General tab
	Profile tab
	Search and Categories tab
	Versions tab
Management Folder	Document Profiles
	Getting Started Help
Misc.	Profile Form
	Help

Office XP	
Enhanced Folders	Check in document
	Check out document
	Open
	Publish by using publishing form
	Save
	Save as
Standard Folders	Check in document
	Check out document
	Open
	Publish by using publishing form
	Save
	Save as Web page
	Save as
Misc.	Create the subscription to folder from the dashboard site instead of from the collaboration toolbar

Area	Feature
Office 2000	
Enhanced Folders	Check in document
	Check out document
	Open
	Publish by using publishing form
	Save
	Save as
Standard Folders	Check in document
	Check out document
	Open
	Publish by using publishing form
	Save
	Save as Web page
	Save as
Misc.	Create the subscription to folder from the dashboard site instead of from the collaboration toolbar

Summary

This chapter provides the procedures to follow if you want to deploy SharePoint Portal Server across an extranet. Once you complete these procedures, you can access your SharePoint Portal Server in both an intranet and an extranet environment. For additional references and information to assist you in deploying SharePoint Portal Server in an extranet environment, see Appendix B, "For More Information."

CHAPTER 13

Searching in a Multilingual Environment

This chapter describes how Microsoft Search (MSSearch), the full-text search component of Microsoft® SharePoint™ Portal Server 2001, functions in a multilingual environment. In addition, it reviews the process that MSSearch applies when crawling, filtering, and querying the full-text index for content. It also provides an explanation of other factors to consider when crawling, filtering, and conducting search queries in a multilingual environment.

A *locale* is defined as the language environment defined for a SharePoint Portal Server computer. A *multilingual environment* is defined as an environment that contains documents in multiple locales. This can include one or more servers with different locales and may also include different client locales. The servers and the clients may be in different locales.

MSSearch Overview

MSSearch provides a series of components that work together to provide full-text access to collections of data. For an detailed overview of MSSearch architecture and technologies, see Chapter 5, "Microsoft Full-Text Search Technologies."

The process for providing full-text access to content follows:

- For a content source, the *Gatherer* instantiates a *Filter Daemon* that contains protocol handlers and filters.

- The *Protocol Handlers* open the content source in its native format, thus making it readable by MSSearch. MSSearch then retrieves the content and makes it accessible to the Filter.

- The *Filter* takes a unit of information such as a document and emits a stream of Unicode characters, which represent both the properties of and the content contained in the document. The Filter returns this stream of characters to MSSearch, where the word breakers then manipulate it.

- *Word breakers* apply language-specific linguistic rules to separate the Unicode stream emitted by the filters into individual words. These words are stored in the index.

- After SharePoint Portal Server creates the index, users can retrieve information by issuing queries through the Search Engine.

SharePoint Portal Server applies word breakers to query terms to break them into individual words. The search engine then expands the query to include the expanded list of terms. It is important that MSSearch uses the same word breaker at both index and query time so that it applies the same linguistic rules and the query returns the most relevant results.

Stemming also occurs at query time. Stemming is a method of mapping a linguistic stem to all matching words to increase the number of relevant results. For example, in English, the stem "buy" matches "bought," "buying," and "buys."

SharePoint Portal Server provides noise word files and thesaurus files that can be customized to account for specific language differences within your organization. A *noise word* is a word such as "the" or "an" that is not useful for searches. A noise word is statistically unimportant for full-text search queries. A list of noise words for a particular language is stored in the noise word file for that language. SharePoint Portal Server provides noise word and thesaurus files for the following languages: Chinese-Simplified, Chinese-Traditional, Dutch, English-International, English-US, French, German, Italian, Japanese, Korean, Spanish, Swedish, and Thai. The thesaurus file is empty by default; you must populate it with selected words and concepts that are relevant to your deployment.

For more information about how to customize MSSearch, see Appendix B, "For More Information."

Overview of Index Creation

When MSSearch crawls a document and includes it in an index, it goes through the following series of steps to apply the proper language resources to that document:

- In filtering the document, MSSearch checks for a valid Language Code Identifier (LCID), a property that contains a standard international abbreviation that uniquely identifies the document locale. MSSearch uses the LCID to identify the appropriate word breaker for that document. Some applications, such as Microsoft Word, emit the language property at the word level. In this case, MSSearch changes the word breaker to ensure that it uses the proper language to read and recognize the word. It only changes to another word breaker when it receives a new language property. If the LCID specifies an unsupported language, MSSearch attempts to find a primary language as an alternate. If the primary language is supported, MSSearch uses that language. For example, if the document uses the English_Australian language, MSSearch uses English_US for the word breaker.

- If the filtered document does not have a language identifier, and the IFilter does not specify the default language for the server, MSSearch uses the neutral word breaker.

- If the filtered document does not have a language identifier, the IFilter may suggest that MSSearch use the default locale specified for the operating system. If that language does not have a supported word breaker, MSSearch uses the neutral word breaker.

- In all instances, MSSearch breaks the following properties using the neutral word breaker.

Properties That Always Use the Neutral Word Breaker

- Filename

- ContentClass

- Shortfilename

- Reverse Filename

- Path

A single installation of MSSearch can crawl documents containing content in multiple languages. The resultant index is language independent and contains words in any language without differentiation.

However, to ensure that SharePoint Portal Server crawls content in multiple languages efficiently and successfully, you must consider the following topics:

- **OS/Locale setup.** When you install Microsoft Windows® 2000, you specify a particular language and locale. The language and locale affect many settings. These settings include numeric format, date format, currency format, uppercase and lowercase mapping, dictionary sort ordering, and others. Although this helps provide excellent localized support for Windows, unintended results can occur within MSSearch.

- **Word breakers.** The first unintended result centers around word breakers for MSSearch. The default language determines the default word breaker. SharePoint Portal Server uses this default word breaker when it builds an index and when it processes search queries. For example, if a server has a default language of Simplified Chinese and SharePoint Portal Server crawls a document that contains no LCID property, MSSearch applies the Simplified Chinese word breaker if the IFilter indicates this default should be used. If this document is actually English, you can imagine that the words extracted from the document and put in the index would be suspect.

- **Noise words.** The second unintended result occurs at the index level. SharePoint Portal Server defines a list of noise words for each language and index. These lists are language specific. Using the wrong language resources, such as word breakers or noise files, can result in strange results. For example, in German, the word "die" is equivalent to the English word "the." However, in English, the word "die" means something entirely different. If MSSearch crawls an English document, and applies the German noise word file, all instances of "die" are ignored and not placed in the index. Thus, a query for "die" does not return this document.

These actions extend to all content included in the index. Although MSSearch can include content stored across multiple servers in the index, it does not include the default language from the server it is crawling. Instead, if the document does not carry LCID properties, MSSearch uses the language setting of the server on which MSSearch is installed. If your deployment includes a server dedicated to the purpose of creating and maintaining indexes, this behavior can dramatically affect the content that MSSearch returns during a search query.

The language specified on the server hosting the index workspace determines how MSSearch includes content in the index. In addition, SharePoint Portal Server installs noise word lists for all languages when it creates an index. You can modify these lists in order to add and remove terms, but any changes will only be in effect for subsequent crawls. For the changes take effect for all documents, you must reset the index and have MSSearch perform a full crawl.

Changes to the noise word list will not be reflected in the index until the index is rebuilt. For example, if you add the word, "Microsoft" to the noise word list, the search engine continues to return results containing "Microsoft" until SharePoint Portal Server performs a full update of the index. If you choose to remove a term from the noise word list, you must follow the same steps.

SharePoint Portal Server includes word breakers for the following languages: Japanese, Simplified Chinese, Traditional Chinese, Korean, Thai, English, Spanish, French, German, Italian, Swedish, and Dutch. If you install SharePoint Portal Server on a server with a language that is not from this list, then MSSearch uses the neutral word breaker. The neutral word breaker derives from the English word breaker. Therefore, the neutral word breaker works best when applied to documents written in western European languages.

Shared Service: MSSearch is a server-based, shared service. This means that any installations of SharePoint Portal Server and Microsoft SQL Server™ that are installed on the same computer use the same version of MSSearch to create indexes and to perform search queries. However, MSSearch creates individual indexes for each application. The service is shared but the data is independent. You can categorize MSSearch and its resources into shared resources and index-specific resources:

Shared Resources

- MSSearch Application
- Word breakers
- Stemmers
- Settings (resource management, failure settings, etc.)

Index-specific

- Index files
- Configuration files (Thesaurus, Noise Word List, etc.)
- Performance settings
- Filter associations

  Important It is important that you read the documentation included with each application that uses MSSearch before installing it on the same server as SharePoint Portal Server in order to ensure that when updating MSSearch, you ensure that each application uses the correct word breaker for creating indexes and search queries.

If you install other applications that use MSSearch, you must ensure that each application uses the same word breaker for creating indexes and for search queries. If you install a newer version of a word breaker, you must reset the index and have MSSearch conduct a full crawl of your content.

SharePoint Portal Server contains the most current version of MSSearch. When you install MSSearch, setup checks the version of the word breakers and always keeps the latest version. So, if you install SQL Server 2000 on a computer running SharePoint Portal Server, MSSearch retains the word breakers from SharePoint Portal Server.

Overview of Querying

Through search queries, MSSearch assists users to find relevant data across large collections of documents. SharePoint Portal Server provides a simple Search Web Part for search queries. You can also customize search for SharePoint Portal Server. This chapter reviews the basic query process included with SharePoint Portal Server. For more information about creating custom queries for SharePoint Portal Server, see Appendix B.

You can describe the basic search query process as follows:

- From the dashboard site, a user enters a search query into the Search text box.

- MSSearch applies word breakers and stemmers to the query.

- MSSearch submits the query to the search engine. The search engine uses a probabilistic algorithm to rank the returned results.

- MSSearch returns the ranked and sorted list to the user. The results list is limited to 2000 results.

Deploying SharePoint Portal Server in a multilingual environment primarily affects the first two steps.

Query Language

In MSSearch there are two basic query predicates:

- **CONTAINS.** Has features for matching words, matching inflectional forms of words, searches using wildcards, and proximity searches. This makes the CONTAINS predicate well suited for finding documents that contain phrases that are "exact" matches to the search terms, or that match them very closely. You can also use attribute weighting in a CONTAINS predicate. This specifies the importance of the columns where you find the search term.

- **FREETEXT.** Has features for finding documents containing combinations of the search terms spread throughout the column. FREETEXT uses the thesaurus and invokes a stemmer on the query text. The result is that the query is run for all permutations of the inflected forms for individual words and phrases in the query text. You can use the FREETEXT predicate to perform exact matches, like the CONTAINS predicate, by placing the query phrase in quotation marks.

For more information about query predicates, see Chapter 24, "Analyzing the Default Query for the Dashboard Site." From a multilingual perspective, you can specify the language of a document by adding the LCID as the last item inside the parenthesis in the query clause for either query predicate:

```
CONTAINS | FREETEXT

( [ <column_identifier> , ] '<content_search_condition>' [, LCID ] )
```

If the query clause does not contain the LCID, MSSearch interprets the language in the following priority:

- **Browser Language.** In a majority of the cases, the best option is to use the language of the browser. When querying from Internet Explorer, it is important that you activate the "Language Auto-Select" option. To activate this in Internet Explorer, on the **View** menu, point to **Encoding**, and then click **Auto-Select**. This causes Internet Explorer to pass the locale to MSSearch as part of the query.

- **Server Default Locale.** If the query language is not passed through LCID or through the browser, MSSearch attempts to use the default locale of the server where the query is performed. The same rules apply as when creating an index. The locale for the server must include an associated word breaker in order to correctly process the query.

- **Neutral Word breaker.** As a last resort, MSSearch uses the neutral word breaker to interpret the query. In a majority of cases, this is the least desirable situation. In general, it is better to use a known language.

In any situation, in order to get predictable results, you must ensure that MSSearch uses the same linguistic resources when creating an index and when users conduct search queries.

Query Interpretation and Transformation

After MSSearch determines the word breaker, the search engine passes the query through the language-specific word breaker to determine each individual term. After breaking the words, the search engine passes the resulting words through a stemmer to generate language-specific inflected forms of each term. The search engine then crawls the index to find matches for the resultant group of words. The use of a word breaker and a stemmer enhances the effectiveness of a search query by generating more relevant alternatives to a user's search query.

Note Stemming is not used in the case of an exact phrase match. In this case, MSSearch breaks the words into multiple terms and then crawls the index.

Other Factors

When deploying SharePoint Portal Server in a multilingual environment, consider the following factors:

Case Sensitivity. MSSearch queries are not case-sensitive. For example, "SELECT" is identical to "Select," "select," and "sELect."

Accent Sensitivity. As a general rule, SharePoint Portal Server is not sensitive to accents. For example, a search for the term "resume" also returns documents containing "résumé." Accents are honored in languages where they are critical, such as Japanese, Chinese, Hebrew, and Farsi.

Katakana Search Terms. SharePoint Portal Server treats full-width Katakana names and half-width Katakana names as the same. Do not create a document or folder with the same full-width Katakana and half-width Katakana names in the same location. By design, SharePoint Portal Server treats the following combinations as the same name:

- Katakana and Hiragana

- Full-width Katakana and half-width Katakana

- Full-width character and half-width character (numeric, alphabetic, sign)

Windows 2000 Locale. If using a non-English locale, SharePoint Portal Server Search returns results only when the administrator is logged in. You can work around this issue by using one of two methods:

- Change the locale of the server to English

- Make the following changes in the registry:

Values for HKEY_USERS\.DEFAULT\Control Panel\International\Locale

Default SharePoint Portal Server Value

00000409   0000041D

Values for HKEY_USERS\.DEFAULT\Control Panel\International\sDecimal

Default SharePoint Portal Server Value

"."   ","

> **Caution** Incorrectly editing the registry may severely damage your system. Back up the current version of the registry before making any changes. You should also back up any valued data on the computer.

Summary

This chapter describes MSSearch, the full-text search component of SharePoint Portal Server, functions in a multilingual environment. In addition, it reviews the process MSSearch applies when crawling, filtering, and querying the full-text index for content. It also provides an explanation of other factors to consider when crawling, filtering, and conducting search queries in a multilingual environment.

CHAPTER 14

Deploying SharePoint Portal Server across Multiple Sites Using RapPort

Rapid Portal (RapPort) allows you to use predefined templates to build intranet portals quickly and inexpensively that take advantage of the search, document management, and collaboration features of Microsoft® SharePoint™ Portal Server 2001. RapPort portals deploy quickly and are easy to maintain. Each portal consists of a SharePoint Portal Server workspace and related dashboard site. Portals can reside on a single dedicated server, or multiple portals can reside on shared data center servers within an organization.

This chapter presents a technical overview of the RapPort deployment. It reviews the process, called *portal provisioning*, required to create multiple intranet portals by using RapPort. In addition, this section provides planning information, installation procedures, administration tasks, and key procedures for using RapPort to deploy SharePoint Portal Server across multiple sites.

> **Note** In this chapter, the words *portal* and *site* are used interchangeably to refer to a Web portal, created using SharePoint Portal Server. A portal creating using SharePoint Portal Server includes a *workspace* and a *dashboard site*. For more information about SharePoint Portal Server, see Chapter 3, "Introducing SharePoint Portal Server."

For more information about the benefits of using RapPort in a corporate environment, see Chapter 28, "KMIT: Deploying SharePoint Portal Server across Multiple Sites." For more information about developing a customized RapPort solution, see Appendix B, "For More Information."

This chapter assumes that the reader is familiar with SharePoint Portal Server, has read the documentation relevant to SharePoint Portal Server, and, ideally, has experience editing Extensible Markup Language (XML) files. In addition, it assumes that the reader has experience modifying settings by using the Registry Editor and Internet Service Manager.

RapPort Architecture

RapPort uses three different servers to deploy SharePoint Portal Server to multiple sites. By using these servers, RapPort automates the process of creating and maintaining intranet portals within an organization. The following list describes the specific function of each of the servers:

- **RapPort Server.** This server is the core of the entire RapPort solution. It handles the request submissions and coordinates the entire portal provisioning process. This server houses a set of configuration files in XML to keep track of all workspace templates, destination servers, and application parameters. It also contains a set of Active Server Pages (ASP) pages used for the submission process and a number of scripts and dynamic-link libraries (DLLs) used to start the provisioning process. In general, you only need one RapPort server per deployment, although you may choose to create additional servers for separate geographical locations.

- **Template Server.** This server stores SharePoint Portal Server workspaces used as templates during the portal provisioning process. RapPort copies the workspace template and related files when creating a new workspace on a destination sever. This server requires SharePoint Portal Server; no RapPort Components are required. For more information about creating workspace templates, see "Creating Workspace Templates."

- **Destination Server.** This server hosts workspaces. You can use one or more destination servers to maintain multiple workspaces. This server contains ASP pages and DLLs used in the portal provisioning process. RapPort uses both of these components to create the workspace and the virtual server.

  You can further classify a destination server into one of two types: *shared* or *dedicated*. A shared server hosts many workspaces. You can control the creation of workspaces on the server by specifying capacity limitations in the configuration files. A dedicated server is used only for the creation of specific workspaces. The user must explicitly specify the name of the server when requesting a workspace. RapPort provides this option so that you can isolate large portals from other workspaces when deploying SharePoint Portal Server. You can locate destination servers anywhere in the organization from a corporate or regional data center to a departmental server in an individual office.

You can use a single server as the RapPort server and the template server. In this case, this server runs the portal provisioning process from the RapPort server and copies all workspace templates from the RapPort server. However, you must deploy at least one destination server. The destination server cannot serve as a RapPort server or a template server.

Figure 14.1 shows a RapPort deployment that uses multiple destination servers:

- Dedicated departmental server (http://Site-1)

- Dedicated data center destination server (http://Site-2)

- Shared destination server A (http://Site-3, http://Site-4)
- Shared destination server B (http://Site-5, http://Site-6, etc.)

  Note Figure 14.1 also shows these portals connected to another SharePoint Portal Server computer dedicated to providing enterprise searching. The workspace templates contain a Web Part on the search dashboard that provides results from the corporate search located on the enterprise search server. This optional deployment configuration illustrates how you can integrate individual sites deployed by using RapPort within an existing SharePoint Portal Server infrastructure.

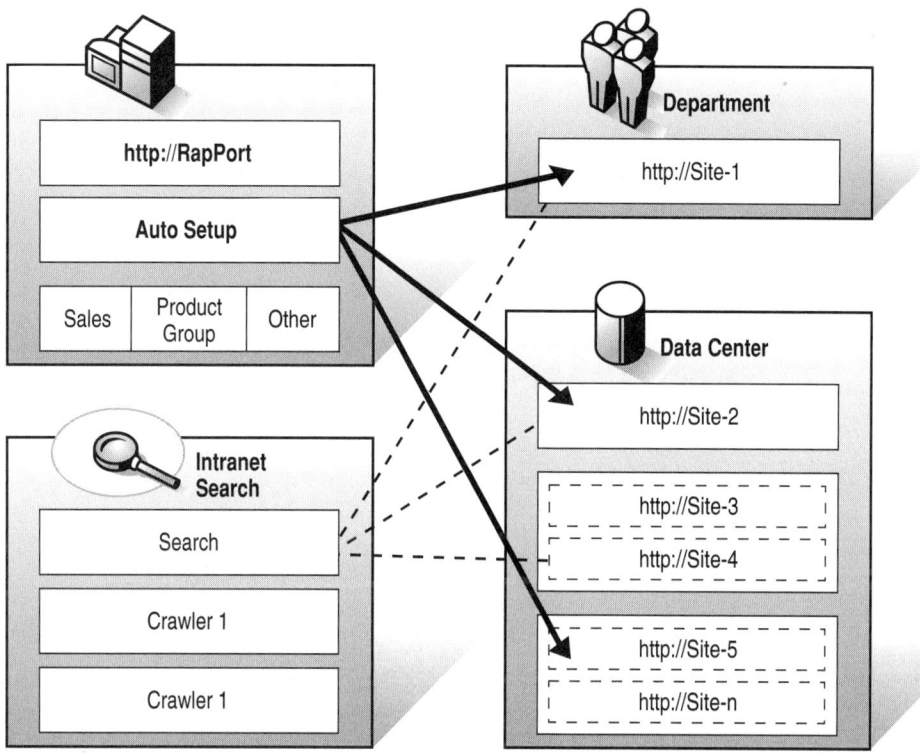

Figure 14.1. RapPort deployment with multiple destination servers

Hardware and Software Requirements

You must use a minimum of two servers to use RapPort to deploy a SharePoint Portal Server workspace. You can use a single server as the RapPort server and the template server. You also need at least one destination server. However, you can modify this architecture by creating multiple template servers, regional RapPort servers, and potentially dozens of destination servers.

The following table shows the recommended hardware capacity in relation to SharePoint Portal Server recommendations.

Capacity Recommendations

Server Type	Hardware Recommendation
The RapPort server. This server experiences moderate load.	• 800-megahertz (MHz) processor minimum recommended. • 512 megabytes (MB) minimum of RAM recommended. • 10 gigabytes (GB) minimum of available disk space. The drive must be formatted as NTFS file system. If combined with the template server: • 800 MHz dual processors minimum recommended. • 512 MB minimum of RAM recommended. • 20 GB minimum of available disk space. The drive must be formatted as NTFS file system.
The template server. This server experiences minimal user activity.	• 500 MHz processor minimum recommended. • 256 MB minimum of RAM recommended. • 10 gigabytes GB minimum of available disk space. The drive must be formatted as NTFS file system.
The destination server. This server experiences variable user activity depending on the number of workspaces.	To estimate destination server capacity, see Chapter 7, "Planning Server Capacity."

RapPort is an application designed to run on a computer running SharePoint Portal Server. Consequently, you must meet the requirements for SharePoint Portal Server in addition to those for RapPort. For more information about these requirements, see Chapter 11, "Installing SharePoint Portal Server." RapPort has three types of requirements—the system requirements for the RapPort servers; requirements for client computers; and requirements of the corporate infrastructure.

RapPort Software Requirements

All servers that participate in the RapPort deployment require the following configuration:

- Microsoft Windows® 2000 Server or Windows 2000 Advanced Server operating system, and Windows 2000 Service Pack 1 (SP1) or later

- Microsoft SharePoint Portal Server 2001

- Hot fixes as specified in Chapter 11, "Installing SharePoint Portal Server"
- Static IP address for the destination server(s)

Client Requirements for Using the RapPort Request Wizard

In order to run the RapPort Setup Wizard, the client computer will require the following configuration:

- Windows 2000 Professional Service Pack 1 (SP1) or later.
- Internet Explorer 5.5 or later. Microsoft Visual Basic® Scripting Edition (VBScript) support is required. This is included in the default installation of Internet Explorer 5.
- Microsoft Office XP.

or

- Microsoft Office 2000 SR-1 and MSXML3 SP1. You can download a copy of MSXML3 SP1 from http://msdn.microsoft.com/.

Infrastructure Dependencies

RapPort is dependent upon several infrastructure components in order to provision portals. These include:

- Name resolution services: Windows Internet Naming Service/Domain Name Server (WINS/DNS).
- Microsoft Active Directory™ directory service.
- Simple Mail Transfer Protocol (SMTP) Service. This is a Windows 2000 Server component.

For client and server environments that differ from the configuration described in this chapter, revisions to the RapPort source code will be necessary. For example, if you do not use Active Directory to manage user objects, you must modify the Request Wizard to accommodate this change. For detailed information about the application structure, see Appendix B.

> **Important** For a list of required service packs, or other required items not specified in this section, see the Readme file in the Tools\RapPort directory on the Microsoft SharePoint Portal Server Resource Kit CD.

Do not create any workspaces on the destination server during installation of SharePoint Portal Server.

Overview of Portal Provisioning Process

RapPort consists of a set of ASP pages, scripts, and ActiveX® DLLs distributed across two or more servers. Figure 14.2 illustrates the provisioning process. The process begins when a user requests a site. The process ends with notification to the user that the site is ready.

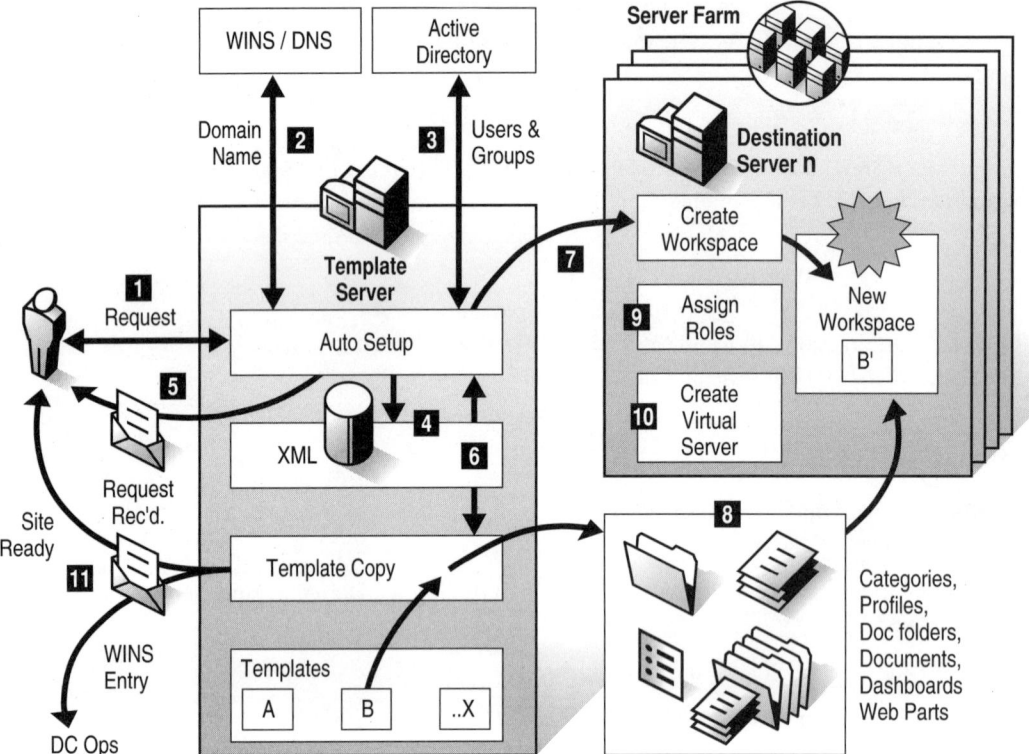

Figure 14.2. Logical Provisioning Process

You can divide the portal provisioning processes into four phases:

- Submitting a request for a site
- Creating a workspace
- Copying the workspace template
- Specifying security and creating a virtual server

The following sections describe each of these phases.

Submitting a Request for a Site

RapPort provides a page for users to submit requests for a site or intranet portal. This site includes a SharePoint Portal Server workspace and its associated dashboard site. This submission page serves as a data collection application that stores all the user input for use later in the provisioning process. Figure 14.3 illustrates the steps in request submission process.

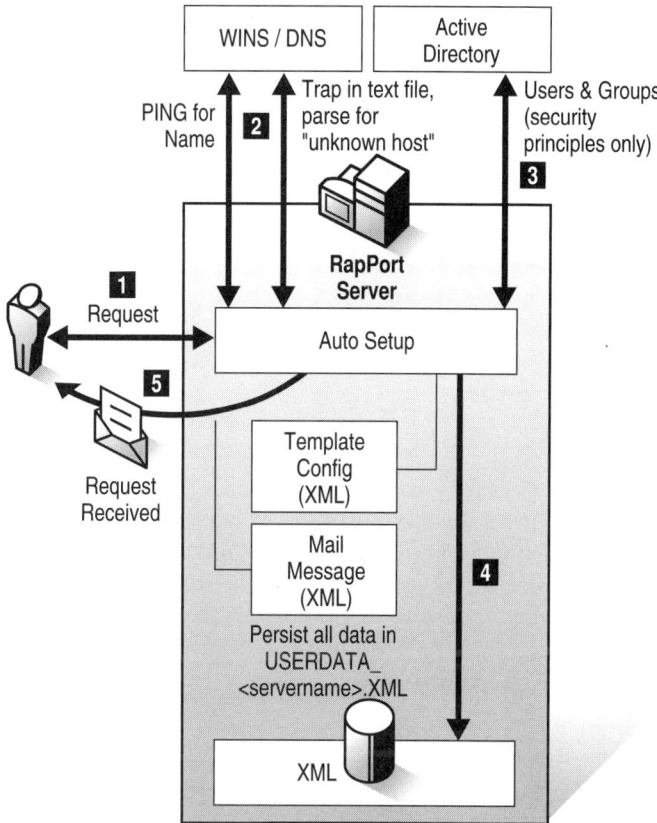

Figure 14.3. Request submission process

The following procedure describes how to request a site.

To submit a request for a site:

1. On the default RapPort home page, click **Request a Site**. The RapPort Setup Wizard opens.

2. Under **Site URL**, type the virtual server name of the portal you want to create.

3. Click **Check Availability**. RapPort checks the availability of the name.

> **Note** If the name is not available, RapPort displays the following message:
>
> "The Site URL requested is already registered. Please specify another URL."

4. Under **Description**, type a brief description of your portal.

5. Under **Domain**, click the domain or region where you want the portal located.

> **Note** You do not need a valid Windows NT domain to deploy RapPort.

6. Under **Template**, click the workspace template you want to apply.

7. Click **Next**.

8. After specifying a name for your portal, you must associate users or groups (security principals) with roles in the workspace. You must assign at least one person to the role of coordinator for each workspace. To do this, under **Permissions**, click **Add**. RapPort displays the **Select Users or Groups Web Page** dialog box.

9. Type the user name or e-mail address of the person you want to add, and then click **Find**.

10. RapPort displays the user name in the list below. Confirm that this is the correct user name. Select the name of the user, and then click **Add**.

11. Click **OK** to close this dialog box and return to the RapPort Setup Wizard.

> **Note** If you have arranged for a dedicated server for your workspace, under **Advanced Settings**, click **Dedicated Server**. This dedicated server must have the destination server components installed or the wizard reports an error. RapPort displays the **Advanced Settings Web Page** dialog box. Type the name of the server where you want to install the workspace. Click **Submit** to submit the server name and close the dialog box. If you have not arranged for a dedicated server for your workspace, RapPort creates your workspace on a shared server by default.

12. To complete the request process, click **Finish**.

RapPort displays a summary request, as shown in Figure 14.4. In addition, RapPort Admin sends an e-mail message confirming the portal request to the user. For more information about e-mail notifications in RapPort, see "Status Messages."

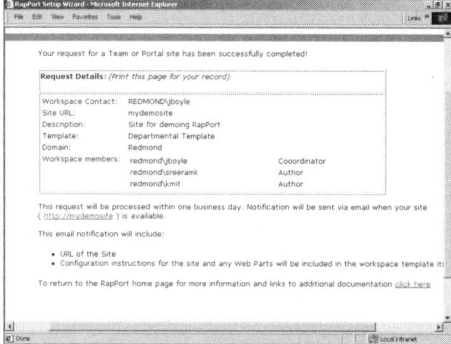

Figure 14.4. RapPort wizard request summary

Creating a Workspace

The workspace creation process creates a new workspace on a destination server. This process begins when RapPort starts AutoSetup on the RapPort server, and ends when it stops and restarts the services on the destination server. Figure 14.5 illustrates this process.

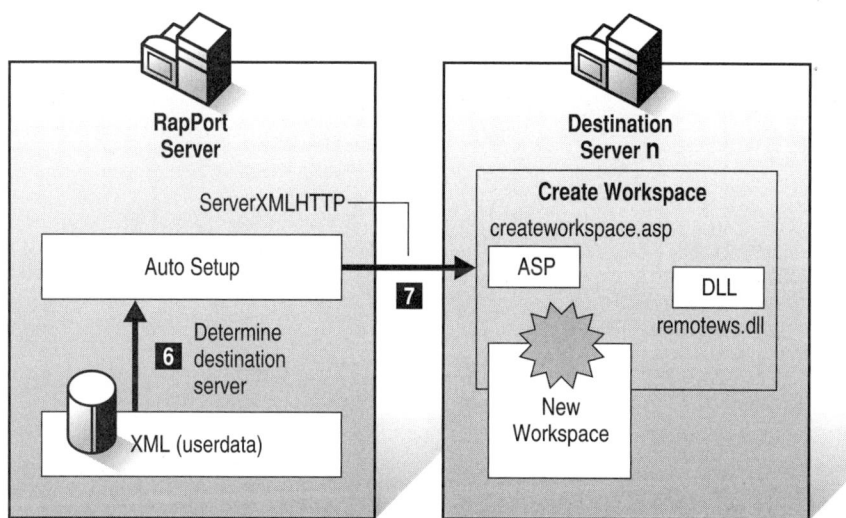

Figure 14.5. Workspace creation process

RapPort runs AutoSetup as a scheduled task on the RapPort server. For optimal performance, it is recommended that you avoid scheduling AutoSetup during peak usage. RapPort always gives the workspace the same name as the virtual server name to ensure a unique identity among all destination servers. In addition, this provides a friendly workspace name for users. AutoSetup determines the destination server to host this workspace by using the first available server based on the region (domain) selected and the current workspace count is less than the capacity defined. RapPort creates the new workspace on the destination server.

Copying the Template

After creating the workspace, RapPort preloads content from the template selected by the user into the new workspace. This process begins after RapPort creates the workspace and ends when RapPort copies all the template content into the new workspace. Figure 14.6 illustrates this process.

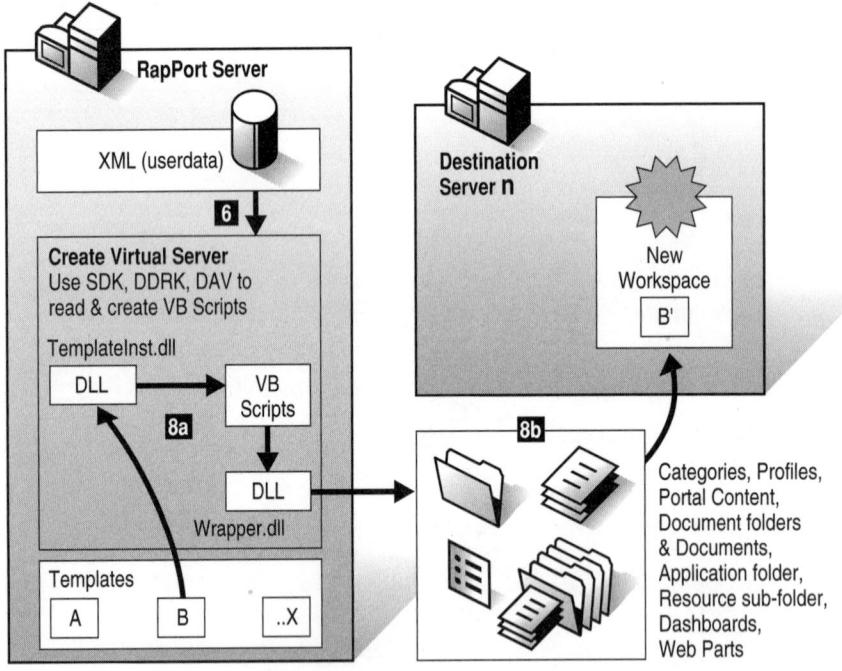

Figure 14.6. Template instantiation process

When applying the template, RapPort deletes any existing content from the new workspace. For example, a standard SharePoint Portal Server workspace contains categories defined as Category 1 through Category 5. RapPort deletes these categories.

Assigning Roles and Creating Virtual Servers

The final stage includes setting security, creating the virtual server, and notifying the appropriate users of the status of the portal request. This process begins after RapPort copies all template content to the new workspace and ends when RapPort sends the notification requesting a WINS/DNS entry for the new virtual server. Figure 14.7 illustrates this process.

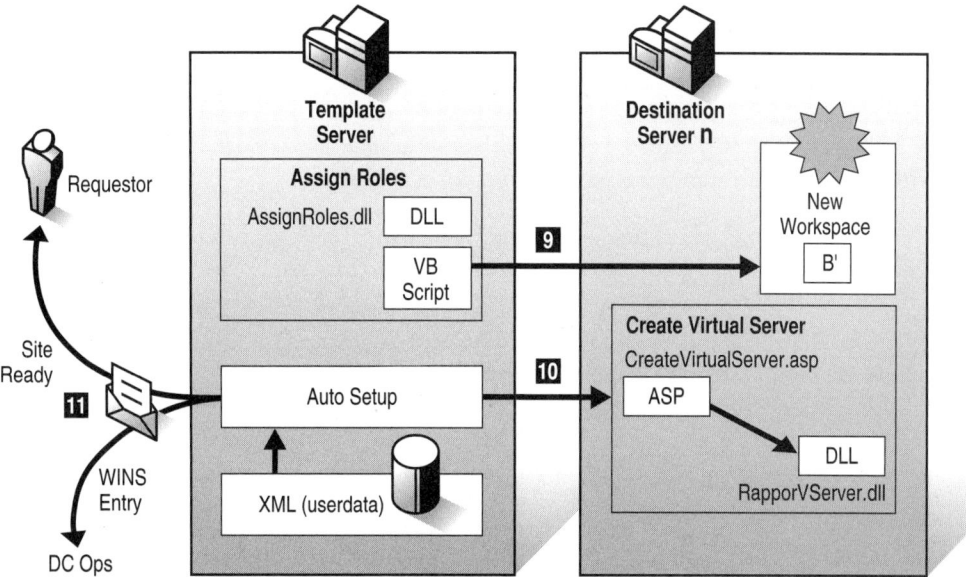

Figure 14.7. Roles, virtual server setup, and notifications

When submitting a request for a site, the person chooses roles to associate with users. The RapPort server uses this information to assign users to roles for the workspace on the destination server. It also creates a new virtual server on the destination server by using the site name as specified by the user who submitted the request. Lastly, it sends two notifications to the appropriate users. First, it sends a message to the address you specify during the RapPort installation for virtual server addressing. This message requests a WINS/DNS entry be created for the new virtual server. The message includes the name and IP address of the server on which it resides. After this person or group completes this entry, users can access the portal at http://*virtual_server_name* instead of http://*server_name/workspace_name*. The RapPort server also sends the user an e-mail notification that the workspace is ready. At this point, the user can begin to add content and customize the workspace as needed. Figure 14.8 shows a sample e-mail.

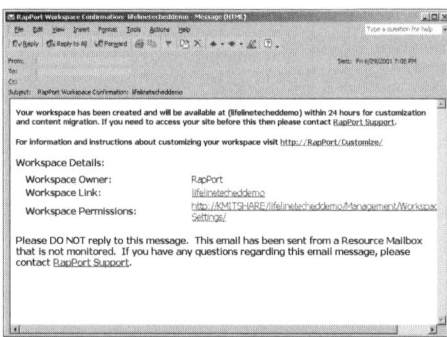

Figure 14.8. E-mail notification that the portal is ready

The RapPort server repeats the process for each request. After the RapPort server completes all requests for new portals, it remotely restarts Microsoft Internet Information Services (IIS) on each destination server that received new portals to clear any inconsistencies or cached data. After they are restarted, the destination servers and their workspaces are available to users. Typically, all of this occurs at night so workspaces are ready the following day by scheduling AutoSetup to run during night.

Deployment Plan

This section reviews all the steps necessary to deploy RapPort. There are four tasks you must perform to use RapPort to deploy SharePoint Portal Server:

- Review the installation requirements.
- Design the architecture.
- Prepare accounts.
- Customize configuration settings based on your architecture.

The following sections describe each of these planning tasks.

Reviewing the Installation Requirements

RapPort is an application designed to run on a computer running SharePoint Portal Server. Consequently, you must meet the requirements for SharePoint Portal Server in addition to those for RapPort.

- Review the hardware and software requirements, including coexistence issues, outlined earlier in this chapter.

Designing the Architecture

Although you can deploy RapPort by using a minimum of two servers, it is recommended that you use a single server for each function for optimal performance. You must have at least one server acting as the RapPort server and template server and at least one destination server.

RapPort Server

In general, you only need one RapPort server per deployment, although you may choose to create additional servers for separate geographical locations. Creating more than one RapPort server per deployment requires careful upfront planning. For more information about this planning, see Appendix B.

Template Server

You can design a template server by using one of three methods:

- You can use a single SharePoint Portal Server computer as the RapPort server and the template server. To do this, you must create the workspace templates on the RapPort server.

- You can use one or more separate SharePoint Portal Server computers to store workspace templates.

- You can use any of your existing SharePoint Portal Server computers as a template server. To do this, you must add an appropriate administrative account as detailed in the following template installation procedure.

Destination Servers

To determine how many destination servers you need, estimate the number of workspaces you predict there will be across your deployment and per region. With this information, determine the number of servers required based on the estimated number of workspaces and locations. For more information about determining server capacity, see Chapter 7, "Planning Server Capacity." This provides the number of destination servers you need.

RapPort supports the concept of regional servers. This allows destination servers to reside closer to the users in order to improve performance. Regional servers typically reside in a regional data center or a similar facility. By using the configuration files, you can present to users a list of these regional locations to select during the request process. RapPort can then create the workspace on a destination server at the appropriate regional location.

Preparing Accounts

During installation, you must provide the following information:

- **User name and password.** This domain account must be a member of the local Administrators group for all servers in this deployment. In addition, you must assign this account to the role of coordinator for each workspace on the template server.

    Note This enables the RapPort server to perform remote calls to the template and destination servers as needed.

- **Two e-mail accounts.** RapPort requires that you specify two e-mail accounts. You can specify these accounts in mails.xml. RapPort uses the first e-mail account to send notifications to users. RapPort uses the second e-mail account to receive status e-mail messages.

    Note For descriptive purposes, this chapter refers to the first e-mail account as *RapPort Admin* and to the second e-mail account as *RapPort Support*.

- **Name of an SMTP server.** RapPort requires an SMTP server to which it can send e-mail notifications.

- **A person or group e-mail account for WINS/DNS entry.** RapPort sends an e-mail message to a person or group requesting a WINS entry for a virtual server name when creating a new workspace. This message includes the name and IP address of the server where the workspace resides. You must determine the appropriate person or group to receive this message.

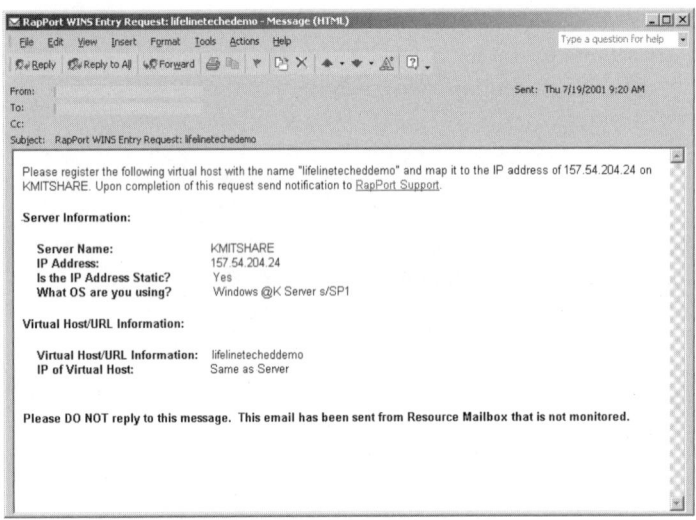

Figure 14.9. Sample WINS e-mail notification

Customizing Configuration Settings

RapPort uses a set of XML files to customize the application for a particular deployment. By default, RapPort stores all configuration files in the following location on the RapPort server:

Drive:\RapPort\AutoSetup\Configuration

Note XML supports the same conventions that the file system supports for naming folders and items. XML files support Unicode characters but should not contain special characters such as those listed here. # : \ ? * < > % / | " ~For a complete list refer to XML specifications available on MSDN.

The following describes each of these files and the required information you must include. For specific procedures to modify these files, see "RapPort Administration and Maintenance."

RapPort Configuration Settings

File Name	Description	Parameters
TemplateConfig.xml	Provides a list of all available templates.	Description Workspace URL
ServerConfig.xml	Provides a list of all servers available to RapPort upon which it can create workspaces.	Server Name Region Type (Shared or Dedicated) Maximum # of workspaces Current # of workspaces Status Comments
RegionCode.xml	List of all regions in which destination servers are available	Name Region Code
Mails.xml	Storage location for all automated RapPort mail messages	Mail ID To, From, CC Subject Body
Constants.xml	Stores RapPort system settings	Timeout Values Paths to components

When editing the XML files, do not delete or change any of the node tags. Change only the text between the > and </ signs for the nodes. Do not add any XML-sensitive special characters (such as &, <, > etc.) while editing the contents in the XML files. Always confirm that the XML file is valid by opening the edited XML file in Microsoft Internet Explorer and confirming that the file opens without errors.

You can customize RapPort for your own deployment. The application, RapPort, maintains all configuration information for the RapPort and destination servers in XML files. You can edit the files to modify these settings. For example, you can add a new destination server by editing ServerConfig.xml, or adjust time-out settings by editing Constants.xml. This section provides procedures for editing these configuration files.

Caution Incorrectly editing the registry may severely damage your system. Back up the current version of the registry before making any changes. You should also back up any valued data on the computer.

To specify e-mail settings:

You must specify the e-mail settings for your RapPort deployment.

- **SMTP Server Configuration.** You can modify the Smart Host name for relaying and delivering e-mail messages from the default SMTP virtual server. For more information, see "RapPort Installations."

- **Mails.xml Configuration.** Located in the RapPort\AutoSetup folder on the RapPort server. This file contains settings for five automated e-mail messages sent by using the RapPortAdmin account. It also includes the SMTP server name. You can identify the beginning of each message by locating the <mail> tag. The "id" attribute of the MAIL element identifies each message by number. The <description> tag identifies the purpose of the message.

  Note You can only modify existing e-mail messages. You cannot add additional boilerplate messages.

To change SMTP mail server name, edit the XML node <smtpservername> and replace it with the appropriate SMTP server name.

You can modify the following parameters for each message in context with the description.

Important Some tags include macros beginning with two underscores, for example, <name>__REQUEST_URL_USER_MAIL__</name>. Do not modify these macros.

- **Name.** The following tags include <name> tags. You can modify the <name> tags as required:

  - <from>

  - <to>

  - <cc>

You can also add additional <name> tags in case you need to notify additional people. Alternatively, you can include names, separated with semicolons, in the same <name> tag.

- **Subject.** You can modify the <subject> tags also.

- **Message Body.** You can modify the <mailbody> tag. This tag includes the body text of the HTML e-mail message.

- **Account.** You must specify the account to which WINS entry requests are sent. To do this, specify the appropriate user or group name in the <to><name> tag.

To change the domain name for notifications, you must edit Constants.xml.

To change the domain name for notifications:

1. In Notepad, open Constants.xml.

2. Modify the domain name in the following node as appropriate:

   <Constant constID="*constMailDomainName*">@adventure-works.com</Constant>

3. Save the file.

4. Edit CreateWorkspace.asp on each destination server.

5. Search for the string "@adventure-works.com" and change the domain name as appropriate.

6. Save the file.

7. Edit FinishPage.asp on the RapPort server.

8. Search for the string "@adventure-works.com".

9. Change the domain name as appropriate.

10. Save the file.

To modify settings in ServerConfig.xml:

- ServerConfig.xml file is located in the **RapPort\AutoSetup\Configuration** folder. The following is a sample configuration:

```
- <root>

- <entry>

 <servertype>shared</servertype>

 <region>R</region>

 <servername>destination_server_name</servername>

 <capacity>10</capacity>

 <current>0</current>

 <available>y</available>

 <comment />

 </entry>

 </root>
```

- **Server Name.** You can modify the names of destination servers from this file. If you add a new server, then copy the entire <entry> node for one server and paste it under <root> node to indicate that server. There is no need to make an entry for the dedicated server. AutoSetup makes an entry on its own to this file if it does not find the dedicated server entry in this file.

- **Workspace Capacity.** The <capacity> tag indicates the maximum number of workspaces that this server can host. Change this value to the appropriate value.

  Note You must enter a numeric value in this field. Do not leave it blank.

- **Server Status.** You modify the availability status of a destination server by using the <available> tag. To change the status, specify Y or N. When you specify Y for the value, AutoSetup uses this destination server when creating workspaces. If the RapPort server marks a destination server as unavailable, then no additional workspaces can be created on it until the status changes to "available." For more information, see "To reset the status of a destination server."

- **Server Type.** By default, the <servertype> tag is set to Shared only.

- **Region.** The <region> tag indicates the region value of the server. You can view the region value in RegionCode.xml.

To modify TemplateConfig.xml:

You can locate TemplateConfig.xml in the **RapPort\RapPortWeb\Configuration** folder. The following is a sample configuration:

```
<template>

<name>Your_Template</name>

<url>http://templateserver/templateworkspace</url>

</template>
```

You can edit this file to add, modify, or remove any workspace templates from your RapPort deployment.

Note Template names should be limited to 50 characters or less, for display purposes in the RapPort Request Wizard.

To modify an existing template:

1. Change the <name> tag to the appropriate value. This value displays in the list of templates in the RapPort Request Wizard.

2. Change the <url> tag to contain the path to the workspace.

3. Save the file.

To create an entry for a new template:

1. To add a new template, copy the entire <template></template> tag and paste it under the <root> tag.

2. Change the <name> tag to the appropriate value. This value displays in the list of templates in the RapPort Request Wizard.

3. Change the <url> tag to contain the path to the workspace.

4. Save the file.

To modify RegionCode.xml:

The RegionCode.xml file is located in the **RapPort\RapPortWeb\Configuration** folder. The following is a sample configuration:

```
<regions>

<region code="R">Redmond</region>

</regions>
```

1. To change the region name modify the text in the <region> tag.

2. To add a new region, insert a new <region> tag and set appropriate code value.

3. When you change the code value for any of the existing regions then you also must modify ServerConfig.xml for all corresponding destination servers.

To modify time-out settings:

RapPort specifies time-out settings for the SERVERXMLHTTP requests in Constants.xml under **RapPort\AutoSetup\Configuration** folder.

Note You should modify time-out settings prior to running AutoSetup.exe. All time-out settings are in milliseconds (ms).

- **ResolveTime.** This value applies to mapping hostnames (such as "www.adventure-works.com") to IP addresses. The default value is 300000 ms.

- **ConnectTime.** The value applies to establishing a communication socket with the target server. The default value is 60000 ms.

- **SendTime.** This value applies to sending an individual packet of request data (if any) on the communication socket to the target server. RapPort typically divides a large request into multiple packets before sending it to a server. The send time-out applies to sending each packet individually. The default value is 300000 ms.

- **ReceiveTime.** This value applies to receiving a packet of response data from the target server. RapPort typically divides large request into multiple packets before sending it to a server. The receive time-out applies to fetching each packet of data off the socket. The default value is 1800000 ms. The following are initial values specified in the constants file:

  - <Constant constID="ResolveTime">300000</Constant>

  - <Constant constID="ConnectTime">60000</Constant>

  - <Constant constID="SendTime">300000</Constant>

  - <Constant constID="ReceiveTime">1800000</Constant>

You can modify the session time-out setting for the RapPort virtual directory.

To modify session time-out:

1. On the **Start** menu, point to **Programs**, point to **Administrative Tools**, and then click **Internet Services Manager**.

2. Expand the server name.

3. Expand **Default Web Site**.

4. Right-click the RapPort virtual directory and then click **Properties**.

5. Click **Configuration**. The **Application Configuration** dialog box appears.

6. Click the **App Options** tab.

7. In **Session Timeout**, type a value.

8. Click **OK**.

9. Click **OK** to close the **Properties** page.

To modify ASP Script time-out:

Change the ASP script time-out settings for the RapPort virtual directory of each destination server. The default value is 600 seconds. You can increase this value if CreateWorkspace.asp is taking too long to execute.

To modify ASP script time-out for the Active Directory virtual directory:

1. On the RapPort Server, click the **Start** button, point to **Programs**, point to **Administrative Tools**, and then click **Internet Services Manager**.

2. Expand the server name.

3. Expand **Default Web Site**.

4. Select the RapPort virtual directory and expand.

5. Select **AD** then right click **Properties**.

6. Click **Configuration**. The **Application Configuration** dialog box appears.

7. Click the **App Options** tab.

8. In **ASP Script timeout**, type a value.

9. Click **OK**.

10. Click **OK** to close the **Properties** page.

> **Note** This value is in Seconds. During the installation, the default for this is set to 600 seconds.

To modify a scheduled task:

1. On the **Start** menu, point to **Settings**, and then click **Control Panel**.

2. Double-click **Scheduled Tasks**.

3. Right-click the RapPort scheduled task, and then click **Properties**.

4. On the **Schedule** tab, modify the schedule as appropriate. You can click **Advanced** to specify advanced schedule options.

5. On the **Task** tab, you can modify the user account and password as required.

   Note You must change the password when the password for this account changes.

6. Click **OK**.

7. Close Scheduled Tasks.

You can modify the user account used for running the COM+ package. The new account must be a member of the local Administrators group on the destination server.

To configure COM+ security settings on the destination server:

1. On the **Start** menu, point to **Programs**, point to **Administrative Tools**, and then click **Component Services**.

2. In **Component Services**, expand the **Component Services** node and its subnodes.

3. Expand COM+ Applications.

4. Right-click **RapPort**, and then click **Properties**.

5. Click the **Identity** tab.

6. Click **This User**.

7. In **User**, enter *username*.

8. In **Password** and **Confirm password**, type *password* for *username*.

9. Click **OK** to close the **Properties** page.

To modify system settings for the destination server:

Caution You can edit the registry by using the Registry Editor (Regedit.exe). Incorrectly editing the registry may severely damage your system. Back up the current version of the registry before making any changes. You should also back up any valued data on the computer.

1. Add the appropriate domain account to the local Administrators group on the destination server.

2. On the **Start** Menu, click **Run**.

3. Type **regedit** and then click **OK**.

4. In **Registry Editor**, navigate to the node:

   HKEY_LOCAL_COMPUTER\SOFTWARE\Microsoft\RapPort

5. Click the node and confirm that all the entries are correctly shown in the right pane. The following values should be configured as outlined:

   • If the IP address of the destination server is changed, modify the IP address as appropriate. For example, "IP"="**192.168.114.201**"

   • Change the name of the proxy server to the new proxy server. For example, "Proxy"="*proxy_server*"

   • Change the proxy port to appropriate value. For example, "ProxyPort"="80"

   • Edit the value of the CommonAdmin to the new domain account, such as *domain\user_account*.

   Important This account must be a member of the local Administrators group on all servers in this deployment.

6. Close Registry Editor.

7. On the destination server, open **Component Services**, and then open property pages for RapPort COM+ application.

8. Click the **Identity** tab and enter the user name and password of the appropriate domain user account.

9. Run Proxycfg prior to running a request as described in "Installing RapPort."

To configure system settings on RapPort server:

Caution Incorrectly editing the registry may severely damage your system. Back up the current version of the registry before making any changes. You should also back up any valued data on the computer.

1. Add appropriate domain account to the local Administrators group on the RapPort server.

2. From the RapPort server, click **Start**, and then click **Run**.

3. Type **regedit** and then click **OK**.

4. In **Registry Editor**, navigate to the node:

   HKEY_LOCAL_COMPUTER\SOFTWARE\Microsoft\RapPort

5. Edit the value of the CommonAdmin to the new domain account, such as *domain\user_account*.

   Important This account must be a member of the local Administrators group on all servers in this deployment.

6. Close Registry Editor.

7. On the RapPort server, open **Component Services**, and then open property pages for RapPort COM+ application.

8. Click the **Identity** tab and enter the user name and password for the appropriate domain account.

9. Run Proxycfg prior to running AutoSetup. For more information, see "Installing RapPort."

To configure the domain account on the template server:

Add appropriate domain account to the local Administrators group on the RapPort server.

To reset passwords when the account password changes:

When any of the accounts used for either the COM+ package or the scheduled job changes, you must manually change the account and password information in two locations. To reset the passwords complete the following steps:

1. On the RapPort server, open **Component Services**, and then open property pages for RapPort COM+ application.

2. Click the **Identity** tab and enter the user name and password for the appropriate domain account.

3. Edit the Scheduled job on the RapPort server.

4. Click the **Set Password** button.

5. Enter the user name and password for the appropriate domain account.

6. Repeat these steps on each of the destination servers.

RapPort Installations

This section provides installation instructions and information about how to remove RapPort. Install RapPort by completing the following steps:

- Review the server hardware and software requirements, including coexistence issues, outlined earlier in this chapter.

- Create the RapPort server.

- Create the template server.

- Create the destination server.

- Create the workspace templates.

The following sections provide detailed instructions on each of these steps.

Installing RapPort

You must create the RapPort server before creating the other servers. This section provides detailed instructions on each installation process.

Install the RapPort Server

This section describes the process of setting up the RapPort server.

Note If RapPort was previously installed on this computer, remove it before beginning the new installation. For more information, see "Removing RapPort."

To set up a domain account as an administrator on the RapPort server:

1. Log on with a user account that is an administrator on the server.

   Note You should use the same domain user account and password on each server in the RapPort deployment. This domain account must be a member of the local Administrators group on each server.

2. On the **Start** menu, point to **Programs**, point to **Administrative Tools**, and then click **Computer Management**.

3. Expand **Local Users and Groups**.

4. Click the **Groups** node.

5. Double-click **Administrators** on the details pane. The **Administrators Properties** dialog box appears.

6. Click **Add**.

7. In the **Select Users or Groups** dialog box, type the name of the appropriate domain account. Add *domain\account_name* to the local Administrators group on the server where *domain* is a valid Windows NT domain name and *account_name* is a valid account.

8. Click **Check Names**.

9. Click **OK**.

10. Click **OK** to close **Administrators Properties**.

11. Close Computer Management.

To confirm SharePoint Portal Server Web Storage System accessibility:

Note This step should be performed before proceeding with further installation.

1. Open Internet Explorer.

2. In **Address**, type **http://*server_name*/public** where *server_name* is the name of the RapPort server.

3. If the public folder is not displayed and the computer stops responding, restart the computer and repeat steps 1 and 2. If the computer still does not respond, the Web Storage System may be corrupted. In this case, rebuild the computer and install SharePoint Portal Server.

To copy RapPort server files:

1. Open Windows Explorer.

2. Copy the RapPortServerFiles.zip file to the root of the local hard disk drive on which the RapPort server is to be installed.

3. Extract all files from this zip file to the root of the local hard disk drive on which the RapPort server is to be installed.

4. Close WinZip.

   Caution Do not move or rename this folder or any subfolder/files.

5. Verify that the following folders and files exist in the folder:

   RapPort

   RapPort\AutoSetup

   • Autosetup.exe

   RapPort\AutoSetup\Components

   • assignRoles.dll

   • SCM.dll

   • TemplateInst.dll

   • WrapperTemplateInst.dll

   RapPort\AutoSetup\Components\XSL

   • convert-dav-to-ddf.xsl

   • import-application-folder-documents.xsl

   • import-application-folders.xsl

   • import-categories.xsl

   • import-document-folders.xsl

   • import-portal.xsl

   • import-portal-content-folders.xsl

   • import-rapportresources-folders.xsl

   • import-schema.xsl

RapPort\AutoSetup\Configuration

- constants.xml

- globalizedStrings.xml

- Mails.xml

- ServerConfig.xml

RapPort\AutoSetup\Logs

- No Files

RapPort\AutoSetup\RegistryEntries

- RapPortServerReg.reg

RapPort\AutoSetup\Temp

- No Files

RapPort\AutoSetup\Utilities

- addauthor.vbs

- addcoordinator.vbs

- addreader.vbs

- RestartIIS.cmd

- sleep.vbs

RapPort\RapPortWeb

- Default.htm

- Global.asa

RapPort\RapPortWeb\Configuration

- RegionCodes.xml

- RegionCodes.xsl

- TemplateConfig.xml

- TemplateConfig.xsl

- todaysServers.xml

RapPort\RapPortWeb\Content (The file list in this folder can change, as it contains the content files for the RapPort Web site, in addition to the files needed for the request creation wizard.)

- BusDivPortal.htm

- Customize.htm

- DeptPortal.htm
- FAQ.htm
- MoreInfo.htm
- Support.htm
- Templates.htm
- 1ptrans.gif
- linenavdns.gif
- new logo.bmp
- ep.css
- expendLeftNav.js
- local.js
- navscrpt.js
- toolbar.js

RapPort\RapPortWeb\Data

RapPort\RapPortWeb\Data\CheckAvailability

- No Files

RapPort\RapPortWeb\Data\History

- No Files

RapPort\RapPortWeb\Data\TemporarySecurityData

- No Files

RapPort\RapPortWeb\Data\UserRequests

- No Files

RapPort\RapPortWeb\Images

- pixel.gif
- settingsicon.gif

RapPort\RapPortWeb\Includes

- CheckAvailability.cmd
- CommonFunction.js
- constants.asp
- constants.inc

- cust.css

- ErrorPage.asp

- errors.js

- messages.inc

RapPort\RapPortWeb\Pages

- advanced.htm

- advancedFrame.asp

- checkURLAvailability.asp

- checkUserRequests.asp

- deleteUserData.asp

- finishPage.asp

- rapportSetup2.asp

- rapportSetup3.asp

- saveTemporarySecurityData.asp

- saveUserData.asp

- saveUserSecurity.asp

- sendTemporarySecurityData.asp

- statusbar.htm

- workspaceRolesContainer.asp

RapPort\RapPortWeb\Pages\AD

- No Files

RapPort\RapPortWeb\Pages\AD\COM

- ActiveDir.dll

RapPort\RapPortWeb\Pages\AD\Components

- No Files

RapPort\RapPortWeb\Pages\AD\Components\UserPicker

- AddressBook.asp

- CommonFunctions.js

- UniCal.css

- UserPicker.asp

- UserPicker.css

- UserPicker.js

RapPort\RapPortWeb\Pages\AD\Images

- No Files

RapPort\RapPortWeb\Pages\AD\Images\UserPicker

- Contact.gif

- Group.gif

To remove the read-only attributes for the files:

1. Open Windows Explorer on the RapPort server.

2. Right-click the **RapPort** folder and then click **Properties**.

3. On the **General** tab, select the **Read-only** check box. If the check box is already selected, go to step eight.

4. Click **OK**.

5. In **Confirm Attribute Changes**, click **Apply changes to this folder, subfolders and files**.

6. Click **OK**.

7. Right-click the **RapPort** folder and then click **Properties**.

8. On the **General** tab, clear the **Read-only** check box.

9. Click **OK**.

10. In **Confirm Attribute Changes**, click **Apply changes to this folder, subfolders and files**.

11. Click **OK**.

> **Caution** When editing the XML files, do not delete or change any of the node tags. Change only the text between the > and </ signs for the nodes.
>
> Do not add any XML-sensitive special characters (such as &, <, > etc.) while editing the contents in the XML files. Always confirm that the XML file is valid by opening the edited XML file in Internet Explorer and confirming that the file opens without errors.
>
> Incorrectly editing the registry may severely damage your system. Back up the current version of the registry before making any changes. You should also back up any valued data on the computer.
>
> When editing the registry (.reg) files, you must enter a single \ as \\ when entering path names, for example, D:\\RapPort\\AutoSetup. Do not remove quotation marks.

To edit RegionCodes.xml:

1. Open Windows Explorer, and then navigate to the following folder on the drive on which the RapPort server is to be installed:

   ..\RapPort\RapPortWeb\Configuration

2. Open **RegionCodes.xml** in Notepad.

3. Copy the XML node <region></region> and paste for each of the region entries you want to make.

4. Edit each XML node <region></region> by adding the actual region name and a unique code for each region. For example, <region code="FE">Far East</region>.

5. Save the file.

6. Close Notepad.

7. Double-click the file to open it in Internet Explorer to confirm that the XML formatting is correct. Internet Explorer should display the file without any errors.

To edit TemplateConfig.xml:

1. In Windows Explorer, and then navigate to the following folder on the drive on which the RapPort server is to be installed:

   ..\RapPort\RapPortWeb\Configuration.

2. Open TemplateConfig.xml in Notepad.

3. Copy the XML node <template></ template> and paste a copy of this node for each of the workspace templates that should be available for copying.

4. Edit the XML node <name></name> under each <template></ template> node by adding the display name of the template. RapPort presents this display name to the user when making a request from the RapPort Web site. For example, <name>Product Group – Portal</name>

   Note A long template name can distort the Web site user interface. It is recommended that you use a reasonable length for the template name. Although there is no limitation on the text for a template name length, 50 characters should be sufficient for displaying properly on the Web site user interface. After entering the name for the template in the XML file, check the Web site user interface for distortion. If the display name distorts, you should shorten the template name so that it can display correctly in the Web site user interface.

5. Edit the XML node <url></url> under each <template></ template> node by adding the complete URL of the corresponding workspace template. For example, <url>http://Adventure-Works/portaltemplate</url>.

6. Save the file.

7. Close Notepad.

8. Double-click the file to open it in Internet Explorer to confirm that the XML formatting is correct. Internet Explorer should display the file without any errors.

To edit ServerConfig.xml:

1. Open Windows Explorer, and then navigate to the following folder on the drive on which the RapPort server is to be installed:

   ..\RapPort\AutoSetup\Configuration

2. Open **ServerConfig.xml** in Notepad.

3. Copy the XML node <entry></entry> and paste for each of the shared destination server entries.

4. Edit the XML node <region></region> under each <entry></entry> node by adding the actual region code for the destination server name. For example, <region>FE</region>. Get the appropriate region code from the RegionCodes.xml file edited in the previous procedure.

5. Edit the XML node <servername></servername> under each <entry></entry> node by adding the actual destination server name. For example, <servername>AdventureWorks</servername>.

6. Edit the XML node <capacity></capacity> node under each <entry></entry> by entering the maximum number of workspaces that can be hosted on this destination server.

7. Edit the XML node <current></current> under each <entry></entry> node by entering the current number of workspaces that are hosted on this destination server.

8. Save the file.

9. Close Notepad.

10. Double-click the file to open it in Internet Explorer to confirm that the XML formatting is correct. Internet Explorer should display the file without any errors.

To edit Mails.xml:

1. Open Windows Explorer, and then navigate to the following folder on the drive on which the RapPort server is to be installed:

   ..\RapPort\AutoSetup\Configuration.

2. Open **Mails.xml** in Notepad.

3. Edit the <smtpservername></smtpservername> node by adding the SMTP server name to be used for sending mail. Typically, this will be the same name as that of the RapPort server, otherwise specify the actual SMTP server name. For example, <smtpservername>AdventureWorks</smtpservername>.

4. Search for the XML node <mail id="4"> in this file.

5. Under this XML node, edit the <to><name></name></to> node by adding the e-mail account to whom the WINS registration entry is sent. For example, <to><name>operations@adventure-works.com</name></to>.

6. Search for **RapAdmin@adventure-works.com**. Replace this account with the e-mail address for the administrator account from which the RapPort application will send e-mails.

7. Search for **RapSupport@adventure-works.com**. Replace this account with the e-mail address for the RapPort Support account that receives mail regarding support.

8. Save the file.

9. Close Notepad.

10. Double-click the file to open it in Internet Explorer to confirm that the XML formatting is correct. Internet Explorer should display the file without any errors.

To change the domain name for notifications:

1. In Notepad, open Constants.xml.

2. Modify the domain name in the following node as appropriate:

   <Constant constID="*constMailDomainName*">@adventure-works.com</Constant>

3. Save the file.

4. Edit FinishPage.asp on the RapPort server.

5. Search for the string "@adventure-works.com."

6. Change the domain name as appropriate.

7. Save the file.

To edit RapPortServerReg.reg:

1. Open Windows Explorer, and then navigate to the following folder on the drive on which the RapPort server is to be installed:

   ..\RapPort\AutoSetup\RegistryEntries

2. Right-click **RapPortServerReg.reg**, and then click **Edit** to open the file in Notepad.

   Caution Incorrectly editing the registry may severely damage your system. Back up the current version of the registry before making any changes. You should also back up any valued data on the computer.

3. Edit the line "Path"="*drive*:\\RapPort" and replace *drive* with the actual drive letter of the drive on which the RapPort server is installed. Do not remove the \\ in the path.

4. Edit the value of "CommonAdmin"= "**domain\\account_name**" and replace it with the user account which is to be used as the administrator account on all RapPort computers.

>   **Important** Use \\ instead of a single \ to specify the account name.

5. Save the file.

6. Close Notepad.

To import the RapPort server registry entries:

>   **Caution** Incorrectly editing the registry may severely damage your system. Follow the instructions below very carefully. Back up the registry before making any changes.

1. Open Windows Explorer, and then navigate to the following folder on the drive on which the RapPort server is to be installed:

>   **..\RapPort\AutoSetup\RegistryEntries**

2. Double-click **RapPortServerReg.reg** to import the registry entries.

3. Click **Yes** to add the information to the registry.

4. Click **OK**.

5. Close Windows Explorer.

To verify that registry entries have been successfully imported:

>   **Caution** Do *not* change any values in the registry. Incorrectly editing the registry may severely damage your system. Back up the current version of the registry before making any changes. You should also back up any valued data on the computer.

1. On the **Start** menu, click **Run**.

2. Type **regedit** and then click **OK**.

3. In **Registry Editor**, navigate to the node:

>   My Computer\HKEY_LOCAL_COMPUTER\SOFTWARE\Microsoft\RapPort

4. Click this node and confirm that all the entries correctly display in the right pane.

5. Close Registry Editor.

To register the RapPort DLLs:

1. On the **Start** menu, click **Run**.

2. Type **regsvr32** *drive*:**\RapPort\AutoSetup\Components\assignRoles.dll** where *drive* is the drive letter for the drive where RapPort server is to be installed.

3. Click **OK**.

4. If the following message does not appear, repeat step 2 until the appropriate message appears:

   "DllRegisterServer in *drive*:\RapPort\AutoSetup\Components\assignRoles.dll succeeded."

5. In the **RegSvr32** dialog box, click **OK**.

6. Repeat steps 1 through 5 for each of the following DLLs, typing the following in step 2:

   - **regsvr32** *drive*:**RapPort\AutoSetup\Components\SCM.dll**

   - **regsvr32** *drive*:**RapPort\AutoSetup\Components\TemplateInst.dll**

   - **regsvr32** *drive*:**RapPort\AutoSetup\Components\WrapperTemplateInst.dll**

   - **regsvr32** *drive*:**RapPort\RapPortWeb\Pages\AD\COM\ActiveDir.dll**

To create a new COM+ application:

1. On the **Start** menu, point to **Programs**, point to **Administrative Tools**, and then click **Component Services**.

2. In **Component Services**, expand the **Component Services** node and its subnodes.

3. Click COM+ Applications.

4. Right-click **COM+ Applications**, point to **New**, and then click **Application**. The Welcome to the COM Application Install Wizard appears.

5. Click **Next**.

6. Click Create an empty application.

7. Enter **RapPort** as the name of the new application, and then select **Server application**.

8. Click **Next**.

9. Click This User.

10. In **User**, enter the name of the appropriate domain account such as *domain\account_name*.

11. In **Password** and **Confirm password**, type the password for the account.

    Note You must change the password for this setting whenever the password for this account changes.

12. Click **Next**.

13. Click **Finish**.

To add components to the new RapPort COM+ application:

1. Expand the **RapPort** node under COM+ Applications.

2. Click **Components** under the **RapPort** node.

3. Right-click **Components**, point to **New**, and then click **Component**. The Welcome to the COM Component Install Wizard appears.

4. Click **Next**.

5. Click Import Component(s) that are already registered.

6. Select **ActiveDir.Helpers** from the list of components.

7. Click **Next**.

8. Click **Finish**.

9. Repeat steps 1 through 8 above for each of the following components, replacing **ActiveDir.Helpers** with the following component names:

   - ActiveDir.QueryGC

   - AssignRoles.Roles

   - SCM.Manager

   - TemplateInst.CodeGenerator

   - WrapperTemplateInst.clsInstantiate.

10. Confirm that all components are visible by expanding the **Components** node.

11. Close Component Services.

To create a new virtual directory in the default Web site:

1. On the **Start** menu, point to **Programs**, point to **Administrative Tools**, and then click **Internet Services Manager**.

2. Expand the server name.

3. Right-click **Default Web Site**, point to **New**, and then click **Virtual Directory**. The Welcome to the Virtual Directory Creation Wizard appears.

4. Click **Next**.

5. On the **Virtual Directory E-mail account** page, type **RapPort** in **E-mail account**, and then click **Next**.

6. On the **Web Site Content Directory** page, click **Browse**, and then navigate to the **RapPort\RapPortWeb** folder on the drive on which the RapPort server is to be installed.

7. Click the **RapPortWeb** folder, and then click **OK**.

8. Click **Next**.

9. On the **Access Permissions** page, click **Next**. Do not change the default access permissions.

10. Click **Finish**.

To configure properties for the Default Web Site:

1. On the **Start** menu, point to **Programs**, point to **Administrative Tools**, and then click **Internet Services Manager**.

2. Expand the server name.

3. Right-click **Default Web Site**, and then click **Properties**.

4. On the **Web Site** tab, select **(All Unassigned) from IP Address**.

5. In **TCP Port**, type **80**. Do not change any other settings.

6. Click the **Directory Security** tab.

7. In **Anonymous access and authentication control**, click **Edit**.

8. In the **Authentication Methods** dialog box, clear all check boxes *except* for the **Integrated Windows authentication** check box.

9. Click **OK**.

10. If the **Inheritance Overrides** dialog box appears, click **RapPort** under **Child Nodes**, and then click **OK**. If the RapPort child node is not displayed in the list, click **OK** without selecting anything.

   Note After clicking **OK**, view the properties of the RapPort virtual directory to ensure that only the Integrated Windows Authentication is specified for the directory security.

11. Click the **Home Directory** tab.

12. Under When connecting to this resource, the content should come from, click **A redirection to a URL**.

13. In **Redirect to**, type **/RapPort**.

14. Under The client will be sent to, click the A directory below this one check box.

15. Click **OK** to close the **Default Web Site Properties** dialog box.

To configure properties for the Active Directory virtual directory under RapPort:

1. On the **Start** menu, point to **Programs**, point to **Administrative Tools**, and then click **Internet Services Manager**.

2. Expand the server name. Typically, the server name is the computer name.

3. Expand the **RapPort** node under **Default Web Site in IIS**, and then expand the **Pages** Web directory.

4. Right-click the **AD** node, and then click **Properties**.

5. On the **Directory** tab, click **Create** under **Application Settings**. Keep other settings at the default values.

6. After creating the Active Directory application, click **Configuration**.

7. In the **Application Configuration** dialog box, click the **App Options** tab.

8. On the **App Options** tab, change the **ASP Script timeout** value to **600** seconds.

9. Click **OK** to close the **Application Configuration** dialog box.

10. Click **OK** button to close **AD Properties**.

To configure properties for the RapPort virtual directory:

1. On the **Start** menu, point to **Programs**, point to **Administrative Tools**, and then click **Internet Services Manager**.

2. Expand the server name.

3. Right-click the **RapPort** node under **Default Web Site**, and then click **Properties**.

4. In the **RapPort Properties** dialog box, click the **HTTP Headers** tab.

5. Click the **Enable Content Expiration** check box.

6. Click **Expire Immediately**.

7. Click **OK** to close RapPort Properties.

To configure the default SMTP virtual server:

1. On the **Start** menu, point to **Programs**, point to **Administrative Tools**, and then click **Internet Services Manager**.

2. Expand the server name.

3. Right-click **Default SMTP Virtual Server**, and then click **Properties**.

4. Click the **Access** tab.

5. Under **Relay restrictions**, click **Relay**. The **Relay Restrictions** dialog box appears.

6. Click **All** except the list below.

7. Select the **Allow all computers which successfully authenticate to relay**, regardless of the list above check box.

8. Click **OK** to close the **Relay Restrictions** dialog box.

9. Click the **Delivery** tab, and then click **Advanced**.

10. In **Smart host**, type the name of the smart host relay server. Do not change any other settings.

11. Click **OK** to close the **Advanced Delivery** dialog box.

12. Click **OK** to close the **Properties** page.

13. Close Internet Information Services.

To create a new scheduled job for AutoSetup.exe:

1. On the **Start** menu, point to **Settings**, and then click **Control Panel**.

2. Double-click **Scheduled Tasks**.

3. In the **Scheduled Tasks** dialog box, double-click **Add Scheduled Task**. The **Scheduled Task Wizard** appears.

4. Click **Next**.

5. Click **Browse**. The **Select Program to Schedule** dialog box appears.

6. Navigate to the **\RapPort\AutoSetup** folder on the drive where the RapPort server is to be installed.

7. Select **AutoSetup.exe**, and then click **Open** to close the **Select Program to Schedule** dialog box.

8. Type **RapPort AutoSetup** as the name of the task.

9. Click **Daily**, and then click **Next**.

10. In **Start time**, enter 12:00AM.

11. Click **Every Day**.

12. In **Start date**, enter the current date, and then click **Next**.

13. Enter the user name of the appropriate domain account, such as *domain\account_name*.

14. In **Password** and **Confirm password**, type the password for the account.

    Note You must change the password when the password for this account changes.

15. Click **Next**.

16. Ensure that the **Open advanced properties for this task** check box is *not* selected.

17. Click **Finish**.

18. Ensure that there is only one task scheduled for AutoSetup.exe.

19. Close Scheduled Tasks.

The default script host should be changed to **cscript** for executing the Microsoft Visual Basic® Scripting Edition (VBScript) files, which have the extension .vbs. This suppresses any dialog boxes shown by *wscript* due to use of the echo command.

To specify the default script host:

1. On the **Start** menu, point to **Programs**, point to **Accessories**, and then click **Command Prompt**.

2. Type **wscript //H:cscript** and then press ENTER.

3. Click **OK** to close the **Windows Script Host** dialog box.

4. Close Command Prompt.

You must configure the proxy settings for SharePoint Portal Server to use fully qualified domain names (FQDNs). You need to perform the following procedure only once.

To configure the proxy settings:

1. On the **Start** menu, point to **Programs**, point to **Accessories**, and then click **Command Prompt**.

2. Change to the SharePoint Portal Server \Bin directory. For example, if you installed SharePoint Portal Server in the Installation directory on drive E, change to E:\Installation\Bin. If you installed SharePoint Portal Server on drive D under Program Files\SharePoint Portal Server, change to D:\Program Files\SharePoint Portal Server\Bin.

3. Type **proxycfg –d –p** *proxy_server_name*:*port_number*"***.***local.domain.name*;**<local>**" and then press ENTER.

For example, if your proxy server name is Proxy1, the port number is 80, and the domain is adventure-works.com, type proxycfg –d –p Proxy1:80 "*.adventure-works.com;<local>"

4. Verify that the correct settings were entered by typing **proxycfg.exe**

5. Close Command Prompt.

To restart the server:

1. Wait for 5 minutes to allow IIS to save settings.

2. Restart the server.

3. Repeat steps in "To check SharePoint Portal Server Web Storage System accessibility" whenever the server is restarted.

Install Template Server

This section describes the process of setting up the RapPort template server.

To configure the appropriate domain account as an administrator:

1. Log on with a user account that is an administrator on the server.

    Note You should use the same domain user account and password on each server in the RapPort deployment. This domain account must be a member of the local Administrators group on each server.

2. On the **Start** menu, point to **Programs**, point to **Administrative Tools**, and then click **Computer Management**.

3. Expand **Local Users and Groups**.

4. Click the **Groups** node.

5. Double-click **Administrators** on the details pane. The **Administrators Properties** dialog box appears.

6. Click **Add**.

7. In the **Select Users or Groups** dialog box, type the name of the appropriate domain account.

8. Click **Check Names**.

9. Click **OK**.

10. Click **OK** to close **Administrators Properties**.

11. Close Computer Management.

To configure appropriate domain account as a coordinator on all template workspaces:

1. On the **Start** menu, point to **Programs**, point to **Administrative Tools**, and then click **SharePoint Portal Server Administration**.

2. Click to expand the server, and then select the workspace template.

3. Right-click the workspace template, and then click **Properties**.

4. Click the **Security** tab, and then click Add.

5. In the **Select Users or Groups** dialog box, type the name of the appropriate domain account.

    Note You should use the same domain user account and password on each server in the RapPort deployment. This domain account must be a member of the local Administrators group on each server.

6. Click **Check Names**.

7. Click **OK**.

8. In **User or Group**, select the appropriate domain account.

9. In Role, click Coordinator.

10. Click **OK**.

11. Repeat steps 3 to 10 for each workspace template.

12. Close SharePoint Portal Server Administration.

Install the Destination Server

This section describes the process of setting up the destination server.

To add the appropriate domain account to the local Administrators group on the server:

1. Log on with a user account that is an administrator on the server.

2. On the **Start** menu, point to **Programs**, point to **Administrative Tools**, and then click **Computer Management**.

3. Expand **Local Users and Groups**.

4. Click the **Groups** node.

5. Double-click **Administrators** in the details pane. The **Administrators Properties** dialog box appears.

6. Click **Add**.

7. In the **Select Users or Groups** dialog box, select the appropriate domain account.

   Note You should use the same domain user account and password on each server in the RapPort deployment. This domain account must be a member of the local Administrators group on each server.

8. Click **Check Names**.

9. Click **OK**.

10. Click **OK** to close the **Administrators Properties** dialog box.

11. Close Computer Management.

To confirm SharePoint Portal Server Web Storage System accessibility:

1. Open Internet Explorer.

2. In **Address**, type **http://**_server_name_**/public** where _server_name_ is the name of the destination server.

3. If the public folder is not displayed and the computer stops responding, restart the computer and repeat steps 1 and 2. If the computer still does not respond, the Web Storage System may be corrupt. In this case, rebuild the computer and install SharePoint Portal Server.

To copy destination server files:

1. Open Windows Explorer.

2. Copy the RapPortDestinationServerFiles.zip file to the root of the local hard disk on which the destination server is to be installed.

3. Extract all files from this zip file to the root of the local hard drive on which the destination server is to be installed.

4. Close WinZip.

   Caution Do not move or rename this folder or any subfolders or files.

5. Verify that the following folders and files exist in the folder:

   RapPort

   - AssignCoordinatorRole-Script.vbs

   - ExecutionPermission-Script.vbs

   - CreateVirtualServer.asp

   - Createworkspace.asp

   RapPort\Components

   - RemoteWS.dll

   - RapPortVServer.dll

   RapPort\Logs

   - No Files

   RapPort\RegistryEntries

   DestinationRegistryEntries.reg

   RapPort\VirtualServers

   - No Files

To remove the read-only attributes for the files:

1. Open Windows Explorer on the destination server.

2. Right-click the **RapPort** folder, and then click **Properties**.

3. On the **General** tab, select the **Read-only** check box. If the check box is already selected, go to step eight.

4. Click **OK**.

5. In the **Confirm Attribute Changes** dialog box, click **Apply changes to this folder,
   subfolders and files**.

6. Click **OK**.

7. Right-click the **RapPort** folder, and then click **Properties**.

8. On the **General** tab, clear the **Read-only** check box.

9. Click **OK**.

10. In the **Confirm Attribute Changes** dialog box, click **Apply changes to this folder,
    subfolders and files**.

11. Click **OK**.

To edit DestinationRegistryEntries.reg:

> **Caution** Incorrectly editing the registry may severely damage your system. Back up
> the current version of the registry before making any changes. You should also back
> up any valued data on the computer.

When editing the registry (.reg) files, you must enter a single \ as \\ when entering
path names, for example, D:\\RapPort\\AutoSetup. Do not remove quotation marks.

1. Open Windows Explorer, and then navigate to the **RapPort\RegistryEntries** folder
   on the drive on which the destination server is to be installed.

2. Right-click **DestinationRegistryEntries.reg**, and then click **Edit** to open the file in
   Notepad.

   > **Note** Do not double-click the file, because this imports the unedited registry en-
   > tries contained in this file into the registry.

3. Edit the line "Domain"="**domain_name**" and replace it with the actual domain for
   this computer.

4. Edit the line "IP"="**192.168.114.201**" and replace the IP address with the actual static
   IP address for this computer.

5. Edit the line "Proxy"="**proxy_server**" and replace the proxy server name with the
   actual proxy server name.

6. Edit the line "ProxyPort"="80" and replace the proxy server port value with the actual proxy server port value. Do not change if the proxy server port is 80.

7. Edit the line "AppPath"="D:\\RapPort" and replace D: with the actual drive letter of
   the drive on which the destination server is installed. Do not remove the \\ in the path.

8. Edit the line "VirtualServersPath"="D:\\RapPort\\VirtualServers" and replace D: with the actual drive letter of the drive on which the destination server is installed. Do not remove the \\ in the path.

9. Edit the line "LogPath"="D:\\RapPort\\Logs" and replace D: with the actual drive letter of the drive on which the destination server is installed. Do not remove the \\ in the path.

10. Save the file.

11. Close Notepad.

To import the RapPort server registry entries:

Caution Incorrectly editing the registry may severely damage your system. Back up the current version of the registry before making any changes. You should also back up any valued data on the computer.

1. Open Windows Explorer, and then navigate to the **\RapPort\RegistryEntries** folder on the drive on which the destination server is to be installed.

2. Double-click **DestinationRegistryEntries.reg** to import the registry entries.

3. Click **Yes** to add the information to the registry.

4. Click **OK**.

5. Close Windows Explorer.

To verify that registry entries have been successfully imported:

1. On the **Start** menu, click **Run**.

2. Type **regedit** and then click **OK**.

3. In **Registry Editor**, navigate to the node:

   My Computer\HKEY_LOCAL_COMPUTER\SOFTWARE\Microsoft\RapPort

4. Click this node and confirm that all the entries are correctly shown in the right pane.

5. Close Registry Editor. Do *not* change any values in the registry.

To register the RapPort DLLs:

1. On the **Start** menu, click **Run**.

2. Type **regsvr32** *drive:***\RapPort\Components\RapPortVServer.dll**
   where *drive* is the drive letter for the drive where destination server is to be installed.

3. Click **OK**.

4. If the following message is not displayed:

>   DllRegisterServer in *drive*:\RapPort\Components\RapPortVServer.dll succeeded

then repeat step 2 until the appropriate message displays. Where *drive* is the drive where RapPort Server is being installed.

5. Click **OK** on the **RegSvr32** dialog box that displays.

6. Repeat steps 1 to 5 above for the following DLL:

>   **regsvr32** *drive*:**\RapPort\Components\RemoteWS.dll**

where *drive* is the drive letter for the drive where destination server is to be installed.

To create a new COM+ application:

1. On the **Start** menu, point to **Programs**, point to **Administrative Tools**, and then click **Component Services**.

2. In **Component Services**, expand the **Component Services** node and its subnodes.

3. Click **COM+ Applications**.

4. Right-click **COM+ Applications**, point to **New**, and then click **Application**. The **Welcome to the COM Application Install Wizard** appears.

5. Click **Next**.

6. Click **Create an empty application**.

7. Enter **RapPort** as the name of the new application, and then select **Server application**.

8. Click **Next**.

9. Click **This user**.

10. In **User**, enter any appropriate domain account that is a member of the local Administrators group.

11. In **Password** and **Confirm password**, type *password* for the account.

    Note You must change this password whenever the password for this account changes.

12. Click **Next**.

13. Click **Finish**.

To add components to the new RapPort COM+ application:

1. Expand the **RapPort** node under COM+ Applications.

2. Click **Components** under the **RapPort** node.

3. Right-click **Components**, point to **New**, and then click **Component**. The **Welcome to the COM Component Install Wizard** appears.

4. Click **Next**.

5. Click **Import component(s) that are already registered**.

6. On the **Choose Components to Import** page, click **RapPortVServer.CreateVServer** from the list of components.

7. Click **Next**.

8. Click **Finish**.

9. Repeat steps 1 through 8 above, replacing RapPortVServer.CreateVServer with **RemoteWS.clsCreateWS**.

10. Confirm that all components are visible by expanding the **Components** node.

11. Close Component Services.

To change the domain name for notifications:

1. Edit CreateWorkspace.asp on the destination server

2. Search for the string "@adventure-works.com".

3. Change the domain name as appropriate.

4. Save the file.

To specify logging properties for the WWW Service:

1. On the **Start** menu, point to **Programs**, point to **Administrative Tools**, and then click **Internet Services Manager**.

2. Right-click the server name, and then click **Properties**.

3. On the **Internet Information Services** tab, in **Master Properties** select **WWW Service**.

4. Click **Edit**. The **WWW Service Master Properties** dialog box appears.

5. On the **Web Site** tab, select the **Enable Logging** check box.

6. In **Active log format**, select **W3C Extended Log File Format**, and then click **Properties**.

7. In the **Extended Logging Properties** dialog box, click the **Extended Properties** tab.

8. Under the **Extended Properties** tree, select the **Referer (cs(Referer))** check box.

9. Click **OK**.

10. If the **Inheritance Overrides** dialog box appears, click **Select All**, and then click **OK**. This dialog box will not appear in all cases.

11. Click **OK** to close the **WWW Service Master Properties** dialog box.

12. Click **OK** to close **Properties** page.

To create a new virtual directory in the Default Web Site:

1. On the **Start** menu, point to **Programs**, point to **Administrative Tools**, and then click **Internet Services Manager**.

2. Expand the server name.

3. Right-click **Default Web Site**, point to **New**, and then click **Virtual Directory**. The Welcome to the Virtual Directory Creation Wizard appears.

4. Click **Next**.

5. On the **Virtual Directory E-mail account** page, type **RapPort** in the **E-mail account** text box, and then click **Next**.

6. On the **Web Site Content Directory** page, click **Browse**, and then navigate to the **\RapPort** folder on the drive on which the Destination server is to be installed.

7. Click the **RapPort** folder, and then click **OK**.

8. Click **Next**.

9. On the **Access Permissions** page, click **Next**. Do not change the default access permissions.

10. Click **Finish**.

To configure properties for the Default Web Site:

1. On the **Start** menu, point to **Programs**, point to **Administrative Tools**, and then click **Internet Services Manager**.

2. Expand the server name.

3. Right-click **Default Web Site**, and then click **Properties**.

4. On the **Web Site** tab, select **(All Unassigned) from IP Address**.

5. In **TCP Port**, type **80**.

To configure properties for the RapPort virtual directory:

1. On the **Start** menu, point to **Programs**, point to **Administrative Tools**, and then click **Internet Services Manager**.

2. Expand the server name. Typically, server name is same as the computer name.

3. Right-click the **RapPort** node under **Default Web Site of IIS**, and then click **Properties**.

4. In the **RapPort Properties** dialog box, click the **HTTP Headers** tab.

5. Select the **Enable Content Expiration** check box.

6. Click **Expire Immediately**.

7. Click the **Virtual Directory** tab.

8. Click **Configuration**.

9. In the **Application Configuration** dialog box, click the **App Options** tab.

10. On the **App Options** tab, change the **ASP Script timeout** value to **3600** seconds.

11. Click **OK** to close the **Application Configuration** dialog box.

12. Click the **Directory Security** tab.

13. In **Anonymous access and authentication control**, click **Edit**.

14. In the **Authentication Methods** dialog box, clear all check boxes *except* for the **Anonymous access** and **Integrated Windows authentication** check box.

15. Click **OK**.

16. If the **Inheritance Overrides** dialog box appears, click **Select All**, and then click **OK**. This dialog box may not display in all cases.

17. Click to close RapPort Properties.

To configure properties for the Default Web Site/SharePoint Portal Server/ Applications virtual directory:

1. On the **Start** menu, point to **Programs**, point to **Administrative Tools**, and then click **Internet Services Manager**.

2. Expand the server name.

3. Expand **Default Web Site**.

4. Expand the **SharePoint Portal Server** virtual directory node.

5. Click the **Applications** virtual directory node.

6. Right-click **Applications**, and then click **Properties**.

7. In the **Applications Properties** dialog box, click the **Directory** tab.

8. In **Execute Permissions**, select **Scripts only**.

9. Click **OK** to close the **Applications Properties** dialog box.

10. Close Internet Services Manager.

The default script host should be changed to **cscript** for executing the VBScript (.vbs) files. This suppresses any dialog boxes shown by *wscript* due to use of the echo command.

To specify the default script host:

1. On the **Start** menu, point to **Programs**, point to **Accessories**, and then click **Command Prompt**.

2. Type **wscript //H:cscript** and then press **Enter**.

3. Click **OK** to close the **Windows Script Host** dialog box.

4. Close Command Prompt.

You must configure the proxy settings for SharePoint Portal Server to use fully qualified domain names (FQDNs).

To configure the proxy settings:

1. On the **Start** menu, point to **Programs**, point to **Accessories**, and then click **Command Prompt**.

2. Change to the SharePoint Portal Server \Bin directory. For example, if you installed SharePoint Portal Server in the Installation directory on drive E, change to E:\Installation\Bin. If you installed SharePoint Portal Server on drive D under Program Files\SharePoint Portal Server, change to the following directory:

    D:\Program Files\SharePoint Portal Server\Bin

3. Type **proxycfg –d –p** *proxy_server_name***:***port_number* **"***.local.domain.name***;<local>"** and then press ENTER.

    For example, if your proxy server name is Proxy1, the port number is 80, and the domain is adventure-works.com, type **proxycfg –d –p Proxy1:80 "*.adventure-works.com;<local>"**.

4. Verify that the correct settings were entered by typing **proxycfg.exe**.

5. Close Command Prompt.

To restart the server:

1. Wait for 5 minutes to allow IIS to save settings.

2. Restart the server.

3. Repeat steps in "To confirm SharePoint Portal Server Web Storage System accessibility" whenever the server is restarted.

Creating Workspace Templates

This section provides tips for creating workspace templates and describes the elements of the workspace that RapPort copies during the portal provisioning process.

A *workspace template* is a SharePoint Portal Server workspace that contains some content. RapPort replicates this workspace so that other workspaces may benefit from the thought and effort put into designing the original content. Although you can use any actual workspace as a template, consider generalizing the content before using it as a template so that the material applies to a more general audience than the original workspace. It is recommended that you limit the number of people with coordinator or author privileges on a workspace template to a small number of people.

A workspace template is stored on the template server. When a user requests a new portal, the RapPort server copies the following elements of a workspace:

- **Categories.** All categories, and associated metadata

- **Schema.** All profiles, attributes, and dictionary values

- **Folder Structure.** All of the following folders and subfolders:

  > http://*server_name*/*workspace_name*/Documents
  > http://*server_name*/*workspace_name*/Portal Content
  > http://*server_name*/*workspace_name*/Portal/Resources/RapPort
  > http://*server_name*/SharePoint Portal Server/Public/Applications/
  > *workspace_name*.

  > **Note** RapPort does not maintain approval routes on folders. You must reapply approval settings on all folders.

- **Security Settings.** RapPort assigns coordinators, authors and readers at the workspace level based on the information provided by the person requesting the portal.

  By default, folders inherit security from the parent folder. Therefore, these settings apply throughout the workspace. It is not recommended that you apply security at the document or individual folder level when creating a template because role settings can vary according to each group's needs.

  > **Important** RapPort does not copy individual document or folder security settings when replicating a template.

- **Documents.** RapPort copies only the latest version of all documents stored in the folders listed previously.

  > **Note** Version history is not copied.

  RapPort identifies all documents as checked-in or published preserving the setting from the workspace template. If a published document is checked out in the template workspace, RapPort copies the latest published version. If a checked-out document in the template workspace was never published, then RapPort copies the last checked-in version. If a document in the template workspace was never checked in, RapPort copies the checked-out version but marks it to checked-in in the new workspace.

- **Dashboard site and Web Parts.** RapPort copies all dashboards and related Web Parts.

  > **Important** RapPort does not copy content source settings. Most organizations do not need to crawl the same content from multiple portals. For more information about using content sources to crawl content, see Chapter 6, "Planning Your Deployment." RapPort also does not copy discussions or subscriptions because the users for the new workspace can differ than those from the template.

To create a workspace template:

1. On the template server, create a new workspace or copy an existing workspace from another SharePoint Portal Server computer.

2. Customize the workspace to reflect the appropriate settings for the template. This may include customizing the dashboard site, creating a category structure, or adding specific content. If you copied an existing workspace, remove all inappropriate content, verify that you checked in, or published all documents, and specifying security at the top of the workspace and modifying inheritance.

For more information about creating workspaces and customizing them, see Appendix B.

Removing RapPort

This section describes the process of removing the RapPort application from your computer.

Remove the RapPort Server

You must log on with the appropriate domain account to perform the following procedures.

To delete the RapPort AutoSetup scheduled job for AutoSetup.exe:

1. On the **Start** menu, point to **Settings**, and then click **Control Panel**.

2. Double-click **Scheduled Tasks**.

3. In the **Scheduled Tasks** window, right-click the scheduled job **RapPort AutoSetup**, and then click **Delete**.

4. In the **Confirm File Delete** dialog box, click **Yes**.

5. Close Scheduled Tasks.

To delete the RapPort COM+ application:

1. On the **Start** menu, point to **Programs**, point to **Administrative Tools**, and then click **Component Services**.

2. In **Component Services**, expand the **Component Services** node and its subnodes.

3. Right-click the **RapPort** application node, and then click **Delete**.

4. In the **Confirm Item Delete** dialog box, click **Yes**.

5. Close Component Services.

To unregister the RapPort DLLs:

1. On the **Start** menu, click **Run**.

2. Type **regsvr32 -u** *drive***:\RapPort\AutoSetup\Components\assignRoles.dll**

   where *drive* is the drive letter for the drive where RapPort server is installed.

3. Click **OK**.

4. In the **RegSvr32** dialog box, click **OK**.

5. Repeat steps 1 through 4 for each of the following DLLs, typing the following in step 2:

   - **regsvr32 -u** *drive***:\RapPort\AutoSetup\Components\SCM.dll**

   - **regsvr32 -u** *drive***:\RapPort\AutoSetup\Components\TemplateInst.dll**

   - **regsvr32 -u** *drive***:\RapPort\AutoSetup\Components\WrapperTemplateInst.dll**

   - **regsvr32 -u** *drive***:\RapPort\RapPortWeb\Pages\AD\COM\ActiveDir.dll**

To delete the virtual directory for RapPort in the default Web site:

1. On the **Start** menu, point to **Programs**, point to **Administrative Tools**, and then click **Internet Services Manager**.

2. Expand the server name.

3. Expand **Default Web Site**.

4. Right-click the RapPort virtual directory, and then click **Delete**.

5. In the **Internet Services Manager** dialog box, click **Yes** to confirm the delete.

6. Close Internet Information Services.

To delete the RapPort server registry entries:

Caution Incorrectly editing the registry may severely damage your system. Back up the current version of the registry before making any changes. You should also back up any valued data on the computer.

1. On the **Start** menu, click **Run**.

2. Type **regedit** and then click OK.

3. In **Registry Editor**, navigate to the node:

   My Computer\HKEY_LOCAL_COMPUTER\SOFTWARE\Microsoft\RapPort

4. Right-click the **RapPort** node, and then click **Delete**.

5. In the **Confirm Key Delete** dialog box, click **Yes**.

6. Close Registry Editor.

To restart the server:

1. Wait five minutes to allow IIS to save settings.

2. Restart the server.

To delete the RapPort folder:

1. Open Windows Explorer.

2. Navigate to the **RapPort** folder on the drive on which the RapPort server is installed.

3. Right-click the **RapPort** folder, and then click **Delete**.

4. In the **Confirm Folder Delete** dialog box, click **Yes**.

5. Close Windows Explorer.

Remove the Template Server

There is no procedure for removing the template server. You can remove the administrator account from each workspace and from the local Administrators group on the template server. You assigned this account to the role of coordinator for the workspace when setting up the template workspace. There is no technical requirement to remove this account.

Remove the Destination Server

This section describes the process of removing RapPort from a destination server.

Removing RapPort from a destination server does not remove any workspaces or virtual servers already created on the destination server.

To delete any RapPort-created site, first delete the virtual server associated with the Web site, and then delete the workspace associated with the Web site.

> **Note** To delete the virtual server associated with this workspace, use Internet Services Manager.

To delete the workspace created by RapPort, use SharePoint Portal Server Administration. For more information about deleting RapPort-created Web sites, see "Delete a workspace and associated virtual server."

When removing RapPort from a destination server, you must manually configure the Home directory redirection property for all existing virtual servers. This is because the folder that contains the redirection default.asp pages for the RapPort created virtual servers is deleted when you remove RapPort. For more information about how to manually configure the redirection, see Chapter 12, "Deploying SharePoint Portal Server in an Extranet Environment."

This section assumes that you installed the Destination server in accordance with the pre-ceding installation instructions.

You must log on with an administrator account to perform the following procedures.

To delete the RapPort COM+ application:

1. On the **Start** menu, point to **Programs**, point to **Administrative Tools**, and then click **Component Services**.

2. In **Component Services**, expand the **Component Services** node and its subnodes.

3. Right-click the **RapPort** application node, and then click **Delete**.

4. In the **Confirm Item Delete** dialog box, click **Yes**.

5. Close Component Services.

To unregister the RapPort DLLs:

1. On the **Start** menu, click **Run**.

2. Type **regsvr32 -u** *drive***:\RapPort\Components\RapPortVServer.dll**

   where *drive* is the drive letter for the drive where destination server is installed.

3. Click **OK**.

4. In the **RegSvr32** dialog box, click **OK**.

5. Repeat steps 1 through 4 for the following DLL, typing the following in step 2:

   - **regsvr32 -u** *drive***:\RapPort\Components\RemoteWS.dll**

To delete the virtual directory for RapPort in the default Web site:

1. On the **Start** menu, point to **Programs**, point to **Administrative Tools**, and then click **Internet Services Manager**.

2. Expand the server name.

3. Expand **Default Web Site**.

4. Right-click the RapPort virtual directory, and then click **Delete**.

5. In the **Internet Services Manager** dialog box, click **Yes** to confirm the delete.

6. Close Internet Information Services.

To delete registry entries:

> **Caution** Incorrectly editing the registry may severely damage your system. Back up the current version of the registry before making any changes. You should also back up any valued data on the computer.

1. On the **Start** menu, click **Run**.

2. Type **regedit** and then click **OK**.

3. In **Registry Editor**, navigate to the node:

    My Computer\HKEY_LOCAL_COMPUTER\SOFTWARE\Microsoft\RapPort

4. Right-click the **RapPort** node, and then click **Delete**.

5. In the **Confirm Key Delete** dialog box, click **Yes**.

6. Close Registry Editor.

To restart the server:

1. Wait five minutes to allow IIS to save settings.

2. Restart the server.

To delete the RapPort folder:

1. Open Windows Explorer.

2. Navigate to the **RapPort** folder on the drive on which the Destination server is installed.

3. Right-click the **RapPort** folder, and then click **Delete**.

4. In the **Confirm Folder Delete** dialog box, click **Yes**.

5. Close Windows Explorer.

RapPort Administration and Maintenance

This section describes monitoring methods to ensure proper operation of RapPort. It also provides possible solutions to issues you may encounter.

RapPort uses SharePoint Portal Server as the underlying platform. Therefore, it assumes that an organization deploying and operating RapPort operates and maintains this environment as outlined in *SharePoint Portal Server Administrator's Help* online. This includes backup, monitoring and performance optimization. RapPort does not require any special backup or optimization of the SharePoint Portal Server environment.

This section focuses on monitoring and maintaining the portal provisioning process by addressing the following topics:

- **Monitoring Initial Operations.** This section reviews possible failures caused by improper installation or configuration.

- **Monitoring Daily Operations.** This section reviews daily tasks and monitoring methods to ensure RapPort operates successfully.

- **Diagnosing Request Problems.** This section describes the failures that may occur during the provisioning process, along with detailed troubleshooting and suggested corrective actions.

- **Resolving Problems.** This section provides detailed procedures for restoring the RapPort application to operation after a provisioning failure.

Monitoring Initial Operations

If the first request submitted to RapPort fails, it is likely the result of an error during installation. The following steps provide a list of items to check to confirm proper installation and setup. In addition, these steps can also assist in diagnosing problems in the event of recent modifications to the RapPort server configuration.

To verify RapPort settings:

Check the following items to confirm proper installation and setup. Please refer to the installation instructions for specific settings.

- Confirm that the same domain account is a member of the local Administrator's group for all servers in this deployment. This account should be the same on the RapPort server, the template server, and any destination servers.

- Confirm the existence of the RapPort virtual directory on the RapPort server and each destination server.

- Check that the proxy configuration on the RapPort server and each destination server is in accordance with the installation instructions for RapPort.

- Confirm that all folders are named properly.

- Ensure that the RapPort folder on the RapPort server and each destination server are not set to Read only.

- The Windows 2000 Everyone group should be granted Full Control NTFS permissions to the RapPort folder.

- Ensure that only one instance of Autosetup.exe occurs in Task Manager on the RapPort server.

- Ensure that you provided the common domain account during installation for Autosetup.exe to use on the RapPort server.

    Note This domain account must be a member of the Local Administrator's group on each server in this deployment.

- Confirm that you registered the COM+ package on the RapPort and destination servers using the appropriate domain account.

- Confirm that you assigned the appropriate domain account to the role of coordinator for all workspaces on the template server.

- In Internet Service Manager, ensure that the following folder specifies "Script Only" on the destination server:

    Default Web Site/Share Point Portal Server/Applications

- Ensure that you configured Cscript as the default Windows scripting host on the RapPort server and each destination server.

- Confirm the DLL registration on the RapPort server and each destination server.

For more information about performing these tasks, see "RapPort Installations."

Monitoring Daily Operations

The RapPort application provides information whenever it receives a request or the provisioning status of a server changes. RapPort logs both successes and failures. RapPort records this information in several places:

- **Mails.** All these events generate mail to the Support e-mail, RapPort Support. This mail includes the details of the activity.

- **Windows 2000 Event Viewer.** These events also generate entries in the RapPort application log of each server.

- **RapPort application log.** The RapPort application log of the RapPort server provides an overview of the status of each execution of AutoSetup.

    You can view the log from the following location on the RapPort server.

    Drive:\RapPort\Autosetup\Logs*ApplicationLog*.txt

- **Request Log.** RapPort creates a request log on the RapPort server and each destination server for each portal request. RapPort names this file request *virtual_server_name*.txt. This log provides a detailed status of the portal provisioning process. You can view the request log at the following locations:

    Drive:\RapPort\Autosetup\Logs*virtual_server_name*.txt on the RapPort server

    Drive:\\RapPort\Logs*virtual_server_name*.txt on the destination server.

- **Request File.** RapPort creates a request file containing the user input when a user requests a new portal. The RapPort server modifies this request file with a code indicating the status of the portal provisioning process as the request goes through various stages during provisioning. You can view the file at the following location on the RapPort server:

  Drive:\RapPort\RapPortWeb\Data\UserRequests\userdata_*virtual_server_name*.xml

  After RapPort successfully completes a request, you can view the file at the following location on the RapPort server:

  Drive:\RapPort\RapPortWeb\Data\History\userdata_*virtual_server_name*.xml

The following table describes the status codes stored in the request file:

Status codes in the request file

Code	Definition
0	Request started, not yet completed
1	Request completed
2	Provisioning Process has started
3	Provisioning Process has failed
4	Provisioning Process has succeeded

Although you can find status information in each of these places, it is recommended that you use e-mail messages sent to the RapPort Support as your primary method of monitoring and troubleshooting processes. This section uses e-mail notification as the primary method of monitoring activity.

Status Messages

Each time a user requests a new portal, you should expect RapPort Support to receive three messages.

- **Request Acknowledgement Notification.** The RapPort server sends an e-mail acknowledging the request for a new portal to the person requesting who submitted the request. The RapPort server sends a copy of this e-mail to RapPort Support.

- **Workspace Creation Notification.** RapPort server sends an e-mail acknowledging that it successfully created the workspace to the person who submitted the request. The RapPort server sends a copy of this e-mail to RapPort Support. If the workspace creation fails, the RapPort server notifies RapPort Support so the problem can be resolved and the process completed.

- **Wins/DNS entry requisition.** After successful creating the virtual server, the RapPort server sends an e-mail message to the appropriate account, requesting a virtual server entry in the WINS/DNS table. The RapPort server sends a copy of this e-mail to RapPort Support.

    Note During setup, you must specify an e-mail account to receive WINS/DNS entry requests. This account can be an individual user or group account.

Unavailable Destination Servers

RapPort makes the destination server(s) status as Unavailable under following conditions:

- When a destination server has reached the specified number of workspaces as defined by the capacity in the ServerConfig.xml, it returns a status of "unavailable."

- If the destination server encounters an failure during workspace creation, it returns a status of "unavailable" to prevent attempting to create additional workspaces on that server.

If the RapPort server marks a destination server as unavailable, then no additional workspaces can be created on it until the status changes to "available."

By marking the server "unavailable," RapPort forces the next portal request to skip that server in the selection process, but continues processing portal requests. RapPort sends an e-mail notifying RapPort Support when a server returns a "server unavailable" status. The message includes information explaining the reason for the status. For information about how to reset the status of a server, see "Resolving Problems."

Daily Checks

The RapPort server sends e-mail to the support team, RapPort Support, at the completion of major tasks. The support team should use these e-mail notifications to conduct the daily checks to verify the system is operating properly or as a starting point to diagnose problem section. The following section summarizes possible failures and potential resolutions.

There are effectively four possible states the administrator may encounter in provisioning a site:

- Confirmation Mail Received, Provisioning Successful

- Confirmation Mail Received, Provisioning Failed

- No Confirmation Mail Received

- Server Unavailable Mail Received

In each of these cases, action may be required. The following sections provide a brief overview of each situation followed by detailed troubleshooting guidance for each situation.

Confirmation Mail Received, Provisioning Successful

If RapPort Support receives all three e-mail messages, including the final confirmation mail with a successful status, you can generally assume that RapPort is operating correctly. However, there are some cases where RapPort may have encountered some problems in the process, but they were not considered significant enough to warrant a failure message.

As an example, RapPort may successfully replicate a workspace template but fail to copy a particular document. In this case, the portal provisioning process completed successfully and RapPort Support receives all three e-mail messages but the final workspace may lack some elements. To resolve this issue, you can manually copy the missing information or delete the workspace and restart the portal provisioning process entirely, depending on the specific instance where the failure occurred.

To determine if RapPort failed to copy or create any items, you must examine the RapPort request logs. For detailed instruction on how to check these logs and resolve any issues, see "Verifying Successful Workspace Creation" under "Diagnosing Request Problems."

Confirmation Mail Received, Provisioning Failed

In cases of outright failure, the e-mail message indicates the cause of the failure. For more information about reviewing any associated logs and resolving any issues see "Confirm Failed Workspace Provisioning" under "Diagnosing Request Problems."

No Confirmation Mail Received

If no confirmation mails are received, then you must use the application log to determine status and determine corrective action. For more information about checking this log and resolving any issues see "Review Application Log" under "Diagnosing Request Problems."

Server Unavailable Mail Received

RapPort sends a message notifying RapPort Support when a server is no longer available to accept requests.

If you receive this mail with a corresponding Workspace Failure e-mail message, see "Confirm Failed Workspace Provisioning" under "Diagnosing Request Problems." Once completed then, you can reset the server status. For information about resetting the server status, see "Reset Destination Server Status" under "Resolving Problems."

If you receive this mail without a corresponding Workspace Failure e-mail message, see "Address Maximum Workspace Capacity" under "Resolving Problems."

Diagnosing Request Problems

This section describes how to diagnose and resolve problems encountered in the provisioning process. It is recommended that you view this section in the context of daily monitoring tasks.

Verify Successful Workspace Creation

To verify that RapPort successfully created a workspace, you must review the request logs. These logs exist on both the RapPort server and the destination server. Scan the request logs for any of the errors or keywords listed below and take the suggested corrective actions.

RapPort names this file request *virtual_server_name*.txt. You can view the request log at the following locations:

Drive:\RapPort\Autosetup\Logs*virtual_server_name*.txt on the RapPort server

Drive:\\RapPort\Logs*virtual_server_name*.txt on the destination server.

To determine the destination server, open the userdata_*virtual_server_name*.xml file in the history folder on the RapPort server and look for the name in the <server> tag.

Keywords: Error, Failed, Permission Denied, 404, 409, 403, 401, unauthorized, timed out, access denied, unable Unauthorized, Timed Out, Access Denied, Unable

Location. *virtual_server_name*.txt on the RapPort server, anywhere in section 4 through 14.

If the item on which the failure occurred is a document, URL link or a shortcut:

1. Copy the item manually from the workspace template into the new workspace.

2. Manually update all the properties associated with the item.

If the item on which the failure occurred is not a document:

1. Create the item manually in the new workspace.

2. Establish any required relationships or associations. For example, if RapPort fails to copy a document profile, then you must create it manually and update the metadata of all documents that are associated with this profile.

Error: Warning!! Unexpected Content Class found

Location. *virtual_server_name*.txt on the RapPort server, section 12.

This indicates that RapPort failed to copy a document or set of documents. To resolve this, perform the following steps:

1. Locate the name of the document in the <source href> portion of the error message in the request log.

2. Copy this document manually from the workspace template to the new workspace.

3. Manually update all the properties associated with the item.

Error: Unable to Create Default.asp file for Redirection.

Location. *virtual_server_name*.txt on the destination server.

RapPort did not create the page, default.asp, used to redirect the virtual server. You must create it manually by performing the following steps:

1. Create a folder with the same name as that of the request URL under
   <Drive>:\RapPort\VirtualServers folder on the destination server and create a new file, called **default.asp**, inside it.

2. Edit this file and put following content in it:

   ```
   <% @Language = "VBScript" %>

   <% Response.Redirect "/workspace_name"%>
   ```

   where *workspace_name* is the name of the workspace.

3. Save the file.

Error: Unable to Enable Discussions On Virtual Server

Location. *virtual_server_name*.txt on the destination server.

If you find this message in the request log, then you must manually enable discussions for that virtual server. For more information about how to enable discussions, see Chapter 12, "Deploying SharePoint Portal Server in an Extranet Environment."

Confirm Failed Workspace Provisioning

When RapPort fails to provision a workspace, RapPort Support receives an e-mail message that indicates the request failed and provides a description of the failure. This sections lists these error messages, the appropriate log and location within the log where you can find additional information. It also provides procedures for diagnosing and resolving the underlying problem.

Error: Creation Of Template Instantiation Component (Tempinst.dll) Failed

Location. *virtual_server_name*.txt on the RapPort server.

Verify that the RapPort COM+ application is properly installed on the RapPort server. If this is not properly installed, then remove and reinstall the COM+ application. If you still receive this error message, remove and reinstall the RapPort server. For more information about removing and reinstalling RapPort, see "Removing RapPort."

To verify the RapPort COM+ application:

1. On the RapPort server, using COM Application Explorer, verify that the RapPort COM+ application package is running under the correct user name and password. To do this, see "To create a new COM+ application."

2. If it is not, edit the COM+ application package properties to enter the appropriate user name and password.

3. Reprocess the request. See "If the Request Failed During the Copy Process, Roles Assignment, or Virtual Server Creation."

If the preceding procedure does not solve the problem, then remove and reinstall the COM+ DLLs by executing the following procedures:

To remove and reinstall the COM+ DLLs:

1. Perform the following procedures:

   - "To delete the RapPort DLLs" under "Removing RapPort."

   - "To create a new COM+ application" under "Install the RapPort Server."

   - "To add components to the new (RapPort) COM+ application" under "Install the RapPort Server."

2. Restart the computer.

3. Reprocess the request as described in "If The Request Failed During The Copy Process, Roles Assignment, Or Virtual Server Creation."

If the previous step does not solve the problem, then remove and reinstall the RapPort server according to the following procedures:

To remove and reinstall the RapPort server:

4. Remove the RapPort server according to the procedure "Removing RapPort."

5. Reinstall the RapPort server according to the procedure "Installing the RapPort Server."

6. Reprocess the request as described in "If The Request Failed During The Copy Process, Roles Assignment, or Virtual Server Creation."

Error: Server Has Been Marked Unavailable As Capacity Is Exhausted

Error: Workspace Capacity On This Server Has Been Reached

Location. *virtual_server_name*.txt on the RapPort server, section 3.

This message indicates that the number of workspaces on this destination server has reached the specified capacity in ServerConfig.xml. To resolve this problem, see "Address Maximum Workspace Capacity." Upon resolving the capacity problem, reset the server status to available. For more information, see "Reset Destination Server Status."

Error: No Server Is Available

Location. *ApplicationLog*.txt on the RapPort server, section 3.

Reprocess this request once you add additional server capacity. To reprocess the request, see "If The Request Fails When No Destination Server Is Available For Request Processing."

Error: Rapport Virtual Directory Is Not Hosted On The Destination Server Or The Required Page (Createworkspace.asp) Is Not Found In The Rapport Virtual Directory

Error: Generation Of Copy Script For Application Folder(s) Copy Failed

Location. *ApplicationLog*.txt on the RapPort server, section 3.

Perform the following steps on the destination server:

1. Verify that IIS is running on the destination server. If not, start IIS.

2. Verify that the RapPort virtual directory is properly configured on the destination server by using the Internet Services Manager. For more information, see "To create a virtual directory for the destination server."

3. Verify that the CreateWorkspace.asp page is present. For more information, see "To copy destination server files."

4. Check network connectivity by pinging the destination server from the RapPort server.

5. Set the server as available. For more information, see "Reset Destination Server Status."

6. Reprocess the request by completing the steps described in "If The Request Fails When The Destination Server On Which The Request Is Being Processed Gets Marked As Unavailable."

Error: Copy ScriptApplication FolderRapPort DLL (RemoteWS.dll) is not Registered on the Destination ServerScript Failed

Location. Failure e-mail messages.

Perform the following procedures on the destination server:

1. Check the COM+ application settings, then try removing and reinstalling the COM+ packages. Finally, remove and reinstall the destination server.

2. Using the COM Application Explorer, check that the RapPort COM+ application package is running under the correct user name and password. For more information, see "To create a new COM+ application."

3. If the application package is not running under the correct user name and password, edit the COM+ application package properties to enter the appropriate user name and password.

4. Set the server as available, see "Reset Destination Server Status."

5. Reprocess the request. See "If The Request Fails When The Destination Server On Which The Request Is Being Processed Gets Marked As Unavailable."

6. If the previous step does not solve the problem, remove and reinstall the DLLs on the destination server, by performing the following procedures:

   - "To delete the RapPort COM+ application" under "Removing the Destination Server."

   - "To unregister the RapPort DLLs" under "Removing the Destination Server."

   - "To register the RapPort DLLs" under "Removing the Destination Server."

   - "To create a new COM+ application" under "Removing the Destination Server."

7. Restart the destination server.

8. Set the server as available by referring to "Resolving Problems: Reset Destination Server Status."

9. Reprocess the request by completing the steps described in "If The Request Fails When The Destination Server On Which The Request Is Being Processed Gets Marked As Unavailable."

10. If the previous step does not solve the problem, then remove and reinstall the destination server according to the following procedures:

    "Remove the Destination Server"

    "Install the Destination Server"

11. Set the server as available, see "Reset Destination Server Status."

12. Reprocess the request, see "If The Request Fails When The Destination Server On Which The Request Is Being Processed Gets Marked As Unavailable."

Error: Copy ScriptSharePoint Portal Server Not Installed on the Destination ServerCategory Failed

Location. E-mail messages only.

Perform the following procedures on the destination server:

1. Check that SharePoint Portal Server is installed on the destination server, and the following registry key exists in the registry of the destination server: "HKEY_LOCAL_COMPUTER\SOFTWARE\Microsoft\SharePoint Portal Server\InstallPath". If not, then remove SharePoint Portal Server and reinstall SharePoint Portal Server.

2. Set the server as available. See "Reset Destination Server Status."

3. Reprocess the request. See "If The Request Fails When The Destination Server On Which The Request Is Being Processed Gets Marked As Unavailable."

Error: Workspace Creation Failed

Location. *virtual_server_name*.txt on the RapPort server, section 1.2.

Perform the following steps on the destination server:

1. Check whether the following services are running on the destination server:

   - W3SVC

   - Msdmserv

   - MSExchangeIS

   - MSSearch

2. If one of the services is not running, start the appropriate service.

3. Check whether SharePoint Portal Server on the destination server is accessible by using SharePoint Portal Server Administration. If it is not accessible, see *SharePoint Portal Server Administrator's Help* online.

4. Set the server as available, see "Reset Destination Server Status."

5. Reprocess the request, see "If The Request Has Failed During Workspace Creation."

Error: Assignment of Common Administrator as Workspace Coordinator Failed on the Server

Error: Execution Permission Setting on Application Folder Failed on the Server

Location. *virtual_server_name*.txt on the RapPort server, section 1.2

Perform the following steps on the destination server:

1. Check whether SharePoint Portal Server on the destination server is accessible by using SharePoint Portal Server Administration. If it is not accessible, see *SharePoint Portal Server Administrator's Help*.

2. Set the server as available, see "Reset Destination Server Status."

3. Reprocess the request, see "If The Request Has Failed After Workspace Has Been Created But Before Copy Is Instantiated."

Error: Virtual Server Creation Failed

Location. *virtual_server_name*.txt on the RapPort server, section 17.2.

Perform the following steps:

1. Check whether IIS is running on the destination server. If it is not running, start IIS.

2. Check that the RapPort virtual directory is properly configured on the destination server by using the Internet Services Manager. See "To create new virtual directory in default web site."

3. Check that the CreateVirtualServer.asp page is present. See "To copy destination server files."

4. Check network connectivity by pinging the destination server from the RapPort server.

5. Reprocess the request. See "If The Request Failed During The Copy Process, Roles Assignment, or Virtual Server Creation."

Error: Error Loading User Request Xml on Destination Server

Location. E-mail messages only.

Perform the following steps.

1. Set the server as available. See "Reset Destination Server Status."

2. Reprocess the request. See "If The Request Fails When No Destination Server Is Available For Request Processing."

Error: Error in the Response from Destination Server

Location. E-mail messages only.

Perform the following steps.

1. Check if IIS is running on destination server. If not start IIS.

2. Check whether the following services are running on the destination server:

   - W3SVC

   - Msdmserv

   - MSExchangeIS

   - MSSearch

3. If one of the services is not running, start the appropriate service.

4. Check whether SharePoint Portal Server on the destination server is accessible by using SharePoint Portal Server Administration. If it is not accessible, see *SharePoint Portal Server Administrator's Help* online.

5. Verify network connectivity by pinging the destination server from the RapPort server, by using the server name.

6. Set the server as available. See "Reset Destination Server Status."

7. Reprocess the request. See "If The Request Has Failed During Workspace Creation."

Error: Copy ScriptFolderWorkspace Creation Request to Destination Server Timed OutFailed

Location. *virtual_server_name*.txt on the RapPort server, section 1.2.

Perform the following steps.

1. Change the ReceiveTime value in the Constants.xml file by increasing it to an appropriate value. Try various configurations to determine the optimal setting. To change the value, see "To modify time-out settings."

3. Change the ASP script time-out settings on the RapPort virtual directory on the destination server to a number greater than or equal to the ReceiveTime set in the step above. To change this value, see "To modify ASP Script time-out."

4. Set the server as available. See "Reset Destination Server Status."

5. Reprocess the request as described under "If The Request Fails When The Destination Server On Which The Request Is Being Processed Gets Marked As Unavailable."

Error: Server Name Or The IP Address Could Not Be Resolved

Error: Server Connection Could Not Be Established

Location. *virtual_server_name*.txt on the RapPort server, section 1.2 or 17.2.

Perform the following steps.

1. Verify network connectivity by pinging the destination server from the RapPort server, by using the server name.

2. Verify the network connectivity and registry entries by pinging the destination server from the RapPort server by using the IP address set in the destination server registry key:

    HKLM\software\Microsoft\RapPort

3. Check whether IIS is running on the destination server. Restart IIS if it is not running.

4. Set the server as available. See "Reset Destination Server Status."

5. Reprocess the request as described under "If The Request Fails When The Destination Server On Which The Request Is Being Processed Gets Marked As Unavailable."

Error: Server Name Or IP Address Could Not Be Resolved While Creating Virtual Server

Error: Failed To Get IP Address From

Location. *virtual_server_name*.txt on the RapPort server, section 17.2.

Perform the following steps.

1. Verify network connectivity by pinging the destination server from the RapPort server, by using the server name.

2. Verify the network connectivity and registry entries by pinging the destination server from the RapPort server by using the IP address set in the destination server registry key:

    HKLM\software\Microsoft\RapPort

3. Check whether IIS is running on the destination server. Restart IIS if it is not running.

4. Reprocess the request, see "If The Request Failed During The Copy Process, Roles Assignment, or Virtual Server Creation."

Error: IIS Reset Failed On

Error: Reset IIS Failed

Location. *ApplicationLog*.txt on the RapPort server, section 4.

Perform the following steps on the destination server on which the request is being processed.

1. Wait for 5 minutes.

2. Restart IIS on the destination server.

3. Open todaysServer.xml on the RapPort server in Notepad.

4. Delete the XML node for this destination server from this todaysServer.xml.

5. Save the file.

Error: Workspace Coordinator(s) Role Assignment Failed

Error: Workspace Author(s) Role Assignment Failed

Location. *virtual_server_name*.txt on the RapPort server, section 15.

Perform the following steps.

1. Check whether SharePoint Portal Server on the destination server is accessible by using the SharePoint Portal Server Administration. If not it is not accessible, see *SharePoint Portal Server Administrator's Help* online.

2. Reprocess the request. See "If The Request Failed During The Copy Process, Roles Assignment, or Virtual Server Creation."

Error: Rapport Registry Key Path Not Found

Location. *ApplicationLog*.txt on the RapPort server, section 4.

1. From the RapPort server, on the **Start** Menu, click **Run**.

2. Type **regedit** and then click **OK**.

3. In **Registry Editor**, navigate to the node:

> **Caution** Incorrectly editing the registry may severely damage your system. Back up the current version of the registry before making any changes. You should also back up any valued data on the computer.

4. Expand HKLM\Software\Microsoft key and check whether the RapPort key exists under it. If it exists, delete and re-create this key. See "To import the RapPort server registry entries."

5. Reprocess the request. See "If The Request Fails When Destination Server On Which The Request Is Being Processed Gets Marked As Unavailable."

Error: Error While Saving File

Location. *virtual_server_name*.txt on the RapPort server or *ApplicationLog*.txt on the RapPort server.

This message indicates that RapPort cannot save one of the XML files typically because the XML files were left as read-only during installation. Perform the following steps.

1. Check that file permissions on RapPort server are **not** read-only, see "To remove the read-only attributes for the files" under "Install the RapPort Server."

2. Check that file permissions on the destination server are **not** read-only, see "To remove the read-only attributes for the files" under "Install the Destination Server."

3. Reprocess the request, see "Restart a Portal Provisioning Request."

Error: Folder Not Found

Error: Error Occurred In Opening Folder

Error: File Not Found

Location. *virtual_server_name*.txt on the RapPort server or *ApplicationLog*.txt on the RapPort server.

One of the folders required by AutoSetup is missing. You must remove and reinstall the RapPort server. Perform the following procedures:

- "Removing RapPort server"

- "Install the RapPort server"

Open completion of the procedures listed above, resubmit the site request.

Error: Invalid Common Administrator Account

Location. *ApplicationLog*.txt on the RapPort server, section 1.

Perform the following steps.

1. Check whether the following registry key exists on the RapPort server:

    HKLM\software\Microsoft\RapPort\CommonAdmin

For more information, see "To verify registry entries have been successfully imported."

Caution Incorrectly editing the registry may severely damage your system. Back up the current version of the registry before making any changes. You should also back up any valued data on the computer.

2. Check whether the user name value in this key is still a valid Windows NT domain account.

3. Reschedule Autosetup.exe to run again.

Error: Error In Parsing Xml

Error: Invalid ServerConfig.xml File

Location. *virtual_server_name*.txt on the RapPort server or *ApplicationLog*.txt on the RapPort server, sections 1.7–1.9, 3.

This error may occur in the event that a configuration file was recently modified and not edited correctly. The error message indicates the name of the XML file that is causing the problem. Perform the following steps.

1. Check the file by opening it in Internet Explorer. Internet Explorer uses its built-in XML parser to analyze XML content and report errors.

2. Correct any problems with the XML file. For more information, see "Customizing Configuration Settings."

3. Check the XML file by opening it in Internet Explorer again.

4. Reschedule Autosetup.exe to run again.

Error: Error Occurred In Sending Rapport E-Mail

Location. *ApplicationLog*.txt on the RapPort server, section 3.

Confirm that the SMTP information and settings in mails.xml are correct. Perform the following steps:

1. Open the file, mails.xml, in Internet Explorer. Internet Explorer uses its built-in XML parser to analyze XML content and report errors.

2. Correct any problems with file, mails.xml. For more information, see "To edit Mails.xml."

3. Check that the SMTP server name specified is correct.

4. Check that the e-mail user names are valid user names.

5. Check that the SMTP server is properly configured. See "To configure the default SMTP virtual server."

6. Check that the SMTP server is actually running by checking with the local operations team.

7. Check the request status. View section 3 of the application log to determine the request status and pertinent error message.

   If the request was successful, send the appropriate confirmation mail to the person who requested the site and RapPort Support. Send the WINS/DNS entry request to the appropriate e-mail account.

   If the request failed, send the appropriate e-mail to RapPort Support indicating the failure and the error message recorded in the application log. Treat this as a standard failure mail, and troubleshoot accordingly.

Error: Error Occurred In Initializing Rapport E-Mail Service

Location. *ApplicationLog*.txt on the RapPort server, section 3.

Confirm that the SMTP information and settings in mails.xml are correct. Perform the following steps:

1. Open the file, mails.xml, in Internet Explorer. Internet Explorer uses its built-in XML parser to analyze XML content and report errors.

2. Correct any problems with file, mails.xml. For more information, see "To edit Mails.xml."

3. Check that the SMTP server name specified is correct.

4. Check that the e-mail user names are valid user names.

5. Check that the SMTP server is properly configured, see "To configure the default SMTP virtual server."

6. Check that the SMTP server is actually running by checking with local operations team.

7. Reschedule Autosetup.exe to run again.

Error: Dedicated Server Unavailable

Location. *ApplicationLog*.txt on the RapPort server, section 3.

This message indicates that the dedicated server against which the request was being processed has been marked as unavailable by the RapPort application. First you must determine the reason for the failure. The reason determines the corrective action you must perform.

To determine the cause of a status "Unavailable":

1. On the RapPort server, open ServerConfig.xml by using Internet Explorer.

2. Locate the <entry></entry> node for the affected destination server.

3. The text in the <comment></comment> provides the reason for the failure. Locate this cause in the following sections and follow the correctives steps provided.

Reason: Rapport Virtual Directory Is Not Hosted On The Destination Server Or The Required Page (Createworkspace.asp) Is Not Found In The Rapport Virtual Directory

1. Check whether IIS is running on the destination server. If it is not running, start IIS.

2. Using the Internet Services Manager, check that the RapPort virtual directory is properly configured on the destination server. For more information, see "To create a virtual directory for the destination sever."

3. Check that the CreateWorkspace.asp page is present, see "To copy destination server files."

4. Check network connectivity by pinging the destination server from the RapPort server.

5. Set the server as available, see "Reset Destination Server Status."

6. Reprocess the request, see "If The Request Fails When Destination Server On Which The Request Is Being Processed Gets Marked As Unavailable."

Reason: Workspace Creation Failed

1. Check whether the following services are running on the destination server:

   - W3SVC

   - Msdmserv

   - MSExchangeIS

   - MSSearch

2. If one of the services is not running, start the appropriate service.

3. Check whether SharePoint Portal Server on the destination server is accessible by using the SharePoint Portal Server Administration. If it is not accessible, see *SharePoint Portal Server Administrator's Help* online.

4. Check that remoteWS.DLL is properly registered on the destination server. For more information, see "To register the RapPort DLLs."

5. Check that Createworkspace.asp exists on the destination server. See "To copy destination server files."

6. Set the server as available. See "Reset destination server Status."

7. Reprocess the request. See "Restart a Portal Provisioning Request: If the request has failed during workspace creation."

Reason: Binding To Folder Using SharePoint Portal Server Software Development Kit (SDK) Failed

1. Check whether the following services are running on the destination server:

   - W3SVC

   - Msdmserv

   - MSExchangeIS

   - MSSearch

2. If one of the services is not running, start the appropriate service.

3. Check whether SharePoint Portal Server on the destination server is accessible by using the SharePoint Portal Server ADMINISTRATION. If it is not accessible, follow the appropriate troubleshooting guidance in *SharePoint Portal Server Administrator's Help* online.

4. Set the server as available, see "Reset Destination Server Status"

5. Reprocess the request, see "Restart a Portal Provisioning Request: If the request has failed after workspace has been created but before copy is instantiated."

Reason: Attempt To Restart SharePoint Portal Server And Other Services Failed

Perform the following steps on the destination server on which the request is being processed:

1. Restart services manually on the destination server. To do this run the following commands on the destination server in the order given below from a command prompt:

```
net stop w3svc

net stop msdmserv

net stop msexchangeIS

net stop mssearch

net start mssearch

net start msexchangeIS

net start msdmserv

net start w3svc
```

2. Check the Windows NT event viewer application log to identify the possible causes of the service(s) failing to start.

3. Check whether SharePoint Portal Server on the destination server is accessible by using SharePoint Portal Server Administration. If it is not accessible, see *SharePoint Portal Server Administrator's Help*.

4. Set the server as available, see "Reset destination server Status."

5. Reprocess the request as specified under "If The Request Has Failed After Workspace Has Been Created But Before Copy Is Instantiated."

Reason: Rapport DLL (Remotews.dll) Is Not Registered On The Destination Server

Perform the following steps on the destination server on which the request is being processed:

1. Check that the RapPort COM+ application package is running under the correct user name and password by using the COM Application Explorer as specified under "To create a new COM+ application."

2. If it is not, edit the COM+ application package properties to enter the appropriate user name and password.

3. Set the server as available as specified under "Reset Destination Server Status."

4. Reprocess the request as specified under "If The Request Fails When Destination Server On Which The Request Is Being Processed Gets Marked As Unavailable."

5. If the previous steps do not solve the problem, then remove and reinstall the DLLs on the destination server, by executing the following procedures:

   - "To delete the RapPort COM+ application"

   - "To unregister the RapPort DLLs"

   - "To register the RapPort DLLs"

   - "To create a new COM+ application"

6. Restart the destination server computer.

7. Set the server as available as specified under "Reset Destination Server Status."

8. Reprocess the request as specified under "Restart a Portal Provisioning Request: If the request fails when destination server on which the request is being processed gets marked as unavailable."

9. If the previous steps do not solve the problem, then uninstall and reinstall the destination server:

   - "Remove the Destination Server"

   - "Install the Destination Server"

10. Set the server as available as specified under "Reset Destination Server Status."

11. Reprocess the request as specified under "If The Request Fails When Destination Server On Which The Request Is Being Processed Gets Marked As Unavailable."

Reason: SharePoint Portal Server Not Installed On The Destination Server

Perform the following steps on the destination server on which the request is being processed:

1. Ensure that SharePoint Portal Server is installed on the destination server, and that the following registry key exists in the registry of the destination server:

   HKEY_LOCAL_COMPUTER\SOFTWARE\Microsoft\SharePoint Portal Server\InstallPath

2. If it is not installed, remove SharePoint Portal Server and reinstall SharePoint Portal Server.

3. Set the server as available. For more information, see "Reset Destination Server Status."

4. Reprocess the request. For more information, see "If The Request Fails When The Destination Server On Which The Request Is Being Processed Gets Marked As Unavailable."

Reason: Error Loading User Request Xml On Destination Server

1. Open the userdata_*virtual_server_name*.xml file by opening it in Internet Explorer. Internet Explorer uses its built-in XML parser to analyze XML content and report errors.

2. Set the server as available, see "Reset Destination Server Status."

3. Reprocess the request, see "Restart a Portal Provisioning Request: If the request fails when the destination server on which the request is being processed gets marked as unavailable."

Reason: Workspace Creation Request To Destination Server Timed Out

Perform the following steps on the destination server:

1. Change the RecieveTime value in the Constants.xml file by increasing it to an appropriate value. Try various configurations to determine the optimal setting. To change the value, see "To modify time-out settings."

2. Change the ASP script time-out settings on the RapPort virtual directory on the destination server to a number greater than or equal to the RecieveTime set in the step above. To change this value, see "To modify ASP Script time-out."

3. Set the server as available. See "Reset Destination Server Status."

4. Reprocess the request as described under "If The Request Fails When The Destination Server On Which The Request Is Being Processed Gets Marked As Unavailable."

Reason: Server Name Or The IP Address Could Not Be Resolved

Reason: Server Connection Could Not Be Established

Perform the following steps on the destination server:

1. Verify network connectivity by pinging the destination server from the RapPort server, by using the name of the server.

2. Verify the network connectivity and registry entries by pinging the destination server from the RapPort server by using the IP address set in the destination server registry key HKLM\software\Microsoft\RapPort.

3. Check whether IIS is running on the destination server. If it is not running, restart IIS.

4. Set the server as available. See "Reset Destination Server Status."

5. Reprocess the request as specified under "If The Request Fails When The Destination Server On Which The Request Is Being Processed Gets Marked As Unavailable."

Reason: Assignment Of Common Administrator As Workspace Coordinator Failed On The Server

Reason: Execution Permission Setting On Application Folder Failed On The Server

Perform the following steps on the destination server on which the request is being processed:

1. Check whether IIS is running on the destination server. If it is not running, restart IIS.

2. Check whether SharePoint Portal Server on the destination server is accessible by using the SharePoint Portal Server Administration. If it is not accessible, see *SharePoint Portal Server Administrator's Help*.

3. Set the server as available as specified under "Reset Destination Server Status."

4. Reprocess the request as specified under "If The Request Has Failed After Workspace Has Been Created But Before Copy Is Instantiated."

All Other Error Messages

Reprocess the request by completing the steps described in the following section: "If The Request Failed During The Copy Process, Roles Assignment, or Virtual Server Creation."

Review Application Log

If you suspect that RapPort has completed a request but did not send an e-mail confirming the request, either success or failure, then you can review the application log on the RapPort server to confirm the status of the request. The application log shows the status of any processed requests and indicates any failures that may have occurred.

The following procedure describes how to check the application log for errors. If you do not find an error and the site request was successful then you must manually send the confirmation e-mail message and WINS/DNS request.

To determine the status of a request:

1. Open the **RapPort application log** and scroll to the end of the log file.

2. Search for the last occurrence of the text string "Starting RapPort AutoSetup" and check the date and time prefixed to it. This date and time should correspond to the **Scheduled Task** for AutoSetup.

   Note To access Scheduled Tasks, on the **Start** menu, point to **Settings**, and then click **Control Panel**. Double-click **Scheduled Tasks**.

3. If the date and time do not correspond, verify the last time AutoSetup executed from **Scheduled Tasks**. If **Last Run Time** does not correspond to the time under **Schedule**, this implies that **AutoSetup** did not execute at the appropriate time.

4. Confirm that you have added **AutoSetup** as a **Scheduled Task**. Specify a new time to process the requests for new portals.

5. If the **Scheduled Task** successfully occurred and there are no corresponding entries in the **RapPort application log**, then the RapPort server is not installed properly.

6. Remove RapPort from the server. For more information about how to do this, see "Removing RapPort."

7. Reinstall the RapPort server. For more information about how to do this, see "Install the RapPort Server."

8. If the last occurrence of the text string "Starting RapPort AutoSetup" has the correct date and time prefixed to it then look for messages in the RapPort application log. For more information, see "Daily Checks" for possible solutions.

9. Search by name for current request file, for example, userdata_*workspace_name*.xml, in the RapPort application log.

   Look for the corresponding string "RapPort Request: *virtual_server_name*", where *virtual_server_name* is the name of the requested portal. Verify the status of the request as success or failed.

10. If the request succeeds, see "Verifying Workspace Creation Successful."

11. If the request fails, see "Workspace Provisioning Failed."

12. If there is no corresponding "RapPort Request: *workspace_name*" string for the current request, then it implies that AutoSetup is unable to complete the request.

13. Restart the server.

14. Follow steps to restart the portal request. For more information, see "Restarting a Portal Request."

The following section discusses possible resolutions based on specific failure messages in the applications log. This section contains a list of keywords or error messages, the log location, and possible resolutions.

Error: Invalid Common Administrator account

Location. *ApplicationLog*.txt on the RapPort server, section 1.

Perform the following steps.

1. Check whether the registry key HKLM\software\Microsoft\RapPort\CommonAdmin exists on the RapPort server. See "To verify Registry Entries have been successfully imported."

    Caution Incorrectly editing the registry may severely damage your system. Back up the current version of the registry before making any changes. You should also back up any valued data on the computer.

2. Check whether the user name value in this key is still a valid Windows NT domain account.

3. Reschedule AutoSetup to run again.

Error: Folder Not Found

Error: File Not Found

Location. *ApplicationLog*.txt on the RapPort server.

One of the folders required by AutoSetup process is missing. Remove and reinstall the RapPort server as described below:

• "Removing RapPort"

• "Install the RapPort server"

• Reprocess the request, see "Restart a Portal Provisioning Request." The specific procedure depends on the step where this error occurred. For example, if this error occurred during workspace creation, see "If the request has failed during workspace creation."

Error: Error In Parsing XML

Error: Invalid ServerConfig.xml File

Location. *ApplicationLog*.txt on the RapPort server, sections 1.7–9, 3, 4.

This error may occur if a configuration file was recently modified and not edited correctly. The error message indicates the name of the file that is causing the problem.

Perform the following steps.

1. Check that file by opening that file in Internet Explorer. Internet Explorer uses its built-in XML parser to analyze XML content and report errors.

2. Correct any problems in the XML file by editing as directed by the original procedure or see the section, "RapPort Administration and Maintenance" for detailed editing instructions.

3. Check the XML file again by using Internet Explorer.

4. Reschedule AutoSetup to run again.

Error: Error Occurred In Initializing Rapport E-Mail Service

Location. *ApplicationLog*.txt on the RapPort server, section 3.

Confirm that the SMTP information and settings in mails.xml are correct by performing the following steps:

1. Open the file, mails.xml, in Internet Explorer. Internet Explorer uses its built-in XML parser to analyze XML content and report errors.

2. Correct any problems with file, mails.xml, by editing as directed in "To edit Mails.xml."

3. Check that the SMTP server name specified is correct.

4. Check that the e-mail user names are valid user names.

5. Check that the SMTP server is properly configured. For detailed procedures, see "To configure the default SMTP virtual server."

6. Check that the SMTP server is actually running by checking with local operations team.

7. Reschedule AutoSetup to run again.

Error: Error Occurred In Sending Rapport E-Mail

Location. *ApplicationLog*.txt on the RapPort server, section 3.

Confirm that the SMTP information and settings in mails.xml are correct by performing the following steps:

1. Open the file, mails.xml, in Internet Explorer. Internet Explorer uses its built-in XML parser to analyze XML content and report errors.

2. Correct any problems with file, mails.xml, by editing as directed in the "To edit Mails.xml."

3. Check that the SMTP server name specified is correct.

4. Check that the e-mail user names are valid user names.

5. Check that the SMTP server is properly configured. See "To configure the default SMTP virtual server."

6. Check that the SMTP server is actually running by checking with the local operations team.

7. Check the request status. View section 3 of the application log to determine the request status and pertinent error message.

8. If the request was successful, send the appropriate confirmation mail to the person who requested the site and RapPort Support. Send the WINS/DNS entry request to the appropriate e-mail account.

9. If the request failed, send the appropriate e-mail to RapPort Support indicating the failure and the error message recorded in the application log. Treat this as a standard failure mail, and troubleshoot accordingly.

Resolving Problems

This section provides procedures to correct RapPort in the event of a failure. It is recommended that you view this section in the context of daily monitoring tasks and diagnosing problems.

View the RapPort Server Configuration

The RapPort application maintains all configuration information in XML files on the RapPort server. These files are in the following directory on the RapPort server:

Drive:\RapPort\AutoSetup\Configuration folder

In many instances after correcting a failure, you must edit one of these files. The following sections describe when, where and how to edit these files to recover from a failure.

Address Maximum Workspace Capacity

When a destination server has reached the specified number of workspaces, it returns a status of unavailable. After a destination server has reached its capacity for workspaces, you have two options. You can increase the limit or you can add additional destination server. Both options require modifying your RapPort configuration.

To extend the capacity of a server:

Using Notepad, open ServerConfig.xml and revise it as follows.

1. Locate the <entry></entry> XML node for this destination server in the file.

2. Within this node, edit the <available>**n**</available> XML node and change the **n** to **y** (<available>**y**</available>), to mark this destination server as available for further workspace creation on it.

   Note The XML tag <available></available> denotes the availability status of each destination server. RapPort marks a destination server as "**y**" in the <available> tag provided it can successfully create workspaces.

3. Within the same <entry></entry> node for the destination server, clear the text within the <comment><comment> node. This clears the reason for the unavailable status.

4. Within the same <entry></entry> node for the destination server, edit the text in the <capacity></capacity> node and replace the text within this node by an appropriate value increased value for the workspace capacity for this destination server depending on the available disk space and other criteria as appropriate.

To add new capacity by adding a new destination server:

1. Leave the availability status and capacity of the current destination server at its current values. This server is no longer available for processing requests.

2. Add an entry for a new destination server in ServerConfig.xml. For more information about how to do this, see "Customizing Configuration Settings."

Reset Destination Server Status

After you resolve the underlying cause for a destination server marked as unavailable, you must reset the status to available.

The following procedure describes how to reset the status of a destination server to available.

To reset the status of a destination server:

Using Notepad, open ServerConfig.xml and revise it as follows.

1. Locate the <entry></entry> XML node for this destination server in the XML file.

2. Within this node, edit the <available>**n**</available> XML node and change the **n** to **y** (<available>**y**</available>), to mark this destination server as available for further workspace creation on it.

   Note The XML tag <available></available> denotes the availability status of each destination server. RapPort marks a destination server as "**y**" in the <available> tag provided it can successfully create workspaces.

3. Within the same <entry></entry> node for the destination server, clear the text within the <comment><comment> node. This clears the reason for the unavailable status.

Delete a Workspace and Associated Settings

In some cases RapPort partially completes a request and then fails. In this case, it may be necessary to remove the failed workspace, so that you can process the request again and create the workspace with the proper name.

Perform the following procedures to delete the registry entries associated with discussions, the virtual server and then finally the workspace:

   Caution Incorrectly editing the registry may severely damage your system. Back up the current version of the registry before making any changes. You should also back up any valued data on the computer.

To delete a workspace and associated settings:

1. On the **Start** menu, click **Run**.

2. In the **Open** text box**,** type **cmd**.

3. Change **Directory** to the following directory:

   %systemroot%\Inetpub\AdminScripts

4. Determine the registry sequence number associated with the virtual server.

   Note The registry manages the virtual servers by sequence number, not by their English names. To determine the sequence number, issue the following command:

   cscript adsutil.vbs enum W3SVC/1

   This returns the name of the first virtual server. Repeat this command incrementing the value (initially "1") until the correct virtual server displays. Note this sequence number as you need it in step 7.

5. Close the Command Prompt.

6. Edit the registry by using **Registry Editor**.

   Caution Incorrectly editing the registry may severely damage your system. Back up the current version of the registry before making any changes. You should also back up any valued data on the computer.

7. Expand the following key:

   HKEY_LOCAL_COMPUTER/SOFTWARE/MICROSOFT/Office/9.0/Web Server/*Number*, where *Number* is the value of the sequence number noted above.

8. Delete this key from the registry.

9. Close Registry Editor.

10. Delete the virtual server by using **Internet Services Manager**.

11. Wait for 5 minutes and then restart IIS.

12. After IIS has successfully restarted, delete the associated workspace by using the SharePoint Portal Administration.

Restart a Portal Provisioning Request

After you resolve a problem stopping RapPort from completing a request for a new portal, you can restart the provisioning process. The following sections review the possible causes and describe how to restart the provisioning process, as this process varies according to the type of failure.

If The Request Has Failed During Workspace Creation:

1. Using SharePoint Portal Server Administration, delete the workspace on the destination server if it exists.

2. In Notepad, open the corresponding request file, userdata_*virtual_server_name*.xml, on the RapPort server and change the request status XML node to "1" (completed request).

3. Save the request file.

4. Double-click the file to open it in Internet Explorer to confirm that the XML formatting is correct. Internet Explorer should display the file without any errors.

5. Follow the steps to change destination server status to available. For more information, see "Reset Destination Server Status."

The RapPort server processes the request the next time AutoSetup runs as a Scheduled Task.

If The Request Has Failed After Workspace Has Been Created But Before Copy Is Instantiated:

1. In SharePoint Portal Server Administration, delete the workspace on the destination server, if it exists.

2. In Notepad, open ServerConfig.xml on the RapPort server and decrement the current workspace count for the destination server within the <current></current> XML node by one. For example, for a given server the Current value may be set to 7, it must be reduced to 6, because the workspace process was started but not successfully completed.

3. Save ServerConfig.xml.

4. In Notepad, open the corresponding request file, userdata_*virtual_server_name*.xml, on the RapPort server and change the request status XML node to "1" (completed request).

5. Save the user request XML file.

6. Double-click the file to open it in Internet Explorer to confirm that the XML formatting is correct. Internet Explorer should display the file without any errors.

7. Follow steps to change destination server status to available. For more information, see "Reset Destination Server Status."

RapPort processes the request the next time AutoSetup runs as a Scheduled Task.

If The Request Failed During The Copy Process, Roles Assignment, Or Virtual Server Creation

1. In SharePoint Portal Server Administration, delete the workspace on the destination server, if it exists.

2. In Notepad, open ServerConfig.xml on the RapPort server and decrement the current workspace count for the destination server within the <current></current> XML node by one. For example, for a given server the Current value may be set to 7, it must be reduced to 6, because the workspace process was started but not successfully completed.

3. Save ServerConfig.xml.

4. In Notepad, open the corresponding request file, userdata_*virtual_server_name*.xml, on the RapPort server and make the following changes:

   - Change the <status> tag to "1" (completed request).

   - Check the request log, *virtual_server_name*.txt, on the RapPort server to determine the server type (Shared or Dedicated). If the server type is Shared then change the <server> tag to "shared."

5. Save the request file.

6. Double-click the file to open it in Internet Explorer to confirm that the XML formatting is correct. Internet Explorer should display the file without any errors.

RapPort processes the request the next time AutoSetup runs as a Scheduled Task.

If The Request Fails When No Destination Server Is Available For Request Processing:

1. Address the capacity limitations of the destination server by either increasing the capacity or adding an additional destination server. For more information, see "Address Maximum Workspace Capacity."

2. Follow steps to change destination server status to available. For more information, see "Reset Destination Server Status."

3. In Notepad, open the corresponding request file, userdata_*virtual_server_name*.xml, on the RapPort server and change the request status XML node to "1" (completed request).

4. Save the request file.

RapPort processes the request the next time AutoSetup runs as a Scheduled Task.

If The Request Fails When The Destination Server On Which The Request Is Being Processed Gets Marked As Unavailable:

1. Follow steps to change destination server status to available. For more information, see "Reset Destination Server Status."

2. In Notepad, open the corresponding request file, userdata_*virtual_server_name*.xml, on the RapPort server and change the request status XML node to "1" (completed request).

3. Save the request file.

RapPort processes the request the next time AutoSetup runs as a Scheduled Task.

If Autosetup.Exe Stops Responding During Request Processing And The Current Request Remains With <Status> = "2" (In Process):

1. Using **Task Manager**, terminate the AutoSetup.exe application.

2. In Notepad, open the corresponding request file, userdata_*virtual_server_name*.xml, on the RapPort server and make the following changes:

   • Change the request status XML node to "1" (completed request).

   • Remove the text, *server_name* from <server>*server_name*</server> XML node.

   Important Do not remove the XML node, only remove the text within the node.

- Remove the complete node <commonadmin></commonadmin>.

  Important Remove the complete node along with the tags, do not remove only the name "Common Admin."

3. Save the request file.

   If copy was in progress and workspace creation was successful when it failed then open ServerConfig.xml on the RapPort server by using Notepad and decrement the current workspace count for the destination server within the <current></current> XML node by one. For example, for a given server the Current value may be set to 7, it must be reduced to 6, because the workspace process was started but not successfully completed.

4. Save ServerConfig.xml.

5. Follow the steps in "Delete a Workspace and Associated Virtual Server" to delete the workspace and the virtual server (if created).

RapPort processes the request the next time AutoSetup runs as a Scheduled Task.

Resolving RapPort Setup Wizard Problems

This section describes errors that may occur when a user requests a new portal by using the RapPort Setup Wizard. This section lists the error messages, possible user action, and suggested resolution. These problems can be organized into two groups.

Non-Critical Errors

These are warnings or errors that may appear in a dialog box to the user when working with the RapPort Wizard. None of these errors are critical to the request process, and most are intermittent. The solution is to simply acknowledge the message and repeat the action, the request then continues. No further troubleshooting is required. These messages are listed as follows:

- An error occurred contacting the server for checking URL availability. Please try again.

- An error occurred contacting the server for saving the request data. Please try again.

- An error occurred contacting the server for deleting the incomplete request data. Please try again.

- An error occurred contacting the server for getting the users/roles data. Please refresh this page to try again.

- An error occurred contacting the server for deleting the incomplete request data. Please try again.

- An error occurred contacting the server for saving the users/roles data. Please try again.

- An error occurred contacting the server for temporary saving of the users/roles data space.

Critical Errors

These errors cause the request process to fail, and consequently the RapPort provisioning process never begins and therefore never creates the workspace. Although there are several errors, only two situations can generate these error messages: The client computer accessing the wizard is missing a component or the server is missing a component. These messages are:

Error: An error occurred creating an MSXML2.DOM Document object. If this occurred after using the **Dedicated Server** dialog box, then the RapPort server is missing the MSXML3.DLL file. This file is installed as part of the SharePoint Portal Server installation.

> **Note** Although the error message reports a problem with MSXML2, the actual problem is with MSXML3.

- Rerun the SharePoint Portal Server installation, and select **Repair**. For more information, see *SharePoint Portal Server Administrator's Help*.

Error: An error occurred checking for URL availability. To resolve this problem, perform the following:

1. Check for the existence of a file named *<virtual_server_name>.txt* in the following directory:

    drive:\RapPort\RapPortWeb\Data\CheckAvailability

2. If it does not exist, using Windows Explorer, check that the Windows 2000 Everyone group is assigned Full permissions on the directory:

    drive:\RapPort\RapPortWeb\Data.

Error: An error occurred creating the MSXML2.ServerXMLHTTP object.
Error: An error occurred creating the MSXML2.XMLHTTP object.
Error: An error occurred creating an MSXML2.DOM Document Object.
The likely cause of these errors is that the client computer is missing the required MSXML3 component. To resolve this problem, perform one of the following actions:

- Install the retail version of Office XP (some Beta versions do not contain the required components).

- Install Office 2000 and MSXML3 SP-1. You can download a copy of MSXML from http://msdn.microsoft.com.

Summary

This chapter presents a technical overview of the RapPort deployment application. It reviews the portal provisions process. In addition, this chapter provides planning information, installation procedures, administration tasks, and key procedures for using RapPort to deploy SharePoint Portal Server to create multiple portals.

For more information about the benefits of using RapPort in a corporate environment, see Chapter 28, "KMIT: Deploying SharePoint Portal Server across Multiple Sites." For more information about developing a customized RapPort solution, see Appendix B.

Optimizing Performance of SharePoint Portal Server

This chapter describes steps for optimizing performance of Microsoft® SharePoint™ Portal Server 2001. In addition to a discussion of appropriate hardware choices, this chapter also provides information about the modifications you can make to your deployment of SharePoint Portal Server. You can modify settings in four areas to improve the performance and increase the scalability of the application:

- Microsoft Web Storage System

- SharePoint Portal Server settings

- Internet Information Services (IIS) settings

- Dashboard and Web Part settings

Hardware Choices

Selecting an appropriate server platform is an extremely important component of a successful portal deployment. The key hardware requirements are the CPU speed, amount of RAM, and hard disk space:

- Increased CPU resources allow SharePoint Portal Server to provide an excellent user experience to large numbers of users during peak usage periods.

- If there are insufficient CPU resources, users experience unacceptable server response times during peak usage periods.

- Additional RAM and hard disk space allow SharePoint Portal Server to provide improved user performance.

- If there is insufficient RAM, users experience unacceptable server response times regardless of the number of active users.

- If there is insufficient hard disk space, users are not able to search for or save additional documents.

An important step in determining your server hardware requirements is establishing clear performance and scalability requirements. For more information about determining your hardware requirements, see Chapter 7, "Planning Server Capacity."

For the purposes of this chapter, use the following guidelines:

Deploying an Enterprise Portal

Characteristics

- Primarily browse and search activity

- 10,000 users

- 10 authors; 10,000 readers

- 2,000,000 or more indexed documents

Hardware

- Quad processor 700-megahertz (MHz) Pentium III with 2 gigabytes (GB) of RAM, 100-GB hard disk (3 spindles).

- A large search site benefits from using a server dedicated to crawling content to improve performance for users of the server dedicated to searching.

Deploying a Business Unit Portal

Characteristics

- Some document management but still a high volume of browse and search activity

- 500–2,000 users

- All author rights

- Multiple workspaces

- 10,000 documents stored; 100,000–200,000 included in the index

Hardware

- Quad processor 700-MHz Pentium III with 2 GB of RAM, 100-GB hard disk (3 spindles).

Deploying a Workgroup Portal

Characteristics

- Document management activities equivalent to browse and search activities

- Fewer than 200 users

- Equal number of authors and readers

- 100,000 indexed documents

Hardware

- Single processor 500-MHz Pentium III with 512 megabytes (MB) of RAM, 20-GB hard disk.

Server Stress Testing

When optimizing an application, it is important to be able to put stress on the server to identify bottlenecks and possible areas for improvement. You can use any tool to put stress on the server. The Microsoft Web Application Stress (WAS) tool lets you create or record a script that can be used to put stress on a server. This application is free of charge and is available for download. For more information about the WAS tool, see Appendix B, "For More Information."

Performance Monitoring

Finding bottlenecks is the key to improving application performance and scalability. Monitoring performance counters is an important part of this process. The most important performance counters to monitor for SharePoint Portal Server are:

- Processor — % Processor Time

    Note The speed of the CPU closely ties to SharePoint Portal Server performance, so monitor this counter closely when putting load on the server. If the CPU spikes consistently, you might need to upgrade your hardware, implement optimization that might reduce the CPU load caching, or move CPU intensive tasks to another server.

- Memory — % Committed bytes in use

- Active Server Pages — ASP Request Execution Time

- Active Server Pages — ASP Request Wait Time

- Active Server Pages — ASP Requests Queued

You can use Microsoft Windows® 2000 Performance Monitor to collect data from these counters, or you can use WAS to collect data while performing a stress test.

Web Storage System Settings

The Web Storage System database and the Store.exe process are at the heart of the SharePoint Portal Server application. They provide the data for the dashboard site itself and the content in the various Web Parts on the dashboards. There is very little manual optimization that you can complete due to improvements in the Store.exe auto-tuning capabilities. However, you can modify some settings. Modification may improve dashboard site performance.

For the Web Storage System included with SharePoint Portal Server, these settings are stored in the registry under

```
HKEY_LOCAL_MACHINE\Software\Microsoft\ESE98\Process\

Information Store\System Parameter Overrides\
```

Modifying the Multi-Heap Registry Setting for Multiple Processors

When SharePoint Portal Server is installed on servers with more than four processors, you may notice high virtual memory usage by the Extensible Storage Engine (ESE) multi-heap. High virtual memory usage can lead to performance problems, especially when the server has multiple gigabytes of memory. Although ESE multi-heaps relate specifically to computers running Microsoft Exchange 2000 Server that have many databases and storage groups configured, modifying this setting may also benefit computers running SharePoint Portal Server. It is recommended that you add the following registry parameter to all servers with more than four processors.

> **Caution** Incorrectly editing the registry may severely damage your system. Back up the current version of the registry before making any changes. You should also back up any valued data on the computer.

Multi-Heap Registry Setting

Location	HKEY_LOCAL_MACHINE\SOFTWARE\Microsoft\ESE98\ Global\OS\Memory
Parameter	MPHeap parallelism (REG_SZ)
Default setting	(Does not exist) = Parallelism set to four times the number of processors installed.
Recommended setting	For 6 to 8 processors, set the value to 0. This value will fix the number of heaps at 11.

> **Note** You must restart the Exchange Information Store process after you adjust the previous registry parameter.

Modifying the MaxSessions Registry Setting

The default number of available database sessions is 40. When running a lot of activities (backups, user sessions, subscription notifications, indexes, etc.) against the server, you can easily run out of database sessions. In this case, you can modify the following registry parameter.

Caution Incorrectly editing the registry may severely damage your system. Back up the current version of the registry before making any changes. You should also back up any valued data on the computer.

MaxSessions Registry Setting

Location	HKEY_LOCAL_MACHINE\SOFTWARE\Microsoft\ ESE98\Process\Information Store\System Parameter Overrides\
Parameter	MaxSessions (REG_SZ)
Default setting	(Does not exist) = 40
Recommended setting	Increase significantly to avoid message in event log and request time-outs. Between 60 and 100.

Modifying the Log Buffers Registry Setting

Web Storage System uses log buffers to store information in memory before writing to the transaction logs. For SharePoint Portal Server, the default value is 84. This value might be too low and could be the cause of excessive disk input/outputs (I/Os) to the transaction log drive. Significant performance degradation is seen if the server is under load or if users are sending large messages. You should increase the default value to 9000 on all servers. The following table summarizes this information.

Caution Incorrectly editing the registry may severely damage your system. Back up the current version of the registry before making any changes. You should also back up any valued data on the computer.

Log Buffers Registry Setting

Location	HKEY_LOCAL_MACHINE\SOFTWARE\Microsoft\ ESE98\Process\Information Store\System Parameter Overrides\
Parameter	LogBuffers (REG_SZ)
Default setting	(Does not exist) = 84
Recommended setting	9000

Modifying the Store Database Cache Size

Exchange 2000 has a 900 MB maximum for the cache size of the store database. SharePoint Portal Server computers with more than 1 GB of memory may benefit from an increase in the size of this cache. Because of virtual address space limitations, this value should never be set higher than 1,200 MB.

> **Note** The 900 MB limit is in place to ensure that the Store.exe process always has ample virtual address (memory) from which to allocate. Increasing this value too much can lead to system instability. For more information about virtual address space, see Appendix B.

Many factors can affect the virtual address space size in the Store.exe process. Some of these factors are:

- Initial allocation of virtual address space on startup

- Number of threads running

- Size of the store database cache

- Number of storage groups and databases on the server (this factor does not affect SharePoint Portal Server computers)

Before increasing the maximum cache size, it is recommended that the administrator use Performance Monitor to monitor the server memory under normal load.

Monitor the following Performance Monitor values:

- Performance Object: Process

- Counter: Virtual Bytes

- Instance: STORE

The information gathered from Performance Monitor gives you an accurate value for the virtual address space that the Store.exe process allocates. On a server with the /3GB switch set in the Boot.ini file, the value seen in Performance Monitor should be below 2.8 GB. On a server without the /3GB switch set in the Boot.ini file, the value should be below 1.8 GB. It is recommended that servers with 1 GB or more of memory have the /3GB switch added to the Boot.ini file. If you see values that are higher than those for either configuration, do not increase the size of your maximum cache size. If you see values that are lower for either configuration, you can safely increase the size of your database maximum cache size. For example, if you have a server configured with the /3GB switch, and Performance Monitor shows the virtual bytes count at 2.5 GB under heavy load, you know you can safely increase your maximum cache size by 300 MB, for a total of 1,200 MB.

SharePoint Portal Server Settings

You can modify settings to improve performance while creating indexes or for performing search queries.

Using Index Workspaces for Creating and Updating Indexes on a Separate Server

Because creating and updating an index is a resource-intensive process, you can choose to have a separate server that is dedicated to creating and updating indexes. The workspace on this server is an index workspace. An index workspace is designed to manage only content sources. The index workspace does not use the document management capabilities of SharePoint Portal Server, such as checking in or checking out documents or versioning, nor does it provide a dashboard site.

Adjusting Index and Search Resource Usage

On the computer hosting the dashboard site, adjust the resource usage of the server to "background."

To adjust the resource usage of the server to background:

1. Open **SharePoint Portal Server Administration**, and right-click the SharePoint Portal Server computer name and choose **Properties**.

2. On the Properties page, click the **General** tab.

3. Adjust the **Search resource usage** and **Indexing resource usage** settings to **Background**.

This ensures that no background index-related tasks consume CPU resources and take away resources from the dashboard site and the Web Storage System. However, if you use your workspace for many search activities, you may want to adjust the **Search resource usage** to **Dedicated** instead. Figure 15.1 illustrates these settings.

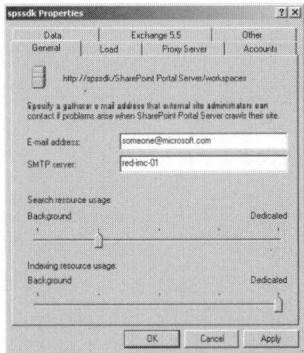

Figure 15.1. Specifying resource usage

Moving Property Store Files to a Different Volume

For high performance, the property store and property store log files must be on separate dedicated physical volumes. You cannot move property store files by using SharePoint Portal Server Administration in Microsoft Management Console (MMC). You must use Catutil.exe to move property store files and to change the location of log files for the property store.

SharePoint Portal Server provides a utility named Catutil.exe that you can use to move index files and property store files and to change the location of the log files for the property store. Property store files contain the metadata from documents. SharePoint Portal Server shares the log files across all workspaces on a server. By default, SharePoint Portal Server stores the property store file and log files in the following directory:

\Data\FTData\SharePointPortalServer

To move the property store file to a new location:

1. Stop the Microsoft Search Service (MSSearch).

2. On the **Start** menu, point to **Programs**, point to **Accessories**, and then click **Command Prompt**.

3. Change to the Program Files\Common Files\Microsoft Shared\MSSearch\Bin folder.

   Note By default, Catutil.exe is stored in the Program Files\Common Files\ Microsoft Shared\MSSearch\Bin folder. However, if you install SharePoint Portal Server on a computer running Microsoft SQL Server™ 7 or SQL Server 2000, Catutil.exe is stored in the Program Files\Common Files\System\MSSearch\B in folder.

4. At the command prompt, type **Catutil.exe PROPSTORE** and then press ENTER. A usage description appears.

5. Type **Catutil.exe PROPSTORE SharePointPortalServer -m** "*path***sps.edb**" and then press ENTER.

- For example, if you want to move the property store to a folder named Store on drive D, you would type:

  Catutil.exe PROPSTORE SharePointPortalServer -m "D:\Store\sps.edb"

- Note that you can change the name of the .edb file from sps.edb to something else. For example, you can type:

  Catutil.exe PROPSTORE SharePointPortalServer -m "D:\Store\MyFileName.edb"

6. Start the MSSearch service.

To specify a new location for the log file:

1. Stop the MSSearch service.

2. On the **Start** menu, point to **Programs**, point to **Accessories**, and then click **Command Prompt**.

3. Change to the Program Files\Common Files\Microsoft Shared\MSSearch\Bin folder.

   Note By default, Catutil.exe is stored in the Program Files\CommonFiles\ Microsoft Shared\MSSearch\Bin folder. However, if you install SharePoint Portal Server on a computer running SQL Server 7 or SQL Server 2000, Catutil.exe is stored in the Program Files\Common Files\System\MSSearch\Bin folder.

4. Type **Catutil.exe PROPSTORE** and then press ENTER. A usage description appears.

5. Type **Catutil.exe PROPSTORE SharePointPortalServer -l** *path* and then press ENTER.

- For example, if the property store file is on drive D, you may want to change the location of the log files to a folder named Logs on drive E to improve performance. You would type:

  Catutil.exe PROPSTORE SharePointPortalServer -l"E:\Log"

6. Start the MSSearch service.

   Important Do not change the location of the log files for the property store to the root of a directory. For example, do not change the location to D:\. MSSearch does not function properly if the files are on a directory root. If you have changed the location to a directory root and MSSearch no longer functions, change the location of the files to a subdirectory instead. For example, change the location to D:\Log Files.

Improving Query Performance

If query performance is slow and the computer has processor memory available, you can increase performance by specifying that MSSearch keep the property store in memory.

Important It is recommended that you do not set the CacheSizeMin to a value more than fifty percent of the available memory. If the CacheSizeMin value is set too high, it causes all queries to the server to fail with the message, "Internal Server Error." In addition, the Subscriptions Summary Web Part displays the following message, "Failed to get subscriptions results." If you encounter either of these errors, set the CacheSizeMin parameter to a lower value and restart the Microsoft Search service.

To increase query performance:

1. On the taskbar, click **Start**, and then click **Run**.

2. Type **regedit** and then click **OK**.

    Caution Incorrectly editing the registry may severely damage your system. Back up the current version of the registry before making any changes. You should also back up any valued data on the computer.

3. In Registry Editor, go to HKEY_LOCAL_MACHINE\SOFTWARE\Microsoft\ Search\1.0\Databases.

4. Right-click **Databases**, point to **New**, and then click **DWORD Value**. A new DWORD value appears.

5. Type **CacheSizeMax** as the name for the new value, and then press ENTER.

6. Right-click **CacheSizeMax**, and then click **Modify**. The **Edit DWORD Value** dialog box appears.

7. In the **Value data** box, type the maximum number of 4,096-byte pages that you want the server to keep in memory. For example, if you want to use 1 GB of RAM, divide $1,024^3$ (1,024 multiplied by 1,024 multiplied by 1,024) by 4,096, and type 262,144 in the **Value data box**.

    Important The total address space for MSSearch is 2 GB. Do not type a value greater than 1.7 GB, even if you have 2 GB or more of RAM.

8. In **Base**, click **Decimal**.

9. Click **OK**.

10. Right-click **Databases**, point to **New**, and then click **DWORD Value**. A new DWORD value appears.

11. Type **CacheSizeMin** as the name for the new value, and then press ENTER.

12. Right-click **CacheSizeMin**, and then click **Modify**. The **Edit DWORD Value** dialog box appears.

13. In the **Value data** box, type the minimum number of 4,096-byte pages that you want the server to keep in memory. This number should be between 50 and 90 percent of CacheSizeMax. For example, if CacheSizeMax is 262144, type a number between 131072 and 235929 in the **Value data box** for CacheSizeMin.

14. In **Base**, click **Decimal**.

15. Click **OK**.

16. Close Registry Editor.

17. Restart MSSearch. To do this:

   - On the taskbar, click **Start**, point to **Programs**, point to **Administrative Tools**, and then click **Services**.

   - Right-click **Microsoft Search**, and then click **Restart**.

Internet Information Server Settings

Both SharePoint Portal Server and the Web Storage System are exposed and accessed through IIS. It is important that you modify IIS to avoid creating a bottleneck. All traffic uses Hypertext Transfer Protocol (HTTP) and IIS, whether originating from the client by using Web Folders or from the browser.

This section contains some general guidelines for optimizing IIS for the dashboard site.

Running the ASP-Engine In-Process

By default, IIS runs with medium application protection. This means that the ASP-engine is pooled and the ASP-applications are using the ASP-engine running outside of the IIS process. This requires significant performance overhead to marshal data and security contexts between processes.

To set the ASP-engine to run in-process with the IIS process:

1. In the Internet Services Manager, right-click the default Web site and select **Properties** from the right-click menu.

2. On the Properties page, click the **Home Directory** tab.

3. Change the Application Protection setting from **Medium (Pooled)** to **Low (IIS Process)**. Figure 15.2 shows this setting changed to Low.

   Caution This modification makes it possible for malfunctioning Web Parts or scripts to take down the entire IIS process. It is recommended that you configure recovery options for the World Wide Web Publishing service to ensure that the process restarts properly if a failure occurs.

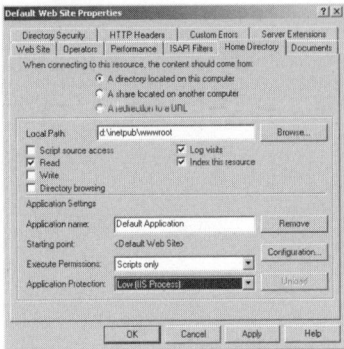

Figure 15.2. Changing the Application Protection setting

Adjusting the ASP Settings

The ASP-engine has several parameters that can be used to increase the performance and scalability of your dashboard site. The need to modify these parameters is determined by your hardware configuration and your assembled set of Web Parts. Closely observe the ASP Request Wait Time and ASP Requests Queued Performance Monitor counters to determine if you can remove any bottlenecks by optimizing the ASP-engine.

The following guidelines originate from KB-article Q253146.

AspProcessorThreadMax

The **AspProcessorThreadMax** metabase property specifies the maximum number of worker threads per processor that IIS creates. The setting can dramatically influence the scalability of your Web applications and the performance of your server in general. Because it defines the maximum number of ASP requests that can run simultaneously, this setting should remain at the default unless your ASP applications are making long-running calls to external components. By default, SharePoint Portal Server sets **AspProcessorThreadMax** to 25.

AspRequestQueueMax

The **AspRequestQueueMax** metabase property specifies the maximum number of concurrent ASP requests that are permitted into the queue. Any client browsers attempting to request ASP files when the queue is full are given an HTTP 500 "Server too busy" error message. By default, SharePoint Portal Server sets **AspRequestQueueMax** to 3,000.

AspQueueConnectionTestTime

IIS places all ASP requests into a queue. If IIS queues the request for longer than the number of seconds specified by the **AspQueueConnectionTestTime** metabase property, ASP checks to determine whether the client is still connected before it executes the request. If the client is no longer connected, the request is not processed and is deleted from the queue. You can use the **AspQueueConnectionTestTime** metabase property to make sure that IIS does not waste time processing a request that has been abandoned by the user. By default, SharePoint Portal Server sets **AspQueueConnectionTestTime** to 3.

AspScriptEngineCacheMax

The **AspScriptEngineCacheMax** property specifies the maximum number of scripting engines that ASP pages will keep cached in memory. By default, SharePoint Portal Server sets **AspScriptEngineCacheMax** to 125.

AspSessionTimeOut

The **AspSessionTimeOut** property specifies the default amount of time (in minutes) that SharePoint Portal Server maintains a session object after the last request associated with the object is made. You can use **AspSessionTimeOut** to optimize your ASP applications. Because session objects consume some memory resources, limiting the lifetime of an individual session with this property makes your applications more scalable. By default, SharePoint Portal Server sets **AspSessionTimeOut** to 20.

> **Caution** Modifying the metabase incorrectly can cause serious problems that may require you to reinstall IIS 5. Microsoft cannot guarantee that problems resulting from incorrectly modifying the metabase can be resolved. Modify the metabase at your own risk.

Run the Adsutil.vbs utility from the *%systemdrive%*\inetpub\adminScripts folder. For example, to reconfigure the **AspRequestQueueMax** metabase property, type the following command:

```
adsutil.vbs set w3svc/AspRequestQueueMax <NewValue>
```

Where <NewValue> is the number of requests that ASP should use per processor.

> **Note** For all entries, these settings change the value at the Master WWW Properties level. All new Web applications and all existing applications inherit these settings unless you explicitly set them at a different value.

Dashboard and Web Part Settings

You can modify settings to improve performance on a specific dashboard or Web Part.

General Guidelines

Ensuring that the Web Parts on your dashboards use caching properly will yield the biggest gain in dashboard performance. By using caching, you may avoid sending costly queries to the Web Storage System and running lengthy ASP-scripts to produce the dynamic output. Instead, the HTML or Extensible Markup Language (XML) content is re-trieved straight from the cache and sent to the client. If you use caching properly, scalability in your dashboard site may increase significantly from handling hundreds of users to thousands of users.

Avoiding the Automatic Refresh for Dashboards

Dashboard refresh is turned off by default, as shown in Figure 15.3. However, it might have been turned on during configuration or the creation of sub-dashboards or personal dashboards. Avoid using the dashboard refresh feature that can automatically refresh it-self after a specified number of seconds. This can create unnecessary traffic when users leave their browsers open and could put significant load on the server for no purpose.

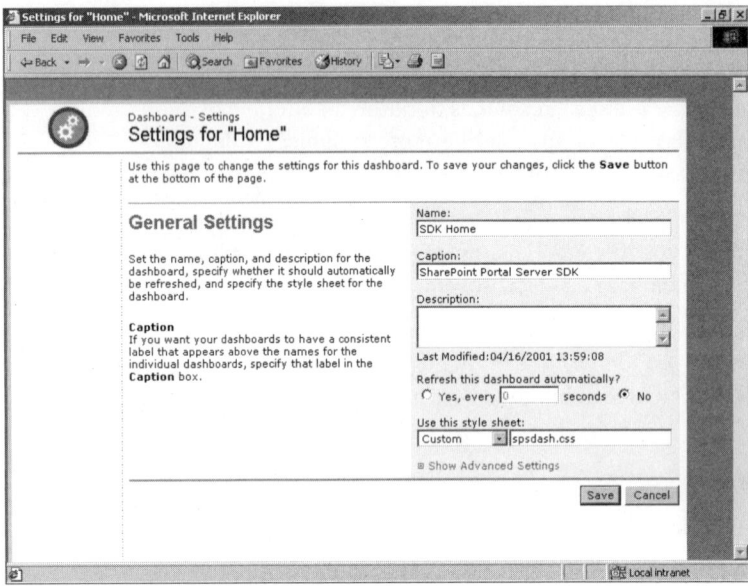

Figure 15.3. Specifying the refresh rate

Using "All Users" Cache for Web Parts

Web Parts support caching on a per-user or per-dashboard basis. Specify the All Users cache setting when possible. This ensures that most requests to see this Web Part are read from the cache and the actual query is not executed. Even for Web Parts that show per-sonal information, consider specifying a cache if the information it provides does not change frequently. These settings also apply to the standard Web Parts that are included with SharePoint Portal Server.

Increasing Refresh Time for Cache Time-Outs

Each Web Part that uses a cache also has a setting specifying how often the cache should be refreshed. Take into consideration the type of information displayed in the Web Part and set the time-out value as high as possible. A high value means less traffic and reduced use of resources.

Additional Development Considerations

The type of search query that you conduct can also affect performance. Consider the following points when assessing query performance.

Avoid Doing DEEP TRAVERSALs on Per-User Web Parts

All the SharePoint Portal Server Web Parts perform queries against the Web Storage System. Some queries, like searching for all recently modified documents in the workspace or all documents checked out to the current user, are extremely costly due to performing a search across the entire Web Storage System and the results being cached only per user. Instead of putting this type of Web Part on the Home page of the dashboard site, consider putting it on a less frequently accessed page.

DEEP TRAVERSALs can work fine on the Home page if you are able to cache the Web Part for all dashboard users and the traversal is not extensive. For example, you should try to avoid doing a deep traversal of all document folders to list the five most recently published documents.

Use Persistent Search Folders

Instead of doing deep traversal or other cross-folder complex queries, use persistent search folders to implement this. This method is far more efficient and consumes fewer resources.

Summary

This chapter describes steps for optimizing SharePoint Portal Server. You can modify settings in four areas in order to improve the performance and increase the scalability of the application. In addition, it is also important to use the appropriate hardware for your deployment goals. By monitoring performance, you can identify potential bottlenecks and address them before performance degrades.

PART 4

Administration and Management

This section provides general strategies for optimizing performance and includes information to add value to your Microsoft® SharePoint™ Portal Server 2001 installation.

CHAPTER 16

Improving Query Performance

This chapter describes factors that affect query latency and provides suggestions for how to improve query performance for your deployment.

Note The information for this chapter originates from the *SharePoint Portal Server Software Development Kit* (SDK). For more information about query performance, see Appendix B, "For More Information."

Factors in Query Latency

Latency in query execution is the amount of time it takes to execute the query and get back a result set. A number of factors affect query latency.

Corpus Size

Size of corpus. The number of documents in the document library and external sources incorporated into the workspace and content from index workspaces can increase query latency.

Query Syntax and Search Terms

The structure of search queries and the search terms that you use can affect query latency. The section describes how specific syntax and terms can impact query performance.

- **Choosing search terms.** Searches over words with few occurrences in the indexare faster than those performed over words with many occurrences. Internet sites often include large documents containing high hit counts for certain words. You can improve performance by determining such files and using site path rules to exclude these files from being crawled. The following query returns the documents with high hit counts for the word "software".

  ```
  SELECT HITCOUNT, PATH FROM SCOPE('DEEP TRAVERSAL OF "http://server01/
  workspace1"')

  WHERE CONTAINS('software') AND HITCOUNT > 500

  ORDER BY HITCOUNT DESC
  ```

- **Choosing query predicates.** Choice of full-text predicates can increase query latency. You can use the CONTAINS predicate to search for exact strings of words or phrases. A query for "SharePoint Portal Server" returns only exact matches on the phrase. In a FREETEXT query on the same search terms, the search engine searches for the words individually as well as the entire phrase. For example, the query for "SharePoint Portal Server" matches documents that contain "SharePoint" OR "Portal" OR "Server". FREETEXT uses the thesaurus and also invokes a stemmer on the query text. The result is that the query runs for all permutations of the inflected forms for individual words and phrases in the query text. FREETEXT also uses a probabilistic ranking algorithm, whereas CONTAINS does not. FREETEXT queries typically return more hits than CONTAINS queries. Consequently, this may increase query latency.

- **Setting query traversal depth.** Deep traversal queries are executed by MSSearch and generally have better performance than shallow traversal queries. This is because deep traversal queries do not check the traversal depth for folders and sub-folders traversed by the query. Checking folder scope using the SCOPE operator increases query latency. Shallow traversal queries, such as Category browsing through the dashboard site, have low latency when they are executed by the SharePoint Portal Server store. For more information about how traversal affects query execution, see Appendix B, "For More Information."

- **Querying over property values of metadata.** Querying over property values of metadata can increase query latency because the value for the property must be read from the property store to confirm that it is an exact match.

- **Limiting result set size.** Specifying a limit on the maximum number of rows returned by the search engine can significantly reduce query latency.

  If you submit a search query through WebDAV, you can specify the maximum number of rows returned by that query by setting the **MS-SEARCH-MAXROWS** header in the WebDAV request. Setting the header to return 200 rows or fewer reduces query latency.

    Note MS-SEARCH-MAXROWS should not exceed 2000.

  For more information, see Appendix B.

- **Managing query time-outs.** You can reduce query latency by specifying a limit on how long to wait before a query is timed out. For information on configuring query time-outs, see Appendix B.

- **Setting the ORDER BY clause.** The ORDER BY clause sorts the query results based on the value of one or more specified columns. Ordering queries by rank does not impact query latency because the Search engine calculates the rank at query time. Ordering queries by anything else causes the query to access the property store to retrieve that value, and, as a result, increasing query latency.

- **Checking equality and regular expressions.** Queries that require the search engine to retrieve property values from the property store have higher latency than other queries. When queries check equality for a property value and when regular expressions are used the search engine retrieves property values from the property store. You use regular expressions in non-full-text predicates, such as LIKE and MATCHES to perform complex pattern matching on text columns. LIKE and MATCHES queries also cause the search engine to access the property store to verify property values and increase the latency for that query. The property store is always accessed when you use the "=" operator to check the value of a property in a query. You can also perform basic pattern matching, such as prefix matching, by using wildcards with full-text-predicates, such as CONTAINS.

Resource Limitations

Server capacity can also affect query latency. This section describes particular resources that can impact query performance.

Managing resource limitations. Query performance improves if components of Microsoft Search (MSSearch) do not compete for resources on the same Microsoft® SharePoint™ Portal Server 2001 computer. One way to improve query performance is to deploy resource-intensive tasks to different servers. For example, you can create an index workspace on a separate server dedicated to creating and maintaining indexes. For more information about configuring a server dedicated to creating and updating indexes, see Appendix B.

Property Store Configuration and Caching

Queries perform best when a high proportion of the property store is loaded into memory. You can control the size of the in-memory cache for the property store through the registry. You can load Properties from the property store into this cache using one of two methods, index propagation or by using a special query.

Registry settings for MSSearch place limits on how much of the property store is loaded and cached in-memory. You can increase the size of this cache by setting the following two registry keys:

> **Caution** Incorrectly editing the registry may severely damage your system. Back up the current version of the registry before making any changes. You should also back up any valued data on the computer.

- **Minimum cache size.** \HKEY_LOCAL_MACHINE\Software\Microsoft\Search\ 1.0\Databases\CacheSizeMin

- **Maximum cache size.** \HKEY_LOCAL_MACHINE\Software\Microsoft\Search\ 1.0\Databases\CacheSizeMax

The value for the key equals the number of 4KB pages of memory, represented in hexa-decimal, which is allocated for the cache. On a system with 2 gigabytes of RAM, setting the minimum cache size to 40000 and the maximum as 48000 allows for a cache that uses between 1 and 1.2 gigabytes of RAM. You must restart MSSearch for the registry settings to take effect.

> **Caution** Setting a substantial difference between minimum and maximum cache size may degrade performance. Setting the maximum cache size to a large percentage of the available RAM degrades performance.

When a property appears in the SELECT clause of a query, the search engine retrieves a property from the property store, and caches that property and its value in memory. The search engine retrieves the value for that property from memory for subsequent queries, thus eliminating disk access to the property store. Query performance can be improved by executing queries that select properties so that the property store is cached into memory. After the scripts finish executing, properties loaded from the property store re-main in memory until the SharePoint Portal Server computer is rebooted or the MSSearch service is restarted.

The property store for MSSearch is cached into memory as a side effect of propagating an index. For more information on how to propagate an index, see Appendix B.

Performance Monitoring

SharePoint Portal Server provides two performance objects to monitor searching on the dashboard site.

- **Microsoft Search object.** You can use the Microsoft Search object to monitor the number and rate the following for the server: failed queries, queries (all), results and successful queries.

- **Microsoft Search Catalogs object.** You can use the Microsoft Search Catalogs ob-ject to monitor the number and rate of the following for each workspace: failed que-ries, queries (all), results and successful queries.

For more information about performance monitors, see Appendix B.

Summary

This chapter described factors that affect query latency and also gave suggestions for how to improve query performance for your deployment. For more information about improving query performance, see Appendix B.

CHAPTER 17

Using Categories

This chapter describes the use of categories in a Microsoft® SharePoint™ Portal Server 2001 workspace. In addition to an overview of designing the category structure, it reviews the methods of categorizing documents and provides recommendations about using the Category Assistant to categorize content automatically.

Although categories are not required to find documents in the workspace, they are valuable for locating documents that relate to a specific subject. Categories help users who do not know where documents are stored to find what they need by allowing them to browse through information by topic. Categories provide a central, easily managed taxonomy of terms that accommodate readers without changing the existing folder structure and processes that the group uses.

Categories serve two purposes. They provide

- A consistent, controlled vocabulary of values that you can apply to documents as metadata.

- A centralized structure for information browsing. Categories direct readers to the information they seek through an organized hierarchy of topics.

Categories provide a flexible way both to *describe* and to *find* documents.

Category browsing is available on the dashboard site and in the Web folder view of the workspace. When you open a category, SharePoint Portal Server displays a list of all the documents that are associated with the category, and any subcategories under it. You can categorize documents from the workspace document library and from crawled content sites.

Categories

Every default workspace contains a category hierarchy. The Categories folder contains a hierarchy of special, folder-like items called categories. Categories do not contain actual documents. Categories contain links to the documents stored in the workspace document library or on crawled sites. The benefit of this design is that you can associate a single document with several categories or remove a document from a category without affecting the document or its association with other categories.

The dashboard site displays the categories in a Web Part on the home page. Each category is a link to an expanded list that shows subcategories, category Best Bets, and documents assigned to the category. To a user browsing the workspace using Microsoft Windows® Explorer, categories work like folders. By using Windows Explorer, a user can expand the category hierarchy and browse through the associated document links for each category. Figure 17.1 illustrates both views.

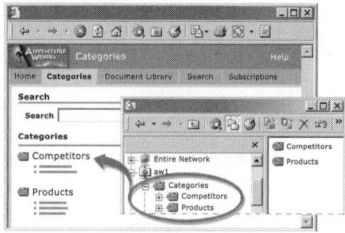

Figure 17.1. Categories viewed on the dashboard site and in Web folders

Using Categories as Metadata

Categories are values that you can apply to documents as metadata. Although they look like folders in the workspace, categories are an extended part of the schema. They function like a list property with a dictionary. Just as there may be a list of values defined for a *Products* property, the list of workspace categories are the dictionary values for the *Categories* property. SharePoint Portal Server keeps the hierarchical category dictionary in the schema synchronized with the set of categories displayed in the workspace. For example, when you add a new category, SharePoint Portal Server creates a corresponding value in the category dictionary.

Using Categories as "Search Folders"

The SharePoint Portal Server implementation of categories provides a convenient way to group documents into folders based on shared metadata such as categories. When a user opens a category folder by using Windows Explorer or browses to a category on the dashboard site, SharePoint Portal Server is actually performing a search query. The category query filters for and then displays documents that have been associated with a particular category value.

Category Planning and Management

Categories are optional—they provide users of a SharePoint Portal Server workspace with an additional way to search for documents. Because you apply categories to individual documents, they do not rely on, or affect, the location of the document in the document library hierarchy. Therefore, a single document can be associated with several categories.

To determine which categories you will need to create, ask users and content owners how their documents are currently organized. Determine the strong and weak points of the current structure, and then develop categories that build on this structure. You can use the existing folder hierarchy as a model for developing a new category hierarchy if it meets the needs of your users.

Determining the number of categories to create depends on the type of organization with which you are working. For example, if you are setting up a workspace for a large manufacturing firm that produces a wide range of diverse products, hundreds of categories may be required to support effective user browsing. However, if you are setting up a workspace for a small consulting firm that specializes in a niche field, fewer than twenty categories may be required.

Designing Your Category Structure

Consider how users choose to organize the content when planning the category structure. For example, do they organize content by department, by project, or by subject matter? If the users organize content by subject matter, what are the top-level categories? How many levels of subcategories do you want users to navigate? You can use SharePoint Portal Server to define as many category levels as you want. However, the more levels you establish, the more likely it is that a user will have difficulty finding content. If you have not organized content in this way before, begin with a shallow structure of one to three levels. You can easily modify the category hierarchy after users have tested the initial category structure.

Note It is recommended that you use no more than 500 categories in a single workspace.

SharePoint Portal Server supports document management by using categories, document profiles, and document folders to organize documents in the workspace. Each of these components has specific issues related to planning. For more information about how to establish a taxonomy and design a category structure, see Chapter 9, "Planning Taxonomies."

Creating Categories

After you determine which categories to add, use Windows Explorer to create your structure in the Categories folder of the workspace. In a SharePoint Portal Server workspace, only a coordinator can create new categories. Each top-level category has its own top-level category folder. A subcategory is a subfolder under the corresponding category folder. When you create a category, SharePoint Portal Server automatically generates the associated category query. At the time you create the category, the SharePoint Portal Server also updates the schema. This enables users to assign the new category value to their documents.

A category must be uniquely identifiable in a workspace. In SharePoint Portal Server, a path identifies each category. The path corresponds to the URL of the category in the workspace. For example, the URL of a category named *Boots* under a top-level category named *Shoes* is:

http://*server_name*/SharePointPortalServer/*workspace_name*/Categories/Shoes/Boots

This category is identified by the category path ":**Shoes:Boots**" on document profiles and in the category query.

Managing Categories

Although categories look like file system folders, they are not the same. You can delete and rename categories, but you cannot move them around in the category hierarchy. When you delete a category, SharePoint Portal Server removes the category and all subcategories but it does not delete the documents associated with the category. It removes the category value from the *Categories* property on all documents in the category. If the name of the category is changed, the new category will contain the same documents. The rename operation initiates a process that updates all the documents with the new category name.

> **Note** Category maintenance is a resource-intensive process. It is recommended that you perform these tasks during maintenance periods.

Categories automatically inherit their security settings from the Categories folder, and thus category security can only be managed at the workspace level. Permission to manage categories is restricted to the coordinators role on the category folders. All other roles have only read access to the categories.

Document Categorization

After you create a category hierarchy, the next step is to categorize the content in the workspace. There are two methods of associating documents with categories:

- Manually assigning categories by editing the document properties (metadata).

- Automatically assigning categories by using the Category Assistant.

Categorizing Documents Manually

There are two ways to assign individual documents to categories:

- Editing the **Search and Categories** tab of the document's Properties page.

- Adding the *Categories* property to the document profile.

In addition to these two methods, this section describes how to apply categories to shortcuts (links) to content stored outside the workspace.

Edit the Properties Page of the Document

You can manually categorize a document by editing the **Search and Categories** tab on the Properties page of the document. By using Windows Explorer, an author or coordinator can select one or more values from the checklist of workspace categories. If the document is stored in an enhanced folder, you must check out the document before you can change the document's category assignments. For a small number of documents, you can use this method of categorization exclusively.

Update the Document Profile

You can also categorize a document by using document profiles. If the coordinator has configured the document profile to display categories, the author will be able to select categories when they check in the document. Adding the *Categories* property to document profiles provides a way to enforce category assignment when authors check in a document. It also distributes the task of document categorization among multiple authors. This method is particularly useful for bulk categorization scenarios, such as when a large set of documents is migrated into the workspace. Both methods are illustrated in the following figure.

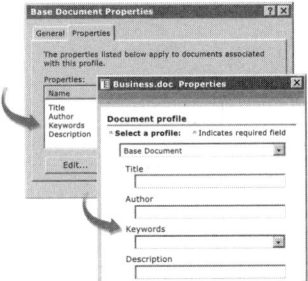

Figure 17.2. Two ways to manually assign categories to a document

Categorize Links to Content Outside the Workspace

When stored in a SharePoint Portal Server folder, shortcuts provide the ability to annotate content stored outside the workspace with metadata. By using shortcuts, you can manually assign categories to information stored outside the workspace. SharePoint Portal Server includes a special document profile called the Web Link profile, which includes a property called *Link*, for this purpose.

When you add a .URL file to a workspace folder and apply the Web Link profile, SharePoint Portal Server uses the *Link* property to determine the target of a shortcut. SharePoint Portal Server automatically updates the *Link* property for a .URL file but not for a .LNK file. To fill in this property, right-click the shortcut to open the profile form and then select **Edit Profile**. When the form opens, SharePoint Portal Server populates the *Link* property. You can close the form by clicking **OK**.

Note If you categorize multiple shortcuts at the same time (bulk edit), SharePoint Portal Server does not automatically update this property. The shortcuts do not display correctly until you open each shortcut individually.

When you add a shortcut to the workspace, the object created in the store is a file called a *stub*. When the *Link* property is set on a stub, two things happen:

- SharePoint Portal Server does a one-page crawl of the link target. As it does this, SharePoint Portal Server applies any properties on the stub automatically to the link target. For example, if you create a shortcut and set the *Link* property on the Web Link profile to http://www.adventure-works.com, and then set the *Categories* property to "Technology," SharePoint Portal Server includes the Web site in the content links that it displays when you browse the Technology category.

- When it displays a stub that has the *Link* property set on it, the dashboard site renders a hyperlink not to the stub (which would be a URL to a shortcut in the workspace), but rather to the target of the *Link* property. In the previous example, when you browse the Technology category, you see a link to http://www.adventure-works.com rather than the shortcut stored in the workspace.

In a folder associated with the Web Link document profile, add a shortcut to the content that you want to categorize and apply the Web Link document profile to the shortcut. Edit the document profile to apply the appropriate categories. Ensure that you fill in the *Link* property correctly before closing the profile form. To preserve the *Link* property of the shortcut when you drag and drop it in the workspace, ensure that the default document profile for the folder includes the *Link* property.

Caution The *Title* property of the Web Link document profile overwrites the actual title of the document retrieved by the shortcut. This is true even if the *Title* property remains empty. To avoid this problem, create a document profile for the shortcuts that includes the *Link* and *Categories* properties but not the *Title* property.

If you crawl a large quantity of content outside the workspace, you can also apply categories automatically. The next section of this chapter describes this method of automatic categorization.

Categorizing Documents Automatically

Efficiently categorizing documents presents a significant challenge to coordinators. Not only can there be a vast amount of information aggregated for the dashboard site but also this information typically lacks inherent structure, making it hard to organize sensibly. To solve this problem, SharePoint Portal Server includes technology that will automatically categorize crawled documents as well as documents published in the workspace. If you plan to use categories for a large number of files, the Category Assistant can efficiently assign categories from your category structure to existing documents and add them automatically to new documents. This reduces the time required to implement categories for your users.

The Category Assistant is based on an adaptive algorithm that can learn the "definition" of a topic if given sufficient training examples. Before using it, you must manually apply categories to a representative selection of documents for the Category Assistant to use as training examples. The Category Assistant compares documents assigned to one category with documents from other categories to identify the most characteristic features (words). Ultimately, the definition of a category is the list of words that best distinguish documents in one category from documents in other categories.

When SharePoint Portal Server updates the index, the Category Assistant compares the category definition to the list of words contained in each new document encountered. More distinguishing words, such as those in the document's title, are given greater weight in the category definitions. The comparison of category definition to document yields a number that represents the confidence with which the Category Assistant would place the document in the given category. SharePoint Portal Server tags the document with the category only if this confidence number is above the precision level set by the coordinator. SharePoint Portal Server can and often does automatically categorize a single document into multiple categories.

SharePoint Portal Server associates documents with categories when it updates the index. For this reason, there may be a delay before you see a document appear in the assigned category. The length of the delay depends on the index method you use and the amount of content that is included in the index.

Extend Category Properties and Views

The Category Assistant categorizes documents by stamping them with metadata. Specifically, there is a hidden property on the base document profile called *Autocategories* (**urn:attributes:autocategories**). The Category Assistant populates this property with the categories that best describe the document. This property is different from the *Categories* property, which users update manually. There are two reasons for this difference:

- To differentiate between a manually categorized and automatically categorized item.

- To enable the Category Assistant to overwrite previous automatic categorization values for a given document without disturbing manual categorizations.

When you enable the Category Assistant, SharePoint Portal Server queries both properties to create category views in Web folders and the dashboard site. When you disable the Category Assistant, SharePoint Portal Server eliminates the query for *Autocategories*, leaving only the query for the *Categories* property. If the Category Assistant is not functioning as the coordinator expects, this makes it easy to turn it off and eliminate all automatically categorized documents from category views.

Configure the Category Assistant

You can access the Category Assistant from the Properties page of the top-level category folder. SharePoint Portal Server enables the feature by default but the Category Assistant does not perform any categorization until you train it.

Consider the following points before training the Category Assistant:

- **Try to provide as many examples as possible.** These examples should encompass as many facets of the category as possible. For example, a category about *Llamas* might include training documents about the evolution of llamas, typical llama habitats, and llama behaviors.

- **Consider applying multiple categories to a document.** You can assign a document to any category that a user might access. For example, if a user wants to find information about a utility that your group uses, she might look under a category called Internal Tools or a category whose name describes the purpose of the tool, such as Archiving.

To configure and train the Category Assistant:

1. On the Category Assistant property page, select the set of documents you want to be automatically categorized. You can select only documents stored in the workspace, only documents stored outside of the workspace, or all documents (default selection).

2. Set the precision level. If you set a high precision level, the Category Assistant will require a more precise match and might categorize fewer documents.

3. Click the **Train Now** button. This button must be clicked in order to create the category definitions. After they are trained, all subsequent documents that are indexed will be subject to automatic categorization.

4. To disable the Category Assistant, clear the **Enable Category Assistant** check box.

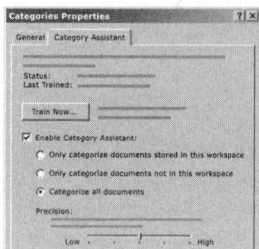

Figure 17.3. Category Assistant property page

Train the Category Assistant

Training the Category Assistant is the most important step in categorizing documents automatically. The Category Assistant needs training examples for each category. Without good training examples, the accuracy of the Category Assistant is limited. It is recommended that you use a minimum of 10 documents per category to train the Category Assistant successfully.

Ideal training documents are

- **All related to the same category topic.** For example, if the category were Product Design, including a document about product specifications would be useful. However, including a training document about product inventory would reduce the Category Assistant's accuracy.

- **Primarily textual.** Word processing documents are excellent training examples. Documents such as spreadsheets do not offer as much text for the Category Assistant to use for categorization.

- **Relatively long.** There must be enough text for the Category Assistant to analyze the documents and identify the keywords that define a category.

Good training examples for each category improve the accuracy of the Category Assistant. The more training examples you provide, the more precise the Category Assistant can be.

You can assign the task of training the Category Assistant to one person or several. Two training models are:

- **Allow authors to categorize documents.** If you want to distribute training responsibilities across a group of authors, you can add the *Categories* property to your document profiles. As authors check in and categorize their documents, they add training examples for the Category Assistant. The benefit of this model is that you use a greater number of documents as training examples. This procedure works best if the authors clearly understand the category structure.

- **Assign training responsibilities to one individual.** If you want to control the Category Assistant training process, you can remove the *Categories* property from your document profiles. You can then assign categories by editing the **Search and Categories** tab of the Properties page of a specific document.

Note that SharePoint Portal Server treats *any* document that you manually categorize as a training example. Therefore, if contributors check in their documents and categorize them on a day-to-day basis, they are implicitly training the Category Assistant. The benefits of this design is that far more documents will be treated as training examples and the coordinator need not worry about managing a special set of training documents.

Override the Category Assistant

At times, you may want to override automatically chosen categories on individual documents. To support this, a property (**urn:content-classes:item::issuggestedcategoryused**) indicates whether the automatically selected categories should be included in category views or not. If it is set to TRUE, then the document will appear in category listings in the Web folder view and on the dashboard site. The property is set by selecting the Display document in suggested categories check box on the **Search and Categories** tab on the Properties page of a document.

If the Category Assistant does not select the appropriate categories for a document, a coordinator can override the Category Assistant by using the following methods:

- **For a single document.** The coordinator may enable the Category Assistant for the workspace but occasionally override automatically chosen categories for specific documents. For example, the Category Assistant may place a document about hats in the Coats category. The coordinator can correct the category assignment by editing the document's Properties page. To do this, clear the Display document in suggested categories check box on the **Search and Categories** tab on the Properties page and manually assign the appropriate categories.

- **For all documents.** If the Category Assistant is not performing as expected, the coordinator can disable it and neutralize all automatically assigned categories. When the Category Assistant categorizes documents, it updates a hidden property on the base document profile called *Autocategories*. When the Category Assistant is disabled, SharePoint Portal Server ignores the *Autocategories* property.

It is difficult to return to an automatic categorization system after you override the Category Assistant for more than a few documents. There is no automated way to do this. If you override the Category Assistant, and then want to undo that action, you must manually update the **Search and Categories** tab on the Properties page of the document. Your changes will take effect at the next index update.

Category Best Bets

Category Best Bets are documents that a coordinator selects as highly relevant to a particular category. For example, the *XML* category might have the XML Homepage as a category Best Bet. SharePoint Portal Server visually promotes Category Best Bets in category listings on the dashboard site, just like keyword Best Bets in search results.

You enable category Best Bets by adding a *Category Best Bets* property to the base document profile. When the dashboard site displays a category, it checks the *Category Best Bets* property to determine if it should visually promote the document.

You can configure category Best Bets on a document using the Search and Categories property page. As you assign the document to categories, SharePoint Portal Server lists those categories as values in the Best Bets area for selection. You can also assign shortcuts to external content as Best Bets. Figure 17.4 illustrates both methods of category assignment.

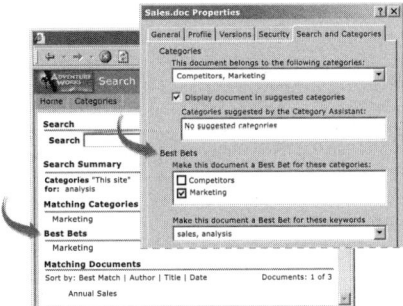

Figure 17.4. Designating a document as a category Best Bet

Summary

This chapter describes the use of categories in a SharePoint Portal Server workspace. In addition to an overview of designing the category structure, it reviews the methods of categorizing documents and provides recommendations about using the Category Assistant to categorize content automatically.

Building a Corporate Portal Using Microsoft Office XP

This chapter presents an overview of the advantages of using Microsoft® SharePoint™ Portal Server 2001 to create a corporate portal. It reviews how Microsoft Office XP can help you quickly and easily customize the default dashboard site to create your own custom portal solution, and how Microsoft SharePoint Team Services can add value to your portal solution. This chapter also provides suggestions for using Office XP, SharePoint Team Services, and SharePoint Portal Server to deploy a total portal solution that facilitates finding, creating, and sharing your mission-critical content from a Web browser or Office XP.

A *portal* is a Web site that gathers information from a variety of sources and displays the information in a single location. In addition, portals typically provide simple Web publishing and search capabilities to users. You can create portals for entire corporations, such as Microsoft, or by departments, such as Marketing, Human Resources, or Sales. Individuals can also create portals, in the form of personalized digital dashboards.

You can extend SharePoint Portal Server and add additional Web application functionality. SharePoint Portal Server is designed around industry and Internet standards, such as OLE DB, Microsoft ActiveX® Data Objects (ADO), Extensible Markup Language (XML), and Microsoft Web Distributed Authoring and Versioning (WebDAV). Because of this support of standards, the use of tools like Microsoft Visual Studio® Professional for Microsoft Windows® allows you to integrate Active Server Pages (ASP) functionality to the dashboard site. For information about how to create custom Web Parts, see Chapter 21, "Creating Custom Web Parts with Office XP Developer." For more information about customization of SharePoint Portal Server, see Appendix B, "For More Information."

When used with Office XP, SharePoint Portal Server makes Office Web publishing and content creation simple and powerful. Office XP becomes a great content development tool that takes advantage of the enterprise-wide search engine, powerful document management, and easy portal customizability features of SharePoint Portal Server to make information available throughout an enterprise.

By using Office XP, you can share and publish information in a corporate portal through Web Parts. You can create these Web Parts and Web applications directly in Office XP. By using Office XP, you can publish Microsoft Excel 2000 PivotTable® reports, Microsoft Word documents, or Microsoft PowerPoint® presentations as Web Parts in your corporate portal by saving to the dashboard site directly from the Office applications. By using SharePoint Portal Server, you can take existing reports and other data from Office or existing Web pages and customize the default dashboard site to share critical, timely information. With the use of other tools, such as Visual Studio, you can further extend your corporate portal to encompass other content.

SharePoint Portal Server and Corporate Portals

SharePoint Portal Server creates a Web portal—known as the *dashboard site*—automatically during installation. The dashboard site offers a centralized access point for finding and managing information. The dashboard site provides access to the key information that you deem critical to your organization. SharePoint Portal Server allows you to:

- **Modify the dashboard site.** The dashboard site is composed of multiple dashboards. Each dashboard is composed of customizable Web Parts. SharePoint Portal Server includes about a dozen default Web Parts, including a Search Web Part, a Categories Web Part, a Best Bets Web Part, and others. This default dashboard site allows you to deploy a portal solution with the initial framework and common portal features in place.

- **Use Web Parts to assist collaboration.** You can use Web Parts to add collaborative applications and tasks, such as group schedules from Microsoft Outlook® or available discussion groups as building blocks for a wide range of business solutions. Office XP allows you to save these Web Parts directly from Office documents.

- **Use ASP and CDO to add Web collaboration.** Develop solutions rapidly. Use Collaboration Data Objects (CDO) to develop applications. CDO is dual-interfaced for programming in C++, Microsoft Visual Basic®, Visual Basic Scripting Edition, Microsoft Jscript®, and Java.

- **Build and host native Web applications.** SharePoint Portal Server includes built-in services for accessing high-performance Web applications, including XML and WebDAV. It also provides support for ASP, custom data access forms, business logic events, and reusable components. With this support, you can build your own native Web applications outside of the SharePoint Portal Server workspace and create a Web Part to link to the application content. For more information about building and hosting native Web applications, see Chapter 19, "Architecting Web Parts for Business Applications."

- **Develop applications with commonly available tools.** You can extend the dashboard site with development tools, such as Visual Studio.

- **Access information by using database technologies.** Data access technologies, such as OLE DB and ADO, enable developers to apply their existing skills and applications when building Web Storage System applications. Your developers can build on existing training and knowledge to create custom solutions for your dashboard site.

- **Use XML to link SharePoint Portal Server to other business servers.** XML support makes it easy to share data from SharePoint Portal Server with other applications within your organization. XML makes integration with other applications seamless.

For more information about how to develop custom applications, see Chapter 19.

Portal Content

With SharePoint Portal Server, information on your dashboard site dynamically changes as users create, modify, and store files in the workspace. With the document management features of SharePoint Portal Server, users participate in developing content for your dashboard site. Office XP users are ready to work with SharePoint Portal Server out of the box. No additional installations are required.

When you use SharePoint Portal Server, you can focus on the accessibility and organization of content, instead of spending time on content preparation. As users add content, you customize and control what content appears on the dashboard site, how it is organized, and to whom it is available. Because SharePoint Portal Server eliminates the extra steps of preparing existing content for the Web, the process of finding, sharing, and publishing information is shorter and easier. When you use them in combination, Office XP and SharePoint Portal Server add value to the user experience by reducing the time to prepare content for the Web.

For Office XP users, the productivity benefits of using Office XP and SharePoint Portal Server together are:

- **Personal dashboard and Web Part development.** With Office XP, you can save Web Parts directly by using the **Save As** feature on the **File** menu. Office XP users can create a personal dashboard. A personal dashboard gives a customized view of information to share information across groups.

- **Integrated search.** Users have a rich search experience from within Office XP. They can look across local servers, SharePoint Portal Server computers, Microsoft Exchange Server computers, or any Web server, making it simple to find and retrieve information regardless of its location. You can search SharePoint Portal Server workspaces directly from within the Office XP applications by using the **Search Pane** feature. During a search, you receive the same results that you would receive from conducting a search query on the dashboard site.

- **Rich built-in document management.** When you use Office XP with SharePoint Portal Server, Office XP users get a rich, secure, and customizable document management experience. SharePoint Portal Server adds check-in, check-out, publishing, and document profiles to the document management process of Office XP. Word, Excel, and PowerPoint applications all have built-in awareness of SharePoint Portal Server for document management. By using My Network Places from Office XP applications, users can check documents in and out of the workspace directly. When users open documents in the workspace from Office XP applications, SharePoint Portal Server automatically prompts them to check out documents before opening them. In addition, Office XP automatically prompts users to check in documents that they have edited when closing them.

- **Smart Tags within Office documents.** Users can use Smart Tags technology within Office XP documents to directly link to categories and searches within SharePoint Portal Server. Users can also access the profile form for a document directly from Office XP applications.

- **One-touch client installation.** You can use Office XP and SharePoint Portal Server together out of the box with a simple, unified installation process. All Office XP applications are native clients for SharePoint Portal Server.

Together, Office XP and SharePoint Portal Server simplify the process of taking information from everyday applications and presenting it on the Web in a central location. Office XP makes creating a Web page as simple as using the **Save As** feature.

The Dashboard Site

With SharePoint Portal Server, you can add additional dashboards to the default dashboard site to customize your dashboard site. In addition, you can enable users to create their own personalized dashboards for collaboration. By using Office XP, you can add Web Parts to any dashboard quickly and easily to provide information to all users. The following figure illustrates how to save an Excel spreadsheet as a Web Part.

Office XP users can save Web Parts by using the **Save As** feature. Office XP users can also create personal dashboards directly from Office XP. Personal dashboards provide customized views of content for sharing across teams.

When a user saves an Office XP document as a Web Part in a personal dashboard folder, SharePoint Portal Server prompts the user to name and describe the Web Part and to indicate the position on the layout of the dashboard. Figure 18.2 shows the Web Part Settings page.

Personal dashboards are dashboards that consist of one or more Web Parts chosen by the creator. By using the Personal Dashboard Web Part that is included with SharePoint Portal Server, users can create customized dashboards to organize and present Web content that is specific to their needs.

For example, a user may want to create a dashboard with information about a specific topic or project, such as a quarterly sales report. Alternatively, a user may want to create a Web site with multiple types of information, such as marketing reports on competitors, competitor product information, and stock market information, that they want to share with others.

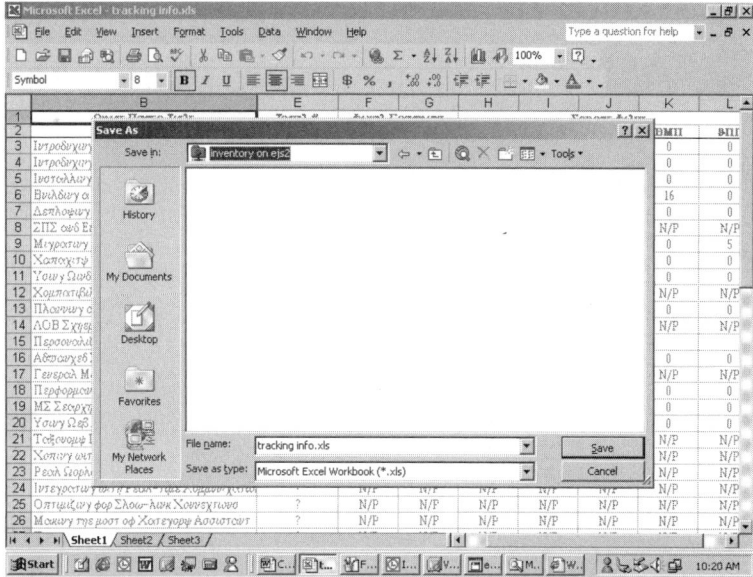

Figure 18.1. Saving an Office XP document as a Web Part

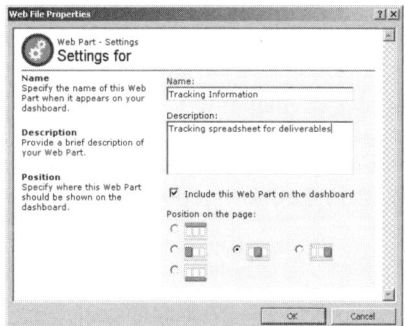

Figure 18.2. Saving a document as a Web Part

The following figure shows a personal dashboard with an Excel spreadsheet that is saved as a Web Part.

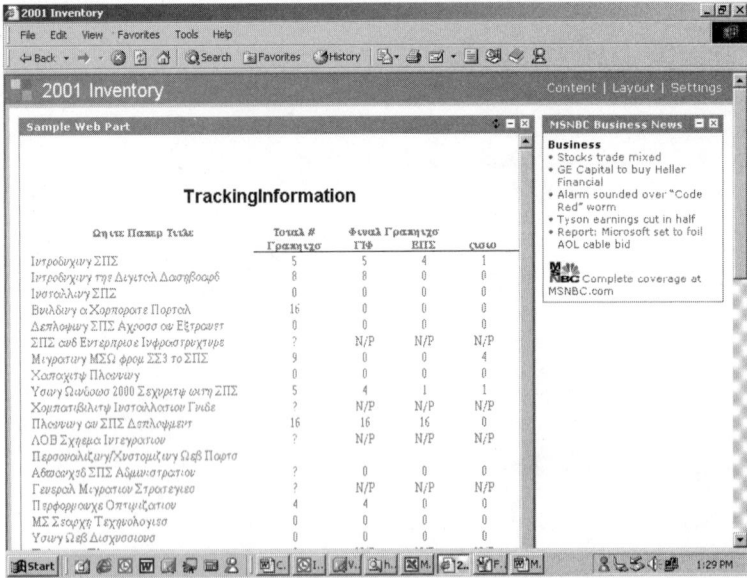

Figure 18.3. Displaying a spreadsheet as a Web Part on a personal dashboard

After you modify the workspace and dashboard site that comes with SharePoint Portal Server, you further customize your portal by adding additional dashboards and Web Parts, such as those available from the Microsoft Web Part Gallery. The example in the preceding figure includes a Microsoft MSN® Encarta® Reference Web Part. In addition, you may choose to allow users to create personal dashboards to publish their own project information. Customization can include:

- Adding custom dashboards to the main dashboard site.

- Creating, importing, or removing Web Parts from dashboards.

- Deciding whether to implement the Personal Dashboards feature of SharePoint Portal Server.

- Organizing and modifying content on the dashboard site as you develop it by using Office XP.

Office XP adds value to SharePoint Portal Server by giving you tools that transform Office XP documents into Web-ready content without the need to reformat and re-create information.

SharePoint Team Services

SharePoint Team Services, which is included with Office XP, gives users the ability to create and contribute to team and project-focused Web sites. SharePoint Portal Server can include documents that are stored in the document libraries of Web sites created by using SharePoint Team Services in the index of a workspace. This makes this content available for searching on the dashboard site.

For more information about using SharePoint Team Services and SharePoint Portal Server together, see Chapter 2, "Introducing SharePoint Technologies."

Custom Web Parts

When you save Office XP documents as Web Parts, your ability to publish content quickly and easily to your dashboard site is enhanced dramatically. By using SharePoint Portal Server and Office XP together, you can personalize your dashboard site to provide the content that your users need. With SharePoint Portal Server and Office XP, publishing documents becomes easier. This section demonstrates how to save an Excel PivotTable report as an interactive Web Part for the dashboard site.

Creating a Web Part from Office XP

With SharePoint Portal Server, you can grant individual users the ability to create their own dashboards, which are stored on the computer running SharePoint Portal Server. After you create a personal dashboard, you can create and import Web parts directly from Office XP. For more information about how to create personal dashboards, see Appendix B.

The following procedure explains how to create a Web Part from an existing Excel document. This process can be modified to create Web Parts from other Office XP documents.

To create a Web Part from an existing Excel document:

1. In Excel, on the **File** menu, click **Open** and select the document you want to save as a Web Part.

2. On the **File** menu, click **Save as Web Page**. The **Save As** dialog box opens.

    Note You can use the **Save as Web Page** command on the **File** menu of any of the Office XP applications.

3. With an Excel PivotTable report, you have the option of selecting interactivity. In the **Save As** dialog box, click to select the **Add interactivity** check box so users can manipulate data in the Web Part.

4. Click **Publish**. The **Publish as Web Page** dialog box opens.

5. Select the **AutoRepublish every time this workbook is saved** check box to have Excel update your Web Part each time someone updates the original file.

6. Under **Viewing options**, select the **Add interactivity with** check box to add interactivity. You can choose between **PivotTable functionality** and **Spreadsheet functionality**.

7. After you select the viewing options, click **Publish**. The **Save As** dialog box opens again. Browse to the personal dashboard folder by using Web Folders.

   Note You must be assigned to the role of Coordinator or Author to save content to a personal dashboard folder.

8. Click the Network Place for the appropriate workspace where the personal dashboard is stored.

9. Click the **Dashboards** folder.

   Note All personal dashboards are stored in the Dashboards folder.

10. Select the appropriate personal dashboard folder.

11. Confirm the file name for the Web Part, and then click **OK**. The **Publish as Web Page** dialog box opens again.

12. Click **Publish**, and the **Web File Properties** dialog box opens in SharePoint Portal Server. SharePoint Portal Server and Office XP recognize that you are saving the file to a folder that is located on a SharePoint Portal Server workspace and not just an ordinary Web folder for Internet publication. SharePoint Portal Server displays a settings page for the new Web Part.

13. Type a name and description for the Web Part and indicate its position on the page. After you type this information, click **OK**.

14. The new Web Part appears automatically when you refresh the personal dashboard in the Web browser.

By using Office XP, users can quickly and easily share and publish information in a dashboard site by using Web Parts.

A Custom Solution Using Office XP

SharePoint Portal Server provides an out-of-the-box corporate portal with a dashboard site as a centralized location for information, a workspace for document management, and role-based security to ensure secure access to information. By using Digital Dashboard technology, you can customize the default dashboard site and create your own customized dashboards. You can also enable other users to create personal dashboards for their own projects and teams within an organization. With Office XP, users can add Office XP documents as Web Parts to any dashboard on the dashboard site. Users can create informal, temporary project Web sites by using SharePoint Team Services. SharePoint Portal Server can include document libraries from these Web sites in the index, making them available for search queries on the dashboard site.

Summary

You can use Office XP and SharePoint Portal Server to provide a powerful and rich portal. This total portal solution centralizes information so that users can search for and share documents regardless of location or format.

Office XP and SharePoint Portal Server simplify Web publishing and content creation. As a content development tool, Office XP takes advantage of the enterprise-wide search engine, powerful document management features, and easy portal customizability of SharePoint Portal Server.

By using SharePoint Portal Server, you can take existing reports and other data from Office XP or existing Web pages and customize the dashboard site to suit your own needs. By using Office XP, customers can share and publish information in a dashboard site through Web Parts. With the use of other tools, such as Visual Studio, you can further extend your dashboard site to encompass other content.

This chapter presents the advantages of using SharePoint Portal Server to create a corporate portal. It reviews how Microsoft Office XP can help you customize the default dashboard site to create your own custom portal solution and how SharePoint Team Services can add further value to your portal solution. It provides suggestions for using Office XP, SharePoint Team Services, and SharePoint Portal Server to deploy a total portal solution that facilitates finding, creating, and sharing all your mission-critical content from a Web browser or Office.

CHAPTER 19

Architecting Web Parts for Business Applications

This chapter describes how to build and deploy Web Parts to distribute mission-critical information from a variety of business applications. This chapter includes information about how to architect a Web Part for business applications, the tools and skill sets needed to build Web Parts, and the challenges that a developer must overcome in the process.

This chapter describes the architecture and related technologies used to create the Microsoft-Avanade Siebel and SAP Toolboxes. A *toolbox* is a collection of Web Parts and related technologies. In this case, the related technologies included COM components and installers. For more information about the SAP and Siebel Toolboxes, see Appendix B, "For More Information."

Readers of this chapter should be familiar with the following technologies:

- Active Server Pages (ASPs).
- Microsoft Visual Basic®.
- COM+ components.
- Microsoft SharePoint™ Portal Server 2001.
- The digital dashboard framework.
- Extensible Markup Language (XML) and Extensible Stylesheet Language Transformations (XSLT).
- Certificates and Public Key Interoperability (PKI).

Effective Web Part Design for Business Applications

Web Parts are sets of properties that wrap around Web-based content. In the context of SharePoint Portal Server, Web Parts provide the Web-based view of content stored in the workspace in addition to any other content you choose to display. You can export and import

Web Parts from SharePoint Portal Server to and from different data sources such as a computer running Microsoft Exchange 2000 or a computer with a Microsoft SQL Server™ 2000 digital dashboard. For more information about exporting Web Parts to different data sources, see Chapter 23, "Deploying Digital Dashboards to Multiple Stores."

When you save a Web Part as XML, Office Developer describes the Web Part in XML format. This stores Web Parts and digital dashboards independent of the schema-capable data source. The XML format is a universal format for representing Web Parts and digital dashboards. It enables the transfer of definitions between different storage platforms. By using this format, you can store definitions in the file system or exchange them among applications. For more information about saving Web Parts in XML format, see Chapter 21, "Creating Custom Web Parts with Office XP Developer."

Because Web Parts adhere to a common standard, you can store them in libraries, and later draw from those libraries to assemble a variety of digital dashboards for your organization. The goal of a digital dashboard is to summarize, synthesize, and reduce the information users see all the time. An effective Web Part should display information in a manner appropriate to a digital dashboard.

An important first step in designing an effective Web Part is to determine what subsets of application data users require in their daily operations. Additionally, the designer should find out if there are any subsets of data that relate to one another. This allows you to design Web Parts that communicate with each other within a digital dashboard application composed of separate components. For example, a Web Part that displays customer names from Siebel could link to a Web Part that displays customer purchase orders from SAP, so that clicking a customer name in the Siebel Web Part displays the purchase orders in the SAP Web Part. Customizable Web Parts, in which the user can sort, filter, and add or remove columns of data, further enhances the user's experience.

Web Part Architecture Design

Designing Web Parts for business applications is similar to designing other distributed enterprise applications. A popular architecture for enterprise applications is the 3-tier, or n-tier, architecture. The 3-tier architecture splits services into Presentation, Business, and Data tiers. The classic 3-tier architecture is a good architecture to start with when building Web Parts for business applications that use SharePoint Portal Server. The following figure describes the three tiers.

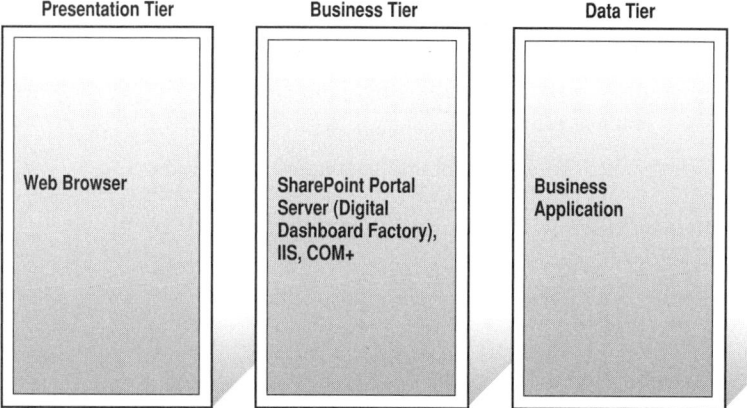

Figure 19.1. Classic 3-tier architecture

The Presentation Tier

Web Parts render in a digital dashboard and require a Web browser on the client computer. Currently, SharePoint Portal Server supports browsers that are HTML 3.2 compliant. Web Parts are, at the risk of oversimplification, like small Web pages. Therefore, developers must address the same issues that are inherent with cross-browser compatibility, including deciding whether to use DHTML, XML, and other client-side technologies in the Web Part.

Developers should be skilled in the variety of technologies associated with traditional Web-based application design. These technologies include HTML, Microsoft JScript, and Visual Basic Scripting Edition (VBScript). To maintain a consistent look and feel among Web Parts, the digital dashboard should use common style sheets created by the user interface developer. At this stage of development, traditional tools such as Microsoft FrontPage® and Microsoft Visual Interdev® can assist HTML and script development.

The digital dashboard also provides a rich set of services that aid in communication and state management. Developers should plan how to take advantage of these services in order to create unique digital dashboard applications that are more than simply the sum of the individual Web Parts. The digital dashboard provides the client-side services through the Digital Dashboard Services Component (DDSC). The presentation tier developer should fully understand the DDSC to create good Web Parts that can communicate with each other.

The Digital Dashboard Services Component (DDSC)

The DDSC is a client-side component that is included in every digital dashboard page as a hidden object. Figure 19.2 illustrates the presentation tier with the DDSC component. This component makes Web Parts reusable and easier to build by providing a standard infrastructure for the following services:

- **Part Discovery.** Allows Web Parts to discover other Web Parts on a digital dashboard.

- **Notification.** Allows Web Parts to respond to external events that occur at the digital dashboard or Web Part level.

- **Session state management.** Allows Web Parts to interchange information and objects within a browser session.

- **State management.** Allows digital dashboards and Web Parts to maintain global state and to persist in this state between activations.

- **Item Retrieval.** Allows Web Parts to retrieve and maintain the state of items in the store module.

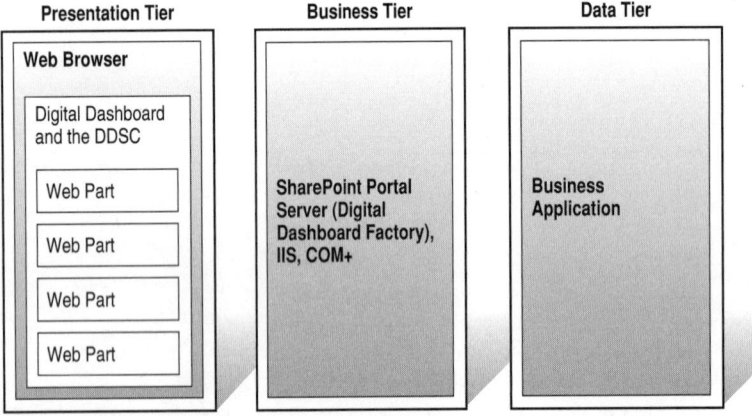

Figure 19.2. Presentation tier with DDSC

For more information about the DDSC and digital dashboard factory, see Appendix B.

The Business Tier

You can separate the business tier into two more logical tiers: the user-centric tier, which manages the delivery of HTML that renders in a client's browser, and the data-centric tier, which handles the complexities of accessing resources in the data tier.

Web Part properties determine how the digital dashboard renders the Web Part.

User-Centric Tier

The digital dashboard factory is a code engine, implemented as an ASP page, or compiled code on the Web server. This server assembles the Web Parts into a layout suitable for rendering Web Parts in a digital dashboard. Web Parts can contain embedded content, including HTML, scripts, Microsoft ActiveX® controls, or XML. They can also contain links pointing to any type of Web-based content in any location.

The factory also exposes a programming object model and a scripting host on the server. Services exposed by this object model include server-side object creation, querying of standard IIS server variables, and querying of factory inspection variables that expose information about the type of factory and environment in which the current part is running. Developers can use the scripting host to build rich Web Part content. Web Parts are defined as an open specification and are meant to run in a platform-independent fashion. Because of this, Web Part authors must use the factory object from the scripting host to ensure portability of the Web Parts.

In an enterprise environment with multiple browsers and devices in the field, the Web Part must detect what type of browser is requesting the data and then send the appropriate Web content for that particular platform. You can accomplish this by using script in a Web Part that queries the factory object for the type of client and then sends the appropriate content.

An effective method for dynamically formatting raw data into Web content is to use XSLT. This technique, coupled with determining the digital dashboard factory browser, allows the developer to take raw XML data, delivered from the data-centric tier, and format it into Web content that can best be viewed in the user's particular environment. By using the scripting host provided by the factory, the developer supplies the Web content by implementing a function called GetContent(). The following figure illustrates the user-centric tier.

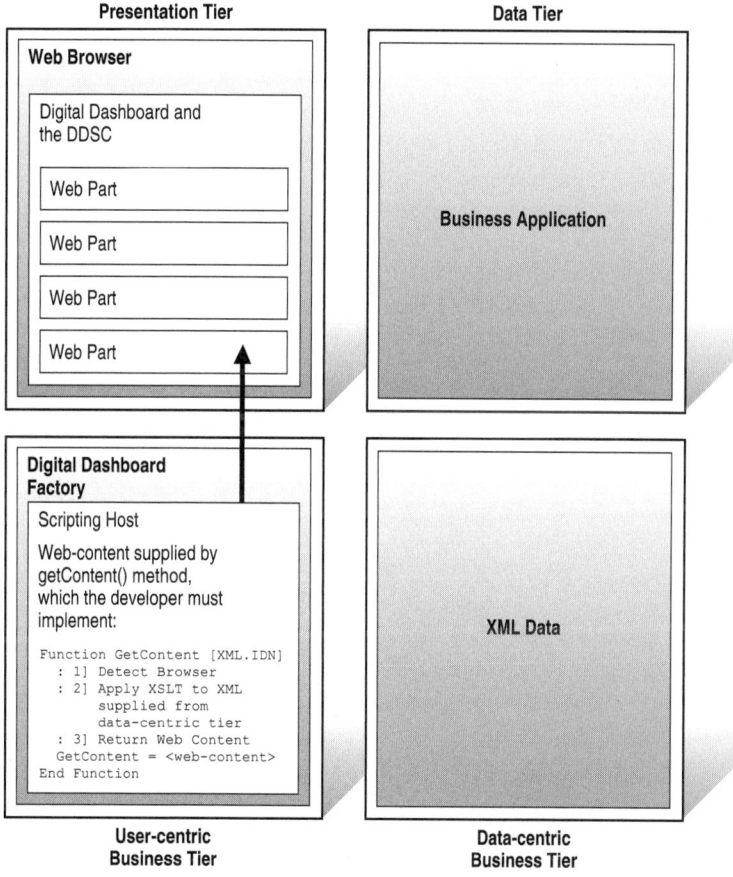

Figure 19.3. User-centric business tier

Data-Centric Tier

Using XML is the most effective technique for passing data from the data-centric tier to the user-centric tier. This gives the user-centric developer the flexibility to format the data into the appropriate Web content.

The first step for the data-centric developer is to build an XML Generator. This is a component wrapper around the application programming interface (API) for the business application. The component wrapper retrieves data and formats it into XML.

The data-centric developer may include an interface for the component that allows the Web Part builder to supply constraints to the information. Filtering and sorting the information from the business application are two examples of such constraints.

Although the work for data-centric developers appears to be relatively straightforward, they have the difficult task of programmatically accessing the data from the business application. This crucial exercise requires extensive knowledge of the business application.

Business applications are inherently intricate. Usually, the data in such applications are contained in data stores whose schema is complex. For example, a full instance of SAP R/3, with all the modules, requires a database that contains over 10,000 tables.

Given the complexity of data stores for business applications, the fact that schemas frequently change, and the fact that most of the data is locked behind a fortress-like application layer, many business application vendors provide published APIs or input/output (I/O) mechanisms for accessing the data. Because Microsoft Windows® is prevalent in most enterprises, many of the application vendors have COM components that expose these APIs. When building Web Parts for the digital dashboard, use of these COM components is the preferred method for accessing business application data.

Because most business and legacy applications are important, the developer must have deep knowledge of the application and the API or I/O mechanism used to access the application to obtain data appropriate for the Web Part. If this is not the case, the development team should consult with experts who have such knowledge.

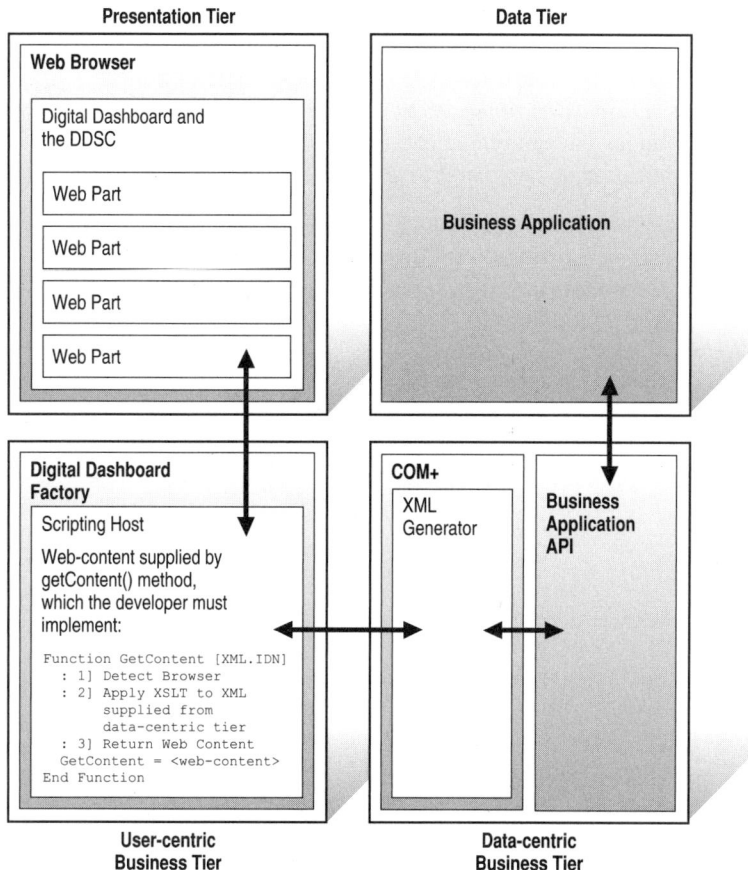

Figure 19.4. Data-centric business tier

Challenges of Web Part Design

This section reviews the particular challenges of designing and deploying Web Parts for business applications within a digital dashboard framework.

Ensuring Authentication

Most business and legacy applications use accounts for authentication into the system separate from those used for Windows authentication. This becomes a challenge for the Web Part builder. Users should not have to enter a user name and password to view each different Web Part on a single page. Each business application should request a user's login information only once, especially if the user needs multiple views of the data.

To give the user a single sign-on experience, you should supply a component to translate a user's authenticated user name (NTLM) and map it to the user name and password for the business application. You must use a signed digital certificate to encrypt the transfer of user name and password to keep the process secure. After the server authenticates a user against the business application, the server should not have to re-authenticate the users when they request data from the same business application by using other Web Parts.

Avanade Security Broker is a utility designed to solve the authentication problem. Avanade Security Broker stores encrypted data, mapping NTLM user names to security authorization schemes of business and legacy applications. Using PKI standards to ensure security encrypts all communications between this utility, the user name/password database, and the calling XML Generator.

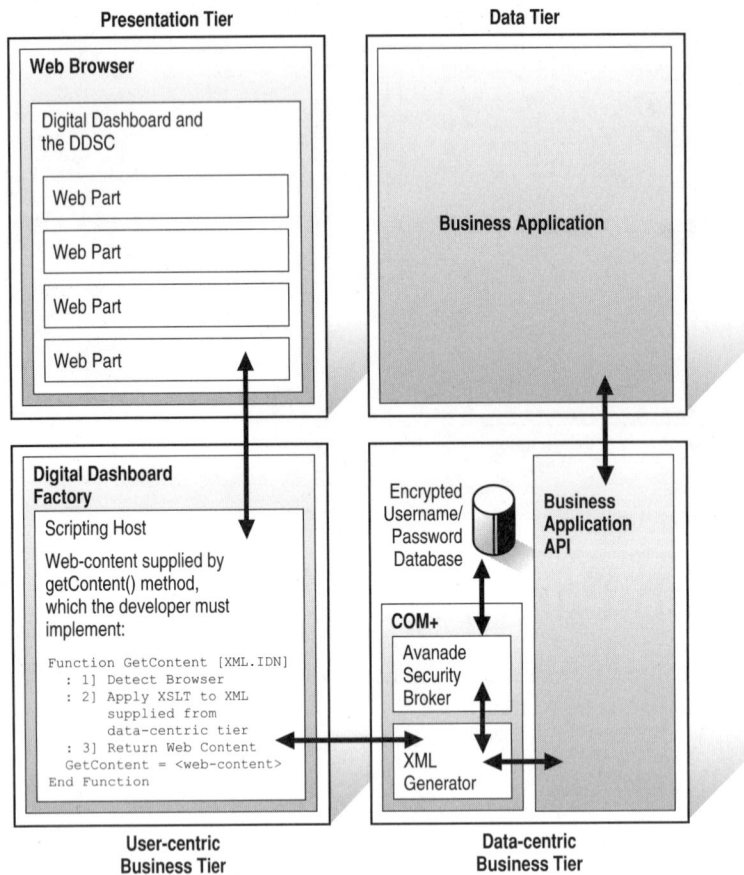

Figure 19.5. Data tier

Addressing LOB Application API Latency

Given the complexity of business applications, it is no surprise that the APIs for those applications can complicate information retrieval. For example, SAP has a rich set of COM APIs that assist the Windows Developer in accessing data from its popular ERP application, R/3. However, many of the function calls that are made to the system are complex and require a strict order with data from one call feeding into the next.

With such complexity, retrieving summary data quickly is a challenge. In such cases, it is helpful to create a staging database that contains summarized data for quick retrieval. By using this technique, the data-centric component of a Web Part operates more efficiently. Ultimately, this increases the usefulness of the component to the user of the Web Part.

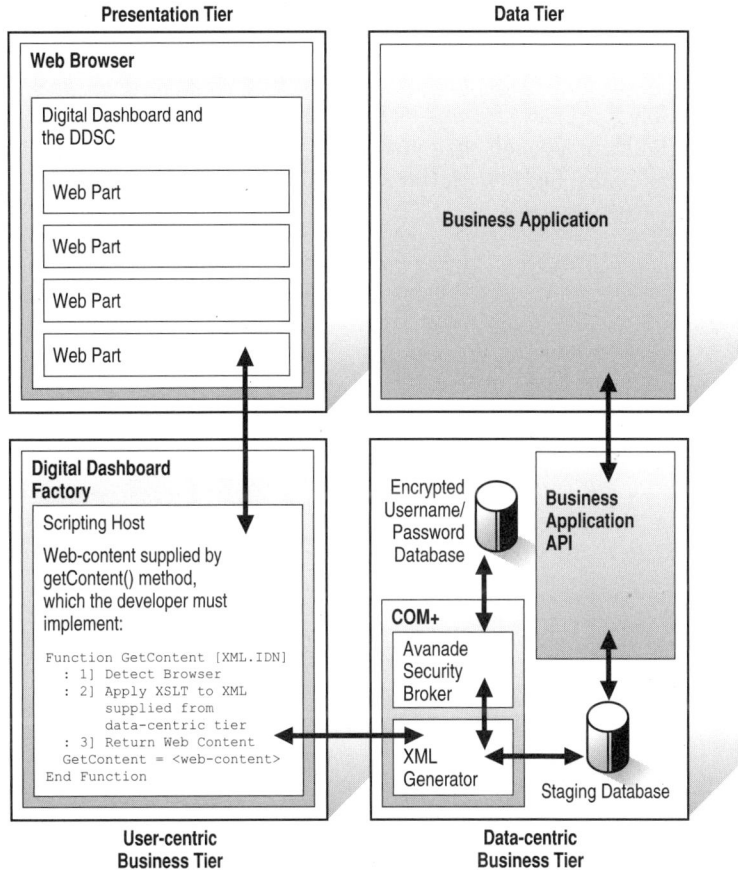

Figure 19.6. Data tier LOB application

Web Part Deployment

Deploying Web Part applications and digital dashboard applications should be easy for an administrator. The examples in this chapter will demonstrate how to construct a Microsoft Installer File (.msi) to use with the Windows Installer application. The installer file will contain instructions on how to install the XML Generator COM+ application and copy Web Parts into a gallery. The installer file will also provide for any business application dependencies. The digital dashboard administrator can allow users in the field to import the Web Parts in a digital dashboard.

Summary

The release of SharePoint Portal Server and the digital dashboard offers the enterprise a powerful, yet simple and cost-effective platform on which to deliver business and legacy application information easily. In addition, third party vendors are building Web Parts that allow companies to pick from pre-built components that quickly plug into a digital dashboard, providing quick, powerful solutions. For more information about creating Web Parts for business applications, see Appendix B.

Creating Web Parts for Multiple Environments

This chapter provides recommendations for creating Web Parts. In addition, it provides a code sample of a stand-alone Web Part by using Active Server Pages (ASP), Microsoft® Visual Basic® Scripting Edition (VBScript), and a code sample of a Web Part to illustrate the recommended strategies. For more information about creating Web Parts, see Appendix B, "For More Information."

General Methodology

The following methodology is recommended when creating Web Parts:

- Always use relative URLs in your HTML, ASP, and VBScript files.

- Generate relative links for any links within your Web Part. If you code the absolute URL in the Web Part or in the creation of the Web Part to a network basic input/output system (NetBIOS) name, your Web Part works only for NetBIOS. URLs that are coded to a NetBIOS name will not work on a computer running Microsoft SharePoint™ Portal Server 2001 deployed across an internal or external fully qualified domain name (FQDN). Using relative links enables you to use the same Web Part for NetBIOS, internal FQDN, and external FQDN.

To use relative links when creating a new Web Part:

1. On the **Settings** page of a Web Part, select the **Get content from the following link** check box.

   Note If you are editing an existing Web Part, click **Show Advanced Settings** to see this check box.

2. Type the URL for the link to the content.

In addition, you can convert the ASP or HTML code to a Web Part. For more information and sample code, see the "Sample Codes" section in this chapter.

   Note To avoid poor and interrupted server performance do not use a stand-alone ASP page as a Web Part.

The threads available for ASPs are computed by adding one to the number of processors. For example, two threads are available on a single processor computer, and three threads are available on a dual processor computer. If you do use a stand-alone ASP page as a Web Part, run it in isolated mode. In this case, there is no increased risk of hangs due to a deadlock.

Note If you use an ASP page as a Web Part and it is not running in isolated mode, it is recommended that you use an ASP page that generates an HTML fragment and not a full page.

A fragment includes only the code that is required to draw the Web Part. It does not include extraneous tags (such as <HTML> </HTML> or <BODY> </BODY>) that may be inserted by your editing application.

Note If you use an ASP page as a Web Part and it is running in isolated mode, it is recommended that the ASP page generate a full HTML page.

- Use Visual Basic scripted files as Web Parts. Using Visual Basic scripted files reduces the load on the server, resulting in increased performance.

- Include copious error handling in the code for Web Parts. Web Parts are difficult to debug once they are in the dashboard framework.

Sample Codes

This section describes two options for Web Parts that use relative URLs: ASP or VBScript code. These options describe a stand-alone Web Part. The ASP and VBScript code samples enable you to use the same Web Part when accessing the server by using NetBIOS, internal FQDN, or external FQDN. The samples contain two relative links and some very basic ASP code.

Note Both code samples perform the same task. The samples are provided to demonstrate two ways to perform the same task.

Using the Sample ASP or VBScript Code

You can create your Web Part from ASP or VBScript code. The advantages of referencing an ASP or VBScript page are:

- You can use existing ASP or VBScript code without changing it.

- All code is executed from the client, reducing the load on the server.

- The Web Part is isolated, preventing any interaction with other Web Parts.

The disadvantages of referencing an ASP page or a VBScript page are:

- The code is not easily portable.

- The Web Part cannot interact with other Web Parts.

- The Web Part cannot function if you are using Netscape Navigator as your browser.

To use sample ASP code as your Web Part:

1. Create a file named **User.asp** containing the following code:

```
<HTML>

<BODY>

<%

Response.write request.servervariables("Logon_User")

%>

<p>

<A Href="../" Target="new">Home</a><p>

<A Href="../Portal/Document%20Library/" Target="new">Document
Library</a>

</BODY>

</HTML>
```

2. Navigate to the **Portal** folder in the workspace.

   Note The Portal folder is a hidden folder.

3. Copy **User.asp** into the **Portal** folder.

4. Navigate to the **Home** page of the dashboard site.

5. Click **Content**.

6. Click **Create a New Web Part**.

7. On the **Settings** page for the Web Part, select the **Get content from the following link** check box.

8. Type /*workspace_name*/**Portal/User.asp** under the **Get content from the following link** check box.

9. Select the **Isolate this Web Part's content from the other Web Parts** check box.

10. Click **Save** to close the **Settings** page for the Web Part.

11. Click **Save** to close the **Content** page for the **Home** page.

Using the Sample Web Part Code

You can create a stand-alone Web Part containing relative links.

The advantages of using a stand-alone Web Part are:

- The code executes more quickly than a non-isolated ASP page or VBScript page.

- The code is portable and reusable on any dashboard.

- The Web Part can interact with other Web Parts.

The disadvantages of using a stand-alone Web Part are:

- The server load increases.

- You must migrate existing code to meet the specification for Web Parts for the digital dashboard.

- The Web Part is difficult to debug once it is deployed. It is recommended that you include copious error handling in your code.

To use a sample Web Part:

1. Create a file named **TestWithRelativeURLs.dwp** containing the following code:

   Note Long commented lines and some code lines wrap to the next line in the following sample. For best results, copy the code sample and paste it directly into Microsoft Notepad.

   ```
   <?xml version="1.0"?>

   <WebPart xmlns="urn:schemas-microsoft-com:webpart:" version="1.0.0">

     <Title>Web Part Sample with relative URLs</Title>

     <Description>How to create a Web Part with relative URLs</
   Description>

     <Content><![CDATA[

   'Generic Web Part Function. REQUIRED.

   Function GetContent(nod)

       Dim strWorkspaceUrl 'Variable to store calculated URL of user
   ```

```
On Error Resume Next

'BEGIN COMMENTS

'NOTE:     ExtractWorkspaceURL and GetServerVariable are function
calls to TahoeUtils.inc.

'          We cannot guarantee backward compatibility with future
SPs or versions of SharePoint Portal Server.

'          It is recommended that you create your own standard
include library to retrieve the URL of the user.

'          Once you create your library, include it in
DashboardExtensions.vbs (see DDRK for more information).

'IMPORTANT: DO NOT modify TahoeUtils.inc in any way. Modifications
may break your portal and are not supported.

'END COMMENTS

strWorkspaceUrl = ExtractWorkspaceUrl(GetDBProtocol() & _

GetServerVariable("SERVER_NAME") & GetServerVariable("URL"))

If Err.Number <> 0 Then Exit Function

strHtmlRet = request.servervariables("Logon_User") & vbCRLF

'Build up HTML output to a string

'Add a relative URL link with strWorkspaceUrl

strHtmlRet = strHtmlRet & "<p>"

strHtmlRet = strHtmlRet & "<a target=new href=""" & _

strWorkspaceUrl & "/Portal"">" & vbCRLF

strHtmlRet = strHtmlRet & "Portal" & vbCRLF

strHtmlRet = strHtmlRet & "</a>" & vbCRLF

'Add another link

strHtmlRet = strHtmlRet & "<p>"

strHtmlRet = strHtmlRet & "<a target=new href=""" & _
```

```
      strWorkspaceUrl & "/Portal/Document Library"">" & vbCRLF

      strHtmlRet = strHtmlRet & "Document Library" & vbCRLF

      strHtmlRet = strHtmlRet & "</a>" & vbCRLF

      'Return string to Dashboard

      GetContent = strHtmlRet

  End Function

]]></Content>

   <ContentType>1</ContentType>

   <IsVisible>1</IsVisible>

   <AllowRemove>1</AllowRemove>

   <HasFrame>1</HasFrame>

   <AllowMinimize>1</AllowMinimize>

   <FrameState>0</FrameState>

   <RequiresIsolation>0</RequiresIsolation>

   <CacheBehavior>0</CacheBehavior>

   <CacheTimeout>0</CacheTimeout>

   <DetailLink></DetailLink>

   <CustomizationLink></CustomizationLink>

   <IsIncluded>1</IsIncluded>

   <PartOrder>0</PartOrder>

   <Zone>3</Zone>

 </WebPart>
```

2. Navigate to the home page of the dashboard site.

3. Click **Content**.

4. Click **Import a Web Part File**.

5. Import **TestWithRelativeURLs.dwp**.

6. Click **Save** to close the **Content** page for the **Home** page.

Summary

This chapter provides recommendations for creating Web Parts. In addition, it provides a code sample of a stand-alone Web Part by using ASP, VBScript, and a code sample of a Web Part to illustrate the recommended strategies.

PART 5

Development

This section provides tools and information for developers who want to customize Microsoft® SharePoint™ Portal Server 2001. It provides key strategies for mapping custom properties, information on how to develop Web Parts for business applications, and information on how to enhance searching.

Creating Custom Web Parts with Office XP Developer

This chapter describes how you can use Microsoft® Office XP Developer to customize Microsoft SharePoint™ Portal Server 2001. It outlines tasks such as creating and adding Web Parts, editing and adding content to Web Parts, exporting and importing Web Parts, adding subdashboards, previewing the workspace, and saving Office XP documents as Web Parts. It also discusses good Web Part coding practices that make it possible for you to write reusable Web Parts. It describes how to save a Web Part as an XML document in order to move it from one store to another.

Overview of Digital Dashboard Technology

SharePoint Portal Server uses Digital Dashboard technology to create a dashboard site. A *dashboard site* is a collection of digital dashboards that provide a Web-based view of the workspace. *A digital dashboard* brings together disparate pieces of information and services and presents them by using Web Parts in a consistent and customizable Web-based view. *Web Parts* are a set of properties that wrap around Web-based content. In the context of SharePoint Portal Server, Web Parts provide the Web-based view of content stored in the workspace in addition to any other content you choose to display.

Office XP Developer is the primary tool for building Web Parts. Although dashboard applications have customization pages you can use to create simple Web Parts, developers can use the rich editing tools in Office XP Developer to build more complex Web Parts for use in the dashboard site for SharePoint Portal Server.

Office XP Developer Environment

You can use a number of methods to customize your digital dashboard from within the Office XP Developer environment. These methods include:

- Opening an existing digital dashboard project in the Microsoft Office XP Developer environment.

- Creating and adding Web Parts.

- Adding content and customizing Web Parts.

- Saving Office XP documents as Web Parts.

- Creating subdashboards.

- Exporting and importing Web Parts as .dwp files.

- Opening a SharePoint Portal Server dashboard site.

Before you can use the Office XP Developer environment to build Web Parts for an existing dashboard site of a SharePoint Portal Server workspace, you must open the workspace in Office XP Developer. Opening the workspace displays the contents of the workspace in the development environment and creates a project file (Portal.ddp) in the Portal folder of the workspace. The Solution Explorer displays the dashboard site, its Web Parts and any resources, and any subdashboards, hierarchically. The Properties Window displays all the properties for the workspace, Web Parts, and subdashboard.

To open the SharePoint Portal Server workspace for the first time and to create the project file:

1. On the **Start** menu, point to **Programs**, point to **Microsoft Office XP Developer**, and then click **Microsoft Development Environment**.

2. On the **File** menu, point to **New**, and then click **Project**.

3. The **New Project** dialog box appears. In the **Project Types** window select **Office Developer Projects**.

4. In the **Templates** window, select the **Dashboard Project** icon.

5. In the **Location** text box, enter **http://**/server_name/workspace_name.

6. In the **Name** text box, enter **Portal**.

   Important All workspaces include a Portal folder that contains all the Web Parts, subdashboards, and the resources for that workspace. In order to open the workspace and to create the project file, you must name the project **Portal**. If you name the project anything else, it will not connect to the workspace.

7. Click **OK**.

The preceding procedure adds a project file, called Portal.ddp, to the Portal folder. In addition, it adds a solution file to your client computer in the following location: *operating_system_drive*\Documents and Settings*user_name*\My Documents\ Office Developer Projects\PortalX\Portal.sln.

The solution file contains references to the projects that are part of that solution. Double-clicking a solution file opens the Office XP Development Environment and loads the referenced projects.

After you create a project and solution file for your workspace, you can open it in the Office XP Developer environment as follows:

To open the SharePoint Portal Server project file in Office XP Developer:

1. On the **Start** menu, point to **Programs**, point to **Microsoft Office XP Developer**, and then click **Microsoft Development Environment**.

2. On the **File** menu, point to **Open**, and then click **Project**.

3. Select the **Portal** project you want to open from the **Open Project** dialog box (for example, Portal.sln).

The project opens in the Office Developer environment. If you do not have the solution file on your computer, you still follow the steps in the following procedure to open an existing dashboard project directly from the workspace:

To open an existing project from the workspace:

1. Create a Web folder to your workspace folder (for example, **http:**//*server_name*/ *workspace_name*/**Portal**).

2. Double-click the **Portal.ddp** file in the **Portal** folder.

The project opens in the Office Developer environment.

Dashboard Site Customization

The following section describes methods you can use to customize your dashboard site, including creating custom Web Parts, creating Web Parts from documents created in Microsoft Word, Microsoft Excel, or Microsoft PowerPoint® or creating additional dashboards and importing or exporting Web Parts. This section provides procedures for each of these tasks.

Creating Web Parts

After you open the project in the Office XP Developer environment, you can customize the dashboard site by adding new Web Parts.

A Web Part can contain any kind of Web-based information. To add Web Parts to a dashboard project, use the Add New Item command. By using this command, you can add an HTML, Microsoft JScript®, Microsoft Visual Basic® Scripting Edition (VBScript), or Extensible Markup Language (XML) Web Part to the dashboard project.

To add a new Web Part to a dashboard:

1. In the **Solution Explorer**, select the dashboard project.

2. Right-click the **Portal** folder, point to **Add** on the **shortcut** menu, and then click **New Item**.

3. Select a Web Part type, and then click **Open**. For this example, select an HTML Web Part type.

When you add a Web Part, Office Developer associates a standard set of properties with the Web Part. To view the properties of a Web Part in the Properties Window, select the Web Part in the Solution Explorer.

Note If the **Properties Window** is not visible, click the **Properties** icon in the Solution Explorer to make it visible or select the **Properties Window** from the **View** menu.

Writing Reusable Web Parts

You can add content to your Web Part using two fundamental coding practices for SharePoint Portal Server:

- To associate a resources folder with a Web Part, you must follow the _Files naming convention. For example, if you name your Web Part *my_Web_Part*.**htm**, then name the associated resources folder for this Web Part *my_Web_Part*_**files**.

- You should use the Web Part Resource (_WPR_) token when referring to the resources folder of a Web Part. For example, if you want to render an image that you imported into the resources folder of a Web Part, then use the following naming convention **<img src= "_WPR_***my_Image*.**jpg">**.

By following these naming conventions, you can write functional and reusable Web Parts.

Adding Content to a Web Part

In this example, you will add content to the HTML Web Part created in the previous procedure. You can edit some properties for the Web Part and display an image in the Web Part.

To add content to a Web Part:

1. To open the Web Part in the code editor, double-click the **Part.htm Web Part** in the **Solution Explorer**.

2. In the body of the Web Part, type **<h1>Hello World</h1>**.

3. Right-click the **Portal** folder, point to **Add** on the **shortcut** menu, and then click **New Folder**. This folder stores resources used for **Part.htm**.

4. Right-click the **Folder1** folder, and then click **Rename** on the shortcut menu.

5. Rename **Folder1** to **Part_Files**.

   Note You also can do this by changing the **Name** property of **Folder1** to **Part_Files**.

6. Right-click **Part_Files**, point to **Add** on the shortcut menu, and then click **Existing Item**.

7. Browse to the location that contains the image resource that you want your Web Part to display (for example, c:\Images\Logo.gif).

   Note You must change the filter **Files of type**: to **All Files (*.*)** to see the resources.

8. Select the image, and then click **Open**.

9. In the code editor for **Part.htm**, type **<img src="_WPR_\Logo.gif">**.

   Your code should look like this:

   ```
   <HTML><BODY>

   <!- Do not edit anything above this comment ->



   <h1>Hello World</h1>

   <img src="_WPR_\Logo.gif">



   <!- Do not edit anything below this comment ->

   </BODY></HTML>
   ```

10. In the **Solution Explorer**, click **Part.htm**.

11. In the **Properties Window**, scroll down to the **Title** property, and change it from **Part** to **Hello World HTM Part**.

12. In the **Properties Window**, find the **Zone** property, and from the drop-down list, change it from **Body** to **Header**.

13. Click **Save All**, or select **Save All** from the **File** menu.

You can use this procedure to add resources of other types. You can preview the dashboard using your Web browser.

Saving Office XP Documents as Web Parts

Office XP provides an easy way to create custom Web Parts for your workspace. You can create a Web Part by saving a document as a Web page into a SharePoint Portal Server workspace folder.

To save an Office XP document as a Web Part:

1. After you finish entering content in your Office XP document, on the **File** menu, click **Save As Web Page**.

2. Type the address of the workspace, including the **Portal** folder and a name for your Web Part:

    http://*server_name*/*workspace_name*/**Portal**/*Web_Part_name*.htm

3. Click **Save**.

4. In the **Web File Properties** form, enter a name, a brief description, and a zone for where you want your Web Part to display.

5. Click **OK**.

6. Close the document.

7. Refresh the workspace view by clicking the **Refresh** button in the **Solution Explorer** to display the new Web Part as part of the workspace. You can now double-click the Web Part and edit its contents from within the Office Developer environment.

Creating Subdashboards

A subdashboard is a digital dashboard that is a child of a parent digital dashboard. You can add subdashboards to your dashboard site to organize the content that you want to display using different levels and sections. You can merge subdashboards and any related dashboards into a single navigation bar by setting the MergeSubDashboards property to True. The navigation bar appears under the title bar of the subdashboard. SharePoint Portal Server optimizes the format of the navigation bar to handle a single root dashboard with one level of child dashboards.

To add subdashboards to your workspace:

1. In the **Solution Explorer**, click the **Portal** folder or a subdashboard (depending on where you want the subdashboard).

2. Right-click, point to **Add**, and then click **New Subdashboard**.

After creating a subdashboard, you can specify the dashboard properties and add Web Parts to it as you would with any other dashboard.

Exporting and Importing Web Parts

SharePoint Portal Server is considered a *schema-capable* data source. You can export and import Web Parts from SharePoint Portal Server to different data sources such as a computer running Microsoft Exchange 2000 computer or a computer with a Microsoft SQL Server™ 2000 dashboard. For more information about exporting Web Parts to different data sources, see Chapter 23, "Deploying Digital Dashboards to Multiple Stores."

When you save a Web Part as XML, Office Developer describes the Web Part in XML format. This stores Web Parts and dashboards independent of the schema-capable data source. XML is a universal format for representing Web Parts and dashboards. It enables the transfer of definitions between different storage platforms. Using this format, you can store definitions in the file system or exchange them among applications. After you click Save, Office Developer saves your Web Part and its properties as an XML document with a DWP extension (.dwp). Office Developer also saves any resources associated with the Web Part to a folder you specify as part of the Save As DWP command. The following steps describe how to export the Web Part that you created in the earlier example.

To export a Web Part from your workspace:

1. In the **Solution Explorer**, click the **Part.htm** Web Part.

2. On the **File** menu, click **Save Copy of Part.HTM As**.

3. In the drop-down list, change the **Save as type** to **DWP file (*.dwp)**.

4. Enter a file name for your Web Part (for example, Part.dwp).

5. Set the **Save in** location to a path on your local file system (for example, C:\DWPFiles).

6. Click **Save**.

When in XML format, a Web Part can be exchanged outside operating systems that manage Web Distributed Authoring and Versioning (WebDAV) properties. Office Developer saves these files in *.dwp format, so there is a common way of representing Web Parts saved as an XML document. When you receive a Web Part as a *.dwp file, you can easily import it into a dashboard. You can import the Web Part to a digital dashboard on a computer running Exchange 2000, SQL Server 2000, or another computer running SharePoint Portal Server. In addition, Office XP Developer provides a catalog of Web Parts. To import a Web Part from this catalog, perform the following steps.

To import a Web Part into your workspace:

1. In the **Solution Explorer**, select the **Portal** folder.

2. Right-click the **Portal** folder, point to **Add**, and then click **Existing Item**.

3. Click the **Web Links.dwp**.

4. Click **Open**.

This adds the Web Links.VBS Web Part to the workspace. Notice that importing the Web Links.dwp added a Web Links.VBS Web Part and a Web Links_Files folder to the workspace. The Web Links_Files folder contains the resources for the Web Links Web Part.

Previewing Your Dashboard

You can preview your dashboard at any time by using your Web browser.

To preview a dashboard:

1. In the **Solution Explorer**, click the **Portal** folder.

2. Right-click the **Portal** folder, and then click **View in Browser** on the **shortcut** menu.

Summary

This chapter describes how you can use Office XP Developer to customize SharePoint Portal Server 2001. It also discusses coding practices for reusable Web Parts, and describes how to save Web Parts in order to move them from SharePoint Portal Server to another application that uses digital dashboards.

By following these procedures, you can open and create a project file for the dashboard site included with SharePoint Portal Server. Using Office Developer, you can customize and extend your dashboard site. For more information on Web Parts and digital dashboards, see Appendix B, "For More Information."

Creating a Corporate Web Part Catalog

After you build or collect a set of Web Parts for your company, you can make them available to your users for use in a digital dashboard for Microsoft® SharePoint™ Portal Server, Microsoft SQL Server™ 2000, or Microsoft Exchange 2000. To do this, you can create a corporate Web Part catalog. This chapter explains how to set up a catalog using SharePoint Portal Server or the SQL Server dashboard that is included in the Digital Dashboard Resource Kit (DDRK) 3.

Overview of Web Part Catalogs

This chapter uses the following terminology:

- **Web Part catalog.** A library of Web Part definition (.dwp) files that you can import into an existing dashboard.

- **Gallery.** A collection of catalogs from which you can import Web Parts into an existing dashboard.

- **Dashboard server.** A server that is running the digital dashboard engine. For the purposes of this chapter, the server is a computer that is running SharePoint Portal Server or a computer that has the SQL Server dashboard installed.

- **Local Web Part catalog.** A Web Part catalog that is stored on a dashboard server. The SQL Server dashboard includes a local catalog as part of its default installation. You must set up a local catalog on a SharePoint Portal Server computer.

- **Web Part catalog server.** A dashboard server that is dedicated to the task of hosting a Web Part catalog. An organization typically deploys a Web Part catalog server as a central distribution point of Web Parts for multiple digital dashboard servers.

Figure 22.1 shows a list of catalogs from which you can import Web Parts to a digital dashboard.

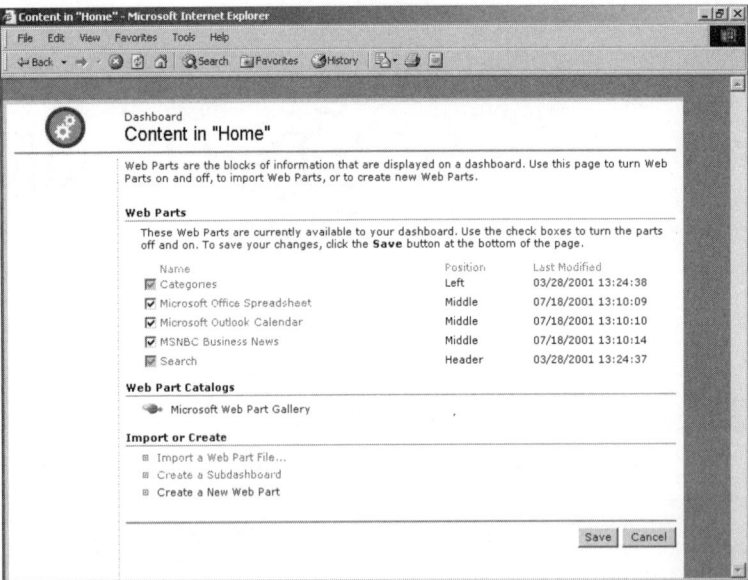

Figure 22.1. Catalogs of Web Parts

Whether you deploy a local Web Part catalog or a dedicated catalog server, use the instructions in the following section. In addition to setting up your own catalog, you can populate your gallery with two additional online Web Parts catalogs.

The Microsoft Web Part Gallery is a public catalog that is available on the Microsoft Web site and contains a variety of Web Parts authored by Microsoft. You can access the Web Part Gallery only from the Contents page of a digital dashboard, by clicking the **Web Part Gallery** link. SharePoint Portal Server and the SQL Server digital dashboard are both linked to this catalog in the Contents management page by default. There is another Web Part Gallery that is available from Microsoft, which includes Web Parts from third-party companies. The Microsoft Web Parts in this gallery are in a self-extracting compressed format. You must download, uncompress, and import these Web Parts into your local catalog or catalog server, or directly into your digital dashboard. For more information about public catalogs that are available from the Microsoft Web site, see Appendix B, "For More Information."

Creating a Catalog

This section outlines the following steps to create a custom catalog:

- Create and collect the Web Parts

- Choose a catalog server

- Populate the catalog and make it accessible

Create and Collect Web Parts

You must assemble a collection of Web Parts for your catalog. You can do this using either of the following methods:

- **Creating.** You can build a set of Web Parts. For more information about tools and instructions on creating Web Parts, see Appendix B.

- **Collecting.** You can collect a set of Web Parts. There are hundreds of available Web Parts that you do not have to create. Before you create a new Web Part, check the Microsoft Online Gallery to look for an existing Web Part. For more information about available Web Parts, see Appendix B, "For More Information."

You can associate a Web Part with multiple files. A Web Part includes an Extensible Markup Language (XML) document with a .dwp file name extension, and associated resources, such as Extensible Stylesheet Language (XSL) files, Graphics Interchange Format (GIF) files, and, style sheets, if they exist. When you collect Web Parts, verify that you have all of the associated resource files. The resources usually reside in the *webpartname_files* subdirectory. In the code of the Web Part, you should see the start <resource> tag, the end </resource> tag, and a reference to the resource files. When you import a Web Part, the Web Part automatically imports the resource files and stores them in the proper location. If the RESOURCE elements exist in the Web Part, confirm that the corresponding files are in the proper location.

Choose a Catalog Server

You can designate a SharePoint Portal Server computer or a computer with the SQL Server dashboard installed to act as a catalog server. A computer with the SQL Server dashboard installed includes a local catalog by default. You must create a local catalog for SharePoint Portal Server.

The advantages and disadvantages of storing the catalog in each location follow:

SharePoint Portal Server. Although you can use SharePoint Portal Server to set up a catalog server quickly and easily, it does not offer categorization of Web Parts. Figure 22.2 shows a catalog setup on a SharePoint Portal Server computer.

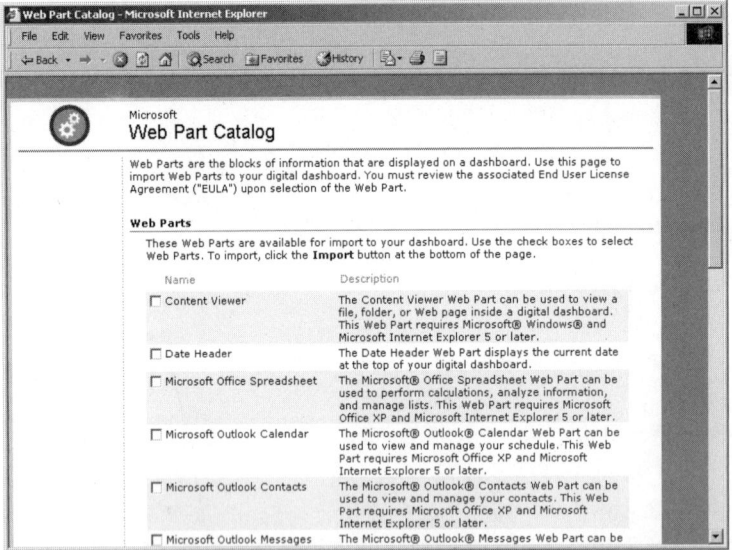

Figure 22.2. Web Part catalog on a SharePoint Portal Server computer

SQL Server Digital Dashboard. Offers categorization of Web Parts. This allows you to group them in meaningful categories such as accounting, personal, Internet, and so on.

You can mix and match catalog servers with dashboard servers. This means that you can use a catalog server (using the SQL Server dashboard) with your SharePoint Portal Server and vice versa. Your needs determine which deployment is most appropriate. If you are setting up a computer that is running SharePoint Portal Server for a small group of users and want to quickly give them a custom catalog, it is easiest to create a local catalog on the same server. If you are setting up a single, large catalog server with hundreds of Web Parts for thousands of dashboards and users, you may want to consider setting up a catalog on a computer with SQL Server dashboard installed because of the increased flexibility of categorization.

Populate the Catalog and Make It Accessible

After you choose a catalog server, you need to populate the catalog and make it available to users. For more information about catalogs, see Appendix B.

Modify Catalogs on a Computer Running SQL Server Digital Dashboard

You can add, modify, or delete the list of Web Parts that are displayed in the local catalog or a custom catalog of a computer with the SQL Server dashboard installed.

To modify the catalog, edit the Wplist.xml file that resides in the Web folder that contains the Web Parts. This file determines which Web Parts are present in the catalog. It also defines the categories that group Web Parts together. You can edit the Wplist.xml file to add new categories or to modify the list of Web Parts that appear in a catalog.

To create a new category, define a new CATEGORY element for it. To add or delete a Web Part, create or delete a WEBPART element.

About CATEGORY Elements

A CATEGORY element defines a specific category that you subsequently use to group Web Parts. It is also a container for the following elements:

- **ID.** The identifier of a category.

- **DESCRIPTION.** A longer string for the category. The value of this element is visible in a dashboard Contents page.

The following example shows the CATEGORY element for Administration Web Parts:

```
<Category>

 <ID>Administration</ID>

 <Description>Dashboard Administration</Description>

</Category>
```

About WEBPART Elements

A WEBPART element defines all of the Web Parts that are contained in a catalog. It is also a container for the following elements:

- **TITLE.** Defines the Web Part title. The value of this element is visible in the Web Part Catalog page that is displayed when a user opens a catalog page.

- **DESCRIPTION.** Defines a long text string that contains information about the Web Part. The value of this element is visible in the Web Part Catalog page.

- **FILENAME.** Defines the Web Part definition (.dwp) of the Web Part.

- **CATEGORYID.** Defines the category in which the Web Part appears. The value of this element must be one of the values defined in the CATEGORY element.

The following example shows the WEBPART element for the Dashboard View Web Part in the Administration dashboard:

```
<Webpart>

  <Title>Dashboard View</Title>

  <Description>The Dashboard Folder View Web Part displays the hierarchy of
  dashboards and folders on the administration dashboard. An administrator
  can remove dashboards or create new ones.</Description>

  <Filename>Dashboard%20View.dwp</Filename>

  <CategoryID>Administration</CategoryID>

</Webpart>
```

To edit the Wplist.xml file:

1. In the **Parts** folder, right-click **Wplist.xml**, and then copy the file to your desktop.

2. Use a text editor to edit the file. You can edit the file by adding, modifying, or removing the CATEGORY and WEBPART elements, and then saving the file to the desktop location.

3. Copy the file back to the **Parts** folder. You can also move the file from Internet Explorer to Windows Explorer by using the drag-and-drop feature.

Make the Catalog Available to Users

The Contents management page of a dashboard renders the local catalog and Web Part Gallery catalog based on XML definitions by default. In addition to these predefined catalogs, you can add custom catalogs that organize Web Parts in different categories, or link to third-party catalogs.

Add and Delete a Catalog on a Computer with the SQL Server Digital Dashboard Installed

To add a new catalog, create a new Web folder in the DAVCatalog root folder. Similar to the Parts folder, use this folder to store the Web Parts you want in the new catalog, and then update the Catalogs.xml file to point to the new catalog. The catalog entries appear in the order in which they appear in the Contents page.

To delete a catalog, remove the definition from the Catalogs.xml file. To modify the contents of the local catalog of a computer with the SQL Server dashboard installed, edit the Wplist.xml file as described previously.

About WEBPARTCATALOG Elements

The WEBPARTCATALOG element defines a specific catalog. It is a container for the following elements:

- **CATALOGNAME.** Defines the catalog title. The value of this element is visible in the Contents page. To create a new catalog, type a new catalog name.

- **HREF.** Defines the source of catalog contents. The source can be the Partcatalog.asp file or another implementation that you provide. If you are creating a new catalog, provide the name of the Web folder to the Partcatalog.asp file.

- **DESCRIPTION.** Defines descriptive text. The catalog does not expose the value of this element by default.

The following example shows how the Catalogs.xml file defines the Local Catalog through the WEBPARTCATALOG element:

```
<DDF:WebPartCatalog>

 <DDF:CatalogName>Local Catalog</DDF:CatalogName>

 <DDF:href>partcatalog.asp?FolderID=_stPortalServer_/_stPortalVRoot_/Parts/
</DDF:href>

 <DDF:Description>Parts available in the Local Catalog.</DDF:Description>

</DDF:WebPartCatalog>
```

Edit the Catalogs.xml File

The Catalogs.xml file is a dashboard factory file that determines which catalogs are present in the Contents management page. You can use any XML editor to modify this file.

To edit the Catalogs.xml:

1. Open the **Catalogs.xml** file. By default, this file is located in the C:\Program Files\SQL Server Digital Dashboard\Factory folder.

2. Edit the file by adding, modifying, or removing the WEBPARTCATALOG element, and then save the file.

Create a Local Catalog on a Computer Running SharePoint Portal Server

SharePoint Portal Server also supports catalog modifications. You can add Web Parts to a catalog on a computer running SharePoint Portal Server.

To add Web Parts to a catalog:

1. Create a personal dashboard to provide the equivalent of a catalog, and then import the Web Parts that you have collected or built. Notice the URL of the new dashboard. For example, a personal dashboard named "Gallery" has the following URL: http://*server_name*/*workspace_name*/dashboards/gallery.

2. Open the Catalogs.xml file. By default, the Catalogs.xml file resides in the http://*server_name*/*workspace_name*/Portal/Resources folder in the workspace.

   Note You must be coordinator of the workspace and enable viewing of hidden files and folders to see the Portal/Resources folder.

3. In the file Catalogs.xml, add a URL to the dashboard site. This URL should include the cmd=catalog parameter as shown in the following example:

   http://*server_name*/*workspace_name*/dashboards/gallery?cmd=catalog

   When the ?cmd=catalog parameter is added to the end of the URL, a catalog view is displayed instead of a dashboard view.

The following example shows an entry in the Catalogs.xml file of a SharePoint Portal Server computer referring to a catalog server that uses the SQL Server dashboard:

```
<?xml version="1.0" ?>

<DDF:CatalogInformation xmlns:DDF="urn:schemas-microsoft-
com:dashboardfactory:">

<DDF:WebPartCatalog>

 <DDF:CatalogName _locID="L_WebPartGallery_Text">My Company's Internal
Catalog</DDF:CatalogName>

 <DDF:href _locID="L_CatalogHREF_Text">http://webparts/dashboard/
partcatalog.asp?FolderID=http://webparts/DAVCatalog/Parts/</DDF:href>

 <DDF:Description _locID="L_GalleryDesc_Text">A collection of sample parts
for use with Microsoft's Digital Dashboard</DDF:Description>

</DDF:WebPartCatalog>

</DDF:CatalogInformation>
```

Summary

This chapter explains how to set up a catalog using SharePoint Portal Server or the SQL Server dashboard included in the Digital Dashboard Resource Kit (DDRK) 3. After building or collecting a set of Web Parts for your company, you can make them available to your users for use in a digital dashboard for SharePoint Portal Server, SQL Server 2000, or Exchange 2000.

CHAPTER 23

Deploying Digital Dashboards to Multiple Stores

This chapter outlines how to facilitate deploying digital dashboards across different stores and deploying Web Parts from one server to another. This chapter describes how to package and deploy Web Storage System dashboards from one server to another. It also shows how to import and export Web Parts from different data sources, such as a Microsoft® SharePoint™ Portal Server 2001, a Microsoft Exchange 2000 computer or a computer running a Microsoft SQL Server™ dashboard.

Deployment Overview

After designing, building, and testing a digital dashboard, the next step is to deploy it to a server. Microsoft Office XP Developer includes the ability to copy dashboard projects from one location to another on the same server. However, Office XP Developer does not support the deployment of digital dashboards from one server to another. To facilitate deployment of dashboard solutions onto a production server, this chapter describes the following two approaches:

- Use the Application Deployment Wizard in the Microsoft Web Storage System Software Development Kit (SDK) to package and deploy the dashboard project onto a server by using digital dashboards.

- Save Web Parts as Extensible Markup Language (XML) Interchange format (.dwp), and import them into a newly created dashboard project on a server by using digital dashboards.

The first approach uses the Application Deployment Wizard. This wizard packages and deploys all items related to a digital dashboard, such as subdashboards and Web Parts, including all of their associated properties, in a simple two-step process. The second approach does not facilitate deployment of a digital dashboard to another server. However, with the second approach, users can save Web Parts to their local file systems in an XML Interchange format (.dwp) and then import them into a new dashboard project on a server that uses digital dashboard technology.

> **Note** With the latter approach, the method does not transfer the associated metadata of the digital dashboard into the newly created project.

This chapter presents both approaches for deploying a digital dashboard from one server to another. By using these methods, you can export and import dashboards from SharePoint Portal Server to different data sources such as an Exchange 2000 computer, a computer running a SQL Server dashboard, or another SharePoint Portal Server computer.

The Application Deployment Wizard

The Application Deployment Wizard packages the Web Storage System application logic and data into a single cabinet (.cab) file. You can deploy this .cab file onto a production server by using the Deploy Application option that is included as part of the same wizard.

Installing the Web Storage System Developer Tools

In order to use the Application Deployment Wizard, you must first download the Web Storage System Developer Tools from the following location:

http://msdn.microsoft.com/downloads/default.asp?URL=/code/sample.asp?URL=/
MSDN-FILES/027/001/557/msdncompositedoc.xml

After installing the Web Storage System Developer Tools, there are two steps remaining to deploy the digital dashboard onto a production server—packaging and deploying.

Packaging the Digital Dashboard

Before deploying a digital dashboard, you must package it into a single .cab file.

To package a digital dashboard into a single .cab file:

1. Click **Start**, point to **Programs**, point to **Web Storage System SDK**, point to **Web Storage System Tools**, and then click **Application Deployment Wizard**.

2. On the **Welcome** screen, click the **Package Application** option, and then click **Next**.

3. On the instruction page, click **Next**.

4. Type the URL of the digital dashboard, including the dashboard folder name; for example, **http://**server_name**/public/**folder_name.

5. Select the **Include all sub-folders** check box to make sure subdashboards and related Web Parts get included in the packaging process, and then click **Next**.

6. Enter the logon information for the server. If the test and production servers are on different domains, then logon information should include domain\user_name.

7. Click the **Package to single CAB file** option. Type a location and name for the .cab file; for example, C:\temp\dashboard.cab, and then click **Next**.

8. Use the default schema filter file **SampleFilter.xml**, and then click **Next** to begin packaging the dashboard application.

Deploying the Digital Dashboard

After packaging the digital dashboard project into a single .cab file, you must deploy it onto a production server.

To deploy the digital dashboard project onto a production server:

1. To launch the Application Deployment Wizard, click **Start**, point to **Programs**, point to **Web Storage System SDK**, point to **Web Storage System Tools**, and then click **Application Deployment Wizard**.

2. On the **Welcome** screen, click the **Deploy Application** option, and then click **Next**.

3. Type the URL of the production server, including the dashboard folder name you want to use; for example, **http:**//*server_name*/**public**/*folder_name*.

4. Click **Next**.

5. Enter the logon information for the server. If the test and production servers are on different domains, then logon information should include *domain*/*user_name*.

6. Click the **Deploy from single CAB file** option, type the location and name of the source .cab file (for example, C:\temp\dashboard.cab), and then click **Next** to begin deployment of the dashboard application.

7. Click **Finish**.

Now that you have deployed the digital dashboard onto the production server, rename the Digital Dashboard Project file (DDP file). Office XP Developer stores this file in the dashboard folder to match the dashboard folder name. For example, if the name of the dashboard folder on the production server is **MyDashboard**, then rename the DDP file inside the MyDashboard folder to **MyDashboard.DDP**. Double-clicking the DDP file now opens the production server dashboard in Office XP Developer and creates a solution file on the client computer.

You can use the Application Deployment Wizard to package and deploy dashboard applications from one server to another. For example, you can copy a dashboard from a computer running Exchange 2000 Server onto a computer running SharePoint Portal Server or from a computer running SharePoint Portal Server to a computer running Exchange 2000 Server.

Web Parts as XML

This approach does not deploy the dashboard to a different server but instead allows you to save Web Parts to the local file system, and then import them into a dashboard project on the production server. After building and testing the Web Parts on the test server, you save the Web Parts on the local file system as **Dashboard Web Part (.dwp)** files, and then import them onto the dashboard on a production server.

To save the Web Parts and then import them onto the dashboard:

1. Use Office XP Developer to create a new dashboard project on the production server.

2. After creating the production server dashboard, use Office XP Developer to open the dashboard project stored on the test server.

3. In the **Solution Explorer**, select the Web Part(s) to save to the production server.

4. On the **File** menu, click **Save Copy of * As** (where * is the name of the Web Part selected).

5. In the **Save Copy As** dialog box, in the **Save as type** list, click **DWP file (*.dwp)**.

6. Type a file name for the Web Part.

7. In the **Save in** box, type a path on the local file system.

8. Click **Save**.

XML is the interchange format for Web Parts. After you click Save, Office XP Developer saves the Web Part and its properties as XML with a DWP extension. It also saves any resources associated with the Web Part to a folder in the destination selected when you save the dashboard.

The following Web Part naming conventions allow you to write reusable and functional Web Parts to export and import from dashboard projects created by using Office XP Developer:

- To associate a resources folder with a Web Part, follow the _Files naming convention. For example, if you name the Web Part MyWebPart.HTM, name the associated resources folder for this Web Part MyWebPart_Files.

- You should use the Web Part Resource (_WPR_) token when referring to the resources folder of a Web Part. For example, if you want to render an image that you have imported into the resources folder of a Web Part, use the following naming convention: <img src= "_WPR_\myImage.jpg">.

Summary

This chapter outlines how to facilitate deploying digital dashboards across different stores and deploying Web Parts from one server to another. This chapter describes how to package and deploy Web Storage System dashboards from one server to another. It also shows how to import and export Web Parts from different data sources, such as a SharePoint Portal Server 2001, Microsoft Exchange 2000 computer or a computer running a Microsoft SQL Server dashboard.

CHAPTER 24

Analyzing the Default Query for the Dashboard Site

This chapter describes the default query for the dashboard site. It reviews the syntax for the query and provides suggestions for how to customize the default query for your deployment.

The default query runs through the Search Web Part on the Microsoft® SharePoint™ Portal Server 2001 dashboard site. It uses the probabilistic ranking feature of the search engine provided in the Search service, in addition to properties exposed through the SharePoint Portal Server schema. Two query strings executed in parallel compose the default query. The first string performs a query on matching categories. The second string performs a query for Best Bets and matching documents.

Introduction

The default query performs matches for both Best Bets and normal document matches. The default query uses coercion functions to rank the Best Bets above other matching documents. The default query also uses attribute weighting to increase the contribution to relevance made by several document properties, such as Subject, Title and Description. The default query returns results that are ranked according to relevance. These results display on the dashboard site according to their rank, with the top five Best Bets appearing first.

The *rank* for a document measures the relevance between the document and a query. On the dashboard site, the determined rank for a document indicates the order in which the document appears in query results. *Attribute weighting* is the ability to adjust ranking relative to the properties specified in the query. For example, with attribute weighting, you can specify that documents that contain a query term in the document title rank higher than those that contain the term only in the document body.

> **Note** The information for this chapter originates from the SharePoint Portal Server Software Development Kit (SDK). For more information and procedures for how to customize Search in SharePoint Portal Server, see Appendix B, "For More Information."

Syntax for Default Query Category Matching

The category portion of the default query searches category name, keywords, subject, title, and description and returns a list of links to relevant category folders. Users can browse categories from the result list on the dashboard site.

The following example, written in SQL with full-text extensions, demonstrates how the default query for the dashboard site performs category matches. In this example the query is searching for categories relevant to the terms "SharePoint Portal Server."

```
SELECT "DAV:href", "DAV:displayname", "DAV:contentclass",

"urn:schemas-microsoft-com:office:office#Category",

"urn:schemas-microsoft-com:office:office#Description"

FROM workspace..SCOPE()

WHERE WITH

("urn:schemas-microsoft-com:office:office#Keywords":1.0,

"urn:schemas-microsoft-com:office:office#Subject":1.0,

"urn:schemas-microsoft-com:office:office#Title":1.0,

"urn:schemas.microsoft.com:fulltextqueryinfo:description":1.0 )

AS #WeightedCatProps

(FREETEXT(#WeightedCatProps, 'SharePoint Portal Server')

OR CONTAINS("DAV:displayname", '"SharePoint Portal Server"'))

AND ("DAV:contentclass" = 'urn:content-classes:categoryfolder')

ORDER BY "urn:schemas-microsoft-com:office:office#Category" ASC
```

The search engine executes the category search against the primary workspace only, and does not include results from index workspaces. This restriction improves category search latency, with no loss of results since the categories should be the same among primary and index workspaces.

Syntax for Default Query Document Matching

The CONTAINS and FREETEXT predicates are part of the WHERE clause, and support searching for words and phrases in text columns. The CONTAINS predicate supports matching words, matching inflectional forms of words, searches using wildcards, and proximity searches. This makes the CONTAINS predicate well suited for performing word or phrase matches. The FREETEXT predicate is better suited for finding documents containing combinations of the search terms spread throughout the document contents and properties. The **BestBetKeyword** property contains the list of search terms for which a document should appear as a Best Bet.

The default query combines CONTAINS and FREETEXT matches on the **BestBetKeyword** property with FREETEXT matches on content and a fixed selection of relevant properties that are assigned attribute weights. The query distinguishes between properties identified as good indicators of content, such as **Title**, **Description**, or **Keywords**, and other properties that appear in the full-text index.

The following table shows the properties used as strong indicators for content in the default query, and the weight they receive.

Note Properties and attribute weights used in the default query for the dashboard site are subject to change.

Properties and Sample Weights

Property	Weight
urn:schemas-microsoft-com:office:office#Author	0.5
urn:schemas-microsoft-com:office:office#Keywords	0.8
urn:schemas-microsoft-com:office:office#Subject	0.8
urn:schemas-microsoft-com:office:office#Title	0.8
urn:schemas.microsoft.com:fulltextqueryinfo:description	0.8

The default query coerces some overlap between the result sets for the three predicates so that it promotes highly relevant matched documents into the Best Bets range displayed on the dashboard site. To avoid intermixing Best Bets with document results, the default query performs the coercion on a predicate basis. The Results Web Part on the dashboard site displays the first five Best Bets with a rank of over 500.

The following table shows the three default query predicates and the rank they receive.

Note Query predicates and rank coercion functions used in the default query for the dashboard site are subject to change.

Predicates and Rank

Predicate	Rank
CONTAINS on **BestBetKeywords**	1000/999
FREETEXT on **BestBetKeywords**	500–999
FREETEXT on document content and selected list of properties	0–600

The default query normalizes the query results and orders them by rank.

The following example, written in Search SQL, demonstrates the Best Bets determined in the document-matching portion of the default query. The query is for "SharePoint Portal Server."

```
SELECT "DAV:href", "DAV:displayname", "DAV:getlastmodified",
"DAV:iscollection", "urn:schemas-microsoft-com:office:office#Title",

"urn:schemas-microsoft-com:office:office#Author",
"urn:schemas.microsoft.com:fulltextqueryinfo:description",

"urn:schemas-microsoft-com:publishing:ShortcutTarget",

"urn:schemas-microsoft-com:publishing:isdoclibrarycontent",

"urn:schemas-microsoft-com:publishing:DiscussionTarget",
"urn:schemas.microsoft.com:fulltextqueryinfo:rank"

FROM SCOPE('DEEP TRAVERSAL OF "/workspace"')

WHERE WITH ( Contents:0.5, "urn:schemas-microsoft-
com:office:office#Author":0.5,

"urn:schemas-microsoft-com:office:office#Keywords":0.8,

"urn:schemas-microsoft-com:office:office#Subject":0.8,

"urn:schemas-microsoft-com:office:office#Title":0.8,
"urn:schemas.microsoft.com:fulltextqueryinfo:description":0.8)

AS #WeightedProps

((CONTAINS("urn:schemas-microsoft-com:publishing:BestBetKeywords",
```

```
'"SharePoint Portal Server"') RANK BY COERCION(absolute, 999))

OR ((FREETEXT("urn:schemas-microsoft-com:publishing:BestBetKeywords",

'SharePoint Portal Server') RANK BY COERCION(multiply, 0.5)) RANK BY
COERCION(add, 500))

OR ((FREETEXT(#WeightedProps, 'SharePoint Portal Server')

OR CONTAINS("DAV:displayname", '"SharePoint Portal Server"'))

RANK BY COERCION(multiply, 0.6)) )

AND NOT ("DAV:contentclass" = 'urn:content-classes:categoryfolder')

AND NOT ("DAV:contentclass" = 'urn:content-classes:rootcategoryfolder')

ORDER BY "urn:schemas.microsoft.com:fulltextqueryinfo:rank" DESC
```

If a document's **BestBetKeyword** property has the value "SharePoint Portal Server," the default query returns that document in the top band as an exact match. If a document's **BestBetKeyword** property contains the value "SharePoint," the default query returns that document in the middle band. If a document has a custom property **Product** with the value "SharePoint Portal Server," or the document contains the words "sharepoint", "portal" or "server", the default query returns the document in the last band. The probabilistic ranking algorithm employed by SharePoint Portal Server ranks documents containing occurrences of all three terms much higher than a document containing only one of the terms.

This portion of the default query excludes category folders from these results, as it includes them in the category portion of the default query.

Default Query Modifications

You can modify limited portions of the default query. For example, you can expand the weighted property list to include custom properties that are meaningful to your data. You can also modify the weight for a given property according to how strong an indicator of content that property is for your data. You can also adjust the rank coercion functions in the default query. For example, you can eliminate the rank coercion on the portion of the query that performs FREETEXT matches on **BestBetKeywords** so that the default query does not promote documents as Best Bets in the query results.

The following table shows the weighted property aliases declared in Portal\resources\ searchConstants.js, with a brief description of modifications that you can make.

Query Variables and Descriptions

Variable	Description
g_strWeightedPropsWhereClauseDeclaration	Modify the properties and weights used in the Best Bets and matching documents portion of the default query.
g_strWeightedCatPropsWhereClauseDeclaration	Modify properties used in the Categories portion of the default query.

You can find the JavaScript code that generates the query at the following path on the dashboard site: Portal\resources\searchFunctions.js.

Caution Changes to the default query are not supported. Any changes made should adhere to the following guidelines:

- Do not remove any properties selected by the query. Doing so interferes with the function of Extensible Stylesheet Language (XSL) style sheets and code on the dashboard site.

- Do not alter the rank of the Best Bets predicates. Doing so interferes with the identification of search results as Best Bets.

- Adding properties to the property list or ordering the query by an attribute other than rank impacts query latency.

Summary

This chapter describes components of the default query for the dashboard site. It provides the syntax for the Best Bets, document matching, and category matching queries that compose the default query. This chapter also gives suggestions for how to customize the default query for your deployment.

Crawling Custom Metadata

This chapter provides the steps necessary to promote metadata from externally crawled content into Microsoft® SharePoint™ Portal Server 2001 content indexes. This chapter also includes a utility script that allows you to automate the process by editing an Extensible Markup Language (XML) file and running a script.

The need to include custom metadata embedded in documents in an index is particularly important to organizations attempting to include content currently crawled by Microsoft Site Server in an index.

SharePoint Portal Server crawls content sources such as file shares and Web sites. In the process, SharePoint Portal Server gathers full-text information from documents and includes it in the index. However, the ability to map metadata to properties of SharePoint Portal Server is restricted to the contents of Lotus Notes databases.

You can map metadata from file share and Web site content sources to properties of SharePoint Portal Server. However, no user interface exists for this mapping. You can write custom code to perform this mapping.

Properties for HTML files are usually stored in <META> tags. Properties for Microsoft Office documents are usually stored in OLE structured storage. You can view most Office properties from within the Office application by clicking **Properties** on the **File** menu.

This chapter assumes that the reader is familiar with SharePoint Portal Server, has read the documentation relevant to searching and creating indexes, and, ideally, has previously configured SharePoint Portal Server to crawl a content source.

This chapter refers to two .zip files containing custom code: C25615624Propmap.zip and C25615624Htmlprop.zip. You can access these .zip files in the \Docs\Samples\ directory on the SharePoint Portal Server Resource Kit CD.

> **Important** The custom code provided is not supported. There is no guarantee that the object model used will be supported in future versions of SharePoint Portal Server.

SharePoint Portal Server supports mapping properties only for Lotus Notes content sources and only by using the user interface provided in SharePoint Portal Server.

Key Terminology

A number of terms used by SharePoint Portal Server differ from the terms used by the underlying Microsoft Web Storage System technology on which SharePoint Portal Server is based. You can usually ignore the Web Storage System terms and use the SharePoint Portal Server counterparts. However, when working with code that uses the automation libraries of SharePoint Portal Server that use the Web Storage System terminology—notably Publishing and Knowledge Management Collaboration Data Objects (PKMCDO)—it is important to keep track of which SharePoint Portal Server terms correspond to which underlying Web Storage System or PKMCDO term. In this document, the following terms are interchangeable.

Terminology Comparison

SharePoint Portal Server term	Web Storage System or PKMCDO term
Document Profile	Content Class
Content Source	KnowledgeStartAddress

In addition, it is important to note how the names of automation component ProgIDs differ depending on whether they are being called using early binding (common in compiled code) or late binding (the only option when using scripting languages). In early binding, most of the automation components of SharePoint Portal Server begin with the prefix PKMCDO, whereas when being called with late binding, they begin with CDO.

Tasks for Mapping Custom Metadata

There are five steps required to configure a SharePoint Portal Server workspace to crawl external content and allow the properties and meta tags in that external content to be promoted as properties in SharePoint Portal Server.

To promote properties from external content into SharePoint Portal Server properties:

1. Create a document profile that includes the list of profile properties that you want to have available through SharePoint Portal Server. This profile can include custom properties.

2. Create a content source that points to the external data. When saving it, do not start creating an index.

3. Modify and apply the property mapping code to map external content meta tags and property tags to the SharePoint Portal Server document profile properties. Example code is provided later.

4. Restart the SharePoint Portal Server services to flush any cached schema.

5. Start the full update for the content source.

The following sections explain these steps in detail.

Document Profile Creation

Create a document profile that includes the list of profile properties that you want to have available through SharePoint Portal Server. You can add custom properties to this profile.

To create a document profile:

1. In the workspace, open the Management folder.

2. In the Management folder, open the Document Profiles subfolder.

3. Double-click **Add Document Profile**. The **Add Document Profile Wizard** opens.

4. Type a descriptive name for the document profile.

5. Select an existing document profile to use as a template. The Base Document Profile is the default template.

6. Click **Next**.

7. Define the properties that make up the fields on the document profile:

   - To add or remove property names from the document profile, select or clear the check boxes next to the property name.

   - To add a new property, click **New**.

   - To edit the attributes of an existing property, select the property by clicking the property name, and then click **Edit**.

8. Click **Next**.

9. To choose the order in which the properties appear on the document profile, select a property, and then use the **Move Up** and **Move Down** arrows.

10. Click **Next**.

11. Review the settings for your new document profile, and then click **Finish**.

When you complete the wizard, the new document profile appears in the Document Profiles folder. The document profile is now available for you to associate with folders in the workspace. After you associate this document profile with a folder, users can select the document profile from a list when checking in a document or editing the properties of a document.

Content Source Creation

Create a content source that points to the external data. When saving it, do not start creating an index.

Propagation of custom metadata is dependent on the creation of and/or modifications to two entries in the workspace: a content source and a site path rule.

To create a content source:

1. Open the Management folder, and then open the Content Sources folder.

2. Double-click **Add Content Source**.

3. The **Add Content Source Wizard** opens. Follow the on-screen instructions to complete the wizard. Do not begin creating or updating an index of the data.

SharePoint Portal Server places the new content source in the Content Sources folder. SharePoint Portal Server includes the information available from the source in the index. After it is included, this information is available for users to search for and view on the dashboard site.

You can modify an existing content source that you created with the SharePoint Portal Server client user interface, or you can create a content source programmatically by using PKMCDO. In either case, you must add the following four properties to the content source:

- An array containing the names of the properties to be read from the source documents.

- An array containing the source data types of those properties.

- An array containing the names of the properties into which the source metadata is stored in the index.

- The document profile that is attributed to the documents found at the content source.

You must add these four properties programmatically. No user interface exists for creating or editing these properties other than for Lotus Notes content sources.

You must create a site path rule that corresponds to this content source. The site path rule should have the same starting address as the content source. In addition, you must programmatically modify the rule so that it contains the following two properties (the included script code does this):

- A reference to the target document profile that is attributed to the documents found through this site path. This reference must be to the same document profile you applied to the content source.

- A URL reference to the content source. The site path rule retrieves its property mapping instructions from the content source entry.

Profile Mapping Code

Modify and apply the property mapping code to map meta tags and property tags from external content to the document profile properties in SharePoint Portal Server. Example code is provided later.

Sample Code

The following code fragment details the required actions to register the propagation of properties and metadata from the external content source into SharePoint Portal Server. This is Microsoft Visual Basic® 6 code, not Microsoft Visual Basic Scripting Edition (VBScript). For VBScript examples, see the included PropMap.wsf script in CrawlingMetadataPropmap.zip. If you add this code to a Visual Basic project, you must include the PKMCDO type library as a reference. The sample that follows makes liberal use of built-in constants for SharePoint Portal Server namespaces.

Note The following code sample shows the path to content sources as /Management/ Content Sources/. If you are running on a non-English system, replace this path with the localized string that contains the name of the content sources folder.

```
Dim objCS As PKMCDO.KnowledgeStartAddress

    Dim objSPR As PKMCDO.IKnowledgeCatalogSitePathRule

    Dim colSitePathRules As IKnowledgeCatalogSitePathRules

    Dim strUrlContentSource As String



    ' Change the following values to reflect the names of your server,

    ' workspace, content source, and target document profile.

    Const MYSERVER = "SharePoint_Portal_Server_computer"

    Const MYWORKSPACE = "SharePoint_Portal_Server_workspace"

    Const MYSOURCE = "FileContentSource"

    Const MYDOCPROFILE = "DocProfileName"



    ' Construct the URL to the Content Sources folder for your workspace.
```

```
    strUrlContentSource = "http://" & MYSERVER & "/" & MYWORKSPACE _

        & «/Management/Content Sources/» & MYSOURCE


' Open the KnowledgeStartAddress (Content Source) item.

    Set objCS = New PKMCDO.KnowledgeStartAddress

objCS.DataSource.Open strUrlContentSource, , adModeReadWrite


' Indicate which content class (Document Profile)

' should be attributed to crawled files.

objCS.Fields(PKMCDO.cdostrURI_TargetContentClass) = _

    PKMCDO.cdostrNS_ContentClasses & MYDOCPROFILE


' All tags will have namespaces prepended to them.

' PKMCDO provides built-in constants for most of these. Change

' the array elements below to the property names you wish to use,

' adding or deleting lines as needed. NOTE: it is important that

' all three of the following arrays match up in terms of number of

' elements and the ordering of property names.


' If you are crawling HTML documents, all properties will have a

' standard HTML namespace prepended to them.  The source namespace

' may vary for other file types.  See below for details.

objCS.Fields(PKMCDO.cdostrURI_SourceProperties) = Array( _

    PKMCDO.cdostrNS_HtmlMetaInfo & "ExternalTag1", _

    PKMCDO.cdostrNS_HtmlMetaInfo & "AnotherTag2", _
```

```
    PKMCDO.cdostrNS_HtmlMetaInfo & "TheLastTag" )


' One data type entry is needed per source property.

objCS.Fields(PKMCDO.cdostrURI_SourceTypes) = Array( _

    "string", _

    "string", _

    "string")


' All SharePoint Portal Server properties are prepended with the
  standard Office

' namespace.  Ensure that they match up in order with their source

' properties.

objCS.Fields(PKMCDO.cdostrURI_TargetProperties) = Array( _

    PKMCDO.cdostrNS_Office & "SharePoint_Portal_Server_Property1", _

    PKMCDO.cdostrNS_Office & "SharePoint_Portal_Server_Property2", _

    PKMCDO.cdostrNS_Office & "SharePoint_Portal_Server_Property3 )


' Adding four properties to the content source definition item

' is not enough. You must also add a site path that corresponds to

' this content source.  You can see these by going to the Content

' Sources management folder and opening the "Additional Settings"

' item, then clicking the "Site Paths" button on the resulting
  dialog box.

Set colSitePathRules = objCS.Workspace.Catalog.SitePathRules
```

```
' NOTE:  This code does NOT check to see if a matching site path

' already exists.  Before you run this code, check to see if matching

' site paths are already present, and if so, delete them.

Set objSPR = colSitePathRules.Add(objCS.Address & "/*", True)

objSPR.ContentClass = objCS.Fields(PKMCDO.cdostrURI_TargetContentClass)

objSPR.PropertyMappingUrl = strUrlContentSource


' Clean up object references and save everything. The site path rule

' item does not need to be explicitly saved, but the content source
  does.

Set colSitePathRules = Nothing

Set objSPR = Nothing


objCS.Fields.Update

objCS.DataSource.Save

Set objCS = Nothing
```

Using Script Files for Property Mapping

The previous sample code illustrates the steps to take when using PKMCDO. The sample that follows, however, is a fully functional application that you can immediately use to configure property mapping. CrawlingMetadataPropmap.zip contains this code.

The CrawlingMetadataPropmap.zip file contains a Microsoft Windows® Scripting Host script file named PropMap.wsf. PropMap.wsf accepts as input an XML file that supplies server, workspace, and content source information, plus property mapping information. An example of the file format expected by this script is provided as PropMap.xml.

You can run the script on any Microsoft Windows 2000–based computer on which you install the SharePoint Portal Server (or client) software (that is, a computer on which you install PKMCDO). The script accepts a single parameter, the path name of the XML file containing the mapping instructions to be processed. If that parameter is missing, the script assumes the file PropMap.xml residing in the same directory as the script file.

The code that follows illustrates the XML document expected by the PropMap.wsf script. The element names describe in detail the information needed to create a property map.

Note This format is not supported and is not suggested as a standard representation. Its scope is restricted to this chapter to add value to the sample custom code included here.

When examining the <targetContentClass> element, note that the script code prepends "urn:content-classes:" to any value that does not have a namespace prepended to it.

When examining the <sourceName> elements, note that the script code prepends "urn:schemas.microsoft.com:htmlinfo:metainfo:" to any value that does not have a namespace prepended to it.

When examining the <targetName> elements, note that the script code prepends "urn:schemas-microsoft-com:office:office#" to any value that does not have a namespace prepended to it.

```xml
<?xml version="1.0"?>

<propertyMap>

<server>

<name>server1</name>

<workspace>

<name>test1</name>

<contentSource>

<name>dogbreeds</name>

<targetContentClass>DogBreed</targetContentClass>

<property>

<sourceName>breedOrigin</sourceName>

<sourceType>string</sourceType>

<targetName>breedOrigin</targetName>

</property>

<property>

<sourceName>breedName</sourceName>
```

```xml
<sourceType>string</sourceType>

<targetName>breedName</targetName>

</property>

<property>

<sourceName>breedFirstBred</sourceName>

<sourceType>dateTime</sourceType>

<targetName>breedFirstBred</targetName>

</property>

<property>

<sourceName>breedWeight</sourceName>

<sourceType>i4</sourceType>

<targetName>breedWeight</targetName>

</property>

<property>

<sourceName>Abstract</sourceName>

<sourceType>string</sourceType>

<targetName>Description</targetName>

</property>

<property>

<sourceName>ContentClass</sourceName>

<sourceType>string</sourceType>

<targetName>DAV:contentclass</targetName>

</property>

<property>

<sourceName>Categories</sourceName>
```

```
<sourceType>string</sourceType>

<targetName>urn:schemas-microsoft-com:publishing:Categories</targetName>

</property>

</contentSource>

</workspace>

</server>

</propertyMap>
```

Using the Modified HTML IFilter Wrapper

An add-on IFilter designed for Index Server is available on Microsoft Software Developers Network (MSDN®). You can register this filter in place of the standard HTML IFilter. The filter works by loading the "true" HTML IFilter, intercepting the <META> tag values it returns, and converting selected values into numbers and/or dates as they are passed to the indexing service.

A series of tests in a SharePoint Portal Server environment showed this IFilter to work properly, with little if any discernable performance penalty.

The original IFilter code is available on MSDN at http://msdn.microsoft.com/library/default.asp?URL=/library/techart/msdn_ismeta.htm. It is strongly recommended that you read this article before proceeding further. It is also recommended that you use the modified copy of that IFilter that is included with this chapter, rather than the code supplied with the original article.

CrawlingMetadataHtmlprop.zip contains the modified version that includes the source. The modified version contains support for the additional date formats mentioned in Knowledge Base article Q240390, specifically:

- Sun Nov 6 08:49:37 1994

- Sun, 06 Nov 1994 08:49:37

- GMT Sunday, 06-Nov-94 08:49:37

- GMT Sun Nov 6 08:49:37 1994

It also supports the more XML and Web Storage System–centric storage format of:

- 1994-11-06T08:49:37.000

The original source code supported a smaller number of formats, which were less standard for HTML content crawling purposes. The original source code required the administrator to indicate in an .ini file which properties to transform into different data types.

While full source code is included, the only files necessary to begin are HTMLProp.dll and HTMLProp.ini. The .ini file contains installation (and removal) information. A ReadMe.txt file provides background context, but a large amount of its content is specific to earlier versions of Index Server. HTMLProp.ini contains all the information needed to install and register HTMLProl.dll.

Service Restart

Restart the following SharePoint Portal Server services to flush any cached schema.

To restart the services:

1. Click **Start**, point to **Programs**, point to **Administrative Tools**, and then click **Services**.

2. Right-click **Microsoft Exchange Information Store**, and then click **Restart**.

3. Right-click **Microsoft Search**, and then click **Restart**.

4. Right-click **SharePoint Portal Server**, and then click **Restart**.

Content Source Updates

Start the full update for the content source.

To start a content source update:

1. In the Management folder, open the Content Sources folder.

2. Right-click the content source that you want to update, and then click **Start Full Update**.

Tips and Troubleshooting

This section presents tips for mapping custom metadata and key steps to help resolve issues you may encounter.

Propagating an Index across Servers

When propagating an index across multiple servers, you must create and run the content source and script on the server dedicated to creating and updating indexes. You must create the document profile and any SharePoint Portal Server custom properties on both the server dedicated to indexes and the server dedicated to searching.

Flushing the Cache

Iterative modifications to the mappings that you define can result in perceived failures. The majority of perceived problems are the result of not flushing the cache between iterative changes to the property mapping information. To prevent these issues, ensure that you stop and start the MSSearch and MSExchangeIS services before each full index update.

Overwriting Site Path Rules

To keep the previous sample code as simple and illustrative as possible, no code is included to check for a matching preexisting site path entry and to delete the entry if it exists. You must do this manually or augment the sample code to perform such a check and delete each time it runs. If you do so, delete and recreate the site path rule. Do not attempt to edit the rule.

The included PropMap.wsf script performs this checking and deletes any such rule before creating a new one.

To view site path rules:

1. In the workspace, open the Management folder, and then open the Content Sources folder.

2. Double-click **Additional Settings**.

3. On the **Rules** tab, click **Site Paths**.

Creating Site Path Rules

When possible, have only one site path rule per content source. Site path restrictions match in top-down order. If the URL of a document matches a site path rule that is not associated with the property mapping, the properties are not mapped and remain empty. It is the site path rule that determines *whether* mapping takes place. SharePoint Portal Server uses the content source entry only to determine *how* to do the mapping.

Viewing Custom Properties for Site Server Documents

Office documents managed by Site Server are usually tagged with custom properties. You cannot view these custom properties in Office, nor can you view them with the PROPDUMP utility. However, the ENUMALL utility can view these custom properties. For more information about these utilities, see Appendix B, "For More Information."

Using both FILTDUMP and IFILTTST, the Site Server custom properties are generated from HTML files but not from Office documents. For more information about these utilities, see Appendix B. This is because the Office IFilter does not directly generate the properties, instead indicating to the calling code that it should use IPropertyStorage to retrieve these additional properties.

Use the following attributes with IFILTTST:
IFILTER_INIT_APPLY_INDEX_ATTRIBUTES and
IFILTER_INIT_APPLY_OTHER_ATTRIBUTES. IFILTTST does not support the
IFILTER_INIT_APPLY_CRAWL_ATTRIBUTES value.

Using Namespaces

Although the properties embedded in HTML and Office documents have no namespace
qualifiers, namespaces are prepended to them during the file crawl. Your property mapping arrays must consider this.

All HTML properties emerge from the crawl with the namespace prefix
"urn:schemas.microsoft.com:htmlinfo:metainfo:", for which PKMCDO provides the constant **cdostrNS_HtmlMetaInfo**.

If the file source being crawled represents documents maintained by Microsoft Site
Server version 3, all .stub files (which are HTML files with embedded redirect state-
ments) also generate properties with this namespace.

If Site Server is managing an Office document, Site Server stamps its own properties into
the document as a separate property set in OLE structured storage. The properties
stamped into the file by the tag tool in Site Server include the previously mentioned
cdostrNS_HtmlMetaInfo namespace prepended to them, even though they are not
HTML documents but are Office documents crawled by Site Server.

Any other Office document properties are prepended with the namespace "urn:schemas-
microsoft-com:office:office", for which PKMCDO provides the constant
cdostrNS_Office. This is the same namespace prepended to all properties that you create
by using the Add Document Profile Wizard in SharePoint Portal Server. The character
"#" is appended to the namespace when followed by a property name.

Avoiding Custom Mappings to the Description

You should avoid custom mappings to the **Description** property unless you are crawling
only HTML files. The **Description** property, specifically urn:schemas-microsoft-
com:office:office#Description, is derived differently depending on the document type.
While mapping the <META> tag of your choice to **Description** works for HTML files
(including Active Server Pages [ASP] files), it does not work for Office documents. For
Office documents, the **Description** field always comes from the embedded **Comments**
property, no matter what you specify in the property map.

Using Many-to-One Mappings

A content source can contain several types of files, and you can find the same target property in different places, with different property names, depending on the source document. Because of this, it is possible to have multiple source properties mapped to the same target property. On a per-document basis, the first property for which SharePoint Portal Server encounters a non-blank value is the one mapped into the target property.

Overriding the Content Source's Target Content Class on a Per-File Basis

If you map a source property, typed as a string, to the target property DAV:contentclass, that property mapping takes precedence over the default target content class you specified for both the content source definition and the site path rule. Note, however, that the value stored in the source file must be a Uniform Resource Name (URN) that matches that of a document profile already registered for this workspace (for example, urn:content-classes:My Content Class).

Categories Can Be Assigned, But Only One Per File

Mapping a source property, typed as a string, to the target property urn:schemas-microsoft-com:publishing:Categories results in SharePoint Portal Server assigning the item to that category. Source values must be valid category names preceded by colons (for example, ":Category 1"). When mapping from META HTML tags, you can map only one value per document. SharePoint Portal Server assigns only a single value to the **Categories** property.

Date and Numeric Data Types Require Additional Handling

Although SharePoint Portal Server supports a **Date** property type (**dateTime**, in Web Storage System terminology), the standard HTML IFilter does not generate date properties from HTML documents as dates.

SharePoint Portal Server conducts no type checking or mapping on the properties. SharePoint Portal Server includes each value in the index as it arrives, in the format returned by the IFilter. In other words, if you map a source property to a target **dateTime** property, but the source value is a string, the content index stores a string value. This can have unforeseen, perhaps error-inducing, effects on the SharePoint Portal Server client user interface.

You can implement date and type checking by using a small amount of extra custom code and by implementing a custom IFilter. For more information on how to add support for non-text properties when crawling external files, see the section "Modified HTML IFilter Wrapper."

Summary

This chapter shows how to map custom metadata from external content sources to your document profiles in SharePoint Portal Server. By following a simple sequence of steps, and by using the scripts provided on the SharePoint Portal Server Resource Kit CD, you can adapt this technique for the custom content in your organization. This allows you to use the Advanced Search Web Part, or your custom search application, to search this external content by using your document profiles and the properties they contain.

PART 6

Case Studies

This section provides specific examples of Microsoft® SharePoint™ Portal Server 2001 as it is deployed in real-world scenarios. These case studies provide ideas and information for how SharePoint Portal Server can assist you to develop a custom portal solution for your own environment.

CHAPTER 26

T-Systems: Technology Center Bids Piles of Files a Final Farewell

Deutsche Telekom Innovationsgesellschaft's Technology Center is one of the first German companies to use Microsoft® SharePoint™ Portal Server 2001 for sophisticated document management. The Center expects significant optimization of project workflow from highly efficient retrieval capabilities and universal transparency throughout the complete document life cycle. Under the terms of an Enterprise Agreement, Microsoft supports the pioneering user with authorized consulting services.

About T-Nova Deutsche Telekom Innovationsgesellschaft mbH

T-Nova Deutsche Telekom Innovationsgesellschaft mbH can now draw on a unique Germany-wide pool of expertise: The Darmstadt Technology Center, with branches in Berlin and eleven other German cities, focuses on highly specialized expertise concerning all types of physical transfer of information. With an eye to customers' current and future needs in networks and related services, the Center offers practical, relevant research and development work that will soon convert the prospects and opportunities arising from the latest technological trends into integrated solutions appropriate for the market.

Innovative network products and top-quality service plans are presently being developed in about 150 company-wide projects simultaneously. These projects involve approximately 1,100 employees. For Dr. Frank Sporleder, the Technology Center's director, the flood of documents, which is rising at a terrific rate, embodies not only a valuable potential source of information, but also collected work—and as such—considerable company capital. About the documents, Dr. Sporleder says, "Their current relevance and availability, along with the related knowledge transfer, are largely responsible for determining the efficiency of our work."

Concerning Web-supported document management, Dr. Sporleder is optimistic of being able to optimize multilayered project work in the customers' interests also. "Performance features such as version and revision management, safeguarding, and archiving of data, controllable access, powerful search and retrieval functions and appropriate workflow capabilities will contribute to this."

Integration Determines Total Cost of Ownership

SharePoint Portal Server arrived on the market at the ideal time for the large-scale document management system (DMS) project. After a thorough examination of the market and detailed product analysis, a team of experts from the Technology Center's KOM (Communication) Department had at first favored a different DMS solution. However, it was determined that SharePoint Portal Server will better ensure the necessary future integration into Deutsche Telekom AG's Microsoft-dominated system. In concrete terms, it was the plans to change the Microsoft Office platform to Office 2000 that revealed, during preliminary stages, the future lack of integration of non-Microsoft products. KOM department head Wilfried Gerfen says, "Office applications are naturally closely connected to the DMS; after all, Word, Excel and PowerPoint® are the sources of the vast majority of the Technology Center's project-related documents."

"Economically speaking, everything pointed to Microsoft's DMS. Every third-party product must inevitably lag behind system and Office-platform upgrades—with a corresponding increase in administrative costs." This is how Uli Grün, who is responsible for KOM's DMS, explains the courageous decision to be the first in Germany to use Microsoft's SharePoint Portal Server. He explains that a favorable price can only be the beginning of an economic feasibility study; the determining factor, however, is the total cost of operating the system, also called the total cost of ownership (TCO). Based on experience, since administrative costs make up a large portion of the TCO, according to Rainer Mack, a Technology Center DMS expert, "The best TCO strategy for the medium and long term is always maximum integration into the system environment."

In the end, a product presentation at Microsoft in Munich convinced Uli Grün's team. The range of functions alone was impressive. However, the completely new, integrative concept of document management was the decisive factor. SharePoint Portal Server comes into play when customers first create documents. It provides complete transparency from a document's first moments of existence until final archiving or deletion at the end of its life cycle. During installation, SharePoint Portal Server also adds appropriate functions to Office applications, which enable check-in and publication of a newly created document in the super ordinate Web Storage System. In Microsoft Office XP, these functions will already be included.

In addition, SharePoint Portal Server uses the same storage technology as Microsoft Exchange Server 2000. For the user this means, among other things, that he can use the new tools and functions with a familiar interface. This reduces administrative costs and limits training expenses. So Rainer Mack need plan only a "basic training day" for users, who will subsequently also be offered an e-mail hotline and further support.

Reduction in Lost Information

With SharePoint Portal Server, every document will be stored together with a series of meaningful, individually definable metadata and profile data so that not only the content, relevant project, and search categories can be determined from the outset, but also the complete workflow for the document and a detailed release schedule. For example, the Technology Center archives documents after two or five years, depending on the project with which they are associated. In the future, this will be a completely automated process. Central safeguarding of all documents will also be automated in the future which, given the T-Nova Technology Center's network approach to project work, is an outstanding advantage that makes the life of IT specialists considerably easier and drastically reduces the loss of information.

In addition, frictional losses during project work, resulting from previously unavoidable inconsistencies between versions, no longer occur. SharePoint Portal Server's complete version and revision management capability allows transparent rollback to any stage of work. A detailed, role-based script determines who has read-only access or writing privileges at which stage of document production, all the way through final release and subsequent intranet publication. Additional collaborative features also offer significant potential for optimization: documents will mesh more closely than ever before with a project's team-oriented work sequence.

For users, another advantage may be even more obvious, namely, SharePoint Portal Server's universal search capabilities. Long searches for information and worries about whether the information found is current no longer deprive Technology Center employees of valuable work time. The highly developed retrieval features are easily available as intranet portals and in the tried and tested design of the digital dashboard. These features also extend to public files in Exchange, intranet, and Internet sites and to non-Microsoft products such as CorelDRAW and Adobe Acrobat.

SharePoint Portal Server is equipped with a complete Software Development Kit (SDK). With the SDK, you can customize SharePoint Portal Server to meet a company's current needs by using scripts. For the Technology Center, developers used these SDKs with Microsoft Visual Basic® 6 to construct a complete conversion tool that consolidates all documents and meta-information from existing systems in SharePoint Portal Server.

The Technology Center obtained the expertise needed for this directly from the source. Under the terms of an Enterprise Agreement, Microsoft Consulting Services is available to the Technology Center for planning and implementation of its sophisticated document management project through an Enterprise Strategy Consultant. This Microsoft consultant serves Deutsche Telekom companies exclusively.

Summary

Deutsche Telekom Innovationsgesellschaft's Technology Center is one of the first German companies to use SharePoint Portal Server for sophisticated document management. The Center expects significant optimization of project workflow from highly efficient retrieval capabilities and universal transparency throughout the complete document life cycle. Under the terms of an Enterprise Agreement, Microsoft is supporting the pioneering user with authorized consulting services.

Microsoft Products Used

- SharePoint Portal Server
- Microsoft Windows® 2000 Server
- Microsoft Project 2000
- Microsoft Windows 2000 Professional
- Visual Basic 6
- Office 2000

Additional Information

For more information about T-Nova Deutsche Telekom Innovationsgesellschaft mbH, see Appendix B, "For More Information."

Migrating from Site Server 3 to SharePoint Portal Server 2001 for Enterprise Search at Microsoft

Approximately 25,000 Microsoft users conduct nearly 125,000 searches each month (which translates to 750,000 queries against the search server) across the corporate intranet, called *corpnet*. Consequently, a small increase in performance can improve the search experience for users.

As Microsoft's Information Technology Group (ITG) approached beta testing of Microsoft® SharePoint™ Portal Server 2001 in the summer of 2000, it used Microsoft Site Server 3 as its enterprise search solution. With Site Server 3, Microsoft employees worldwide could easily find and aggregate information from across the enterprise.

Migrating to SharePoint Portal Server yielded two key benefits:

More relevant and timely search results delivered to users.

- Latency, or response time, improved by 22 percent.

- Indexes updated nightly by using adaptive updates.

Improved crawling performance.

- Full update of an index nearly three times faster than Site Server 3.

- Adaptive update of an index seven times faster than Site Server 3.

Microsoft employees now enjoy more relevant and timely search results because of the improvements in performance, nightly updates to the content indexes, and the new probabilistic ranking algorithm used for relevancy ranking.

This chapter describes the ITG deployment plan of SharePoint Portal Server and the subsequent results. It provides detailed information and recommendations based on this deployment. It includes technical information on the existing environment, design decisions, deployment steps, and testing considerations. It concludes with a summary of recommendations based on this experience.

> **Note** This is not intended to serve as a procedural guide. The intranet site names provided are for illustration only and do not necessarily reflect actual names.

Planning

The migration from Site Server 3 to SharePoint Portal Server for intranet search at Microsoft included the following stages: Planning, Analysis and Design, Deployment, and Management.

Identifying Deployment Goals

In addition to running the enterprise IT utility, ITG plays a strategic role as one of Microsoft's early adopters, testing and deploying Microsoft software before customer release. All ITG early adoption efforts must show tangible business benefits to Microsoft beyond testing for scale and load in a real-world production environment. This was true for the SharePoint Portal Server beta deployments.

Among other benefits and services, this deployment extends the "Microsoft software as a service" model to continue to provide:

- A customer-specific, service-level agreement for each portal owner that defined the service and clearly stated the procedures for support and maintenance over time.

- Search across multiple (even disparate) content sets.

- Better performance and more timely and relevant results.

- The inclusion of existing content and additional content in the index.

The project team established one key metric to measure their success. The team had to ensure that the system handled the stress of crawling about 6 million documents in a time frame that matched their existing results. The existing enterprise search solution included only about 3 million documents in an index. The team also planned to add additional intranet content to the indexes. In addition, ITG required additional room for the growth of content over time.

To verify that SharePoint Portal Server would handle the same load as Site Server 3, the team ran both products in parallel for 30 days before retiring the Site Server 3 solution.

Establishing a Project Timeline

ITG began planning in the summer of 2000 to test SharePoint Portal Server as an enterprise index and search technology through all interim releases, including Beta 1, Beta 2, Release Candidates, and the final release-to-manufacturing (RTM) version.

The team divided the project into the following four phases:

Planning

- Establish the team.
- Collect information on the current environment.
- Develop a project plan.

Analysis and Design

- Create the architecture and select the hardware.
- Review and redefine the catalogs.

Deploying

- Install the hardware and software.
- Configure servers running SharePoint Portal Server.
- Create workspaces.
- Set up content sources and site rules.
- Complete property mapping from custom document properties to the SharePoint Portal Server schema.
- Modify Active Server Pages (ASPs) for searching and for returning results.
- Test crawling.
- Test searching.
- Operate Site Server 3 and SharePoint Portal Server in parallel.

Managing

- Make the transition to production.
- Manage operations and perform maintenance.

The team spent about nine months on this effort from beginning to end, working part-time. From midsummer when the team was formed until the end of the year 2000, the team spent most of its time testing the index and search capabilities of SharePoint Portal Server and optimizing for the goal of 6 million documents, as shown in Figure 27.1.

The migration to production began in early January 2001 with development of the search page and completion of the final tests of crawling. In mid-February, ITG set up the parallel environment. Before RTM in mid-March, SharePoint Portal Server replaced Site Server 3 for search queries on the primary corporate portal, called *MSWeb*, and the Product Group Portal. After RTM, ITG began converting all major portals at Microsoft to SharePoint Portal Server for search. When this process is complete, Microsoft will retire the Site Server 3 solution throughout the corporate intranet.

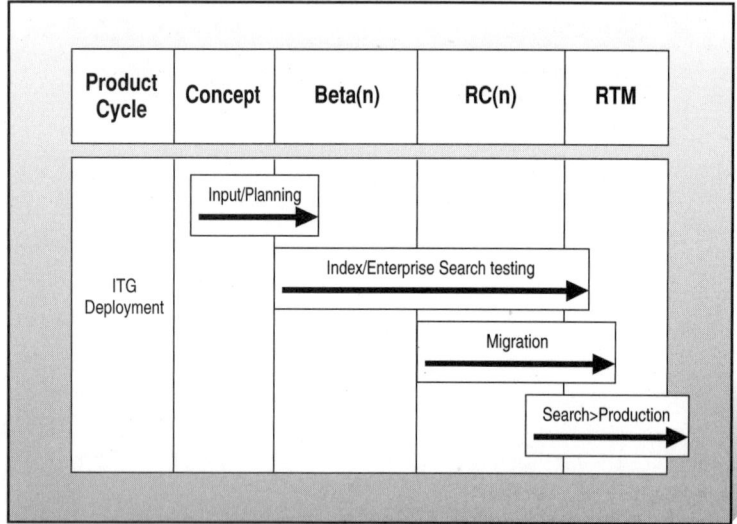

Figure 27.1. Project and development timeline

Based on its experience, the team estimates that a typical enterprise customer migration of similar scale might take approximately three months, as illustrated in the following table.

Typical Enterprise Project Timeline

	Month 1	Month 2	Month 3
1. Planning	1 week		
2. Catalog review (optional) Note: can parallel activities 3 and 4	1–4 weeks		
3. Hardware installation and setup	1 week		
4. Configuration of servers and workspaces, and setup of site rules	1 week		
5. Test of crawling operations		2 weeks	
6. Modify existing custom ASP pages		1 week	
7. Test of search page		1 week	
8. Parallel operations			2–4 weeks
9. Ongoing catalog and index review			

Collecting Information

The next part of the planning process included collecting critical information about the existing environment, including several critical components.

Hardware Specifications

Hardware specifications for both crawl and search servers:

- Specify similar hardware for test comparison.

- Comply with upgrades in accordance with ITG hardware standards.

Architecture Diagrams

Architecture diagrams, indicating:

- Hardware, network, propagation paths

Catalog Information

List of all Site Server 3 catalogs, including:

- The server on which the catalogs are stored

- Who owns the catalogs

- How frequently the catalogs are crawled

- What start addresses and site rules are contained in the catalogs

- Whether complex URLs are enabled

Key metrics for each individual catalog and across all catalogs:

- For index (per catalog): number of site rules, number of documents, catalog size, time to crawl, and propagation time

- For search (total and per catalog): number of queries per month and at peak load

Network Environment

Network factors, including:

- Networking protocols

- Firewall configuration

The project team examined the existing network environment for possible factors that would affect deployment, but determined that they did not need to make any configuration changes.

User Environment

Unique environmental factors including:

- The Microsoft corpnet spans the world. Consequently, SharePoint Portal Server must crawl documents in multiple languages for inclusion in the content indexes and must allow users to submit queries in multiple languages. SharePoint Portal Server allows users to submit queries in English, French, Italian, German, Swedish, Spanish, Dutch, Japanese, Chinese Simplified, Chinese Traditional, Korean, and Thai.

- Corpnet is in use worldwide 24 hours a day, 7 days a week, 365 days a year.

- Security is enforced per document at the file share level.

Analysis and Design

After collecting information and creating a deployment plan, the project team synthesized information to provide a description of the existing infrastructure and a vision of the new infrastructure.

Searching Using Site Server

Originally, most sites within Microsoft did not offer any type of search. Individual departments or groups built their own sites, and the overhead of setting up, running, and maintaining a search capability on each site was burdensome. The major business division portals—such as IT, HR, Product, Finance, Sales, Support, Legal, Operations, and Microsoft Corporate—offered some search capability. The basic problem was that they all set up their own environments and often crawled each other's sites, resulting in duplication of efforts, sometimes three or four times over.

Site Server 3 became the backbone of this centralized search solution. It was set up with dedicated servers for crawling and searching. Site Server created a catalog for each site. The owner of each site or portal specified what content to include or exclude from the catalog for its site, in addition to what, if any, content on its site should not be crawled.

After developing the process for including content in an index, ITG created a set of custom ASP pages—one for querying and one for returning results. ITG modified these pages to fit each portal's needs for custom query capabilities and custom results sets. One by one, the major portals moved to this search solution because they could get better search capabilities for less effort. After all the major intranet sites had migrated, a number of second-tier sites also implemented this search solution.

Site Server 3 Infrastructure

The Site Server 3 architecture at Microsoft consisted of one search server and two crawl servers. The crawl servers included content in their indexes from their respective catalogs, and then propagated the information from the catalogs to the search server. This architecture, shown in Figure 27.2, ensured that the search capability was always available to users.

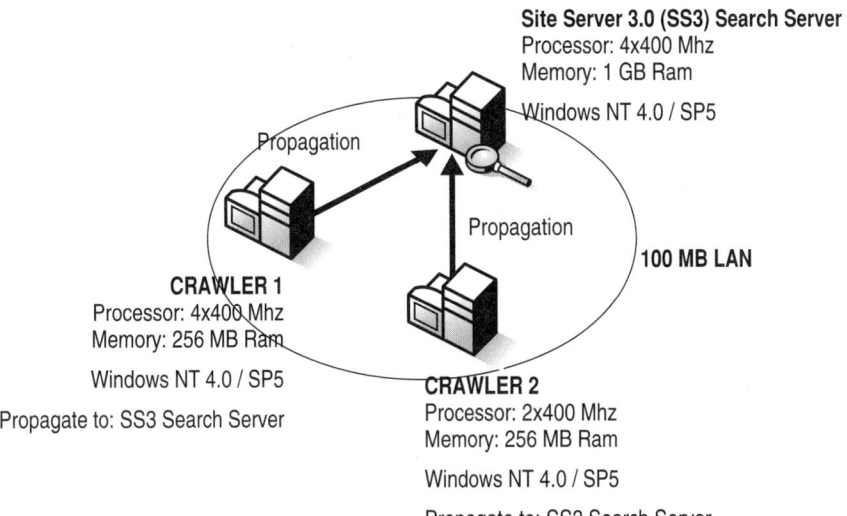

Figure 27.2. Site Server 3 search solution architecture

This solution crawled about 3 million corporate intranet documents and files, handling nearly 30,000 queries per day. There were 48 catalogs on these servers, and many sites requested that their searches include several of these catalogs.

Searching with SharePoint Portal Server

SharePoint Portal Server is a complete solution—integrated document management, corporate portal, and search. However, this deployment implements only the search and index creation aspects of SharePoint Portal Server. Because this migration does not include the dashboard site and document management features, separate teams started projects to test those features.

The project team modeled the new design largely on the existing Site Server 3 design. The team modified the existing set of custom search and results pages to handle SharePoint Portal Server in addition to Site Server 3. In this design, as each portal migrates to SharePoint Portal Server, the portals simply change their Web forms to point to the new query page on the SharePoint Portal Server computer.

SharePoint Portal Server Propagation Model

The propagation model includes two servers dedicated to creating and maintaining indexes and one server dedicated to searching as part of the centralized search service, as illustrated in Figure 27.3.

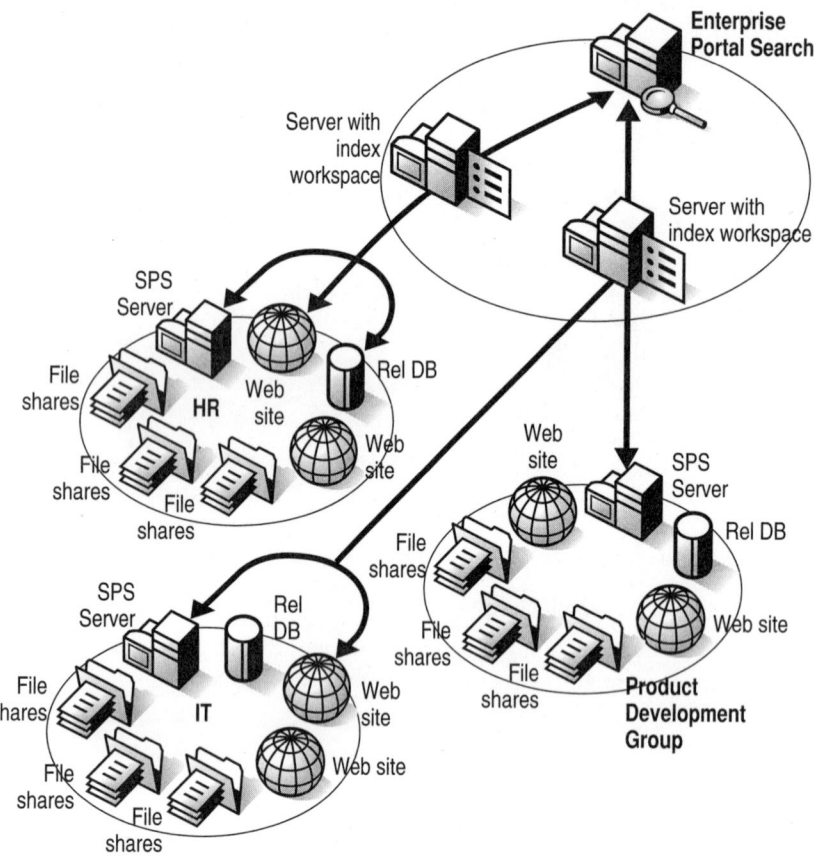

Figure 27.3. Enterprise search tiered server architecture

The server dedicated to searching stores a copy of the index propagated from the index workspaces of the servers dedicated to creating indexes.

> **Note** The task of creating an index is resource intensive. Consequently, with SharePoint Portal Server, you can create an index workspace on a separate server to isolate the tasks associated with creating and maintaining indexes from other SharePoint Portal Server tasks. After you create the index, SharePoint Portal Server propagates it to the server dedicated to searching. SharePoint Portal Server propagates the index immediately after creating it, or you can schedule the creation of the index to coincide with times of low network traffic.

For more information about this scenario, see Chapter 3, "Introducing SharePoint Portal Server: Configuration Flexibility."

Architecture Comparison

The migration to SharePoint Portal Server did not change the basic architecture for searching across the corpnet. The Site Server 3 architecture used two servers dedicated to crawling content and one search server. The hardware configuration for the Site Server 3 architecture included one server with four processors, used for searching, and one server with two processors, both used for crawling. The largest Site Server 3 catalog existed on a server with four processors. The SharePoint Portal Server architecture uses the same architecture as Site Server except that both servers used for creating and maintaining indexes use four processors. This difference in hardware configuration did not affect the results because most performance measures were made by using the largest catalog.

The project team estimated that additional RAM might also help performance. A *master merge* is an MSSearch process in which separate content index sub-files are merged into a single content index file. Because SharePoint Portal Server performs master merges less frequently while updating indexes, performance on the server used for creating and maintaining indexes improves with additional memory. Previous tests of additional RAM on the servers running Site Server 3 and Microsoft Windows NT® 4 did not show significant performance gains. However, the ITG corporate server standard for operating systems changed from Windows NT 4 to Microsoft Windows® 2000 Advanced Server. Windows 2000 makes better use of additional memory than Windows NT 4. Therefore, the project team doubled RAM to 512 megabytes (MB) on each server that hosted an index workspace.

The project team estimated hard disk size requirements based on the index size in Site Server 3 and added room for growth. After determining this number, they doubled it to hold a backup copy of the indexes on the server. The ITG standard hard disk configuration for running SharePoint Portal Server places the document store that includes documents and associated metadata on one hard disk, the content indexes on a second disk, and the logs on a third disk to minimize bottlenecks and maximize input/output (I/O) throughput.

Server Configurations

The following table lists the server configurations that ITG used for this project.

Enterprise Search Hardware Configurations

Hardware configuration	Enterprise search	Index 1	Index 2
Processor	4 X 550 megahertz (MHz)	4 X 550 MHz	4 X 400 MHz
Memory (initial)	512 MB RAM	512 MB RAM	512 MB RAM

continued

Enterprise Search Hardware Configurations *continued*

Hardware configuration	Enterprise search	Index 1	Index 2
Memory (final)	2 gigabytes (GB) RAM	2 GB RAM	512 MB RAM
Disk space	92 GB	68 GB	35 GB
OS	Windows 2000 Advanced Server SP1	Windows 2000 Advanced Server SP1	Windows 2000 Advanced Server SP1

Note As the table shows, the team increased RAM in one of the crawl servers to test scalability; this nearly doubled the crawl speed. The team also increased RAM in the search server to provide approximately 1 GB for the server to cache the property store. This reduced latency.

SharePoint Portal Server Architecture

Figure 27.4 shows the current architecture at Microsoft for enterprise search.

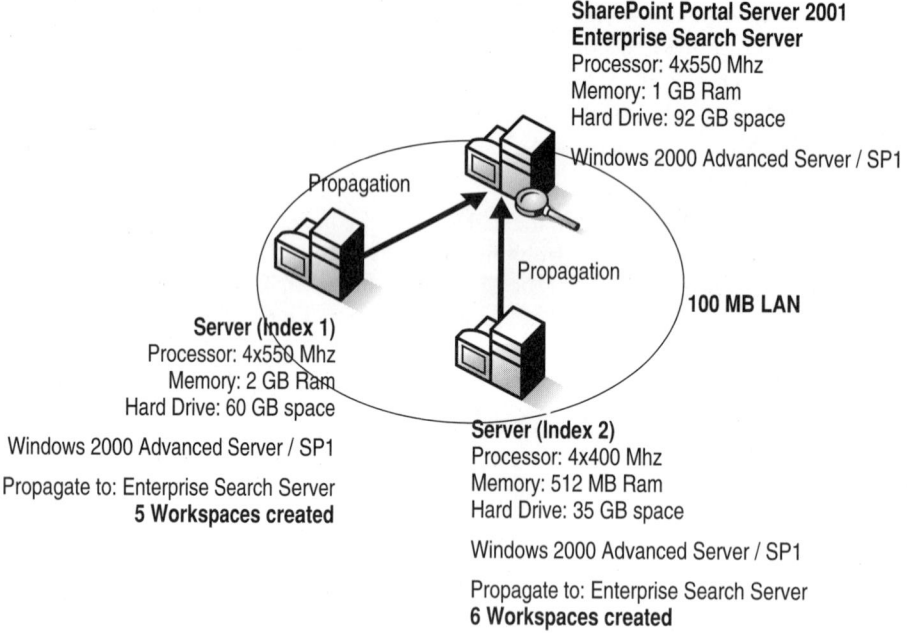

**SharePoint Portal Server 2001
Enterprise Search Server**
Processor: 4x550 Mhz
Memory: 1 GB Ram
Hard Drive: 92 GB space
Windows 2000 Advanced Server / SP1

Propagation

Propagation

100 MB LAN

Server (Index 1)
Processor: 4x550 Mhz
Memory: 2 GB Ram
Hard Drive: 60 GB space

Windows 2000 Advanced Server / SP1

Propagate to: Enterprise Search Server
5 Workspaces created

Server (Index 2)
Processor: 4x400 Mhz
Memory: 512 MB Ram
Hard Drive: 35 GB space

Windows 2000 Advanced Server / SP1

Propagate to: Enterprise Search Server
6 Workspaces created

Figure 27.4. SharePoint Portal Server architecture

Reviewing the Catalog

Site Server 3 creates catalogs to enable searching of content. SharePoint Portal Server creates indexes. An *index* is a resource that is built to enable full-text search of documents, document properties, and content stored outside the workspace but made available through content sources. A *workspace* can include multiple propagated indexes. When you create the workspace, SharePoint Portal Server automatically creates one index. You can propagate indexes only from index workspaces and only to a single destination workspace on another server (usually a server that is used primarily for searching). A destination workspace can accept indexes from up to four index workspaces. An index workspace is designed to manage only content sources.

The review identified 48 catalogs in the Site Server 3 environment. The primary intranet catalog included approximately 2.5 million documents; the remaining half million documents were spread across the other 47 catalogs.

Search Scopes

There were two main reasons to redefine the catalogs using search scopes. First, many of these catalogs wasted resources crawling the same content. Second, because the SharePoint Portal Server search service is multi-threaded, it was possible for the SharePoint Portal Server to have two threads crawling the same content at the same time.

Search scopes in SharePoint Portal Server offer the ability to restrict searching to a subset of an index. Scopes label entries in the full-text index so that they can be quickly identified by queries to deliver faster and more relevant information. The design of the index handles the search scopes by ensuring that the server passes the correct catalog parameters to the custom search page.

The project team created search scopes to help classify content for a single index without having to create additional workspaces. For example, suppose that Human Resources Web and Legal Web wanted to offer search of their own sites, but both wanted to include the Policy site. Instead of having two separate workspaces for each and crawling the Policy site twice, the team created a single workspace with three search scopes. The team created a scope of the content source pointing to the Policy site called "Policy" and then created a scope for all the content sources pointing to the Legal sites called "Legal." They also created a scope, called "HR," for all the content sources pointing to the Human Resources site. This reduced the number of index workspaces from three to one and prevented crawling the Policy site twice. From the Human Resources site, users can also search the Human Resources and Policy sites by using the different search scopes. Likewise, from the Legal site, users can also search the Policy and Legal sites by using the different search scopes. The queries return more relevant query results by using only the relevant search scopes.

Query Performance

Another consideration in catalog review and redesign was query performance and load balancing. Although search scopes are useful, overusing them can cause performance issues. One logical extension of search scopes includes crawling everything in one workspace, and creating scopes for each content source accordingly. In that case, using the index from the single workspace with many scopes performs all queries. However, as the number of search scopes increases, query performance declines and the index size increases. Because of this, the project team decided to limit search scopes to only two or three, and mainly in smaller workspaces.

An alternative approach is to create a workspace for each site or group of sites on the intranet, and then create a query that spans both workspaces. This also causes query performance to decline as you increase the number of index workspaces included in the query, so the team also decided to limit these types of queries to include only two or three workspaces.

Duplication

The team reviewed the existing catalog structure to eliminate redundant crawling. They reviewed the content sources and created a better design. During the process, the team closely examined scopes or queries across index workspaces that might compromise performance. In certain cases, performance was improved by crawling the same content twice from different workspaces and having search run a query against one workspace rather than having multiple dashboard sites query only one workspace.

To conduct the review of the catalogs, the team described each Site Server 3 catalog in a Microsoft Excel spreadsheet, as shown in the following tables.

Reviewing Content Sources

Content source	Hops and depth	Adaptive	Scope	Schedule
\\server01\d$\ Inetpub\handbook	This folder and all subfolders	Yes	Handbook	None
\\server01\d$\ Inetpub\ humanresourcesWeb	This folder and all subfolders	Yes	None	None
http://search1/sas/ dir.asp?setid=1	1 page hop, 0 site hops	No	None	Weekly

Reviewing Site Path Rules

Site path rules		Crawl account	Complex URLs
Avoid	file://server01/d$\inetpub\handbook*_vti**		
Crawl	file://server01/d$\inetpub\handbook*	default	Yes
Avoid	file://server01/d$\inetpub\humanresourcesrweb*_vti**		
Crawl	file://server01/d$\inetpub\hrweb*	default	No

Reviewing Catalog Information

Source	Display Mappings
\\server01\d$\Inetpub\handbook	http://corphandbook/
\\server01\d$\Inetpub\hrweb	http://hrwebsite/

The team then compared and identified catalogs to consolidate. The initial examination reduced more than half the number of catalogs, from 48 to 20. After several iterations, the team reduced the number of catalogs to 11.

Consolidation and Workspace Creation

As an outcome of this exercise, the team decided to create a one-to-one correspondence between remaining catalogs and workspaces. Figure 27.4 shows the final layout of the servers and workspaces.

Identifying Key Points

The key points learned in the Analysis and Design phase were:

- Deployment requires no significant hardware change. Additional memory or processors improve performance.

- Migration is a great time to review and clean up catalogs.

- Catalog redesign requires a variety of approaches:

  - Remove duplicate crawls of content where possible.

  - Limit searches to no more than two or three scopes or workspaces.

Deployment

The deployment phase included installing hardware and software, modifying settings, and testing. After deploying the SharePoint Portal Server environment, ITG ran it in parallel with Site Server 3.

Installing and Modifying Settings

This section reviews the installation and configuration for the workspaces. In particular, it reviews the process for creating content sources.

Install Hardware and Operating Systems

The project team installed the hardware for the SharePoint Portal Server deployment in the same data center as the Site Server 3 environment, so network connectivity and other environmental variables remained the same.

Next, the team installed the operating system. For more information about installation requirements, see Chapter 11, "Installing SharePoint Portal Server." You must deploy a server dedicated to searching before deploying a server dedicated to index workspaces. When you create an index workspace, you must specify the destination workspace, as shown in Figure 27.5. Therefore, the project team began by first configuring the server dedicated to searching and then configuring the servers that would host index workspaces.

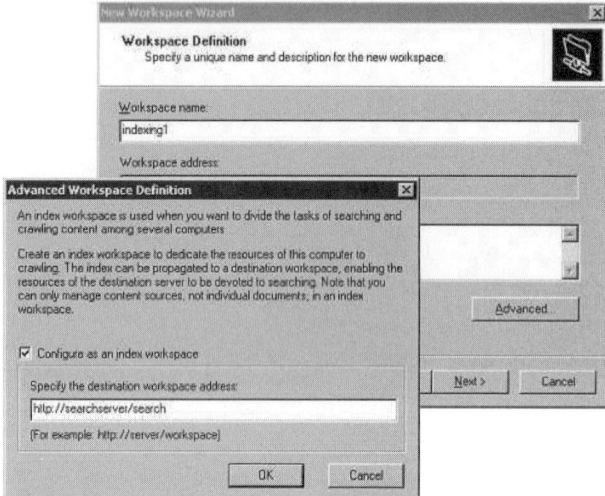

Figure 27.5. Creating an index workspace

Specify Workspace Settings

The team specified the settings as detailed in the following table.

Workspace configuration settings

	Enterprise search	Index 1	Index 2
Catalog Name	All catalogs propagate to the Enterprise Search server	BestbetsCorpPortal, HumanResourcesWeb, corporate portal, WebCat2, WindowsUA	ITG portal, KBInt portal, corporate portal param, Product Group Portal, SAP portal, MSWordTest
General			
Indexing Resource Usage	1 (Background)	5 (Dedicated)	5 (Dedicated)
Search Resource Usage	5 (Dedicated)	1 (Background)	1 (Background)
Site Hit Frequency Rules	None	None	None
Proxy Server			
Do not connect using a proxy server	Disable	Enable	Enable
Use the proxy server settings of the default content access account	Enable	Disable	Disable
Use the proxy server specification below	Disable	Disable	Disable
Default File Types in Site Server 3 removed from catalog	asp, doc, htm, html, ppt, xls, txt, exch,	asp, doc, htm, html, ppt, xls, txt, exch	asp, doc, htm, html, ppt, xls, txt, exch
Removed from Enterprise Search:	nsf, xml, odc, tiff, eml, dot, tif, mht	nsf, xml, odc, tiff, eml, dot, tif, mht	nsf, xml, odc, tiff, eml, dot, tif, mht

The team specified a System Resource Usage of 5 as the default for the servers hosting index workspaces. This allows full system resource usage when the server crawls content.

Note SharePoint Portal Server provides resource usage controls for searching and index creation, the two resource-intensive processes that are commonly performed on SharePoint Portal Server computers.

It is recommended that you balance resource usage to optimize performance depending on your server configuration. If you distribute searching and index creation across multiple servers, dedicate resources on each computer to the specific task that each computer performs. If you use one server to perform both index creation and searching, balance resource usage evenly between the two processes.

By design, this enterprise search solution does not crawl content outside the firewall. To allow SharePoint Portal Server to crawl only internal sites but without having to specify many rules (for example, exclude all *.com, *.edu, *.org), the team disabled the proxy server on each of the servers that hosted index workspaces. This prevented crawling anything outside the corporate environment.

To minimize unnecessary security changes, SharePoint Portal Server uses the same accounts to crawl and propagate content as Site Server 3. As with Site Server 3, SharePoint Portal Server respects Access Control Lists (ACLs). The use of ACLs maintains security as implemented in each of the original content sites.

Create Workspaces

The team created one workspace to correspond to each Site Server 3 catalog. After creating all the workspaces, the team created the content sources. Figure 27.6 shows an example of the content sources (called start address in Site Server 3) in one workspace.

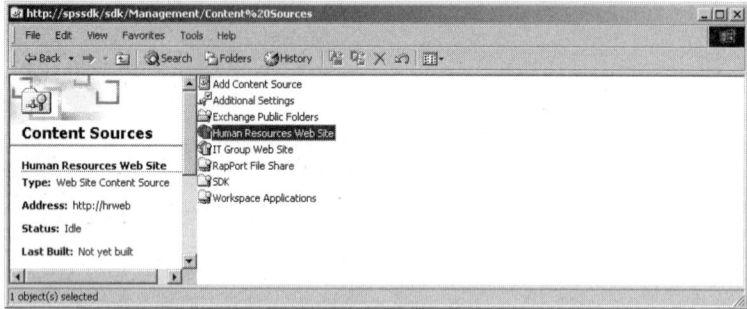

Figure 27.6. Example of content sources

Most workspaces contained several content types. A single content source cannot refer to different content types, but you can refer to multiple content types in a workspace.

During testing, the team discovered the following tips for properly configuring hops and depth:

- To crawl this entire site, set SiteHops to 0 and set page depth to unlimited.

- To crawl a single page, set SiteHops to 0 and set page depth to 0.

- Custom: Manual setup for the number of sites and hops.

For tracking purposes, the project team created a matrix showing which workspaces and sites used complex URLs and which content sources used which protocols, as shown in the following table.

Note The team restricted the use of complex URLs to well-known parameterized URLs, to minimize the risk of crawling URLs that continued to generate additional links without end.

Tracking Spreadsheet

Workspace name	Complex URL	Protocol		
		File	HTTP	Exchange
bestbetsCorporatePortal (Index 1)	Y	N	Y	N
Corporate Portal Intranet (Index 1)	N	Y	Y	Y
HumanResourcesWeb (Index 1)	Y	Y	Y	N
WebCatalog2 (Index 1)	Y	N	Y	N
WindowsUA (Index 1)	Y	Y	Y	Y
Corporate Portal Param (Index 2)	Y	Y	Y	Y
ITG portal (Index 2)	Y	Y	Y	Y
KBInt portal (Index 2)	N	Y	N	N
Product Group Portal (Index 2)	N	Y	Y	Y
SAPWeb (Index 2)	Y	Y	Y	Y
MSWordTest (Index 2)	Y	Y	Y	Y

Modify Additional Settings

The team specified three additional settings when configuring content sources: site path rules, Access/Display mappings, and file types.

Figure 27.7 shows the properties page for modifying site path rules in a single workspace.

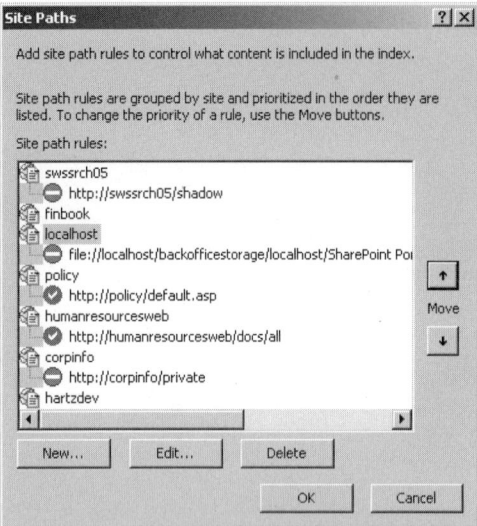

Figure 27.7. Example of site path rules

The spreadsheet of catalogs created during the Analysis and Design phase contained the site path rules and mappings. It is critically important that the site path rules be set exactly as intended. For more information about adding content sources, see Appendix B, "For More Information."

Create Content Sources

The following principles can assist you when you need to create content sources:

- Site path rules match in order from the top down.

- Use the asterisk (*) character with care. For example, an inclusion rule for http://searchserver/* crawls all subdirectories on the site. By contrast, an inclusion rule for http://searchserver/ crawls only the home page of that server.

- Enable complex URLs to crawl links with parameters following a question mark (?) in the link; for example, default.asp?name=abc.

- To exclude a protocol, add a site restriction as follows:

    File:*

    http://*

    Exch:*

Map Properties across Workspaces

SharePoint Portal Server crawls the text content of a Microsoft Office document and standard Office summary properties. If you want to include additional properties, you must create a document profile in the workspace with those properties. SharePoint Portal Server includes the metadata from the document profile in the index.

Important When SharePoint Portal Server propagates the indexes to a server dedicated to searching, the destination server must possess the same document profiles.

You must map properties of HTML documents or custom metadata of external documents to a document profile. This allows SharePoint Portal Server to crawl the additional properties. HTML files usually store custom properties in <META> tags. For more information about mapping custom properties, see Chapter 25, "Crawling Custom Metadata."

To map properties between servers, the project team performed the following procedure.

To map properties between servers:

1. Create document profiles for each index workspace.

    The team created a document profile called "Search Custom Tags" for each index workspace. Each workspace included additional metadata, as shown in the following table.

Example of property mapping for index workspaces

Workspace: bestbetsCorporatePortal	Workspace: CorporatePortal
META_Categories	META_Categories
META_PageURL	META_PageURL
META_XMLTerms	META_XMLTerms
META_Keyword	META_Keyword
Keywords	Keywords
Description	Description
Title	Title
Author	Author

Workspace: HumanResourcesWeb	Workspace: LibraryCatalog
META_Categories	META_MainAuthor
META_PageURL	META_itemtype
META_XMLTerms	META_pubdate
META_Keyword	META_subtitle
Keywords	Keywords
Description	Description
Title	Title
Author	Author

2. Create a document profile on the server dedicated to searching.

The team created a document profile with the same name used in step 1 on the server dedicated to searching. This document profile includes all the properties of the document profiles from each index workspace, as shown in the following table.

Example of property mapping for server dedicated to searching

Server dedicated to searching

META_Categories	META_PageURL
META_XMLTerms	META_Keyword
META_MainAuthor	META_itemtype
META_pubdate	META_subtitle
Keywords	Description
Title	Author

Note The document profile on the server dedicated to searching must contain the union of the properties of all the document profiles on the servers that host index workspaces. Any properties that are mapped and crawled on the server that maintains indexes, but are not present in the document profile on the server dedicated to searching, are not available in the index workspace that propagates to the search server.

3. Run the property mapping script.

The team ran the property mapping script for each index workspace. For more information about this script, see Chapter 25.

Note It is important to note that the account credentials under which the property mapping script runs must have administrator rights on the server and coordinator roles on the workspace.

4. Restart services on the servers.

To flush the caches, the team restarted the following services on the servers hosting index workspaces:

- SharePoint Portal Server

- Microsoft Exchange Information Store

- Microsoft Search

5. Start a full update of the index.

After restarting the services, the team reset the index and began a full update.

Modify Search Pages

The existing search solution allowed customized query and results sets for each portal. Because of this, the team chose not to use the default dashboard site provided as part of SharePoint Portal Server.

By contrast, many customers may have only a single centralized search page to which all internal sites link. These customers could simply replace the existing page with the Search dashboard from SharePoint Portal Server and avoid creating custom search pages.

From each portal, a user uses a search box to submit queries. After submission, the user is redirected to a hosted ASP page on the server dedicated to searching. Site Server 3 takes the following steps during this process:

1. Accepts the query from the referring site

2. Executes the search by using Site Server 3 Component Object Model (COM) objects

3. Receives the results set

4. Converts the results into Extensible Markup Language (XML)

5. Returns the XML to the user's browser (Microsoft uses Microsoft Internet Explorer 5.5 and passes XML to the client)

The transition from Site Server 3 to SharePoint Portal Server required the project team to modify step 2 and step 4 of the preceding process. For step 2, the team changed the query so that it used the Structured Query Language (SQL) syntax with full-text extensions instead of native Site Server 3 COM objects.

The following example illustrates a SELECT statement using WebDAV in SharePoint Portal Server.

```
SELECT "urn:schemas-microsoft-com:office:office#Office", "DAV:parentname",
"DAV:href", "urn:schemas-microsoft-com:office:office#Title",
"urn:schemas.microsoft.com:fulltextqueryinfo:description", "urn:schemas-
microsoft-com:office:office#META_PageURL","urn:schemas-microsoft-
com:office:office#META_Categories", rank, "DAV:getcontentlength",
"DAV:getcontenttype", "DAV:getlastmodified"

FROM TABLE corpportal..SCOPE()

WHERE WITH ("urn:schemas-microsoft-com:office:office#Title",
"urn:schemas.microsoft.com:fulltextqueryinfo:description",
"urn:schemas.microsoft.com:fulltextqueryinfo:contents") AS #DocDesc
(FREETEXT (#DocDesc, '401k')

RANK BY COERCION ABSOLUTE , 1000)) ORDER BY rank DESC
```

Note The SELECT list returns the mapped meta properties (in the Office namespace).

The team used the workspace-level scope to restrict results to one of the index workspaces. They also used group aliasing in addition to freetext and rank coercion. For more information about restricting search results, see Appendix B.

To modify step 4 in the preceding process, the team modified the process for formatting results. Originally, the page used a custom routine to create XML from the results set for

Site Server 3, but SharePoint Portal Server returns XML natively. This eliminated the need to convert results to XML. The team simply applied an Extensible Stylesheet Language (XSL) transformation to achieve the formatting they wanted.

Samples of the ASP pages for Site Server 3 and SharePoint Portal Server are provided in the following code.

Site Server 3 Search ASP Page Sample Code

This is a sample of the Site Server 3 ASP code.

```
<%@LANGUAGE="VBScript" %>

<% ' Copyright 1997-1998 Microsoft Corporation. All rights reserved. %>

<%

   DisplayText=Request("q1")

   RecordNum=Request("RecordNum")

   if RecordNum= "" then RecordNum=1

%>



<html>

<head><title>Search Page</title>

   <meta http-equiv=content-type content="text/html; charset=iso-8859-1">

   <meta http-equiv=»content-language» content=»EN»>

</head>

<body text="#000000" link="#000000" alink="#000000" vlink="#000000"
topmargin=17 leftmargin=15 bgcolor="ffffff">



<form method=get>Search:

   <input type=Text name="q1" value="<%=DisplayText%>" size="23">

   <input type=submit name="Search" value="Go">

   <input type=hidden name="ct" value="MyCatalog">
```

```
</form>


<%

If DisplayText <> "" Then

    %>Searching for <b><%=DisplayText%></b>

    <%

      ' Set query and utility objects, and define query object properties.

            set util = Server.CreateObject("MSSearch.util")

            set Q = Server.CreateObject("MSSearch.Query")

            Q.SetQueryFromURL(Request.QueryString)

            Q.MaxRecords = 25

            Q.SortBy = "Rank[d],DocTitle"

            Q.Columns = "DocTitle, DocAddress, FileWrite, Size, Description,
FileName, DocSignature, Rank, DetectedLanguage, MimeType, SiteName,
NNTP_MessageID"


      ' Create the recordset holding the search results.

      on error resume next

      set RS = Q.CreateRecordSet("sequential")

      if err then

      createerror = err.description

      createerrnumber = err.number

      end if


      ' Error description.

            if err then
```

```
                    Response.write createerror

    ' Display results

        else

        Response.write "<table><tr><td><font size = 2>"

                ' Set up number found.

                NumberFound= RS.Properties("RowCount")

                if RS.Properties("RowLimitExceeded") = true then

                 NumberFound = "More than " & NumberFound

                end if



                ' Set up loop to iterate through results.
                Do while not RS.EOF



                ' Set up title for links, providing an alternative if
DocTitle is blank.
                if RS("DocTitle") <> "" then

                        Title = RS("DocTitle")

                else

                        Title = "No title: " & RS("DocAddress")

                end if



                ' Set up link itself.

                        Link = RS("DocAddress")



                ' One table is used for each search result.
```

```
                Response.write "</font></td></tr><tr><td> </td></
tr></table>"

                Response.write "<table cellpadding=0 cellspacing=0>"

                Response.write "<tr><td width=21><font size=2><p>"

                Response.write "<table cellpadding=1 cellspacing=1
border=0><tr><td align=top>"

                    Response.Write "<font size='2'>" & RS("Rank") & "</
font>"

                %>

                </td></tr></table>

                <%

                Response.Write "</font></td>"

                Response.Write "<td bgcolor='#80BBDD'><font size=2>"

                %>

                <a <% = LinkTarget %> href='<% = Link %>'><% = Title
%></a>

                </font></td></tr><tr><td></td><td><font size=2>

                <% Response.write
util.TruncateToWhiteSpace(RS(«Description»),250) %>

                </font></td></tr>

                <tr><td></td><td height=5></td></tr>

                <tr><td></td><td>

                <font color=808080 size=1>[<% =
util.TruncateToWhiteSpace(RS("FileWrite"), 12 ) %>]

                <% iSize = CInt(CLng(RS("Size"))/1024) %>

                  (<% = iSize %>k)  

                </font>

        <%
```

```
           ' Increment the results.

                  RS.MoveNext

                  RecordNum = RecordNum + 1

                  Loop

                  Response.write "</font></td></tr></table>"



           ' If there are more results pages, set up the "More Results"
  link.

                  if RS.Properties("MoreRows") = true then

                  Q.StartHit = RS.Properties("NextStartHit")

                  ' Repeat query with new start hit.

                         L_MoreResults_link = "More Results"

                         MoreLink = "<a href=?" & Q.QueryToURL & "&" _

                         & "DisplayText=" & Server.URLEncode(DisplayText)
  & "&" _

                         & "RecordNum=" & RecordNum _

                         & ">" & L_MoreResults_link & "</a>"

                  end if

           %><% = MoreLink %>

            </font></td>

            </tr>

            </table>

      <%

      End if

  End If

  %>
```

SharePoint Portal Server Search ASP Page Sample Code

This is a sample of the SharePoint Portal Server ASP code.

```asp
<%@LANGUAGE="VBScript" %>

<% ' Copyright 2001 Microsoft Corporation. All rights reserved. %>

<%

    DisplayText=Request("q1")

    ct=Request("ct")



    If DisplayText = "" Then %>

        <html>

        <head><title>Search Page</title>

            <meta http-equiv=content-type content="text/html;
charset=iso-8859-1">

            <meta http-equiv="content-language" content="EN">

        </head>

        <body text="#000000" link="#000000" alink="#000000"
vlink="#000000" topmargin=17 leftmargin=15 bgcolor="ffffff">

        <form method=get>Search:

            <input type=Text name="q1" value="<%=DisplayText%>"
size="23">

            <input type=submit name="Search" value="Go">

            <input type=hidden name="ct" value="MyCatalog">

        </form>

        <%

    Else

        Response.ContentType = "text/xml"
```

```
            Response.Write("<?xml version='1.0' encoding='ISO-8859-1'?>" &
vbCRLF)

            Response.Write("<Results xmlns:dt='urn:schemas-microsoft-
com:datatypes'>")



            set oProc = Application("StyleTransform").createProcessor

            Set xh = Server.CreateObject("Msxml2.SERVERXMLHTTP")



            strQuery = "<?xml version=""1.0"" encoding=""utf-
8""?><a:searchrequest xmlns:a=""DAV:""><a:sql>" &_

                "SELECT ""rank"", ""DAV:href"", ""urn:schemas-microsoft-
com:office:office#Title"",
""urn:schemas.microsoft.com:fulltextqueryinfo:description"",
""DAV:getcontentlength"", ""DAV:getlastmodified""" &_

                "FROM " & ct & "..SCOPE() " &_

                "WHERE WITH (""urn:schemas-microsoft-
com:office:office#Title"",
""urn:schemas.microsoft.com:fulltextqueryinfo:description"",
""urn:schemas.microsoft.com:fulltextqueryinfo:contents"") AS #DocDesc
(FREETEXT (#DocDesc, '" & DisplayText & "')) " &_

                "ORDER BY ""rank"" DESC</a:sql></a:searchrequest>"



            'Make DAV request

            xh.setTimeouts 0, 6000, 6000, 0

            xh.open "SEARCH", "http://myServer/myWorkspace", False

            xh.setRequestHeader "content-type", "text/xml"

            xh.setRequestHeader "range", "rows=0-9"

            xh.setRequestHeader "MS-Search-MaxRows", 200

            xh.setRequestHeader "MS-Search-UseContentIndex", "t"

            xh.send strQuery
```

```
            'Process DAV response

        if xh.Status <> 207 then

                Response.Write "<error>Status: " & xh.Status & ". Status
Text: " & xh.statusText & "</error>"

                Response.Write "<errorReason><![CDATA[" & xh.responseText
& "]]></errorReason>"

        else

                if xh.responseXML.parseError.errorCode <> 0 then

                Response.Write "<error>XML response error code = " &
xh.responseXML.parseError.errorCode & " " &
xh.responseXML.parseError.reason & "</error>"

                end if



                'Display results

                if
xh.responseXML.selectSingleNode("a:multistatus").haschildnodes = false then

                Response.Write("<ResultSet totalhits='0'><error>No
documents match your query.</error></ResultSet>")

                else

                oProc.input = xh.responseXML.documentElement

                oProc.transform

                Response.Write(oProc.output)

                end if

        end if

    Response.Write "</Results>"

End If

%>
```

Testing

Testing included two tasks. The project team verified that SharePoint Portal Server met the criteria for creating and maintaining indexes for the identified content. In addition, they verified that SharePoint Portal Server met the criteria for searching, including the criteria for workspace propagation process and speed, basic functionality, and the custom search page.

Index Testing

The team identified two goals for testing the process of creating an index:

- SharePoint Portal Server can crawl all the content crawled by using Site Server 3.

- SharePoint Portal Server can crawl up to 6 million documents.

The second goal verified the scalability of the SharePoint Portal Server search solution. ITG's goal was 6 million documents. That number was based on 3 million documents in the index at the beginning of the test, plus additional occasional sources, and an additional number used as a growth factor.

To measure crawl performance, the test team established several metrics. The following table shows these metrics according to source.

Index Test Metrics

Data collection	Found at
Number of documents	Event viewer, SharePoint Portal Server Administration in Microsoft Management Console (MMC), ASP event log
Crawl status	SharePoint Portal Server Administration in MMC, Web folders view
Crawl start time	Event viewer application log
Crawl end time	Event viewer application log
Crawl duration	Manual calculation using the preceding data
Catalog size	SharePoint Portal Server Administration in MMC
Property store **Note** Property store size is applied at server level and *not* at catalog level	Folder <...\SharePoint Portal Server\FTData\ SharepointPortalServer\sps.edb>, by using Windows Explorer

The team executed each crawl several times. They refined the rules until they were satisfied the proper content was actually being included in the index. They used the dashboard search on the server dedicated to searching to assist with this check.

The team used the event viewer and gatherer log viewer from SharePoint Portal Server to examine the system to ensure that the index was operating normally and without problems. Figure 27.8 shows an example of the event viewer entries for starting and stopping the index.

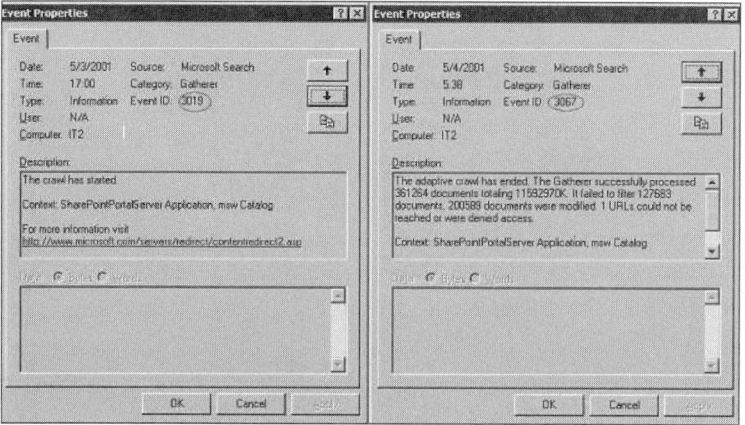

Figure 27.8. Example event viewer entries

The following table shows an example of the data collected to track crawls.

Example Index Test Metrics

Catalog name **Full crawl**

	# of docs	Crawl duration	Prop. duration	Catalog size	Property store size
bestbetsCorpPortal (Index 1)	851	1 min	1 min	1 MB	4.61 GB
Corporate Portal Intranet (Index 1)	2,920,178	3,127 min	65 min	5,081 MB	
HumanResourcesWeb (Index 1)	3,927	24 min	1 min	4 MB	
WebCatalog2 (Index 1)	17,882	24 min	1 min	14 MB	
WindowsUA (Index 1)	14,198	8 min	1 min	14 MB	
CorpPortal Param (Index 2)	694	3 min	1 min	1 MB	1.04 GB
ITG portal (Index 2)	13,250	37 min	1 min	13 MB	
KBInt portal (Index 2)	226,474	269 min	15 min	325 MB	
Product Group Portal (Index 2)	159,257	224 min	19 min	605 MB	
SAPWeb (Index 2)	3,609	47 min	1 min	3 MB	
MSWordTest (Index 2)	15,233	11 min	1 min	24 MB	

SharePoint Portal Server completed the full crawls with satisfactory results at a volume of about 3 million documents. ITG added more content sources for scale testing. Eventually, SharePoint Portal Server crawled just over 6 million documents. Crawl performance did not drop off due to the size of the index.

Next, the team tested incremental updates on each of the catalogs. The incremental crawls took about half the time of the original full index and proved successful.

Finally, the team tested adaptive crawling on the largest catalogs in multiple passes until the number of documents modified converged. In doing so, the team discovered that convergence took about eight passes for the largest workspace. In these passes, crawl time was reduced from 51 hours for a full index to less than 8 hours for the shortest adaptive crawl, a nearly sevenfold improvement. Figure 27.9 shows the index times per pass.

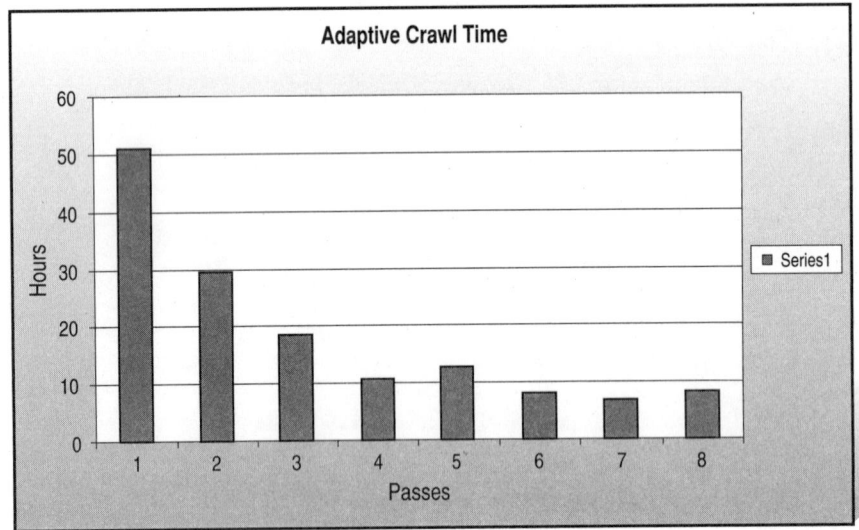

Figure 27.9. Adaptive crawl times

The testing process involved the following steps:

- Perform a full index: n days

- Perform an incremental index: day $n+1$

- Perform an adaptive update and track the number of documents changed: each night

When an index reaches a steady state of number of documents updated or crawl time, it has converged. After convergence, the crawl time remains approximately the same each night, unless SharePoint Portal Server detects a large change in content such as a new site coming online.

Search Testing

ITG tested three additional features. First, they tested the workspace propagation process and times. Next, they tested the basic searching by using the dashboard site. Finally, they tested the custom search page.

When examining propagation, it is important to determine that propagation completes successfully. In addition, ITG needed an estimate of how long the propagation took to complete. The following table outlines the metrics and their sources.

> **Note** You should measure the duration of propagation, from the start of the process on the server hosting the index workspace to the end of the process on the search server.

Search Test Metrics

Data collection	Currently found at
Propagation status	SharePoint Portal Server Administration in MMC, Event Viewer
Propagation start time	Event Viewer (on both servers)
Propagation end time	Event Viewer (on search server)
Propagation duration	Manual calculation from data collected

The ITG team tested the results for simple full-text queries that used SharePoint Portal Server. After performing queries, they compared the results seen in Site Server 3 queries with those in SharePoint Portal Server to ensure that crawling returned the proper documents and appropriately followed the rules.

Finally, after completing the custom ASP page modifications, they tested the ASP pages. The test involved both the query and results pages. Final tests measured performance and accuracy of the results sets.

For query latency, the ASP page recorded the exact time of the request and the exact time of the response in an SQL database, along with other relevant data used to track usage metrics. The team created a set of 47 queries, most of them from the top 100 queries run the previous month. This set included one-term and two-term phrases and some unusual queries. They ran this set of queries on Site Server 3 and then on SharePoint Portal Server. The data collected included the time of the first request of a query and then the results of the next four queries for the same term. These latency times, in seconds, are shown in the following table.

ASP Page Performance Testing

Product	Initial	#2	#3	#4	#5
Site Server 3	1.11	0.84	0.81	0.81	0.86
SharePoint Portal Server	4.28	0.65	0.65	0.65	0.65

ITG determined the disparity between initial response times with SharePoint Portal Server and Site Server 3 to be the cache. Because Site Server 3 was already in use and taking queries, many queries and terms were already loaded into memory. This helped reduce the initial response time. SharePoint Portal Server had none of the terms in memory, so all queries required reading from the disk. Subsequent queries with SharePoint Portal Server were 22 percent faster than Site Server 3.

In addition to faster query rates with SharePoint Portal Server, tests determined that the server dedicated to searching was capable of taking advantage of additional memory. When the team increased RAM from 1 GB to 2 GB on this server, latency time dropped. They allowed 1 GB of RAM for running the operating system and SharePoint Portal Server and 1 GB of RAM for caching the property store. Loading a large part of the property store helped improve performance by speeding access to data used in search queries. The numbers in the previous table were from the testing once the team added the additional memory, but before they ran the "warm-up" script.

To facilitate this pre-loading or "warm up" of the cache, the team developed a script that runs immediately after crawling completes and propagates. This script loads the cache with data, so the cache is ready when the service enters production. For more information about this script, see Appendix B.

> **Note** If you set the maximum cache size too high, you can leave insufficient memory for SharePoint Portal Server, the operating system and any other applications on your server. A good rule-of-thumb is to leave at least 0.5 GB for use by SharePoint Portal Server and the operating system. For example, on a server with 2 GB of physical memory, set the minimum cache size to 1 GB and the maximum cache size to 1.5 GB (or less, if you have other applications running).

You must leave enough memory for other processes and for monitoring Microsoft Search objects in Performance Monitor.

Results of Testing

The search tests yielded the following results:

- Average latency time was reduced by 22 percent (after the cache was pre-loaded).

- On the server dedicated to searching, you can improve performance when caching the property store by adding additional memory.

- To maintain NTLM credentials, ASP pages must be on the search server.

After developing the custom ASP pages, the team validated the search results through testing. They added a link to the results page for Site Server 3, asking users to try the new search page that relied on SharePoint Portal Server. From this process, the team monitored the following data:

- Query string and number of times it was requested

- Total number of queries

- Total number of unique users

- Average response times

Key Points

The key points learned during the Deployment phase and index testing were:

- The test crawled about 3 million documents, with the largest catalog averaging 970 documents per minute. This represented a nearly threefold increase over 330 documents per minute with Site Server 3. In addition, SharePoint Portal Server crawled a larger number of documents and more diverse file types.

- Although comparable, the SharePoint Portal Server deployment used hardware that is more powerful.

- Adaptive crawling reduced crawling time from 51 hours to less than 8 hours. This represents a sevenfold increase.

- By using adaptive crawling, SharePoint Portal Server updates the largest index nightly instead of weekly. This results in more timely and relevant information.

- Additional RAM and processors make a significant difference in crawl performance with SharePoint Portal Server.

- To improve performance, optimize the site rules and content sources.

Management

To transition a portal that uses Site Server 3 for searching to SharePoint Portal Server, ITG modified the URL on the page where users perform search queries to point to the SharePoint Portal Server computer dedicated to searching. For example:

- Existing URL: http://siteserver3/search/default.asp

- New URL: http://spsearch/search/default.asp

First, the team modified the URL for searching on the primary corporate portal, MSWeb, to point to the SharePoint Portal Server computer. As expected, the load immediately increased from a few thousand queries per week to nearly 30,000 per day.

Next, the team modified the URL for searching on the Product Group Portal to point to the SharePoint Portal Server computer. This portal used the dashboard site included with SharePoint Portal Server for searching, instead of a custom ASP page. The team simply added a new Web Part to the search dashboard. This site handles about 2,000 searches per month.

The team continued this process for each of the major business portals across the corporate intranet. In addition to completing the transition to SharePoint Portal Server, ITG must continue to monitor performance for SharePoint Portal Server and to implement a disaster recovery plan that is compatible with SharePoint Portal Server. The next section reviews these steps.

Monitoring Performance

Through effective monitoring, ITG has determined that this deployment meets performance expectations. ITG also captures monitoring data for trend analysis to predict future problems and fine-tune alert thresholds.

Note Although separate administration is possible, ITG administers Windows 2000 and SharePoint Portal Server together.

Server activity for SharePoint Portal Server generates performance data that Windows 2000 can track and log on the system. The data is described as a performance object and is typically named for the component generating the data. Every performance object provides counters that represent data on specific aspects of the object. ITG monitors standard Windows 2000 Advanced Server performance objects, along with several specific objects for SharePoint Portal Server. For example, to monitor MSSearch, select the performance object called Microsoft Gatherer and the Heartbeats counter.

The performance objects to monitor for enterprise search include:

- Microsoft Gatherer
- Microsoft Gatherer Projects
- Microsoft Search
- Microsoft Search Catalogs
- Microsoft Search Indexer Catalogs

The following table describes the counters that ITG routinely monitors.

Monitoring Performance Objects

Performance object	Counter	Explanation
Microsoft Gatherer	Documents Filtered (and Rate)	Number of documents attempted to be crawled since the service started.
	Documents Successfully Filtered (and Rate)	Number of documents successfully crawled since the service started.
	Documents Delayed Retry	Non-0 means the Microsoft Web Storage System is having problems; by default, retries until cleared.

Performance object	Counter	Explanation
Microsoft Gatherer *(continued)*	Reason to Back off	Non-0 means crawling is paused, because of high disk I/O, low memory, etc.
	Server objects	Number of servers crawled.
	Time outs	Too high means network problems.
	Adaptive Crawl Accepts	Documents accepted by adaptive update.
	Adaptive Crawl Error Samples	Documents accessed for error sampling.
	Adaptive Crawl Errors	Documents that adaptive update incorrectly rejects.
	Adaptive Crawl Excludes	Documents that adaptive update excludes.
	Adaptive Crawl False Positives	Number of false positives that occur when the adaptive update has predicted that a document has changed when it has not. If this number is high, the adaptive update algorithm is not modeling the changes in the documents correctly.
	Adaptive Crawl Total	Documents to which adaptive update logic was applied.
Microsoft Gatherer Projects	Crawls In progress	Number of concurrent crawls.
	Status Success (and Rate)	Number of documents successfully filtered for this workspace.
	Status Error	Number of errors.
	URLs in History	Number of URLs covered in all crawls.
	Waiting Documents	Gatherer queue length— 0 means idle.
Microsoft Search	Failed Queries	Number of failed queries.
	Successful Queries (and Rate)	Number of successful queries.

continued

Monitoring Performance Objects *continued*

Performance object	Counter	Explanation
Microsoft Search Indexer Catalogs	Merge progress 0–100%	Non-100 means indexes are currently being merged—crawl can be paused during that time.
	Number of Documents	Number of documents in the catalog included in the index.
	Index Size	Size of the index in megabytes

Planning for Disaster Recovery

The backup and restore process represents the only substantial change in the operation of SharePoint Portal Server over Site Server 3. SharePoint Portal Server provides a built-in script for backing up the entire server with all the workspace and catalog information to an image file. You can then restore this image on another server.

ITG uses the MSDMBACK utility installed with SharePoint Portal Server to copy the backup files to disk each night, and then uses Windows 2000 Backup to back up those files to tape.

Important This output from MSDMBACK must be saved to a local drive.

Because Windows 2000 Backup attempts to lock the files while backing up, which prevents crawls from continuing, servers that host index workspaces must be set to exclude the following directory from the Windows 2000 backup:

operating_system_drive\Program Files\SharePoint Portal
Server\Data\FTData\SharepointPortalServer

The MSDMBACK utility takes a snapshot of all necessary SharePoint Portal Server data directories as part of its backup.

Each night, ITG runs the backup process on each server that hosts an index workspace and the enterprise portal server. MSDMBACK is run, backing up the data to another partition according to the following steps:

1. From the directory: *operating_system_drive*\Program Files\SharePoint Portal Server\Bin, run the following command:

    cscript msdmback.vbs /b "*path_to_backup_file_name*"

    where the *path_to_backup_file_name* parameter is the name of the backup file to be created.

2. The preceding command is entered into a .cmd file that is scheduled to run by using the Windows 2000 task scheduler. Note that the start in parameter specifies *operating_system_drive*\Program Files\SharePoint Portal Server\Bin.

> **Note** The script/schedule task must be run under the context of an account that has administrator privileges on each server.

3. Run a full Windows 2000 backup to tape every night for each server.

It is important to note that the backup process stores passwords for content sources in encrypted form in the backup image. The optional password used for the backup image (provided during backup) encrypts only the passwords. Use of the optional password does not encrypt the remainder of the backup image, including the documents and metadata. If the administrator loses the password that was used to create the backup image, and attempts to restore, the restoration succeeds, but the restored information for the content source access account is invalid. In addition, subsequent crawls of this content source may fail because of authentication failures.

The backup process also stores user name and password pairs that are used for content sources in encrypted registry files. The optional password provided during restoration decrypts only the user name and password pairs. If the administrator loses the password that was used to create the backup image, and then tries to restore the image, the restoration succeeds but leaves the user name and password pairs for content sources blank.

Identifying Key Points

Organizations that want to make the transition from Site Server 3 to SharePoint Portal Server may find the approach taken by Microsoft's ITG group (outlined in the following list) to be helpful:

- Run a test server to learn how the new technology operates.

- Take the opportunity to examine site rules, property mappings, and catalogs; make necessary changes for enhanced performance.

- Build a custom ASP page if the SharePoint Portal Server dashboard site user interface is not used.

- Run Site Server 3 and SharePoint Portal Server in parallel to test performance.

- When the acceptance criteria have been met, remove the old environment and leave the SharePoint Portal Server environment.

Summary

Migrating to SharePoint Portal Server yielded two key benefits, including:

More relevant and timely search results delivered to users.

- Latency, or response time, improved by 22 percent.

- Indexes updated nightly by using adaptive updates.

Improved crawling performance.

- Full update of an index nearly three times faster than Site Server 3

- Adaptive update of an index seven times faster than Site Server 3

In addition to these benefits, ITG identified the following key points:

The migration process is straightforward. Migrating to SharePoint Portal Server is not complex. SharePoint Portal Server can use the same architecture as, and similar hardware to, Site Server 3. You can begin the catalog review process while ordering hardware and learning the product. Modifying existing ASP pages is simple, and you can use the built-in user interface included with SharePoint Portal Server. You encounter few changes in day-to-day operation from administering Site Server 3.

It is recommended that you review and refine existing catalogs. The appropriate time to review existing catalogs is before implementation. Over time, your catalogs have probably lost accuracy. Start addresses do not exist anymore; your servers crawl the same content multiple times; some catalogs are redundant or unnecessary. As you review catalog definitions, you can also review your internal customer requirements. Customers now have the opportunity to redefine and refine their requirements for searching.

SharePoint Portal Server gives improved full update performance and adaptive crawling benefits. With SharePoint Portal Server, you can crawl more content in the same amount of time as Site Server 3, using similar hardware. This provides room for growth. Alternatively, you can crawl existing content with less hardware than Site Server 3. This allows you to buy less expensive hardware. In addition, you can update existing content more frequently than Site Server 3, using similar hardware. This provides more timely and relevant results to your users.

Adding memory improves performance. Adding memory provides a quicker and less expensive way to improve performance than adding servers to your infrastructure.

This chapter describes the ITG deployment plan of SharePoint Portal Server and its subsequent results. It provides detailed information and recommendations based on this deployment. It includes technical information on the existing environment, design decisions, deployment steps, and testing considerations. It concludes with a summary of recommendations based on this experience.

CHAPTER 28

KMIT: Deploying SharePoint Portal Server across Multiple Sites

Intranet Web sites, or *portals*, are expensive to create, difficult to update and maintain, and inefficient for finding information quickly. Microsoft® SharePoint™ Portal Server 2001 offers solutions to assist organizations in finding, sharing, and publishing information. With Rapid Portal (RapPort), the process of creating and customizing a corporate portal that uses SharePoint Portal Server takes only a few days.

RapPort Overview

Rapid Portal, called "RapPort," offers Microsoft's internal users predefined templates to quickly and inexpensively build intranet portals that take advantage of the search, document management, and collaboration features of SharePoint Portal Server. RapPort portals deploy quickly and are easy to maintain.

RapPort and SharePoint Portal Server bring significant benefits to Microsoft's internal groups:

- **Self-Provisioning of Intranet sites.** Creates sites with content from predefined templates.

- **Reduces the time and cost to build and manage a site.** Cost to build a site dropped from $68,500 to $3,750. Maintenance effort cut by 80 percent.

Intranet portals often fail to map to day-to-day work. For example, information might be stored in multiple places without a consistent taxonomy. Tools may focus on individual work instead of sharing and collaboration. In addition, intranet portals rarely include tools to help with mostly manual day-to-day tasks. This is true even inside Microsoft.

To address those issues, in June 2000, the Knowledge Management Information Technology group (KMIT) inside Microsoft set out to look at knowledge management and collaboration in departments within Microsoft, and to create solutions that eased those problems.

The Knowledge Management Information Technology Group

KMIT has several unique charters within Microsoft:

- Drive creation of knowledge management and collaborative solutions on emerging Microsoft Technologies.

- Provide real-world feedback to the product teams while solving real business and user problems.

They discovered that Microsoft's 40,000 employees, like other knowledge workers in worldwide enterprises, were generally dissatisfied with existing capabilities in the areas of site creation, search, document collaboration and management, and maintainability.

Some groups were using Microsoft Office Server Extensions (OSE), for document publishing, discussion and subscription capabilities. Version tracking presented a challenge, however, as did site navigation. Within a group, different sub-groups wanted to organize documents differently. Consequently, the "one view fits all" folder hierarchy view was unsatisfactory. Also, these groups usually handled their calendars and contact management needs with applications separate from the document collaboration space.

Other groups created their own custom Web sites with custom applications. This provided them with great control over the look, feel, and navigation features. However, these solutions were time consuming to build, hard to maintain, and impossible to share with other groups. The resources dedicated to building and maintaining these solutions were not available for Microsoft's primary mission, building and providing innovative software and solutions.

RapPort and SharePoint Portal Server

In order to solve these problems, the KMIT team envisioned a template-based, rapid deployment tool to create collaborative sites easily and quickly. These sites needed to support intergroup and intragroup collaboration as well as function as a central location for group members to see and do their work. KMIT chose to build RapPort on SharePoint Portal Server because of its out-of-the-box capabilities, including:

- **Document management.** Document profiles, check-in and check-out, versioning, and simple approval and publishing, along with seamless Office XP integration.

- **Customizable portal.** Easy-to-customize dashboard site using Web Parts. Includes category browsing for information organization.

- **Search.** Crawls full content and metadata of documents stored locally or on other platforms including Web sites, file shares, and Microsoft Exchange public folders for inclusion in an index.

- **Collaboration features.** Notifications when content in documents, folders, categories, search results change; searchable, document based discussions.

RapPort Portals

With RapPort, once employees decide they need an intranet site, they simply fill out a two-page Web form, and the site is ready the next business day. On the second day they configure the site, which resides in the corporate data center, and then load their documents and other content. The site is deployed by the third day, instead of weeks later.

The contents of a RapPort site are pre-loaded at the time a user creates each site. RapPort copies the content of the master template the user selected to the new site. The templates are the key to RapPort success. A template is simply a pre-built SharePoint workspace, and includes:

- **Virtual server name.** The site is known as http://my_site for ease of use.

- **Categories, document profiles, and attributes.** These features form the basis of a consistent taxonomy implementation.

- **Document folder structure and documents.** Users can preload content such as templates or samples to promote best practices.

- **Web Parts, dashboards, and applications.** These technologies provide a way to customize the interface. They provide meaningful functionality based on the audience. For example, a product development group portal receives a view of bug database information; sales offices portals receive sales data from Siebel.

RapPort currently includes templates for department and business unit portals for product development and sales organizations. Experts from each of these groups helped build this set of templates. KMIT continues to refine and extend templates as adoption accelerates. The architecture for RapPort supports an unlimited number of templates.

Figure 28.1 shows the architecture of RapPort. The RapPort server stores both the RapPort application and the templates. The AUTOSETUP component creates the sites and populates them on any one of a number of servers based on simple allocation rules. Finally, Microsoft uses SharePoint Portal Server as the enterprise search solution. RapPort offers a Web Part that enables each RapPort site to "plug in" to the enterprise search solution.

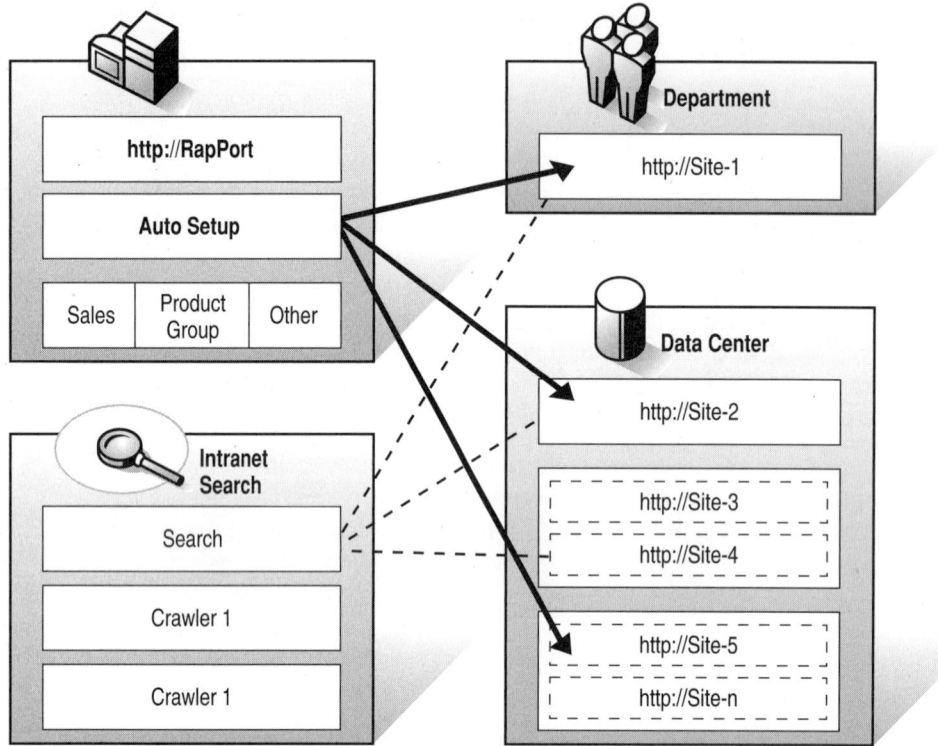

Figure 28.1. RapPort architecture

Benefits of RapPort Deployment

RapPort provides three key benefits to corporate intranet portals. The first benefit is *self-provisioning*, the ability for users to do a self-service request for a site. The second is *preloading* the workspace with content from a predefined template. Instead of users starting with a blank workspace, they receive a site that has been preconfigured with components tailored to their business. The third key benefit is *ease of maintenance*. RapPort includes Web Parts that ease content management for daily tasks and assist quickly restructuring sites when people, organizations, or projects change.

In addition, RapPort presents significant reduction in time and costs for deploying a corporate intranet portal. The Business Tools Division (BTD) used RapPort with SharePoint Portal Server to create its marketing Web site. The group saw tremendous improvements in time and costs. The following table shows a nearly $65,000 savings between creating the original site and the one based using RapPort and SharePoint Portal Server 2001.

Time and Cost Comparisons

Task	BTD Web Site	BTD RapPort Site
Development	12 calendar weeks $38,500 contractor	2 days
Implementation	2 weeks	4 days
Content Loading	2 weeks	2.5 days
Total Implementation	15 weeks	2 weeks
Total Costs	$68,500	$3,750

In March 2001, the Product Group portal, which aggregates content from the more than 400 Product Development sites inside Microsoft, migrated to SharePoint by using RapPort. The following table shows the nearly 80 percent reduction in labor required to manage the site. Equally important, RapPort eliminated the need for developer resources to maintain the site, freeing that resource to focus on other activities.

Maintenance Comparison

Task	Role	OLD PG Portal (IIS/ ASP / SQL)	(SHAREPOINT / RapPort) New PG Portal
Routine Tasks	PM	74 hours per month	21 hours per month
	Dev	16 hours per month	None
Re-organizations	PM	1.5 hours per month	1 hour per month
	Dev	10.5 hours per month	None

Summary

Intranet Web sites can be expensive to create, difficult to update and maintain, and inefficient for finding information quickly. SharePoint Portal Server offers solutions for how organizations find, share, and publish information. With RapPort, the process of creating and customizing a corporate portal that uses SharePoint Portal Server takes only a few days.

Microsoft Products and Technologies Used

- Microsoft Windows® 2000, Server, Advanced Server Service Pack 1

- SharePoint Portal Server 2001

- RapPort

Benefits

RapPort and SharePoint Portal Server brought significant benefits to Microsoft's internal groups:

- For the IT group, it automates site creation. This reduces labor, and speeds implementation. RapPort creates sites on Datacenter servers, making them easier to manage.

- For the business, creating a template once and replicating it many times, saves enormous costs. Consistent sites in terms of look, functionality, and taxonomy across groups, improve collaboration and speeds communications.

- For internal customers, it provides a rich set of features including document management, a dashboard site, and powerful search capabilities. The templates provide business-specific, useful applications and a one-stop location for users to work.

For more information about how to deploy SharePoint Portal Server by using RapPort, see Chapter 14, "Deploying SharePoint Portal Server across Multiple Sites Using RapPort."

CHAPTER 29

Cairn Energy: Using the Category Assistant to Optimize Document Management

The Category Assistant provides an automatic process to categorize documents quickly and efficiently regardless of their storage location. With the Category Assistant, employees can use the company vocabulary to structure existing content for portal users.

This chapter describes using the Category Assistant by Cairn Energy to categorize corporate documents.

Cairn Energy faced two challenges when it came to categorizing documents in Microsoft® SharePoint™ Portal Server 2001:

- Manually categorizing large numbers of documents is time consuming because someone has to go through each document. Cairn Energy did not want to burden an internal resource in this way.

- Manually categorizing any number of external documents is not possible because you cannot check in external documents. Cairn Energy did not want to populate the dashboard site at the beginning of the project with large numbers of documents.

About Cairn Energy

Cairn Energy PLC is an oil and gas exploration company with offices in Scotland, the Netherlands, India, and Bangladesh. Information the company relies on is spread across the world and key decision makers need access to this information wherever they are located. Drilling and exploration operations generate large amounts of information that needs to be distributed, analyzed, and preserved. High-value investment decisions often need to be made with short notice. These decisions can only be made through collaboration between globally distributed teams. These decisions rely in part on access to the intellectual property amassed from previous exploration projects. Moreover, the results of these decisions frequently demand the rapid provision of corporate information services to remote locations. Therefore, Cairn Energy PLC requires a flexible infrastructure to facilitate the effective capture of information and its subsequent organization and distribution.

Automatic Categorization

Automatic categorization with the Category Assistant is composed of two parts. First, you must "train" the Category Assistant to recognize documents belonging to particular categories. Second, SharePoint Portal Server crawls documents for inclusion in an index. During this latter process, SharePoint Portal Server associates documents with categories based on information from the training documents.

When using the Category Assistant, consider the following factors:

- You must provide the Category Assistant with training documents. To do this, you check documents in to the workspace. During check-in, you specify at least one category. After check-in, you must publish the documents before they can be included in an index. You can also include external documents in the set of training documents by creating Web links in the workspace to the documents.

- You can use the Category Assistant to categorize any document included in the index no matter where it resides. SharePoint Portal Server creates an index of searchable information that includes all workspace content. It can also include a variety of information stored outside the workspace on other SharePoint Portal Server workspaces, Web sites, file systems, Microsoft Exchange Servers, and Lotus Notes databases. When indexed, documents are categorized by the Category Assistant. The Category Assistant's precision can be controlled so that more or fewer documents are categorized.

After evaluating the Category Assistant in a test environment, the Cairn Energy project team decided that in order to ensure the most accurate results, careful planning was in order. The following sections outline the planning process. In addition, they describe how this team developed training documents.

Selecting Training Documents

The project team attributes the quality of categorization achieved by the Category Assistant to the quality of the training documents used. Although finding good training documents is time consuming, it greatly reduced the amount of time spent categorizing documents overall.

The team found that understanding how the Category Assistant learns was useful when choosing training documents. The training process builds a list of definitive terms for each category by comparing training documents in a single category to those in other categories. The Category Assistant identifies the top 300 shared features among the training documents for a category. The Category Assistant then applies an algorithm to all documents included in the index to determine the proposed category membership.

The project team chose ten categories for training from the overall list of categories. Each category included a minimum of 20 training documents.

The project team found the following points useful for selecting training documents:

- Explain how the Category Assistant works to the people supplying the training documents.

- Create at least ten categories for the Category Assistant to learn.

- Use training documents that contain a minimum of 2,000 words each.

- Choose documents with a large number of words per file. For example, Microsoft Excel spreadsheets and Microsoft PowerPoint® presentations frequently did not make good training documents. Files with high word counts, such as Microsoft Word documents, Adobe Acrobat files, and files in the Tagged Image File Format (TIFF) format make good training documents.

- Use training documents that represent a broad range of examples from the subject category.

- Use training documents that cover the category subject throughout the document. Even though documents may start on the subject, if much of the content is not relevant, this lowers accuracy.

- You can use training documents that belong to multiple categories.

Adding Training Documents

The team found that dragging documents into the workspace by using Web folders was the most efficient way to add documents. The team created document profiles that included the Categories attribute. After they added documents to the workspace, they checked them in and published them using the new document profile. The team used these documents as representative samples for training the Category Assistant.

Cairn Energy found that adding training documents individually was time consuming. With SharePoint Portal Server, you can check in multiple documents at once to speed the process. SharePoint Portal Server only includes published documents in the index so you must ensure approval and publishing of documents used for training before running the Category Assistant.

If you do not want to add a document to the workspace but you do want to use it as a training document, you can create a Web link that points to the external document. To do this, create a blank document in the workspace to represent the external document and apply the Web link document profile. You can add the Categories attribute to the Web link profile. When you check in and publish the document in the workspace, you can assign the appropriate category to it. When SharePoint Portal Server crawls the workspace, it also crawls the URL associated with the Web link and crawls the metadata included on the document profile. This includes this document in the index, but leaves it in the original location. By following this process, you can include external documents in the set of training documents.

The team developed the following process:

- Add multiple documents to the workspace by using Web folders.

- Categorize documents in the workspace by using the document profile.

- Add Web links in the workspace to external documents.

- Categorize the external documents by using the Web Link document profile.

After completing these steps, you can begin training the Category Assistant.

Training the Category Assistant

To categorize documents automatically, you must complete two tasks. First, train the Category Assistant with a set of documents that represent your categories. Second, apply the newly learned categories to all the documents included in the index. You can train the Category Assistant first and then schedule SharePoint Portal Server to perform a full crawl at the next appropriate time. At Cairn Energy, the team found this useful because categorization and crawling affect overall performance of SharePoint Portal Server.

Note To access the Category Assistant, in the workspace, right-click the **Categories** folder, and then click **Properties**.

Monitoring Training

You can monitor the training process by using the Microsoft Windows® 2000 Event Viewer Log.

If insufficient training documents are available, SharePoint Portal Server generates an error message in the Application log as MSSearch Gatherer Event 3065 *workspace name_train$$$ Catalog.*

When you initiate a training session, SharePoint Portal Server enters a message in the Application log as MSSearch Gatherer Event 3035 *workspace name_train$$$ Catalog.*

Upon successful completion of the training, SharePoint Portal Server generates a message in the Application log as MSSearch Gatherer Event 3018 *workspace name_train$$$ Catalog.*

All documents that you categorize using the document profile during check-in are potential training documents. It is important to maintain the accuracy of categories applied to documents in this way. If you retrain the Category Assistant by using poor quality training documents, you affect the accuracy of the automatic categorization performed by the Category Assistant. Cairn Energy only trained the Category Assistant when the high quality of training documents was certain.

Categorizing Documents

After you complete the training, you can manually start the crawl process so that SharePoint Portal Server includes the documents in the index. Alternatively, you can defer the crawl until the next scheduled time. Each time SharePoint Portal Server performs a full update, it also categorizes the documents included in the index.

You can limit the documents you automatically categorize to documents stored in the workspace, or you can choose to include documents stored outside the workspace. Cairn Energy automatically categorized all documents regardless of their location.

The team initially set the Category Assistant to "High Precision" when training it. You can update the index by using the same training documents. Cairn Energy found that reducing the precision increases the number of documents suggested by the Category Assistant. In addition, the quality of the training documents affects the accuracy of the suggested categories. Cairn Energy experimented with reducing precision, but the team decided that including fewer documents with higher accuracy was more suitable to their deployment.

After SharePoint Portal Server categorizes a document, you can view the proposed category structure.

To view the proposed category structure:

1. In Web folders, right-click the document you want to view, and then click **Properties**.

2. Click the **Search and Categories** tab.

The categories are listed under **Categories suggested by the Category Assistant**. SharePoint Portal Server displays documents from external content sources in the **Categories** folder in the workspace.

If the Category Assistant generates inaccurate results, you can override the suggested categories for documents stored within the workspace.

To override the categories suggested by the Category Assistant:

1. Open the properties page for the document for which you want to override the suggested categories.

2. On the **Search and Categories** tab, clear the **Show Suggested Categories** check box.

You cannot override this setting for documents stored outside of the workspace. Therefore, it is very important to use good training documents to achieve the highest possible levels of accuracy.

Results

Cairn Energy measured the accuracy of the Category Assistant by looking at the documents displayed in the Categories folder and assessing the relevance.

The following section summarizes the deployment environment and the results from the Category Assistant. The project team estimates the Category Assistant to be about 90 percent accurate. The Category Assistant retained accuracy after the initial testing and categorization phase into the second phase. The team automatically categorized only a small proportion of the overall company documents. With the addition of further training documents, it is expected that the Category Assistant will continue with the same level of accuracy.

Index Statistics

The following table provides information about the documents included in the index for Cairn Energy.

Index Statistics

Sources	Number of Documents	Size	Health
Intranet	2,315	500 megabytes (MB)	99 percent
Public folder	5,477	500 MB	99 percent
Share one	4,295	500 MB	99 percent
Share two	9,986	4 GB	98 percent
Share three	60,765	16 GB	97 percent

Document Types

Document types for the Cairn Energy deployment break into the following percentages:

- 70 percent Word
- 15 percent Excel
- 5 percent Portable Document Format (PDF)
- 5 percent PowerPoint
- 5 percent TIFF

All documents are in English.

Category Assistant Configuration

The project team set the Category Assistant prevision level to High Precision. They also enabled the Category Assistant to categorize all documents, regardless of their storage location.

Category Assistant Results

The following table summarizes the results after training the category assistant. The first update shows the number of training documents and the suggested category results after updating the index the first time. The second update shows the results after updating the index a second time.

Results of the Category Assistant

Training Categories	First Update		Second Update	
	Number of Training documents	Number of Suggested Category	Number of Training Documents	Number of Suggested Category
Finance	21	303	48	3,712
HSE	24	62	24	62
IM	20	50	39	140
Procurement	20	1,920	20	1,920
Risk	21	128	21	128
Procedures	0	0	27	176
Asset1	10	25	10	25
Asset2	10	39	15	101
Asset3	0	11	24	11
Asset4	23	105	30	170
Asset5	0	0	30	597

The Procurement and Finance categories present the most impressive results. The Category Assistant identified documents as purchase orders and categorized them all appropriately. With the Category Assistant set to "High Precision," categorization was highly accurate and resulted in very few ineffective results.

Summary

The Category Assistant is an extremely valuable tool for rapidly applying structure to information when deploying SharePoint Portal Server. It is essential that you plan effectively and identify suitable categories and representative training documents.

Appendixes

This section provides additional relevant information for use in planning, deploying, and maintaining Microsoft® SharePoint™ Portal Server 2001. It includes a description of the CD-ROM contents including the tools and a list of additional resources that are available to further assist you.

Tools, Samples, eBooks, and More

This appendix describes the contents of the CD that accompanies the Microsoft®
SharePoint™ Portal Server 2001 Resource Kit. The CD includes an electronic version of
the printed book, samples for use with SharePoint Portal Server, and a number of tools
and Web Parts.

Resource Kit CD Contents

You can find the following files and directories on the CD:

File	Contents
SPSRK.chm	The eBook version of the *Microsoft SharePoint Portal Server 2001 Resource Kit*.
Autorun.inf	An autorun menu for linking to the resources on the resource kit CD.
Readme.htm	A description of the contents of the CD and any late-breaking information relevant to this resource kit..

For more information about installing and using these files, see Readme.txt on the CD.

This resource kit CD includes four directories:

- Docs
- Support
- Tools
- WebParts

The following sections describe the contents of each directory.

Docs

This directory contains supplemental documentation for the resource kit. The following
tools also include supplemental documentation:

Electronic Version of the Printed Book

The complete text of the original print book is contained on this CD in a fully searchable electronic version. To install the eBook, run AUTORUN.EXE on the root directory of the CD. Microsoft Internet Explorer 5.01 or later and the proper HTML Help components are required to view the eBook. If your computer does not have Microsoft Internet Explorer 5.01 or later installed, the setup program will offer to install Internet Explorer 5.5 for you. The setup program has been configured to install the minimum files necessary to view the eBook, and it will not change your current settings or associations.

If your computer runs on Microsoft Windows NT® 4 or Microsoft Windows® 2000, you will need administrative privileges to install the eBook.

For more information about the eBook installation, refer to the Readme.txt file on the root directory of the CD. The eBook file, SPSRK.chm, is located on the root directory of the CD, and contains information from this resource kit.

Archive Tool

The Archive Tool includes additional documentation, called SPSUTIL Documentation.htm. This document provides specific procedures for use with this tool. A copy of this document is located in the \Docs directory of the CD and in the \Tools\Archive directory of the CD.

Import/Export

The Import/Export tool includes additional documentation, called SPS XML and Import Tool.doc. This document provides information about how to customize the tool for Extensible Markup Language (XML) import formats. A copy of this document is located in the \Docs directory of the CD and in the \Tools\spsimex\import directory of the CD.

Samples

Code samples discussed in the book are included on this CD in the \Docs\Samples folder. To copy all the sample files to your hard disk, double-click the sample file in the \Docs\Samples folder and extract the sample according to instructions. The samples require about 350 KB of hard disk space. If you are using a computer running Windows NT or Windows 2000, you will need administrative privileges to install the sample files.

To remove the sample files, locate the files on your hard drive by using Windows Explorer. Select the files, and then press Delete on the keyboard.

Chapter 25, "Crawling Custom Metadata" contains extensive code examples. You can copy and paste code examples from the text file without having to enter them from the keyboard.

C25615624Htmlprop.zip

This file contains code samples associated with Chapter 25. This file is located under \Docs\Samples on the resource kit CD.

C25615624Propmap.zip

This file contains code samples associated with Chapter 25. This file contains a Windows Scripting Host script file named PropMap.wsf. PropMap.wsf accepts as input an XML file that supplies server, workspace, and content source information, plus property mapping information. An example of the file format expected by this script is provided as PropMap.xml. This file is located under \Docs\Samples on the resource kit CD.

Support Symbols

The Support\Symbols directory contains the following symbols used for debugging:

File name	Description	Location on CD
rtffilt.pdb	Debug symbols for the RTF filter.	\Support\Symbols\dll
XMLFilter.pdb	Debug symbols for the XML filter.	\Support\Symbols\dll
RunAsSystem.pdb	Debug symbols for the RunAsSystem utility used in the Undelete Web Part.	\Support\Symbols\exe

Tools

The tools listed below are available on the CD to help you more effectively use, manage, and develop applications for Microsoft SharePoint Portal Server 2001.

Tools are located on the CD in the Tools folder. A short name is provided in parentheses for each tool or sample listed below; this short name is the name of the folder on the CD that contains the item. You can find detailed information about each tool in the file Readme.txt in the \Tools*ShortName* folder on the CD.

You can find the following tools on the CD:

Workspace Archive Tool (archive)

The archive tool enables you to archive content from a SharePoint Portal Server workspace. By default, the archived content is stored in a file directory, and the metadata is stored in a stub XML file. This architecture is extensible and enables you to write custom code to process archived items.

This tool is located under \Tools\archive on the resource kit CD. The following files are included in this directory:

- archive.bat
- archive.vbs
- Readme.txt
- SPSUTIL Documentation.htm
- SPSUtil.dll
- \source\archive.bat
- \source\Archive.cls
- \source\archive.vbs
- \source\iProcess.cls
- \source\MoveDelete.cls
- \source\m_globals.bas
- \source\SPSUtil.vbp

Category Smart Tags Component (smart_tag)

This smart tag enables users of Microsoft Office XP to access information quickly from categories in SharePoint Portal Server workspaces while viewing and authoring documents in Office.

This tool is located under \Tools\smart_Tag on the resource kit CD. The following files are included in this directory:

- Readme.txt
- SPSCategories.dll
- SPSCategories.reg
- \source\SmartTagAction.cls
- \source\SmartTagRecognizer.cls
- \source\SPSCategories.vbp

Category Sort Order Tool (category_sort)

This tool sorts the values for the Categories property in a workspace into alphabetical order. The order of these values determines the order in which the category list displays when a user categorizes a document.

This tool is located under \Tools\category_sort on the resource kit CD. The following files are included in this directory:

- Readme.txt

- sort_categories.vbs

Document Usage Tracking Tool (doc_usage)

The tool uses the information in the Internet Information Services (IIS) logs to determine the number of times documents have been accessed in the workspace. You can use the results to determine which documents in the workspace users access most frequently. The tool uses the information in the Internet Information Services (IIS) logs to determine the number of times a document has been accessed.

This tool is located under \Tools\doc_usage on the resource kit CD. The following files are included in this directory:

- doc_usage.vbs

- Readme.txt

Edit File Tool (edit_file)

This style sheet adds an Edit action to the listing for each document in the document library of SharePoint Portal Server. If you are running Microsoft Office XP or later, you can click the Edit link to open the document in the appropriate Microsoft Office application.

This tool is located under \Tools\edit_file on the resource kit CD. The following files are included in this directory:

- FolderItemsPart.xsl

- Readme.txt

Extranet Configuration Tool (spsextranet)

This tool automates many of the tasks described in Chapter 12, "Deploying SharePoint Portal Server in an Extranet Environment," of the resource kit and in the white paper titled "Deploying Microsoft SharePoint Portal Server 2001 across an Extranet." This tool configures your SharePoint Portal Server computer to work with additional host names, including fully qualified domain names. This tool is located under \Tools\spsextranet on the resource kit CD. The following files are included in this directory:

- Readme.txt

- spsconfig.wsf

FTP Protocol Handler (FTPph)

You can use SharePoint Portal Server to crawl File Transfer Protocol (FTP) servers by installing the FTP protocol handler and creating a content source for the FTP site. This tool is located under \Tools\FTPph on the resource kit CD. The following files are included in this directory:

- Readme.txt

- ftpph.dll

Import and Export Tools (spsimex)

These tools enable you to import and export content and schema into a new or existing SharePoint Portal Server workspace from an existing workspace.

Import

The import utility enables you to import content and schema into a new or existing SharePoint Portal Server workspace. Content and schema must exist in a file system folder and an XML manifest file, respectively. To ensure that the XML manifest file and content are properly formatted, use the export utility.

This tool is located under \Tools\spsimex\import on the resource kit CD. The following files are included in this directory:

- Readme.txt

- Setup.exe

- Setup.lst

- SPS XML and Import Tool.doc

- SPSIMEXImport.cab

- SPSIMEXImport.exe

- \Source\Form1.frm

- \Source\form1.frx

- \Source\guidgen.bas

- \Source\log.bas

- \Source\modImport.bas

- \Source\SPSIMEX.vbp

- \Source\SPSIMEXImport.gif

- \Source\WinAPI.bas

Export

The export utility enables you to persist a SharePoint Portal Server workspace to a fixed format XML file with the actual content being stored locally.

This tool is located under \Tools\spsimex\export on the resource kit CD. The following files are included in this directory:

- Readme.txt
- SPSExport.dll
- SPSIMEXExport.exe
- \Source\SPSExport.cls
- \Source\SPSExport.vbp
- \Source\SPSExport_form.frm
- \Source\spsexport_form.frx
- \Source\SPSExport_form.vbp
- \Source\SPSIMEX.vbg
- \Source\SPSIMEXExport.gif
- \Source\WinAPI.bas

Index Active Directory Content Tool (index_ad)

This tool enables SharePoint Portal Server to return users from the Windows Active Directory™ directory service in search results.

This tool is located under \Tools\index_ad on the resource kit CD. The following files are included in this directory:

- ad_generator.asp
- ad_lookup.asp
- Readme.txt

Rapid Portal, a Web-Based Workspace Provisioning Tool (RapPort)

Rapid Portal (RapPort) is a self-service, template-based, automated provisioning solution for SharePoint Portal Server workspaces. RapPort enables you to easily create portals from a set of templates containing schema, content, and business applications implemented as dashboards and Web Parts.

This tool is located under \Tools\RapPort on the resource kit CD. The following files are included in this directory:

- RapPortDestinationServerFiles.zip

- RapPortServerFiles.zip

- Readme.txt

- Source\Destination Server

- Source\Destination Server\Components

- Source\Destination Server\Components\Virtual Server Creation

- Source\Destination Server\Components\Virtual Server Creation\CreateVServer.cls

- Source\Destination Server\Components\Virtual Server Creation\modRegistryDefines.bas

- Source\Destination Server\Components\Virtual Server Creation\RapportVServer.dll

- Source\Destination Server\Components\Virtual Server Creation\RapportVServer.exp

- Source\Destination Server\Components\Virtual Server Creation\RapportVServer.lib

- Source\Destination Server\Components\Virtual Server Creation\RapportVServer.tlb

- Source\Destination Server\Components\Virtual Server Creation\RapportVServer.vbp

- Source\Destination Server\Components\WorkSpace Creation

- Source\Destination Server\Components\WorkSpace Creation\clsCreateWS.cls

- Source\Destination Server\Components\WorkSpace Creation\modConstants.bas

- Source\Destination Server\Components\WorkSpace Creation\modUtils.bas

- Source\Destination Server\Components\WorkSpace Creation\RegistryKey.bas

- Source\Destination Server\Components\WorkSpace Creation\RegistryKeyDefines.bas

- Source\Destination Server\Components\WorkSpace Creation\RemoteWS.dll

- Source\Destination Server\Components\WorkSpace Creation\RemoteWS.exp

- Source\Destination Server\Components\WorkSpace Creation\RemoteWS.lib

- Source\Destination Server\Components\WorkSpace Creation\RemoteWS.TLB

- Source\Destination Server\Components\WorkSpace Creation\RemoteWS.vbp

- Source\Destination Server\RegistryEntries

- Source\Destination Server\RegistryEntries\DestinationRegistryEntries.reg

- Source\Destination Server\Scripts And Pages

- Source\Destination Server\Scripts And Pages\AssignCoordinatorRole-Script.vbs

- Source\Destination Server\Scripts And Pages\CreateVirtualServer.asp

- Source\Destination Server\Scripts And Pages\createworkspace.asp

- Source\Destination Server\Scripts And Pages\ExecutionPermission-Script.vbs

- Source\RapPort Server

- Source\RapPort Server\AutoSetup

- Source\RapPort Server\AutoSetup\Autosetup Exe

- Source\RapPort Server\AutoSetup\Autosetup Exe\Autosetup.exe

- Source\RapPort Server\AutoSetup\Autosetup Exe\Autosetup.vbp

- Source\RapPort Server\AutoSetup\Autosetup Exe\modIISUtils.bas

- Source\RapPort Server\AutoSetup\Autosetup Exe\modLogging.bas

- Source\RapPort Server\AutoSetup\Autosetup Exe\modRapportMails.bas

- Source\RapPort Server\AutoSetup\Autosetup Exe\moduleAutosetup.bas

- Source\RapPort Server\AutoSetup\Autosetup Exe\moduleGlbConstants.bas

- Source\RapPort Server\AutoSetup\Autosetup Exe\modUtils.bas

- Source\RapPort Server\AutoSetup\Components

- Source\RapPort Server\AutoSetup\Components\AssignRoles

- Source\RapPort Server\AutoSetup\Components\AssignRoles\assignRoles.dll

- Source\RapPort Server\AutoSetup\Components\AssignRoles\assignRoles.exp

- Source\RapPort Server\AutoSetup\Components\AssignRoles\assignRoles.lib

- Source\RapPort Server\AutoSetup\Components\AssignRoles\assignRoles.TLB

- Source\RapPort Server\AutoSetup\Components\AssignRoles\assignRoles.vbp

- Source\RapPort Server\AutoSetup\Components\AssignRoles\Roles.cls

- Source\RapPort Server\AutoSetup\Components\SCM

- Source\RapPort Server\AutoSetup\Components\SCM\cls

- Source\RapPort Server\AutoSetup\Components\SCM\SCM.dll

- Source\RapPort Server\AutoSetup\Components\SCM\SCM.exp

- Source\RapPort Server\AutoSetup\Components\SCM\SCM.lib

- Source\RapPort Server\AutoSetup\Components\SCM\SCM.TLB

- Source\RapPort Server\AutoSetup\Components\SCM\SCM.vbp

- Source\RapPort Server\AutoSetup\Components\SCM\cls\Manager.cls

- Source\RapPort Server\AutoSetup\Components\Template Instantiation

- Source\RapPort Server\AutoSetup\Components\Template Instantiation\TemplateInst.dll

- Source\RapPort Server\AutoSetup\Components\Template Instantiation\TemplateInst.exp

- Source\RapPort Server\AutoSetup\Components\Template Instantiation\TemplateInst.lib

- Source\RapPort Server\AutoSetup\Components\Template Instantiation\
  TemplateInst.TLB

- Source\RapPort Server\AutoSetup\Components\Template Instantiation\TemplateInst.vbp

- Source\RapPort Server\AutoSetup\Components\Template Instantiation\BAS

- Source\RapPort Server\AutoSetup\Components\Template Instantiation\BAS\
  modApplicationFolderDocuments.bas

- Source\RapPort Server\AutoSetup\Components\Template Instantiation\BAS\
  modApplicationFolders.bas

- Source\RapPort Server\AutoSetup\Components\Template Instantiation\BAS\
  modCategories.bas

- Source\RapPort Server\AutoSetup\Components\Template Instantiation\BAS\
  modConstants.bas

- Source\RapPort Server\AutoSetup\Components\Template Instantiation\BAS\
  modCopyDocs.bas

- Source\RapPort Server\AutoSetup\Components\Template Instantiation\BAS\
  modDashboard.bas

- Source\RapPort Server\AutoSetup\Components\Template Instantiation\BAS\
  modDocumentFolders.bas

- Source\RapPort Server\AutoSetup\Components\Template Instantiation\BAS\
  modDocuments.bas

- Source\RapPort Server\AutoSetup\Components\Template Instantiation\BAS\modErr.bas

- Source\RapPort Server\AutoSetup\Components\Template Instantiation\BAS\
  modGen.bas

- Source\RapPort Server\AutoSetup\Components\Template Instantiation\BAS\
  modGlobals.bas

- Source\RapPort Server\AutoSetup\Components\Template Instantiation\BAS\
  modMain.bas

- Source\RapPort Server\AutoSetup\Components\Template Instantiation\BAS\
  modPortalContentDocuments.bas

- Source\RapPort Server\AutoSetup\Components\Template Instantiation\BAS\
  modPortalContentFolders.bas

- Source\RapPort Server\AutoSetup\Components\Template Instantiation\BAS\ modRapPortResourcesDocuments.bas

- Source\RapPort Server\AutoSetup\Components\Template Instantiation\BAS\ modRapPortResourcesFolders.bas

- Source\RapPort Server\AutoSetup\Components\Template Instantiation\BAS\ modSchema.bas

- Source\RapPort Server\AutoSetup\Components\Template Instantiation\BAS\ modUtilXML.bas

- Source\RapPort Server\AutoSetup\Components\Template Instantiation\CLS

- Source\RapPort Server\AutoSetup\Components\Template Instantiation\CLS\ CodeGenerator.cls

- Source\RapPort Server\AutoSetup\Components\Template Instantiation\CLS\ NamespacePrefixes.cls

- Source\RapPort Server\AutoSetup\Components\Template Instantiation\XSL

- Source\RapPort Server\AutoSetup\Components\Template Instantiation\XSL\ convert-dav-to-ddf.xsl

- Source\RapPort Server\AutoSetup\Components\Template Instantiation\XSL\ import-application-folder-documents.xsl

- Source\RapPort Server\AutoSetup\Components\Template Instantiation\XSL\ import-application-folders.xsl

- Source\RapPort Server\AutoSetup\Components\Template Instantiation\XSL\ import-categories.xsl

- Source\RapPort Server\AutoSetup\Components\Template Instantiation\XSL\ import-document-folders.xsl

- Source\RapPort Server\AutoSetup\Components\Template Instantiation\XSL\ import-portal-content-folders.xsl

- Source\RapPort Server\AutoSetup\Components\Template Instantiation\XSL\ import-portal.xsl

- Source\RapPort Server\AutoSetup\Components\Template Instantiation\XSL\ import-rapportresources-folders.xsl

- Source\RapPort Server\AutoSetup\Components\Template Instantiation\XSL\ import-schema.xsl

- Source\RapPort Server\AutoSetup\Components\WrapperTemplateInst

- Source\RapPort Server\AutoSetup\Components\WrapperTemplateInst\clsInstantiate.cls

- Source\RapPort Server\AutoSetup\Components\WrapperTemplateInst\ TemplateInstantiation.vbp

- Source\RapPort Server\AutoSetup\Components\WrapperTemplateInst\ WrapperTemplateInst.dll

- Source\RapPort Server\AutoSetup\Components\WrapperTemplateInst\ WrapperTemplateInst.exp

- Source\RapPort Server\AutoSetup\Components\WrapperTemplateInst\ WrapperTemplateInst.lib

- Source\RapPort Server\AutoSetup\Components\WrapperTemplateInst\ WrapperTemplateInst.TLB

- Source\RapPort Server\AutoSetup\Configuration

- Source\RapPort Server\AutoSetup\Configuration\constants.xml

- Source\RapPort Server\AutoSetup\Configuration\globalizedStrings.xml

- Source\RapPort Server\AutoSetup\Configuration\Mails.xml

- Source\RapPort Server\AutoSetup\Configuration\serverConfig.xml

- Source\RapPort Server\AutoSetup\RegistryEntries

- Source\RapPort Server\AutoSetup\RegistryEntries\RapPortServerReg.reg

- Source\RapPort Server\AutoSetup\Utilities

- Source\RapPort Server\AutoSetup\Utilities\addauthor.vbs

- Source\RapPort Server\AutoSetup\Utilities\addcoordinator.vbs

- Source\RapPort Server\AutoSetup\Utilities\addreader.vbs

- Source\RapPort Server\AutoSetup\Utilities\RestartIIS.cmd

- Source\RapPort Server\AutoSetup\Utilities\sleep.vbs

- Source\RapPort Server\RapPortWeb

- Source\RapPort Server\RapPortWeb\default.htm

- Source\RapPort Server\RapPortWeb\Global.asa

- Source\RapPort Server\RapPortWeb\Configuration

- Source\RapPort Server\RapPortWeb\Configuration\regionCodes.xml

- Source\RapPort Server\RapPortWeb\Configuration\regionCodes.xsl

- Source\RapPort Server\RapPortWeb\Configuration\templateConfig.xml

- Source\RapPort Server\RapPortWeb\Configuration\templateConfig.xsl

- Source\RapPort Server\RapPortWeb\Configuration\todaysServers.xml

- Source\RapPort Server\RapPortWeb\Content

- Source\RapPort Server\RapPortWeb\Content\1ptrans.gif

- Source\RapPort Server\RapPortWeb\Content\BusDivPortal.htm

- Source\RapPort Server\RapPortWeb\Content\Customize.htm

- Source\RapPort Server\RapPortWeb\Content\DeptPortal.htm

- Source\RapPort Server\RapPortWeb\Content\ep.css

- Source\RapPort Server\RapPortWeb\Content\expendLeftNav.js

- Source\RapPort Server\RapPortWeb\Content\FAQ.htm

- Source\RapPort Server\RapPortWeb\Content\linenavdns.gif

- Source\RapPort Server\RapPortWeb\Content\local.js

- Source\RapPort Server\RapPortWeb\Content\MoreInfo.htm

- Source\RapPort Server\RapPortWeb\Content\navscrpt.js

- Source\RapPort Server\RapPortWeb\Content\new logo.bmp

- Source\RapPort Server\RapPortWeb\Content\Templates.htm

- Source\RapPort Server\RapPortWeb\Content\toolbar.js

- Source\RapPort Server\RapPortWeb\Images

- Source\RapPort Server\RapPortWeb\Images\pixel.gif

- Source\RapPort Server\RapPortWeb\Images\settingsicon.gif

- Source\RapPort Server\RapPortWeb\Includes

- Source\RapPort Server\RapPortWeb\Includes\CheckAvailability.cmd

- Source\RapPort Server\RapPortWeb\Includes\CommonFunction.js

- Source\RapPort Server\RapPortWeb\Includes\constants.asp

- Source\RapPort Server\RapPortWeb\Includes\constants.inc

- Source\RapPort Server\RapPortWeb\Includes\cust.css

- Source\RapPort Server\RapPortWeb\Includes\ErrorPage.asp

- Source\RapPort Server\RapPortWeb\Includes\errors.js

- Source\RapPort Server\RapPortWeb\Includes\messages.inc

- Source\RapPort Server\RapPortWeb\Pages

- Source\RapPort Server\RapPortWeb\Pages\advanced.htm

- Source\RapPort Server\RapPortWeb\Pages\advancedFrame.asp

- Source\RapPort Server\RapPortWeb\Pages\checkURLAvailability.asp

- Source\RapPort Server\RapPortWeb\Pages\checkUserRequests.asp

- Source\RapPort Server\RapPortWeb\Pages\deleteUserData.asp

- Source\RapPort Server\RapPortWeb\Pages\finishPage.asp

- Source\RapPort Server\RapPortWeb\Pages\rapportSetup2.asp

- Source\RapPort Server\RapPortWeb\Pages\rapportSetup3.asp

- Source\RapPort Server\RapPortWeb\Pages\saveTemporarySecurityData.asp

- Source\RapPort Server\RapPortWeb\Pages\saveUserData.asp

- Source\RapPort Server\RapPortWeb\Pages\saveUserSecurity.asp

- Source\RapPort Server\RapPortWeb\Pages\sendTemporarySecurityData.asp

- Source\RapPort Server\RapPortWeb\Pages\statusbar.htm

- Source\RapPort Server\RapPortWeb\Pages\workspaceRolesContainer.asp

- Source\RapPort Server\RapPortWeb\Pages\AD

- Source\RapPort Server\RapPortWeb\Pages\AD\COM

- Source\RapPort Server\RapPortWeb\Pages\AD\COM\ActiveDir.dll

- Source\RapPort Server\RapPortWeb\Pages\AD\COM\ActiveDir.lib

- Source\RapPort Server\RapPortWeb\Pages\AD\COM\ActiveDir.vbp

- Source\RapPort Server\RapPortWeb\Pages\AD\COM\Helpers.cls

- Source\RapPort Server\RapPortWeb\Pages\AD\COM\QueryGC.cls

- Source\RapPort Server\RapPortWeb\Pages\AD\images

- Source\RapPort Server\RapPortWeb\Pages\AD\images\UserPicker

- Source\RapPort Server\RapPortWeb\Pages\AD\images\UserPicker\Contact.gif

- Source\RapPort Server\RapPortWeb\Pages\AD\images\UserPicker\Group.gif

- Source\RapPort Server\RapPortWeb\Pages\AD\Components

- Source\RapPort Server\RapPortWeb\Pages\AD\Components\UserPicker

- Source\RapPort Server\RapPortWeb\Pages\AD\Components\UserPicker\
AddressBook.asp

- Source\RapPort Server\RapPortWeb\Pages\AD\Components\UserPicker\
CommonFunctions.js

- Source\RapPort Server\RapPortWeb\Pages\AD\Components\UserPicker\UniCal.css

- Source\RapPort Server\RapPortWeb\Pages\AD\Components\UserPicker\
UserPicker.asp

- Source\RapPort Server\RapPortWeb\Pages\AD\Components\UserPicker\
UserPicker.css

- Source\RapPort Server\RapPortWeb\Pages\AD\Components\UserPicker\UserPicker.js

RTF IFilter (filters\RTF)

This tool reports the time it takes to access a document stored in a SharePoint Portal Server workspace. Use this tool to determine how load is affecting performance of the server. Use this tool as a simple test to verify that the server is functioning normally. The output of the access attempt is reported to help you to diagnose any failures that occur.

This tool is located under \Tools\server_latency on the resource kit CD. The following files are included in this directory:

- Readme.txt

- rtffilt.dll

Server Document Access Latency Reporting Tool (server_latency)

This tool reports the time it takes to access a document stored in a SharePoint Portal Server workspace. Use this tool to determine how load is affecting performance of the server. Use this tool as a simple test to verify that the server is functioning normally. The output of the access attempt is reported to help you to diagnose any failures that occur.

This tool is located under \Tools\server_latency on the resource kit CD. The following files are included in this directory:

- Readme.txt

- sps_ping.htm

SharePoint Portal Server Integrity Checker (spsinteg)

This tool verifies the integrity of SharePoint Portal Server workspaces.

This tool is located under \Tools\spsinteg on the resource kit CD. The following files are included in this directory:

- Readme.txt
- spsinteg.vbs

XML IFilter (filters\XML)

The XML content filter enables crawling of documents that have an .xml extension so they may be accessed in search results.

This tool is located under \Tools\filters\XML on the resource kit CD. The following files are included in this directory:

- Readme.txt
- XMLFilter.dll

Web Parts

The Web Parts listed below are available on the CD to help you more effectively use, manage, and deploy applications for Microsoft SharePoint Portal Server 2001.

Web Parts are located on the CD in the WebParts folder. A short name is provided in parentheses for each Web Part listed below; this short name is the name of the folder on the CD that contains the item. You can find detailed information about each Web Part in the file Readme.txt in the \WebParts*ShortName* folder on the CD.

You can find the following Web Parts on the CD:

Add a Link to Document Library (add_a_link)

This Web Part enables users to create Web links within the document library without the need for the client components of SharePoint Portal Server. Users may customize data on the Web link profile and publish links directly from the dashboard site.

This Web Part is located under \WebParts\add_a_link on the resource kit CD. The following files are included in this directory:

- Add a Link.dwp
- Readme.txt

Add a News, Announcements or Quick Link to Home (add_link_to_home)

You can use this Web Part to add news, announcements, and quick links to the home page of the dashboard site for SharePoint Portal Server.

This Web Part is located under \WebParts\add_link_to_home on the resource kit CD. The following files are included in this directory:

- Add a Link to the Dashboard Site Home Page.dwp

- Readme.txt

Announcements Authoring Tool (announcements)

This Web Part enables authors to create content for the Announcements Web Part without the need for Microsoft FrontPage® or Microsoft Word. The user experience has been modeled after Microsoft SharePoint Team Services. The Announcements Web Part is designed to replace the standard Announcements Web Part that ships with SharePoint Portal Server.

This Web Part is located under \WebParts\announcements on the resource kit CD. The following files are included in this directory:

- Announcements.dwp

- Readme.txt

- \Announcements_Files\absmode.gif

- \Announcements_Files\abspos.gif

- \Announcements_Files\AddItem.gif

- \Announcements_Files\ADDLISTITEM.ASP

- \Announcements_Files\addlistitems.xsl

- \Announcements_Files\announce.xml

- \Announcements_Files\bgcolor.gif

- \Announcements_Files\Bold.gif

- \Announcements_Files\borders.gif

- \Announcements_Files\Break.gif

- \Announcements_Files\bullist.gif

- \Announcements_Files\calendar.gif

- \Announcements_Files\Center.gif

- \Announcements_Files\Copy.gif
- \Announcements_Files\Cut.gif
- \Announcements_Files\DeIndent.gif
- \Announcements_Files\delcell.gif
- \Announcements_Files\delcol.gif
- \Announcements_Files\delrow.gif
- \Announcements_Files\End.gif
- \Announcements_Files\exportevent.asp
- \Announcements_Files\fgcolor.gif
- \Announcements_Files\Find.gif
- \Announcements_Files\font.gif
- \Announcements_Files\fullscrn.gif
- \Announcements_Files\HTMLEditor.htm
- \Announcements_Files\iframe.htm
- \Announcements_Files\image.gif
- \Announcements_Files\inindent.gif
- \Announcements_Files\inscell.gif
- \Announcements_Files\inscol.gif
- \Announcements_Files\insrow.gif
- \Announcements_Files\instable.gif
- \Announcements_Files\instable.htm
- \Announcements_Files\Italic.gif
- \Announcements_Files\left.gif
- \Announcements_Files\Link.gif
- \Announcements_Files\listitemutils.asp
- \Announcements_Files\Lock.gif
- \Announcements_Files\mrgcell.gif
- \Announcements_Files\mycontent.asp

- \Announcements_Files\mycontent.xsl
- \Announcements_Files\newdoc.gif
- \Announcements_Files\newlink.gif
- \Announcements_Files\Newproj.gif
- \Announcements_Files\numlist.gif
- \Announcements_Files\Open.gif
- \Announcements_Files\ows.css
- \Announcements_Files\ows.js
- \Announcements_Files\owsbrows.js
- \Announcements_Files\Paste.gif
- \Announcements_Files\pixel.gif
- \Announcements_Files\print.gif
- \Announcements_Files\project.gif
- \Announcements_Files\props.gif
- \Announcements_Files\reddot.gif
- \Announcements_Files\Redo.gif
- \Announcements_Files\right.gif
- \Announcements_Files\Save.gif
- \Announcements_Files\SaveAll.gif
- \Announcements_Files\SaveAs.gif
- \Announcements_Files\saveitem.gif
- \Announcements_Files\selcolor.htm
- \Announcements_Files\snapgrid.gif
- \Announcements_Files\spltcell.gif
- \Announcements_Files\Start.gif
- \Announcements_Files\TaskList.gif
- \Announcements_Files\under.gif
- \Announcements_Files\Undo.gif

Category Management (category_management)

This Web Part allows a workspace coordinator to create, edit, and delete categories from the dashboard site without using the client components of SharePoint Portal Server.

This Web Part is located under \WebParts\category_management on the resource kit CD. The following files are included in this directory:

- category_management.dwp

- Readme.txt

Workspace Content Source Status Reporting (cs_status)

This Web Part provides status reporting for all content sources in a workspace. It shows basic status information for each content source including the number of items indexed, the number of errors reported, and the last time the content source was updated.

This Web Part is located under \WebParts\cs_status on the resource kit CD. The following files are included in this directory:

- Content Source Status.dwp

- Readme.txt

Server Content Source Status Reporting (cs_status_server)

This Web Part provides status reporting for all content sources in all workspaces on a server. It is designed for use by administrators who have coordinator access to all workspaces on the server. It shows basic status for each content source including the number of items indexed, the number of errors reported, and the last time the content source was updated.

This Web Part is located under \WebParts\cs_status_server on the resource kit CD. The following files are included in this directory:

- Content Source Status (Server).dwp

- Readme.txt

Centralized Workspace Coordinator Management (coordinator_management)

This Web Part provides central access to workspace management tasks. From the dashboard site, it provides links to manage categories, document profiles, content sources, portal content, and workspace settings.

This Web Part is located under \WebParts\coordinator_management on the resource kit CD. The following files are included in this directory:

- Manage Your Workspace.dwp

- Readme.txt

Personalized Document Status Report (doc_status)

This Web Part shows each user the documents that are checked out to him, documents awaiting his approval, and documents pending the approval of others. Before use, an administrator must run a setup script on the server.

This Web Part is located under \WebParts\doc_status on the resource kit CD. The following files are included in this directory:

- Doc Status.dwp

- doc_status_install.vbs

- Readme.txt

Create Documents from Office XP Templates (document_templates)

These Web Parts enable you to create documents from templates. You must have Office XP installed to use these Web Parts.

There are two different Web Parts for creating documents from templates:

- New document.dwp

- Create document from template.dwp

New document.dwp is designed to run from the Home page of the dashboard site. Create document from template.dwp is designed to be run from within the Document Library dashboard.

These Web Parts are located under \WebParts\document_templates on the resource kit CD. The following files are included in this directory:

- Create document from template.dwp
- CreateTemplate.vbs
- New Document.dwp
- Readme.txt

Events Authoring Tool (events)

This Web Part enables authors to create content for the Events Web Part without the need for special authoring tools such as FrontPage or Microsoft Word. The user experience has been modeled after SharePoint Team Services.

This Web Part is located under \WebParts\events on the resource kit CD. The following files are included in this directory:

- CreateEvents.vbs
- Events.dwp
- Readme.txt
- \Events_Files\absmode.gif
- \Events_Files\abspos.gif
- \Events_Files\AddItem.gif
- \Events_Files\ADDLISTITEM.ASP
- \Events_Files\addlistitems.xsl
- \Events_Files\bgcolor.gif
- \Events_Files\Bold.gif
- \Events_Files\borders.gif
- \Events_Files\Break.gif
- \Events_Files\bullist.gif
- \Events_Files\calendar.gif
- \Events_Files\Center.gif
- \Events_Files\Copy.gif

- \Events_Files\Cut.gif
- \Events_Files\DeIndent.gif
- \Events_Files\delcell.gif
- \Events_Files\delcol.gif
- \Events_Files\delrow.gif
- \Events_Files\End.gif
- \Events_Files\event.xml
- \Events_Files\exportevent.asp
- \Events_Files\fgcolor.gif
- \Events_Files\Find.gif
- \Events_Files\font.gif
- \Events_Files\fullscrn.gif
- \Events_Files\HTMLEditor.htm
- \Events_Files\iframe.htm
- \Events_Files\image.gif
- \Events_Files\inindent.gif
- \Events_Files\inscell.gif
- \Events_Files\inscol.gif
- \Events_Files\insrow.gif
- \Events_Files\instable.gif
- \Events_Files\instable.htm
- \Events_Files\Italic.gif
- \Events_Files\left.gif
- \Events_Files\Link.gif
- \Events_Files\listitemutils.asp
- \Events_Files\Lock.gif
- \Events_Files\mrgcell.gif
- \Events_Files\mycontent.asp

- \Events_Files\mycontent.xsl
- \Events_Files\newdoc.gif
- \Events_Files\newlink.gif
- \Events_Files\Newproj.gif
- \Events_Files\numlist.gif
- \Events_Files\Open.gif
- \Events_Files\ows.css
- \Events_Files\ows.js
- \Events_Files\owsbrows.js
- \Events_Files\Paste.gif
- \Events_Files\pixel.gif
- \Events_Files\print.gif
- \Events_Files\project.gif
- \Events_Files\props.gif
- \Events_Files\reddot.gif
- \Events_Files\Redo.gif
- \Events_Files\right.gif
- \Events_Files\Save.gif
- \Events_Files\SaveAll.gif
- \Events_Files\SaveAs.gif
- \Events_Files\saveitem.gif
- \Events_Files\selcolor.htm
- \Events_Files\snapgrid.gif
- \Events_Files\spltcell.gif
- \Events_Files\Start.gif
- \Events_Files\TaskList.gif
- \Events_Files\under.gif
- \Events_Files\Undo.gif

Personal Dashboard Status Reporting (personal_dashboard_status)

This Web Part provides coordinators or administrators with a list of all personal dashboards in a workspace and the date when each dashboard was last modified. In addition, it provides links to the dashboards and their management folders.

This Web Part is located under \WebParts\personal_dashboard_status on the resource kit CD. The following files are included in this directory:

- Personal Dashboards Status.dwp

- Readme.txt

Advanced Search Property List Browser (property_browser)

This Web Part extends the Advanced search feature of Microsoft SharePoint Portal Server 2001. The Advanced search feature enables you to search for documents based upon properties. This Web Part expands that capability by allowing you to search for documents based upon properties and by providing the values for properties of list type.

This Web Part is located under \WebParts\property_browser on the resource kit CD. The following files are included in this directory:

- Property Browser.dwp

- Readme.txt

Document Library Contents Undelete Tool (undelete)

This Web Part displays a list of all the documents deleted from a particular folder. In addition to the display name of the deleted document, this Web Part contains an Undelete link. When you click this link, the document is returned to the folder from which it was deleted.

This Web Part is located under \WebParts\undelete on the resource kit CD. The following files are included in this directory:

- ConfigureFolder.wsf

- Readme.txt

- RunAsSystem.exe

- SetUndelete.cmd

- UnDelete.dwp

- UnDelete.vbs

- UnDelete.xsl

For More Information

The following resources provide additional information about the topics in this resource kit, Microsoft® SharePoint™ Portal Server 2001, and related Microsoft products and technologies.

For more information about SharePoint Portal Server, including documentation that shipped with the product, see http://www.microsoft.com/SharePoint/.

Chapter 2: Introducing SharePoint Technologies

This chapter presents an overview of the features of SharePoint Portal Server 2001 and Microsoft SharePoint Team Services, in addition to an overview of how the SharePoint technologies are best used together to provide the appropriate level of information management across an enterprise.

For more information about SharePoint Team Services, see http://www.microsoft.com/technet/.

Chapter 4: Introducing the Dashboard Site

This chapter introduces the default dashboard site and presents information about customizing the dashboard site. It reviews the components of the dashboard site and describes the primary management tasks and security issues associated with it.

See the *SharePoint Portal Server Software Development Kit (SDK)*, available at http://msdn.microsoft.com/, for more information about the following topics:

- Developing additional solutions for SharePoint Portal Server.
- Creating custom search queries.
- Using the thesaurus to expand a search query.

See the *Digital Dashboard Resource Kit*, available at http://msdn.microsoft.com/, for more information about the following topics:

- Digital Dashboard technology
- Creating Web Parts.

See the Dashboard Site Help for SharePoint Portal Server, available from the Help link in the upper right corner of the dashboard site, for more information about the following topics:

- Creating personal dashboards.
- Changing dashboard settings.
- Customizing dashboard content.
- Adding content to default Web Parts.
- Modifying Web Parts.

Chapter 5: Introducing Microsoft Full-Text Search Technologies

This chapter describes full-text search technology that is used in a variety of Microsoft products. This chapter can help you to choose the Microsoft products that are best suited for your information retrieval needs.

See the *Microsoft Platform Software Development Kit (SDK)* available at http://msdn.microsoft.com/ for more information about the following topics:

- API, see the white paper "Using Custom Filters with Indexing Service."
- Query dialects
- A list of features new to Indexing Service 3 included with Microsoft Windows® 2000 is available in the Platform SDK.
- The ranking formulae used in Indexing Service.
- HTTPDAV protocol and DASL.

See Microsoft Research at http://research.microsoft.com/ for more information about the following topics:

- The ranking formula developed by Microsoft Researcher and City University Professor Stephen Robertson, winner of the prestigious Association for Computing Machinery Special Interest Group on Information Retrieval (ACM SIGIR) 2000 Salton Award.

See the SQL Web site at http://www.microsoft.com/sql for more information about the following topics:

- Microsoft SQL Server™ 2000

- Full-text search in SQL 7.0, see the white paper, "Textual Searches on Database Data Using SQL Server 7.0."

- Combining file system and SQL table searches using SQL Server full-text search, see the white paper "Textual Searches on File Data Using Microsoft SQL Server 7.0."

See the Site Server Web site at http://www.microsoft.com/siteserver/ for more information about the following topics:

- Site Server object model

See the Exchange Web site at http://www.microsoft.com/exchange/ for more information about the following topics:

- Microsoft Exchange Server 2000

- Full-Text Indexing in Exchange, see the white paper "Best Practices for Deploying Full-Text Indexing."

See the Microsoft Office Web site at http://www.microsoft.com/office/ for more information about the following topics:

- Office extensibility and programmability

For information about Microsoft E-Commerce Business Solutions and Microsoft Site Server 3 Commerce Edition, see http://www.microsoft.com/business/ecommerce/.

Chapter 7: Planning Server Capacity

This chapter identifies the technical boundaries of SharePoint Portal Server to assist you in planning for maximum capacity usage. It also provides suggestions about where to increase resources to scale SharePoint Portal Server to maintain optimal performance.

For more information about setting resource usage for searching and index creation, see MMC Help in the SharePoint Portal Server Administration console (Administrator's Help).

See the *SharePoint Portal Server SDK* for more information about the **SharePoint Portal Document Management Server** object, *Successful Checkins Latency*, *Successful Copies Latency*, and *Successful Publishes Latency* counters.

Chapter 8: Planning Security

This chapter presents an overview of the advantages of using Windows 2000 security features with SharePoint Portal Server. It reviews the elements of Windows 2000 security that allow you to secure access to content on your corporate portal and the role-based security model for SharePoint Portal Server. It presents an overview of SharePoint Portal Server security architecture, including the publishing model and provides suggestions for securing content for search and content aggregation.

See the *Windows 2000 Platform SDK*, available at http://www.microsoft.com/windows2000/, for more information about the following topics:

- PKI and Public Key cryptography, see the white paper "Microsoft Windows 2000 Public Key Infrastructure."

- Kerberos, see the white paper "Security Support Provider Interface/About SSPI/Overview of the Kerberos Protocol."

- Microsoft Windows 2000 Active Directory™ directory service, see the white paper, "Microsoft Windows NT Active Directory Technical Summary."

- Trust relationships in a Microsoft Windows NT 4.0 environment, see the white paper, "Domain Planning Guide."

See the *Windows 2000 Deployment Planning Guide*, available at http://www.microsoft.com/windows2000/ for more information about the following topics:

- Trust relationships in native and mixed mode environments, see "Chapter 10: Determining Domain Migration Strategies."

See the Microsoft Security Web site at http://www.microsoft.com/security/ for more information about the following topics:

- Microsoft Internet security.

For more information about Windows 2000 and Windows NT Server, see http://www.microsoft.com/ntserver/ and the Windows NT Server Forum on the Microsoft Network (GO WORD: MSNTS).

Chapter 9: Planning Taxonomies

This chapter describes the tools available in SharePoint Portal Server that help organize information for delegated coordination, collaboration, and browsing. This chapter also presents a method that coordinators can use to import an existing folder hierarchy into a workspace in a way that takes advantage of the capabilities provided by SharePoint Portal Server.

See the *SharePoint Portal Server Software Development Kit (SDK)*, available at http://msdn.microsoft.com/, for more information about the following topics:

- Creating scripts to build a workspace taxonomy, import content, and apply metadata

Chapter 10: Planning Web Discussions

This chapter describes how to implement and use Web discussions with SharePoint Portal Server. This chapter describes the relationships among Office, your existing Web browser, and SharePoint Portal Server, and assists you in troubleshooting and addressing any incompatibilities.

See "IFS Drive and the Microsoft Web Storage System" in the Readme file, located on the SharePoint Portal Server installation disc, for more information about the following topics:

- Mounting the Web Storage System drive

See the *SharePoint Portal Server Software Development Kit (SDK)*, available at http://msdn.microsoft.com/, for more information about the following topics:

- Deleting discussions by using Microsoft ActiveX® Data Objects (ADO)

Chapter 11: Installing SharePoint Portal Server

This chapter provides installation procedures and troubleshooting information. In addition, this chapter provides information about the operating system and browser support, the installable file system (IFS) drive and the Microsoft Web Storage System, and proxy server settings used by SharePoint Portal Server.

For more information about planning your deployment, see *Planning and Installation* and *Managing Content,* located on the SharePoint Portal Server installation disk.

Chapter 12: Deploying SharePoint Portal Server in an Extranet Environment

This chapter provides the procedures to follow if you want to deploy SharePoint Portal Server across an extranet. Once you complete these procedures, you can access your SharePoint Portal Server in both an intranet and an extranet environment.

For more information about Domain Name System (DNS), see MMC Help in the DNS console.

For the latest information about implementing IIS security configurations to secure your server, see http://www.microsoft.com/SharePoint.

For more information about the Web Storage System Explorer, see the *Web Storage System SDK*, available at http://msdn.microsoft.com/.

Chapter 13: Searching in a Multilingual Environment

This chapter describes MSSearch, the full-text search component of SharePoint Portal Server, functions in a multilingual environment. In addition, it reviews the process MSSearch applies when crawling, filtering, and querying the full-text index for content. It also provides an explanation of other factors to consider when crawling, filtering, and conducting search queries in a multilingual environment.

See the *SharePoint Portal Server Software Development Kit (SDK)*, available at http://msdn.microsoft.com/, for more information about the following topics:

- Detailed explanation of MS Search technology

- Extending MS Search features and functionality in an sharepoint Portal Server deployment scenario

- Extending SharePoint Portal Server through custom queries

Chapter 14: Deploying SharePoint Portal Server across Multiple Sites Using RapPort

This chapter presents a technical overview of the RapPort deployment. It reviews the process, called *portal provisioning*, required to create multiple intranet portals by using RapPort. In addition, this section provides planning information, installation procedures, administration tasks, and key procedures for using RapPort to deploy SharePoint Portal Server across multiple sites.

For detailed information on the application structure, see the white paper "RapPort Application Component Details" available at http://www.microsoft.com/SharePoint/.

For more information about creating workspaces and customizing them, see SharePoint Portal Server Administrator's Help.

Chapter 15: Optimizing Performance of SharePoint Portal Server

This chapter describes steps for optimizing SharePoint Portal Server. You can modify settings in four areas in order to improve the performance and increase the scalability of the application. In addition, it is also important to use the appropriate hardware for your deployment goals. By monitoring performance, you can identify potential bottlenecks and address them before performance degrades.

See Microsoft Knowledge Base (KB) article Q266096, "XGEN: Exchange 2000 Requires /3GB Switch with More Than 1 Gigabyte of Physical RAM." For more information about the following topics:

- Increasing virtual address space

See the *Web Storage System Software Development Kit (SDK)* available at http://msdn.microsoft.com/ for more information about the following topics:

- How to create and use a persistent search folder

See Microsoft Web Application Stress tool at http://msdn.microsoft.com/ for information about the following:

- The Microsoft Web Application Stress (WAS) tool lets you create or record a script that can used to put stress on a server.

See the Exchange Web site at http://www.microsoft.com/Exchange/ for more information about the following topics:

- Optimizing Exchange see Exchange 2000 Internals: Quick Tuning Guide.

See Microsoft Product Support Services at http://support.microsoft.com/ for more information about the following topics:

- Tuning the Performance and Scalability of ASP Web Applications

Chapter 16: Improving Query Performance

This chapter described factors that affect query latency and also gave suggestions for how to improve query performance for your deployment.

See the *SharePoint Portal Server Software Development Kit (SDK)*, available at http://msdn.microsoft.com/, for more information about the following topics:

- Query performance
- How traversal affects query execution (see "Search Query Path")
- Using WebDAV features (see "WebDAV/DASL Request and Response Syntax")
- Cache Document Properties

See *Planning and Installation,* located on the SharePoint Portal Server installation disk, for more information about the following topics:

- Configuring a server dedicated to indexing

- Client, Server, and Network Planning

- Multiple Server Scenarios

See *SharePoint Portal Server Administrator's Help* for more information about the following topics:

- Configuring query time-outs

- Propagating an index

- Performance monitors

Chapter 18: Building a Corporate Portal Using Microsoft Office XP

This chapter presents the advantages of using SharePoint Portal Server to create a corporate portal. It reviews how Microsoft Office XP can help you customize the default dashboard site to create your own custom portal solution and how SharePoint Team Services can add further value to your portal solution.

See the Dashboard Site Help for SharePoint Portal Server, available from the Help link in the upper right corner of the dashboard site, for more information about the following topics:

- Creating personal dashboards

Chapter 19: Architecting Web Parts for Business Applications

This chapter describes how to build and deploy Web Parts to distribute mission-critical information from a variety of business applications. This chapter includes information about how to architect a Web Part for business applications, the tools and skill sets needed to build Web Parts, and the challenges that a developer must overcome in the process. This chapter was prepared in conjunction with Avanade.

See the Digital Dashboard Web site at http://www.microsoft.com/digitaldashboard/ for more information about the following topics:

- Instructions to download and install the SAP and Siebel Toolboxes from the Microsoft Web Part Gallery

- The latest versions of Web Parts and tools, including the Microsoft Avanade SAP and Siebel Web Parts, in the online Web Parts Gallery.

See the *Digital Dashboard Resource Kit*, including the *Web Parts Development Kit*, available at http://msdn.microsoft.com/ for more information about the following topics:

- The DDSC and digital dashboard factory.

- Creating Web Parts.

Chapter 20: Creating Web Parts for Multiple Environments

This chapter provides recommendations for creating Web Parts. In addition, it provides a code sample of a stand-alone Web Part by using Active Server Pages (ASP), Microsoft Visual Basic® Scripting Edition (VBScript), and a code sample of a Web Part to illustrate the recommended strategies.

See the *Digital Dashboard Resource Kit*, including the *Web Parts Development Kit*, available at http://msdn.microsoft.com/ for more information about creating Web Parts.

Chapter 21: Creating Custom Web Parts with Office XP Developer

This chapter describes how you can use Office XP Developer to customize SharePoint Portal Server 2001. It also discusses coding practices for reusable Web Parts, and describes how to save Web Parts in order to move them from SharePoint Portal Server to another application that uses digital dashboards.

See the *Digital Dashboard Resource Kit*, including the *Web Parts Development Kit*, available at http://msdn.microsoft.com for more information about the following topics:

- Web Parts

- Digital dashboards

See the MSDN Office Developer Center at http://msdn.microsoft.com/office for the updated information about Web Parts and digital dashboards.

Chapter 22: Creating a Corporate Web Part Catalog

After you build or collect a set of Web Parts for your company, you can make them available to your users for use in a digital dashboard for SharePoint Portal Server, SQL Server 2000, or Exchange 2000. To do this, you can create a corporate Web Part catalog. This chapter explains how to set up a catalog using SharePoint Portal Server or the SQL Server dashboard that is included in the Digital Dashboard Resource Kit (DDRK) 3.0.

See the *Digital Dashboard Resource Kit*, including the *Web Parts Development Kit*, available at http://msdn.microsoft.com/ for more information about the following topics:

- Tools and instructions on building Web Parts.

- Creating Web Part catalog, see "Working with Catalogs."

Chapter 23: Deploying Digital Dashboards to Multiple Stores

This chapter outlines how to facilitate deploying digital dashboards across different stores and deploying Web Parts from one server to another. This chapter describes how to package and deploy Web Storage System dashboards from one server to another. It also shows how to import and export Web Parts from different data sources such as a SharePoint Portal Server, Exchange 2000 computer or a computer running a SQL Server dashboard.

See the Web Storage System Developer Tools, available from http://msdn.microsoft.com/ for use with the Application Deployment Wizard.

Chapter 24: Analyzing the Default Query for the Dashboard Site

This chapter describes the default query for the dashboard site. It reviews the syntax for the query and provides suggestions for how to customize the default query for your deployment.

See the *SharePoint Portal Server Software Development Kit (SDK)*, available at http://msdn.microsoft.com/, for more information about the following topics:

- Customizing Search for SharePoint Portal Server

- Search SQL Syntax used to write queries for SharePoint Portal Server, see the "SharePoint Portal Server Search SQL Syntax."

- Advanced search applications, see "Searching SharePoint Portal Server."

See Microsoft Research at http://research.microsoft.com/ for more information about the following topics:

- Rank coercion algorithms

Chapter 25: Crawling Custom Metadata

This chapter provides the steps necessary to promote metadata from externally crawled content into SharePoint Portal Server content indexes. This chapter also includes a utility script that allows you to automate the process by editing an Extensible Markup Language (XML) file and running a script.

See the *Platform Software Development Kit* (SDK) available from http://msdn.microsoft.com/ for the following tools:

- PROPDUMP utility

- ENUMALL utility

- FILTDUMP utility

- IFILTTST utility

Chapter 26: T-Systems: Technology Center Bids Piles of Files a Final Farewell

Deutsche Telekom Innovationsgesellschaft's Technology Center is one of the first German company to use the new SharePoint Portal Server for sophisticated document management. The Center expects significant optimization of project workflow from highly efficient retrieval capabilities and universal transparency throughout the complete document life cycle. Under the terms of an Enterprise Agreement, Microsoft is supporting the pioneering user with authorized consulting services.

For more information about T-Systems and the T-Nova Deutsche Telekom Innovationsgesellschaft mbH, contact:

Technologiezentrum [Technology Center]
64307 Darmstadt
Mr. Uli Grün
Telephone: +49 6151 83-8375
Fax: +49 6151 83-5570
E-mail: uli.gruen@t-systems.de

Chapter 27: Migrating from Site Server 3 to SharePoint Portal Server 2001 for Enterprise Search at Microsoft

This chapter describes the Information Technology Group (ITG) deployment plan of SharePoint Portal Server and the subsequent results in the Microsoft corporate environment. It provides detailed information and recommendations based on this deployment. It includes technical information on the existing environment, design decisions, deployment steps, and testing considerations. It concludes with a summary of recommendations based on this experience.

See *Microsoft Official Curriculum Course 2095: Implementing Microsoft SharePoint Portal Server 2001* for additional background on the design of proper rules.

See the *SharePoint Portal Server User's Help* for more information about adding content sources.

See the *SharePoint Portal Server Software Development Kit (SDK)*, available at http://msdn.microsoft.com/, for more information about the following topics:

- Mapping the HTML META tags to SharePoint Portal Server properties for inclusion in the index workspace (sample script)

- Using workspace level scope to restrict results to one of the index workspaces

- Group aliasing

- Freetext and rank coercion

- Sample scripts

For questions, comments, or suggestions about this document, or to obtain additional information about Microsoft Information Technology (IT) Showcase, please send e-mail to showcase@microsoft.com. To view additional IT Showcase material, see http://www.microsoft.com/technet/showcase/.

Table of Figures

This table lists the figures used as illustrations in each chapter of this book.

Chapter 8: Planning Security

Chapter 9: Planning Taxonomies

Chapter 14: Deploying SharePoint Portal Server across Multiple Sites Using RapPort

Chapter 15: Optimizing Performance of SharePoint Portal Server

Chapter 17: Using Categories

Chapter 18: Building a Corporate Portal Using Microsoft Office XP

Chapter 19: Architecting Web Parts for Business Applications

Chapter 22: Creating a Corporate Web Part Catalog

Chapter 27: Migrating from Site Server 3 to SharePoint Portal Server 2001 for Enterprise Search at Microsoft

Chapter 28: KMIT: Deploying SharePoint Portal Server across Multiple Sites

Glossary

A

administrator

A user who has permission to set up, configure, and maintain servers; manage server resources; create and update indexes; and control security at the top level of the workspace.

Applications folder

A folder containing a subfolder for each workspace that is automatically added to the index for that workspace. The subfolders can include applications designed for the Microsoft Web Storage System, making these applications searchable by Microsoft SharePoint Portal Server 2001.

approval process

The process of reviewing a document before publishing the document.

approval route

The path through which a document is approved.

approve

An option during an approval process to allow a document to be published.

See also: approval process, publish, reject

approver

A user who has permission to approve or reject documents in a specified folder.

author

A user who has permission to add, edit, delete, or read all documents in a folder. Authors can also create, rename, and delete folders, but cannot set the security policy on a folder. In an enhanced folder, authors can also submit any document for publishing.

B

Best Bet

A document property that designates a document as highly relevant to a specific category or keyword search.

C

categories

Groups of related content, organized hierarchically by subject matter.

Categories folder

A folder that coordinators use to organize categories.

Category Assistant

A tool used to categorize workspace documents automatically.

check in

To add or return a document to an enhanced folder. Releases the editing reservation on a document, allowing others to open and edit the document.

See also: check out, enhanced folder, check-in form

check-in form

A form that appears when a user checks in a document. It contains check-in comments, an option to publish a document, and a drop-down menu for selecting a document profile.

check out

To create a writable version of a document while preventing other users from editing the same document.

See also: check in, enhanced folder

comment

A brief text description that provides additional information or context about the document to which it is attached.

content source

The starting point for crawling a file system, database, or Web site in order to include content in an index.

See also: crawl, full-text index

coordinator

A user who has permission to configure user roles on a folder and to perform all author tasks. In an enhanced folder, coordinators can select an approval process, undo the check-out of a document, or end the publishing process by using the Cancel Publishing or Bypass Approval actions.

Coordinators at the workspace level can also manage content sources, document profiles, categories, and subscriptions, and can customize the dashboard site.

crawl

To search content to include it in an index.

See also: content source, inclusion/exclusion rules, update

D

dashboard

See definition for: digital dashboard

dashboard application

A dashboard plus all the support pieces, customization pages, and custom Web Part forms.

dashboard site

A Web site created by using Microsoft Digital Dashboard technology. The dashboard site contains a number of pages, or dashboards, and includes customization pages and custom Web Part forms. The dashboard site is used to distribute information to workspace users through a Web browser.

See also: digital dashboard, Web Part

dashboard view

A visual presentation of the information in a Web Part folder, in a format suitable for viewing on a Web browser.

DASL

See definition for: Distributed Authoring Search and Location (DASL)

DAV

See definition for: Distributed Authoring and Versioning (DAV)

default version

The version selected when a particular version is not specified.

demote

To automatically copy the property values found in a SharePoint Portal Server document profile to the properties of a Microsoft Office document. For example, the author name entered in the Author property on the document profile is copied to the Author field on a Properties page in a Microsoft Word document.

See also: promote

depth

A measure of folder enumeration, such as how many links to follow from the content source.

See also: scope

dictionary

A defined list of values for a property.

digital dashboard

A page on a dashboard site. Each dashboard contains a collection of Web Parts in a modular view that can be presented to users in a Web browser.

See also: dashboard site, Web Part

discussions

A feature for adding threaded remarks about a document.

Distributed Authoring and Versioning (DAV)

An extension to the HTTP protocol, DAV enables a client to perform file system-type operations on a remote server, allowing the creation of Web-based document management applications.

Distributed Authoring Search and Location (DASL)

Defines the SEARCH operation implemented in DAV. The body of the SEARCH operation contains the request or criteria for the search.

document

A discrete unit of content and its associated metadata.

document library

The storage location for documents in the workspace.

See also: Documents folder

document profile

A set of properties applied to similar documents.

Documents folder

A folder that is used to store documents in the workspace.

draft

An unpublished version of a document stored in the workspace.

See also: publish

E

enhanced folder

A document storage folder that supports document management tasks such as check-in, check-out, versioning, approval, and publishing.

exclusion rules

See definition for: inclusion/exclusion rules

F

folder policy

Restrictions placed on a folder that limit access to it, or that limit operations that can be performed on the folder.

folder tree

A hierarchical display of folder organization.

full-text index

A resource that is compiled to enable full-text search of documents, document properties, and content stored outside the workspace but made available through content sources. The full-text index contains all text content and properties retrieved from the document through indexing filters (IFilters).

See also: full-text search, search

full-text search

Search of documents, document properties, and content through the use of full-text search predicates.

See also: search

G

There are no glossary terms that begin with this letter.

H

There are no glossary terms that begin with this letter.

I

inclusion/exclusion rules

Rules that determine what content should be included or excluded when specific sites are crawled.

See also: crawl

index

See definition for: full-text index

index workspace

A workspace that manages only content sources.

J

There are no glossary terms that begin with this letter.

K

keywords

A list that represents terms a user might use in a search query.

L

There are no glossary terms that begin with this letter.

M

Management folder

A folder that contains the tools for managing document profiles, search resources, and workspace settings.

metadata

Data about data. For example, the title, subject, author, and size of a file constitute metadata about the file.

Microsoft Management Console (MMC)

A management display framework that hosts administration tools and applications. By using MMC, you can create, save, and open collections of tools and applications. Saved collections of tools and applications are called consoles.

multi-valued

A property that can hold more than one value.

See also: property value

N

namespace

A prefix applied to Uniform Resource Identifiers (URIs), Uniform Resource Names (URNs), and Extensible Markup Language (XML) entities to prevent naming conflicts.

O

OLE/DB

A set of OLE interfaces that provide applications with uniform access to data stored in diverse information sources. These interfaces support the amount of database management system (DBMS) functionality appropriate to the data source, enabling the data source to share its data.

P

permission

Authorization for a user to perform an action, such as sending e-mail for another user or posting items in a public folder.

Portal Content folder

A folder that contains content for the digital dashboard.

profile

See definition for: document profile

profile form

The form in which properties of a document are displayed, and values specific to the document are selected and stored.

promote

To automatically copy the property values found in a Microsoft Office document to the properties of a SharePoint Portal Server document profile. For example, the author name entered in the Author field of a Word document's Properties page is copied to the Author property on the document profile.

See also: demote

property

An element of metadata for a document profile. Each document profile has multiple properties. Properties can be system defined, such as file size or creation date, or can be user defined, such as title or keywords.

See also: metadata

property definition

The scope and behavior for a single element of metadata that can be applied to a resource. It can have an allowed list of values (a dictionary) that is restrictive or unrestrictive for the setting of the value. It can be either optional or required to contain data. All required property values must have a valid value assigned to them before they can be successfully submitted to the SharePoint Portal Server store. A property definition can also be specified as either single valued or multi-valued, and simple ranges can be set for validity checking.

See also: metadata, property

property store

The table of properties and their values used and maintained by the Search service. Each row in the table corresponds to a document in the full-text index.

property value

The value of a single element of metadata that has been applied to a resource. It can be either single valued or multi-valued.

See also: resource, single valued, multi-valued

property weighting

The ability to manipulate the rank of a search result by assigning more importance to particular property values. For example, a file that matches a search term in the title might rank higher than a file that matches the search term only in the text.

See also: rank coercion

publish

To make a document visible to readers.

See also: approve, draft, reject

Q

There are no glossary terms that begin with this letter.

R

rank

The relevance of a file to a search query.

rank coercion

The ability to rank a file at the top of search results for a given search query.

See also: property weighting

reader

A user who can search for and read documents but cannot add them to the workspace. By default, all folder users have reader permissions. In an enhanced folder, readers can view only folders and published versions of documents. A reader cannot check out, edit, or delete workspace documents and cannot view draft document versions.

reject

An option during an approval process to prevent the publication of a document.

See also: approve, approval process, publish

resource

Data, metadata, a collection of data, or a collection of metadata accessed as a content item. Examples: a document, a database table, a content class.

roles

Logical sets of permissions, similar to groups, that determine access to documents in the workspace.

S

schema

The configuration of stored metadata. Schema also refers to a particular language for describing the nature and particulars of the structure of stored metadata.

scope

The range and depth of a search on the dashboard site. For example, when searching for the term "fiscal reports," you can narrow the scope of your search to a particular category, such as "Earnings."

See also: depth

search

The functionality of finding information in documents based on keywords found in the text of those documents or related to the properties of the documents. This is commonly referred to as full-text search. You must create full-text indexes to use full-text search.

See also: full-text search, full-text index

silent installation

An installation that runs unattended and does not require any user input after it has been started.

single valued

A property that can hold only one value.

See also: property value

stemming

A method of mapping a linguistic stem to all matching words. For example, in English, the stem "buy" matches "bought," "buying," and "buys."

subscription

A request for notification when changes are made to a document, the contents of a folder, a category, or a list of search results.

T

There are no glossary terms that begin with this letter.

U

undo check-out

Neutralizes any changes since check-out and returns the document to a checked-in state.

update

The process through which MSSearch crawls content and compiles an index of the content. Full updates include all content; incremental updates include only content that has changed. Adaptive updates (or crawls) include only content that is likely to have changed based on an analysis of historical information.

See also: crawl

V

version history

The (reverse) chronological listing of revisions that have been made to an item, and any associated comments.

version label

A number or other text that indicates the version of an item.

vocabulary

All of the values associated with documents in a workspace. These may include property values, document profiles, categories, and other keywords.

W

Web folder

A folder that provides an interface for managing files on a remote Web server. Web folders provide document storage and publishing functionality.

See also: dashboard site, digital dashboard, document profile, Web Part

Web Part

A customizable, reusable component used to display specific information on a dashboard. Web Parts are used to associate Web-based content (such as XML, HTML, and scripting) with a specific set of properties in an organizational framework.

See also: dashboard site, digital dashboard, Web Part folder

Web Part folder

A workspace folder, under the Portal Content folder, that is associated with a specific Web Part on the dashboard site. The Web Part folder applies a specific document profile to the documents it contains. For example, the Quick Links folder is associated with the Quick Links Web Part, and applies the Quick Links document profile to all the documents it contains.

See also: dashboard site, digital dashboard, Web Part

Web Storage System

A storage platform that provides a single repository for managing multiple types of unstructured information in one infrastructure. The Web Storage System combines the features and functionality of the file system, the Web, and a collaboration server (such as Microsoft Exchange Server) through a single, URL-addressable location. This location can be used for storing, accessing, and managing information, in addition to building and running applications. The Web Storage System is based on the technology that drives Exchange Server Information Store.

word breaking

A search technology used to separate text into individual words for implementing search queries.

workspace

An organized collection of documents, content sources, management folders, categories, document profiles, subscriptions, and discussions. It provides a central location to organize, manage, and publish content.

X

There are no glossary terms that begin with this letter.

Y

There are no glossary terms that begin with this letter.

Z

There are no glossary terms that begin with this letter.

Index

Microsoft Press® Resource Kits

powerhouse

resources to minimize costs
while maximizing performance

Deploy and support your enterprise business systems using the expertise and tools of those who know the technology best—the Microsoft product groups. Each RESOURCE KIT packs precise technical reference, installation and rollout tactics, planning guides, upgrade strategies, and essential utilities on CD-ROM. They're everything you need to help maximize system performance as you reduce ownership and support costs!

Microsoft® Windows® 2000 Server Resource Kit
ISBN 1-57231-805-8
U.S.A. $299.99   Canada $460.99

Microsoft Windows 2000 Professional Resource Kit
ISBN 1-57231-808-2
U.S.A. $69.99   Canada $107.99

Microsoft Office XP Resource Kit
ISBN 0-7356-1403-2
U.S.A. $69.99   Canada $99.99

Microsoft Small Business Server 2000 Resource Kit
ISBN 0-7356-1252-8
U.S.A. $69.99   Canada $99.99

Microsoft SQL Server™ 2000 Resource Kit
ISBN 0-7356-1266-8
U.S.A. $69.99   Canada $99.99

Microsoft Exchange 2000 Server Resource Kit
ISBN 0-7356-1017-7
U.S.A. $69.99   Canada $99.99

Microsoft Application Center 2000 Resource Kit
ISBN 0-7356-1023-1
U.S.A. $69.99   Canada $99.99

Microsoft Commerce Server 2000 Resource Kit
ISBN 0-7356-1128-9
U.S.A. $69.99   Canada $99.99

Microsoft Host Integration Server 2000 Resource Kit
ISBN 0-7356-1182-3
U.S.A. $69.99   Canada $99.99

***Microsoft*®**

mspress.microsoft.com

Practical, portable guides for IT administrators

For immediate answers that will help you administer Microsoft products efficiently, get ADMINISTRATOR'S POCKET CONSULTANTS. Ideal at the desk or on the go from workstation to workstation, these hands-on, fast-answers reference guides focus on what needs to be done in specific scenarios to support and manage mission-critical products.

Microsoft® Windows® 2000 Administrator's Pocket Consultant
ISBN 0-7356-0831-8

Microsoft Windows NT® Server 4.0 Administrator's Pocket Consultant
ISBN 0-7356-0574-2

Microsoft SQL Server™ 2000 Administrator's Pocket Consultant
ISBN 0-7356-1129-7

Microsoft Exchange 2000 Server Administrator's Pocket Consultant
ISBN 0-7356-0962-4

Microsoft Windows 2000 and IIS 5.0 Administrator's Pocket Consultant
ISBN 0-7356-1024-X

Microsoft®
mspress.microsoft.com

In-depth. Focused.
And
ready for work.

Get the technical drilldown you need to deploy and support Microsoft products more effectively with the MICROSOFT TECHNICAL REFERENCE series. Each guide focuses on a specific aspect of the technology—weaving in-depth detail with on-the-job scenarios and practical how-to information for the IT professional. Get focused—and take technology to its limits—with MICROSOFT TECHNICAL REFERENCES.

Microsoft®
mspress.microsoft.com

Get a **Free**
*e-mail newsletter, updates,
special offers, links to related books,
and more when you*

register on line!

Register your Microsoft Press® title on our Web site and you'll get a FREE subscription to our e-mail newsletter, *Microsoft Press Book Connections.* You'll find out about newly released and upcoming books and learning tools, online events, software downloads, special offers and coupons for Microsoft Press customers, and information about major Microsoft® product releases. You can also read useful additional information about all the titles we publish, such as detailed book descriptions, tables of contents and indexes, sample chapters, links to related books and book series, author biographies, and reviews by other customers.

Registration is easy. Just visit this Web page and fill in your information:

http://www.microsoft.com/mspress/register

Microsoft®

END USER LICENSE AGREEMENT
FOR MICROSOFT SHAREPOINT PORTAL SERVER 2001 RESOURCE KIT

IMPORTANT—READ CAREFULLY: This Microsoft End-User License Agreement ("EULA") is a legal agreement between you (either an individual person or a single legal entity, who will be referred to in this EULA as "You") and Microsoft Corporation for the Microsoft software product that accompanies this EULA, including any associated media, printed materials and electronic documentation (the "Software Product"). The Software Product also includes any software updates, add-on components, web services and/or supplements that Microsoft may provide to You or make available to You after the date You obtain Your initial copy of the Software Product to the extent that such items are not accompanied by a separate license agreement or terms of use. By installing, copying, downloading, accessing or otherwise using the Software Product, You agree to be bound by the terms of this EULA. If You do not agree to the terms of this EULA, do not install, access or use the Software Product; instead, You should return it to Your place of purchase for a full refund.

SOFTWARE PRODUCT LICENSE

The Software Product is protected by intellectual property laws and treaties. The Software Product is licensed, not sold.

1. **GRANT OF LICENSE.** This Section of the EULA describes Your general rights to install and use the Software Product The license rights described in this Section are subject to all other terms and conditions of this EULA.

   General License Grant to Install and Use Software Product. You may install and use an unlimited number of copies of the Software Product on computers, devices, workstations, terminals, or other digital electronic or analog devices ("Device") physically residing at a single geographical location.

   Additional License Grant for Media Elements. The Software Product may include certain photographs, clip art, animations, sounds, music and video clips (together "Media Elements"). If so, the following terms describe Your rights to the Media Elements:

   - Except as specified in the next Section, You may use, copy and modify the Media Elements and distribute copies of the Media Elements, along with Your modifications, as part of Your software product(s) and service(s), including Your web site(s).

   - You are not licensed to do any of the following:

   - You may not sell, license or distribute copies of the Media Elements on a stand-alone basis or as part of any collection, product or service where the primary value of the product or service are the Media Elements.

   - You may not use or distribute any of the Media Elements that include representations of identifiable individuals, governments, logos, initials, emblems, trademarks, or entities for any commercial purposes or to express or imply any endorsement or association with any product, service, entity, or activity.

   - You may not create obscene or scandalous works, as defined by federal law at the time the work is created, using the Media Elements.

   - You must indemnify, hold harmless, and defend Microsoft from and against any claims or lawsuits, including attorneys' fees, that arise from or result from the use or distribution of Media Elements as modified by You.

   - You must include Your own valid copyright notice on Your products and services that include copies of the Media Elements, which notice shall be sufficient to protect Microsoft's copyright in the Software Product. You will not remove or obscure any copyright, trademark or patent notices that appear on the Software Product as delivered to You.

   - You may not permit third parties to distribute copies of the Media Elements except as part of Your product or service.

   Additional License Grant for Samples and Redistributable Code. The Software Product may include "samples" of documents, software programs and/or web pages that are listed in a file called "samples.txt." The Software Product also may include "redistributable" components in object code form that are listed in a file called "redist.txt." Except as specified in the next Section of this EULA, the following terms describe Your rights to the samples and redistributable components included in the Software Product:

   - <u>Samples.</u> You may modify the "samples" listed in the samples.txt file of the Software Product and distribute copies of such samples, including Your modifications, in object code form, provided You comply with the distribution requirements described below.

   - <u>Redistributable Code.</u> You may reproduce and distribute copies of the programs and files listed in the redist.txt file of the Software Product and distribute such redistributable components in object code form as part of Your value added products and/or services, provided You comply with the distribution requirements described below. For purposes of this Section, a "value added product or service" means a software product or service, including a web page, which adds significant and primary functionality to the redistributable component.

- • Distribution Requirements. You may only distribute the sample and redistributable code if You comply with the requirements above and You (a) do not use Microsoft's name, logo or trademarks to market or identify any of Your products or services, unless You are party to a separate agreement giving You such rights, (b) indemnify, hold harmless, and defend Microsoft from and against any claims or lawsuits, including attorneys' fees, that arise from or result from the use or distribution of modified samples and Your value added products and services, (c) include Your own valid copyright notice on Your products and services that include the modified samples and value added products and services that include redistributable components, which notice shall be sufficient to protect Microsoft's copyrights, (d) do not remove or obscure any copyright, trademark or patent notices that appear on the Software Product as delivered to You, (e) do not permit further redistribution of the redistributable components by third parties except as part of Your value added products and services, (f) do not use the samples or redistributable code to create, or as part of, any product that, in the reasonable opinion of Microsoft, competes with Microsoft or enables users to migrate from a Microsoft product to a competing product, (f) otherwise comply with the terms of this EULA.

Reservation of Rights. All rights not expressly granted are reserved by Microsoft.

2. DESCRIPTION OF OTHER RIGHTS AND LIMITATIONS.

Academic Edition Software. If the Software Product is identified as "Academic Edition" or "AE," You must be a "Qualified Educational User" to use the Software Product. If You are not a Qualified Educational User, You have no rights under this EULA. To determine whether You are a Qualified Educational User, please contact the Microsoft Sales Information Center/One Microsoft Way/Redmond, WA 98052-6399 or the Microsoft subsidiary serving Your country.

Mandatory Activation. You may not be able to exercise Your rights to the Software Product under this EULA after a finite number of product launches unless You activate Your copy of the Software Product in the manner described during the launch sequence.

Copy Protection. The Software Product may include copy protection technology to prevent the unauthorized copying of the Software Product or may require original media for use of the Software Product on the Device. It is illegal to make unauthorized copies of the Software Product or to circumvent any copy protection technology included in the Software Product.

Not for Resale Software. If the Software Product is labeled "Not For Resale" or "NFR," then, notwithstanding other sections of this EULA, Your use of the Software Product is limited to use for demonstration, test, or evaluation purposes and You may not resell, or otherwise transfer for value, the Software Product.

Limitations on Reverse Engineering, Decompilation, and Disassembly. You may not reverse engineer, decompile, or disassemble the Software Product, except and only to the extent that such activity is expressly permitted by applicable law notwithstanding this limitation.

Separation of Component Parts. The Software Product is licensed as a single product. Its component parts may not be separated for use on more than one Device unless expressly permitted by this EULA.

Trademarks. This EULA does not grant You any rights in connection with any trademarks or service marks of Microsoft.

No rental, leasing or commercial hosting. You may not rent, lease, lend or provide commercial hosting services to third parties with the Software Product.

Support Services. Microsoft may provide You with support services related to the Software Product ("Support Services"). Use of Support Services is governed by the Microsoft policies and programs described in the user manual, in "online" documentation, or in other Microsoft-provided materials. Any supplemental software code provided to You as part of the Support Services are considered part of the Software Product and subject to the terms and conditions of this EULA. You acknowledge and agree that Microsoft may use technical information You provide to Microsoft as part of the Support Services for its business purposes, including for product support and development. Microsoft will not utilize such technical information in a form that personally identifies You.

Software Transfer. Except as specified in this Section, the initial licensee of the Software Product may make a one-time permanent transfer of this EULA and Software Product only directly to an end user. This transfer must include all of the Software Product (including all component parts, the media and printed materials, any upgrades, this EULA, and, if applicable, the Certificate of Authenticity). Such transfer may not be by way of consignment or any other indirect transfer. The transferee of such one-time transfer must agree to comply with the terms of this EULA, including the obligation not to further transfer this EULA and Software Product. Subscription Products are non-transferable.

Termination. Without prejudice to any other rights, Microsoft may terminate this EULA if You fail to comply with the terms and conditions of this EULA. In such event, You must destroy all copies of the Software Product and all of **its component parts.**

3. INTELLECTUAL PROPERTY RIGHTS. All title and intellectual property rights in and to the Software Product (including but not limited to any images, photographs, animations, video, audio, music, text, and "applets" incorporated into the Software Product), the accompanying printed materials, and any copies of the Software Product are owned by Microsoft or its suppliers. All title and intellectual property rights in and to the content that is not contained in the Software Product, but may be accessed through use of the Software Product, is the property of the respective content owners and may be protected by applicable copyright or other intellectual property laws and treaties. This EULA grants You no rights to use such content. If this Software Product contains documentation that is provided only in electronic form, you may print one copy of such electronic documentation. You may not copy the printed materials accompanying the Software Product.

4. **BACKUP COPY.** After installation of one copy of the Software Product pursuant to this EULA, you may keep the original media on which the Software Product was provided by Microsoft solely for backup or archival purposes. If the original media is required to use the Software Product on the Device, you may make one copy of the Software Product solely for backup or archival purposes. Except as expressly provided in this EULA, you may not otherwise make copies of the Software Product or the printed materials accompanying the Software Product.

5. **U.S. GOVERNMENT LICENSE RIGHTS.** All Software Product provided to the U.S. Government pursuant to solicitations issued on or after December 1, 1995 is provided with the commercial license rights and restrictions described elsewhere herein. All Software Product provided to the U.S. Government pursuant to solicitations issued prior to December 1, 1995 is provided with RESTRICTED RIGHTS as provided for in FAR, 48 CFR 52.227-14 (JUNE 1987) or DFAR, 48 CFR 252.227-7013 (OCT 1988), as applicable.

6. **EXPORT RESTRICTIONS.** You acknowledge that the Software Product is of U.S. origin. You agree to comply with all applicable international and national laws that apply to the Software Product, including the U.S. Export Administration Regulations, as well as end-user, end-use and destination restrictions issued by U.S. and other governments. For additional information, see http://www.microsoft.com/exporting/.

7. **APPLICABLE LAW.**

If you acquired this Software Product in the United States, this EULA is governed by the laws of the State of Washington.

If you acquired this Software Product in Canada, unless expressly prohibited by local law, this EULA is governed by the laws in force in the Province of Ontario, Canada; and, in respect of any dispute which may arise hereunder, you consent to the jurisdiction of the federal and provincial courts sitting in Toronto, Ontario. If this Software Product was acquired outside the United States, then local law may apply.

Should you have any questions concerning this EULA, or if you desire to contact Microsoft for any reason, please contact the Microsoft subsidiary serving your country, or write: Microsoft Sales Information Center/One Microsoft Way/Redmond, WA 98052-6399.

8. **LIMITED WARRANTY.**

LIMITED WARRANTY FOR SOFTWARE PRODUCTS ACQUIRED IN THE US AND CANADA. Microsoft warrants that the Software Product will perform substantially in accordance with the accompanying materials for a period of ninety (90) days from the date of receipt.

If an implied warranty or condition is created by your state/jurisdiction and federal or state/provincial law prohibits disclaimer of it, you also have an implied warranty or condition, BUT ONLY AS TO DEFECTS DISCOVERED DURING THE PERIOD OF THIS LIMITED WARRANTY (NINETY DAYS). AS TO ANY DEFECTS DISCOVERED AFTER THE NINETY (90) DAY PERIOD, THERE IS NO WARRANTY OR CONDITION OF ANY KIND. Some states/jurisdictions do not allow limitations on how long an implied warranty or condition lasts, so the above limitation may not apply to you.

Any supplements or updates to the SOFTWARE PRODUCT, including without limitation, any (if any) service packs or hot fixes provided to you after the expiration of the ninety (90) day Limited Warranty period are not covered by any warranty or condition, express, implied or statutory.

LIMITATION ON REMEDIES; NO CONSEQUENTIAL OR OTHER DAMAGES. Your exclusive remedy for any breach of this Limited Warranty is as set forth below. Except for any refund elected by Microsoft, YOU ARE NOT ENTITLED TO ANY DAMAGES, INCLUDING BUT NOT LIMITED TO CONSEQUENTIAL DAMAGES, if the SOFTWARE PRODUCT does not meet Microsoft's Limited Warranty, and, to the maximum extent allowed by applicable law, even if any remedy fails of its essential purpose. The terms of Section 11 below ("Exclusion of Incidental, Consequential and Certain Other Damages") are also incorporated into this Limited Warranty. Some states/jurisdictions do not allow the exclusion or limitation of incidental or consequential damages, so the above limitation or exclusion may not apply to you. This Limited Warranty gives you specific legal rights. You may have others which vary from state/jurisdiction to state/jurisdiction.

YOUR EXCLUSIVE REMEDY. Microsoft's and its suppliers' entire liability and your exclusive remedy shall be, at Microsoft's option from time to time exercised subject to applicable law, (a) return of the price paid (if any) for the Software Product, or (b) repair or replacement of the Software Product, that does not meet this Limited Warranty and that is returned to Microsoft with a copy of your receipt. You will receive the remedy elected by Microsoft without charge, except that you are responsible for any expenses you may incur (e.g. cost of shipping the Software Product to Microsoft). This Limited Warranty is void if failure of the Software Product has resulted from accident, abuse, misapplication, abnormal use or a virus. Any replacement Software Product will be warranted for the remainder of the original warranty period or thirty (30) days, whichever is longer. Outside the United States or Canada, neither these remedies nor any product support services offered by Microsoft are available without proof of purchase from an authorized international source. To exercise your remedy, contact: Microsoft, Attn. Microsoft Sales Information Center/One Microsoft Way/Redmond, WA 98052-6399, or the Microsoft subsidiary serving your country.

LIMITED WARRANTY FOR SOFTWARE PRODUCTS ACQUIRED OUTSIDE THE US AND CANADA. FOR THE LIMITED WARRANTIES AND SPECIAL PROVISIONS PERTAINING TO YOUR PARTICULAR JURISDICTION, PLEASE REFER TO YOUR WARRANTY BOOKLET INCLUDED WITH THIS PACKAGE OR PROVIDED WITH THE SOFTWARE PRODUCT PRINTED MATERIALS.

9. **DISCLAIMER OF WARRANTIES.** The Limited Warranty that appears above is the only express warranty made to you and is provided in lieu of any other express warranties (if any) created by any documentation or packaging. Except for the Limited Warranty and to the maximum extent permitted by applicable law, Microsoft and its suppliers provide the SOFTWARE Product and support services (if any) *AS IS AND WITH ALL FAULTS*, and hereby disclaim all other warranties and conditions, either express, implied or statutory, including, but not limited to, any (if any) implied warranties, duties or conditions of merchantability, of fitness for a particular purpose, of accuracy or completeness of responses, of results, of workmanlike effort, of lack of viruses, and of lack of negligence, all with regard to the SOFTWARE Product, and the provision of or failure to provide support services. ALSO, THERE IS NO WARRANTY OR CONDITION OF TITLE, QUIET ENJOYMENT, QUIET POSSESSION, CORRESPONDENCE TO DESCRIPTION OR NON-INFRINGEMENT WITH REGARD TO THE SOFTWARE Product.

10. **EXCLUSION OF INCIDENTAL, CONSEQUENTIAL AND CERTAIN OTHER DAMAGES.** TO THE MAXIMUM EXTENT PERMITTED BY APPLICABLE LAW, IN NO EVENT SHALL MICROSOFT OR ITS SUPPLIERS BE LIABLE FOR ANY SPECIAL, INCIDENTAL, INDIRECT, OR CONSEQUENTIAL DAMAGES WHATSOEVER (INCLUDING, BUT NOT LIMITED TO, DAMAGES FOR LOSS OF PROFITS OR CONFIDENTIAL OR OTHER INFORMATION, FOR BUSINESS INTERRUPTION, FOR PERSONAL INJURY, FOR LOSS OF PRIVACY, FOR FAILURE TO MEET ANY DUTY INCLUDING OF GOOD FAITH OR OF REASONABLE CARE, FOR NEGLIGENCE, AND FOR ANY OTHER PECUNIARY OR OTHER LOSS WHATSOEVER) ARISING OUT OF OR IN ANY WAY RELATED TO THE USE OF OR INABILITY TO USE THE SOFTWARE PRODUCT, THE PROVISION OF OR FAILURE TO PROVIDE SUPPORT SERVICES, OR OTHERWISE UNDER OR IN CONNECTION WITH ANY PROVISION OF THIS EULA, EVEN IN THE EVENT OF THE FAULT, TORT (INCLUDING NEGLIGENCE), STRICT LIABILITY, BREACH OF CONTRACT OR BREACH OF WARRANTY OF MICROSOFT OR ANY SUPPLIER, AND EVEN IF MICROSOFT OR ANY SUPPLIER HAS BEEN ADVISED OF THE POSSIBILITY OF SUCH DAMAGES.

11. **LIMITATION OF LIABILITY AND REMEDIES.** Notwithstanding any damages that you might incur for any reason whatsoever (including, without limitation, all damages referenced above and all direct or general damages), the entire liability of Microsoft and any of its suppliers under any provision of this EULA and your exclusive remedy for all of the foregoing (except for any remedy of repair or replacement elected by Microsoft with respect to any breach of the Limited Warranty) shall be limited to the greater of the amount actually paid by you for the SOFTWARE Product or U.S.$5.00. The foregoing limitations, exclusions and disclaimers (including Sections 9, 10 and 11 above) shall apply to the maximum extent permitted by applicable law, even if any remedy fails its essential purpose.

12. **ENTIRE AGREEMENT.** This EULA (including any addendum or amendment to this EULA which is included with the Software Product) is the entire agreement between you and Microsoft relating to the Software Product and the support services (if any) and they supersede all prior or contemporaneous oral or written communications, proposals and representations with respect to the Software Product or any other subject matter covered by this EULA. To the extent the terms of any Microsoft policies or programs for support services conflict with the terms of this EULA, the terms of this EULA shall control.

Si vous avez acquis votre produit Microsoft au CANADA, la garantie limitée suivante vous concerne :

GARANTIE LIMITÉE

Microsoft garantit que le Produit fonctionnera conformément aux documents inclus pendant une période de 90 jours suivant la date de réception.

Si une garantie ou condition implicite est créée par votre État ou votre territoire et qu'une loi fédérale ou provinciale ou État en interdit le déni, vous jouissez également d'une garantie ou condition implicite, MAIS UNIQUEMENT POUR LES DÉFAUTS DÉCOUVERTS DURANT LA PÉRIODE DE LA PRÉSENTE GARANTIE LIMITÉE (QUATRE-VINGT-DIX JOURS). IL N'Y A AUCUNE GARANTIE OU CONDITION DE QUELQUE NATURE QUE CE SOIT QUANT AUX DÉFAUTS DÉCOUVERTS APRÈS CETTE PÉRIODE DE QUATRE-VINGT-DIX JOURS. Certains États ou territoires ne permettent pas de limiter la durée d'une garantie ou condition implicite de sorte que la limitation ci-dessus peut ne pas s'appliquer à vous.

Tous les suppléments ou toutes les mises à jour relatifs au Produit, notamment, les ensembles de services ou les réparations à chaud (le cas échéant) qui vous sont fournis après l'expiration de la période de quatre-vingt-dix jours de la garantie limitée ne sont pas couverts par quelque garantie ou condition que ce soit, expresse ou implicite.

LIMITATION DES RECOURS; ABSENCE DE DOMMAGES INDIRECTS OU AUTRES. Votre recours exclusif pour toute violation de la présente garantie limitée est décrit ci-après. Sauf pour tout remboursement au choix de Microsoft, si le Produit ne respecte pas la garantie limitée de Microsoft et, dans la mesure maximale permise par les lois applicables, même si tout recours n'atteint pas son but essentiel, VOUS N'AVEZ DROIT À AUCUNS DOMMAGES, NOTAMMENT DES DOMMAGES INDIRECTS. Les modalités de la clause «Exclusion des dommages accessoires, indirects et de certains autres dommages » sont également intégrées à la présente garantie limitée. Certains États ou territoires ne permettent pas l'exclusion ou la limitation des dommages indirects ou accessoires de sorte que la limitation ou l'exclusion ci-dessus peut ne pas s'appliquer à vous. La présente garantie limitée vous donne des droits légaux spécifiques. Vous pouvez avoir d'autres droits qui peuvent varier d'un territoire ou d'un État à un autre. VOTRE RECOURS EXCLUSIF. L'obligation intégrale de Microsoft et de ses fournisseurs et votre recours exclusif seront, selon le choix de Microsoft de temps à autre sous réserve de toute loi applicable, a) le remboursement du prix payé, le cas échéant, pour le Produit ou b) la réparation ou le remplacement du Produit qui ne respecte pas la présente garantie limitée et qui est retourné à Microsoft avec une copie de votre reçu. Vous recevrez la compensation choisie par Microsoft, sans frais, sauf que vous êtes responsable des dépenses que vous pourriez engager (p. ex., les frais d'envoi du Produit à Microsoft). La présente garantie limitée est nulle si la défectuosité du Produit est causée par un accident, un usage abusif, une mauvaise application, un usage anormal ou un virus. Tout Produit de remplacement sera garanti pour le reste de la période de garantie initiale ou pendant trente (30) jours, selon la plus longue entre ces deux périodes. À l'extérieur des États-Unis ou du Canada, ces recours ou l'un quelconque des services de soutien technique offerts par Microsoft ne sont pas disponibles sans preuve d'achat d'une source internationale autorisée. Pour exercer votre recours, vous devez communiquer avec Microsoft et vous adresser au Microsoft Sales Information Center/One Microsoft Way/Redmond, WA 98052-6399, ou à la filiale de Microsoft de votre pays.

DÉNI DE GARANTIES. La garantie limitée mentionnée ci-dessus constitue la seule garantie expresse qui vous est donnée et remplace toutes autres garanties expresses (s'il en est) mentionnées dans un document ou sur un emballage. Sauf en ce qui a trait à la garantie limitée et dans la mesure maximale permise par les lois applicables, le Produit et les services de soutien technique (le cas échéant) sont fournis *TELS QUELS ET AVEC TOUS LES DÉFAUTS* par Microsoft et ses fournisseurs, lesquels par les présentes dénient toutes autres garanties et conditions expresses, implicites ou en vertu de la loi, notamment (le cas échéant) les garanties, devoirs ou conditions implicites de qualité marchande, d'adaptation à un usage particulier, d'exactitude ou d'exhaustivité des réponses, des résultats, des efforts déployés selon les règles de l'art, d'absence de virus et de négligence, le tout à l'égard du Produit et de la prestation des services de soutien technique ou de l'omission d'une telle prestation. PAR AILLEURS, IL N'Y A AUCUNE GARANTIE OU CONDITION QUANT AU TITRE DE PROPRIÉTÉ, À LA JOUISSANCE OU LA POSSESSION PAISIBLE, À LA CONCORDANCE À UNE DESCRIPTION NI QUANT À UNE ABSENCE DE CONTREFAÇON CONCERNANT LE PRODUIT.

EXCLUSION DES DOMMAGES ACCESSOIRES, INDIRECTS ET DE CERTAINS AUTRES DOMMAGES. DANS LA MESURE MAXIMALE PERMISE PAR LES LOIS APPLICABLES, EN AUCUN CAS MICROSOFT OU SES FOURNISSEURS NE SERONT RESPONSABLES DES DOMMAGES SPÉCIAUX, CONSÉCUTIFS, ACCESSOIRES OU INDIRECTS DE QUELQUE NATURE QUE CE SOIT (NOTAMMENT, LES DOMMAGES À L'ÉGARD DU MANQUE À GAGNER OU DE LA DIVULGATION

DE RENSEIGNEMENTS CONFIDENTIELS OU AUTRES, DE LA PERTE D'EXPLOITATION, DE BLESSURES CORPORELLES, DE LA VIOLATION DE LA VIE PRIVÉE, DE L'OMISSION DE REMPLIR TOUT DEVOIR, Y COMPRIS D'AGIR DE BONNE FOI OU D'EXERCER UN SOIN RAISONNABLE, DE LA NÉGLIGENCE ET DE TOUTE AUTRE PERTE PÉCUNIAIRE OU AUTRE PERTE DE QUELQUE NATURE QUE CE SOIT) SE RAPPORTANT DE QUELQUE MANIÈRE QUE CE SOIT À L'UTILISATION DU PRODUIT OU À L'INCAPACITÉ DE S'EN SERVIR, À LA PRESTATION OU À L'OMISSION D'UNE TELLE PRESTATION DE SERVICES DE SOUTIEN TECHNIQUE OU AUTREMENT AUX TERMES DE TOUTE DIS-POSITION DU PRÉSENT EULA OU RELATIVEMENT À UNE TELLE DISPOSITION, MÊME EN CAS DE FAUTE, DE DÉLIT CIVIL (Y COMPRIS LA NÉGLIGENCE), DE RESPONSABILITÉ STRICTE, DE VIOLATION DE CONTRAT OU DE VIOLA-TION DE GARANTIE DE MICROSOFT OU DE TOUT FOURNISSEUR ET MÊME SI MICROSOFT OU TOUT FOURNISSEUR A ÉTÉ AVISÉ DE LA POSSIBILITÉ DE TELS DOMMAGES.

LIMITATION DE RESPONSABILITÉ ET RECOURS. Malgré les dommages que vous puissiez subir pour quelque motif que ce soit (notamment, tous les dommages susmentionnés et tous les dommages directs ou généraux), l'obligation intégrale de Microsoft et de l'un ou l'autre de ses fournisseurs aux termes de toute disposition du présent EULA et votre recours exclusif à l'égard de tout ce qui précède (sauf en ce qui concerne tout recours de réparation ou de remplacement choisi par Microsoft à l'égard de tout manquement à la garantie limitée) se limite au plus élevé entre les montants suivants : le montant que vous avez réellement payé pour le Produit ou 5,00 $US. Les limites, exclusions et dénis qui précèdent (y compris les clauses ci-dessus), s'appliquent dans la mesure maximale permise par les lois applicables, même si tout recours n'atteint pas son but essentiel.

La présente Convention est régie par les lois de la province d'Ontario, Canada. Chacune des parties à la présente reconnaît irrévocablement la compétence des tribunaux de la province d'Ontario et consent à instituer tout litige qui pourrait découler de la présente auprès des tribunaux situés dans le district judiciaire de York, province d'Ontario.

Au cas où vous auriez des questions concernant cette licence ou que vous désiriez vous mettre en rapport avec Microsoft pour quelque raison que ce soit, veuillez contacter la succursale Microsoft desservant votre pays, dont l'adresse est fournie dans ce produit, ou écrivez à : Microsoft Sales Information Center, One Microsoft Way, Redmond, Washington 98052-6399.

System Requirements

To use the *Microsoft SharePoint Portal Server 2001 Resource Kit* CD-ROM, you need a computer equipped with the following minimum configuration:

- PC with a Pentium III or higher processor.

- Microsoft Windows 2000 Server with Windows 2000 Service Pack 1 or later, or Windows 2000 Advanced Server with Service Pack 1 or later operating system.

- Minimum of 256 MB of RAM.

- Minimum of 550 MB of available hard-disk space. The drive must be formatted as NTFS file system.

- Simple Mail Transfer Protocol (SMTP) Service. This is a Windows 2000 Server component.

- Microsoft Internet Information Services (IIS) 5.0.

- Microsoft Internet Explorer 4.01 or later, or Netscape Communicator 4.75 or later, running on the Windows operating system. Internet Explorer 5.5 is included with the eBook and will be installed on the user's machine automatically if necessary. The Internet Explorer setup has been configured to install the minimum necessary files and will not change the user's current settings or associations.

- Microsoft Office 2000 or later is required to use SharePoint Portal Server Office extensions.

- CD-ROM drive.

- Network adapter card.

- Keyboard.

- VGA, Super VGA, or video graphics adapter compatible with Windows Server or Windows 2000 Advanced Server.

- Microsoft Mouse, Microsoft IntelliMouse, or compatible pointing device (optional).

Actual requirements will vary based on your system configuration and the applications and features you choose to install.